THE CIVITAS ANTHOLOGY OF

AFRICAN AMERICAN SLAVE NARRATIVES

OTHER BOOKS FROM CIVITAS

Pioneers of the Black Atlantic:
Five Slave Narratives from
the Enlightenment, 1772–1815
edited by Henry Louis Gates Jr.
and William L. Andrews

Black Saga: The African American
Experience: A Chronology
by Charles M. Christian

The Ordeal of Integration:
Progress and Resentment in
America's "Racial" Crisis
by Orlando Patterson

Rituals of Blood: Consequences of Slavery
in Two American Centuries
by Orlando Patterson

THE CIVITAS ANTHOLOGY OF AFRICAN AMERICAN SLAVE NARRATIVES

Edited by
William L. Andrews
Henry Louis Gates Jr.

CIVITAS
COUNTERPOINT
Washington, D.C.

Library of Congress Cataloging-in-Publication Data

The Civitas anthology of African American slave narratives /
edited by William L. Andrews, Henry Louis Gates, Jr.
p.   cm.
1. Slaves—United States—Biography.   2. Afro-Americans—Biography.
3. Slaves' writings, American.   I. Andrews, William L., 1946–   .
II. Gates, Henry Louis.
E444.C44   1999
973'.0496073'00922—dc21   98-49051
CIP

ISBN 1-58243-019-5 (alk. paper)

Book design by David Bullen
Composition by Wilsted & Taylor Publishing Services

Printed in the United States of America on acid-free paper that meets the
American National Standards Institute Z39-48 Standard.

CIVITAS/COUNTERPOINT
P.O. Box 65793
Washington, D.C. 20035-5793

Counterpoint is a member of the Perseus Books Group.

10 9 8 7 6 5 4 3 2 1

FIRST PRINTING

CONTENTS

PREFACE

Henry Louis Gates Jr.

THE SPECTER OF the enslavement of black human beings from the African continent—on a scale unprecedented in savagery and brutality in human history—has haunted African American discourse for the past two centuries. Anxiety, anger, bitterness, regret, sadness, complicity, shame, the urge to forget as well as the urge to remember and glorify—these are only a few in the range of emotions that African Americans have expressed in their writings about the slave past, about the complex heritage of a system of slavery that constituted for us what T. S. Eliot called "the dissociation of sensibility" that he claimed World War I was for the Western world.

One reason for ambivalence and ambiguity about slavery in the African American consciousness, especially in the nineteenth and early twentieth centuries, was a deep-seated anger over the role of Europeans and Americans in the slave trade, particularly their failure to acknowledge its immense scale of devastation on the lives and cultures of Africans taken to the New World as well as those Africans left behind. Another reason was bitterness over the role of black Africans in the trade itself. No one put this more bluntly than Frederick Douglass, who railed against "the savage chiefs of the western coasts of Africa, who for ages have been accustomed to selling their captives into bondage, and pocketing the ready cash for them." Richard Wright, in his book *Black Power* (1954), could not write objectively about the emergence of the nation that would be known as Ghana because of his anger at the role of the Asante in the slave trade.

Still another source of anxiety was a vague embarrassment over the idea that, somehow, our ancestors may have been weaker than they should have been, less resistant, less "manly"—to use the word that often appeared in the nineteenth century—than their African captors, since so many were prisoners of war, the conquered and defeated. Others have wondered if Africa herself was cursed because of the apparent willingness of so many African societies to participate in the slave trade, bartering what to us appears to be their sisters and brothers for a mess of pottage. Still others have written extensively about the moral corruption that slavery entailed for white Europe and America.

But most of all, I believe the difficulties that we often had in coming to grips with the history of our enslavement is related fundamentally to the larger pattern of denial about the crucial shaping role of slavery—and its horrific, inhuman nature—that is reflected in the pattern of understatement, omission, and amnesia that has characterized so much of the white American attitude toward the history of slavery.

So exasperated was Booker T. Washington that, writing in 1900, he urged his kinsmen to "turn away from the slave past" and create "a New Negro for a New Century." Slavery, he argued, was best forgotten. Not everyone, fortunately, heeded this sort of advice, or yielded to this kind of anxiety. (Just two years later, Washington would remember the role of the institution of slavery in the shaping of his own life in his masterful autobiography, *Up From Slavery*.) W. E. B. Du Bois, for one, repeatedly addressed the matter of slavery, from its suppression, in his Ph.D. thesis, and the radical opposition to it, in his biography of John Brown, to his estimation of the number of slaves "stolen" frm Africa's shores, a figure that, in his classic work, *Darkwater* (1920), he placed at 100 million.

I believe that Du Bois arrived at that figure in order to dramatize the depth of his anguish at the unprecedented scale of the African slave trade, in an attempt to force his American readers to begin to accept responsibility for its devastation. Toni Morrison, for similar reasons, I believe, arrived at a figure of "60 millions, and more" in her classic novel, *Beloved*. Other large estimates, such as that by the scholar Walter Rodney, are equally reflective of a strategy to dramatize slavery's horror by embracing extraordinarily large numbers to do so.

Thanks to the W. E. B. Du Bois Institute's "Trans-Atlantic Slave Trade Data Base," directed by David Eltis and derived from the work of several other scholars, such as Philip Curtin and Patrick Manning, we can reasonably estimate that between the fifteenth and the late nineteenth centuries approximately twelve million people were shipped from the coast of West Africa across the Atlantic to the New World. It is also estimated that two million slaves were shipped from East African ports across the Sahara Desert, while "five million more were taken from the savanna to the forest in the internal trade," according to Anthony Appiah. Indeed, "By the end of the nineteenth century, between a third and a half of the population, living in 'the great swathe of Sahelian grasslands extending from the Atlantic coast of Senegal to the shores of Lake Chad,' were slaves" (Appiah, quoting John Reader).

What is so curious about the history of Africans enslaved in Great Britain and the United States is that they created a genre of literature writing about—and railing against—their enslavement. This genre of literature—known as the slave narratives—would become the fundament upon which both the Anglo-African and the African American literary traditions would be constructed. No group in the long and cruel history of human enslavement has ever written about slavery as extensively, elegantly, compassionately, and compellingly as have African American slaves.

William Andrews and I have attempted to gather here the slave narratives that we believe most fully exemplify the genre, in all of its complexity and various forms. Literature, as Samuel Johnson used the term, denoted an acquaintance with letters or books; it also connoted polite or humane learning and literary culture. While it is true that the slaves who had managed to steal some learning (in Frederick Douglass's phrase) were keen to demonstrate an acquaintance with letters or books to a skeptical public, it is difficult to claim that slave literature was meant to exemplify polite or humane learning, or to serve as evidence of a black literary culture. Indeed, it is more accurate to say that these narratives represent impolite learning, and that they rail against the arbitrary and inhuman learning that masters foisted upon slaves in order to reinforce a perverse fiction of the natural order of things. The slave wrote not only to demonstrate humane letters, but also to demonstrate his or her own membership in the human community. To a remarkable extent, the works we have collected here express a broad "concord of sensibilities" shared in the nineteenth century by persons of African descent in the Western Hemisphere, works that continue to be strangely resonant, and relevant, as the twenty-first century draws near.

The canon of the slave narratives begins to unveil the horror and the heroism, the courage and the vacillations, the betrayers and the betrayed, that are the human legacy of slavery. What, finally, do these narratives tell us, what wisdom do they impart for the twenty-first-century reader? That, in the face of treachery and evil, simply to survive and endure is enough; but to thrive and bear witness to the contours of human experience—which is, at once, black and universal—is sublime.

THE TEXTS in this volume have been edited, but not abridged, to facilitate contemporary reading. We have modernized and/or emended the spelling of words in some of these texts to conform to contemporary American English usage. Thus words such as "labour," "coloured," "staid," "shew," "manoeuvres," "spectres," "defence," "calk," and "sympathise" in the original texts are emended to read "labor," "colored," "stayed," "show," "maneuvers," "specters," "defense," "caulk," and "sympathize," respectively. Italicized words and passages in the original texts have been preserved in italics in this edition, but some unitalicized terms that are normally italicized in today's usage—such as the names of ships or the titles of books and newspapers—have been italicized in this edition as an aid to the reader. Obvious inconsistencies in spelling within a given text have been silently corrected. Single words such as "maybe," "anyone," "eavesdrop," and "goodbye" that appear as two words in some of these texts are printed in accordance with twentieth-century usage.

We have not attempted to regularize inconsistencies in capitalization within or among the texts, nor have we imposed contemporary capitalization style on these texts. Some terms normally capitalized today, such as Negro or the North, often appear in lower case in these texts. Punctuation practices in these texts sometimes diverge from contemporary practices, such as in the placement of commas and apostrophes and the use of dashes. We have left punctuation in these texts unaltered. Grammatical practices that differ from those of today have not been corrected. Quotations from the Bible in these texts have not been emended.

William L. Andrews

THE CIVITAS ANTHOLOGY OF AFRICAN AMERICAN SLAVE NARRATIVES

INTRODUCTION

William L. Andrews

THE NARRATIVES OF fugitive slaves form the bedrock tradition of African American literature. Some of the biggest selling and most influential novels of American literature, from Harriet Beecher Stowe's *Uncle Tom's Cabin* (1852) and Mark Twain's *Adventures of Huckleberry Finn* (1884) to William Styron's *Confessions of Nat Turner* (1967) and Toni Morrison's *Beloved* (1987), owe much of their power and social resonance to their participation in the slave narrative tradition. From late-eighteenth-century narratives by Africans who endured the nightmarish Middle Passage and came of age in England or the Americas, through the classic American fugitive slave narratives of the mid-nineteenth century, up to the thousands of oral histories of former slaves gathered by the Federal Writers' Project in the 1920s and 1930s, slave narratives have provided some of the most graphic and damning documentary evidence of the horrors of America's "peculiar institution." The personal witness of slaves has appeared on broadsides, in newspaper interviews, magazines, pamphlets, government reports, gift books, biographies, histories, and in autobiographies of various lengths, some as long as five hundred pages. Aside from the countless short biographical accounts of and interviews with fugitive slaves in various eighteenth- and nineteenth-century periodicals, approximately seventy slave narratives were published as books in the United States and Great Britain before slavery was officially abolished in the United States in 1865. At least fifty more narratives by former slaves came out in book form in the United States between 1865 and 1930. To affirm the dedication of the ex-slave population to mutual progress for whites and blacks alike, Booker T. Washington wrote *Up from Slavery* (1901), which many critics and historians regard as the last of the great American slave narratives. From Frederick Douglass through Booker T. Washington, most of the major writers of African American literature before World War I launched their literary careers via some form of the slave narrative.

The earliest slave narratives emerged in England, not North America, the product of British antislavery work. The first slave narrative published in book form in English, *A Narrative of the Most Remarkable*

Particulars in the Life of James Albert Ukawsaw Gronniosaw, An African Prince, appeared in London in 1772. Including North American and Irish editions, Gronniosaw's narrative was reprinted at least a dozen times before the end of the century. Gronniosaw's more famous successor, Olaudah Equiano, published his two-volume *Interesting Narrative of the Life of Olaudah Equiano, or Gustavus Vassa, the African* in London in 1789. Equiano's *Narrative* went through nine British editions and two American printings in his lifetime, not to mention German, Dutch, and Russian translations. The most representative and influential early slave narratives, including those by Equiano and Gronniosaw, have been collected in *Pioneers of the Black Atlantic: Five Slave Narratives of the Enlightenment, 1772–1815* (Counterpoint, 1998), edited by the two editors of this volume.

London was also the site of the publication of the first female slave narrative to emerge from the Americas, *The History of Mary Prince, a West Indian Slave* (1831), which was dictated by Prince to a white Englishwoman to support a petition for freedom that Prince and her antislavery friends had presented to Parliament on her behalf. Prince's *History* was also remarkable in broaching the topic of the sexual exploitation of slave women, which many even in the antislavery movement were unsure of how to discuss publicly because of the delicacy of the whole issue of female sexuality in the nineteenth century. Throughout the international heyday of the slave narrative in the mid-nineteenth century, publishers in Great Britain fed a lively market in their country for slave writing, printing numerous editions of slave narratives often in the wake of lecture tours by celebrated American fugitive slaves such as Douglass, William Wells Brown, and William and Ellen Craft. Some of the most popular slave narratives not only enjoyed a wide audience in Great Britain and the United States but were translated into French, German, Dutch, Celtic, Russian, and Spanish.

With the rise of the militant antislavery movement in the United States in the 1830s came a demand for slave narratives that would explicitly highlight the harsh realities of slavery, thereby supporting the movement's call for immediate and unconditional emancipation. Radical "immediatist" abolitionists such as William Lloyd Garrison were convinced that the eyewitness testimony of former slaves against slavery would touch the hearts and change the minds of many in the northern population of the United States who were either ignorant of or indifferent to the plight of African Americans in the South. The immediatist turn in American abolitionism encouraged fugitive slaves who had previously kept their northern identities hidden to prevent recapture to step forward and speak out publicly against their former masters and the institution of slavery. In the late 1830s and early 1840s the first of this new brand of outspokenly antislavery slave narratives found their way into print under such titles as *Slavery in the United States: A Narrative of the Life and Adventures of Charles Ball* (1836) and *A Narrative of the Adventures and Escape of Moses Roper, from American Slavery* (1838). These set the mold for what would become by midcentury a form of autobiography that blended personal memory and a rhetorical attack on slavery to produce a powerful expressive tool both as literature and as propaganda.

In July 1849, Ephraim Peabody, a Boston Unitarian minister and abolitionist, wrote the first review of the American fugitive slave narrative, praising it as "a new department in the literature of civilization," though America could claim but "a mournful honor" for having created the conditions that engendered it (Davis and Gates, 19). Occupying some thirty pages of *The Christian Examiner*, a quarterly of moderately progressive opinion, Peabody's "Narratives of Fugitive Slaves" analyzed the thought and careers of some of the most influential fugitive slave writers of the 1840s, a decade in which increasing public agitation over slavery gave fugitive slaves their first real opportunity to speak and write in a national forum. Focusing a great deal of attention on the *Narrative of the Life of Frederick Douglass, an American Slave* (1845) and the *Narrative of William W. Brown, an American Slave* (1847), Peabody stressed the impact that this new African American literary genre had made on public opinion in the United States and Europe.

Fugitive slave narratives had amassed an "immense circulation" throughout "the whole of the North," Peabody observed. Douglass's autobiography, the first of the best-selling slave narratives of the decade, "has in this country alone passed through seven editions, and is, we are told, now out of print" (Davis and Gates, 20). As for Brown's *Narrative*, "not less than eight thousand copies have already sold." Peabody was probably unaware of the eleven thousand copies of Brown's *Narrative*, revised in 1848 and expanded in 1849, that had sold in England by the end of 1849. By 1850, Douglass's *Narrative*, available not only in the United States but also in England, Ireland, and in a French translation, had sold thirty thousand copies internationally, a sales record that only the most popular American novels, such as those by James Fenimore Cooper, could match. "We place these volumes without hesitation among the most remarkable productions of the age," Peabody asserted, "remarkable as being pictures of slavery by the slave, remarkable as disclosing under a new light the mixed elements of American civilization, and not less remarkable as a vivid exhibition of the force and working of the native love of freedom in the individual mind." There was something epic about the struggles of men like Douglass and Brown. "We know not where one who wished to write a modern Odyssey could find a better subject than in the adventures of a fugitive slave" (Davis and Gates, 19).

Ephraim Peabody was by no means alone among white American intellectuals in awarding this kind of literary distinction to the slave narrative. The prominent transcendentalist clergyman and social activist Theodore Parker considered slave narratives the only truly indigenous American literary form. "All the original romance of Americans is in them," Parker insisted in an 1849 commencement address, "not in the white man's novel" (Andrews, *To Tell a Free Story*, 98). A review of the *Narrative of the Life and Adventures of Henry Bibb, an American Slave* (1849), which rivals the works of Douglass and Brown in thrilling storytelling, facility of style, and distinctiveness of personal voice, shows how much white Americans were impressed by the human drama as well as the political force of the great slave narratives of the 1840s and 1850s. "This fugitive slave literature is destined to be a powerful lever," asserted the Boston *Chronotype* in 1849. "We see in it [fugitive slave literature] the easy and infallible means of abolitionizing the free states. Argument provokes argument, reason is met by sophistry; but narratives of slaves go right to the heart of men. We defy any man to think with patience or tolerance of slavery after reading Bibb's narrative. . . . Put a dozen copies of this book into every school, district, or neighbourhood in the free states, and you might sweep the whole north on a thorough-going liberty platform for abolishing slavery, everywhere and anywhere" (Foster, 20).

Important American feminist literary pioneers such as Lydia Maria Child, Margaret Fuller, and Harriet Beecher Stowe applauded slave narratives for their advocacy of human equality and their revelation of the plight of African American women in bondage. In a *New York Tribune* review of Douglass's *Narrative,* Fuller pronounced it "an excellent piece of writing," adding, "we have never read one more simple, true, coherent, and warm with genuine feeling" (Andrews, ed., *Critical Essays on Frederick Douglass,* 21). In her *Key to Uncle Tom's Cabin* (1853), published as a source book to *Uncle Tom's Cabin* (1852) after the latter became a controversial international best-seller, Stowe stated that she had modeled several of the major African American characters in her novel, including Uncle Tom himself, on the protagonists of slave narratives by Douglass and other black contemporaries and on her personal acquaintance with several female runaways. Child's belief in the importance of slave narratives both as antislavery propaganda and as human documents led her to assist Harriet Jacobs, a fugitive from North Carolina, in the publication of the first narrative authored by a female slave from the American South, *Incidents in the Life of a Slave Girl* (1861). Jacobs's frank treatment of interracial sex along with her story of a near-incredible struggle to escape her master and attain her freedom has made *Incidents* one of the most widely read slave narratives in the twentieth century. Yet Jacobs's autobiography received comparatively little notice when it first appeared, in part because of its explosive portrayal of sex but primarily because the looming shadow of civil war tended to obscure everything else in the eyes of readers in the United States. Had Child and Jacobs found a publisher a year or two earlier, *Incidents* might have rivaled William and Ellen Craft's riveting escape narrative *Running a Thousand Miles for Freedom*, published in London in 1860. In England, where the Crafts fled to avoid capture after their daring flight from Georgia to Philadelphia in 1848, their appearances and speaking engagements were heavily attended and widely reported. People from the towns and cities, commoners and royalty, turned out to hear a woman, to all appearances "white," and her dark-skinned husband describe their lives together as slaves and as hunted fugitives. Successful lecture tours in Great Britain and on the European continent by Douglass and Brown as well as the Crafts gave international prominence in the 1840s and 1850s to these expatriate writers and brought them into contact with progressive European writers and intellectuals, who in turn used their talents to spread the fame of these literary fugitives.

"This growing sympathy for the slave is more to be dreaded by the South than bullets and guns combined," wrote one supporter to William Lloyd Garrison, the leader of radical abolitionism in America during the peak of the antislavery crusade in the United States (Starling, 236). As the war of words between slave narrators and the defenders of slavery heated up in the 1840s and 1850s, Christian pacifists like Garrison clung to a nonviolent line, hoping that slavery could be extirpated from American soil by moral force, not armed conflict. Nevertheless, on the eve of the Civil War, few Garrisonians could forget the violent event that galvanized their crusade into a national movement thirty years earlier. The same year in which *Incidents in the Life of a Slave Girl* was published, Thomas Wentworth Higginson, contemplating the national conflict that would elevate him to command an all-black regiment in the Union army, recalled the career of Nat Turner, leader of the bloodiest slave revolt in U.S. history. In August 1861, exactly thirty years after Turner's uprising, Higginson described Turner in the *Atlantic Monthly* as a living "memory of terror and a symbol of retribution triumphant." Higginson estimated that Turner's autobiography, *The Confessions of Nat Turner,* published barely a week after Turner's execution on November 11, 1831, had sold some fifty thousand copies. Today we remember that brief narrative, recorded by a white Virginian who claimed to have worked from Prophet Nat's dictation, as the initiating text of the classic American slave narratives of the 1840s and 1850s. Almost all the great slave narrators of the American antislavery crusade ultimately incorporated Turner in some form or other into their own writing. In *My Bondage and My Freedom* (1855), his revised and expanded slave narrative, Douglass recalled a white man who threatened him with Turner's fate if the young slave kept teaching a Sabbath school for his fellow slaves. William Wells Brown made Nat Turner a heroic figure in the 1849 edition of the *Narrative of William W. Brown.* A year after the publication of his own narrative, Henry Bibb published a pamphlet, *Slave Insurrection in Southampton County, Virginia* (1850), keeping alive the story of Turner. Harriet Jacobs devoted an entire chapter of *Incidents in the Life of a Slave Girl* to her recollections of the response in her hometown of Edenton, North Carolina, to the news of the Turner revolt. With the exception of Mary Prince, who saw her story into print in London a few months before the Southampton slave revolt and who seems never to have visited North America, the writers of the great mid-nineteenth-century slave narratives not only looked back to Turner as a precursor but looked to one another for mutual support and inspiration through shared correspondence, laudatory introductions on the abolitionist lecture platform, and encouragement of one another's writing efforts.

The great nineteenth-century slave narratives typically carry a black message inside a white envelope. Prefatory (and sometimes appended) matter by whites, such as Garrison's preface to Douglass's *Narrative* or Amy Post's letter of recommendation appending Jacobs's *Incidents in the Life of a Slave Girl,* attests to the reliability and good character of the narrator. Sometimes these "authenticating documents" shed light on the conditions under which the narrative was composed and written. The texts that set the tone for the classic slave narratives of the 1830–1865 era—*The History of Mary Prince* (1831) and *The Confessions of Nat Turner* (1831)—begin with detailed commentary on the circumstances of composition as well as the character and bearing of the slave himself or herself. Thomas R. Gray, the Virginia lawyer who interviewed Turner before his execution for his part in the greatest slave revolt in U.S. history, reports: "By permission of the Jailor, I have had ready access to [Turner], and finding that he was willing to make a full and free confession of the origin, progress and consummation of the insurrectory movements of the slaves of which he was the contriver and head; I determined for the gratification of public curiosity to commit his statements to writing, and publish them, with little or no variation, from his own words. That this is a faithful record of his confessions, the annexed certificate of the County Court of Southampton, will attest." Thomas Pringle, the British reformer who financed the publication of *The History of Mary Prince,* explains in his preface: "The narrative was taken down from Mary's own lips by a lady who happened to be at the time residing in my family as a visitor. It was written out fully, with all the narrator's repetitions and prolixities, and afterwards pruned into its present shape; retaining, as far as was practicable, Mary's exact expressions and peculiar phraseology. No fact of importance has been omitted, and not a single circumstance or sentiment has been added."

Moving past the white-authored prefaces and recommendation letters to the actual narrative supplied by the fugitive slave, we find a story that centers on a rite of passage from slavery (usually in the South) to freedom (usually in the North, though sometimes the quest does not end until the fugitive's arrival in Canada or Great Britain). Usually the antebellum slave narrator portrays slavery as a condition of extreme physical, intellectual, emotional, and spiritual deprivation, a kind of hell on earth. Precipitating the narrator's decision to escape is some sort of personal crisis, such as the sale of a loved one or a dark night of the soul in which hope contends with despair for the spirit of the slave. Impelled by faith in God and a commitment to liberty and human dignity comparable, the North American slave narrator often stresses, to that of the Founding Fathers of the United States, the slave undertakes an arduous quest for freedom that climaxes in his or her arrival in the North. In many antebellum narratives, the attainment of freedom is signaled not simply by reaching the free states but by re-naming oneself and dedicating one's future to antislavery activism. Douglass and Brown provide particularly memorable accounts of the act of self-naming and their discovery of a profession in antislavery activism, lecturing, and writing.

To ensure the absolute factuality of slave narratives and to rebut charges from defenders of slavery that the narratives were distorted by biased abolitionist editors and ghostwriters, the antislavery movement in the mid-1840s made a priority of publishing narratives by slaves who could write their own stories. Although Frederick Douglass was by no means the first fugitive slave to write his own narrative, his was among the first to feature the subtitle *Written by Himself* on the title page of his *Narrative.* One of the reasons why Douglass's *Narrative* became the epitome of the slave narrative in the antebellum era was its powerful evocation of the idea of literacy as the key to individual dignity, freedom, and opportunity. After Douglass's *Narrative,* the presence of the subtitle *Written by Himself* on slave narratives such as Brown's and Bibb's, and *Written by Herself* in the case of Jacobs's, testified to the African American author's dedication to literary self-determination. Thus the quest for physical freedom became inter-twined in the work of a Douglass or Jacobs with the emergence from ignorance and unself-consciousness to knowledge and a sense of mission and social purpose.

One reason for identifying Mary Prince as a harbinger of the classic American slave narrator is her narrative's eloquent testimony to the tenacious integrity of her own selfhood despite overwhelming efforts to subvert it and brutalize her. The extensive detailing of atrocities suffered by Prince from her earliest childhood, on which so much of the *History* focuses, reminds us that this narrative was published by an English antislavery society and undoubtedly was intended to serve the society's propaganda interests. As her sponsor and editor, Thomas Pringle, comments in his preface, personal statements like Prince's guaranteed that "good people in England might hear from a slave what a slave had felt and suffered," instead of depending solely on what anti-slavery agitators thought about slavery and the slave. But more re-markable in Prince's *History* than her patience with and endurance of the wrongs done to her by a succession of West Indian masters is her gradual resistance, both verbal and physical, to her oppressors. The *History* shows how Prince refused the role of victim, choosing instead a series of strategies that would enable her to gain her freedom.

As important as Prince's example is in inaugurating black women's autobiography in the Americas, her active pursuit of freedom and the opportunity to voice her protest against slavery through the publication of her story underline the importance of this text to the evolution of the slave narrative tradition. Readers should note the fact that Prince approached her editor, Thomas Pringle, with the specific suggestion of writing her history. Hers was among the earliest slave narratives designed to tell the ugly but necessary truth about a socioeconomic system in the British West Indies that few people in England understood apart from the propaganda of the slaveowners. The way Prince tells that truth, both in the detail with which she recounts atrocities and in the frankness with which she speaks of many West Indian whites, must have surprised, if not shocked, many of her readers. Women, particularly those of Prince's caste and class, were not expected to speak out so bluntly in public, especially about their supposed betters. According to the prevailing standards of "true womanhood" in the early nineteenth century, a white woman would risk the charge of "unsexing" herself, of deserting her proper station in life and becoming something unnatural and morally perverse, by speaking out publicly against well-placed and presumably respectable men and women. A black woman who assailed her supposed betters risked even worse reprisals from whites. The racist mythology of the era did not treat black women as women but as breeding animals who had no right to even the limited degree of self-regard that white women were allowed in a male-dominated culture.

Mary Prince argues implicitly against this mythology by showing how cruel whites pushed her to the limits of her endurance. Only by talking back, saying no, and finally refusing to live any longer with her last master and mistress, the abusive Mr. and Mrs. John Woods, could Prince hope to preserve her physical and mental health and someday return to her husband. Her story concludes with a notable assertion from a black woman: "I know what slaves feel—I can tell by myself what other slaves feel, and by what they have told me. The man that says slaves be quite happy in slavery—that they don't want to be free—that man is either ignorant or a lying person." In this remark a black female slave declares herself to be a more reliable authority on slavery than any white man and to be fully capable of speaking for all her fellow slaves, both male and female, against any white man. The implication of this declaration should not be underestimated, since it constitutes the first claim in the African American autobiographical tradition for the black woman's authority as a spokesperson for *all* black people, regardless of sex, on the subject of "what slaves feel" about the morality of slavery.

The Confessions of Nat Turner was the first North American slave narrative to receive wide attention in the United States and particularly in the South. Unlike later classic slave narratives of the antislavery crusade, however, Turner's *Confessions* was not written by someone sympathetic to the slave in question or to the cause of emancipation in general. Turner's amanuensis, Thomas R. Gray, was a Virginia lawyer and one-time slaveowner who published the *Confessions* partly to enrich himself and partly to quell the rumors of impending servile insurrection that had whipsawed the South since Turner's actual uprising. In the first sentence of the *Confessions,* Gray announces, "The late insurrection in Southampton has greatly excited the public mind, and led to a thousand idle, exaggerated and mischievous reports," which he intends to dispel by enabling whites "to understand the origin and progress of this dreadful conspiracy, and the motives which influence its diabolical actors." By naming Turner's action an "insurrection" and a "conspiracy," Gray aims from the start to prejudice his readers as to who Turner was and how he should be understood. As an insurrectionist, Turner was by definition the leader of an unwarranted revolt against civil authority and the constituted government of the land.

Yet the first time the condemned slave gets a chance to speak in the *Confessions,* in the opening statement of what is purportedly Turner's oral narrative, we read: "SIR,—You have asked me to give a history of the motives which induced me to undertake the late insurrection, *as you call it*" (emphasis added). Replying to Gray in this way sets the tone for the entire narrative, in which Turner and Gray vie for the power to define Turner. Gray has the first and last word, we might say, because he writes the prefatory and concluding documents, leaving Turner with the narrative middle, which is not, of course, a text one can regard without some skepticism since Gray wrote this part of the text too. Still in reading Turner's narrative it is important to recognize the ways in which the condemned man attempted to represent himself according to his own lights, so that his sense of self and his understanding of his mission and its justification would not be buried under the weight of Gray's hostile rhetoric.

According to a dominant stereotype of "the Negro" in the early nineteenth century, one maintained by major European philosophers such as Georg Wilhelm Friedrich Hegel and David Hume, the African was an inveterate child, incapable of change, except for the worse, unless carefully supervised by whites. Hegel called Africa the land of perpetual childhood whose denizens were "capable of no development or culture." "As we see them at this day, such have they always been." "No change of their nature can be expected to result" from any efforts to elevate them from slavery to freedom, argued an early defender of slavery in the United States, and plenty of antebellum American writers echoed the notion that blacks were predestined to occupy their peculiar station in the scheme of things, both ethnologically and socioeconomically (Gates, 19–21).

The Confessions of Nat Turner plainly challenged this image of the Negro as a constant, lacking the motive or potential for change unless and until factored into the white man's equation. We should not overlook the important fact that the *Confessions* contains the first significant chronology of an African American life in the literature of the American South. The simple but unprecedented import of the "confession" Turner recounts lies in his making a history of *himself*, when all Gray asked him for was "a history of the motives" that led to his uprising. From the outset of his portion of the *Confessions*, Turner announces that to give a proper accounting of his motives, "I must go back to the days of my infancy, and even before I was born." Turner then makes a crucial statement that interjects him irreversibly into history: "I was thirty-one years of age the 2nd of October last, and born the property of Benj. Turner, of this county." What follows is Turner's personal story, carried through a discernible beginning, middle, and end, and bearing an authority and conviction that left Gray both appalled and fascinated: "The calm, deliberate composure with which he spoke of his late deeds and intentions, the expression of his fiend-like face when excited by enthusiasm, still bearing the stains of the blood of helpless innocence about him; clothed with rags and covered with chains; yet daring to raise his manacled hands to heaven, with a spirit soaring above the attributes of man; I looked on him and my blood curdled in my veins." In the end, Gray tries to explain Turner away with labels such as "fanatic," "madman," and "fiend." But Turner remains elusive; something about him is masked and unfathomable. "He is a complete fanatic, or plays his part most admirably," Gray admits. Thus we are left to wonder, even as Gray seems to have wondered, if Turner's *Confessions* is really a confession at all. Gray hoped he was recording the confession of a crime. But many readers today think it sounds more like a confession of faith, the faith of a man convinced that he was about to be martyred for having led a divinely sanctioned holy war. These tensions within the text are one of the main reasons why Turner and his *Confessions* remain so provocative in the American national imagination as well as in the slave narrative tradition.

Frederick Douglass, author of the most influential African American text of his era, rose through the ranks of the antislavery movement in the 1840s and 1850s to become the most electrifying speaker and commanding writer produced by black America in the nineteenth century. With the publication in 1845 of the *Narrative of the Life of Frederick Douglass, an American Slave, Written by Himself,* the antebellum slave narrative reached its epitome. Among slave narratives only Turner's *Confessions* challenged Douglass's *Narrative* for best-seller status in nineteenth-century America. In his own time Douglass's readership far outstripped that of such well-known white autobiographical writers as Henry David Thoreau, Margaret Fuller, and Walt Whitman. Douglass's writing, which eventually comprised three autobiographies, a short novel, and a substantial amount of journalism and oratory, was devoted primarily to the creation of a heroic image of himself designed to elevate the image of the slave in white Americans' eyes, to demonstrate the full potential of black people for freedom and a productive life as American citizens, and to inspire in African Americans the belief that color need not be a permanent bar to their achievement of the American Dream.

William Lloyd Garrison, Douglass's abolitionist mentor, introduced his *Narrative* by stressing how representative Douglass's experience of slavery had been. But Garrison could not help but note the extraordinary individuality of this black author's manner of rendering that experience. It is Douglass's style of self-presentation, through which he recreated the slave as an evolving self bound for mental as well as physical freedom, that has made his autobiography so memorable. In Douglass's *Narrative* the interlocking themes of freedom and literacy are given classic expression in African American literature. In the narratives of less gifted fugitive slaves, freedom is portrayed as a physical place—the North, or Canada or Great Britain—or, most pragmatically, as an economic condition, in which the African American can finally achieve self-sufficiency and dignity through independent work. Douglass's *Narrative* adds to these notions of freedom a more idealized dimension—freedom is a state of mind and spirit characterized by unrestrained self-expression through language, both spoken and written. This is why Douglass's *Narrative* does not conclude with his successful flight to the North but with his first foray onto the antislavery lecture platform several years thereafter. To Douglass the power to use language to change the minds of others is the greatest power that an individual can exert and the most compelling sign of that individual's freedom. Ultimate freedom inheres in the power of self-expression—to speak freely what is on one's mind and in one's heart. Douglass's *Narrative* testifies to this freedom both in its climactic portrayal of its protagonist freely speaking out against slavery and in the demonstrated fact of Douglass's having become a writer who authors his own story and thus participates in the great tradition of American literary individualism through autobiography.

In the history of African American literature, Douglass's importance and influence are virtually immeasurable. His *Narrative* gave the English-speaking world the most compelling and sophisticated rendition of an African American selfhood ever fashioned by a black writer up to that time. Douglass's literary artistry invested this model of selfhood with a moral and political authority that all aspirants to the role of African American culture hero—from Booker T. Washington to Malcolm X—have had to come to terms with in their own autobiographies and in their public careers.

Like Douglass, William Wells Brown, whether on the platform or in print, proved expert at capitalizing on his inherently interesting life and developing a rhetorically sophisticated style of self-representation. The edition of Brown's autobiography that appears in *The Civitas Anthology of African American Slave Narratives* is the longest of the four versions of his narrative published during the antebellum era; it appeared in London in 1849 under the title *Narrative of William W. Brown, an American Slave, Written by Himself.* Although packaged especially for a British reading audience, the fourth edition of the *Narrative* preserves the essence of Brown's story launched in 1847 when Brown's *Narrative* challenged Douglass's in popularity and sales.

The *Narrative of William W. Brown* typifies in its subject matter and development the basic plot structure of the antebellum slave narrative. Brown begins with three chapters on his childhood and gradual initiation into the horrors of slavery. In chapters 4 through 7 he comes to a mature realization of his condition as a slave, which leads to his resolution to try to seize his freedom. Chapter 8 ends with a failed escape attempt that testifies not only to Brown's dedication to freedom but also to his commitment to his mother. Brown then recalls a kind of dark night of the soul in chapter 9, occasioned by his visit to his mother just before she is to be sold away from him forever. Although profoundly desperate over the loss of his mother and sister, Brown still does not give up hope. Instead he plots his climactic escape, which is recounted in suspenseful detail in chapters 10 and 11. With freedom attained and a new name adopted, Brown concludes by noting his active engagement in antislavery work as a lecturer for William Lloyd Garrison's American Anti-Slavery Society. Demonstrating his commitment to this work, Brown added a chapter to the 1849 edition of his *Narrative* that recounts his participation in the violent but successful rescue of a fugitive slave family near Buffalo in the autumn of 1836.

Although in many ways Brown's story may be read as a paradigm of the genre in which he wrote, his manner of telling that story is more distinctively his own. Compared to the highly self-conscious rhetorical flourishes of Frederick Douglass's *Narrative,* Brown's decidedly understated, restrained, almost deadpan manner of recounting his life seems artless, though it is carefully crafted. Brown's portrayal of himself in his *Narrative* also represents a distinct departure from the self-image Douglass cultivates in *Narrative of the Life of Frederick Douglass.* More than any previous slave narrator, Douglass subscribes to what some have called the heroic fugitive school of American literature, in which a black rugged individualist struggles against the oppressiveness of bondage, dedicates himself singlemindedly to freedom, and overcomes all obstacles that stand between him and the goal of his indomitable striving. The turning point of Douglass's story evokes the traditional heroic ideal of male combat: the teenage Douglass battles hand to hand with the malicious slave breaker Edward Covey. Having wrested his sense of potential, pride, and worthiness for freedom from the tyrannical white man, the formerly humiliated slave is transformed into a heroic resister, a man with a mission that must inevitably triumph.

Brown seems to have almost deliberately refused to identify himself according to Douglass's myth of the heroic resister. From the outset of Brown's *Narrative,* the reader encounters admirable black men who pit themselves physically and morally against ruthless slaveowners in an effort to attain human dignity. Yet almost invariably they fail. The slaves who succeed against these overwhelming odds are those who learn how to use guile and deception to protect and advance their interests. Brown makes it clear that he too was a slave trickster, savvy enough to profess to his master's wife a matrimonial desire for a slave woman whom he did not love in order to divert his owners' attention away from his much stronger attachment to the idea of freedom. Even after an abortive escape attempt, when confronted with an exasperated, threatening master, Brown refuses to back down from a combat of wits. When his master demands to know why he has run away, Brown reminds the white man that he himself had authorized the slave to seek out a "good master" to whom he could hire his time for wages. So, with uppity logic, the slave maintains that he had done just that. "I had acted according to his orders. He had told me to look for a master, and I had been to look for one."

In sparring matches like this one, where the slave uses his wits to assert that he is and must be his own master, Brown testifies to a key element of real-world, day-to-day master-slave relationships. Only rarely did a violent physical confrontation resolve the tensions that underlay the slave's and the master's perpetual struggle for authority and power on the plantation. Much more typically the slave used a kind of mental jujitsu, similar to the tactics of the slaves' folk hero, Brer Rabbit, to deceive or divert his oppressors, thereby seizing mastery of the moment and gaining a measure of opportunity and freedom. Thus it is often the ordinary, the representative, and the nonheroic—even the antiheroic—that come to the fore in Brown's *Narrative*. Yet in Brown's willingness to focus on himself as a slave trickster and to explore a slave's survival ethic, we discover in his *Narrative* a striking brand of realism.

Henry Bibb extended this realism into one of the most absorbing picaresque road narratives published in African American or American literature of the nineteenth century. The *Narrative of the Life and Adventures of Henry Bibb, an American Slave, Written by Himself* (1849) details more candidly than any slave narrative of its time what Bibb termed "my manner of living on the road," by which he meant not only the road to freedom but also the road back into slavery. Bibb traveled them both five times between 1837 and 1841 in the process of attempting to free not only himself but his slave wife and child. Instead of focusing on his experience as a slave on plantations in Kentucky and Louisiana and among the Cherokees, Bibb chose to characterize his life as a harrowing pattern of flight and pursuit, capture and escape, as he struggled repeatedly despite enormous odds to rescue his entire family from bondage. This decision made Bibb's *Narrative* unusual not only for its treatment of his "life on the road"; it also made him the most memorable family man among the classic slave narrators. Bibb's love of freedom and devotion to his wife, Malinda, and his daughter, Mary Frances, placed him in some of the most heartrending conflicts ever depicted in the slave narrative.

In a remarkable letter from his master, Silas Gatewood, which forms part of the preface to his *Narrative,* Bibb allows himself to be labeled "a notorious liar, and a rogue." In numerous instances in his *Narrative,* Bibb both avows and vigorously defends his transgressions of conventional morality while engaged in either making his escape from slavery or returning to the South to effect the escape of his wife and daughter. Bibb admits that he lied to potential purchasers about his past, faked sorrow over the death of a master while plotting to run away, passed for white to trick a group of Irishmen into buying him a steamboat ticket to freedom, stole various articles from Gatewood (including a mule and a bowie knife), and robbed strangers of their horses to speed him on his getaways. His justification is this: "It is useless for a poor helpless slave, to resist a white man in a slaveholding State." Thus "the only weapon of self defense that I could use successfully was that of deception." To a white reader who would censure his robbing and horse thieving Bibb demands, "Who would not do the same thing to rescue a wife, child, father, or mother?" Bibb has no intention of yielding the moral high ground to any white reader of his *Narrative.* He is determined to show that as a father, husband, and slave he was caught in excruciating dilemmas that conventional moral standards could not resolve. He had to develop his own brand of "moral courage."

Who can tell how many Henry Bibbs there must have been among the fugitive slaves, men who either tried and failed to escape with their families or who escaped individually and then had to deal with the guilt and sense of obligation that their freedom brought with it? Bibb's dilemmas touch our sympathies in ways that Douglass and Brown, who seem to assimilate and succeed in the North without so much as a longing look backward, do not move us. Bibb's *Narrative* offers a strikingly emotional self-portrait of a man caught between two worlds, a slave past that he could not cast off or forget and a future in freedom to which he urgently desired to commit himself. The manner in which Bibb ultimately finds closure to his sense of obligation to his wife and child in slavery makes *Narrative of the Life and Adventures of Henry Bibb* a uniquely poignant autobiography in the slave narrative tradition.

As the slave narrative evolved in the crisis years of the 1850s and early 1860s, it addressed the problem of slavery with unprecedented candor, unmasking as never before the moral and social complexities of the American caste and class system in the North as well as the South. No slave narrator outdid William Craft in denouncing slavery and all those associated with it. In the opening pages of *Running a Thousand Miles for Freedom; or, The Escape of William and Ellen Craft from Slavery* (1860), Craft pronounced that in the American South "there is a greater want of humanity and high principle amongst the whites than among any other civilized people in the world." As proof of southern degeneracy, Craft accused whites in the South of trafficking in the persons of free white girls so as to satisfy the lust of slavery for more and more marketable bodies. "I have known worthless white people," Craft insisted, "to sell their own free children into slavery." By the time he had brought his astounding narrative to its end, Craft had roundly condemned all white Americans, northern as well as southern, for their bigotry and racial injustice. "It is well known in England, if not all over the world, that the Americans, as a people, are notoriously mean and cruel towards all colored persons, whether they are bond or free." Whereas most slave narratives, especially Douglass's and Brown's, tended to excoriate the South as a corrupt slavocracy while idealizing the North as a land of freedom and democracy, William Craft injected into *Running a Thousand Miles for Freedom* a criticism of American racism that knew no boundaries, neither those between North and South nor those between the United States and Canada. *Running a Thousand Miles for Freedom* is most often remembered for telling the inside story of the most sensational and unlikely escape two American slaves ever made to freedom. But Craft's narrative is also a powerful indictment of the Fugitive Slave Law of 1850, which made escaped slaves like the Crafts perpetual fugitives even after they had arrived in the so-called free states. Although the most famous element of their story was their one-thousand-mile flight from Georgia to Boston, just as important, after 1850, was the revelation by Craft of what happened to force his wife and him to leave Boston for Canada and why Canada proved to be no safe haven either. Because they could not feel safe until they reached England, where they resided from 1850 until well after slavery was abolished in the United States, William and Ellen Craft might well have titled their narrative "Running Two Thousand Miles for Freedom." Their saga of cross-dressing, racial imposture, and consummate role-playing places the Crafts among the most renowned con men and women in American literature. Readers have appreciated their story not only for its wonderful suspense but also for its humor, predicated on the ease with which these two wily slaves could dupe whites, southern and northern, simply by exploiting their delusions of racial superiority.

Harriet Jacobs, author of *Incidents in the Life of a Slave Girl* (1861), brought the era of the classic slave narrative to a close with the boldest and most provocative indictment of "the patriarchal institution" ever written by an American slave. Thirty years earlier Mary Prince had alluded to the sexual exploitation of slave women as one of the moral abominations of slavery. Challenging societal injunctions against women, black or white, speaking out on such matters, Jacobs undertook the arduous task of telling the suppressed truth about both the exploitation of slave women and their efforts to resist it. Previous male fugitive slave narrators such as Douglass and Brown had called attention to the sexual victimization of slave women by white men. But these men had said little about how slave women resisted victimhood or tried to exercise a measure of freedom within the restrictions of their oppression. Although she knew that she risked losing her readers' respect by speaking out, Jacobs refused to censor her account of her own sexual exploitation in slavery or her story of how she used her sexuality as a weapon against such exploitation. Writing an unprecedented mixture of confession, self-justification, and societal exposé, Jacobs turned her autobiography into a unique analysis of the myths and the realities that defined the situation of the African American woman and her relationship to the nineteenth century's "cult of true womanhood." As a result, *Incidents in the Life of a Slave Girl* occupies a crucial place in the history of both African American and American women's literature.

Incidents in the Life of a Slave Girl bears the classic subtitle *Written by Herself*, yet until the 1980s, when research confirmed its authorship and reliability, the authenticity of this autobiography has been doubted, partly because the title page of *Incidents* does not bear the name of its author. Nowhere in *Incidents*, in fact, does its author disclose her own identity. Instead, Jacobs calls herself Linda Brent and masks the important places and persons in her narrative in the manner of a novelist. "I had no motive for secrecy on my own account," the author insists in her preface to *Incidents*, but given the harrowing and sensational story she had to tell, the one-time fugitive felt she had little alternative but to shield herself from a readership whose understanding and empathy she could not take for granted. Still, as Jacobs states more than once in her story, her primary motive in writing *Incidents* was to enlist white women of the North on behalf of thousands of "slave mothers that are still in bondage" in the South.

One natural way of appealing to white women in the North was on the basis of a common experience of motherhood, for Jacobs was the mother of two children born in slavery. The crux of her problem, however, in claiming such commonality between herself and her readers was that Jacobs's two children had been the progeny of an illicit and clandestine liaison between herself and a white man, indeed, a North Carolina congressman. This man, Jacobs freely admits, was not her master, nor does she claim that he coerced her into submitting to his desires. "I knew what I did," Jacobs states evenly, "and I did it with deliberate calculation." But having acknowledged her share of responsibility for transgressing the most fundamental standard of proper womanly behavior in the nineteenth century, how could the narrator of *Incidents in the Life of a Slave Girl* ask respectable white women of the North to empathize with her? Jacobs decided to recount in candid detail the factors that led her to "plunge into the abyss" of proscribed interracial sex. She places heavy stress on the ways in which her master so harassed and abused her that, out of desperation, she turned to another white man as her lover, a man powerful and seemingly concerned enough to purchase their children's freedom, if not hers. Pausing to address her white female reader in chapter 10, Jacobs begs her "pity" and "pardon"—"I know I did wrong"—but adds, almost defiantly, "in looking back, calmly, on the events of my life, I feel that the slave woman ought not to be judged by the same standard as others," that is, as other women in freedom. Thus *Incidents in the Life of a Slave Girl* attacks slavery's subversion of the institutions of marriage, motherhood, and family by exposing the essential incompatibility between the social reality lived by enslaved black women in the South and the traditional sexual morality espoused by free white women of the North. The moral corruption of the South—Jacobs's pervasive theme in *Incidents*—is not the fault of the female slave but of the patriarchal system that makes her an object of male desire without giving her the right or the freedom to love or marry whom she chooses.

"Reader, my story ends with freedom; not in the usual way, with marriage," Jacobs writes in the conclusion of her narrative. Unlike the heroines of most nineteenth-century white women's novels and autobiographies, Jacobs never had the luxury of regarding marriage as the ultimate goal and source of fulfillment in her life. For Jacobs genuine freedom and "a home of my own" are more important. For freedom she was willing to endure seven years in hiding in a crawl space above a storeroom in her grandmother's house in Edenton, North Carolina, before escaping to the North in 1842. For her own and her children's freedom, she worked and saved as a seamstress and a nurse in the North, dodging slave catchers and moving her family from New York to Boston to Rochester to escape detection. In 1852, against her will, a white employer bought Jacobs's freedom. With it came a measure of relief from the rootless life and incessant anxieties of recapture that had plagued her for ten years. Yet in the end, Jacobs could not say she had achieved her lifelong goal of freedom. Freedom seemed tainted by its having been purchased, and it remained compromised by the North's racism and complicity with the slave power. Real freedom had become inextricably bound up in the idea of home, which did not mean a husband or some sort of domestic ideal but rather a defined physical as well as emotional space where an African American woman could exercise social and economic self-sufficiency and independence. On this remarkably feminist—or perhaps womanist—note of continued purposeful struggle, Jacobs concluded *Incidents in the Life of a Slave Girl,* dedicating herself, in effect, to what Virginia Woolf later phrased so famously as "a room of one's own."

Regardless of how Harriet Jacobs's individual quest for a home turned out, *Incidents in the Life of a Slave Girl* has made a room of its own on the ground floor of the African American slave narrative tradition. Douglass's *Narrative* and Jacobs's *Incidents* are now the two most widely studied and read slave narratives in America. Douglass fashioned the male fugitive slave into an African American hero in quest of freedom and knowledge. Jacobs pioneered the image of the fugitive slave woman as an articulate resister and survivor, a dedicated mother determined to redefine the very idea of home for African Americans in freedom. Yet all of their most important contemporaries—Mary Prince, Nat Turner, William Wells Brown, Henry Bibb, and William and Ellen Craft—played important roles in the antislavery literary campaign and in the establishment of models for black manhood and womanhood that could liberate white Americans from their prejudice and fear and inspire renewing cultural ideals of selfhood and community among African Americans. Today when we read prize-winning books such as Richard Wright's *Black Boy (American Hunger)* (1945), Ralph Ellison's *Invisible Man* (1952), *The Autobiography of Malcolm X* (1965), Margaret Walker's *Jubilee* (1965), Alex Haley's *Roots* (1976), Sherley Anne Williams's *Dessa Rose* (1986), Toni Morrison's *Beloved*

(1987), and Charles Johnson's *Middle Passage* (1990), we are reminded of the ongoing vitality of the classic slave narrative tradition of the antebellum era in contemporary African American letters.

REFERENCES

William L. Andrews, ed., *Critical Essays on Frederick Douglass* (Boston: G. K. Hall, 1991).

———, *To Tell a Free Story: The First Century of Afro-American Autobiography, 1760–1865* (Urbana: University of Illinois Press, 1986).

Joanne M. Braxton, *Black Women Writing Autobiography* (Philadelphia: Temple University Press, 1989).

Vincent Carretta, ed., *Unchained Voices: An Anthology of Black Authors in the English-Speaking World of the 18th Century* (Lexington: University Press of Kentucky, 1996).

Charles T. Davis and Henry Louis Gates Jr., *The Slave's Narrative* (New York: Oxford University Press, 1985).

William Edward Farrison, *William Wells Brown, Author and Reformer* (Chicago: University of Chicago Press, 1969).

Frances Smith Foster, *Witnessing Slavery: The Development of Ante-bellum Slave Narratives*, 2nd ed. (Madison: University of Wisconsin Press, 1994).

Henry Louis Gates Jr., *Figures in Black* (New York: Oxford University Press, 1987).

Harriet A. Jacobs, *Incidents in the Life of a Slave Girl*, ed. Jean Fagan Yellin (Cambridge: Harvard University Press, 1987).

William S. McFeely, *Frederick Douglass* (New York: W. W. Norton, 1991).

Marion Wilson Starling, *The Slave Narrative: Its Place in American History* (Washington, D.C.: Howard University Press, 1988).

Henry Irving Tragle, *The Southampton Slave Revolt of 1831* (Amherst: University of Massachusetts Press, 1971).

THE

HISTORY OF MARY PRINCE,

A WEST INDIAN SLAVE.

RELATED BY HERSELF.

___

WITH A SUPPLEMENT BY THE EDITOR.

___

To which is added,

THE NARRATIVE OF ASA-ASA,

A CAPTURED AFRICAN.

___

"By our sufferings, since ye brought us
To the man-degrading mart,—
All sustain'd by patience, taught us
Only by a broken heart,—
Deem our nation brutes no longer,
Till some reason ye shall find
Worthier of regard, and stronger
Than the colour of our kind." COWPER.

___

LONDON:
PUBLISHED BY F. WESTLEY AND A. H. DAVIS,
STATIONERS' HALL COURT;
AND BY WAUGH & INNES, EDINBURGH.

___

1831.

I

THE HISTORY OF

MARY PRINCE,

A WEST INDIAN SLAVE, RELATED BY HERSELF,

TO WHICH IS ADDED, THE NARRATIVE OF

ASA-ASA,

A CAPTURED AFRICAN

PREFACE.

THE IDEA OF writing Mary Prince's history was first suggested by herself. She wished it to be done, she said, that good people in England might hear from a slave what a slave had felt and suffered; and a letter of her late master's, which will be found in the Supplement, induced me to accede to her wish without further delay. The more immediate object of the publication will afterwards appear.

The narrative was taken down from Mary's own lips by a lady who happened to be at the time residing in my family as a visitor. It was written out fully, with all the narrator's repetitions and prolixities, and afterwards pruned into its present shape; retaining, as far as was practicable, Mary's exact expressions and peculiar phraseology. No fact of importance has been omitted, and not a single circumstance or sentiment has been added. It is essentially her own, without any material alteration further than was requisite to exclude redundancies and gross grammatical errors, so as to render it clearly intelligible.

After it had been thus written out, I went over the whole, carefully examining her on every fact and circumstance detailed; and in all that relates to her residence in Antigua I had the advantage of being assisted in this scrutiny by Mr. Joseph Phillips, who was a resident in that colony during the same period, and had known her there.

The names of all the persons mentioned by the narrator have been printed in full, except those of Capt. I——— and his wife, and that of Mr. D———, to whom conduct of peculiar atrocity is ascribed. These three individuals are now gone to answer at a far more awful tribunal than that of public opinion, for the deeds of which their former bond-woman accuses them; and to hold them up more openly to human reprobation could no longer affect themselves, while it might deeply lacerate the feelings of their surviving and perhaps innocent relatives, without any commensurate public advantage.

Without detaining the reader with remarks on other points which will be adverted to more conveniently in the Supplement, I shall here merely notice further, that the Anti-Slavery Society has no concern whatever with this publication, nor are they in any degree responsible for the statements it contains. I have published the tract, not as their

Secretary, but in my private capacity; and any profits that may arise from the sale will be exclusively appropriated to the benefit of Mary Prince herself.

THO. PRINGLE.

7, Solly Terrace, Claremont Square,

January 25, 1831.

P.S. Since writing the above, I have been furnished by my friend Mr. George Stephen, with the interesting narrative of Asa-Asa, a captured African, now under his protection; and have printed it as a suitable appendix to this little history.

T. P.

THE HISTORY OF MARY PRINCE,

A WEST INDIAN SLAVE.

(Related by herself.)

I WAS BORN at Brackish-Pond, in Bermuda, on a farm belonging to Mr. Charles Myners. My mother was a household slave; and my father, whose name was Prince, was a sawyer belonging to Mr. Trimmingham, a ship-builder at Crow-Lane. When I was an infant, old Mr. Myners died, and there was a division of the slaves and other property among the family. I was bought along with my mother by old Captain Darrel, and given to his grandchild, little Miss Betsey Williams. Captain Williams, Mr. Darrel's son-in-law, was master of a vessel which traded to several places in America and the West Indies, and he was seldom at home long together.

Mrs. Williams was a kind-hearted good woman, and she treated all her slaves well. She had only one daughter, Miss Betsey, for whom I was purchased, and who was about my own age. I was made quite a pet of by Miss Betsey, and loved her very much. She used to lead me about by the hand, and call me her little nigger. This was the happiest period of my life; for I was too young to understand rightly my condition as a slave, and too thoughtless and full of spirits to look forward to the days of toil and sorrow.

My mother was a household slave in the same family. I was under her own care, and my little brothers and sisters were my play-fellows and companions. My mother had several fine children after she came to Mrs. Williams,—three girls and two boys. The tasks given out to us children were light, and we used to play together with Miss Betsey, with as much freedom almost as if she had been our sister.

My master, however, was a very harsh, selfish man; and we always dreaded his return from sea. His wife was herself much afraid of him; and, during his stay at home, seldom dared to show her usual kindness to the slaves. He often left her, in the most distressed circumstances, to reside in other female society, at some place in the West Indies of which I have forgot the name. My poor mistress bore his ill-treatment with great patience, and all her slaves loved and pitied her. I was truly

27

attached to her, and, next to my own mother, loved her better than any creature in the world. My obedience to her commands was cheerfully given: it sprung solely from the affection I felt for her, and not from fear of the power which the white people's law had given her over me.

I had scarcely reached my twelfth year when my mistress became too poor to keep so many of us at home; and she hired me out to Mrs. Pruden, a lady who lived about five miles off, in the adjoining parish, in a large house near the sea. I cried bitterly at parting with my dear mistress and Miss Betsey, and when I kissed my mother and brothers and sisters, I thought my young heart would break, it pained me so. But there was no help; I was forced to go. Good Mrs. Williams comforted me by saying that I should still be near the home I was about to quit, and might come over and see her and my kindred whenever I could obtain leave of absence from Mrs. Pruden. A few hours after this I was taken to a strange house, and found myself among strange people. This separation seemed a sore trial to me then; but oh! 'twas light, light to the trials I have since endured!—'twas nothing—nothing to be mentioned with them; but I was a child then, and it was according to my strength.

I knew that Mrs. Williams could no longer maintain me; that she was fain to part with me for my food and clothing; and I tried to submit myself to the change. My new mistress was a passionate woman; but yet she did not treat me very unkindly. I do not remember her striking me but once, and that was for going to see Mrs. Williams when I heard she was sick, and staying longer than she had given me leave to do. All my employment at this time was nursing a sweet baby, little Master Daniel; and I grew so fond of my nursling that it was my greatest delight to walk out with him by the sea-shore, accompanied by his brother and sister, Miss Fanny and Master James.—Dear Miss Fanny! She was a sweet, kind young lady, and so fond of me that she wished me to learn all that she knew herself; and her method of teaching me was as follows:—Directly she had said her lessons to her grandmamma, she used to come running to me, and make me repeat them one by one after her; and in a few months I was able not only to say my letters but to spell many small words. But this happy state was not to last long. Those days were too pleasant to last. My heart always softens when I think of them.

At this time Mrs. Williams died. I was told suddenly of her death, and my grief was so great that, forgetting I had the baby in my arms, I ran away directly to my poor mistress's house; but reached it only in time to see the corpse carried out. Oh, that was a day of sorrow,—a heavy day! All the slaves cried. My mother cried and lamented her sore; and I (foolish creature!) vainly entreated them to bring my dear mistress back to life. I knew nothing rightly about death then, and it seemed a hard thing to bear. When I thought about my mistress I felt as if the world was all gone wrong; and for many days and weeks I could think of nothing else. I returned to Mrs. Pruden's; but my sorrow was too great to be comforted, for my own dear mistress was always in my mind. Whether in the house or abroad, my thoughts were always talking to me about her.

I stayed at Mrs. Pruden's about three months after this; I was then sent back to Mr. Williams to be sold. Oh, that was a sad sad time! I recollect the day well. Mrs. Pruden came to me and said, "Mary, you will have to go home directly; your master is going to be married, and he means to sell you and two of your sisters to raise money for the wedding." Hearing this I burst out a crying,—though I was then far from being sensible of the full weight of my misfortune, or of the misery that waited for me. Besides, I did not like to leave Mrs. Pruden, and the dear baby, who had grown very fond of me. For some time I could scarcely believe that Mrs. Pruden was in earnest, till I received orders for my immediate return.—Dear Miss Fanny! how she cried at parting with me, whilst I kissed and hugged the baby, thinking I should never see him again. I left Mrs. Pruden's, and walked home with a heart full of sorrow. The idea of being sold away from my mother and Miss Betsey was so frightful, that I dared not trust myself to think about it. We had been bought of Mr. Myners, as I have mentioned, by Miss Betsey's grandfather, and given to her, so that we were by right *her* property, and I never thought we should be separated or sold away from her.

When I reached the house, I went in directly to Miss Betsey. I found her in great distress; and she cried out as soon as she saw me, "Oh, Mary! my father is going to sell you all to raise money to marry that wicked woman. You are *my* slaves, and he has no right to sell you; but it is all to please her." She then told me that my mother was living with her father's sister at a house close by, and I went there to see her. It was a sorrowful meeting; and we lamented with a great and sore crying our unfortunate situation. "Here comes one of my poor picaninnies!" she said, the moment I came in, "one of the poor slave-brood who are to be sold tomorrow."

Oh dear! I cannot bear to think of that day,—it is too much.—It recalls the great grief that filled my heart, and the woeful thoughts that passed to and fro through my mind, whilst listening to the pitiful words of my poor mother, weeping for the loss of her children. I wish I could find words to tell you all I then felt and suffered. The great God above alone knows the thoughts of the poor slave's heart, and the bitter pains which follow such separations as these. All that we love taken away from us—Oh, it is sad, sad! and sore to be borne!—I got no sleep that night for thinking of the morrow; and dear Miss Betsey was scarcely less distressed. She could not bear to part with her old play-mates, and she cried sore and would not be pacified.

The black morning at length came; it came too soon for my poor mother and us. Whilst she was putting on us the new osnaburgs in which we were to be sold, she said, in a sorrowful voice, (I shall never forget it!) "See, I am *shrouding* my poor children; what a task for a mother!"—She then called Miss Betsey to take leave of us. "I am going to carry my little chickens to market," (these were her very words,) "take your last look of them; maybe you will see them no more." "Oh, my poor slaves! my own slaves!" said dear Miss Betsey, "you belong to me; and it grieves my heart to part with you."—Miss Betsey kissed us all, and, when she left us, my mother called the rest of the slaves to bid us goodbye. One of them, a woman named Moll, came with her infant in her arms. "Ay!" said my mother, seeing her turn away and look at her child with the tears in her eyes, "your turn will come next." The slaves could say nothing to comfort us; they could only weep and lament with us. When I left my dear little brothers and the house in which I had been brought up, I thought my heart would burst.

Our mother, weeping as she went, called me away with the children Hannah and Dinah, and we took the road that led to Hamble Town, which we reached about four o'clock in the afternoon. We followed my mother to the market-place, where she placed us in a row against a large house, with our backs to the wall and our arms folded across our breasts. I, as the eldest, stood first, Hannah next to me, then Dinah; and our mother stood beside, crying over us. My heart throbbed with grief and terror so violently, that I pressed my hands quite tightly across my breast, but I could not keep it still, and it continued to leap as though it would burst out of my body. But who cared for that? Did one of the many bystanders, who were looking at us so carelessly, think of the pain that wrung the hearts of the negro woman and her young ones? No, no! They were not all bad, I dare say, but slavery hardens white people's hearts towards the blacks; and many of them were not slow to make their remarks upon us aloud, without regard to our grief—though their light words fell like cayenne on the fresh wounds of our hearts. Oh those white people have small hearts who can only feel for themselves.

At length the vendue master, who was to offer us for sale like sheep or cattle, arrived, and asked my mother which was the eldest. She said nothing, but pointed to me. He took me by the hand, and led me out into the middle of the street, and, turning me slowly round, exposed me to the view of those who attended the vendue. I was soon surrounded by strange men, who examined and handled me in the same manner that a butcher would a calf or a lamb he was about to purchase, and who talked about my shape and size in like words—as if I could no more understand their meaning than the dumb beasts. I was then put up to sale. The bidding commenced at a few pounds, and gradually rose to fifty-seven,* when I was knocked down to the highest bidder; and the people who stood by said that I had fetched a great sum for so young a slave.

I then saw my sisters led forth, and sold to different owners; so that we had not the sad satisfaction of being partners in bondage. When the sale was over, my mother hugged and kissed us, and mourned over us, begging of us to keep up a good heart, and do our duty to our new masters. It was a sad parting; one went one way, one another, and our poor mammy went home with nothing.†

*Bermuda currency; about £38 sterling.
†Let the reader compare the above affecting account, taken down from the mouth of this negro woman, with the following description of a vendue of slaves at the Cape of Good Hope, published by me in 1826, from the letter of a friend,—and mark their similarity in several characteristic circumstances. The resemblance is easily accounted for: slavery wherever it prevails produces similar effects.—"Having heard that there was to be a sale of cattle, farm stock, &c. by auction, at a Veld-Cornet's in the vicinity, we halted our waggon one day for the purpose of procuring a fresh spann of oxen. Among the stock of the farm sold, was a female slave and her three children. The two eldest children were girls, the one about thirteen years of age, and the other about eleven; the youngest was a boy. The whole family were exhibited together, but they were sold separately, and to different purchasers. The farmers examined them as if they had been so many head of cattle. While the sale was going on, the mother and her children were exhibited on a table, that they might be seen by the company, which was very large. There could not have been a finer subject for an able painter than this unhappy group. The tears, the anxiety, the anguish of the mother, while she met the gaze of the multitude, eyed the different countenances of the bidders, or cast a heart-rending look upon the children; and the simplicity and touching sorrow of the young ones, while they clung to their distracted parent, wiping their eyes, and half concealing their faces,—contrasted with the marked insensibility and jocular countenances of the spectators and purchasers,—furnished a striking commentary on the miseries of slavery, and its debasing effects upon the hearts of its abettors. While the woman was in this distressed situation

My new master was a Captain I——, who lived at Spanish Point. After parting with my mother and sisters, I followed him to his store, and he gave me into the charge of his son, a lad about my own age, Master Benjy, who took me to my new home. I did not know where I was going, or what my new master would do with me. My heart was quite broken with grief, and my thoughts went back continually to those from whom I had been so suddenly parted. "Oh, my mother! my mother!" I kept saying to myself, "Oh, my mammy and my sisters and my brothers, shall I never see you again!"

Oh, the trials! the trials! they make the salt water come into my eyes when I think of the days in which I was afflicted—the times that are gone; when I mourned and grieved with a young heart for those whom I loved.

It was night when I reached my new home. The house was large, and built at the bottom of a very high hill; but I could not see much of it that night. I saw too much of it afterwards. The stones and the timber were the best things in it; they were not so hard as the hearts of the owners.*

Before I entered the house, two slave women, hired from another owner, who were at work in the yard, spoke to me, and asked who I belonged to? I replied, "I am come to live here." "Poor child, poor child!" they both said; "you must keep a good heart, if you are to live here."— When I went in, I stood up crying in a corner. Mrs. I—— came and took off my hat, a little black silk hat Miss Pruden made for me, and said in a rough voice, "You are not come here to stand up in corners and cry, you are come here to work." She then put a child into my arms, and, tired as I was, I was forced instantly to take up my old occupation of a nurse.—I could not bear to look at my mistress, her countenance was so stern. She was a stout tall woman with a very dark complexion, and her brows were always drawn together into a frown. I thought of the words of the two slave women when I saw Mrs. I——, and heard the harsh sound of her voice.

The person I took the most notice of that night was a French Black called Hetty, whom my master took in privateering from another vessel, and made his slave. She was the most active woman I ever saw, and

---

she was asked, 'Can you feed sheep?' Her reply was so indistinct that it escaped me; but it was probably in the negative, for her purchaser rejoined, in a loud and harsh voice, 'Then I will teach you with the sjamboc,' (a whip made of the rhinoceros' hide.) The mother and her three children were sold to three separate purchasers; and they were literally torn from each other."—*Ed.*

*These strong expressions, and all of a similar character in this little narrative, are given verbatim as uttered by Mary Prince.—*Ed.*

she was tasked to her utmost. A few minutes after my arrival she came in from milking the cows, and put the sweet-potatoes on for supper. She then fetched home the sheep, and penned them in the fold; drove home the cattle, and staked them about the pond side;* fed and rubbed down my master's horse, and gave the hog and the fed cow† their suppers; prepared the beds, and undressed the children, and laid them to sleep. I liked to look at her and watch all her doings, for hers was the only friendly face I had as yet seen, and I felt glad that she was there. She gave me my supper of potatoes and milk, and a blanket to sleep upon, which she spread for me in the passage before the door of Mrs. I———'s chamber.

I got a sad fright, that night. I was just going to sleep, when I heard a noise in my mistress's room; and she presently called out to inquire if some work was finished that she had ordered Hetty to do. "No, Ma'am, not yet," was Hetty's answer from below. On hearing this, my master started up from his bed, and just as he was, in his shirt, ran down stairs with a long cow-skin‡ in his hand. I heard immediately after, the cracking of the thong, and the house rang to the shrieks of poor Hetty, who kept crying out, "Oh, Massa! Massa! me dead. Massa! have mercy upon me—don't kill me outright."—This was a sad beginning for me. I sat up upon my blanket, trembling with terror, like a frightened hound, and thinking that my turn would come next. At length the house became still, and I forgot for a little while all my sorrows by falling fast asleep.

The next morning my mistress set about instructing me in my tasks. She taught me to do all sorts of household work; to wash and bake, pick cotton and wool, and wash floors, and cook. And she taught me (how can I ever forget it!) more things than these; she caused me to know the exact difference between the smart of the rope, the cart-whip, and the cow-skin, when applied to my naked body by her own cruel hand. And there was scarcely any punishment more dreadful than the blows I received on my face and head from her hard heavy fist. She was a fearful woman, and a savage mistress to her slaves.

There were two little slave boys in the house, on whom she vented her bad temper in a special manner. One of these children was a mulatto, called Cyrus, who had been bought while an infant in his moth-

---

*The cattle on a small plantation in Bermuda are, it seems, often thus staked or tethered, both night and day, in situations where grass abounds.
†A cow fed for slaughter.
‡A thong of hard twisted hide, known by this name in the West Indies.

er's arms; the other, Jack, was an African from the coast of Guinea, whom a sailor had given or sold to my master. Seldom a day passed without these boys receiving the most severe treatment, and often for no fault at all. Both my master and mistress seemed to think that they had a right to ill-use them at their pleasure; and very often accompanied their commands with blows, whether the children were behaving well or ill. I have seen their flesh ragged and raw with licks.—Lick—lick—they were never secure one moment from a blow, and their lives were passed in continual fear. My mistress was not contented with using the whip, but often pinched their cheeks and arms in the most cruel manner. My pity for these poor boys was soon transferred to myself; for I was licked, and flogged, and pinched by her pitiless fingers in the neck and arms, exactly as they were. To strip me naked—to hang me up by the wrists and lay my flesh open with the cow-skin, was an ordinary punishment for even a slight offense. My mistress often robbed me too of the hours that belong to sleep. She used to sit up very late, frequently even until morning; and I had then to stand at a bench and wash during the greater part of the night, or pick wool and cotton; and often I have dropped down overcome by sleep and fatigue, till roused from a state of stupor by the whip, and forced to start up to my tasks.

Poor Hetty, my fellow slave, was very kind to me, and I used to call her my Aunt; but she led a most miserable life, and her death was hastened (at least the slaves all believed and said so,) by the dreadful chastisement she received from my master during her pregnancy. It happened as follows. One of the cows had dragged the rope away from the stake to which Hetty had fastened it, and got loose. My master flew into a terrible passion, and ordered the poor creature to be stripped quite naked, notwithstanding her pregnancy, and to be tied up to a tree in the yard. He then flogged her as hard as he could lick, both with the whip and cow-skin, till she was all over streaming with blood. He rested, and then beat her again and again. Her shrieks were terrible. The consequence was that poor Hetty was brought to bed before her time, and was delivered after severe labor of a dead child. She appeared to recover after her confinement, so far that she was repeatedly flogged by both master and mistress afterwards; but her former strength never returned to her. Ere long her body and limbs swelled to a great size; and she lay on a mat in the kitchen, till the water burst out of her body and she died. All the slaves said that death was a good thing for poor Hetty; but I cried very much for her death. The manner of it filled me with horror. I could not bear to think about it; yet it was always present to my mind for many a day.

After Hetty died all her labors fell upon me, in addition to my own. I had now to milk eleven cows every morning before sunrise, sitting among the damp weeds; to take care of the cattle as well as the children; and to do the work of the house. There was no end to my toils— no end to my blows. I lay down at night and rose up in the morning in fear and sorrow; and often wished that like poor Hetty I could escape from this cruel bondage and be at rest in the grave. But the hand of that God whom then I knew not, was stretched over me; and I was mercifully preserved for better things. It was then, however, my heavy lot to weep, weep, weep, and that for years; to pass from one misery to another, and from one cruel master to a worse. But I must go on with the thread of my story.

One day a heavy squall of wind and rain came on suddenly, and my mistress sent me round the corner of the house to empty a large earthen jar. The jar was already cracked with an old deep crack that divided it in the middle, and in turning it upside down to empty it, it parted in my hand. I could not help the accident, but I was dreadfully frightened, looking forward to a severe punishment. I ran crying to my mistress, "O mistress, the jar has come in two." "You have broken it, have you?" she replied; "come directly here to me." I came trembling: she stripped and flogged me long and severely with the cow-skin; as long as she had strength to use the lash, for she did not give over till she was quite tired.—When my master came home at night, she told him of my fault; and oh, frightful! how he fell a swearing. After abusing me with every ill name he could think of, (too, too bad to speak in England,) and giving me several heavy blows with his hand, he said, "I shall come home tomorrow morning at twelve, on purpose to give you a round hundred." He kept his word—Oh sad for me! I cannot easily forget it. He tied me up upon a ladder, and gave me a hundred lashes with his own hand, and master Benjy stood by to count them for him. When he had licked me for some time he sat down to take breath; then after resting, he beat me again and again, until he was quite wearied, and so hot (for the weather was very sultry), that he sank back in his chair, almost like to faint. While my mistress went to bring him drink, there was a dreadful earthquake. Part of the roof fell down, and everything in the house went—clatter, clatter, clatter. Oh I thought the end of all things near at hand; and I was so sore with the flogging, that I scarcely cared whether I lived or died. The earth was groaning and shaking; everything tumbling about; and my mistress and the slaves were shrieking and crying out, "The earthquake! the earthquake!" It was an awful day for us all.

During the confusion I crawled away on my hands and knees, and laid myself down under the steps of the piazza, in front of the house. I was in a dreadful state—my body all blood and bruises, and I could not help moaning piteously. The other slaves, when they saw me, shook their heads and said, "Poor child! poor child!"—I lay there till the morning, careless of what might happen, for life was very weak in me, and I wished more than ever to die. But when we are very young, death always seems a great way off, and it would not come that night to me. The next morning I was forced by my master to rise and go about my usual work, though my body and limbs were so stiff and sore, that I could not move without the greatest pain.—Nevertheless, even after all this severe punishment, I never heard the last of that jar; my mistress was always throwing it in my face.

Some little time after this, one of the cows got loose from the stake, and eat one of the sweet-potato slips. I was milking when my master found it out. He came to me, and without any more ado, stooped down, and taking off his heavy boot, he struck me such a severe blow in the small of my back, that I shrieked with agony, and thought I was killed; and I feel a weakness in that part to this day. The cow was frightened at his violence, and kicked down the pail and spilt the milk all about. My master knew that this accident was his own fault, but he was so enraged that he seemed glad of an excuse to go on with his ill usage. I cannot remember how many licks he gave me then, but he beat me till I was unable to stand, and till he himself was weary.

After this I ran away and went to my mother, who was living with Mr. Richard Darrel. My poor mother was both grieved and glad to see me; grieved because I had been so ill used, and glad because she had not seen me for a long, long while. She dared not receive me into the house, but she hid me up in a hole in the rocks near, and brought me food at night, after everybody was asleep. My father, who lived at Crow-Lane, over the salt-water channel, at last heard of my being hid up in the cavern, and he came and took me back to my master. Oh I was loth, loth to go back; but as there was no remedy, I was obliged to submit.

When we got home, my poor father said to Capt. I———, "Sir, I am sorry that my child should be forced to run away from her owner; but the treatment she has received is enough to break her heart. The sight of her wounds has nearly broke mine.—I entreat you, for the love of God, to forgive her for running away, and that you will be a kind master to her in future." Capt. I——— said I was used as well as I deserved, and that I ought to be punished for running away. I then took courage and said that I could stand the floggings no longer; that I was weary of my life, and therefore I had run away to my mother; but mothers could only weep and mourn over their children, they could not save them from cruel masters—from the whip, the rope, and the cow-skin. He told me to hold my tongue and go about my work, or he would find a way to settle me. He did not, however, flog me that day.

For five years after this I remained in his house, and almost daily received the same harsh treatment. At length he put me on board a sloop, and to my great joy sent me away to Turk's Island. I was not permitted to see my mother or father, or poor sisters and brothers, to say goodbye, though going away to a strange land, and might never see them again. Oh the Buckra people who keep slaves think that black people are like cattle, without natural affection. But my heart tells me it is far otherwise.

We were nearly four weeks on the voyage, which was unusually long. Sometimes we had a light breeze, sometimes a great calm, and the ship made no way; so that our provisions and water ran very low, and we were put upon short allowance. I should almost have been starved had it not been for the kindness of a black man called Anthony, and his wife, who had brought their own victuals, and shared them with me.

When we went ashore at the Grand Quay, the captain sent me to the house of my new master, Mr. D———, to whom Captain I——— had sold me. Grand Quay is a small town upon a sandbank; the houses low and built of wood. Such was my new master's. The first person I saw, on my arrival, was Mr. D———, a stout sulky looking man, who carried me through the hall to show me to his wife and children. Next day I was put up by the vendue master to know how much I was worth, and I was valued at one hundred pounds currency.

My new master was one of the owners or holders of the salt ponds, and he received a certain sum for every slave that worked upon his premises, whether they were young or old. This sum was allowed him out of the profits arising from the salt works. I was immediately sent to work in the salt water with the rest of the slaves. This work was perfectly new to me. I was given a half barrel and a shovel, and had to stand up to my knees in the water, from four o'clock in the morning till nine, when we were given some Indian corn boiled in water, which we were obliged to swallow as fast as we could for fear the rain should come on and melt the salt. We were then called again to our tasks, and worked through the heat of the day; the sun flaming upon our heads like fire, and raising salt blisters in those parts which were not completely covered. Our feet and legs, from standing in the salt water for so many hours, soon became full of dreadful boils, which eat down in some cases to the very bone, afflicting the sufferers with great torment. We came home at twelve; ate our corn soup, called *blawly*, as fast as we could, and went back to our employment till dark at night. We then shovelled up the salt in large heaps, and went down to the sea, where we washed the pickle from our limbs, and cleaned the barrows and shovels from the salt. When we returned to the house, our master gave us each our allowance of raw Indian corn, which we pounded in a mortar and boiled in water for our suppers.

We slept in a long shed, divided into narrow slips, like the stalls used for cattle. Boards fixed upon stakes driven into the ground, without mat or covering, were our only beds. On Sundays, after we had washed the salt bags, and done other work required of us, we went into the bush and cut the long soft grass, of which we made trusses for our legs and feet to rest upon, for they were so full of the salt boils that we could get no rest lying upon the bare boards.

Though we worked from morning till night, there was no satisfying Mr. D———. I hoped, when I left Capt. I———, that I should have been better off, but I found it was but going from one butcher to another. There was this difference between them: my former master used to beat me while raging and foaming with passion; Mr. D——— was usually quite calm. He would stand by and give orders for a slave to be cruelly whipped, and assist in the punishment, without moving a muscle of his face; walking about and taking snuff with the greatest composure. Nothing could touch his hard heart—neither sighs, nor tears, nor prayers, nor streaming blood; he was deaf to our cries, and careless of our sufferings.—Mr. D——— has often stripped me naked, hung me up by the wrists, and beat me with the cow-skin, with his own hand, till my body was raw with gashes. Yet there was nothing very remarkable in this; for it might serve as a sample of the common usage of the slaves on that horrible island.

Owing to the boils in my feet, I was unable to wheel the barrow fast through the sand, which got into the sores, and made me stumble at every step; and my master, having no pity for my sufferings from this cause, rendered them far more intolerable, by chastising me for not being able to move so fast as he wished me. Another of our employments was to row a little way off from the shore in a boat, and dive for large stones to build a wall round our master's house. This was very hard work; and the great waves breaking over us continually, made us often so giddy that we lost our footing, and were in danger of being drowned.

Ah, poor me!—my tasks were never ended. Sick or well, it was work—work—work!—After the diving season was over, we were sent to the South Creek, with large bills, to cut up mangoes to burn lime with. Whilst one party of slaves were thus employed, another were sent to the other side of the island to break up coral out of the sea.

When we were ill, let our complaint be what it might, the only medicine given to us was a great bowl of hot salt water, with salt mixed with it, which made us very sick. If we could not keep up with the rest of the gang of slaves, we were put in the stocks, and severely flogged the next morning. Yet, not the less, our master expected, after we had thus been kept from our rest, and our limbs rendered stiff and sore with ill usage, that we should still go through the ordinary tasks of the day all the same.—Sometimes we had to work all night, measuring salt to load a vessel; or turning a machine to draw water out of the sea for the salt-making. Then we had no sleep—no rest—but were forced to work as fast as we could, and go on again all next day the same as usual. Work—work—work—Oh that Turk's Island was a horrible place! The people in England, I am sure, have never found out what is carried on there. Cruel, horrible place!

Mr. D——— had a slave called old Daniel, whom he used to treat in the most cruel manner. Poor Daniel was lame in the hip, and could not keep up with the rest of the slaves; and our master would order him to be stripped and laid down on the ground, and have him beaten with a rod of rough briar till his skin was quite red and raw. He would then call for a bucket of salt, and fling upon the raw flesh till the man writhed on the ground like a worm, and screamed aloud with agony. This poor man's wounds were never healed, and I have often seen them full of maggots, which increased his torments to an intolerable degree. He was an object of pity and terror to the whole gang of slaves, and in his wretched case we saw, each of us, our own lot, if we should live to be as old.

Oh the horrors of slavery!—How the thought of it pains my heart!

But the truth ought to be told of it; and what my eyes have seen I think it is my duty to relate; for few people in England know what slavery is. I have been a slave—I have felt what a slave feels, and I know what a slave knows; and I would have all the good people in England to know it too, that they may break our chains, and set us free.

Mr. D——— had another slave called Ben. He being very hungry, stole a little rice one night after he came in from work, and cooked it for his supper. But his master soon discovered the theft; locked him up all night; and kept him without food till one o'clock the next day. He then hung Ben up by his hands, and beat him from time to time till the slaves came in at night. We found the poor creature hung up when we came home; with a pool of blood beneath him, and our master still licking him. But this was not the worst. My master's son was in the habit of stealing the rice and rum. Ben had seen him do this, and thought he might do the same, and when master found out that Ben had stolen the rice and swore to punish him, he tried to excuse himself by saying that Master Dickey did the same thing every night. The lad denied it to his father, and was so angry with Ben for informing against him, that out of revenge he ran and got a bayonet, and whilst the poor wretch was suspended by his hands and writhing under his wounds, he run it quite through his foot. I was not by when he did it, but I saw the wound when I came home, and heard Ben tell the manner in which it was done.

I must say something more about this cruel son of a cruel father.— He had no heart—no fear of God; he had been brought up by a bad father in a bad path, and he delighted to follow in the same steps. There was a little old woman among the slaves called Sarah, who was nearly past work; and, Master Dickey being the overseer of the slaves just then, this poor creature, who was subject to several bodily infirmities, and was not quite right in her head, did not wheel the barrow fast enough to please him. He threw her down on the ground, and after beating her severely, he took her up in his arms and flung her among the prickly-pear bushes, which are all covered over with sharp venomous prickles. By this her naked flesh was so grievously wounded, that her body swelled and festered all over, and she died a few days after. In telling my own sorrows, I cannot pass by those of my fellow-slaves— for when I think of my own griefs, I remember theirs.

I think it was about ten years I had worked in the salt ponds at Turk's Island, when my master left off business, and retired to a house he had in Bermuda, leaving his son to succeed him in the island. He took me with him to wait upon his daughters; and I was joyful, for I was sick, sick of Turk's Island, and my heart yearned to see my native place again, my mother, and my kindred.

I had seen my poor mother during the time I was a slave in Turk's Island. One Sunday morning I was on the beach with some of the slaves, and we saw a sloop come in loaded with slaves to work in the salt water. We got a boat and went aboard. When I came upon the deck I asked the black people, "Is there any one here for me?" "Yes," they said, "your mother." I thought they said this in jest—I could scarcely believe them for joy; but when I saw my poor mammy my joy was turned to sorrow, for she had gone from her senses. "Mammy," I said, "is this you?" She did not know me. "Mammy," I said, "what's the matter?" She began to talk foolishly, and said that she had been under the vessel's bottom. They had been overtaken by a violent storm at sea. My poor mother had never been on the sea before, and she was so ill, that she lost her senses, and it was long before she came quite to herself again. She had a sweet child with her—a little sister I had never seen, about four years of age, called Rebecca. I took her on shore with me, for I felt I should love her directly; and I kept her with me a week. Poor little thing! hers has been a sad life, and continues so to this day. My mother worked for some years on the island, but was taken back to Bermuda some time before my master carried me again thither.*

After I left Turk's Island, I was told by some negroes that came over from it, that the poor slaves had built up a place with boughs and leaves, where they might meet for prayers, but the white people pulled it down twice, and would not allow them even a shed for prayers. A flood came down soon after and washed away many houses, filled the place with sand, and overflowed the ponds: and I do think that this was for their wickedness; for the Buckra men† there were very wicked. I saw and heard much that was very very bad at that place.

I was several years the slave of Mr. D—— after I returned to my native place. Here I worked in the grounds. My work was planting and

---

*Of the subsequent lot of her relatives she can tell but little. She says, her father died while she and her mother were at Turk's Island; and that he had been long dead and buried before any of his children in Bermuda knew of it, they being slaves on other estates. Her mother died after Mary went to Antigua. Of the fate of the rest of her kindred, seven brothers and three sisters, she knows nothing further than this—that the eldest sister, who had several children to her master, was taken by him to Trinidad; and that the youngest, Rebecca, is still alive, and in slavery in Bermuda. Mary herself is now about forty-three years of age.—*Ed.*

†Negro term for white people.

hoeing sweet-potatoes, Indian corn, plaintains, bananas, cabbages, pumpkins, onions, &c. I did all the household work, and attended upon a horse and cow besides,—going also upon all errands. I had to curry the horse—to clean and feed him—and sometimes to ride him a little. I had more than enough to do—but still it was not so very bad as Turk's Island.

My old master often got drunk, and then he would get in a fury with his daughter, and beat her till she was not fit to be seen. I remember on one occasion, I had gone to fetch water, and when I was coming up the hill I heard a great screaming; I ran as fast as I could to the house, put down the water, and went into the chamber, where I found my master beating Miss D——— dreadfully. I strove with all my strength to get her away from him; for she was all black and blue with bruises. He had beat her with his fist, and almost killed her. The people gave me credit for getting her away. He turned round and began to lick me. Then I said, "Sir, this is not Turk's Island." I can't repeat his answer, the words were too wicked—too bad to say. He wanted to treat me the same in Bermuda as he had done in Turk's Island.

He had an ugly fashion of stripping himself quite naked, and ordering me then to wash him in a tub of water. This was worse to me than all the licks. Sometimes when he called me to wash him I would not come, my eyes were so full of shame. He would then come to beat me. One time I had plates and knives in my hand, and I dropped both plates and knives, and some of the plates were broken. He struck me so severely for this, that at last I defended myself, for I thought it was high time to do so. I then told him I would not live longer with him, for he was a very indecent man—very spiteful, and too indecent; with no shame for his servants, no shame for his own flesh. So I went away to a neighboring house and sat down and cried till the next morning, when I went home again, not knowing what else to do.

After that I was hired to work at Cedar Hills, and every Saturday night I paid the money to my master. I had plenty of work to do there—plenty of washing; but yet I made myself pretty comfortable. I earned two dollars and a quarter a week, which is twenty pence a day.

During the time I worked there, I heard that Mr. John Wood was going to Antigua. I felt a great wish to go there, and I went to Mr. D———, and asked him to let me go in Mr. Wood's service. Mr. Wood did not then want to purchase me; it was my own fault that I came under him, I was so anxious to go. It was ordained to be, I suppose; God led me there. The truth is, I did not wish to be any longer the slave of my indecent master.

Mr. Wood took me with him to Antigua, to the town of St. John's, where he lived. This was about fifteen years ago. He did not then know whether I was to be sold; but Mrs. Wood found that I could work, and she wanted to buy me. Her husband then wrote to my master to inquire whether I was to be sold? Mr. D—— wrote in reply, "that I should not be sold to anyone that would treat me ill." It was strange he should say this, when he had treated me so ill himself. So I was purchased by Mr. Wood for 300 dollars, (or £100 Bermuda currency.)*

My work there was to attend the chambers and nurse the child, and to go down to the pond and wash clothes. But I soon fell ill of the rheumatism, and grew so very lame that I was forced to walk with a stick. I got the Saint Anthony's fire, also, in my left leg, and became quite a cripple. No one cared much to come near me, and I was ill a long long time; for several months I could not lift the limb. I had to lie in a little old out-house, that was swarming with bugs and other vermin, which tormented me greatly; but I had no other place to lie in. I got the rheumatism by catching cold at the pond side, from washing in the fresh water; in the salt water I never got cold. The person who lived in next yard, (a Mrs. Greene,) could not bear to hear my cries and groans. She was kind, and used to send an old slave woman to help me, who sometimes brought me a little soup. When the doctor found I was so ill, he said I must be put into a bath of hot water. The old slave got the bark of some bush that was good for the pains, which she boiled in the hot water, and every night she came and put me into the bath, and did what she could for me: I don't know what I should have done, or what would have become of me, had it not been for her.—My mistress, it is true, did send me a little food; but no one from our family came near me but the cook, who used to shove my food in at the door, and say, "Molly, Molly, there's your dinner." My mistress did not care to take any trouble about me; and if the Lord had not put it into the hearts of the neighbors to be kind to me, I must, I really think, have lain and died.

It was a long time before I got well enough to work in the house. Mrs. Wood, in the meanwhile, hired a mulatto woman to nurse the child; but she was such a fine lady she wanted to be mistress over me. I thought it very hard for a colored woman to have rule over me because

*About £67. 10s. sterling.

I was a slave and she was free. Her name was Martha Wilcox; she was a saucy woman, very saucy; and she went and complained of me, without cause, to my mistress, and made her angry with me. Mrs. Wood told me that if I did not mind what I was about, she would get my master to strip me and give me fifty lashes: "You have been used to the whip," she said, "and you shall have it here." This was the first time she threatened to have me flogged; and she gave me the threatening so strong of what she would have done to me, that I thought I should have fallen down at her feet, I was so vexed and hurt by her words. The mulatto woman was rejoiced to have power to keep me down. She was constantly making mischief; there was no living for the slaves—no peace after she came.

I was also sent by Mrs. Wood to be put in the Cage one night, and was next morning flogged, by the magistrate's order, at her desire; and this all for a quarrel I had about a pig with another slave woman. I was flogged on my naked back on this occasion: although I was in no fault after all; for old Justice Dyett, when we came before him, said that I was in the right, and ordered the pig to be given to me. This was about two or three years after I came to Antigua.

When we moved from the middle of the town to the Point, I used to be in the house and do all the work and mind the children, though still very ill with the rheumatism. Every week I had to wash two large bundles of clothes, as much as a boy could help me to lift; but I could give no satisfaction. My mistress was always abusing and fretting after me. It is not possible to tell all her ill language.—One day she followed me foot after foot scolding and rating me. I bore in silence a great deal of ill words: at last my heart was quite full, and I told her that she ought not to use me so;—that when I was ill I might have lain and died for what she cared; and no one would then come near me to nurse me, because they were afraid of my mistress. This was a great affront. She called her husband and told him what I had said. He flew into a passion: but did not beat me then; he only abused and swore at me; and then gave me a note and bade me go and look for an owner. Not that he meant to sell me; but he did this to please his wife and to frighten me. I went to Adam White, a cooper, a free black, who had money, and asked him to buy me. He went directly to Mr. Wood, but was informed that I was not to be sold. The next day my master whipped me.

Another time (about five years ago) my mistress got vexed with me, because I fell sick and I could not keep on with my work. She complained to her husband, and he sent me off again to look for an owner. I went to a Mr. Burchell, showed him the note, and asked him to buy me for my own benefit; for I had saved about 100 dollars, and hoped, with a little help, to purchase my freedom. He accordingly went to my master:—"Mr. Wood," he said, "Molly has brought me a note that she wants an owner. If you intend to sell her, I may as well buy her as another." My master put him off and said that he did not mean to sell me. I was very sorry at this, for I had no comfort with Mrs. Wood, and I wished greatly to get my freedom.

The way in which I made my money was this.—When my master and mistress went from home, as they sometimes did, and left me to take care of the house and premises, I had a good deal of time to myself, and made the most of it. I took in washing, and sold coffee and yams and other provisions to the captains of ships. I did not sit still idling during the absence of my owners; for I wanted, by all honest means, to earn money to buy my freedom. Sometimes I bought a hog cheap on board ship, and sold it for double the money on shore; and I also earned a good deal by selling coffee. By this means I by degrees acquired a little cash. A gentleman also lent me some to help to buy my freedom—but when I could not get free he got it back again. His name was Captain Abbot.

My master and mistress went on one occasion into the country, to Date Hill, for change of air, and carried me with them to take charge of the children, and to do the work of the house. While I was in the country, I saw how the field negroes are worked in Antigua. They are worked very hard and fed but scantily. They are called out to work before daybreak, and come home after dark; and then each has to heave his bundle of grass for the cattle in the pen. Then, on Sunday morning, each slave has to go out and gather a large bundle of grass; and, when they bring it home, they have all to sit at the manager's door and wait till he come out: often have they to wait there till past eleven o'clock, without any breakfast. After that, those that have yams or potatoes, or fire-wood to sell, hasten to market to buy a dog's worth* of salt fish, or pork, which is a great treat for them. Some of them buy a little pickle out of the shad barrels, which they call sauce, to season their yams and Indian corn. It is very wrong, I know, to work on Sunday or go to market; but will not God call the Buckra men to answer for this on the great day of judgment—since they will give the slaves no other day?

*A dog is the 72nd part of a dollar.

While we were at Date Hill Christmas came; and the slave woman who had the care of the place (which then belonged to Mr. Roberts the marshal), asked me to go with her to her husband's house, to a Methodist meeting for prayer, at a plantation called Winthorps. I went; and they were the first prayers I ever understood. One woman prayed; and then they all sung a hymn; then there was another prayer and another hymn; and then they all spoke by turns of their own griefs as sinners. The husband of the woman I went with was a black driver. His name was Henry. He confessed that he had treated the slaves very cruelly; but said that he was compelled to obey the orders of his master. He prayed them all to forgive him, and he prayed that God would forgive him. He said it was a horrid thing for a ranger* to have sometimes to beat his own wife or sister; but he must do so if ordered by his master.

I felt sorry for my sins also. I cried the whole night, but I was too much ashamed to speak. I prayed God to forgive me. This meeting had a great impression on my mind, and led my spirit to the Moravian church; so that when I got back to town, I went and prayed to have my name put down in the Missionaries' book; and I followed the church earnestly every opportunity. I did not then tell my mistress about it; for I knew that she would not give me leave to go. But I felt I *must* go. Whenever I carried the children their lunch at school, I ran round and went to hear the teachers.

The Moravian ladies (Mrs. Richter, Mrs. Olufsen, and Mrs. Sauter) taught me to read in the class; and I got on very fast. In this class there were all sorts of people, old and young, grey headed folks and children; but most of them were free people. After we had done spelling, we tried to read in the Bible. After the reading was over, the missionary gave out a hymn for us to sing. I dearly loved to go to the church, it was so solemn. I never knew rightly that I had much sin till I went there. When I found out that I was a great sinner, I was very sorely grieved, and very much frightened. I used to pray God to pardon my sins for Christ's sake, and forgive me for everything I had done amiss; and when I went home to my work, I always thought about what I had heard from the missionaries, and wished to be good that I might go to heaven. After a while I was admitted a candidate for the holy Communion.—I had been baptized long before this, in August 1817, by the Rev. Mr. Curtin, of the English Church, after I had been taught to repeat the Creed and the Lord's Prayer. I wished at that time to attend a

*The head negro of an estate—a person who has the chief superintendence under the manager.

Sunday School taught by Mr. Curtin, but he would not receive me without a written note from my master, granting his permission. I did not ask my owner's permission, from the belief that it would be refused; so that I got no further instruction at that time from the English Church.*

Some time after I began to attend the Moravian Church, I met with Daniel James, afterwards my dear husband. He was a carpenter and cooper to his trade; an honest, hard-working, decent black man, and a widower. He had purchased his freedom of his mistress, old Mrs. Baker, with money he had earned whilst a slave. When he asked me to marry him, I took time to consider the matter over with myself, and would not say yes till he went to church with me and joined the Moravians. He was very industrious after he bought his freedom; and he had hired a comfortable house, and had convenient things about him. We were joined in marriage, about Christmas 1826, in the Moravian Chapel at Spring Gardens, by the Rev. Mr. Olufsen. We could not be married in the English Church. English marriage is not allowed to slaves; and no free man can marry a slave woman.

When Mr. Wood heard of my marriage, he flew into a great rage, and sent for Daniel, who was helping to build a house for his old mistress. Mr. Wood asked him who gave him a right to marry a slave of his? My husband said, "Sir, I am a free man, and thought I had a right to choose a wife; but if I had known Molly was not allowed to have a husband, I should not have asked her to marry me." Mrs. Wood was more vexed about my marriage than her husband. She could not forgive me for getting married, but stirred up Mr. Wood to flog me dreadfully with the horsewhip. I thought it very hard to be whipped at my time of life for getting a husband—I told her so. She said that she would not have nigger men about the yards and premises, or allow a nigger man's clothes to be washed in the same tub where hers were washed. She was fearful, I think, that I should lose her time, in order to wash and do things for my husband: but I had then no time to wash for myself; I was obliged to put out my own clothes, though I was always at the wash-tub.

*She possesses a copy of Mrs. Trimmer's "Charity School Spelling Book," presented to her by the Rev. Mr. Curtin, and dated August 30, 1817. In this book her name is written "Mary, Princess of Wales"—an appellation which, she says, was given her by her owners. It is a common practice with the colonists to give ridiculous names of this description to their slaves; being, in fact, one of the numberless modes of expressing the habitual contempt with which they regard the negro race.—In printing this narrative we have retained Mary's paternal name of Prince.—*Ed.*

I had not much happiness in my marriage, owing to my being a slave. It made my husband sad to see me so ill-treated. Mrs. Wood was always abusing me about him. She did not lick me herself, but she got her husband to do it for her, whilst she fretted the flesh off my bones. Yet for all this she would not sell me. She sold five slaves whilst I was with her; but though she was always finding fault with me, she would not part with me. However, Mr. Wood afterwards allowed Daniel to have a place to live in our yard, which we were very thankful for.

After this, I fell ill again with the rheumatism, and was sick a long time; but whether sick or well, I had my work to do. About this time I asked my master and mistress to let me buy my own freedom. With the help of Mr. Burchell, I could have found the means to pay Mr. Wood; for it was agreed that I should afterwards serve Mr. Burchell awhile, for the cash he was to advance for me. I was earnest in the request to my owners; but their hearts were hard—too hard to consent. Mrs. Wood was very angry—she grew quite outrageous—she called me a black devil, and asked me who had put freedom into my head. "To be free is very sweet," I said: but she took good care to keep me a slave. I saw her change color, and I left the room.

About this time my master and mistress were going to England to put their son to school, and bring their daughters home; and they took me with them to take care of the child. I was willing to come to England: I thought that by going there I should probably get cured of my rheumatism, and should return with my master and mistress, quite well, to my husband. My husband was willing for me to come away, for he had heard that my master would free me,—and I also hoped this might prove true; but it was all a false report.

The steward of the ship was very kind to me. He and my husband were in the same class in the Moravian Church. I was thankful that he was so friendly, for my mistress was not kind to me on the passage; and she told me, when she was angry, that she did not intend to treat me any better in England than in the West Indies—that I need not expect it. And she was as good as her word.

When we drew near to England, the rheumatism seized all my limbs worse than ever, and my body was dreadfully swelled. When we landed at the Tower, I showed my flesh to my mistress, but she took no great notice of it. We were obliged to stop at the tavern till my master got a house; and a day or two after, my mistress sent me down into the wash-house to learn to wash in the English way. In the West Indies we wash with cold water—in England with hot. I told my mistress I was afraid that putting my hands first into the hot water and then into the cold, would increase the pain in my limbs. The doctor had told my mistress long before I came from the West Indies, that I was a sickly body and the washing did not agree with me. But Mrs. Wood would not release me from the tub, so I was forced to do as I could. I grew worse, and could not stand to wash. I was then forced to sit down with the tub before me, and often through pain and weakness was reduced to kneel or to sit down on the floor, to finish my task. When I complained to my mistress of this, she only got into a passion as usual, and said washing in hot water could not hurt anyone;—that I was lazy and insolent, and wanted to be free of my work; but that she would make me do it. I thought her very hard on me, and my heart rose up within me. However I kept still at that time, and went down again to wash the child's things; but the English washerwomen who were at work there, when they saw that I was so ill, had pity upon me and washed them for me.

After that, when we came up to live in Leigh Street, Mrs. Wood sorted out five bags of clothes which we had used at sea, and also such as had been worn since we came on shore, for me and the cook to wash. Elizabeth the cook told her, that she did not think that I was able to stand to the tub, and that she had better hire a woman. I also said myself, that I had come over to nurse the child, and that I was sorry I had come from Antigua, since mistress would work me so hard, without compassion for my rheumatism. Mr. and Mrs. Wood, when they heard this, rose up in a passion against me. They opened the door and bade me get out. But I was a stranger, and did not know one door in the street from another, and was unwilling to go away. They made a dreadful uproar, and from that day they constantly kept cursing and abusing me. I was obliged to wash, though I was very ill. Mrs. Wood, indeed once hired a washerwoman, but she was not well treated, and would come no more.

My master quarrelled with me another time, about one of our great washings, his wife having stirred him up to do so. He said he would compel me to do the whole of the washing given out to me, or if I again refused, he would take a short course with me: he would either send me down to the brig in the river, to carry me back to Antigua, or he would turn me at once out of doors, and let me provide for myself. I said I would willingly go back, if he would let me purchase my own freedom. But this enraged him more than all the rest: he cursed and swore at me dreadfully, and said he would never sell my freedom—if I wished to be free, I was free in England, and I might go and try what freedom would do for me, and be d———d. My heart was very sore with this treatment, but I had to go on. I continued to do my work, and did all I could to give satisfaction, but all would not do.

Shortly after, the cook left them, and then matters went on ten times worse. I always washed the child's clothes without being commanded to do it, and anything else that was wanted in the family; though still I was very sick—very sick indeed. When the great washing came round, which was every two months, my mistress got together again a great many heavy things, such as bed-ticks, bed-coverlets, &c. for me to wash. I told her I was too ill to wash such heavy things that day. She said, she supposed I thought myself a free woman, but I was not; and if I did not do it directly I should be instantly turned out of doors. I stood a long time before I could answer, for I did not know well what to do. I knew that I was free in England, but I did not know where to go, or how to get my living; and therefore, I did not like to leave the house. But Mr. Wood said he would send for a constable to thrust me out; and at last I took courage and resolved that I would not be longer thus treated, but would go and trust to Providence. This was the fourth time they had threatened to turn me out, and, go where I might, I was determined now to take them at their word; though I thought it very hard, after I had lived with them for thirteen years, and worked for them like a horse, to be driven out in this way, like a beggar. My only fault was being sick, and therefore unable to please my mistress, who thought she never could get work enough out of her slaves; and I told them so: but they only abused me and drove me out. This took place from two to three months, I think, after we came to England.

When I came away, I went to the man (one Mash) who used to black the shoes of the family, and asked his wife to get somebody to go with me to Hatton Garden to the Moravian Missionaries: these were the only persons I knew in England. The woman sent a young girl with me to the mission house, and I saw there a gentleman called Mr. Moore. I told him my whole story, and how my owners had treated me, and asked him to take in my trunk with what few clothes I had. The missionaries were very kind to me—they were sorry for my destitute situation, and gave me leave to bring my things to be placed under their care. They were very good people, and they told me to come to the church.

When I went back to Mr. Wood's to get my trunk, I saw a lady, Mrs. Pell, who was on a visit to my mistress. When Mr. and Mrs. Wood heard me come in, they set this lady to stop me, finding that they had gone too far with me. Mrs. Pell came out to me, and said, "Are you really going to leave, Molly? Don't leave, but come into the country with me." I believe she said this because she thought Mrs. Wood would easily get me back again. I replied to her, "Ma'am, this is the fourth time my master and mistress have driven me out, or threatened to drive me—and I will give them no more occasion to bid me go. I was not willing to leave them, for I am a stranger in this country, but now I must go—I can stay no longer to be so used." Mrs. Pell then went upstairs to my mistress, and told that I would go, and that she could not stop me. Mrs. Wood was very much hurt and frightened when she found I was determined to go out that day. She said, "If she goes the people will rob her, and then turn her adrift." She did not say this to me, but she spoke it loud enough for me to hear; that it might induce me not to go, I suppose. Mr. Wood also asked me where I was going to. I told him where I had been, and that I should never have gone away had I not been driven out by my owners. He had given me a written paper some time before, which said that I had come with them to England by my own desire; and that was true. It said also that I left them of my own free will, because I was a free woman in England; and that I was idle and would not do my work—which was not true. I gave this paper afterwards to a gentleman who inquired into my case.*

I went into the kitchen and got my clothes out. The nurse and the servant girl were there, and I said to the man who was going to take out my trunk, "Stop, before you take up this trunk, and hear what I have to say before these people. I am going out of this house, as I was ordered; but I have done no wrong at all to my owners, neither here nor in the West Indies. I always worked very hard to please them, both by night and day; but there was no giving satisfaction, for my mistress could never be satisfied with reasonable service. I told my mistress I was sick, and yet she has ordered me out of doors. This is the fourth time; and now I am going out."

And so I came out, and went and carried my trunk to the Moravians. I then returned back to Mash the shoe-black's house, and begged his wife to take me in. I had a little West Indian money in my trunk; and they got it changed for me. This helped to support me for a little while. The man's wife was very kind to me. I was very sick, and she boiled nourishing things up for me. She also sent for a doctor to see

*See page 55.

me, and he sent me medicine, which did me good, though I was ill for a long time with the rheumatic pains. I lived a good many months with these poor people, and they nursed me, and did all that lay in their power to serve me. The man was well acquainted with my situation, as he used to go to and fro to Mr. Wood's house to clean shoes and knives; and he and his wife were sorry for me.

About this time, a woman of the name of Hill told me of the Anti-Slavery Society, and went with me to their office, to inquire if they could do anything to get me my freedom, and send me back to the West Indies. The gentlemen of the Society took me to a lawyer, who examined very strictly into my case; but told me that the laws of England could do nothing to make me free in Antigua.* However they did all they could for me: they gave me a little money from time to time to keep me from want; and some of them went to Mr. Wood to try to persuade him to let me return a free woman to my husband; but though they offered him, as I have heard, a large sum for my freedom, he was sulky and obstinate, and would not consent to let me go free.

This was the first winter I spent in England, and I suffered much from the severe cold, and from the rheumatic pains, which still at times torment me. However, Providence was very good to me, and I got many friends—especially some Quaker ladies, who hearing of my case, came and sought me out, and gave me good warm clothing and money. Thus I had great cause to bless God in my affliction.

When I got better I was anxious to get some work to do, as I was unwilling to eat the bread of idleness. Mrs. Mash, who was a laundress, recommended me to a lady for a charwoman. She paid me very handsomely for what work I did, and I divided the money with Mrs. Mash; for though very poor, they gave me food when my own money was done, and never suffered me to want.

In the spring, I got into service with a lady, who saw me at the house where I sometimes worked as a charwoman. This lady's name was Mrs. Forsyth. She had been in the West Indies, and was accustomed to Blacks, and liked them. I was with her six months, and went with her to Margate. She treated me well, and gave me a good character when she left London.†

After Mrs. Forsyth went away, I was again out of place, and went to

---

*She came first to the Anti-Slavery Office in Aldermanbury, about the latter end of November 1828; and her case was referred to Mr. George Stephen to be investigated. More of this hereafter.—Ed.

†She refers to a written certificate which will be inserted afterwards.

lodgings, for which I paid two shillings a week, and found coals and candle. After eleven weeks, the money I had saved in service was all gone, and I was forced to go back to the Anti-Slavery office to ask a supply, till I could get another situation. I did not like to go back—I did not like to be idle. I would rather work for my living than get it for nothing. They were very good to give me a supply, but I felt shame at being obliged to apply for relief whilst I had strength to work.

At last I went into the service of Mr. and Mrs. Pringle, where I have been ever since, and am as comfortable as I can be while separated from my dear husband, and away from my own country and all old friends and connections. My dear mistress teaches me daily to read the word of God, and takes great pains to make me understand it. I enjoy the great privilege of being enabled to attend church three times on the Sunday: and I have met with many kind friends since I have been here, both clergymen and others. The Rev. Mr. Young, who lives in the next house, has shown me much kindness, and taken much pains to instruct me, particularly while my master and mistress were absent in Scotland. Nor must I forget, among my friends, the Rev. Mr. Mortimer, the good clergyman of the parish, under whose ministry I have now sat for upwards of twelve months. I trust in God I have profited by what I have heard from him. He never keeps back the truth, and I think he has been the means of opening my eyes and ears much better to understand the word of God. Mr. Mortimer tells me that he cannot open the eyes of my heart, but that I must pray to God to change my heart, and make me to know the truth, and the truth will make me free.

I still live in the hope that God will find a way to give me my liberty, and give me back to my husband. I endeavor to keep down my fretting, and to leave all to Him, for he knows what is good for me better than I know myself. Yet, I must confess, I find it a hard and heavy task to do so.

I am often much vexed, and I feel great sorrow when I hear some people in this country say, that the slaves do not need better usage, and do not want to be free.* They believe the foreign people,† who deceive them, and say slaves are happy. I say, Not so. How can slaves be happy when they have the halter round their neck and the whip upon their back? and are disgraced and thought no more of than beasts?—and are separated from their mothers, and husbands, and children, and sis-

---

*The whole of this paragraph especially, is given as nearly as was possible in Mary's precise words.
†She means West Indians.

ters, just as cattle are sold and separated? Is it happiness for a driver in the field to take down his wife or sister or child, and strip them, and whip them in such a disgraceful manner?—women that have had children exposed in the open field to shame! There is no modesty or decency shown by the owner to his slaves; men, women, and children are exposed alike. Since I have been here I have often wondered how English people can go out into the West Indies and act in such a beastly manner. But when they go to the West Indies, they forget God and all feeling of shame, I think, since they can see and do such things. They tie up slaves like hogs—moor★ them up like cattle, and they lick them, so as hogs, or cattle, or horses never were flogged;—and yet they come home and say, and make some good people believe, that slaves don't want to get out of slavery. But they put a cloak about the truth. It is not so. All slaves want to be free—to be free is very sweet. I will say the truth to English people who may read this history that my good friend, Miss S———, is now writing down for me. I have been a slave myself—I know what slaves feel—I can tell by myself what other slaves feel, and by what they have told me. The man that says slaves be quite happy in slavery—that they don't want to be free—that man is either ignorant or a lying person. I never heard a slave say so. I never heard a Buckra man say so, till I heard tell of it in England. Such people ought to be ashamed of themselves. They can't do without slaves, they say. What's the reason they can't do without slaves as well as in England? No slaves here—no whips—no stocks—no punishment, except for wicked people. They hire servants in England; and if they don't like them, they send them away: they can't lick them. Let them work ever so hard in England, they are far better off than slaves. If they get a bad master, they give warning and go hire to another. They have their liberty. That's just what *we* want. We don't mind hard work, if we had proper treatment, and proper wages like English servants, and proper time given in the week to keep us from breaking the Sabbath. But they won't give it: they will have work—work—work, night and day, sick or well, till we are quite done up; and we must not speak up nor look amiss, however much we be abused. And then when we are quite done up, who cares for us, more than for a lame horse? This is slavery. I tell it, to let English people know the truth; and I hope they will never leave off to pray God, and call loud to the great King of England, till all the poor blacks be given free, and slavery done up for evermore.

★A West Indian phrase: to fasten or tie up.

SUPPLEMENT TO THE

HISTORY OF MARY PRINCE.

BY THE EDITOR.

LEAVING MARY'S NARRATIVE, for the present, without comment
to the reader's reflections, I proceed to state some circumstances connected with her case which have fallen more particularly under my
own notice, and which I consider it incumbent now to lay fully before
the public.

About the latter end of November, 1828, this poor woman found
her way to the office of the Anti-Slavery Society in Aldermanbury, by
the aid of a person who had become acquainted with her situation, and
had advised her to apply there for advice and assistance. After some
preliminary examination into the accuracy of the circumstances related by her, I went along with her to Mr. George Stephen, solicitor,
and requested him to investigate and draw up a statement of her case,
and have it submitted to counsel, in order to ascertain whether or not,
under the circumstances, her freedom could be legally established on
her return to Antigua. On this occasion, in Mr. Stephen's presence
and mine, she expressed, in very strong terms, her anxiety to return
thither if she could go as a free person, and, at the same time, her extreme apprehensions of the fate that would probably await her if she returned as a slave. Her words were, "I would rather go into my grave
than go back a slave to Antigua, though I wish to go back to my husband very much—very much—very much! I am much afraid my owners would separate me from my husband, and use me very hard, or
perhaps sell me for a field negro;—and slavery is too too bad. I would
rather go into my grave!"

The paper which Mr. Wood had given her before she left his house,
was placed by her in Mr. Stephen's hands. It was expressed in the following terms:—

"I have already told Molly, and now give it her in writing, in order
that there may be no misunderstanding on her part, that as I brought
her from Antigua at her own request and entreaty, and that she is

consequently now free, she is of course at liberty to take her baggage and go where she pleases. And, in consequence of her late conduct, she must do one of two things—either quit the house, or return to Antigua by the earliest opportunity, as she does not evince a disposition to make herself useful. As she is a stranger in London, I do not wish to turn her out, or would do so, as two female servants are sufficient for my establishment. If after this she does remain, it will be only during her good behavior: but on no consideration will I allow her wages or any other remuneration for her services.

"JOHN A. WOOD."

"London, August 18, 1828."

This paper, though not devoid of inconsistencies, which will be apparent to any attentive reader, is craftily expressed; and was well devised to serve the purpose which the writer had obviously in view, namely, to frustrate any appeal which the friendless black woman might make to the sympathy of strangers, and thus prevent her from obtaining an asylum, if she left his house, from any respectable family. As she had no one to refer to for a character in this country except himself, he doubtless calculated securely on her being speedily driven back, as soon as the slender fund she had in her possession was expended, to throw herself unconditionally upon his tender mercies; and his disappointment in this expectation appears to have exasperated his feelings of resentment towards the poor woman, to a degree which few persons alive to the claims of common justice, not to speak of christianity or common humanity, could easily have anticipated. Such, at least, seems the only intelligible inference that can be drawn from his subsequent conduct.

The case having been submitted, by desire of the Anti-Slavery Committee, to the consideration of Dr. Lushington and Mr. Sergeant Stephen, it was found that there existed no legal means of compelling Mary's master to grant her manumission; and that if she returned to Antigua, she would inevitably fall again under his power, or that of his attorneys, as a slave. It was, however, resolved to try what could be effected for her by amicable negotiation; and with this view Mr. Ravenscroft, a solicitor, (Mr. Stephen's relative,) called upon Mr. Wood, in order to ascertain whether he would consent to Mary's manumission on any reasonable terms, and to refer, if required, the amount of compensation for her value to arbitration. Mr. Ravenscroft with some difficulty obtained one or two interviews, but found Mr. Wood so full of animosity against the woman, and so firmly bent against any arrangement having her freedom for its object, that the negotiation was soon broken off as hopeless. The angry slave-owner declared "that he would not move a finger about her in this country, or grant her manumission on any terms whatever; and that if she went back to the West Indies, she must take the consequences."

This unreasonable conduct of Mr. Wood, induced the Anti-Slavery Committee, after several other abortive attempts to effect a compromise, to think of bringing the case under the notice of Parliament. The heads of Mary's statement were accordingly engrossed in a Petition, which Dr. Lushington offered to present, and to give notice at the same time of his intention to bring in a Bill to provide for the entire emancipation of all slaves brought to England with the owner's consent. But before this step was taken, Dr. Lushington again had recourse to negotiation with the master; and, partly through the friendly intervention of Mr. Manning, partly by personal conference, used every persuasion in his power to induce Mr. Wood to relent and let the bondwoman go free. Seeing the matter thus seriously taken up, Mr. Wood became at length alarmed,—not relishing, it appears, the idea of having the case publicly discussed in the House of Commons; and to avert this result he submitted to temporize—assumed a demeanor of unwonted civility, and even hinted to Mr. Manning (as I was given to understand) that if he was not driven to utter hostility by the threatened exposure, he would probably meet our wishes "in his own time and way." Having gained time by these maneuvers, he adroitly endeavored to cool the ardor of Mary's new friends, in her cause, by representing her as an abandoned and worthless woman, ungrateful towards him, and undeserving of sympathy from others; allegations which he supported by the ready affirmation of some of his West India friends, and by one or two plausible letters procured from Antigua. By these and like artifices he appears completely to have imposed on Mr. Manning, the respectable West India merchant whom Dr. Lushington had asked to negotiate with him; and he prevailed so far as to induce Dr. Lushington himself (actuated by the benevolent view of thereby best serving Mary's cause,) to abstain from any remarks upon his conduct when the petition was at last presented in Parliament. In this way he dextrously contrived to neutralize all our efforts, until the close of the Session of 1829; soon after which he embarked with his family for the West Indies.

Every exertion for Mary's relief having thus failed; and being fully convinced from a twelvemonth's observation of her conduct, that she was really a well-disposed and respectable woman; I engaged her, in December 1829, as a domestic servant in my own family. In this capacity she has remained ever since; and I am thus enabled to speak of her conduct and character with a degree of confidence I could not have otherwise done. The importance of this circumstance will appear in the sequel.

From the time of Mr. Wood's departure to Antigua, in 1829, till June or July last, no further effort was attempted for Mary's relief. Some faint hope was still cherished that this unconscionable man would at length relent, and "in his own time and way," grant the prayer of the exiled negro woman. After waiting, however, nearly twelve-months longer, and seeing the poor woman's spirits daily sinking under the sickening influence of hope deferred, I resolved on a final attempt in her behalf, through the intervention of the Moravian Missionaries, and of the Governor of Antigua. At my request, Mr. Edward Moore, agent of the Moravian Brethren in London, wrote to the Rev. Joseph Newby, their Missionary in that island, empowering him to negotiate in his own name with Mr. Wood for Mary's manumission, and to procure his consent, if possible, upon terms of ample pecuniary compensation. At the same time the excellent and benevolent William Allen, of the Society of Friends, wrote to Sir Patrick Ross, the Governor of the Colony, with whom he was on terms of friendship, soliciting him to use his influence in persuading Mr. Wood to consent: and I confess I was sanguine enough to flatter myself that we should thus at length prevail. The result proved, however, that I had not yet fully appreciated the character of the man we had to deal with.

Mr. Newby's answer arrived early in November last, mentioning that he had done all in his power to accomplish our purpose, but in vain; and that if Mary's manumission could not be obtained without Mr. Wood's consent, he believed there was no prospect of its ever being effected.

A few weeks afterwards I was informed by Mr. Allen, that he had received a letter from Sir Patrick Ross, stating that he also had used his best endeavors in the affair, but equally without effect. Sir Patrick at the same time inclosed a letter, addressed by Mr. Wood to his Secretary, Mr. Taylor, assigning his reasons for persisting in this extraordinary course. This letter requires our special attention. Its tenor is as follows:—

"My dear Sir,

"In reply to your note relative to the woman Molly, I beg you will have the kindness to oblige me by assuring his Excellency that I regret exceedingly my inability to comply with his request, which under other circumstances would afford me very great pleasure.

"There are many and powerful reasons for inducing me to refuse my sanction to her returning here in the way she seems to wish. It would be to reward the worst species of ingratitude, and subject myself to insult whenever she came in my way. Her moral character is very bad, as the police records will show; and she would be a very troublesome character should she come here without any restraint. She is not a native of this country, and I know of no relation she has here. I induced her to take a husband, a short time before she left this, by providing a comfortable house in my yard for them, and prohibiting her going out after 10 to 12 o'clock (our bed-time) without special leave. This she considered the greatest, and indeed the only, grievance she ever complained of, and all my efforts could not prevent it. In hopes of inducing her to be steady to her husband, who was a free man, I gave him the house to occupy during our absence; but it appears the attachment was too loose to bind her, and he has taken another wife: so on that score I do her no injury.—In England she made her election, and quitted my family. This I had no right to object to; and I should have thought no more of it, but not satisfied to leave quietly, she gave every trouble and annoyance in her power, and endeavored to injure the character of my family by the most vile and infamous falsehoods, which was embodied in a petition to the House of Commons, and would have been presented, had not my friends from this island, particularly the Hon. Mr. Byam and Dr. Coull, come forward, and disproved what she had asserted.

"It would be beyond the limits of an ordinary letter to detail her baseness, though I will do so should his Excellency wish it; but you may judge of her depravity by one circumstance, which came out before Mr. Justice Dyett, in a quarrel with another female.

    *   *   *   *   *   *   *

"Such a thing I could not have believed possible.*

"Losing her value as a slave in a pecuniary point of view I con-

---

*I omit the circumstance here mentioned, because it is too indecent to appear in a publication likely to be perused by females. It is, in all probability, a vile calumny; but even if it were perfectly true, it would not serve Mr. Wood's case one straw.—Any reader who wishes it, may see the passage referred to, in the autograph letter in my possession. T. P.

sider of no consequence; for it was our intention, had she conducted herself properly and returned with us, to have given her freedom. She has taken her freedom; and all I wish is, that she would enjoy it without meddling with me.

"Let me again repeat, if his Excellency wishes it, it will afford me great pleasure to state such particulars of her, and which will be incontestably proved by numbers here, that I am sure will acquit me in his opinion of acting unkind or ungenerous towards her. I'll say nothing of the liability I should incur, under the Consolidated Slave Law, of dealing with a free person as a slave.

"My only excuse for entering so much into detail must be that of my anxious wish to stand justified in his Excellency's opinion.

"I am, my dear Sir,
Yours very truly,
John A. Wood.
"20th Oct. 1830."

"Charles Taylor, Esq.
&c. &c. &c.

"I forgot to mention that it was at her own special request that she accompanied me to England—and also that she had a considerable sum of money with her, which she had saved in my service. I knew of £36 to £40, at least, for I had some trouble to recover it from a white man, to whom she had lent it.

"J. A. W."

Such is Mr. Wood's justification of his conduct in thus obstinately refusing manumission to the Negro-woman who had escaped from his "house of bondage."

Let us now endeavor to estimate the validity of the excuses assigned, and the allegations advanced by him, for the information of Governor Sir Patrick Ross, in this deliberate statement of his case.

1. To allow the woman to return home free, would, he affirms "be to reward the worst species of ingratitude."

He assumes, it seems, the sovereign power of pronouncing a virtual sentence of banishment, for the alleged crime of ingratitude. Is this then a power which any man ought to possess over his fellow-mortal? or which any good man would ever wish to exercise? And, besides, there is no evidence whatever, beyond Mr. Wood's mere assertion, that Mary Prince owed him or his family the slightest mark of gratitude. Her account of the treatment she received in his service, *may* be incorrect; but her simple statement is at least supported by minute and feasible details, and, unless rebutted by positive facts, will certainly command credence from impartial minds more readily than his angry accusation, which has something absurd and improbable in its very front. Moreover, is it not absurd to term the assertion of her *natural rights* by a slave,—even supposing her to have been kindly dealt with by her "owners," and treated in every respect the reverse of what Mary affirms to have been her treatment by Mr. Wood and his wife,—"the *worst* species of ingratitude?" This may be West Indian ethics, but it will scarcely be received as sound doctrine in Europe.

2. To permit her return would be "to subject himself to insult whenever she came in his way."

This is a most extraordinary assertion. Are the laws of Antigua then so favorable to the free blacks, or the colonial police so feebly administered, that there are no sufficient restraints to protect a rich colonist like Mr. Wood,—a man who counts among his familiar friends the Honorable Mr. Byam, and Mr. Taylor the Government Secretary,—from being insulted by a poor Negro-woman? It is preposterous.

3. Her moral character is so bad, that she would prove very troublesome should she come to the colony "without any restraint."

"Any restraint?" Are there no restraints (supposing them necessary) short of absolute slavery to keep "troublesome characters" in order? But this, I suppose, is the *argumentum ad gubernatorem*—to frighten the governor. She is such a termagant, it seems, that if she once gets back to the colony *free,* she will not only make it too hot for poor Mr. Wood, but the police and courts of justice will scarce be a match for her! Sir Patrick Ross, no doubt, will take care how he intercedes further for so formidable a virago! How can one treat such arguments seriously?

4. She is not a native of the colony, and he knows of no relation she has there.

True: But was it not her home (so far as a slave can have a home) for thirteen or fourteen years? Were not the connections, friendships, and associations of her mature life formed there? Was it not there she hoped to spend her latter years in domestic tranquillity with her husband, free from the lash of the taskmaster? These considerations may appear light to Mr. Wood, but they are everything to this poor woman.

5. He induced her, he says, to take a husband, a short time before she left Antigua, and gave them a comfortable house in his yard, &c.&c.

This paragraph merits attention. He *"induced her to take a husband?"* If the fact were true, what brutality of mind and manners does it not indicate among these slave-holders? They refuse to legalize the marriages of their slaves, but *induce* them to form such temporary connections as may suit the owner's conveniency, just as they would pair the lower animals; and this man has the effrontery to tell us so! Mary, however, tells a very different story, (see page 47;) and her assertion, independently of other proof, is at least as credible as Mr. Wood's. The reader will judge for himself as to the preponderance of internal evidence in the conflicting statements.

6. He alleges that she was, before marriage, licentious, and even depraved in her conduct, and unfaithful to her husband afterwards.

These are serious charges. But if true, or even partially true, how comes it that a person so correct in his family hours and arrangements as Mr. Wood professes to be, and who expresses so edifying a horror of licentiousness, could reconcile it to his conscience to keep in the bosom of his family so *depraved,* as well as so *troublesome* a character for at least thirteen years, and confide to her for long periods too the charge of his house and the care of his children—for such I shall show to have been the facts? How can he account for not having rid himself with all speed, of so disreputable an inmate—he who values her loss so little "in a pecuniary point of view?" How can he account for having sold *five other slaves* in that period, and yet have retained this shocking woman—nay, even have refused to sell her, on more than one occasion, when offered her full value? It could not be from ignorance of her character, for the circumstance which he adduces as a proof of her shameless depravity, and which I have omitted on account of its indecency, occurred, it would appear, not less than *ten years ago.* Yet, notwithstanding her alleged ill qualities and habits of gross immorality, he has not only constantly refused to part with her; but after thirteen long years, brings her to England as an attendant on his wife and children, with the avowed intention of carrying her back along with his maiden daughter, a young lady returning from school! Such are the extraordinary facts; and until Mr. Wood shall reconcile these singular inconsistencies between his actions and his allegations, he must not be surprised if we in England prefer giving credit to the former rather than the latter; although at present it appears somewhat difficult to say which side of the alternative is the more creditable to his own character.

7. Her husband, he says, has taken another wife: "so that on that score," he adds, "he does her no injury."

Supposing this fact be true, (which I doubt, as I doubt every mere assertion from so questionable a quarter,) I shall take leave to put a question or two to Mr. Wood's conscience. Did he not write from England to his friend Mr. Darrel, soon after Mary left his house, directing him to turn her husband, Daniel James, off his premises, on account of her offense; telling him to inform James at the same time that his wife had *taken up* with another man, who had robbed her of all she had—a calumny as groundless as it was cruel? I further ask if the person who invented this story (whoever he may be,) was not likely enough to impose similar fabrications on the poor negro man's credulity, until he may have been induced to prove false to his marriage vows, and to "take another wife," as Mr. Wood coolly expresses it? But withal, I strongly doubt the fact of Daniel James' infidelity; for there is now before me a letter from himself to Mary, dated in April 1830, couched in strong terms of conjugal affection; expressing his anxiety for her speedy return, and stating that he had lately "received a grace" (a token of religious advancement) in the Moravian church, a circumstance altogether incredible if the man were living in open adultery, as Mr. Wood's assertion implies.

8. Mary, he says, endeavored to injure the character of his family by infamous falsehoods, which were embodied in a petition to the House of Commons, and would have been presented, had not his friends from Antigua, the Hon. Mr. Byam, and Dr. Coull, disproved her assertions.

I can say something on this point from my own knowledge. Mary's petition contained simply a brief statement of her case, and, among other things, mentioned the treatment she had received from Mr. and Mrs. Wood. Now the principal facts are corroborated by other evidence, and Mr. Wood must bring forward very different testimony from that of Dr. Coull before well-informed persons will give credit to his contradiction. The value of that person's evidence in such cases will be noticed presently. Of the Hon. Mr. Byam I know nothing, and shall only at present remark that it is not likely to redound greatly to his credit to appear in such company. Furthermore, Mary's petition *was* presented, as Mr. Wood ought to know; though it was not discussed, nor his conduct exposed as it ought to have been.

9. He speaks of the liability he should incur, under the Consolidated Slave Law, of dealing with a free person as a slave.

Is not this pretext hypocritical in the extreme? What liability could he possibly incur by voluntarily resigning the power, conferred on him by an iniquitous colonial law, of re-imposing the shackles of slavery on the bondwoman from whose limbs they had fallen when she touched the free soil of England?—There exists no liability from which he might not have been easily secured, or for which he would not have been fully compensated.

He adds in a postscript that Mary had a considerable sum of money with her,—from £36 to £40 at least, which she had saved in his service. The fact is, that she had at one time 113 dollars in cash; but only a very small portion of that sum appears to have been brought by her to England, the rest having been partly advanced, as she states, to assist her husband, and partly lost by being lodged in unfaithful custody.

Finally, Mr. Wood repeats twice that it will afford him great pleasure to state for the governor's satisfaction, if required, such particulars of "the woman Molly," upon incontestable evidence, as he is sure will acquit him in his Excellency's opinion "of acting unkind or ungenerous towards her."

This is well: and I now call upon Mr. Wood to redeem his pledge;—to bring forward facts and proofs fully to elucidate the subject;—to reconcile, if he can, the extraordinary discrepancies which I have pointed out between his assertions and the actual facts, and especially between his account of Mary Prince's character and his own conduct in regard to her. He has now to produce such a statement as will acquit him not only in the opinion of Sir Patrick Ross, but of the British public. And in this position he has spontaneously placed himself, in attempting to destroy, by his deliberate criminatory letter, the poor woman's fair fame and reputation,—an attempt but for which the present publication would probably never have appeared.

HERE PERHAPS we might safely leave the case to the judgment of the public; but as this negro woman's character, not the less valuable to her because her condition is so humble, has been so unscrupulously blackened by her late master, a party so much interested and inclined to place her in the worst point of view,—it is incumbent on me, as her advocate with the public, to state such additional testimony in her behalf as I can fairly and conscientiously adduce.

My first evidence is Mr. Joseph Phillips, of Antigua. Having submitted to his inspection Mr. Wood's letter and Mary Prince's narrative, and requested his candid and deliberate sentiments in regard to the actual facts of the case, I have been favored with the following letter from him on the subject:—

"London, January 18, 1831.
"Dear Sir,

"In giving you my opinion of Mary Prince's narrative, and of Mr. Wood's letter respecting her, addressed to Mr. Taylor, I shall first mention my opportunities of forming a proper estimate of the conduct and character of both parties.

"I have known Mr. Wood since his first arrival in Antigua in 1803. He was then a poor young man, who had been brought up as a ship carpenter in Bermuda. He was afterwards raised to be a clerk in the Commissariat department, and realized sufficient capital to commence business as a merchant. This last profession he has followed successfully for a good many years, and is understood to have accumulated very considerable wealth. After he entered into trade, I had constant intercourse with him in the way of business; and in 1824 and 1825, I was regularly employed on his premises as his clerk; consequently, I had opportunities of seeing a good deal of his character both as a merchant and as a master of slaves. The former topic I pass over as irrelevant to the present subject: in reference to the latter, I shall merely observe that he was not, in regard to ordinary matters, more severe than the ordinary run of slave owners; but, if seriously offended, he was not of a disposition to be easily appeased, and would spare no cost or sacrifice to gratify his vindictive feelings. As regards the exaction of work from domestic slaves, his wife was probably more severe than himself—it was almost impossible for the slaves ever to give her entire satisfaction.

"Of their slave Molly (or Mary) I know less than of Mr. and Mrs. Wood; but I saw and heard enough of her, both while I was constantly employed on Mr. Wood's premises, and while I was there occasionally on business, to be quite certain that she was viewed by her owners as their most respectable and trustworthy female slave. It is within my personal knowledge that she had usually the charge of the house in their absence, was entrusted with the keys, &c.; and was always considered by the neighbors and visitors as their confidential household servant, and as a person in whose integrity they placed unlimited confidence,—although when Mrs. Wood was at home, she was no doubt kept pretty closely at washing and other hard work. A decided proof of the estimation in which she was held by her owners exists in the fact that Mr. Wood uniformly refused to part with her, whereas he sold five other slaves while she was with them. Indeed, she always appeared to me to be a slave of superior intelligence and respectability; and I always understood such to be her general character in the place.

"As to what Mr. Wood alleges about her being frequently before the police, &c. I can only say I never heard of the circumstance before; and as I lived for twenty years in the same small town, and in the vicinity of their residence, I think I could scarcely have failed to become acquainted with it, had such been the fact. She might, however, have been occasionally before the magistrate in consequence of little disputes among the slaves, without any serious imputation on her general respectability. She says she was twice summoned to appear as a witness on such occasions; and that she was once sent by her mistress to be confined in the Cage, and was afterwards flogged by her desire. This cruel practice is very common in Antigua; and, in my opinion, is but little creditable to the slave owners and magistrates by whom such arbitrary punishments are inflicted, frequently for very trifling faults. Mr. James Scotland is the only magistrate in the colony who invariably refuses to sanction this reprehensible practice.

"Of the immoral conduct ascribed to Molly by Mr. Wood, I can say nothing further than this—that I have heard she had at a former period (previous to her marriage) a connection with a white person, a Capt. ———— , which I have no doubt was broken off when she became seriously impressed with religion. But, at any rate, such connections are so common, I might almost say universal, in our slave colonies, that except by the missionaries and a few serious persons, they are considered, if faults at all, so very venial as scarcely to deserve the name of immorality. Mr. Wood knows this colonial estimate of such connections as well as I do; and, however false such an estimate must be allowed to be, especially when applied to their own conduct by persons of education, pretending to adhere to the pure Christian rule of morals,—yet when he ascribes to a negro slave, to whom legal marriage was denied, such great criminality for laxity of this sort, and professes to be so exceedingly shocked and amazed at the tale he himself relates, he must, I am confident, have had a further object in view than the information of Mr. Taylor or Sir Patrick Ross. He must, it is evident, have been aware that his letter would be sent to Mr. Allen, and accordingly adapted it, as more important documents from the colonies are often adapted, *for effect in England.* The tale of the slave Molly's immoralities, be assured, was not intended for Antigua so much as for Stoke Newington, and Peckham, and Aldermanbury.

"In regard to Mary's narrative generally, although I cannot speak to the accuracy of the details, except in a few recent particulars, I can with safety declare that I see no reason to question the truth of a single fact stated by her, or even to suspect her in any instance of intentional exaggeration. It bears in my judgment the genuine stamp of truth and nature. Such is my unhesitating opinion, after a residence of twenty-seven years in the West Indies.

To T. Pringle, Esq.

"I remain, &c.

"Joseph Phillips."

"P. S. As Mr. Wood refers to the evidence of Dr. T. Coull in opposition to Mary's assertions, it may be proper to enable you justly to estimate the worth of that person's evidence in cases connected with the condition and treatment of slaves. You are aware that in 1829, Mr. M'Queen of Glasgow, in noticing a Report of the "Ladies' Society of Birmingham for the relief of British Negro Slaves," asserted with his characteristic audacity, that the statement which it contained respecting distressed and deserted slaves in Antigua was "an abominable falsehood." Not contented with this, and with insinuating that I, as agent of the society in the distribution of their charity in Antigua, had fraudulently duped them out of their money by a fabricated tale of distress, Mr. M'Queen proceeded to libel me in the most opprobrious terms, as "a man of the most worthless and abandoned character."* Now I know from good authority that it was

---

*In elucidation of the circumstances above referred to, I subjoin the following extracts from the Report of the Birmingham Ladies' Society for 1830:—

"As a portion of the funds of this association has been appropriated to assist the benevolent efforts of a society which has for fifteen years afforded relief to distressed and deserted slaves in Antigua, it may not be uninteresting to our friends to learn the manner in which the agent of this society has been treated for simply obeying the command of our Savior, by ministering, like the good Samaritan, to the distresses of the helpless and the desolate. The society's proceedings being adverted to by a friend of Africa, at one of the public meetings held in this country, a West Indian planter, who was present, wrote over to his friends in Antigua, and represented the conduct of the distributors of this charity in such a light, that it was deemed worthy of the cognizance of the House of Assembly. Mr. Joseph Phillips, a resident of the island, who had most kindly and disinterestedly exerted himself in the distribution of the money from England among the poor deserted slaves, was brought before the Assembly, and most severely interrogated: on his refusing to

upon Dr. Coull's information that Mr. M'Queen founded this impudent contradiction of notorious facts, and this audacious libel of my personal character. From this single circumstance you may judge of the value of his evidence in the case of Mary Prince. I can furnish further information respecting Dr. Coull's colonial proceedings, both private and judicial, should circumstances require it."

"J. P."

I leave the preceding letter to be candidly weighed by the reader in opposition to the inculpatory allegations of Mr. Wood—merely re-

deliver up his private correspondence with his friends in England, he was thrown into a loathsome jail, where he was kept for nearly five months; while his loss of business, and the oppressive proceedings instituted against him, were involving him in poverty and ruin. On his discharge by the House of Assembly, he was seized in their lobby for debt, and again imprisoned."

"In our report for the year 1826, we quoted a passage from the 13th Report of the Society for the relief of deserted Slaves in the island of Antigua, in reference to a case of great distress. This statement fell into the hands of Mr. M'Queen, the Editor of the *Glasgow Courier*. Of the consequences resulting from this circumstance we only gained information through the *Leicester Chronicle*, which had copied an article from the *Weekly Register* of Antigua, dated St. John's, September 22, 1829. We find from this that Mr. M'Queen affirms, that 'with the exception of the fact that the society is, as it deserves to be, duped out of its money, the whole tale' (of the distress above referred to) 'is an abominable falsehood.' This statement, which we are informed has appeared in many of the public papers, is COMPLETELY REFUTED in our Appendix, No. 4, to which we refer our readers. Mr. M'Queen's statements, we regret to say, would lead many to believe that there are no deserted Negroes to assist; and that the case mentioned was a perfect fabrication. He also distinctly avers, that the disinterested and humane agent of the society, Mr. Joseph Phillips, is 'a man of the most worthless and abandoned character.' In opposition to this statement, we learn the good character of Mr. Phillips from those who have long been acquainted with his laudable exertions in the cause of humanity, and from the Editor of the *Weekly Register* of Antigua, who speaks, on his own knowledge, of more than twenty years back; confidently appealing at the same time to the inhabitants of the colony in which he resides for the truth of his averments, and producing a testimonial to Mr. Phillips's good character signed by two members of the Antigua House of Assembly, and by Mr. Wyke, the collector of his Majesty's customs, and by Antigua merchants, as follows—'that they have been acquainted with him the last four years and upwards, and he has always conducted himself in an upright becoming manner—his character we know to be unimpeached, and his morals unexceptionable.'

(Signed) "Thomas Saunderson	John D. Taylor
John A. Wood	George Wyke
Samuel L. Darrel	Giles S. Musson
	Robert Grant."

"St. John's, Antigua, June 28, 1825."

In addition to the above testimonies, Mr. Phillips has brought over to England with him others of a more recent date, from some of the most respectable persons marking that Mr. Wood will find it somewhat difficult to impugn the evidence of Mr. Phillips, whose "upright," "unimpeached," and "unexceptionable" character, he has himself vouched for in unqualified terms, by affixing his signature to the testimonial published in the, *Weekly Register* of Antigua in 1825. (See Note previous page.)

The next testimony in Mary's behalf is that of Mrs. Forsyth, a lady in whose service she spent the summer of 1829.—(See page 52.) This lady, on leaving London to join her husband, voluntarily presented Mary with a certificate, which, though it relates only to a recent and short period of her history, is a strong corroboration of the habitual respectability of her character. It is in the following terms:—

"Mrs. Forsyth states, that the bearer of this paper (Mary James,) has been with her for the last six months: that she has found her an excellent character, being honest, industrious, and sober; and that she parts with her on no other account than this—that being obliged to travel with her husband, who has lately come from abroad in bad health, she has no further need of a servant. Any person wishing to engage her, can have her character in full from Miss Robson, 4, Keppel Street, Russel Square, whom Mrs. Forsyth has requested to furnish particulars to anyone desiring them.

"4, Keppel Street, 28th Sept. 1829."

In the last place, I add my own testimony in behalf of this negro woman. Independently of the scrutiny, which, as Secretary of the Anti-Slavery Society, I made into her case when she first applied for assistance, at 18, Aldermanbury, and the watchful eye I kept upon her conduct for the ensuing twelvemonths, while she was the occasional pensioner of the Society, I have now had the opportunity of closely observing her conduct for fourteen months, in the situation of a domestic servant in my own family; and the following is the deliberate opinion of Mary's character, formed not only by myself, but also by my wife and sister-in-law, after this ample period of observation. We have found her perfectly honest and trustworthy in all respects; so that we have no hesitation in leaving everything in the house at her disposal. She had the entire charge of the house during our absence in Scotland for three months last autumn, and conducted herself in that charge with the utmost discretion and fidelity. She is not, it is true, a very ex-

---

in Antigua—sufficient to cover with confusion all his unprincipled calumniators. See also his account of his own case in the Anti-Slavery Reporter, No. 74, p. 69.

pert housemaid, nor capable of much hard work, (for her constitution appears to be a good deal broken,) but she is careful, industrious, and anxious to do her duty and to give satisfaction. She is capable of strong attachments, and feels deep, though unobtrusive, gratitude for real kindness shown her. She possesses considerable natural sense, and has much quickness of observation and discrimination of character. She is remarkable for *decency* and *propriety* of conduct—and her *delicacy*, even in trifling minutiae, has been a trait of special remark by the females of my family. This trait, which is obviously quite unaffected, would be a most inexplicable anomaly, if her former habits had been so indecent and depraved as Mr. Wood alleges. Her chief faults, so far as we have discovered them, are, a somewhat violent and hasty temper, and a considerable share of natural pride and self-importance; but these defects have been but rarely and transiently manifested, and have scarcely occasioned an hour's uneasiness at any time in our household. Her religious knowledge, notwithstanding the pious care of her Moravian instructors in Antigua, is still but very limited, and her views of christianity indistinct; but her profession, whatever it may have of imperfection, I am convinced, has nothing of insincerity. In short, we consider her on the whole as respectable and well-behaved a person in her station, as any domestic, white or black, (and we have had ample experience of both colors,) that we have ever had in our service.

But after all, Mary's character, important though its exculpation be to her, is not really the point of chief practical interest in this case. Suppose all Mr. Wood's defamatory allegations to be true—suppose him to be able to rake up against her out of the records of the Antigua police, or from the veracious testimony of his brother colonists, twenty stories as bad or worse than what he insinuates—suppose the whole of her own statement to be false, and even the whole of her conduct since she came under our observation here to be a tissue of hypocrisy;—suppose all this—and leave the negro woman as black in character as in complexion,*—yet it would affect not the main facts—which are

---

*If it even were so, how strong a plea of palliation might not the poor negro bring, by adducing the neglect of her various owners to afford religious instruction or moral discipline, and the habitual influence of their evil *example* (to say the very least,) before her eyes? What moral good could she possibly learn—what moral evil could she easily escape, while under the uncontrolled power of such masters as she describes Captain I———— and Mr. D———— of Turk's Island? All things considered, it is indeed wonderful to find her such as she now is. But as she has herself piously expressed it, "that God whom then she knew not mercifully preserved her for better things."

these.—1. Mr. Wood, not daring in England to punish this woman arbitrarily, as he would have done in the West Indies, drove her out of his house, or left her, at least, only the alternative of returning instantly to Antigua, with the certainty of severe treatment there, or submitting in silence to what she considered intolerable usage in his household. 2. He has since obstinately persisted in refusing her manumission, to enable her to return home in security, though repeatedly offered more than ample compensation for her value as a slave; and this on various frivolous pretexts, but really, and indeed not unavowedly, in order to *punish* her for leaving his service in England, though he himself had professed to give her that option. These unquestionable facts speak volumes.*

*Since the preceding pages were printed off, I have been favored with a communication from the Rev. J. Curtin, to whom among other acquaintances of Mr. Wood's in this country, the entire proof sheets of this pamphlet had been sent for inspection. Mr. Curtin corrects some omissions and inaccuracies in Mary Prince's narrative (see page 46,) by stating, 1. That she was baptized, not in August, but on the 6th of April, 1817; 2. That sometime before her baptism, on her being admitted a catechumen, preparatory to that holy ordinance, she brought a note from her owner, Mr. Wood, recommending her for religious instruction, &c.; 3. That it was his usual practice, when any adult slaves came on *week days* to school, to require their owners' permission for their attendance; but that on *Sundays* the chapel was open indiscriminately to all.—Mary, after a personal interview with Mr. Curtin, and after hearing his letter read by me, still maintains that Mr. Wood's note recommended her for baptism merely, and that she never received any religious instruction whatever from Mr. and Mrs. Wood, or from anyone else at that period beyond what she has stated in her narrative. In regard to her non-admission to the Sunday school without permission from her owners, she admits that she may possibly have mistaken the clergyman's meaning on that point, but says that such was certainly her impression at the time, and the actual cause of her non-attendance.

Mr. Curtin finds in his books some reference to Mary's connection with a Captain ———, (the individual, I believe, alluded to by Mr. Phillips at page 66); but he states that when she attended his chapel she was always decently and becomingly dressed, and appeared to him to be in a situation of trust in her mistress's family.

Mr. Curtin offers no comment on any other part of Mary's statement; but he speaks in very favorable, though general terms of the respectability of Mr. Wood, whom he had known for many years in Antigua; and of Mrs. Wood, though she was not personally known to him, he says, that he had "heard her spoken of by those of her acquaintance, as a lady of very mild and amiable manners."

Another friend of Mr. and Mrs. Wood, a lady who had been their guest both in Antigua and England, alleges that Mary has grossly misrepresented them in her narrative; and says that she "can vouch for their being the most benevolent, kind-hearted people that can possibly live." She has declined, however, to furnish me with any written correction of the misrepresentations she complains of, although I offered to insert her testimony in behalf of her friends, if sent to me in time. And having already kept back the publication a fortnight waiting for communications of this sort, I will not delay it longer. Those who have withheld their strictures have only themselves to blame.

Of the general character of Mr. and Mrs. Wood, I would not designedly give any *unfair* impression. Without implicitly adopting either the *ex parte* view of Mary Prince, or

The case affords a most instructive illustration of the true spirit of the slave system, and of the pretensions of the slaveholders to assert, not merely their claims to a "vested right" in the *labor* of their bondmen, but to an indefeasible property in them as their "absolute chattels." It furnishes a striking practical comment on the assertions of the West Indians that self-interest is a sufficient check to the indulgence of vindictive feelings in the master; for here is a case where a man (a *respectable* and *benevolent* man as his friends aver,) prefers losing entirely the full price of the slave, for the mere satisfaction of preventing a poor black woman from returning home to her husband! If the pleasure of thwarting the benevolent wishes of the Anti-Slavery Society in behalf of the deserted negro, be an additional motive with Mr. Wood, it will not much mend his wretched plea.

I MAY HERE ADD a few words respecting the earlier portion of Mary Prince's narrative. The facts there stated must necessarily rest entirely,—since we have no collateral evidence,—upon their intrinsic claims to probability, and upon the reliance the reader may feel disposed, after perusing the foregoing pages, to place on her veracity. To my judgment, the internal evidence of the truth of her narrative appears remarkably strong. The circumstances are related in a tone of natural sincerity, and are accompanied in almost every case with characteristic and minute details, which must, I conceive, carry with them full conviction to every candid mind that this negro woman has actually seen, felt, and suffered all that she so impressively describes; and that the picture she has given of West Indian slavery is not less true than it is revolting.

But there may be some persons into whose hands this tract may fall, so imperfectly acquainted with the real character of Negro Slavery, as to be shocked into partial, if not absolute incredulity, by the acts of inhuman oppression and brutality related of Capt. I——— and his wife,

---

the unmeasured encomiums of their friends, I am willing to believe them to be, on the whole, fair, perhaps favorable, specimens of colonial character. Let them even be rated, if you will, in the very highest and most benevolent class of slaveholders; and, laying everything else entirely out of view, let Mr. Wood's conduct in this affair be tried exclusively by the facts established beyond dispute, and by his own statement of the case in his letter to Mr. Taylor. But then, I ask, if the very *best* and *mildest* of your slave-owners can act as Mr. Wood is proved to have acted, what is to be expected of persons whose mildness, or equity, or common humanity no one will dare to vouch for? If such things are done in the green tree, what will be done in the dry?—And what else then can Colonial Slavery possibly be, even in its best estate, but a system incurably evil and iniquitous?—I require no other data—I need add no further comment.

and of Mr. D———, the salt manufacturer of Turk's Island. Here, at least, such persons may be disposed to think, there surely must be *some* exaggeration; the facts are too shocking to be credible. The facts are indeed shocking, but unhappily not the less credible on that account. Slavery is a curse to the oppressor scarcely less than to the oppressed: its natural tendency is to brutalize both. After a residence myself of six years in a slave colony, I am inclined to doubt whether, as regards its *demoralizing* influence, the master is not even a greater object of compassion than his bondman. Let those who are disposed to doubt the atrocities related in this narrative, on the testimony of a sufferer, examine the details of many cases of similar barbarity that have lately come before the public, on unquestionable evidence. Passing over the reports of the Fiscal of Berbice,* and the Mauritius horrors recently unveiled,[†] let them consider the case of Mr. and Mrs. Moss, of the Bahamas, and their slave Kate, so justly denounced by the Secretary for the Colonies;[‡]—the cases of Eleanor Mead,[§]—of Henry Williams,[||]— and of the Rev. Mr. Bridges and Kitty Hylton,** in Jamaica. These cases alone might suffice to demonstrate the inevitable tendency of slavery as it exists in our colonies, to brutalize the master to a truly frightful degree—a degree which would often cast into the shade even the atrocities related in the narrative of Mary Prince; and which are sufficient to prove, independently of all other evidence, that there is nothing in the revolting character of the facts to affect their credibility; but that on the contrary, similar deeds are at this very time of frequent occurrence in almost every one of our slave colonies. The system of coercive labor may vary in different places; it may be more destructive to human life in the cane culture of Mauritius and Jamaica, than in the predial and domestic bondage of Bermuda or the Bahamas,—but the spirit and character of slavery are everywhere the same, and cannot fail to produce similar effects. Wherever slavery prevails, there will inevitably be found cruelty and oppression. Individuals who have preserved humane, and amiable, and tolerant dispositions towards their black dependents, may doubtless be found among slaveholders; but even where a happy instance of this sort occurs, such as Mary's first mistress, the kind-hearted Mrs. Williams, the favored condition of the

*See Anti-Slavery Reporter, Nos. 5 and 16.
[†]Ibid, No. 44.
[‡]Ibid, No. 47.
[§]Ibid, No. 64, p. 345; No. 71, p. 481.
[||]Ibid, No. 65, p. 356; No. 69, p. 431.
**Anti-Slavery Reporter, Nos. 66, 69, and 76.

slave is still as precarious as it is rare: it is every moment at the mercy of events; and must always be held by a tenure so proverbially uncertain as that of human prosperity, or human life. Such examples, like a feeble and flickering streak of light in a gloomy picture, only serve by contrast to exhibit the depth of the prevailing shades. Like other exceptions, they only prove the general rule: the unquestionable tendency of the system is to vitiate the best tempers, and to harden the most feeling hearts. "Never be kind, nor speak kindly to a slave," said an accomplished English lady in South Africa to my wife: "I have now," she added, "been for some time a slave-owner, and have found, from vexatious experience in my own household, that nothing but harshness and hauteur will do with slaves."

I might perhaps not inappropriately illustrate this point more fully by stating many cases which fell under my own personal observation, or became known to me through authentic sources, at the Cape of Good Hope—a colony where slavery assumes, as it is averred, a milder aspect than in any other dependency of the empire where it exists; and I could show, from the judicial records of that colony, received by me within these few weeks, cases scarcely inferior in barbarity to the worst of those to which I have just specially referred; but to do so would lead me too far from the immediate purpose of this pamphlet, and extend it to an inconvenient length. I shall therefore content myself with quoting a single short passage from the excellent work of my friend Dr. Walsh, entitled *Notices of Brazil*,—a work which, besides its other merits, has vividly illustrated the true spirit of Negro Slavery, as it displays itself not merely in that country, but wherever it has been permitted to open its Pandora's box of misery and crime.

Let the reader ponder on the following just remarks, and compare the facts stated by the Author in illustration of them, with the circumstances related at pages 33 and 34 of Mary's narrative:—

"If then we put out of the question the injury inflicted on others, and merely consider the deterioration of feeling and principle with which it operates on ourselves, ought it not to be a sufficient, and, indeed, unanswerable argument, against the permission of Slavery?

"The exemplary manner in which the paternal duties are performed at home, may mark people as the most fond and affectionate parents; but let them once go abroad, and come within the contagion of slavery, and it seems to alter the very nature of a man; and the father has sold, and still sells, the mother and his children, with as little compunction as he would a sow and her litter of pigs; and he often disposes of them together.

"This deterioration of feeling is conspicuous in many ways among the Brazilians. They are naturally a people of a humane and good-natured disposition, and much indisposed to cruelty or severity of any kind. Indeed, the manner in which many of them treat their slaves is a proof of this, as it is really gentle and considerate; but the natural tendency to cruelty and oppression in the human heart, is continually evolved by the impunity and uncontrolled license in which they are exercised. I never walked through the streets of Rio, that some house did not present to me the semblance of a bridewell, where the moans and the cries of the sufferers, and the sounds of whips and scourges within, announced to me that corporal punishment was being inflicted. Whenever I remarked this to a friend, I was always answered that the refractory nature of the slave rendered it necessary, and no house could properly be conducted unless it was practiced. But this is certainly not the case; and the chastisement is constantly applied in the very wantonness of barbarity, and would not, and dared not, be inflicted on the humblest wretch in society, if he was not a slave, and so put out of the pale of pity.

"Immediately joining our house was one occupied by a mechanic, from which the most dismal cries and moans constantly proceeded. I entered the shop one day, and found it was occupied by a saddler, who had two negro boys working at his business. He was a tawny, cadaverous-looking man, with a dark aspect; and he had cut from his leather a scourge like a Russian knout, which he held in his hand, and was in the act of exercising on one of the naked children in an inner room: and this was the cause of the moans and cries we heard every day, and almost all day long.

"In the rear of our house was another, occupied by some women of bad character, who kept, as usual, several negro slaves. I was awoke early one morning by dismal cries, and looking out of the window, I saw in the back yard of the house, a black girl of about fourteen years old; before her stood her mistress, a white woman, with a large stick in her hand. She was undressed except her petticoat and chemise, which had fallen down and left her shoulders and bosom bare. Her hair was streaming behind, and every fierce and malevolent passion was depicted in her face. She too, like my hostess at Governo [another striking illustration of the *dehumanizing* effects of Slavery,] was the very representation of a fury. She was striking the poor girl, whom she had driven up into a corner, where she was on her knees appealing for mercy. She showed her none, but continued to strike her on the head and thrust the stick into her face, till she was herself exhausted, and her poor victim covered with blood. This scene was renewed every morning, and the cries and moans of the poor suffering blacks, announced that they were enduring the penalty of slavery, in being the objects on which the irritable and malevolent passions of the whites are allowed to vent themselves with impunity; nor could I help deeply deploring that state of society in which the vilest characters in the community are allowed an almost uncontrolled power of life and death, over their innocent, and far more estimable fellow-creatures."—(*Notices of Brazil*, vol. ii, p. 354–356.)

In conclusion, I may observe that the history of Mary Prince furnishes a corollary to Lord Stowell's decision in the case of the slave Grace, and that it is most valuable on this account. Whatever opinions may be held by some readers on the grave question of immediately abolishing Colonial Slavery, nothing assuredly can be more repugnant to the feelings of Englishmen than that the system should be permitted to extend its baneful influence to this country. Yet such is the case, when the slave landed in England still only possesses that qualified degree of freedom, that a change of domicile will determine it. Though born a British subject, and resident within the shores of England, he is cut off from his dearest natural rights by the sad alternative of regaining them at the expense of liberty, and the certainty of severe treatment. It is true that he has the option of returning; but it is a cruel mockery to call it a voluntary choice, when upon his return depend his means of subsistence and his reunion with all that makes life valuable. Here he has tasted "the sweets of freedom," to quote the words of the unfortunate Mary Prince; but if he desires to restore himself to his family, or to escape from suffering and destitution, and the other evils of a climate uncongenial to his constitution and habits, he must abandon the enjoyment of his late-acquired liberty, and again subject himself to the arbitrary power of a vindictive master.

The case of Mary Prince is by no means a singular one; many of the same kind are daily occurring: and even if the case were singular, it would still loudly call for the interference of the legislature. In instances of this kind no injury can possibly be done to the owner by confirming to the slave his resumption of his natural rights. It is the master's spontaneous act to bring him to this country; he knows when he brings him that he divests himself of his property; and it is, in fact, a minor species of slave trading, when he has thus enfranchised his slave, to *re-capture* that slave by the necessities of his condition, or by working upon the better feelings of his heart. Abstractedly from all legal technicalities, there is no real difference between thus compelling the return of the enfranchised negro, and trepanning a free native of England by delusive hopes into perpetual slavery. The most ingenious casuist could not point out any essential distinction between the two cases. Our boasted liberty is the dream of imagination, and no longer the characteristic of our country, if its bulwarks can thus be thrown down by colonial special pleading. It would well become the character of the present Government to introduce a Bill into the Legislature making perpetual that freedom which the slave has acquired by his passage here, and thus to declare, in the most ample sense of the words, (what indeed we had long fondly believed to be the fact, though it now appears that we have been mistaken,) THAT NO SLAVE CAN EXIST WITHIN THE SHORES OF GREAT BRITAIN.

Narrative of Louis Asa-Asa,

A CAPTURED AFRICAN.

THE FOLLOWING interesting narrative is a convenient supplement to the history of Mary Prince. It is given, like hers, as nearly as possible in the narrator's words, with only so much correction as was necessary to connect the story, and render it grammatical. The concluding passage in inverted commas, is entirely his own.

While Mary's narrative shows the disgusting character of colonial slavery, this little tale explains with equal force the horrors in which it originates.

It is necessary to explain that Louis came to this country about five years ago, in a French vessel called the Pearl. She had lost her reckoning, and was driven by stress of weather into the port of St. Ives, in Cornwall. Louis and his four companions were brought to London upon a writ of Habeas Corpus at the instance of Mr. George Stephen; and, after some trifling opposition on the part of the master of the vessel, were discharged by Lord Wynford. Two of his unfortunate fellow-sufferers died of the measles at Hampstead; the other two returned to Sierra Leone; but poor Louis, when offered the choice of going back to Africa, replied, "Me no father, no mother now; me stay with you." And here he has ever since remained; conducting himself in a way to gain the good will and respect of all who know him. He is remarkably intelligent, understands our language perfectly, and can read and write well. The last sentences of the following narrative will seem almost too peculiar to be his own; but it is not the first time that in conversation with Mr. George Stephen, he has made similar remarks. On one occasion in particular, he was heard saying to himself in the kitchen, while sitting by the fire apparently in deep thought, "Me think,—me think—" A fellow-servant inquired what he meant; and he added, "Me think what a good thing I came to England! Here, I know what God is, and read my Bible; in my country they have no God, no Bible."

How severe and just a reproof to the guilty wretches who visit his country only with fire and sword! How deserved a censure upon the not less guilty men, who dare to vindicate the state of slavery, on the lying pretext, that its victims are of an inferior nature! And scarcely less deserving of reprobation are those who have it in their power to prevent these crimes, but who remain inactive from indifference, or are dissuaded from throwing the shield of British power over the victim of oppression, by the sophistry, and the clamor, and the avarice of the oppressor. It is the reproach and the sin of England. May God avert from our country the ruin which this national guilt deserves!

We lament to add, that the Pearl which brought these negroes to our shore, was restored to its owners at the instance of the French Government, instead of being condemned as a prize to Lieut. Rye, who, on his own responsibility, detained her, with all her manacles and chains and other detestable proofs of her piratical occupation on board. We trust it is not yet too late to demand investigation into the reasons for restoring her.

The Negro Boy's Narrative.

My father's name was Clashoquin; mine is Asa-Asa. He lived in a country called Bycla, near Egie, a large town. Egie is as large as Brighton; it was some way from the sea. I had five brothers and sisters. We all lived together with my father and mother; he kept a horse, and was respectable, but not one of the great men. My uncle was one of the great men at Egie: he could make men come and work for him: his name was Otou. He had a great deal of land and cattle. My father sometimes worked on his own land, and used to make charcoal. I was too little to work; my eldest brother used to work on the land; and we were all very happy.

A great many people, whom we called Adinyés, set fire to Egie in the morning before daybreak; there were some thousands of them. They killed a great many, and burnt all their houses. They stayed two days, and then carried away all the people whom they did not kill.

They came again every now and then for a month, as long as they could find people to carry away. They used to tie them by the feet, except when they were taking them off, and then they let them loose; but if they offered to run away, they would shoot them. I lost a great many friends and relations at Egie; about a dozen. They sold all they carried away, to be slaves. I know this because I afterwards saw them as slaves on the other side of the sea. They took away brothers, and sisters, and husbands, and wives; they did not care about this. They were sold for cloth or gunpowder, sometimes for salt or guns; sometimes they got four or five guns for a man: they were English guns, made like my master's that I clean for his shooting. The Adinyés burnt a great many places besides Egie. They burnt all the country wherever they found villages; they used to shoot men, women, and children, if they ran away.

They came to us about eleven o'clock one day, and directly they came they set our house on fire. All of us had run away. We kept together, and went into the woods, and stopped there two days. The Adinyés then went away, and we returned home and found everything burnt. We tried to build a little shed, and were beginning to get comfortable again. We found several of our neighbors lying about wounded; they had been shot. I saw the bodies of four or five little children whom they had killed with blows on the head. They had carried away their fathers and mothers, but the children were too small for slaves, so they killed them. They had killed several others, but these were all that I saw. I saw them lying in the street like dead dogs.

In about a week after we got back, the Adinyés returned, and burnt all the sheds and houses they had left standing. We all ran away again; we went to the woods as we had done before.—They followed us the next day. We went farther into the woods, and stayed there about four days and nights; we were half starved; we only got a few potatoes. My uncle Otou was with us. At the end of this time, the Adinyés found us. We ran away. They called my uncle to go to them; but he refused, and they shot him immediately: they killed him. The rest of us ran on, and they did not get at us till the next day. I ran up into a tree: they followed me and brought me down. They tied my feet. I do not know if they found my father and mother, and brothers and sisters: they had run faster than me, and were half a mile farther when I got up into the tree: I have never seen them since.—There was a man who ran up into the tree with me: I believe they shot him, for I never saw him again.

They carried away about twenty besides me. They carried us to the sea. They did not beat us: they only killed one man, who was very ill and too weak to carry his load: they made all of us carry chickens and meat for our food; but this poor man could not carry his load, and they ran him through the body with a sword.—He was a neighbor of ours. When we got to the sea they sold all of us, but not to the same person. They sold us for money; and I was sold six times over, sometimes for money, sometimes for cloth, and sometimes for a gun. I was about thirteen years old. It was about half a year from the time I was taken, before I saw the white people.

We were taken in a boat from place to place, and sold at every place we stopped at. In about six months we got to a ship, in which we first saw white people: they were French. They bought us. We found here a great many other slaves; there were about eighty, including women and children. The Frenchmen sent away all but five of us into another very large ship. We five stayed on board till we got to England, which was about five or six months. The slaves we saw on board the ship were chained together by the legs below deck, so close they could not move. They were flogged very cruelly: I saw one of them flogged till he died; we could not tell what for. They gave them enough to eat. The place they were confined in below deck was so hot and nasty I could not bear to be in it. A great many of the slaves were ill, but they were not attended to. They used to flog me very bad on board the ship: the captain cut my head very bad one time.

"I am very happy to be in England, as far as I am very well;—but I have no friend belonging to me, but God, who will take care of me as he has done already. I am very glad I have come to England, to know who God is. I should like much to see my friends again, but I do not now wish to go back to them: for if I go back to my own country, I might be taken as a slave again. I would rather stay here, where I am free, than go back to my country to be sold. I shall stay in England as long as (please God) I shall live. I wish the King of England could know all I have told you. I wish it that he may see how cruelly we are used. We had no king in our country, or he would have stopt it. I think the king of England might stop it, and this is why I wish him to know it all. I have heard say he is good; and if he is, he will stop it if he can. I am well off myself, for I am well taken care of, and have good bed and good clothes; but I wish my own people to be as comfortable."

"LOUIS ASA-ASA."

"London, January 31, 1831."

THE
CONFESSIONS

OF

NAT TURNER,

THE LEADER OF THE LATE

INSURRECTION IN SOUTHAMPTON, VA.

As fully and voluntarily made to

THOMAS R. GRAY,

In the prison where he was confined, and acknowledged by
him to be such when read before the Court of Southampton; with the certificate, under seal of
the Court convened at Jerusalem,
Nov. 5, 1831, for his trial.

ALSO, AN AUTHENTIC

ACCOUNT OF THE WHOLE INSURRECTION,

WITH LISTS OF THE WHITES WHO WERE MURDERED,

AND OF THE NEGROES BROUGHT BEFORE THE COURT OF
SOUTHAMPTON, AND THERE SENTENCED, &c.

Baltimore:
PUBLISHED BY THOMAS R. GRAY.
Lucas & Deaver, print.
1831.

2

THE CONFESSIONS OF

NAT TURNER,

THE LEADER OF THE LATE INSURRECTION

IN SOUTHAMPTON, VA.,

AS FULLY AND VOLUNTARILY MADE

TO THOMAS R. GRAY

Be it remembered, That on this tenth day of November, Anno Domini, eighteen hundred and thirty-one, Thomas R. Gray of the said District, deposited in this office the title of a book, which is in the words as following:

"The Confessions of Nat Turner, the leader of the late insurrection in Southampton, Virginia, as fully and voluntarily made to Thomas R. Gray, in the prison where he was confined, and acknowledged by him to be such when read before the Court of Southampton; with the certificate, under seal, of the Court convened at Jerusalem, November 5, 1831, for his trial. Also, an authentic account of the whole insurrection, with lists of the whites who were murdered, and of the negroes brought before the Court of Southampton, and there sentenced, &c. the right whereof he claims as proprietor, in conformity with an Act of Congress, entitled "An act to amend the several acts respecting Copy Rights."

TO THE PUBLIC

The late insurrection in Southampton has greatly excited the public mind, and led to a thousand idle, exaggerated and mischievous reports. It is the first instance in our history of an open rebellion of the slaves, and attended with such atrocious circumstances of cruelty and destruction, as could not fail to leave a deep impression, not only upon the minds of the community where this fearful tragedy was wrought, but throughout every portion of our country, in which this population is to be found. Public curiosity has been on the stretch to understand the origin and progress of this dreadful conspiracy, and the motives which influence its diabolical actors. The insurgent slaves had all been destroyed, or apprehended, tried, and executed, (with the exception of the leader,) without revealing anything at all satisfactory, as to the motives which governed them, or the means by which they expected to accomplish their object. Everything connected with this sad affair was wrapt in mystery, until Nat Turner, the leader of this ferocious band, whose name has resounded throughout our widely extended empire, was captured. This "great Bandit" was taken by a single individual, in a cave near the residence of his late owner, on Sunday, the thirtieth of October, without attempting to make the slightest resistance, and on the following day safely lodged in the jail of the County. His captor was Benjamin Phipps, armed with a shot gun well charged. Nat's only weapon was a small light sword which he immediately surrendered, and begged that his life might be spared. Since his confinement, by permission of the Jailor, I have had ready access to him, and finding that he was willing to make a full and free confession of the origin, progress and consummation of the insurrectory movements of the slaves of which he was the contriver and head; I determined for the gratification of public curiosity to commit his statements to writing, and publish them, with little or no variation, from his own words. That this is a faithful record of his confessions, the annexed certificate of the County Court of Southampton, will attest. They certainly bear one stamp of truth and sincerity. He makes no attempt (as all the other insurgents who were examined did,) to exculpate himself, but frankly acknowledges his full participation in all the guilt of the transaction. He was not only the contriver of the conspiracy, but gave the first blow towards its execution.

It will thus appear, that whilst everything upon the surface of society wore a calm and peaceful aspect; whilst not one note of preparation was heard to warn the devoted inhabitants of woe and death, a gloomy fanatic was revolving in the recesses of his own dark, bewildered, and overwrought mind, schemes of indiscriminate massacre to the whites. Schemes too fearfully executed as far as his fiendish band proceeded in their desolating march. No cry for mercy penetrated their flinty bosoms. No acts of remembered kindness made the least impression upon these remorseless murderers. Men, women and children, from hoary age to helpless infancy were involved in the same cruel fate. Never did a band of savages do their work of death more unsparingly. Apprehension for their own personal safety seems to have been the only principle of restraint in the whole course of their bloody proceedings. And it is not the least remarkable feature in this horrid transaction, that a band actuated by such hellish purposes, should have resisted so feebly, when met by the whites in arms. Desperation alone, one would think, might have led to greater efforts. More than twenty of them attacked Dr. Blunt's house on Tuesday morning, a little before daybreak, defended by two men and three boys. They fled precipitately at the first fire; and their future plans of mischief, were entirely disconcerted and broken up. Escaping thence, each individual sought his own safety either in concealment, or by returning home, with the hope that his participation might escape detection, and all were shot down in the course of a few days, or captured and brought to trial and punishment. Nat has survived all his followers, and the gallows will speedily close his career. His own account of the conspiracy is submitted to the public, without comment. It reads an awful, and it is hoped, a useful lesson, as to the operations of a mind like his, endeavoring to grapple with things beyond its reach. How it first became bewildered and confounded, and finally corrupted and led to the conception and perpetration of the most atrocious and heart-rending deeds. It is calculated also to demonstrate the policy of our laws in restraint of this class of our population, and to induce all those entrusted with their execution, as well as our citizens generally, to see that they are strictly and rigidly enforced. Each particular community should look to its own safety, whilst the general guardians of the laws, keep a watchful eye over all. If Nat's statements can be relied on, the insurrection in this county was entirely local, and his designs confided but to a few, and these in his immediate vicinity. It was not instigated by motives of revenge or sudden anger, but the results of long deliberation, and a settled purpose of mind. The offspring of gloomy fanaticism, acting upon materials but too well prepared for such impressions. It will be long remembered in the annals of our country, and many a mother as she presses her infant darling to her bosom, will shudder at the recollection of Nat Turner, and his band of ferocious miscreants.

Believing the following narrative, by removing doubts and conjectures from the public mind which otherwise must have remained, would give general satisfaction, it is respectfully submitted to the public by their ob't serv't,

T. R. Gray.

Jerusalem, Southampton, Va., Nov. 5, 1831.
We the undersigned, members of the Court convened at Jerusalem, on Saturday, the 5th day of Nov. 1831, for the trial of Nat, *alias* Nat Turner, a negro slave, late the property of Putnam Moore, deceased, do hereby certify, that the confessions of Nat, to Thomas R. Gray, was read to him in our presence, and that Nat acknowledged the same to be full, free, and voluntary; and that furthermore, when called upon by

the presiding Magistrate of the Court, to state if he had anything to say, why sentence of death should not be passed upon him, replied he had nothing further than he had communicated to Mr. Gray. Given under our hands and seals at Jerusalem, this 5th day of November, 1831.

Jeremiah Cobb,	[Seal.]
Thomas Pretlow,	[Seal.]
James W. Parker,	[Seal.]
Carr Bowers,	[Seal.]
Samuel B. Hines,	[Seal.]
Orris A. Browne,	[Seal.]

State of Virginia, Southampton County, to wit:
I, James Rochelle, Clerk of the County Court of Southampton in the State of Virginia, do hereby certify, that Jeremiah Cobb, Thomas Pretlow, James W. Parker, Carr Bowers, Samuel B. Hines, and Orris A. Browne, esqr's are acting Justices of the Peace, in and for the County aforesaid, and were members of the Court which convened at Jerusalem, on Saturday the 5th day of November, 1831, for the trial of Nat *alias* Nat Turner, a negro slave, late the property of Putnam Moore, deceased, who was tried and convicted, as an insurgent in the late insurrection in the county of Southampton aforesaid, and that full faith and credit are due, and ought to be given to their acts as Justices of the peace aforesaid.

In testimony whereof, I have hereunto set my hand and caused the seal of the Court aforesaid, to be affixed this 5th day of November, 1831.
James Rochelle, C. S. C. C.

CONFESSION
Agreeable to his own appointment, on the evening he was committed to prison, with permission of the jailer, I visited NAT on Tuesday the 1st November, when, without being questioned at all, he commenced his narrative in the following words:—

SIR,—You have asked me to give a history of the motives which induced me to undertake the late insurrection, as you call it—To do so I must go back to the days of my infancy, and even before I was born. I was thirty-one years of age the 2d of October last, and born the property of Benj. Turner, of this county. In my childhood a circumstance occurred which made an indelible impression on my mind, and laid the ground work of that enthusiasm, which has terminated so fatally to many, both white and black, and for which I am about to atone at the gallows. It is here necessary to relate this circumstance—trifling as it may seem, it was the commencement of that belief which has grown with time, and even now, sir, in this dungeon, helpless and forsaken as I am, I cannot divest myself of. Being at play with other children, when three or four years old, I was telling them something, which my mother overhearing, said it had happened before I was born—I stuck to my story, however, and related somethings which went, in her opinion, to confirm it—others being called on were greatly astonished, knowing that these things had happened, and caused them to say in my hearing, I surely would be a prophet, as the Lord had shown me things that had happened before my birth. And my father and mother strengthened me in this my first impression, saying in my presence, I was intended for some great purpose, which they had always thought from certain marks on my head and breast—[a parcel of excrescences which I believe are not at all uncommon, particularly among negroes, as I have seen several with the same. In this case he has either cut them off or they have nearly disappeared]—My grandmother, who was very religious, and to whom I was much attached—my master, who belonged to the church, and other religious persons who visited the house, and whom I often saw at prayers, noticing the singularity of my manners, I suppose, and my uncommon intelligence for a child, remarked I had too much sense to be raised, and if I was, I would never be of any service to anyone as a slave—To a mind like mine, restless, inquisitive and observant of everything that was passing, it is easy to suppose that religion was the subject to which it would be directed, and although this subject principally occupied my thoughts—there was nothing that I saw or heard of to which my attention was not directed—The manner in which I learned to read and write, not only had great influence on my own mind, as I acquired it with the most perfect ease, so much so, that I have no recollection whatever of learning the alphabet—but to the astonishment of the family, one day, when a book was shown me to keep me from crying, I began spelling the names of different objects—this was a source of wonder to all in the neighborhood, particularly the blacks—and this learning was constantly improved at all opportunities—when I got large enough to go to work, while employed, I was reflecting on many things that would present themselves to my imagination, and whenever an opportunity occurred of looking at a book, when the school children were getting their lessons, I would find many things that the fertility of my own imagination had depicted to me before; all my time, not devoted to my master's service, was spent either in prayer, or in making experiments in casting different things in moulds made of earth, in attempting to make paper, gun-powder, and many other experiments, that although I could not perfect, yet convinced me of its practicability if I had the means.* I was not addicted to stealing in my youth, nor have ever been—Yet such was the confidence of the negroes in the neighbor-hood, even at this early period of my life, in my superior judgment, that they would often carry me with them when they were going on any roguery, to plan for them. Growing up among them, with this confi-dence in my superior judgment, and when this, in their opinions, was perfected by Divine inspiration, from the circumstances already al-luded to in my infancy, and which belief was ever afterwards zealously inculcated by the austerity of my life and manners, which became the subject of remark by white and black.—Having soon discovered to be great, I must appear so, and therefore studiously avoided mixing in so-ciety, and wrapped myself in mystery, devoting my time to fasting and prayer—By this time, having arrived to man's estate, and hearing the scriptures commented on at meetings, I was struck with that particu-lar passage which says: "Seek ye the kingdom of Heaven and all things shall be added unto you." I reflected much on this passage, and prayed daily for light on this subject—As I was praying one day at my plough, the spirit spoke to me, saying "Seek ye the kingdom of Heaven and all things shall be added unto you." *Question*—what do you mean by the Spirit. *Ans.* The Spirit that spoke to the prophets in former days—and I was greatly astonished, and for two years prayed continually, when-ever my duty would permit—and then again I had the same revelation, which fully confirmed me in the impression that I was ordained for some great purpose in the hands of the Almighty. Several years rolled round, in which many events occurred to strengthen me in this my be-lief. At this time I reverted in my mind to the remarks made of me in my childhood, and the things that had been shown me—and as it had been said of me in my childhood by those by whom I had been taught to pray, both white and black, and in whom I had the greatest confi-dence, that I had too much sense to be raised, and if I was, I would never be of any use to anyone as a slave. Now finding I had arrived to

*When questioned as to the manner of manufacturing those different articles, he was found well informed on the subject.

man's estate, and was a slave, and these revelations being made known to me, I began to direct my attention to this great object, to fulfil the purpose for which, by this time, I felt assured I was intended. Knowing the influence I had obtained over the minds of my fellow servants, (not by the means of conjuring and such like tricks—for to them I always spoke of such things with contempt) but by the communion of the Spirit whose revelations I often communicated to them, and they believed and said my wisdom came from God. I now began to prepare them for my purpose, by telling them something was about to happen that would terminate in fulfilling the great promise that had been made to me—About this time I was placed under an overseer, from whom I ranaway—and after remaining in the woods thirty days, I returned, to the astonishment of the negroes on the plantation, who thought I had made my escape to some other part of the country, as my father had done before. But the reason of my return was, that the Spirit appeared to me and said I had my wishes directed to the things of this world, and not to the kingdom of Heaven, and that I should return to the service of my earthly master—"For he who knoweth his Master's will, and doeth it not, shall be beaten with many stripes, and thus have I chastened you." And the negroes found fault, and murmured against me, saying that if they had my sense they would not serve any master in the world. And about this time I had a vision—and I saw white spirits and black spirits engaged in battle, and the sun was darkened—the thunder rolled in the Heavens, and blood flowed in streams—and I heard a voice saying, "Such is your luck, such you are called to see, and let it come rough or smooth, you must surely bear it." I now withdrew myself as much as my situation would permit, from the intercourse of my fellow servants, for the avowed purpose of serving the Spirit more fully—and it appeared to me, and reminded me of the things it had already shown me, and that it would then reveal to me the knowledge of the elements, the revolution of the planets, the operation of tides, and changes of the seasons. After this revelation in the year 1825, and the knowledge of the elements being made known to me, I sought more than ever to obtain true holiness before the great day of judgment should appear, and then I began to receive the true knowledge of faith. And from the first steps of righteousness until the last, was I made perfect; and the Holy Ghost was with me, and said, "Behold me as I stand in the Heavens"—and I looked and saw the forms of men in different attitudes—and there were lights in the sky to which the children of darkness gave other names than what they really were—for they were the lights of the Savior's hands, stretched forth from east to west, even as they were extended on the cross on Calvary for the redemption of sinners. And I wondered greatly at these miracles, and prayed to be informed of a certainty of the meaning thereof—and shortly afterwards, while laboring in the field, I discovered drops of blood on the corn as though it were dew from heaven—and I communicated it to many, both white and black, in the neighborhood—and I then found on the leaves in the woods hieroglyphic characters, and numbers, with the forms of men in different attitudes, portrayed in blood, and representing the figures I had seen before in the heavens. And now the Holy Ghost had revealed itself to me, and made plain the miracles it had shown me—For as the blood of Christ had been shed on this earth, and had ascended to heaven for the salvation of sinners, and was now returning to earth again in the form of dew—and as the leaves on the trees bore the impression of the figures I had seen in the heavens, it was plain to me that the Savior was about to lay down the yoke he had borne for the sins of men, and the great day of judgment was at hand. About this time I told these things to a white man, (Etheldred T. Brantley) on whom it had a wonderful effect—and he ceased from his wickedness, and was attacked immediately with a cutaneous eruption, and blood oozed from the pores of his skin, and after praying and fasting nine days, he was healed, and the Spirit appeared to me again, and said, as the Savior had been baptised so should we be also—and when the white people would not let us be baptised by the church, we went down into the water together, in the sight of many who reviled us, and were baptised by the Spirit—After this I rejoiced greatly, and gave thanks to God. And on the 12th of May, 1828, I heard a loud noise in the heavens, and the Spirit instantly appeared to me and said the Serpent was loosened, and Christ had laid down the yoke he had borne for the sins of men, and that I should take it on and fight against the Serpent, for the time was fast approaching when the first should be last and the last should be first. *Ques.* Do you not find yourself mistaken now? *Ans.* Was not Christ crucified. And by signs in the heavens that it would make known to me when I should commence the great work—and until the first sign appeared, I should conceal it from the knowledge of men—And on the appearance of the sign, (the eclipse of the sun last February) I should arise and prepare myself, and slay my enemies with their own weapons. And immediately on the sign appearing in the heavens, the seal was removed from my lips, and I communicated the great work laid out for me to do, to four in whom I had the greatest confidence, (Henry, Hark, Nelson, and Sam)—it was intended by us to have begun the work of death on the 4th July last— Many were the plans formed and rejected by us, and it affected my mind to such a degree, that I fell sick, and the time passed without our coming to any determination how to commence—Still forming new schemes and rejecting them, when the sign appeared again, which determined me not to wait longer.

Since the commencement of 1830, I had been living with Mr. Joseph Travis, who was to me a kind master, and placed the greatest confidence in me; in fact, I had no cause to complain of his treatment to me. On Saturday evening, the 20th of August, it was agreed between Henry, Hark and myself, to prepare a dinner the next day for the men we expected, and then to concert a plan, as we had not yet determined on any. Hark, on the following morning, brought a pig, and Henry brandy, and being joined by Sam, Nelson, Will and Jack, they prepared in the woods a dinner, where, about three o'clock, I joined them.

Q. Why were you so backward in joining them.

A. The same reason that had caused me not to mix with them for years before.

I saluted them on coming up, and asked Will how came he there, he answered, his life was worth no more than others, and his liberty as dear to him. I asked him if he thought to obtain it? He said he would, or lose his life. This was enough to put him in full confidence. Jack, I knew, was only a tool in the hands of Hark, it was quickly agreed we should commence at home (Mr. J. Travis') on that night, and until we had armed and equipped ourselves, and gathered sufficient force, neither age nor sex was to be spared, (which was invariably adhered to.) We remained at the feast, until about two hours in the night, when we went to the house and found Austin; they all went to the cider press and drank, except myself. On returning to the house, Hark went to the door with an axe, for the purpose of breaking it open, as we knew we were strong enough to murder the family, if they were awaked by the noise; but reflecting that it might create an alarm in the neighborhood, we determined to enter the house secretly, and murder them whilst sleeping. Hark got a ladder and set it against the chimney, on which I ascended, and hoisting a window, entered and came downstairs, unbarred the door, and removed the guns from their places. It was then observed that I must spill the first blood. On which, armed with a hatchet, and accompanied by Will, I entered my master's chamber, it being dark, I could not give a death blow, the hatchet glanced from his head, he sprang from the bed and called his wife, it was his last word, Will laid him dead, with a blow of his axe, and Mrs. Travis shared the same fate, as she lay in bed. The murder of this family, five in number, was the work of a moment, not one of them awoke; there was a little infant sleeping in a cradle, that was forgotten, until we had left the house and gone some distance, when Henry and Will returned and killed it; we got here, four guns that would shoot, and several old muskets, with a pound or two of powder. We remained some time at the barn, where we paraded; I formed them in a line as soldiers, and after carrying them through all the maneuvers I was master of, marched them off to Mr. Salathiel Francis', about six hundred yards distant. Sam and Will went to the door and knocked. Mr. Francis asked who was there, Sam replied it was him, and he had a letter for him, on which he got up and came to the door; they immediately seized him, and dragging him out a little from the door, he was dispatched by repeated blows on the head; there was no other white person in the family. We started from there for Mrs. Reese's, maintaining the most perfect silence on our march, where finding the door unlocked, we entered, and murdered Mrs. Reese in her bed, while sleeping; her son awoke, but it was only to sleep the sleep of death, he had only time to say who is that, and he was no more. From Mrs. Reese's we went to Mrs. Turner's, a mile distant, which we reached about sunrise, on Monday morning. Henry, Austin, and Sam, went to the still, where, finding Mr. Peebles, Austin shot him, and the rest of us went to the house; as we approached, the family discovered us, and shut the door. Vain hope! Will, with one stroke of his axe, opened it, and we entered and found Mrs. Turner and Mrs. Newsome in the middle of a room, almost frightened to death. Will immediately killed Mrs. Turner, with one blow of his axe. I took Mrs. Newsome by the hand, and with the sword I had when I was apprehended, I struck her several blows over the head, but not being able to kill her, as the sword was dull. Will turning around and discovering it, dispatched her also. A general destruction of property and search for money and ammunition, always succeeded the murders. By this time my company amounted to fifteen, and nine men mounted, who started for Mrs. Whitehead's, (the other six were to go through a by-way to Mr. Bryant's, and rejoin us at Mrs. Whitehead's,) as we approached the house we discovered Mr. Richard Whitehead standing in the cotton patch, near the lane fence; we called him over into the lane, and Will, the executioner, was near at hand, with his fatal axe, to send him to an untimely grave. As we pushed on to the house, I discovered someone run round the garden, and thinking it was some of the white family, I pursued them, but finding it was a servant girl belonging to the house, I returned to commence the work of death, but they whom I left, had not been idle; all the family were already murdered, but Mrs. Whitehead and her daughter Margaret. As I came round to the door I saw Will pulling Mrs. Whitehead out of the house, and at the step he nearly severed her head from her body, with his broad axe. Miss Margaret, when I discovered her, had concealed herself in the corner, formed by the projection of the cellar cap from the house; on my approach she fled, but was soon overtaken, and after repeated blows with a sword, I killed her by a blow on the head, with a fence rail. By this time, the six who had gone by Mr. Bryant's, rejoined us, and informed me they had done the work of death assigned them. We again divided, part going to Mr. Richard Porter's, and from thence to Nathaniel Francis', the others to Mr. Howell Harris', and Mr. T. Doyle's. On my reaching Mr. Porter's, he had escaped with his family. I understood there, that the alarm had already spread, and I immediately returned to bring up those sent to Mr. Doyle's, and Mr. Howell Harris'; the party I left going on to Mr. Francis', having told them I would join them in that neighborhood. I met these sent to Mr. Doyle's and Mr. Harris' returning, having met Mr. Doyle on the road and killed him; and learning from some who joined them, that Mr. Harris was from home, I immediately pursued the course taken by the party gone on before; but knowing they would complete the work of death and pillage, at Mr. Francis' before I could get there, I went to Mr. Peter Edwards', expecting to find them there, but they had been here also. I then went to Mr. John T. Barrow's, they had been here and murdered him. I pursued on their track to Capt. Newit Harris', where I found the greater part mounted, and ready to start; the men now amounting to about forty, shouted and hurraed as I rode up, some were in the yard, loading their guns, others drinking. They said Captain Harris and his family had escaped, the property in the house they destroyed, robbing him of money and other valuables. I ordered them to mount and march instantly, this was about nine or ten o'clock, Monday morning. I proceeded to Mr. Levi Waller's, two or three miles distant. I took my station in the rear, and as it 'twas my object to carry terror and devastation wherever we went, I placed fifteen or twenty of the best armed and most to be relied on, in front, who generally approached the houses as fast as their horses could run; this was for two purposes, to prevent their escape and strike terror to the inhabitants—on this account I never got to the houses, after leaving Mrs. Whitehead's, until the murders were committed, except in one case. I sometimes got in sight in time to see the work of death completed, viewed the mangled bodies as they lay, in silent satisfaction, and immediately started in quest of other victims—Having murdered Mrs. Waller and ten children, we started for Mr. William Williams'—having killed him and two little boys that were there; while engaged in this, Mrs. Williams fled and got some distance from the house, but she was pursued, overtaken, and compelled to get up behind one of the company, who brought her back, and after showing her the mangled body of her lifeless husband, she was told to get down and lay by his side, where she was shot dead. I then started for Mr. Jacob Williams, where the family were murdered—Here we found a young man named Drury, who had come on business with Mr. Williams—he was pursued, overtaken and shot. Mrs. Vaughan was the next place we visited—and after murdering the family here, I determined on starting for Jerusalem—Our number amounted now to fifty or sixty, all mounted and armed with guns, axes, swords and clubs—On reaching Mr. James W. Parker's gate, immediately on the road leading to Jerusalem, and about three miles distant, it was proposed to me to call there, but I objected, as I knew he was gone to Jerusalem, and my object was to reach there as soon as possible; but some of the men having relations at Mr. Parker's it was agreed that they might call and get his people. I remained at the gate on the road, with seven or eight; the others going across the field to the house, about half a mile off. After waiting some time for them, I became impatient, and started to the house for them, and on our return we were met by a party of white men, who had pursued our blood-stained track, and who had fired on those at the gate, and dispersed them, which I knew nothing of, not having been at that time rejoined by any of them—Immediately on discovering the whites, I ordered my men to halt and form, as they appeared to be alarmed—The white men, eighteen in number, approached us in about one hundred yards, when one of them fired, (this was against the positive orders of Captain Alexander P. Peete, who commanded, and who had directed the men to reserve their fire until within thirty paces)—And I discovered about half of them retreating, I then ordered my men to fire and rush on them; the few remaining stood their ground until we approached within fifty yards, when they fired and retreated. We pursued and overtook some of them who we thought we left dead; (they were not killed) after pursuing them about two hundred yards, and rising a little hill, I discovered they were met by another party, and had halted, and were reloading their guns, (this was a small party from Jerusalem who knew the negroes were in the field, and had just tied their horses to await their return to the road, knowing that Mr. Parker and family were in Jerusalem, but knew nothing of the party that had gone in with Captain Peete; on hearing the firing they immediately rushed to the spot and arrived just in time to arrest the progress of these barbarous villains, and save the lives of their friends and fellow citizens.) Thinking that those who retreated first, and the party who fired on us at fifty or sixty yards distant, had all only fallen back to meet others with ammunition. As I saw them reloading their guns, and more coming up than I saw at first, and several of my bravest men being wounded, the others became panic struck and squandered over the field; the white men pursued and fired on us several times. Hark had his horse shot under him, and I caught another for him as it was running by me; five or six of my men were wounded, but none left on the field; finding myself defeated here I instantly determined to go through a private way, and cross the Nottoway river at the Cypress Bridge, three miles below Jerusalem, and attack that place in the rear, as I expected they would look for me on the other road, and I had a great desire to get there to procure arms and ammunition. After going a short distance in this private way, accompanied by about twenty men, I overtook two or three who told me the others were dispersed in every direction. After trying in vain to collect a sufficient force to proceed to Jerusalem, I determined to return, as I was sure they would make back to their old neighborhood, where they would rejoin me, make new recruits, and come down again. On my way back, I called at Mrs. Thomas's, Mrs. Spencer's, and several other places, the white families having fled, we found no more victims to gratify our thirst for blood, we stopped at Maj. Ridley's quarter for the night, and being joined by four of his men, with the recruits made since my defeat, we mustered now about forty strong. After placing out sentinels, I laid down to sleep, but was quickly roused by a great racket; starting up, I found some mounted, and others in great confusion; one of the sentinels having given the alarm that we were about to be attacked, I ordered some to ride round and reconnoiter, and on their return the others being more alarmed, not knowing who they were, fled in different ways, so that I was reduced to about twenty again; with this I determined to attempt to recruit, and proceed on to rally in the neighborhood, I had left. Dr. Blunt's was the nearest house, which we reached just before day; on riding up the yard, Hark fired a gun. We expected Dr. Blunt and his family were at Maj. Ridley's, as I knew there was a company of men there; the gun was fired to ascertain if any of the family were at home; we were immediately fired upon and retreated, leaving several of my men. I do not know what became of them, as I never saw them afterwards. Pursuing our course back and coming in sight of Captain Harris', where we had been the day before, we discovered a party of white men at the house, on which all deserted me but two, (Jacob and Nat,) we concealed ourselves in the woods until near night, when I sent them in search of Henry, Sam, Nelson, and Hark, and directed them to rally all they could, at the place we had had our dinner the Sunday before, where they would find me, and I accordingly returned there as soon as it was dark and remained until Wednesday evening, when discovering white men riding around the place as though they were looking for someone, and none of my men joining me, I concluded Jacob and Nat had been taken, and compelled to betray me. On this I gave up all hope for the present; and on Thursday night after having supplied myself with provisions from Mr. Travis's, I scratched a hole under a pile of fence rails in a field, where I concealed myself for six weeks, never leaving my hiding place but for a few minutes in the dead of night to get water which was very near; thinking by this time I could venture out, I began to go about in the night and eavesdrop the houses in the neighborhood; pursuing this course for about a fortnight and gathering little or no intelligence, afraid of speaking to any human being, and returning every morning to my cave before the dawn of day. I know not how long I might have led this life, if accident had not betrayed me, a dog in the neighborhood passing by my hiding place one night while I was out, was attracted by some meat I had in my cave, and crawled in and stole it, and was coming out just as I returned. A few nights after, two negroes having started to go hunting with the same dog, and passed that way, the dog came again to the place, and having just gone out to walk about, discovered me and barked, on which thinking myself discovered, I spoke to them to beg concealment. On making myself known they fled from me. Knowing then they would betray me, I immediately left my hiding place, and was pursued almost incessantly until I was taken a fortnight afterwards by Mr. Benjamin Phipps, in a little hole I had dug out with my sword, for the purpose of concealment, under the top of a fallen tree. On Mr. Phipps' discovering the place of my concealment, he cocked his gun and aimed at me. I requested him not to shoot and I would give up, upon which he demanded my sword. I delivered it to him, and he brought me to prison. During the time I was pursued, I had many hair breadth escapes, which your time will not permit you to relate. I am here loaded with chains, and willing to suffer the fate that awaits me.

I here proceeded to make some inquiries of him, after assuring him of the certain death that awaited him, and that concealment would only bring destruction on the innocent as well as guilty, of his own color, if he knew of any extensive or concerted plan. His answer was, I do not. When I questioned him as to the insurrection in North Carolina happening about the same time, he denied any knowledge of it; and when I looked him in the face as though I would search his inmost thoughts, he replied, "I see sir, you doubt my word; but can you not think the same ideas, and strange appearances about this time in the heavens might prompt others, as well as myself, to this undertaking." I now had much conversation with and asked him many questions, having forborne to do so previously, except in the cases noted in parenthesis; but during his statement, I had, unnoticed by him, taken notes as to some particular circumstances, and having the advantage of his statement before me in writing, on the evening of the third day that I had been with him, I began a cross examination, and found his statement corroborated by every circumstance coming within my own knowledge or the confessions of others whom had been either killed or executed, and whom he had not seen nor had any knowledge since 22d of August last, he expressed himself fully satisfied as to the impracticability of his attempt. It has been said he was ignorant and cowardly, and that his object was to murder and rob for the purpose of obtaining money to make his escape. It is notorious, that he was never known to have a dollar in his life; to swear an oath, or drink a drop of spirits. As to his ignorance, he certainly never had the advantages of education, but he can read and write, (it was taught him by his parents,) and for natural intelligence and quickness of apprehension, is surpassed by few men I have ever seen. As to his being a coward, his reason as given for not resisting Mr. Phipps, shows the decision of his character. When he saw Mr. Phipps present his gun, he said he knew it was impossible for him to escape as the woods were full of men; he therefore thought it was better to surrender, and trust to fortune for his escape. He is a complete fanatic, or plays his part most admirably. On other subjects he possesses an uncommon share of intelligence, with a mind capable of attaining anything; but warped and perverted by the influence of early impressions. He is below the ordinary stature, though strong and active, having the true negro face, every feature of which is strongly marked. I shall not attempt to describe the effect of his narrative, as told and commented on by himself, in the condemned hole of the prison. The calm, deliberate composure with which he spoke of his late deeds and intentions, the expression of his fiend-like face when excited by enthusiasm, still bearing the stains of the blood of helpless innocence about him; clothed with rags and covered with chains; yet daring to raise his manacled hands to heaven, with a spirit soaring above the attributes of man; I looked on him and my blood curdled in my veins.

I will not shock the feelings of humanity, nor wound afresh the bosoms of the disconsolate sufferers in this unparalleled and inhuman massacre, by detailing the deeds of their fiend-like barbarity. There were two or three who were in the power of these wretches, had they known it, and who escaped in the most providential manner. There were two whom they thought they left dead on the field at Mr. Parker's, but who were only stunned by the blows of their guns, as they did not take time to reload when they charged on them. The escape of a little girl who went to school at Mr. Waller's, and where the children were collecting for that purpose, excited general sympathy. As their teacher had not arrived, they were at play in the yard, and seeing the negroes approach, she ran up on a dirt chimney, (such as are common to log houses,) and remained there unnoticed during the massacre of the eleven that were killed at this place. She remained on her hiding place till just before the arrival of a party, who were in pursuit of the murderers, when she came down and fled to a swamp, where, a mere child as she was, with the horrors of the late scene before her, she lay concealed until the next day, when seeing a party go up to the house, she came up, and on being asked how she escaped, replied with the utmost simplicity, "The Lord helped her." She was taken up behind a gentleman of the party, and returned to the arms of her weeping mother. Miss Whitehead concealed herself between the bed and the mat that supported it, while they murdered her sister in the same room, without discovering her. She was afterwards carried off, and concealed for protection by a slave of the family, who gave evidence against several of them on their trial. Mrs. Nathaniel Francis, while concealed in a closet heard their blows, and the shrieks of the victims of these ruthless savages; they then entered the closet where she was concealed, and went out without discovering her. While in this hiding place, she heard two of her women in a quarrel about the division of her clothes. Mr. John T. Barron, discovering them approaching his house, told his wife to make her escape, and scorning to fly, fell fighting on his own threshold. After firing his rifle, he discharged his gun at them, and then broke it over the villain who first approached him, but he was overpowered, and slain. His bravery, however, saved from the hands of these monsters, his lovely and amiable wife, who will long lament a husband so deserving of her love. As directed by him, she attempted to escape through the garden, when she was caught and held by one of her servant girls, but another coming to her rescue, she fled to the woods, and concealed herself. Few indeed, were those who escaped their work of death. But fortunate for society, the hand of retributive justice has overtaken them; and not one that was known to be concerned has escaped.

THE COMMONWEALTH VS. NAT TURNER.

Charged with making insurrection, and plotting to take away the lives of divers free white persons, &c. on the 22d of August, 1831.
The court composed of————, having met for the trial of Nat Turner, the prisoner was brought in and arraigned, and upon his arraignment pleaded *Not guilty*; saying to his counsel, that he did not feel so.

On the part of the Commonwealth, Levi Waller was introduced, who being sworn, deposed as follows: (agreeably to Nat's own Confession.) Col. Trezvant* was then introduced, who being sworn, narrated Nat's Confession to him, as follows: (his Confession as given to Mr. Gray.) The prisoner introduced no evidence, and the case was submitted without argument to the court, who having found him guilty, Jeremiah Cobb, Esq. Chairman, pronounced the sentence of the court, in the following words: "Nat Turner! Stand up. Have you anything to say why sentence of death should not be pronounced against you?"

Ans. I have not, I have made a full confession to Mr. Gray, and I have nothing more to say.

Attend then to the sentence of the Court. You have been arraigned and tried before this court, and convicted of one of the highest crimes in our criminal code. You have been convicted of plotting in cold blood, the indiscriminate destruction of men, of helpless women, and of infant children. The evidence before us leaves not a shadow of doubt, but that your hands were often imbrued in the blood of the innocent; and your own confession tells us that they were stained with the blood of a master; in your own language, "too indulgent." Could I stop here, your crime would be sufficiently aggravated. But the origi-

*The committing Magistrate.

nal contriver of a plan, deep and deadly, one that never can be effected, you managed so far to put it into execution, as to deprive us of many of our most valuable citizens; and this was done when they were asleep, and defenseless; under circumstances shocking to humanity. And while upon this part of the subject, I cannot but call your attention to the poor misguided wretches who have gone before you. They are not few in number—they were your bosom associates; and the blood of all cries aloud, and calls upon you, as the author of their misfortune. Yes! You forced them unprepared, from Time to Eternity. Borne down by this load of guilt, your only justification is, that you were led away by fanaticism. If this be true, from my soul I pity you; and while you have my sympathies, I am, nevertheless called upon to pass the sentence of the court. The time between this and your execution, will necessarily be very short; and your only hope must be in another world. The judgment of the court is, that you be taken hence to the jail from whence you came, thence to the place of execution, and on Friday next, between the hours of 10 A.M. and 2 P.M. be hung by the neck until you are dead! dead! dead and may the Lord have mercy upon your soul.

A list of persons murdered in the Insurrection,
on the 21st and 22d of August, 1831.

Joseph Travers and wife and three children, Mrs. Elizabeth Turner, Hartwell Prebles, Sarah Newsome, Mrs. P. Reese and son William, Trajan Doyle, Henry Bryant and wife and child, and wife's mother, Mrs. Catharine Whitehead, son Richard and four daughters and grandchild, Salathiel Francis, Nathaniel Francis' overseer and two children, John T. Barrow, George Vaughan, Mrs. Levi Waller and ten children, William Williams, wife and two boys, Mrs. Caswell Worrell and child, Mrs. Rebecca Vaughan, Ann Eliza Vaughan, and son Arthur, Mrs. John K. Williams and child, Mrs. Jacob Williams and three children, and Edwin Drury—amounting to fifty-five.

A List of Negroes brought before the Court of Southampton,
with their owners' names, and sentence.

Daniel,	Richard Porter,	Convicted.
Moses,	J. T. Barrow,	Do.
Tom,	Caty Whitehead,	Discharged.
Jack and Andrew,	Caty Whitehead,	Con. and transported.
Jacob,	Geo. H. Charlton,	Disch'd without trial.
Isaac,	Ditto,	Convi. and transported.

Jack,	Everett Bryant,	Discharged.
Nathan,	Benj. Blunt's estate,	Convicted.
Nathan, Tom, and Davy, (boys,)	Nathaniel Francis,	Convicted and transported.
Davy,	Elizabeth Turner,	Convicted.
Curtis,	Thomas Ridley,	Do.
Stephen,	Do.	Do.
Hardy and Isham,	Benjamin Edwards,	Convicted and transp'd.
Sam,	Nathaniel Francis,	Convicted.
Hark,	Joseph Travis' estate.	Do.
Moses, (a boy,)	Do.	Do. and transported.
Davy,	Levi Waller,	Convicted.
Nelson,	Jacob Williams,	Do.
Nat,	Edm'd Turner's estate,	Do.
Jack,	Wm. Reese's estate,	Do.
Dred,	Nathaniel Francis,	Do.
Arnold, Artist, (free,)		Discharged.
Sam,	J. W. Parker,	Acquitted.
Ferry and Archer,	J. W. Parker,	Disch'd without trial.
Jim,	William Vaughan,	Acquitted.
Bob,	Temperance Parker,	Do.
Davy,	Joseph Parker,	
Daniel,	Solomon D. Parker,	Disch'd without trial.
Thomas Haithcock, (free,)		Sent on for further trial.
Joe,	John C. Turner,	Convicted.
Lucy,	John T. Barrow,	Do.
Matt,	Thomas Ridley,	Acquitted.
Jim,	Richard Porter,	Do.
Exum Artes, (free,)		Sent on for further trial.
Joe,	Richard P. Briggs.	Disch'd without trial.
Bury Newsome, (free,)		Sent on for further trial.
Stephen,	James Bell,	Acquitted.
Jim and Isaac,	Samuel Champion,	Convicted and trans'd.
Preston,	Hannah Williamson,	Acquitted.
Frank,	Solomon D. Parker,	Convi'd and transp'd.
Jack and Shadrach,	Nathaniel Simmons,	Acquitted.
Nelson,	Benj. Blunt's estate,	Do.
Sam,	Peter Edwards,	Convicted.
Archer,	Arthur G. Reese,	Acquitted.
Isham Turner, (free,)		Sent on for further trial.
Nat Turner,	Putnam Moore, dec'd,	Convicted.

NARRATIVE

OF THE

LIFE

OF

FREDERICK DOUGLASS,

AN AMERICAN SLAVE.

WRITTEN BY HIMSELF.

BOSTON:
PUBLISHED AT THE ANTI-SLAVERY OFFICE,
NO. 25 CORNHILL

1845.

3

NARRATIVE OF THE LIFE OF

FREDERICK DOUGLASS,

AN AMERICAN SLAVE,

WRITTEN BY HIMSELF

PREFACE.

In the month of August, 1841, I attended an anti-slavery convention in Nantucket, at which it was my happiness to become acquainted with Frederick Douglass, the writer of the following Narrative. He was a stranger to nearly every member of that body; but, having recently made his escape from the southern prison-house of bondage, and feeling his curiosity excited to ascertain the principles and measures of the abolitionists,—of whom he had heard a somewhat vague description while he was a slave,—he was induced to give his attendance, on the occasion alluded to, though at that time a resident in New Bedford.

Fortunate, most fortunate occurrence!—fortunate for the millions of his manacled brethren, yet panting for deliverance from their awful thraldom!—fortunate for the cause of negro emancipation, and of universal liberty!—fortunate for the land of his birth, which he has already done so much to save and bless!—fortunate for a large circle of friends and acquaintances, whose sympathy and affection he has strongly secured by the many sufferings he has endured, by his virtuous traits of character, by his ever-abiding remembrance of those who are in bonds, as being bound with them!—fortunate for the multitudes, in various parts of our republic, whose minds he has enlightened on the subject of slavery, and who have been melted to tears by his pathos, or roused to virtuous indignation by his stirring eloquence against the enslavers of men!—fortunate for himself, as it at once brought him into the field of public usefulness, "gave the world assurance of a man," quickened the slumbering energies of his soul, and consecrated him to the great work of breaking the rod of the oppressor, and letting the oppressed go free!

I shall never forget his first speech at the convention—the extraordinary emotion it excited in my own mind—the powerful impression it created upon a crowded auditory, completely taken by surprise—the applause which followed from the beginning to the end of his felicitous remarks. I think I never hated slavery so intensely as at that moment; certainly, my perception of the enormous outrage which is inflicted by it, on the godlike nature of its victims, was rendered far more clear than ever. There stood one, in physical proportion and stature commanding and exact—in intellect richly endowed—in natural eloquence a prodigy—in soul manifestly "created but a little lower than the angels"—yet a slave, ay, a fugitive slave,—trembling for his safety, hardly daring to believe that on the American soil, a single white person could be found who would befriend him at all hazards, for the love of God and humanity! Capable of high attainments as an intellectual and moral being—needing nothing but a comparatively small amount of cultivation to make him an ornament to society and a blessing to his race—by the law of the land, by the voice of the people, by the terms of the slave code, he was only a piece of property, a beast of burden, a chattel personal, nevertheless!

A beloved friend from New Bedford prevailed on Mr. DOUGLASS to address the convention. He came forward to the platform with a hesitancy and embarrassment, necessarily the attendants of a sensitive mind in such a novel position. After apologizing for his ignorance, and reminding the audience that slavery was a poor school for the human intellect and heart, he proceeded to narrate some of the facts in his own history as a slave, and in the course of his speech gave utterance to many noble thoughts and thrilling reflections. As soon as he had taken his seat, filled with hope and admiration, I rose, and declared that PATRICK HENRY, of revolutionary fame, never made a speech more eloquent in the cause of liberty, than the one we had just listened to from the lips of that hunted fugitive. So I believed at that time—such is my belief now. I reminded the audience of the peril which surrounded this self-emancipated young man at the North,—even in Massachusetts, on the soil of the Pilgrim Fathers, among the descendants of revolutionary sires; and I appealed to them, whether they would ever allow him to be carried back into slavery,—law or no law, constitution or no constitution. The response was unanimous and in thunder-tones—"NO!" "Will you succor and protect him as a brother-man—a resident of the old Bay State?" "YES!" shouted the whole mass, with an energy so startling, that the ruthless tyrants south of Mason and Dixon's line might almost have heard the mighty burst of feeling, and recognized it as the pledge of an invincible determination, on the part of those who gave it, never to betray him that wanders, but to hide the outcast, and firmly to abide the consequences.

It was at once deeply impressed upon my mind, that, if Mr. DOUGLASS could be persuaded to consecrate his time and talents to the promotion of the anti-slavery enterprise, a powerful impetus would be given to it, and a stunning blow at the same time inflicted on northern prejudice against a colored complexion. I therefore endeavored to instil hope and courage into his mind, in order that he might dare to engage in a vocation so anomalous and responsible for a person in his situation; and I was seconded in this effort by warm-hearted friends, especially by the late General Agent of the Massachusetts Anti-Slavery Society, Mr. JOHN A. COLLINS, whose judgment in this instance entirely coincided with my own. At first, he could give no encouragement; with unfeigned diffidence, he expressed his conviction that he was not adequate to the performance of so great a task; the path marked out was wholly an untrodden one; he was sincerely apprehensive that he should do more harm than good. After much deliberation, however, he consented to make a trial; and ever since that period, he has acted as a lecturing agent, under the auspices either of the American or the Massachusetts Anti-Slavery Society. In labors he has been most abundant; and his success in combating prejudice, in gaining proselytes, in agitating the public mind, has far surpassed the most sanguine expectations that were raised at the commencement of his brilliant career. He has borne himself with gentleness and meekness, yet with true manliness of character. As a public speaker, he excels in pathos, wit, comparison, imitation, strength of reasoning, and fluency of language. There is in him that union of head and heart, which is indispensable to an enlightenment of the heads and a winning of the hearts of others. May his strength continue to be equal to his day! May he continue to "grow in grace, and in the knowledge of God," that he may be increasingly serviceable in the cause of bleeding humanity, whether at home or abroad!

It is certainly a very remarkable fact, that one of the most efficient advocates of the slave population, now before the public, is a fugitive slave, in the person of FREDERICK DOUGLASS; and that the free colored population of the United States are as ably represented by one of their own number, in the person of CHARLES LENOX REMOND, whose eloquent appeals have extorted the highest applause of multitudes on both sides of the Atlantic. Let the calumniators of the colored race despise themselves for their baseness and illiberality of spirit, and henceforth cease to talk of the natural inferiority of those who require nothing but time and opportunity to attain to the highest point of human excellence.

It may, perhaps, be fairly questioned, whether any other portion of the population of the earth could have endured the privations, sufferings and horrors of slavery, without having become more degraded in the scale of humanity than the slaves of African descent. Nothing has been left undone to cripple their intellects, darken their minds, debase their moral nature, obliterate all traces of their relationship to mankind; and yet how wonderfully they have sustained the mighty load of a most frightful bondage, under which they have been groaning for centuries! To illustrate the effect of slavery on the white man,—to show that he has no powers of endurance, in such a condition, superior to those of his black brother,—DANIEL O'CONNELL, the distinguished advocate of universal emancipation, and the mightiest champion of prostrate but not conquered Ireland, relates the following anecdote in a speech delivered by him in the Conciliation Hall, Dublin, before the Loyal National Repeal Association, March 31, 1845. "No matter," said Mr. O'CONNELL, "under what specious term it may disguise itself, slavery is still hideous. *It has a natural, an inevitable tendency to brutalize every noble faculty of man.* An American sailor, who was cast away on the shore of Africa, where he was kept in slavery for three years, was, at the expiration of that period, found to be imbruted and stultified—he had lost all reasoning power; and having forgotten his native language, could only utter some savage gibberish between Arabic and English, which nobody could understand, and which even he himself found difficulty in pronouncing. So much for the humanizing influence of THE DOMESTIC INSTITUTION!" Admitting this to have been an extraordinary case of mental deterioration, it proves at least that the white slave can sink as low in the scale of humanity as the black one.

Mr. DOUGLASS has very properly chosen to write his own Narrative, in his own style, and according to the best of his ability, rather than to employ someone else. It is, therefore, entirely his own production; and, considering how long and dark was the career he had to run as a slave,—how few have been his opportunities to improve his mind since he broke his iron fetters,—it is, in my judgment, highly creditable to his head and heart. He who can peruse it without a tearful eye, a heaving breast, an afflicted spirit,—without being filled with an unutterable abhorrence of slavery and all its abettors, and animated with a determination to seek the immediate overthrow of that execrable system,—without trembling for the fate of this country in the hands of a righteous God, who is ever on the side of the oppressed, and whose arm is not shortened that it cannot save,—must have a flinty heart, and be qualified to act the part of a trafficker "in slaves and the souls of men." I am confident that it is essentially true in all its statements; that nothing has been set down in malice, nothing exaggerated, nothing drawn from the imagination; that it comes short of the reality, rather than overstates a single fact in regard to SLAVERY AS IT IS. The experience of FREDERICK DOUGLASS, as a slave, was not a peculiar one; his lot was not especially a hard one; his case may be regarded as a very fair specimen of the treatment of slaves in Maryland, in which State it is conceded that they are better fed and less cruelly treated than in Georgia, Alabama, or Louisiana. Many have suffered incomparably more, while very few on the plantations have suffered less, than himself. Yet how deplorable was his situation! what terrible chastisements were inflicted upon his person! what still more shocking outrages were perpetrated upon his mind! with all his noble powers and sublime aspirations, how like a brute was he treated, even by those professing to have the same mind in them that was in Christ Jesus! to what dreadful liabilities was he continually subjected! how destitute of friendly counsel and aid, even in his greatest extremities! how heavy was the midnight of woe which shrouded in blackness the last ray of hope, and filled the future with terror and gloom! what longings after freedom took possession of his breast, and how his misery augmented, in proportion as he grew reflective and intelligent,—thus demonstrating that a happy slave is an extinct man! how he thought, reasoned, felt, under the lash of the driver, with the chains upon his limbs! what perils he encountered in his endeavors to escape from his horrible doom! and how signal have been his deliverance and preservation in the midst of a nation of pitiless enemies!

This Narrative contains many affecting incidents, many passages of great eloquence and power; but I think the most thrilling one of them all is the description DOUGLASS gives of his feelings, as he stood soliloquizing respecting his fate, and the chances of his one day being a freeman, on the banks of the Chesapeake Bay—viewing the receding vessels as they flew with their white wings before the breeze, and apostrophizing them as animated by the living spirit of freedom. Who can read that passage, and be insensible to its pathos and sublimity? Compressed into it is a whole Alexandrian library of thought, feeling, and sentiment—all that can, all that need be urged, in the form of expostulation, entreaty, rebuke, against that crime of crimes,—making man the property of his fellow-man! O, how accursed is that system, which entombs the godlike mind of man, defaces the divine image, reduces those who by creation were crowned with glory and honor to a level with four-footed beasts, and exalts the dealer in human flesh above all that is called God! Why should its existence be prolonged one hour? Is it not evil, only evil, and that continually? What does its presence imply but the absence of all fear of God, all regard for man, on the part of the people of the United States? Heaven speed its eternal overthrow!

So profoundly ignorant of the nature of slavery are many persons, that they are stubbornly incredulous whenever they read or listen to any recital of the cruelties which are daily inflicted on its victims. They do not deny that the slaves are held as property; but that terrible fact seems to convey to their minds no idea of injustice, exposure to outrage, or savage barbarity. Tell them of cruel scourgings, of mutilations and brandings, of scenes of pollution and blood, of the banishment of all light and knowledge, and they affect to be greatly indignant at such enormous exaggerations, such wholesale misstatements, such abominable libels on the character of the southern planters! As if all these direful outrages were not the natural results of slavery! As if it were less cruel to reduce a human being to the condition of a thing, than to give him a severe flagellation, or to deprive him of necessary food and clothing! As if whips, chains, thumb-screws, paddles, bloodhounds, overseers, drivers, patrols, were not all indispensable to keep the slaves down, and to give protection to their ruthless oppressors! As if, when the marriage institution is abolished, concubinage, adultery, and incest, must not necessarily abound; when all the rights of humanity are annihilated, any barrier remains to protect the victim from the fury of the spoiler; when absolute power is assumed over life and liberty, it will not be wielded with destructive sway! Skeptics of this character abound in society. In some few instances, their incredulity arises from a want of reflection; but, generally, it indicates a hatred of the light, a desire to shield slavery from the assaults of its foes, a contempt of the colored race, whether bond or free. Such will try to discredit the shocking tales of slaveholding cruelty which are recorded in this truthful Narrative; but they will labor in vain. Mr. DOUGLASS has frankly disclosed the place of his birth, the names of those who claimed ownership in his body and soul, and the names also of those who committed the crimes which he has alleged against them. His statements, therefore, may easily be disproved, if they are untrue.

In the course of his Narrative, he relates two instances of murderous cruelty,—in one of which a planter deliberately shot a slave belonging to a neighboring plantation, who had unintentionally gotten within his lordly domain in quest of fish; and in the other, an overseer blew out the brains of a slave who had fled to a stream of water to escape a bloody scourging. Mr. DOUGLASS states that in neither of these instances was anything done by way of legal arrest or judicial investigation. *The Baltimore American,* of March 17, 1845, relates a similar case of atrocity, perpetrated with similar impunity—as follows:— "*Shooting a Slave.*—We learn, upon the authority of a letter from Charles county, Maryland, received by a gentleman of this city, that a young man, named Matthews, a nephew of General Matthews, and whose father, it is believed, holds an office at Washington, killed one of the slaves upon his father's farm by shooting him. The letter states that young Matthews had been left in charge of the farm; that he gave an order to the servant, which was disobeyed, when he proceeded to the house, *obtained a gun, and, returning, shot the servant.* He immediately, the letter continues, fled to his father's residence, where he still remains unmolested."—Let it never be forgotten, that no slaveholder or overseer can be convicted of any outrage perpetrated on the person of a slave, however diabolical it may be, on the testimony of colored witnesses, whether bond or free. By the slave code, they are adjudged to be as incompetent to testify against a white man, as though they were indeed a part of the brute creation. Hence, there is no legal protection in fact, whatever there may be in form, for the slave population; and any amount of cruelty may be inflicted on them with impunity. Is it possible for the human mind to conceive of a more horrible state of society?

The effect of a religious profession on the conduct of southern masters is vividly described in the following Narrative, and shown to be anything but salutary. In the nature of the case, it must be in the highest degree pernicious. The testimony of Mr. DOUGLASS, on this point, is sustained by a cloud of witnesses, whose veracity is unimpeachable. "A slaveholder's profession of Christianity is a palpable imposture. He is a felon of the highest grade. He is a man-stealer. It is of no importance what you put in the other scale."

Reader! are you with the man-stealers in sympathy and purpose, or on the side of their down-trodden victims? If with the former, then are you the foe of God and man. If with the latter, what are you prepared to do and dare in their behalf? Be faithful, be vigilant, be untiring in your efforts to break every yoke, and let the oppressed go free. Come what may—cost what it may—inscribe on the banner which you un-

furl to the breeze, as your religious and political motto—"No Compromise with Slavery! No Union with Slaveholders!"

> *Wm. Lloyd Garrison.*
> Boston,
> May 1, 1845.

LETTER
From Wendell Phillips, Esq.

Boston, April 22, 1845.

My Dear Friend:

You remember the old fable of "The Man and the Lion," where the
lion complained that he should not be so misrepresented "when the
lions wrote history."

I am glad the time has come when the "lions write history." We have
been left long enough to gather the character of slavery from the involuntary evidence of the masters. One might, indeed, rest sufficiently
satisfied with what, it is evident, must be, in general, the results of such
a relation, without seeking further to find whether they have followed
in every instance. Indeed, those who stare at the half-peck of corn a
week, and love to count the lashes on the slave's back, are seldom the
"stuff" out of which reformers and abolitionists are to be made. I remember that, in 1838, many were waiting for the results of the West
India experiment, before they could come into our ranks. Those "results" have come long ago; but, alas! few of that number have come
with them, as converts. A man must be disposed to judge of emancipation by other tests than whether it has increased the produce of
sugar,—and to hate slavery for other reasons than because it starves
men and whips women,—before he is ready to lay the first stone of his
anti-slavery life.

I was glad to learn, in your story, how early the most neglected of
God's children waken to a sense of their rights, and of the injustice
done them. Experience is a keen teacher; and long before you had mas-
tered your A B C, or knew where the "white sails" of the Chesapeake
were bound, you began, I see, to gauge the wretchedness of the slave,
not by his hunger and want, not by his lashes and toil, but by the cruel
and blighting death which gathers over his soul.

In connection with this, there is one circumstance which makes
your recollections peculiarly valuable, and renders your early insight

the more remarkable. You come from that part of the country where
we are told slavery appears with its fairest features. Let us hear, then,
what it is at its best estate—gaze on its bright side, if it has one; and then
imagination may task her powers to add dark lines to the picture, as she
travels southward to that (for the colored man) Valley of the Shadow
of Death, where the Mississippi sweeps along.

Again, we have known you long, and can put the most entire confidence in your truth, candor, and sincerity. Everyone who has heard
you speak has felt, and, I am confident, everyone who reads your book
will feel, persuaded that you give them a fair specimen of the whole
truth. No one-sided portrait,—no wholesale complaints,—but strict
justice done, whenever individual kindliness has neutralized, for a
moment, the deadly system with which it was strangely allied. You
have been with us, too, some years, and can fairly compare the twilight
of rights, which your race enjoy at the North, with that "noon of night"
under which they labor south of Mason and Dixon's line. Tell us
whether, after all, the half-free colored man of Massachusetts is worse
off than the pampered slave of the rice swamps!

In reading your life, no one can say that we have unfairly picked out
some rare specimens of cruelty. We know that the bitter drops, which
even you have drained from the cup, are no incidental aggravations, no
individual ills, but such as must mingle always and necessarily in the
lot of every slave. They are the essential ingredients, not the occasional
results, of the system.

After all, I shall read your book with trembling for you. Some years
ago, when you were beginning to tell me your real name and birth-
place, you may remember I stopped you, and preferred to remain ignorant of all. With the exception of a vague description, so I continued,
till the other day, when you read me your memoirs. I hardly knew, at
the time, whether to thank you or not for the sight of them, when I reflected that it was still dangerous, in Massachusetts, for honest men to
tell their names! They say the fathers, in 1776, signed the Declaration
of Independence with the halter about their necks. You, too, publish
your declaration of freedom with danger compassing you around. In
all the broad lands which the Constitution of the United States over-
shadows, there is no single spot,—however narrow or desolate,—
where a fugitive slave can plant himself and say, "I am safe." The whole
armory of Northern Law has no shield for you. I am free to say that, in
your place, I should throw the MS. into the fire.

You, perhaps, may tell your story in safety, endeared as you are to so many warm hearts by rare gifts, and a still rarer devotion of them to the service of others. But it will be owing only to your labors, and the fearless efforts of those who, trampling the laws and Constitution of the country under their feet, are determined that they will "hide the outcast," and that their hearths shall be, spite of the law, an asylum for the oppressed, if, some time or other, the humblest may stand in our streets, and bear witness in safety against the cruelties of which he has been the victim.

Yet it is sad to think, that these very throbbing hearts which welcome your story, and form your best safeguard in telling it, are all beating contrary to the "statute in such case made and provided." Go on, my dear friend, till you, and those who, like you, have been saved, so as by fire, from the dark prison-house, shall stereotype these free, illegal pulses into statutes; and New England, cutting loose from a bloodstained Union, shall glory in being the house of refuge for the oppressed;—till we no longer merely "*hide* the outcast," or make a merit of standing idly by while he is hunted in our midst; but, consecrating anew the soil of the Pilgrims as an asylum for the oppressed, proclaim our *welcome* to the slave so loudly, that the tones shall reach every hut in the Carolinas, and make the broken-hearted bondman leap up at the thought of old Massachusetts.

God speed the day!

Till then, and ever,
Yours truly,
Wendell Phillips.

[FREDERICK DOUGLASS.]

Narrative of the Life

of Frederick Douglass.

Chapter I

I was born in Tuckahoe, near Hillsborough, and about twelve miles from Easton, in Talbot county, Maryland. I have no accurate knowledge of my age, never having seen any authentic record containing it. By far the larger part of the slaves know as little of their ages as horses know of theirs, and it is the wish of most masters within my knowledge to keep their slaves thus ignorant. I do not remember to have ever met a slave who could tell of his birthday. They seldom come nearer to it than planting-time, harvest-time, cherry-time, spring-time, or fall-time. A want of information concerning my own was a source of unhappiness to me even during childhood. The white children could tell their ages. I could not tell why I ought to be deprived of the same privilege. I was not allowed to make any inquiries of my master concerning it. He deemed all such inquiries on the part of a slave unproper and impertinent, and evidence of a restless spirit. The nearest estimate I can give makes me now between twenty-seven and twenty-eight years of age. I come to this, from hearing my master say, some time during 1835, I was about seventeen years old.

My mother was named Harriet Bailey. She was the daughter of Isaac and Betsey Bailey, both colored, and quite dark. My mother was of a darker complexion than either my grandmother or grandfather.

My father was a white man. He was admitted to be such by all I ever heard speak of my parentage. The opinion was also whispered that my master was my father; but of the correctness of this opinion, I know nothing; the means of knowing was withheld from me. My mother and I were separated when I was but an infant—before I knew her as my mother. It is a common custom, in the part of Maryland from which I ran away, to part children from their mothers at a very early age. Frequently, before the child has reached its twelfth month, its mother is taken from it, and hired out on some farm a considerable distance off, and the child is placed under the care of an old woman, too old for field labor. For what this separation is done, I do not know, unless it be to hinder the development of the child's affection toward its mother, and to blunt and destroy the natural affection of the mother for the child. This is the inevitable result.

I never saw my mother, to know her as such, more than four or five times in my life; and each of these times was very short in duration, and at night. She was hired by a Mr. Stewart, who lived about twelve miles from my home. She made her journeys to see me in the night, travelling the whole distance on foot, after the performance of her day's work. She was a field hand, and a whipping is the penalty of not being in the field at sunrise, unless a slave has special permission from his or her master to the contrary—a permission which they seldom get, and one that gives to him that gives it the proud name of being a kind master. I do not recollect of ever seeing my mother by the light of day. She was with me in the night. She would lie down with me, and get me to sleep, but long before I waked she was gone. Very little communication ever took place between us. Death soon ended what little we could have while she lived, and with it her hardships and suffering. She died when I was about seven years old, on one of my master's farms, near Lee's Mill. I was not allowed to be present during her illness, at her death, or burial. She was gone long before I knew anything about it. Never having enjoyed, to any considerable extent, her soothing presence, her tender and watchful care, I received the tidings of her death with much the same emotions I should have probably felt at the death of a stranger.

Called thus suddenly away, she left me without the slightest intimation of who my father was. The whisper that my master was my father, may or may not be true; and, true or false, it is of but little consequence to my purpose whilst the fact remains, in all its glaring odiousness, that slaveholders have ordained, and by law established, that the children of slave women shall in all cases follow the condition of their mothers; and this is done too obviously to administer to their own lusts, and make a gratification of their wicked desires profitable as well as pleasurable; for by this cunning arrangement, the slaveholder, in cases not a few, sustains to his slaves the double relation of master and father.

I know of such cases; and it is worthy of remark that such slaves invariably suffer greater hardships, and have more to contend with, than others. They are, in the first place, a constant offense to their mistress. She is ever disposed to find fault with them; they can seldom do anything to please her; she is never better pleased than when she sees them under the lash, especially when she suspects her husband of showing to his mulatto children favors which he withholds from his black slaves. The master is frequently compelled to sell this class of his slaves, out of deference to the feelings of his white wife; and, cruel as the deed may strike anyone to be, for a man to sell his own children to human flesh-mongers, it is often the dictate of humanity for him to do so; for, unless he does this, he must not only whip them himself, but must stand by and see one white son tie up his brother, of but few shades darker complexion than himself, and ply the gory lash to his naked back; and if he lisp one word of disapproval, it is set down to his parental partiality, and only makes a bad matter worse, both for himself and the slave whom he would protect and defend.

Every year brings with it multitudes of this class of slaves. It was doubtless in consequence of a knowledge of this fact, that one great statesman of the south predicted the downfall of slavery by the inevitable laws of population. Whether this prophecy is ever fulfilled or not, it is nevertheless plain that a very different-looking class of people are springing up at the south, and are now held in slavery, from those originally brought to this country from Africa; and if their increase will do no other good, it will do away the force of the argument, that God cursed Ham, and therefore American slavery is right. If the lineal descendants of Ham are alone to be scripturally enslaved, it is certain that slavery at the south must soon become unscriptural; for thousands are ushered into the world, annually, who, like myself, owe their existence to white fathers, and those fathers most frequently their own masters.

I have had two masters. My first master's name was Anthony. I do not remember his first name. He was generally called Captain Anthony—a title which, I presume, he acquired by sailing a craft on the Chesapeake Bay. He was not considered a rich slaveholder. He owned two or three farms, and about thirty slaves. His farms and slaves were under the care of an overseer. The overseer's name was Plummer. Mr. Plummer was a miserable drunkard, a profane swearer, and a savage monster. He always went armed with a cowskin and a heavy cudgel. I have known him to cut and slash the women's heads so horribly, that even master would be enraged at his cruelty, and would threaten to whip him if he did not mind himself. Master, however, was not a humane slaveholder. It required extraordinary barbarity on the part of an overseer to affect him. He was a cruel man, hardened by a long life of slaveholding. He would at times seem to take great pleasure in whipping a slave. I have often been awakened at the dawn of day by the most heart-rending shrieks of an own aunt of mine, whom he used to tie up to a joist, and whip upon her naked back till she was literally covered with blood. No words, no tears, no prayers, from his gory victim, seemed to move his iron heart from its bloody purpose. The louder she screamed, the harder he whipped; and where the blood ran fastest, there he whipped longest. He would whip her to make her scream, and whip her to make her hush; and not until overcome by fatigue, would he cease to swing the blood-clotted cowskin. I remember the first time I ever witnessed this horrible exhibition. I was quite a child, but I well remember it. I never shall forget it whilst I remember anything. It was the first of a long series of such outrages, of which I was doomed to be a witness and a participant. It struck me with awful force. It was the blood-stained gate, the entrance to the hell of slavery, through which I was about to pass. It was a most terrible spectacle. I wish I could commit to paper the feelings with which I beheld it.

This occurrence took place very soon after I went to live with my old master, and under the following circumstances. Aunt Hester went out one night,—where or for what I do not know,—and happened to be absent when my master desired her presence. He had ordered her not to go out evenings, and warned her that she must never let him catch her in company with a young man, who was paying attention to her, belonging to Colonel Lloyd. The young man's name was Ned Roberts, generally called Lloyd's Ned. Why master was so careful of her, may be safely left to conjecture. She was a woman of noble form, and of graceful proportions, having very few equals, and fewer superiors, in personal appearance, among the colored or white women of our neighborhood.

Aunt Hester had not only disobeyed his orders in going out, but had been found in company with Lloyd's Ned; which circumstance, I found, from what he said while whipping her, was the chief offense. Had he been a man of pure morals himself, he might have been thought interested in protecting the innocence of my aunt; but those who knew him will not suspect him of any such virtue. Before he commenced whipping Aunt Hester, he took her into the kitchen, and stripped her from neck to waist, leaving her neck, shoulders, and back, entirely naked. He then told her to cross her hands, calling her at the same time a d———d b———h. After crossing her hands, he tied them with a strong rope and led her to a stool under a large hook in the joist, put in for the purpose. He made her get upon the stool, and tied her hands to the hook. She now stood fair for his infernal purpose. Her arms were stretched up at their full length, so that she stood upon the ends of her toes. He then said to her, "Now, you d——d b——h, I'll learn you how to disobey my orders!" and after rolling up his sleeves, he commenced to lay on the heavy cowskin, and soon the warm, red blood (amid heart-rending shrieks from her, and horrid oaths from him) came dripping to the floor. I was so terrified and horror-stricken at the sight, that I hid myself in a closet, and dared not venture out till long after the bloody transaction was over. I expected it would be my turn next. It was all new to me. I had never seen anything like it before. I had always lived with my grandmother on the outskirts of the plantation, where she was put to raise the children of the younger women. I had therefore been, until now, out of the way of the bloody scenes that often occurred on the plantation.

Chapter II

M Y MASTER'S FAMILY consisted of two sons, Andrew and Richard; one daughter, Lucretia, and her husband, Captain Thomas Auld. They lived in one house, upon the home plantation of Colonel Edward Lloyd. My master was Colonel Lloyd's clerk and superintendent. He was what might be called the overseer of the overseers. I spent two years of childhood on this plantation in my old master's family. It was here that I witnessed the bloody transaction recorded in the first chapter; and as I received my first impressions of slavery on this plantation, I will give some description of it, and of slavery as it there existed. The plantation is about twelve miles north of Easton, in Talbot county, and is situated on the border of Miles River. The principal products raised upon it were tobacco, corn, and wheat. These were raised in great abundance; so that, with the products of this and the other farms belonging to him, he was able to keep in almost constant employment a large sloop, in carrying them to market at Baltimore. This sloop was named *Sally Lloyd*, in honor of one of the colonel's daughters. My master's son-in-law, Captain Auld, was master of the vessel; she was otherwise manned by the colonel's own slaves. Their names were Peter, Isaac, Rich, and Jake. These were esteemed very highly by the other slaves, and looked upon as the privileged ones of the plantation; for it was no small affair, in the eyes of the slaves, to be allowed to see Baltimore.

Colonel Lloyd kept from three to four hundred slaves on his home plantation, and owned a large number more on the neighboring farms

belonging to him. The names of the farms nearest to the home plantation were Wye Town and New Design. "Wye Town" was under the
overseership of a man named Noah Willis. New Design was under
the overseership of a Mr. Townsend. The overseers of these, and all
the rest of the farms, numbering over twenty, received advice and direction from the managers of the home plantation. This was the great
business place. It was the seat of government for the whole twenty
farms. All disputes among the overseers were settled here. If a slave
was convicted of any high misdemeanor, became unmanageable, or
evinced a determination to run away, he was brought immediately
here, severely whipped, put on board the sloop, carried to Baltimore,
and sold to Austin Woolfolk, or some other slave-trader, as a warning
to the slaves remaining.

Here, too, the slaves of all the other farms received their monthly allowance of food, and their yearly clothing. The men and women slaves
received, as their monthly allowance of food, eight pounds of pork, or
its equivalent in fish, and one bushel of corn meal. Their yearly clothing consisted of two coarse linen shirts, one pair of linen trousers, like
the shirts, one jacket, one pair of trousers for winter, made of coarse
negro cloth, one pair of stockings, and one pair of shoes; the whole of
which could not have cost more than seven dollars. The allowance of
the slave children was given to their mothers, or the old women having
the care of them. The children unable to work in the field had neither
shoes, stockings, jackets, nor trousers, given to them; their clothing
consisted of two coarse linen shirts per year. When these failed them,
they went naked until the next allowance-day. Children from seven to
ten years old, of both sexes, almost naked, might be seen at all seasons
of the year.

There were no beds given the slaves, unless one coarse blanket be
considered such, and none but the men and women had these. This,
however, is not considered a very great privation. They find less
difficulty from the want of beds, than from the want of time to sleep;
for when their day's work in the field is done, the most of them having
their washing, mending, and cooking to do, and having few or none of
the ordinary facilities for doing either of these, very many of their
sleeping hours are consumed in preparing for the field the coming
day; and when this is done, old and young, male and female, married
and single, drop down side by side, on one common bed,—the cold,
damp floor,—each covering himself or herself with their miserable
blankets; and here they sleep till they are summoned to the field by the

driver's horn. At the sound of this, all must rise, and be off to the field. There must be no halting; everyone must be at his or her post; and woe betides them who hear not this morning summons to the field; for if they are not awakened by the sense of hearing, they are by the sense of feeling: no age nor sex finds any favor. Mr. Severe, the overseer, used to stand by the door of the quarter, armed with a large hickory stick and heavy cowskin, ready to whip anyone who was so unfortunate as not to hear, or, from any other cause, was prevented from being ready to start for the field at the sound of the horn.

Mr. Severe was rightly named: he was a cruel man. I have seen him whip a woman, causing the blood to run half an hour at the time; and this, too, in the midst of her crying children, pleading for their mother's release. He seemed to take pleasure in manifesting his fiendish barbarity. Added to his cruelty, he was a profane swearer. It was enough to chill the blood and stiffen the hair of an ordinary man to hear him talk. Scarce a sentence escaped him but that was commenced or concluded by some horrid oath. The field was the place to witness his cruelty and profanity. His presence made it both the field of blood and of blasphemy. From the rising till the going down of the sun, he was cursing, raving, cutting, and slashing among the slaves of the field, in the most frightful manner. His career was short. He died very soon after I went to Colonel Lloyd's; and he died as he lived, uttering, with his dying groans, bitter curses and horrid oaths. His death was regarded by the slaves as the result of a merciful providence.

Mr. Severe's place was filled by a Mr. Hopkins. He was a very different man. He was less cruel, less profane, and made less noise, than Mr. Severe. His course was characterized by no extraordinary demonstrations of cruelty. He whipped, but seemed to take no pleasure in it. He was called by the slaves a good overseer.

The home plantation of Colonel Lloyd wore the appearance of a country village. All the mechanical operations for all the farms were performed here. The shoemaking and mending, the blacksmithing, cartwrighting, coopering, weaving, and grain-grinding, were all performed by the slaves on the home plantation. The whole place wore a business-like aspect very unlike the neighboring farms. The number of houses, too, conspired to give it advantage over the neighboring farms. It was called by the slaves the *Great House Farm*. Few privileges were esteemed higher, by the slaves of the out-farms, than that of being selected to do errands at the Great House Farm. It was associated in their minds with greatness. A representative could not be prouder of his election to a seat in the American Congress, than a slave on one of the out-farms would be of his election to do errands at the Great House Farm. They regarded it as evidence of great confidence reposed in them by their overseers; and it was on this account, as well as a constant desire to be out of the field from under the driver's lash, that they esteemed it a high privilege, one worth careful living for. He was called the smartest and most trusty fellow, who had this honor conferred upon him the most frequently. The competitors for this office sought as diligently to please their overseers, as the office-seekers in the political parties seek to please and deceive the people. The same traits of character might be seen in Colonel Lloyd's slaves, as are seen in the slaves of the political parties.

The slaves selected to go to the Great House Farm, for the monthly allowance for themselves and their fellow-slaves, were peculiarly enthusiastic. While on their way, they would make the dense old woods, for miles around, reverberate with their wild songs, revealing at once the highest joy and the deepest sadness. They would compose and sing as they went along, consulting neither time nor tune. The thought that came up, came out—if not in the word, in the sound;—and as frequently in the one as in the other. They would sometimes sing the most pathetic sentiment in the most rapturous tone, and the most rapturous sentiment in the most pathetic tone. Into all of their songs they would manage to weave something of the Great House Farm. Especially would they do this, when leaving home. They would then sing most exultingly the following words:—

"I am going away to the Great House Farm!
O, yea! O, yea! O!"

This they would sing, as a chorus, to words which to many would seem unmeaning jargon, but which, nevertheless, were full of meaning to themselves. I have sometimes thought that the mere hearing of those songs would do more to impress some minds with the horrible character of slavery, than the reading of whole volumes of philosophy on the subject could do.

I did not, when a slave, understand the deep meaning of those rude and apparently incoherent songs. I was myself within the circle; so that I neither saw nor heard as those without might see and hear. They told a tale of woe which was then altogether beyond my feeble comprehension; they were tones loud, long, and deep; they breathed the prayer and complaint of souls boiling over with the bitterest anguish. Every tone was a testimony against slavery, and a prayer to God for deliverance from chains. The hearing of those wild notes always depressed my spirit, and filled me with ineffable sadness. I have frequently found myself in tears while hearing them. The mere recurrence to those songs, even now, afflicts me; and while I am writing these lines, an expression of feeling has already found its way down my cheek. To those songs I trace my first glimmering conception of the dehumanizing character of slavery. I can never get rid of that conception. Those songs still follow me, to deepen my hatred of slavery, and quicken my sympathies for my brethren in bonds. If anyone wishes to be impressed with the soul-killing effects of slavery, let him go to Colonel Lloyd's plantation, and, on allowance-day, place himself in the deep pine woods, and there let him, in silence, analyze the sounds that shall pass through the chambers of his soul,—and if he is not thus impressed, it will only be because "there is no flesh in his obdurate heart."

I have often been utterly astonished, since I came to the north, to find persons who could speak of the singing, among slaves, as evidence of their contentment and happiness. It is impossible to conceive of a greater mistake. Slaves sing most when they are most unhappy. The songs of the slave represent the sorrows of his heart; and he is relieved by them, only as an aching heart is relieved by its tears. At least, such is my experience. I have often sung to drown my sorrow, but seldom to express my happiness. Crying for joy, and singing for joy, were alike uncommon to me while in the jaws of slavery. The singing of a man cast away upon a desolate island might be as appropriately considered as evidence of contentment and happiness, as the singing of a slave; the songs of the one and of the other are prompted by the same emotion.

Chapter III

COLONEL LLOYD kept a large and finely cultivated garden, which afforded almost constant employment for four men, besides the chief gardener, (Mr. M'Durmond.) This garden was probably the greatest attraction of the place. During the summer months, people came from far and near—from Baltimore, Easton, and Annapolis—to see it. It abounded in fruits of almost every description, from the hardy apple of the north to the delicate orange of the south. This garden was not the least source of trouble on the plantation. Its excellent fruit was quite a temptation to the hungry swarms of boys, as well as the older slaves, belonging to the colonel, few of whom had the virtue or the vice to resist it. Scarcely a day passed, during the summer, but that some slave had to take the lash for stealing fruit. The colonel had to resort to all kinds of stratagems to keep his slaves out of the garden. The last and most successful one was that of tarring his fence all around; after which, if a slave was caught with any tar upon his person, it was deemed sufficient proof that he had either been into the garden, or had tried to get in. In either case, he was severely whipped by the chief gardener. This plan worked well; the slaves became as fearful of tar as of the lash. They seemed to realize the impossibility of touching *tar* without being defiled.

The colonel also kept a splendid riding equipage. His stable and carriage-house presented the appearance of some of our large city livery establishments. His horses were of the finest form and noblest blood. His carriage-house contained three splendid coaches, three or four gigs, besides dearborns and barouches of the most fashionable style.

This establishment was under the care of two slaves—old Barney and young Barney—father and son. To attend to this establishment was their sole work. But it was by no means an easy employment; for in nothing was Colonel Lloyd more particular than in the management of his horses. The slightest inattention to these was unpardonable, and was visited upon those, under whose care they were placed, with the severest punishment; no excuse could shield them, if the colonel only suspected any want of attention to his horses—a supposition which he frequently indulged, and one which, of course, made the office of old and young Barney a very trying one. They never knew when they were safe from punishment. They were frequently whipped when least deserving, and escaped whipping when most deserving it. Everything depended upon the looks of the horses, and the state of Colonel Lloyd's own mind when his horses were brought to him for use. If a horse did not move fast enough, or hold his head high enough, it was owing to some fault of his keepers. It was painful to stand near the stable-door, and hear the various complaints against the keepers when a horse was taken out for use. "This horse has not had proper attention. He has not been sufficiently rubbed and curried, or he has not been properly fed; his food was too wet or too dry; he got it too soon or too late; he was too hot or too cold; he had too much hay, and not enough of grain; or he had too much grain, and not enough of hay; instead of old Barney's attending to the horse, he had very improperly left it to his son." To all these complaints, no matter how unjust, the slave must answer never a word. Colonel Lloyd could not brook any contradiction from a slave. When he spoke, a slave must stand, listen, and tremble; and such was literally the case. I have seen Colonel Lloyd make old Barney, a man between fifty and sixty years of age, uncover his bald head, kneel down upon the cold, damp ground, and receive upon his naked and toil-worn shoulders more than thirty lashes at the time. Colonel Lloyd had three sons—Edward, Murray, and Daniel,—and three sons-in-law, Mr. Winder, Mr. Nicholson, and Mr. Lowndes. All of these lived at the Great House Farm, and enjoyed the luxury of whipping the servants when they pleased, from old Barney down to William Wilkes, the coach-driver. I have seen Winder make one of the house-servants stand off from him a suitable distance to be touched with the end of his whip, and at every stroke raise great ridges upon his back.

To describe the wealth of Colonel Lloyd would be almost equal to describing the riches of Job. He kept from ten to fifteen house-servants. He was said to own a thousand slaves, and I think this estimate quite within the truth. Colonel Lloyd owned so many that he did not know them when he saw them; nor did all the slaves of the out-farms know him. It is reported of him, that, while riding along the road one day, he met a colored man, and addressed him in the usual manner of speaking to colored people on the public highways of the south: "Well, boy, whom do you belong to?" "To Colonel Lloyd," replied the slave. "Well, does the colonel treat you well?" "No, sir," was the ready reply. "What, does he work you too hard?" "Yes, sir." "Well, don't he give you enough to eat?" "Yes, sir, he gives me enough, such as it is."

The colonel, after ascertaining where the slave belonged, rode on; the man also went on about his business, not dreaming that he had been conversing with his master. He thought, said, and heard nothing more of the matter, until two or three weeks afterwards. The poor man was then informed by his overseer that, for having found fault with his master, he was now to be sold to a Georgia trader. He was immediately chained and handcuffed; and thus, without a moment's warning, he was snatched away, and forever sundered, from his family and friends, by a hand more unrelenting than death. This is the penalty of telling the truth, of telling the simple truth, in answer to a series of plain questions.

It is partly in consequence of such facts, that slaves, when inquired of as to their condition and the character of their masters, almost universally say they are contented, and that their masters are kind. The slaveholders have been known to send in spies among their slaves, to ascertain their views and feelings in regard to their condition. The frequency of this has had the effect to establish among the slaves the maxim, that a still tongue makes a wise head. They suppress the truth rather than take the consequences of telling it, and in so doing prove themselves a part of the human family. If they have anything to say of their masters, it is generally in their masters' favor, especially when speaking to an untried man. I have been frequently asked, when a slave, if I had a kind master, and do not remember ever to have given a negative answer; nor did I, in pursuing this course, consider myself as uttering what was absolutely false; for I always measured the kindness of my master by the standard of kindness set up among slaveholders around us. Moreover, slaves are like other people, and imbibe prejudices quite common to others. They think their own better than that of others. Many, under the influence of this prejudice, think their own masters are better than the masters of other slaves; and this, too, in some cases, when the very reverse is true. Indeed, it is not uncommon for slaves even to fall out and quarrel among themselves about the relative goodness of their masters, each contending for the superior goodness of his own over that of the others. At the very same time, they mutually execrate their masters when viewed separately. It was so on our plantation. When Colonel Lloyd's slaves met the slaves of Jacob Jepson, they seldom parted without a quarrel about their masters; Colonel Lloyd's slaves contending that he was the richest, and Mr. Jepson's slaves that he was the smartest, and most of a man. Colonel Lloyd's slaves would boast his ability to buy and sell Jacob Jepson. Mr. Jepson's slaves would boast his ability to whip Colonel Lloyd. These quarrels would almost always end in a fight between the parties, and those that whipped were supposed to have gained the point at issue. They seemed to think that the greatness of their masters was transferable to themselves. It was considered as being bad enough to be a slave; but to be a poor man's slave was deemed a disgrace indeed!

Chapter IV

MR. HOPKINS remained but a short time in the office of overseer. Why his career was so short, I do not know, but suppose he lacked the necessary severity to suit Colonel Lloyd. Mr. Hopkins was succeeded by Mr. Austin Gore, a man possessing, in an eminent degree, all those traits of character indispensable to what is called a first-rate overseer. Mr. Gore had served Colonel Lloyd, in the capacity of overseer, upon one of the out-farms, and had shown himself worthy of the high station of overseer upon the home or Great House Farm.

Mr. Gore was proud, ambitious, and persevering. He was artful, cruel, and obdurate. He was just the man for such a place, and it was just the place for such a man. It afforded scope for the full exercise of all his powers, and he seemed to be perfectly at home in it. He was one of those who could torture the slightest look, word, or gesture, on the part of the slave, into impudence, and would treat it accordingly. There must be no answering back to him; no explanation was allowed a slave, showing himself to have been wrongfully accused. Mr. Gore acted fully up to the maxim laid down by slaveholders,—"It is better that a dozen slaves suffer under the lash, than that the overseer should be convicted, in the presence of the slaves, of having been at fault." No matter how innocent a slave might be—it availed him nothing, when accused by Mr. Gore of any misdemeanor. To be accused was to be convicted, and to be convicted was to be punished; the one always following the other with immutable certainty. To escape punishment was to escape accusation; and few slaves had the fortune to do either, under the overseership of Mr. Gore. He was just proud enough to demand the most debasing homage of the slave, and quite servile enough to crouch, himself, at the feet of the master. He was ambitious enough to be contented with nothing short of the highest rank of overseers, and persevering enough to reach the height of his ambition. He was cruel enough to inflict the severest punishment, artful enough to descend to the lowest trickery, and obdurate enough to be insensible to the voice of a reproving conscience. He was, of all the overseers, the most dreaded by the slaves. His presence was painful; his eye flashed confusion; and seldom was his sharp, shrill voice heard, without producing horror and trembling in their ranks.

Mr. Gore was a grave man, and, though a young man, he indulged in no jokes, said no funny words, seldom smiled. His words were in perfect keeping with his looks, and his looks were in perfect keeping with his words. Overseers will sometimes indulge in a witty word, even with the slaves; not so with Mr. Gore. He spoke but to command, and commanded but to be obeyed; he dealt sparingly with his words, and bountifully with his whip, never using the former where the latter would answer as well. When he whipped, he seemed to do so from a sense of duty, and feared no consequences. He did nothing reluctantly, no matter how disagreeable; always at his post, never inconsistent. He never promised but to fulfil. He was, in a word, a man of the most inflexible firmness and stone-like coolness.

His savage barbarity was equalled only by the consummate coolness with which he committed the grossest and most savage deeds upon the slaves under his charge. Mr. Gore once undertook to whip one of Colonel Lloyd's slaves, by the name of Demby. He had given Demby but few stripes, when, to get rid of the scourging, he ran and plunged himself into a creek, and stood there at the depth of his shoulders, refusing to come out. Mr. Gore told him that he would give him three calls, and that, if he did not come out at the third call, he would shoot him. The first call was given. Demby made no response, but stood his ground. The second and third calls were given with the same result. Mr. Gore then, without consultation or deliberation with anyone, not even giving Demby an additional call, raised his musket to his face, taking deadly aim at his standing victim, and in an instant poor Demby was no more. His mangled body sank out of sight, and blood and brains marked the water where he had stood.

A thrill of horror flashed through every soul upon the plantation, excepting Mr. Gore. He alone seemed cool and collected. He was asked by Colonel Lloyd and my old master, why he resorted to this extraordinary expedient. His reply was, (as well as I can remember,) that Demby had become unmanageable. He was setting a dangerous example to the other slaves,—one which, if suffered to pass without some such demonstration on his part, would finally lead to the total subversion of all rule and order upon the plantation. He argued that if one slave refused to be corrected, and escaped with his life, the other slaves would soon copy the example; the result of which would be, the freedom of the slaves, and the enslavement of the whites. Mr. Gore's defense was satisfactory. He was continued in his station as overseer upon the home plantation. His fame as an overseer went abroad. His horrid crime was not even submitted to judicial investigation. It was committed in the presence of slaves, and they of course could neither institute a suit, nor testify against him; and thus the guilty perpetrator of one of the bloodiest and most foul murders goes unwhipped of justice, and uncensured by the community in which he lives. Mr. Gore lived in St. Michael's, Talbot county, Maryland, when I left there; and if he is still alive, he very probably lives there now; and if so, he is now, as he was then, as highly esteemed and as much respected as though his guilty soul had not been stained with his brother's blood.

I speak advisedly when I say this,—that killing a slave, or any colored person, in Talbot county, Maryland, is not treated as a crime, either by the courts or the community. Mr. Thomas Lanman, of St. Michael's, killed two slaves, one of whom he killed with a hatchet, by knocking his brains out. He used to boast of the commission of the awful and bloody deed. I have heard him do so laughingly, saying, among other things, that he was the only benefactor of his country in the company, and that when others would do as much as he had done, we should be relieved of "the d———d niggers."

The wife of Mr. Giles Hick, living but a short distance from where I used to live, murdered my wife's cousin, a young girl between fifteen and sixteen years of age, mangling her person in the most horrible manner, breaking her nose and breastbone with a stick, so that the poor girl expired in a few hours afterward. She was immediately buried, but had not been in her untimely grave but a few hours before she was taken up and examined by the coroner, who decided that she had come to her death by severe beating. The offense for which this girl was thus murdered was this:—She had been set that night to mind Mrs. Hick's baby, and during the night she fell asleep, and the baby cried. She, having lost her rest for several nights previous, did not hear the crying. They were both in the room with Mrs. Hicks. Mrs. Hicks, finding the girl slow to move, jumped from her bed, seized an oak stick of wood by the fireplace, and with it broke the girl's nose and breastbone, and thus ended her life. I will not say that this most horrid murder produced no sensation in the community. It did produce sensation, but not enough to bring the murderess to punishment. There was a warrant issued for her arrest, but it was never served. Thus she escaped not only punishment, but even the pain of being arraigned before a court for her horrid crime.

Whilst I am detailing bloody deeds which took place during my stay on Colonel Lloyd's plantation, I will briefly narrate another, which occurred about the same time as the murder of Demby by Mr. Gore.

Colonel Lloyd's slaves were in the habit of spending a part of their nights and Sundays in fishing for oysters, and in this way made up the deficiency of their scanty allowance. An old man belonging to Colonel Lloyd, while thus engaged, happened to get beyond the limits of Colonel Lloyd's, and on the premises of Mr. Beal Bondly. At this trespass, Mr. Bondly took offense, and with his musket came down to the shore, and blew its deadly contents into the poor old man.

Mr. Bondly came over to see Colonel Lloyd the next day, whether to pay him for his property, or to justify himself in what he had done, I know not. At any rate, this whole fiendish transaction was soon hushed up. There was very little said about it at all, and nothing done. It was a common saying, even among little white boys, that it was worth a half-cent to kill a "nigger," and a half-cent to bury one.

Chapter V

As to my own treatment while I lived on Colonel Lloyd's plantation, it was very similar to that of the other slave children. I was not old enough to work in the field, and there being little else than field work to do, I had a great deal of leisure time. The most I had to do was to drive up the cows at evening, keep the fowls out of the garden, keep the front yard clean, and run of errands for my old master's daughter, Mrs. Lucretia Auld. The most of my leisure time I spent in helping Master Daniel Lloyd in finding his birds, after he had shot them. My connection with Master Daniel was of some advantage to me. He became quite attached to me, and was a sort of protector of me. He would not allow the older boys to impose upon me, and would divide his cakes with me.

I was seldom whipped by my old master, and suffered little from anything else than hunger and cold. I suffered much from hunger, but much more from cold. In hottest summer and coldest winter, I was kept almost naked—no shoes, no stockings, no jacket, no trousers, nothing on but a coarse tow linen shirt, reaching only to my knees. I had no bed. I must have perished with cold, but that, the coldest nights, I used to steal a bag which was used for carrying corn to the mill. I would crawl into this bag, and there sleep on the cold, damp, clay floor, with my head in and feet out. My feet have been so cracked with the frost, that the pen with which I am writing might be laid in the gashes.

We were not regularly allowanced. Our food was coarse corn meal boiled. This was called *mush*. It was put into a large wooden tray or trough, and set down upon the ground. The children were then called, like so many pigs, and like so many pigs they would come and devour the mush; some with oyster-shells, others with pieces of shingle, some with naked hands, and none with spoons. He that ate fastest got most; he that was strongest secured the best place; and few left the trough satisfied.

I was probably between seven and eight years old when I left Colonel Lloyd's plantation. I left it with joy. I shall never forget the ecstasy with which I received the intelligence that my old master (Anthony) had determined to let me go to Baltimore, to live with Mr. Hugh Auld, brother to my old master's son-in-law, Captain Thomas Auld. I received this information about three days before my departure. They were three of the happiest days I ever enjoyed. I spent the most part of all these three days in the creek, washing off the plantation scurf, and preparing myself for my departure.

The pride of appearance which this would indicate was not my own. I spent the time in washing, not so much because I wished to, but because Mrs. Lucretia had told me I must get all the dead skin off my feet and knees before I could go to Baltimore; for the people in Baltimore were very cleanly, and would laugh at me if I looked dirty. Besides, she was going to give me a pair of trousers, which I should not put on unless I got all the dirt off me. The thought of owning a pair of trousers was great indeed! It was almost a sufficient motive, not only to make me take off what would be called by pig-drovers the mange, but the skin itself. I went at it in good earnest, working for the first time with the hope of reward.

The ties that ordinarily bind children to their homes were all suspended in my case. I found no severe trial in my departure. My home was charmless; it was not home to me; on parting from it, I could not feel that I was leaving anything which I could have enjoyed by staying. My mother was dead, my grandmother lived far off, so that I seldom saw her. I had two sisters and one brother, that lived in the same house with me; but the early separation of us from our mother had well nigh blotted the fact of our relationship from our memories. I looked for home elsewhere, and was confident of finding none which I should relish less than the one which I was leaving. If, however, I found in my new home hardship, hunger, whipping, and nakedness, I had the consolation that I should not have escaped any one of them by staying. Having already had more than a taste of them in the house of my old master, and having endured them there, I very naturally inferred my ability to endure them elsewhere, and especially at Baltimore; for I had something of the feeling about Baltimore that is expressed in the proverb, that "being hanged in England is preferable to dying a natural death in Ireland." I had the strongest desire to see Baltimore. Cousin Tom, though not fluent in speech, had inspired me with that desire by his eloquent description of the place. I could never point out any thing at the Great House, no matter how beautiful or powerful, but that he had seen something at Baltimore far exceeding, both in beauty and strength, the object which I pointed out to him. Even the Great House itself, with all its pictures, was far inferior to many buildings in Baltimore. So strong was my desire, that I thought a gratification of it would fully compensate for whatever loss of comforts I should sustain by the exchange. I left without a regret, and with the highest hopes of future happiness.

We sailed out of Miles River for Baltimore on a Saturday morning. I remember only the day of the week, for at that time I had no knowledge of the days of the month, nor the months of the year. On setting sail, I walked aft, and gave to Colonel Lloyd's plantation what I hoped would be the last look. I then placed myself in the bows of the sloop, and there spent the remainder of the day in looking ahead, interesting myself in what was in the distance rather than in things nearby or behind.

In the afternoon of that day, we reached Annapolis, the capital of the State. We stopped but a few moments, so that I had no time to go on shore. It was the first large town that I had ever seen, and though it would look small compared with some of our New England factory villages, I thought it a wonderful place for its size—more imposing even than the Great House Farm!

We arrived at Baltimore early on Sunday morning, landing at Smith's Wharf, not far from Bowley's Wharf. We had on board the sloop a large flock of sheep; and after aiding in driving them to the slaughterhouse of Mr. Curtis on Louden Slater's Hill, I was conducted by Rich, one of the hands belonging on board of the sloop, to my new home in Alliciana Street, near Mr. Gardner's ship-yard, on Fells Point.

Mr. and Mrs. Auld were both at home, and met me at the door with their little son Thomas, to take care of whom I had been given. And here I saw what I had never seen before; it was a white face beaming with the most kindly emotions; it was the face of my new mistress, Sophia Auld. I wish I could describe the rapture that flashed through my soul as I beheld it. It was a new and strange sight to me, brightening up my pathway with the light of happiness. Little Thomas was told, there was his Freddy,—and I was told to take care of little Thomas; and thus

I entered upon the duties of my new home with the most cheering prospect ahead.

I look upon my departure from Colonel Lloyd's plantation as one of the most interesting events of my life. It is possible, and even quite probable, that but for the mere circumstance of being removed from that plantation to Baltimore, I should have today, instead of being here seated by my own table, in the enjoyment of freedom and the happiness of home, writing this Narrative, been confined in the galling chains of slavery. Going to live at Baltimore laid the foundation, and opened the gateway, to all my subsequent prosperity. I have ever regarded it as the first plain manifestation of that kind providence which has ever since attended me, and marked my life with so many favors. I regarded the selection of myself as being somewhat remarkable. There were a number of slave children that might have been sent from the plantation to Baltimore. There were those younger, those older, and those of the same age. I was chosen from among them all, and was the first, last, and only choice.

I may be deemed superstitious, and even egotistical, in regarding this event as a special interposition of divine Providence in my favor. But I should be false to the earliest sentiments of my soul, if I suppressed the opinion. I prefer to be true to myself, even at the hazard of incurring the ridicule of others, rather than to be false, and incur my own abhorrence. From my earliest recollection, I date the entertainment of a deep conviction that slavery would not always be able to hold me within its foul embrace; and in the darkest hours of my career in slavery, this living word of faith and spirit of hope departed not from me, but remained like ministering angels to cheer me through the gloom. This good spirit was from God, and to him I offer thanksgiving and praise.

Chapter VI

MY NEW mistress proved to be all she appeared when I first met her at the door,—a woman of the kindest heart and finest feelings. She had never had a slave under her control previously to myself, and prior to her marriage she had been dependent upon her own industry for a living. She was by trade a weaver; and by constant application to her business, she had been in a good degree preserved from the blighting and

dehumanizing effects of slavery. I was utterly astonished at her goodness. I scarcely knew how to behave towards her. She was entirely unlike any other white woman I had ever seen. I could not approach her
as I was accustomed to approach other white ladies. My early instruction was all out of place. The crouching servility, usually so acceptable
a quality in a slave, did not answer when manifested toward her. Her
favor was not gained by it; she seemed to be disturbed by it. She did not
deem it impudent or unmannerly for a slave to look her in the face. The
meanest slave was put fully at ease in her presence, and none left without feeling better for having seen her. Her face was made of heavenly
smiles, and her voice of tranquil music.

But, alas! this kind heart had but a short time to remain such. The
fatal poison of irresponsible power was already in her hands, and soon
commenced its infernal work. That cheerful eye, under the influence
of slavery, soon became red with rage; that voice, made all of sweet accord, changed to one of harsh and horrid discord; and that angelic face
gave place to that of a demon.

Very soon after I went to live with Mr. and Mrs. Auld, she very
kindly commenced to teach me the A, B, C. After I had learned this,
she assisted me in learning to spell words of three or four letters. Just at
this point of my progress, Mr. Auld found out what was going on, and
at once forbade Mrs. Auld to instruct me further, telling her, among
other things, that it was unlawful, as well as unsafe, to teach a slave to
read. To use his own words, further, he said, "If you give a nigger an
inch, he will take an ell. A nigger should know nothing but to obey his
master—to do as he is told to do. Learning would *spoil* the best nigger
in the world. Now," said he, "if you teach that nigger (speaking of myself) how to read, there would be no keeping him. It would forever unfit him to be a slave. He would at once become unmanageable, and of
no value to his master. As to himself, it could do him no good, but a
great deal of harm. It would make him discontented and unhappy."
These words sank deep into my heart, stirred up sentiments within
that lay slumbering, and called into existence an entirely new train of
thought. It was a new and special revelation, explaining dark and mys-
terious things, with which my youthful understanding had struggled,
but struggled in vain. I now understood what had been to me a most
perplexing difficulty—to wit, the white man's power to enslave the
black man. It was a grand achievement, and I prized it highly. From
that moment, I understood the pathway from slavery to freedom. It
was just what I wanted, and I got it at a time when I the least expected

it. Whilst I was saddened by the thought of losing the aid of my kind mistress, I was gladdened by the invaluable instruction which, by the merest accident, I had gained from my master. Though conscious of the difficulty of learning without a teacher, I set out with high hope, and a fixed purpose, at whatever cost of trouble, to learn how to read. The very decided manner with which he spoke, and strove to impress his wife with the evil consequences of giving me instruction, served to convince me that he was deeply sensible of the truths he was uttering. It gave me the best assurance that I might rely with the utmost confidence on the results which, he said, would flow from teaching me to read. What he most dreaded, that I most desired. What he most loved, that I most hated. That which to him was a great evil, to be carefully shunned, was to me a great good, to be diligently sought; and the argument which he so warmly urged, against my learning to read, only served to inspire me with a desire and determination to learn. In learning to read, I owe almost as much to the bitter opposition of my master, as to the kindly aid of my mistress. I acknowledge the benefit of both.

I had resided but a short time in Baltimore before I observed a marked difference, in the treatment of slaves, from that which I had witnessed in the country. A city slave is almost a freeman, compared with a slave on the plantation. He is much better fed and clothed, and enjoys privileges altogether unknown to the slave on the plantation. There is a vestige of decency, a sense of shame, that does much to curb and check those outbreaks of atrocious cruelty so commonly enacted upon the plantation. He is a desperate slaveholder, who will shock the humanity of his nonslaveholding neighbors with the cries of his lacerated slave. Few are willing to incur the odium attaching to the reputation of being a cruel master; and above all things, they would not be known as not giving a slave enough to eat. Every city slaveholder is anxious to have it known of him, that he feeds his slaves well; and it is due to them to say, that most of them do give their slaves enough to eat. There are, however, some painful exceptions to this rule. Directly opposite to us, on Philpot Street, lived Mr. Thomas Hamilton. He owned two slaves. Their names were Henrietta and Mary. Henrietta was about twenty-two years of age, Mary was about fourteen; and of all the mangled and emaciated creatures I ever looked upon, these two were the most so. His heart must be harder than stone, that could look upon these unmoved. The head, neck, and shoulders of Mary were literally cut to pieces. I have frequently felt her head, and found it nearly covered with festering sores, caused by the lash of her cruel mistress. I do not know that her master ever whipped her, but I have been an eye-witness to the cruelty of Mrs. Hamilton. I used to be in Mr. Hamilton's house nearly every day. Mrs. Hamilton used to sit in a large chair in the middle of the room, with a heavy cowskin always by her side, and scarce an hour passed during the day but was marked by the blood of one of these slaves. The girls seldom passed her without her saying, "Move faster, you *black gip!*" at the same time giving them a blow with the cowskin over the head or shoulders, often drawing the blood. She would then say, "Take that, you *black gip!*"—continuing, "If you don't move faster, I'll move you!" Added to the cruel lashings to which these slaves were subjected, they were kept nearly half-starved. They seldom knew what it was to eat a full meal. I have seen Mary contending with the pigs for the offal thrown into the street. So much was Mary kicked and cut to pieces, that she was oftener called *"pecked"* than by her name.

Chapter VII

I LIVED in Master Hugh's family about seven years. During this time, I succeeded in learning to read and write. In accomplishing this, I was compelled to resort to various stratagems. I had no regular teacher. My mistress, who had kindly commenced to instruct me, had, in compli-ance with the advice and direction of her husband, not only ceased to instruct, but had set her face against my being instructed by anyone else. It is due, however, to my mistress to say of her, that she did not adopt this course of treatment immediately. She at first lacked the de-pravity indispensable to shutting me up in mental darkness. It was at least necessary for her to have some training in the exercise of irre-sponsible power, to make her equal to the task of treating me as though I were a brute.

My mistress was, as I have said, a kind and tender-hearted woman; and in the simplicity of her soul she commenced, when I first went to live with her, to treat me as she supposed one human being ought to treat another. In entering upon the duties of a slaveholder, she did not seem to perceive that I sustained to her the relation of a mere chattel, and that for her to treat me as a human being was not only wrong, but dangerously so. Slavery proved as injurious to her as it did to me. When I went there, she was a pious, warm, and tender-hearted woman. There was no sorrow or suffering for which she had not a tear. She had bread for the hungry, clothes for the naked, and comfort for every mourner that came within her reach. Slavery soon proved its ability to divest her of these heavenly qualities. Under its influence, the tender heart became stone, and the lamblike disposition gave way to one of tiger-like fierceness. The first step in her downward course was in her ceasing to instruct me. She now commenced to practice her husband's precepts. She finally became even more violent in her opposition than her husband himself. She was not satisfied with simply doing as well as he had commanded; she seemed anxious to do better. Nothing seemed to make her more angry than to see me with a newspaper. She seemed to think that here lay the danger. I have had her rush at me with a face made all up of fury, and snatch from me a newspaper, in a manner that fully revealed her apprehension. She was an apt woman; and a little experience soon demonstrated, to her satisfaction, that education and slavery were incompatible with each other.

From this time I was most narrowly watched. If I was in a separate room any considerable length of time, I was sure to be suspected of having a book, and was at once called to give an account of myself. All this, however, was too late. The first step had been taken. Mistress, in teaching me the alphabet, had given me the *inch,* and no precaution could prevent me from taking the *ell.*

The plan which I adopted, and the one by which I was most successful, was that of making friends of all the little white boys whom I met in the street. As many of these as I could, I converted into teachers. With their kindly aid, obtained at different times and in different places, I finally succeeded in learning to read. When I was sent of errands, I always took my book with me, and by going one part of my errand quickly, I found time to get a lesson before my return. I used also to carry bread with me, enough of which was always in the house, and to which I was always welcome; for I was much better off in this regard than many of the poor white children in our neighborhood. This bread I used to bestow upon the hungry little urchins, who, in return, would give me that more valuable bread of knowledge. I am strongly tempted to give the names of two or three of those little boys, as a testimonial of the gratitude and affection I bear them; but prudence forbids;—not that it would injure me, but it might embarrass them; for it is almost an unpardonable offense to teach slaves to read in this Christian country. It is enough to say of the dear little fellows, that they lived on Philpot Street, very near Durgin and Bailey's ship-yard. I used to talk this matter of slavery over with them. I would sometimes say to them, I wished

I could be as free as they would be when they got to be men. "You will be free as soon as you are twenty-one, *but I am a slave for life!* Have not I as good a right to be free as you have?" These words used to trouble them; they would express for me the liveliest sympathy, and console me with the hope that something would occur by which I might be free.

I was now about twelve years old, and the thought of being *a slave for life* began to bear heavily upon my heart. Just about this time, I got hold of a book entitled *The Columbian Orator*. Every opportunity I got, I used to read this book. Among much of other interesting matter, I found in it a dialogue between a master and his slave. The slave was represented as having run away from his master three times. The dialogue represented the conversation which took place between them, when the slave was retaken the third time. In this dialogue, the whole argument in behalf of slavery was brought forward by the master, all of which was disposed of by the slave. The slave was made to say some very smart as well as impressive things in reply to his master—things which had the desired though unexpected effect; for the conversation resulted in the voluntary emancipation of the slave on the part of the master.

In the same book, I met with one of Sheridan's mighty speeches on and in behalf of Catholic emancipation. These were choice documents to me. I read them over and over again with unabated interest. They gave tongue to interesting thoughts of my own soul, which had frequently flashed through my mind, and died away for want of utterance. The moral which I gained from the dialogue was the power of truth over the conscience of even a slaveholder. What I got from Sheridan was a bold denunciation of slavery, and a powerful vindication of human rights. The reading of these documents enabled me to utter my thoughts, and to meet the arguments brought forward to sustain slavery; but while they relieved me of one difficulty, they brought on another even more painful than the one of which I was relieved. The more I read, the more I was led to abhor and detest my enslavers. I could regard them in no other light than a band of successful robbers, who had left their homes, and gone to Africa, and stolen us from our homes, and in a strange land reduced us to slavery. I loathed them as being the meanest as well as the most wicked of men. As I read and contemplated the subject, behold! that very discontentment which Master Hugh had predicted would follow my learning to read had already come, to torment and sting my soul to unutterable anguish. As I writhed under it, I would at times feel that learning to read had been a curse rather than a blessing. It had given me a view of my wretched condition, without the remedy. It opened my eyes to the horrible pit, but to no ladder upon which to get out. In moments of agony, I envied my fellow-slaves for their stupidity. I have often wished myself a beast. I preferred the condition of the meanest reptile to my own. Anything, no matter what, to get rid of thinking! It was this everlasting thinking of my condition that tormented me. There was no getting rid of it. It was pressed upon me by every object within sight or hearing, animate or inanimate. The silver trump of freedom had roused my soul to eternal wakefulness. Freedom now appeared, to disappear no more forever. It was heard in every sound, and seen in everything. It was ever present to torment me with a sense of my wretched condition. I saw nothing without seeing it, I heard nothing without hearing it, and felt nothing without feeling it. It looked from every star, it smiled in every calm, breathed in every wind, and moved in every storm.

I often found myself regretting my own existence, and wishing myself dead; and but for the hope of being free, I have no doubt but that I should have killed myself, or done something for which I should have been killed. While in this state of mind, I was eager to hear anyone speak of slavery. I was a ready listener. Every little while, I could hear something about the abolitionists. It was some time before I found what the word meant. It was always used in such connections as to make it an interesting word to me. If a slave ran away and succeeded in getting clear, or if a slave killed his master, set fire to a barn, or did anything very wrong in the mind of a slaveholder, it was spoken of as the fruit of *abolition*. Hearing the word in this connection very often, I set about learning what it meant. The dictionary afforded me little or no help. I found it was "the act of abolishing;" but then I did not know what was to be abolished. Here I was perplexed. I did not dare to ask anyone about its meaning, for I was satisfied that it was something they wanted me to know very little about. After a patient waiting, I got one of our city papers, containing an account of the number of petitions from the north, praying for the abolition of slavery in the District of Columbia, and of the slave trade between the States. From this time I understood the words *abolition* and *abolitionist,* and always drew near when that word was spoken, expecting to hear something of importance to myself and fellow-slaves. The light broke in upon me by degrees. I went one day down on the wharf of Mr. Waters; and seeing two Irishmen unloading a scow of stone, I went, unasked, and helped them. When we had finished, one of them came to me and asked me if I were a slave. I told him I was. He asked, "Are ye a slave for life?" I told him that I was. The good Irishman seemed to be deeply affected by the statement. He said to the other that it was a pity so fine a little fellow as myself should be a slave for life. He said it was a shame to hold me. They both advised me to run away to the north; that I should find friends there, and that I should be free. I pretended not to be interested in what they said, and treated them as if I did not understand them; for I feared they might be treacherous. White men have been known to encourage slaves to escape, and then, to get the reward, catch them and return them to their masters. I was afraid that these seemingly good men might use me so; but I nevertheless remembered their advice, and from that time I resolved to run away. I looked forward to a time at which it would be safe for me to escape. I was too young to think of doing so immediately; besides, I wished to learn how to write, as I might have occasion to write my own pass. I consoled myself with the hope that I should one day find a good chance. Meanwhile, I would learn to write.

The idea as to how I might learn to write was suggested to me by being in Durgin and Bailey's ship-yard, and frequently seeing the ship carpenters, after hewing, and getting a piece of timber ready for use, write on the timber the name of that part of the ship for which it was intended. When a piece of timber was intended for the larboard side, it would be marked thus—"L." When a piece was for the starboard side, it would be marked thus—"S." A piece for the larboard side forward, would be marked thus—"L. F." When a piece was for starboard side forward, it would be marked thus—"S. F." For larboard aft, it would be marked thus—"L. A." For starboard aft, it would be marked thus— "S. A." I soon learned the names of these letters, and for what they were intended when placed upon a piece of timber in the ship-yard. I immediately commenced copying them, and in a short time was able to make the four letters named. After that, when I met with any boy who I knew could write, I would tell him I could write as well as he. The next word would be, "I don't believe you. Let me see you try it." I would then make the letters which I had been so fortunate as to learn, and ask him to beat that. In this way I got a good many lessons in writing, which it is quite possible I should never have gotten in any other way. During this time, my copy-book was the board fence, brick wall, and pavement; my pen and ink was a lump of chalk. With these, I learned mainly how to write. I then commenced and continued copying the Italics in *Webster's Spelling Book,* until I could make them all without looking on the book. By this time, my little Master Thomas had gone to school, and learned how to write, and had written over a number of copy-books. These had been brought home, and shown to some of our near neighbors, and then laid aside. My mistress used to go to class meeting at the Wilk Street meeting-house every Monday afternoon, and leave me to take care of the house. When left thus, I used to spend the time in writing in the spaces left in Master Thomas's copy-book, copying what he had written. I continued to do this until I could write a hand very similar to that of Master Thomas. Thus, after a long, tedious effort for years, I finally succeeded in learning how to write.

Chapter VIII

IN A VERY short time after I went to live at Baltimore, my old master's youngest son Richard died; and in about three years and six months after his death, my old master, Captain Anthony, died, leaving only his son, Andrew, and daughter, Lucretia, to share his estate. He died while on a visit to see his daughter at Hillsborough. Cut off thus unexpectedly, he left no will as to the disposal of his property. It was therefore necessary to have a valuation of the property, that it might be equally divided between Mrs. Lucretia and Master Andrew. I was immediately sent for, to be valued with the other property. Here again my feelings rose up in detestation of slavery. I had now a new conception of my degraded condition. Prior to this, I had become, if not insensible to my lot, at least partly so. I left Baltimore with a young heart overborne with sadness, and a soul full of apprehension. I took passage with Captain Rowe, in the schooner *Wild Cat,* and, after a sail of about twenty-four hours, I found myself near the place of my birth. I had now been absent from it almost, if not quite, five years. I, however, remembered the place very well. I was only about five years old when I left it, to go and live with my old master on Colonel Lloyd's plantation; so that I was now between ten and eleven years old.

We were all ranked together at the valuation. Men and women, old and young, married and single, were ranked with horses, sheep, and swine. There were horses and men, cattle and women, pigs and children, all holding the same rank in the scale of being, and were all subjected to the same narrow examination. Silvery-headed age and sprightly youth, maids and matrons, had to undergo the same indelicate inspection. At this moment, I saw more clearly than ever the brutalizing effects of slavery upon both slave and slaveholder.

After the valuation, then came the division. I have no language to express the high excitement and deep anxiety which were felt among us poor slaves during this time. Our fate for life was now to be decided. We had no more voice in that decision than the brutes among whom we were ranked. A single word from the white men was enough—against all our wishes, prayers, and entreaties—to sunder forever the dearest friends, dearest kindred, and strongest ties known to human beings. In addition to the pain of separation, there was the horrid dread of falling into the hands of Master Andrew. He was known to us all as being a most cruel wretch,—a common drunkard, who had, by his reckless mismanagement and profligate dissipation, already wasted a large portion of his father's property. We all felt that we might as well be sold at once to the Georgia traders, as to pass into his hands; for we knew that that would be our inevitable condition,—a condition held by us all in the utmost horror and dread.

I suffered more anxiety than most of my fellow-slaves. I had known what it was to be kindly treated; they had known nothing of the kind. They had seen little or nothing of the world. They were in very deed men and women of sorrow, and acquainted with grief. Their backs had been made familiar with the bloody lash, so that they had become callous; mine was yet tender; for while at Baltimore I got few whippings, and few slaves could boast of a kinder master and mistress than myself; and the thought of passing out of their hands into those of Master Andrew—a man who, but a few days before, to give me a sample of his bloody disposition, took my little brother by the throat, threw him on the ground, and with the heel of his boot stamped upon his head till the blood gushed from his nose and ears—was well calculated to make me anxious as to my fate. After he had committed this savage outrage upon my brother, he turned to me, and said that was the way he meant to serve me one of these days,—meaning, I suppose, when I came into his possession.

Thanks to a kind Providence, I fell to the portion of Mrs. Lucretia, and was sent immediately back to Baltimore, to live again in the family of Master Hugh. Their joy at my return equalled their sorrow at my departure. It was a glad day to me. I had escaped a worse than lion's jaws. I was absent from Baltimore, for the purpose of valuation and division, just about one month, and it seemed to have been six.

Very soon after my return to Baltimore, my mistress, Lucretia, died, leaving her husband and one child, Amanda; and in a very short time after her death, Master Andrew died. Now all the property of my old master, slaves included, was in the hands of strangers,—strangers who had had nothing to do with accumulating it. Not a slave was left free. All remained slaves, from the youngest to the oldest. If any one thing in my experience, more than another, served to deepen my conviction of the infernal character of slavery, and to fill me with unutterable loathing of slaveholders, it was their base ingratitude to my poor old grandmother. She had served my old master faithfully from youth to old age. She had been the source of all his wealth; she had peopled his plantation with slaves; she had become a great-grandmother in his service. She had rocked him in infancy, attended him in childhood, served him through life, and at his death wiped from his icy brow the cold death-sweat, and closed his eyes forever. She was nevertheless left a slave—a slave for life—a slave in the hands of strangers; and in their hands she saw her children, her grandchildren, and her great-grandchildren, divided, like so many sheep, without being gratified with the small privilege of a single word, as to their or her own destiny. And, to cap the climax of their base ingratitude and fiendish barbarity, my grandmother, who was now very old, having outlived my old master and all his children, having seen the beginning and end of all of them, and her present owners finding she was of but little value, her frame already racked with the pains of old age, and complete helplessness fast stealing over her once active limbs, they took her to the woods, built her a little hut, put up a little mud-chimney, and then made her welcome to the privilege of supporting herself there in perfect loneliness; thus virtually turning her out to die! If my poor old grandmother now lives, she lives to suffer in utter loneliness; she lives to remember and mourn over the loss of children, the loss of grandchildren, and the loss of great-grandchildren. They are, in the language of the slave's poet, Whittier,—

> "Gone, gone, sold and gone
> To the rice swamp dank and lone,
> Where the slave-whip ceaseless swings,
> Where the noisome insect stings,
> Where the fever-demon strews
> Poison with the falling dews,
> Where the sickly sunbeams glare

Through the hot and misty air:—
Gone, gone, sold and gone
To the rice swamp dank and lone,
From Virginia hills and waters—
Woe is me, my stolen daughters!"

The hearth is desolate. The children, the unconscious children, who once sang and danced in her presence, are gone. She gropes her way, in the darkness of age, for a drink of water. Instead of the voices of her children, she hears by day the moans of the dove, and by night the screams of the hideous owl. All is gloom. The grave is at the door. And now, when weighed down by the pains and aches of old age, when the head inclines to the feet, when the beginning and ending of human existence meet, and helpless infancy and painful old age combine together—at this time, this most needful time, the time for the exercise of that tenderness and affection which children only can exercise towards a declining parent—my poor old grandmother, the devoted mother of twelve children, is left all alone, in yonder little hut, before a few dim embers. She stands—she sits—she staggers—she falls—she groans—she dies—and there are none of her children or grandchildren present, to wipe from her wrinkled brow the cold sweat of death, or to place beneath the sod her fallen remains. Will not a righteous God visit for these things?

In about two years after the death of Mrs. Lucretia, Master Thomas married his second wife. Her name was Rowena Hamilton. She was the eldest daughter of Mr. William Hamilton. Master now lived in St. Michael's. Not long after his marriage, a misunderstanding took place between himself and Master Hugh; and as a means of punishing his brother, he took me from him to live with himself at St. Michael's. Here I underwent another most painful separation. It, however, was not so severe as the one I dreaded at the division of property; for, during this interval, a great change had taken place in Master Hugh and his once kind and affectionate wife. The influence of brandy upon him, and of slavery upon her, had effected a disastrous change in the characters of both; so that, as far as they were concerned, I thought I had little to lose by the change. But it was not to them that I was attached. It was to those little Baltimore boys that I felt the strongest attachment. I had received many good lessons from them, and was still receiving them, and the thought of leaving them was painful indeed. I was leaving, too, without the hope of ever being allowed to return.

Master Thomas had said he would never let me return again. The barrier betwixt himself and brother he considered impassable.

I then had to regret that I did not at least make the attempt to carry out my resolution to run away; for the chances of success are tenfold greater from the city than from the country.

I sailed from Baltimore for St. Michael's in the sloop *Amanda*, Captain Edward Dodson. On my passage, I paid particular attention to the direction which the steamboats took to go to Philadelphia. I found, instead of going down, on reaching North Point they went up the bay, in a north-easterly direction. I deemed this knowledge of the utmost importance. My determination to run away was again revived. I resolved to wait only so long as the offering of a favorable opportunity. When that came, I was determined to be off.

Chapter IX

I HAVE now reached a period of my life when I can give dates. I left Baltimore, and went to live with Master Thomas Auld, at St. Michael's, in March, 1832. It was now more than seven years since I lived with him in the family of my old master, on Colonel Lloyd's plantation. We of course were now almost entire strangers to each other. He was to me a new master, and I to him a new slave. I was ignorant of his temper and disposition; he was equally so of mine. A very short time, however, brought us into full acquaintance with each other. I was made acquainted with his wife not less than with himself. They were well matched, being equally mean and cruel. I was now, for the first time during a space of more than seven years, made to feel the painful gnawings of hunger—a something which I had not experienced before since I left Colonel Lloyd's plantation. It went hard enough with me then, when I could look back to no period at which I had enjoyed a sufficiency. It was tenfold harder after living in Master Hugh's family, where I had always had enough to eat, and of that which was good. I have said Master Thomas was a mean man. He was so. Not to give a slave enough to eat, is regarded as the most aggravated development of meanness even among slaveholders. The rule is, no matter how coarse the food, only let there be enough of it. This is the theory; and in the part of Maryland from which I came, it is the general practice,—though there are many exceptions. Master Thomas gave us enough of neither coarse nor fine food. There were four slaves of us in the kitchen—my sister Eliza, my aunt Priscilla, Henny, and myself; and we were allowed less than a half of a bushel of corn-meal per week, and very little else, either in the shape of meat or vegetables. It was not enough for us to subsist upon. We were therefore reduced to the wretched necessity of living at the expense of our neighbors. This we did by begging and stealing, whichever came handy in the time of need, the one being considered as legitimate as the other. A great many times have we poor creatures been nearly perishing with hunger, when food in abundance lay mouldering in the safe and smoke-house, and our pious mistress was aware of the fact; and yet that mistress and her husband would kneel every morning, and pray that God would bless them in basket and store!

Bad as all slaveholders are, we seldom meet one destitute of every element of character commanding respect. My master was one of this rare sort. I do not know of one single noble act ever performed by him. The leading trait in his character was meanness; and if there were any other element in his nature, it was made subject to this. He was mean; and, like most other mean men, he lacked the ability to conceal his meanness. Captain Auld was not born a slaveholder. He had been a poor man, master only of a Bay craft. He came into possession of all his slaves by marriage; and of all men, adopted slaveholders are the worst. He was cruel, but cowardly. He commanded without firmness. In the enforcement of his rules, he was at times rigid, and at times lax. At times, he spoke to his slaves with the firmness of Napoleon and the fury of a demon; at other times, he might well be mistaken for an inquirer who had lost his way. He did nothing of himself. He might have passed for a lion, but for his ears. In all things noble which he attempted, his own meanness shone most conspicuous. His airs, words, and actions, were the airs, words, and actions of born slaveholders, and, being assumed, were awkward enough. He was not even a good imitator. He possessed all the disposition to deceive, but wanted the power. Having no resources within himself, he was compelled to be the copyist of many, and being such, he was forever the victim of inconsistency; and of consequence he was an object of contempt, and was held as such even by his slaves. The luxury of having slaves of his own to wait upon him was something new and unprepared for. He was a slaveholder without the ability to hold slaves. He found himself incapable of managing his slaves either by force, fear, or fraud. We seldom called him "master;" we generally called him "Captain Auld," and were hardly disposed to title him at all. I doubt not that our conduct

had much to do with making him appear awkward, and of consequence fretful. Our want of reverence for him must have perplexed
him greatly. He wished to have us call him master, but lacked the
firmness necessary to command us to do so. His wife used to insist
upon our calling him so, but to no purpose. In August, 1832, my master attended a Methodist camp-meeting held in the Bay-side, Talbot
county, and there experienced religion. I indulged a faint hope that his
conversion would lead him to emancipate his slaves, and that, if he did
not do this, it would, at any rate, make him more kind and humane. I
was disappointed in both these respects. It neither made him to be humane to his slaves, nor to emancipate them. If it had any effect on his
character, it made him more cruel and hateful in all his ways; for I believe him to have been a much worse man after his conversion than before. Prior to his conversion, he relied upon his own depravity to shield
and sustain him in his savage barbarity; but after his conversion, he
found religious sanction and support for his slaveholding cruelty.
He made the greatest pretensions to piety. His house was the house of
prayer. He prayed morning, noon, and night. He very soon distinguished himself among his brethren, and was soon made a class-leader
and exhorter. His activity in revivals was great, and he proved himself
an instrument in the hands of the church in converting many souls.
His house was the preachers' home. They used to take great pleasure
in coming there to put up; for while he starved us, he stuffed them. We
have had three or four preachers there at a time. The names of those
who used to come most frequently while I lived there, were Mr. Storks,
Mr. Ewery, Mr. Humphry, and Mr. Hickey. I have also seen Mr.
George Cookman at our house. We slaves loved Mr. Cookman. We believed him to be a good man. We thought him instrumental in getting
Mr. Samuel Harrison, a very rich slaveholder, to emancipate his slaves;
and by some means got the impression that he was laboring to effect
the emancipation of all the slaves. When he was at our house, we were
sure to be called in to prayers. When the others were there, we were
sometimes called in and sometimes not. Mr. Cookman took more notice of us than either of the other ministers. He could not come among
us without betraying his sympathy for us, and, stupid as we were, we
had the sagacity to see it.

While I lived with my master in St. Michael's, there was a white
young man, a Mr. Wilson, who proposed to keep a Sabbath school for
the instruction of such slaves as might be disposed to learn to read the
New Testament. We met but three times, when Mr. West and Mr.

Fairbanks, both class-leaders, with many others, came upon us with sticks and other missiles, drove us off, and forbade us to meet again. Thus ended our little Sabbath school in the pious town of St. Michael's.

I have said my master found religious sanction for his cruelty. As an example, I will state one of many facts going to prove the charge. I have seen him tie up a lame young woman, and whip her with a heavy cowskin upon her naked shoulders, causing the warm red blood to drip; and, in justification of the bloody deed, he would quote this passage of Scripture—"He that knoweth his master's will, and doeth it not, shall be beaten with many stripes."

Master would keep this lacerated young woman tied up in this horrid situation four or five hours at a time. I have known him to tie her up early in the morning, and whip her before breakfast; leave her, go to his store, return at dinner, and whip her again, cutting her in the places already made raw with his cruel lash. The secret of master's cruelty toward "Henny" is found in the fact of her being almost helpless. When quite a child, she fell into the fire, and burned herself horribly. Her hands were so burnt that she never got the use of them. She could do very little but bear heavy burdens. She was to master a bill of expense; and as he was a mean man, she was a constant offense to him. He seemed desirous of getting the poor girl out of existence. He gave her away once to his sister; but, being a poor gift, she was not disposed to keep her. Finally, my benevolent master, to use his own words, "set her adrift to take care of herself." Here was a recently-converted man, holding on upon the mother, and at the same time turning out her helpless child, to starve and die! Master Thomas was one of the many pious slaveholders who hold slaves for the very charitable purpose of taking care of them.

My master and myself had quite a number of differences. He found me unsuitable to his purpose. My city life, he said, had had a very pernicious effect upon me. It had almost ruined me for every good purpose, and fitted me for everything which was bad. One of my greatest faults was that of letting his horse run away, and go down to his father-in-law's farm, which was about five miles from St. Michael's. I would then have to go after it. My reason for this kind of carelessness, or carefulness, was, that I could always get something to eat when I went there. Master William Hamilton, my master's father-in-law, always gave his slaves enough to eat. I never left there hungry, no matter how great the need of my speedy return. Master Thomas at length said he would stand it no longer. I had lived with him nine months, during which time he had given me a number of severe whippings, all to no good purpose. He resolved to put me out, as he said, to be broken; and, for this purpose, he let me for one year to a man named Edward Covey. Mr. Covey was a poor man, a farm-renter. He rented the place upon which he lived, as also the hands with which he tilled it. Mr. Covey had acquired a very high reputation for breaking young slaves, and this reputation was of immense value to him. It enabled him to get his farm tilled with much less expense to himself than he could have had it done without such a reputation. Some slaveholders thought it not much loss to allow Mr. Covey to have their slaves one year, for the sake of the training to which they were subjected, without any other compensation. He could hire young help with great ease, in consequence of this reputation. Added to the natural good qualities of Mr. Covey, he was a professor of religion—a pious soul—a member and a class-leader in the Methodist church. All of this added weight to his reputation as a "nigger-breaker." I was aware of all the facts, having been made acquainted with them by a young man who had lived there. I nevertheless made the change gladly; for I was sure of getting enough to eat, which is not the smallest consideration to a hungry man.

Chapter X

I LEFT Master Thomas's house, and went to live with Mr. Covey, on the 1st of January, 1833. I was now, for the first time in my life, a field hand. In my new employment, I found myself even more awkward than a country boy appeared to be in a large city. I had been at my new home but one week before Mr. Covey gave me a very severe whipping, cutting my back, causing the blood to run, and raising ridges on my flesh as large as my little finger. The details of this affair are as follows: Mr. Covey sent me, very early in the morning of one of our coldest days in the month of January, to the woods, to get a load of wood. He gave me a team of unbroken oxen. He told me which was the in-hand ox, and which the off-hand one. He then tied the end of a large rope around the horns of the in-hand ox, and gave me the other end of it, and told me, if the oxen started to run, that I must hold on upon the rope. I had never driven oxen before, and of course I was very awkward. I, however, succeeded in getting to the edge of the woods with little difficulty; but I had got a very few rods into the woods, when the oxen took fright, and started full tilt, carrying the cart against trees, and over stumps, in the most frightful manner. I expected every moment that my brains would be dashed out against the trees. After running thus for a considerable distance, they finally upset the cart, dashing it with great force against a tree, and threw themselves into a dense thicket. How I escaped death, I do not know. There I was, entirely alone, in a thick wood, in a place new to me. My cart was upset and shattered, my oxen were entangled among the young trees, and there was none to help me. After a long spell of effort, I succeeded in getting my cart righted, my oxen disentangled, and again yoked to the cart. I now proceeded with my team to the place where I had, the day before, been chopping wood, and loaded my cart pretty heavily, thinking in this way to tame my oxen. I then proceeded on my way home. I had now consumed one half of the day. I got out of the woods safely, and now felt out of danger. I stopped my oxen to open the woods gate; and just as I did so, before I could get hold of my ox-rope, the oxen again started, rushed through the gate, catching it between the wheel and the body of the cart, tearing it to pieces, and coming within a few inches of crushing me against the gate-post. Thus twice, in one short day, I escaped death by the merest chance. On my return, I told Mr. Covey what had happened, and how it happened. He ordered me to return to the woods again immediately. I did so, and he followed on after me. Just as I got into the woods, he came up and told me to stop my cart, and that he would teach me how to trifle away my time, and break gates. He then went to a large gum-tree, and with his axe cut three large switches, and, after trimming them up neatly with his pocket-knife, he ordered me to take off my clothes. I made him no answer, but stood with my clothes on. He repeated his order. I still made him no answer, nor did I move to strip myself. Upon this he rushed at me with the fierceness of a tiger, tore off my clothes, and lashed me till he had worn out his switches, cutting me so savagely as to leave the marks visible for a long time after. This whipping was the first of a number just like it, and for similar offenses.

I lived with Mr. Covey one year. During the first six months, of that year, scarce a week passed without his whipping me. I was seldom free from a sore back. My awkwardness was almost always his excuse for whipping me. We were worked fully up to the point of endurance. Long before day we were up, our horses fed, and by the first approach of day we were off to the field with our hoes and ploughing teams. Mr. Covey gave us enough to eat, but scarce time to eat it. We were often less than five minutes taking our meals. We were often in the field from the first approach of day till its last lingering ray had left us; and at saving-fodder time, midnight often caught us in the field binding blades.

Covey would be out with us. The way he used to stand it, was this. He would spend the most of his afternoons in bed. He would then come out fresh in the evening, ready to urge us on with his words, example, and frequently with the whip. Mr. Covey was one of the few slaveholders who could and did work with his hands. He was a hard-working man. He knew by himself just what a man or a boy could do. There was no deceiving him. His work went on in his absence almost as well as in his presence; and he had the faculty of making us feel that he was ever present with us. This he did by surprising us. He seldom approached the spot where we were at work openly, if he could do it secretly. He always aimed at taking us by surprise. Such was his cunning, that we used to call him, among ourselves, "the snake." When we were at work in the cornfield, he would sometimes crawl on his hands and knees to avoid detection, and all at once he would rise nearly in our midst, and scream out, "Ha, ha! Come, come! Dash on, dash on!" This being his mode of attack, it was never safe to stop a single minute. His comings were like a thief in the night. He appeared to us as being ever at hand. He was under every tree, behind every stump, in every bush, and at every window, on the plantation. He would sometimes mount his horse, as if bound to St. Michael's, a distance of seven miles, and in half an hour afterwards you would see him coiled up in the corner of the wood-fence, watching every motion of the slaves. He would, for this purpose, leave his horse tied up in the woods. Again, he would sometimes walk up to us, and give us orders as though he was upon the point of starting on a long journey, turn his back upon us, and make as though he was going to the house to get ready; and, before he would get half way thither, he would turn short and crawl into a fence-corner, or behind some tree, and there watch us till the going down of the sun.

Mr. Covey's *forte* consisted in his power to deceive. His life was devoted to planning and perpetrating the grossest deceptions. Everything he possessed in the shape of learning or religion, he made conform to his disposition to deceive. He seemed to think himself equal to deceiving the Almighty. He would make a short prayer in the morning, and a long prayer at night; and, strange as it may seem, few men would at times appear more devotional than he. The exercises of his family devotions were always commenced with singing; and, as he was a very poor singer himself, the duty of raising the hymn generally came upon me. He would read his hymn, and nod at me to commence. I would at times do so; at others, I would not. My non-compliance would almost always produce much confusion. To show himself independent of me, he would start and stagger through with his hymn in the most discordant manner. In this state of mind, he prayed with more than ordinary spirit. Poor man! such was his disposition, and success at deceiving, I do verily believe that he sometimes deceived himself into the solemn belief, that he was a sincere worshipper of the most high God; and this, too, at a time when he may be said to have been guilty of compelling his woman slave to commit the sin of adultery. The facts in the case are these: Mr. Covey was a poor man; he was just commencing in life; he was only able to buy one slave; and, shocking as is the fact, he bought her, as he said, for *a breeder*. This woman was named Caroline. Mr. Covey bought her from Mr. Thomas Lowe, about six miles from St. Michael's. She was a large, able-bodied woman, about twenty years old. She had already given birth to one child, which proved her to be just what he wanted. After buying her, he hired a married man of Mr. Samuel Harrison, to live with him one year; and him he used to fasten up with her every night! The result was, that, at the end of the year, the miserable woman gave birth to twins. At this result Mr. Covey seemed to be highly pleased, both with the man and the wretched woman. Such was his joy, and that of his wife, that nothing they could do for Caroline during her confinement was too good, or too hard, to be done. The children were regarded as being quite an addition to his wealth.

If at any one time of my life more than another, I was made to drink the bitterest dregs of slavery, that time was during the first six months of my stay with Mr. Covey. We were worked in all weathers. It was never too hot or too cold; it could never rain, blow, hail, or snow, too hard for us to work in the field. Work, work, work, was scarcely more the order of the day than of the night. The longest days were too short for him, and the shortest nights too long for him. I was somewhat unmanageable when I first went there, but a few months of this discipline tamed me. Mr. Covey succeeded in breaking me. I was broken in body, soul, and spirit. My natural elasticity was crushed, my intellect languished, the disposition to read departed, the cheerful spark that lingered about my eye died; the dark night of slavery closed in upon me; and behold a man transformed into a brute!

Sunday was my only leisure time. I spent this in a sort of beast-like stupor, between sleep and wake, under some large tree. At times I would rise up, a flash of energetic freedom would dart through my soul, accompanied with a faint beam of hope, that flickered for a moment, and then vanished. I sank down again, mourning over my wretched condition. I was sometimes prompted to take my life, and that of Covey, but was prevented by a combination of hope and fear. My sufferings on this plantation seem now like a dream rather than a stern reality.

Our house stood within a few rods of the Chesapeake Bay, whose broad bosom was ever white with sails from every quarter of the habitable globe. Those beautiful vessels, robed in purest white, so delightful to the eye of freemen, were to me so many shrouded ghosts, to terrify and torment me with thoughts of my wretched condition. I have often, in the deep stillness of a summer's Sabbath, stood all alone upon the lofty banks of that noble bay, and traced, with saddened heart and tearful eye, the countless number of sails moving off to the mighty ocean. The sight of these always affected me powerfully. My thoughts would compel utterance; and there, with no audience but the Almighty, I would pour out my soul's complaint, in my rude way, with an apostrophe to the moving multitude of ships:—

"You are loosed from your moorings, and are free; I am fast in my chains, and am a slave! You move merrily before the gentle gale, and I sadly before the bloody whip! You are freedom's swift-winged angels, that fly round the world; I am confined in bands of iron! O that I were free! O, that I were on one of your gallant decks, and under your protecting wing! Alas! betwixt me and you, the turbid waters roll. Go on, go on. O that I could also go! Could I but swim! If I could fly! O, why was I born a man, of whom to make a brute! The glad ship is gone; she hides in the dim distance. I am left in the hottest hell of unending slavery. O God, save me! God, deliver me! Let me be free! Is there any God? Why am I a slave? I will run away. I will not stand it. Get caught, or get clear, I'll try it. I had as well die with ague as the fever. I have only one life to lose. I had as well be killed running as die standing. Only think of it; one hundred miles straight north, and I am free! Try it? Yes! God helping me, I will. It cannot be that I shall live and die a slave. I will take to the water. This very bay shall yet bear me into freedom. The steamboats steered in a north-east course from North Point. I will do the same; and when I get to the head of the bay, I will turn my canoe adrift, and walk straight through Delaware into Pennsylvania. When I get there, I shall not be required to have a pass; I can travel without being disturbed. Let but the first opportunity offer, and, come what will, I am off. Meanwhile, I will try to bear up under the yoke. I am not the only slave in the world. Why should I fret? I can bear as much as any of them. Besides, I am but a boy, and all boys are bound to someone. It may be that my misery in slavery will only increase my happiness when I get free. There is a better day coming."

Thus I used to think, and thus I used to speak to myself; goaded almost to madness at one moment, and at the next reconciling myself to my wretched lot.

I have already intimated that my condition was much worse, during the first six months of my stay at Mr. Covey's, than in the last six. The circumstances leading to the change in Mr. Covey's course toward me form an epoch in my humble history. You have seen how a man was made a slave; you shall see how a slave was made a man. On one of the hottest days of the month of August, 1833, Bill Smith, William Hughes, a slave named Eli, and myself, were engaged in fanning wheat. Hughes was clearing the fanned wheat from before the fan, Eli was turning, Smith was feeding, and I was carrying wheat to the fan. The work was simple, requiring strength rather than intellect; yet, to one entirely unused to such work, it came very hard. About three o'clock of that day, I broke down; my strength failed me; I was seized with a violent aching of the head, attended with extreme dizziness; I trembled in every limb. Finding what was coming, I nerved myself up, feeling it would never do to stop work. I stood as long as I could stagger to the hopper with grain. When I could stand no longer, I fell, and felt as if held down by an immense weight. The fan of course stopped; everyone had his own work to do; and no one could do the work of the other, and have his own go on at the same time.

Mr. Covey was at the house, about one hundred yards from the treading-yard where we were fanning. On hearing the fan stop, he left immediately, and came to the spot where we were. He hastily inquired what the matter was. Bill answered that I was sick, and there was no one to bring wheat to the fan. I had by this time crawled away under the side of the post and rail-fence by which the yard was enclosed, hoping to find relief by getting out of the sun. He then asked where I was. He was told by one of the hands. He came to the spot, and, after looking at me awhile, asked me what was the matter. I told him as well as I could, for I scarce had strength to speak. He then gave me a savage kick in the side, and told me to get up. I tried to do so, but fell back in the attempt. He gave me another kick, and again told me to rise. I again tried, and succeeded in gaining my feet; but, stooping to get the tub with which I was feeding the fan, I again staggered and fell. While down in this situation, Mr. Covey took up the hickory slat with which Hughes had been striking off the half-bushel measure, and with it gave me a heavy blow upon the head, making a large wound, and the blood ran freely; and with this again told me to get up. I made no effort to comply, having now made up my mind to let him do his worst. In a short time after receiving this blow, my head grew better. Mr. Covey had now left me to my fate. At this moment I resolved, for the first time, to go to my master, enter a complaint, and ask his protection. In order to this, I must that afternoon walk seven miles; and this, under the circumstances, was truly a severe undertaking. I was exceedingly feeble; made so as much by the kicks and blows which I received, as by the severe fit of sickness to which I had been subjected. I, however, watched my chance, while Covey was looking in an opposite direction, and started for St. Michael's. I succeeded in getting a considerable distance on my way to the woods, when Covey discovered me, and called after me to come back, threatening what he would do if I did not come. I disregarded both his calls and his threats, and made my way to the woods as fast as my feeble state would allow; and thinking I might be overhauled by him if I kept the road, I walked through the woods, keeping far enough from the road to avoid detection, and near enough to prevent losing my way. I had not gone far before my little strength again failed me. I could go no farther. I fell down, and lay for a considerable time. The blood was yet oozing from the wound on my head. For a time I thought I should bleed to death; and think now that I should have done so, but that the blood so matted my hair as to stop the wound. After lying there about three quarters of an hour, I nerved myself up again, and started on my way, through bogs and briers, barefooted and bareheaded, tearing my feet sometimes at nearly every step; and after a journey of about seven miles, occupying some five hours to perform it, I arrived at master's store. I then presented an appearance enough to affect any but a heart of iron. From the crown of my head to my feet, I was covered with blood. My hair was all clotted with dust and blood; my shirt was stiff with blood. My legs and feet were torn in sundry places with briers and thorns, and were also covered with blood. I suppose I looked like a man who had escaped a den of wild beasts, and barely escaped them. In this state I appeared before my master, humbly entreating him to interpose his authority for my protection. I told him all the circumstances as well as I could, and it seemed, as I spoke, at times to affect him. He would then walk the floor, and seek to justify Covey by saying he expected I deserved it. He asked me what I wanted. I told him, to let me get a new home; that as sure as I lived with Mr. Covey again, I should live with but to die with him; that Covey would surely kill me; he was in a fair way for it. Master Thomas ridiculed the idea that there was any danger of Mr. Covey's killing me, and said that he knew Mr. Covey; that he was a good man, and that he could not think of taking me from him; that, should he do so, he would lose the whole year's wages; that I belonged to Mr. Covey for one year, and that I must go back to him, come what might; and that I must not trouble him with any more stories, or that he would himself *get hold of me*. After threatening me thus, he gave me a very large dose of salts, telling me that I might remain in St. Michael's that night, (it being quite late,) but that I must be off back to Mr. Covey's early in the morning; and that if I did not, he would *get hold of me*, which meant that he would whip me. I remained all night, and, according to his orders, I started off to Covey's in the morning, (Saturday morning,) wearied in body and broken in spirit. I got no supper that night, or breakfast that morning. I reached Covey's about nine o'clock; and just as I was getting over the fence that divided Mrs. Kemp's fields from ours, out ran Covey with his cowskin, to give me another whipping. Before he could reach me, I succeeded in getting to the cornfield; and as the corn was very high, it afforded me the means of hiding. He seemed very angry, and searched for me a long time. My behavior was altogether unaccountable. He finally gave up the chase, thinking, I suppose, that I must come home for something to eat; he would give himself no further trouble in looking for me. I spent that day mostly in the woods, having the alternative before me,—to go home and be whipped to death, or stay in the woods and be starved to death. That night, I fell in with Sandy Jenkins, a slave with whom I was somewhat acquainted. Sandy had a free wife who lived about four miles from Mr. Covey's; and it being Saturday, he was on his way to see her. I told him my circumstances, and he very kindly invited me to go home with him. I went home with him, and talked this whole matter over, and got his advice as to what course it was best for me to pursue. I found Sandy an old adviser. He told me, with great solemnity, I must go back to Covey; but that before I went, I must go with him into another part of the woods, where there was a certain *root*, which, if I would take some of it with me, carrying it *always on my right side,* would render it impossible for Mr. Covey, or any other white man, to whip me. He said he had carried it for years; and since he had done so, he had never received a blow, and never expected to while he carried it. I at first rejected the idea, that the simple carrying of a root in my pocket would have any such effect as he had said, and was not disposed to take it; but Sandy impressed the necessity with much earnestness, telling me it could do no harm, if it did no good. To please him, I at length took the root, and, according to his direction, carried it upon my right side. This was Sunday morning. I immediately started for home; and upon entering the yard gate, out came Mr. Covey on his way to meeting. He spoke to me very kindly, bade me drive the pigs from a lot nearby, and passed on towards the church. Now, this singular conduct of Mr. Covey really made me begin to think that there was something in the *root* which Sandy had given me; and had it been on any other day than Sunday, I could have attributed the conduct to no other cause than the influence of that root; and as it was, I was half inclined to think the *root* to be something more than I at first had taken it to be. All went well till Monday morning. On this morning, the virtue of the *root* was fully tested. Long before daylight, I was called to go and rub, curry, and feed, the horses. I obeyed, and was glad to obey. But whilst thus engaged, whilst in the act of throwing down some blades from the loft, Mr. Covey entered the stable with a long rope; and just as I was half out of the loft, he caught hold of my legs, and was about tying me. As soon as I found what he was up to, I gave a sudden spring, and as I did so, he holding to my legs, I was brought sprawling on the stable floor. Mr. Covey seemed now to think he had me, and could do what he pleased; but at this moment—from whence came the spirit I don't know—I resolved to fight; and, suiting my action to the resolution, I seized Covey hard by the throat; and as I did so, I rose. He held on to me, and I to him. My resistance was so entirely unexpected, that Covey seemed taken all aback. He trembled like a leaf. This gave me assurance, and I held him uneasy, causing the blood to run where I touched him with the ends of my fingers. Mr. Covey soon called out to Hughes for help. Hughes came, and, while Covey held me, attempted to tie my right hand. While he was in the act of doing so, I watched my chance, and gave him a heavy kick close under the ribs. This kick fairly sickened Hughes, so that he left me in the hands of Mr. Covey. This kick had the effect of not only weakening Hughes, but Covey also. When he saw Hughes bending over with pain, his courage quailed. He asked me if I meant to persist in my resistance. I told him I did, come what might; that he had used me like a brute for six months, and that I was determined to be used so no longer. With that, he strove to drag me to a stick that was lying just out of the stable door. He meant to knock me down. But just as he was leaning over to get the stick, I seized him with both hands by his collar, and brought him by a sudden snatch to the ground. By this time, Bill came. Covey called upon him for assistance. Bill wanted to know what he could do. Covey said, "Take hold of him, take hold of him!" Bill said his master hired him out to work, and not to help to whip me; so he left Covey and myself to fight our own battle out. We were at it for nearly two hours. Covey at length let me go, puffing and blowing at a great rate, saying that if I had not resisted, he would not have whipped me half so much. The truth was, that he had not whipped me at all. I considered him as getting entirely the worst end of the bargain; for he had drawn no blood from me, but I had from him. The whole six months afterwards, that I spent with Mr. Covey, he never laid the weight of his finger upon me in anger. He would occasionally say, he didn't want to get hold of me again. "No," thought I, "you need not; for you will come off worse than you did before."

This battle with Mr. Covey was the turning-point in my career as a slave. It rekindled the few expiring embers of freedom, and revived within me a sense of my own manhood. It recalled the departed self-confidence, and inspired me again with a determination to be free. The gratification afforded by the triumph was a full compensation for whatever else might follow, even death itself. He only can understand the deep satisfaction which I experienced, who has himself repelled by force the bloody arm of slavery. I felt as I never felt before. It was a glorious resurrection, from the tomb of slavery, to the heaven of freedom. My long-crushed spirit rose, cowardice departed, bold defiance took its place; and I now resolved that, however long I might remain a slave in form, the day had passed forever when I could be a slave in fact. I did not hesitate to let it be known of me, that the white man who expected to succeed in whipping, must also succeed in killing me.

From this time I was never again what might be called fairly whipped, though I remained a slave four years afterwards. I had several fights, but was never whipped.

It was for a long time a matter of surprise to me why Mr. Covey did not immediately have me taken by the constable to the whipping-post, and there regularly whipped for the crime of raising my hand against a white man in defense of myself. And the only explanation I can now think of does not entirely satisfy me; but such as it is, I will give it. Mr. Covey enjoyed the most unbounded reputation for being a first-rate overseer and negro-breaker. It was of considerable importance to him.

That reputation was at stake; and had he sent me—a boy about sixteen years old—to the public whipping-post, his reputation would have been lost; so, to save his reputation, he suffered me to go unpunished.

My term of actual service to Mr. Edward Covey ended on Christmas day, 1833. The days between Christmas and New Year's day are allowed as holidays; and, accordingly, we were not required to perform any labor, more than to feed and take care of the stock. This time we regarded as our own, by the grace of our masters; and we therefore used or abused it nearly as we pleased. Those of us who had families at a distance, were generally allowed to spend the whole six days in their society. This time, however, was spent in various ways. The staid, sober, thinking and industrious ones of our number would employ themselves in making corn-brooms, mats, horse-collars, and baskets; and another class of us would spend the time in hunting opossums, hares, and coons. But by far the larger part engaged in such sports and merriments as playing ball, wrestling, running foot-races, fiddling, dancing, and drinking whisky; and this latter mode of spending the time was by far the most agreeable to the feelings of our masters. A slave who would work during the holidays was considered by our masters as scarcely deserving them. He was regarded as one who rejected the favor of his master. It was deemed a disgrace not to get drunk at Christmas; and he was regarded as lazy indeed, who had not provided himself with the necessary means, during the year, to get whisky enough to last him through Christmas.

From what I know of the effect of these holidays upon the slave, I believe them to be among the most effective means in the hands of the slaveholder in keeping down the spirit of insurrection. Were the slaveholders at once to abandon this practice, I have not the slightest doubt it would lead to an immediate insurrection among the slaves. These holidays serve as conductors, or safety-valves, to carry off the rebellious spirit of enslaved humanity. But for these, the slave would be forced up to the wildest desperation; and woe betide the slaveholder, the day he ventures to remove or hinder the operation of those conductors! I warn him that, in such an event, a spirit will go forth in their midst, more to be dreaded than the most appalling earthquake.

The holidays are part and parcel of the gross fraud, wrong, and inhumanity of slavery. They are professedly a custom established by the benevolence of the slaveholders; but I undertake to say, it is the result of selfishness, and one of the grossest frauds committed upon the down-trodden slave. They do not give the slaves this time because they would not like to have their work during its continuance, but because they know it would be unsafe to deprive them of it. This will be seen by the fact, that the slaveholders like to have their slaves spend those days just in such a manner as to make them as glad of their ending as of their beginning. Their object seems to be, to disgust their slaves with freedom, by plunging them into the lowest depths of dissipation. For instance, the slaveholders not only like to see the slave drink of his own accord, but will adopt various plans to make him drunk. One plan is, to make bets on their slaves, as to who can drink the most whisky without getting drunk; and in this way they succeed in getting whole multitudes to drink to excess. Thus, when the slave asks for virtuous freedom, the cunning slaveholder, knowing his ignorance, cheats him with a dose of vicious dissipation, artfully labelled with the name of liberty. The most of us used to drink it down, and the result was just what might be supposed: many of us were led to think that there was little to choose between liberty and slavery. We felt, and very properly too, that we had almost as well be slaves to man as to rum. So, when the holidays ended, we staggered up from the filth of our wallowing, took a long breath, and marched to the field,—feeling, upon the whole, rather glad to go, from what our master had deceived us into a belief was freedom, back to the arms of slavery.

I have said that this mode of treatment is a part of the whole system of fraud and inhumanity of slavery. It is so. The mode here adopted to disgust the slave with freedom, by allowing him to see only the abuse of it, is carried out in other things. For instance, a slave loves molasses; he steals some. His master, in many cases, goes off to town, and buys a large quantity; he returns, takes his whip, and commands the slave to eat the molasses, until the poor fellow is made sick at the very mention of it. The same mode is sometimes adopted to make the slaves refrain from asking for more food than their regular allowance. A slave runs through his allowance, and applies for more. His master is enraged at him; but, not willing to send him off without food, gives him more than is necessary, and compels him to eat it within a given time. Then, if he complains that he cannot eat it, he is said to be satisfied neither full nor fasting, and is whipped for being hard to please! I have an abundance of such illustrations of the same principle, drawn from my own observation, but think the cases I have cited sufficient. The practice is a very common one.

On the first of January, 1834, I left Mr. Covey, and went to live with Mr. William Freeland, who lived about three miles from St. Michael's.

I soon found Mr. Freeland a very different man from Mr. Covey. Though not rich, he was what would be called an educated southern gentleman. Mr. Covey, as I have shown, was a well-trained negro-breaker and slave-driver. The former (slaveholder though he was) seemed to possess some regard for honor, some reverence for justice, and some respect for humanity. The latter seemed totally insensible to all such sentiments. Mr. Freeland had many of the faults peculiar to slaveholders, such as being very passionate and fretful; but I must do him the justice to say, that he was exceedingly free from those degrading vices to which Mr. Covey was constantly addicted. The one was open and frank, and we always knew where to find him. The other was a most artful deceiver, and could be understood only by such as were skillful enough to detect his cunningly-devised frauds. Another advantage I gained in my new master was, he made no pretensions to, or profession of, religion; and this, in my opinion, was truly a great advantage. I assert most unhesitatingly, that the religion of the south is a mere covering for the most horrid crimes,—a justifier of the most appalling barbarity,—a sanctifier of the most hateful frauds,—and a dark shelter under, which the darkest, foulest, grossest, and most infernal deeds of slaveholders find the strongest protection. Were I to be again reduced to the chains of slavery, next to that enslavement, I should regard being the slave of a religious master the greatest calamity that could befall me. For of all slaveholders with whom I have ever met, religious slaveholders are the worst. I have ever found them the meanest and basest, the most cruel and cowardly, of all others. It was my unhappy lot not only to belong to a religious slaveholder, but to live in a community of such religionists. Very near Mr. Freeland lived the Rev. Daniel Weeden, and in the same neighborhood lived the Rev. Rigby Hopkins. These were members and ministers in the Reformed Methodist Church. Mr. Weeden owned, among others, a woman slave, whose name I have forgotten. This woman's back, for weeks, was kept literally raw, made so by the lash of this merciless, *religious* wretch. He used to hire hands. His maxim was, Behave well or behave ill, it is the duty of a master occasionally to whip a slave, to remind him of his master's authority. Such was his theory, and such his practice.

Mr. Hopkins was even worse than Mr. Weeden. His chief boast was his ability to manage slaves. The peculiar feature of his government was that of whipping slaves in advance of deserving it. He always managed to have one or more of his slaves to whip every Monday morning. He did this to alarm their fears, and strike terror into those who escaped. His plan was to whip for the smallest offenses, to prevent the commission of large ones. Mr. Hopkins could always find some excuse for whipping a slave. It would astonish one, unaccustomed to a slave-holding life, to see with what wonderful ease a slaveholder can find things, of which to make occasion to whip a slave. A mere look, word, or motion,—a mistake, accident, or want of power,—are all matters for which a slave may be whipped at any time. Does a slave look dissatisfied? It is said, he has the devil in him, and it must be whipped out. Does he speak loudly when spoken to by his master? Then he is getting high-minded, and should be taken down a button-hole lower. Does he forget to pull off his hat at the approach of a white person? Then he is wanting in reverence, and should be whipped for it. Does he ever venture to vindicate his conduct, when censured for it? Then he is guilty of impudence,—one of the greatest crimes of which a slave can be guilty. Does he ever venture to suggest a different mode of doing things from that pointed out by his master? He is indeed presumptuous, and getting above himself; and nothing less than a flogging will do for him. Does he, while ploughing, break a plough,—or, while hoeing, break a hoe? It is owing to his carelessness, and for it a slave must always be whipped. Mr. Hopkins could always find something of this sort to justify the use of the lash, and he seldom failed to embrace such opportunities. There was not a man in the whole county, with whom the slaves who had the getting their own home, would not prefer to live, rather than with this Rev. Mr. Hopkins. And yet there was not a man anywhere round, who made higher professions of religion, or was more active in revivals,—more attentive to the class, love-feast, prayer and preaching meetings, or more devotional in his family,—that prayed earlier, later, louder, and longer,—than this same reverend slave-driver, Rigby Hopkins.

But to return to Mr. Freeland, and to my experience while in his employment. He, like Mr. Covey, gave us enough to eat; but, unlike Mr. Covey, he also gave us sufficient time to take our meals. He worked us hard, but always between sunrise and sunset. He required a good deal of work to be done, but gave us good tools with which to work. His farm was large, but he employed hands enough to work it, and with ease, compared with many of his neighbors. My treatment, while in his employment, was heavenly, compared with what I experienced at the hands of Mr. Edward Covey.

Mr. Freeland was himself the owner of but two slaves. Their names were Henry Harris and John Harris. The rest of his hands he hired.

These consisted of myself, Sandy Jenkins,★ and Handy Caldwell. Henry and John were quite intelligent, and in a very little while after I went there, I succeeded in creating in them a strong desire to learn how to read. This desire soon sprang up in the others also. They very soon mustered up some old spelling-books, and nothing would do but that I must keep a Sabbath school. I agreed to do so, and accordingly devoted my Sundays to teaching these my loved fellow-slaves how to read. Neither of them knew his letters when I went there. Some of the slaves of the neighboring farms found what was going on, and also availed themselves of this little opportunity to learn to read. It was understood, among all who came, that there must be as little display about it as possible. It was necessary to keep our religious masters at St. Michael's unacquainted with the fact, that, instead of spending the Sabbath in wrestling, boxing, and drinking whisky, we were trying to learn how to read the will of God; for they had much rather see us engaged in those degrading sports, than to see us behaving like intellectual, moral, and accountable beings. My blood boils as I think of the bloody manner in which Messrs. Wright Fairbanks and Garrison West, both class-leaders, in connection with many others, rushed in upon us with sticks and stones, and broke up our virtuous little Sabbath school, at St. Michael's—all calling themselves Christians! humble followers of the Lord Jesus Christ! But I am again digressing.

I held my Sabbath school at the house of a free colored man, whose name I deem it imprudent to mention; for should it be known, it might embarrass him greatly, though the crime of holding the school was committed ten years ago. I had at one time over forty scholars, and those of the right sort, ardently desiring to learn. They were of all ages, though mostly men and women. I look back to those Sundays with an amount of pleasure not to be expressed. They were great days to my soul. The work of instructing my dear fellow-slaves was the sweetest engagement with which I was ever blessed. We loved each other, and to leave them at the close of the Sabbath was a severe cross indeed. When I think that these precious souls are today shut up in the prison-house of slavery, my feelings overcome me, and I am almost ready to ask, "Does a righteous God govern the universe? and for what does he hold

---

★This is the same man who gave me the roots to prevent my being whipped by Mr. Covey. He was "a clever soul." We used frequently to talk about the fight with Covey, and as often as we did so, he would claim my success as the result of the roots which he gave me. This superstition is very common among the more ignorant slaves. A slave seldom dies but that his death is attributed to trickery.

the thunders in his right hand, if not to smite the oppressor, and deliver the spoiled out of the hand of the spoiler?" These dear souls came not to Sabbath school because it was popular to do so, nor did I teach them because it was reputable to be thus engaged. Every moment they spent in that school, they were liable to be taken up, and given thirty-nine lashes. They came because they wished to learn. Their minds had been starved by their cruel masters. They had been shut up in mental darkness. I taught them, because it was the delight of my soul to be doing something that looked like bettering the condition of my race. I kept up my school nearly the whole year I lived with Mr. Freeland; and, beside my Sabbath school, I devoted three evenings in the week, during the winter, to teaching the slaves at home. And I have the happiness to know, that several of those who came to Sabbath school learned how to read; and that one, at least, is now free through my agency.

The year passed off smoothly. It seemed only about half as long as the year which preceded it. I went through it without receiving a single blow. I will give Mr. Freeland the credit of being the best master I ever had, *till I became my own master.* For the ease with which I passed the year, I was, however, somewhat indebted to the society of my fellow-slaves. They were noble souls; they not only possessed loving hearts, but brave ones. We were linked and interlinked with each other. I loved them with a love stronger than anything I have experienced since. It is sometimes said that we slaves do not love and confide in each other. In answer to this assertion, I can say, I never loved any or confided in any people more than my fellow-slaves, and especially those with whom I lived at Mr. Freeland's. I believe we would have died for each other. We never undertook to do anything, of any importance, without a mutual consultation. We never moved separately. We were one; and as much so by our tempers and dispositions, as by the mutual hardships to which we were necessarily subjected by our condition as slaves.

At the close of the year 1834, Mr. Freeland again hired me of my master, for the year 1835. But, by this time, I began to want to live *upon free land* as well as *with Freeland;* and I was no longer content, therefore, to live with him or any other slaveholder. I began, with the commencement of the year, to prepare myself for a final struggle, which should decide my fate one way or the other. My tendency was upward. I was fast approaching manhood, and year after year had passed, and I was still a slave. These thoughts roused me—I must do something. I therefore resolved that 1835 should not pass without witnessing an attempt, on my part, to secure my liberty. But I was not willing to cherish this determination alone. My fellow-slaves were dear to me. I was anxious to have them participate with me in this, my life-giving determination. I therefore, though with great prudence, commenced early to ascertain their views and feelings in regard to their condition, and to imbue their minds with thoughts of freedom. I bent myself to devising ways and means for our escape, and meanwhile strove, on all fitting occasions, to impress them with the gross fraud and inhumanity of slavery. I went first to Henry, next to John, then to the others. I found, in them all, warm hearts and noble spirits. They were ready to hear, and ready to act when a feasible plan should be proposed. This was what I wanted. I talked to them of our want of manhood, if we submitted to our enslavement without at least one noble effort to be free. We met often, and consulted frequently, and told our hopes and fears, recounted the difficulties, real and imagined, which we should be called on to meet. At times we were almost disposed to give up, and try to content ourselves with our wretched lot; at others, we were firm and unbending in our determination to go. Whenever we suggested any plan, there was shrinking—the odds were fearful. Our path was beset with the greatest obstacles; and if we succeeded in gaining the end of it, our right to be free was yet questionable—we were yet liable to be returned to bondage. We could see no spot, this side of the ocean, where we could be free. We knew nothing about Canada. Our knowledge of the north did not extend farther than New York; and to go there, and be forever harassed with the frightful liability of being returned to slavery—with the certainty of being treated tenfold worse than before—the thought was truly a horrible one, and one which it was not easy to overcome. The case sometimes stood thus: At every gate through which we were to pass, we saw a watchman—at every ferry a guard—on every bridge a sentinel—and in every wood a patrol. We were hemmed in upon every side. Here were the difficulties, real or imagined—the good to be sought, and the evil to be shunned. On the one hand, there stood slavery, a stern reality, glaring frightfully upon us,—its robes already crimsoned with the blood of millions, and even now feasting itself greedily upon our own flesh. On the other hand, away back in the dim distance, under the flickering light of the north star, behind some craggy hill or snow-covered mountain, stood a doubtful freedom—half frozen—beckoning us to come and share its hospitality. This in itself was sometimes enough to stagger us; but when we permitted ourselves to survey the road, we were frequently appalled. Upon either side we saw grim death, assuming the most horrid shapes. Now it was starvation, causing us to eat our own flesh;—now we were contending with the waves, and were drowned;—now we were overtaken, and torn to pieces by the fangs of the terrible blood-hound. We were stung by scorpions, chased by wild beasts, bitten by snakes, and finally, after having nearly reached the desired spot,—after swimming rivers, encountering wild beasts, sleeping in the woods, suffering hunger and nakedness,—we were overtaken by our pursuers, and, in our resistance, we were shot dead upon the spot! I say, this picture sometimes appalled us, and made us

> "rather bear those ills we had,
> Than fly to others, that we knew not of."

In coming to a fixed determination to run away, we did more than Patrick Henry, when he resolved upon liberty or death. With us it was a doubtful liberty at most, and almost certain death if we failed. For my part, I should prefer death to hopeless bondage.

Sandy, one of our number, gave up the notion, but still encouraged us. Our company then consisted of Henry Harris, John Harris, Henry Bailey, Charles Roberts, and myself. Henry Bailey was my uncle, and belonged to my master. Charles married my aunt: he belonged to my master's father-in-law, Mr. William Hamilton.

The plan we finally concluded upon was, to get a large canoe belonging to Mr. Hamilton, and upon the Saturday night previous to Easter holidays, paddle directly up the Chesapeake Bay. On our arrival at the head of the bay, a distance of seventy or eighty miles from where we lived, it was our purpose to turn our canoe adrift, and follow the guidance of the north star till we got beyond the limits of Maryland. Our reason for taking the water route was, that we were less liable to be suspected as runaways; we hoped to be regarded as fishermen; whereas, if we should take the land route, we should be subjected to interruptions of almost every kind. Anyone having a white face, and being so disposed, could stop us, and subject us to examination.

The week before our intended start, I wrote several protections, one for each of us. As well as I can remember, they were in the following words, to wit:—

"THIS is to certify that I, the undersigned, have given the bearer, my servant, full liberty to go to Baltimore, and spend the Easter holidays. Written with mine own hand, &c., 1835.

"WILLIAM HAMILTON,
"Near St. Michael's, in Talbot county, Maryland."

We were not going to Baltimore; but, in going up the bay, we went toward Baltimore, and these protections were only intended to protect us while on the bay.

As the time drew near for our departure, our anxiety became more and more intense. It was truly a matter of life and death with us. The strength of our determination was about to be fully tested. At this time, I was very active in explaining every difficulty, removing every doubt, dispelling every fear, and inspiring all with the firmness indispensable to success in our undertaking; assuring them that half was gained the instant we made the move; we had talked long enough; we were now ready to move; if not now, we never should be; and if we did not intend to move now, we had as well fold our arms, sit down, and acknowledge ourselves fit only to be slaves. This, none of us were prepared to acknowledge. Every man stood firm; and at our last meeting, we pledged ourselves afresh, in the most solemn manner, that, at the time appointed, we would certainly start in pursuit of freedom. This was in the middle of the week, at the end of which we were to be off. We went, as usual, to our several fields of labor, but with bosoms highly agitated with thoughts of our truly hazardous undertaking. We tried to conceal our feelings as much as possible; and I think we succeeded very well.

After a painful waiting, the Saturday morning, whose night was to witness our departure, came. I hailed it with joy, bring what of sadness it might. Friday night was a sleepless one for me. I probably felt more anxious than the rest, because I was, by common consent, at the head of the whole affair. The responsibility of success or failure lay heavily upon me. The glory of the one, and the confusion of the other, were alike mine. The first two hours of that morning were such as I never experienced before, and hope never to again. Early in the morning, we went, as usual, to the field. We were spreading manure; and all at once, while thus engaged, I was overwhelmed with an indescribable feeling, in the fullness of which I turned to Sandy, who was nearby, and said, "We are betrayed!" "Well," said he, "that thought has this moment struck me." We said no more. I was never more certain of anything.

The horn was blown as usual, and we went up from the field to the house for breakfast. I went for the form, more than for want of anything to eat that morning. Just as I got to the house, in looking out at the lane gate, I saw four white men, with two colored men. The white men were on horseback, and the colored ones were walking behind, as if tied. I watched them a few moments till they got up to our lane gate.

Here they halted, and tied the colored men to the gate-post. I was not yet certain as to what the matter was. In a few moments, in rode Mr. Hamilton, with a speed betokening great excitement. He came to the door, and inquired if Master William was in. He was told he was at the barn. Mr. Hamilton, without dismounting, rode up to the barn with extraordinary speed. In a few moments, he and Mr. Freeland returned to the house. By this time, the three constables rode up, and in great haste dismounted, tied their horses, and met Master William and Mr. Hamilton returning from the barn; and after talking awhile, they all walked up to the kitchen door. There was no one in the kitchen but myself and John. Henry and Sandy were up at the barn. Mr. Freeland put his head in at the door, and called me by name, saying, there were some gentlemen at the door who wished to see me. I stepped to the door, and inquired what they wanted. They at once seized me, and, without giving me any satisfaction, tied me—lashing my hands closely together. I insisted upon knowing what the matter was. They at length said, that they had learned I had been in a "scrape," and that I was to be examined before my master; and if their information proved false, I should not be hurt.

In a few moments, they succeeded in tying John. They then turned to Henry, who had by this time returned, and commanded him to cross his hands. "I won't!" said Henry, in a firm tone, indicating his readiness to meet the consequences of his refusal. "Won't you?" said Tom Graham, the constable. "No, I won't!" said Henry, in a still stronger tone. With this, two of the constables pulled out their shining pistols, and swore, by their Creator, that they would make him cross his hands or kill him. Each cocked his pistol, and, with fingers on the trigger, walked up to Henry, saying, at the same time, if he did not cross his hands, they would blow his damned heart out. "Shoot me, shoot me!" said Henry; "you can't kill me but once. Shoot, shoot,— and be damned! *I won't be tied!*" This he said in a tone of loud defiance; and at the same time, with a motion as quick as lightning, he with one single stroke dashed the pistols from the hand of each constable. As he did this, all hands fell upon him, and, after beating him some time, they finally overpowered him, and got him tied.

During the scuffle, I managed, I know not how, to get my pass out, and, without being discovered, put it into the fire. We were all now tied; and just as we were to leave for Easton jail, Betsy Freeland, mother of William Freeland, came to the door with her hands full of biscuits, and divided them between Henry and John. She then delivered herself of a speech, to the following effect:—addressing herself to me, she said, "*You devil! You yellow devil!* it was you that put it into the heads of Henry and John to run away. But for you, you long-legged mulatto devil! Henry nor John would never have thought of such a thing." I made no reply, and was immediately hurried off towards St. Michael's. Just a moment previous to the scuffle with Henry, Mr. Hamilton suggested the propriety of making a search for the protections which he had understood Frederick had written for himself and the rest. But, just at the moment he was about carrying his proposal into effect, his aid was needed in helping to tie Henry; and the excitement attending the scuffle caused them either to forget, or to deem it unsafe, under the circumstances, to search. So we were not yet convicted of the intention to run away.

When we got about half way to St. Michael's, while the constables having us in charge were looking ahead, Henry inquired of me what he should do with his pass. I told him to eat it with his biscuit, and own nothing; and we passed the word around, *"Own nothing;"* and *"Own nothing!"* said we all. Our confidence in each other was unshaken. We were resolved to succeed or fail together, after the calamity had befallen us as much as before. We were now prepared for anything. We were to be dragged that morning fifteen miles behind horses, and then to be placed in the Easton jail. When we reached St. Michael's, we underwent a sort of examination. We all denied that we ever intended to run away. We did this more to bring out the evidence against us, than from any hope of getting clear of being sold; for, as I have said, we were ready for that. The fact was, we cared but little where we went, so we went together. Our greatest concern was about separation. We dreaded that more than anything this side of death. We found the evidence against us to be the testimony of one person; our master would not tell who it was; but we came to a unanimous decision among ourselves as to who their informant was. We were sent off to the jail at Easton. When we got there, we were delivered up to the sheriff, Mr. Joseph Graham, and by him placed in jail. Henry, John, and myself, were placed in one room together—Charles, and Henry Bailey, in another. Their object in separating us was to hinder concert.

We had been in jail scarcely twenty minutes, when a swarm of slave traders, and agents for slave traders, flocked into jail to look at us, and to ascertain if we were for sale. Such a set of beings I never saw before! I felt myself surrounded by so many fiends from perdition. A band of pirates never looked more like their father, the devil. They laughed and grinned over us, saying, "Ah, my boys! we have got you, haven't we?" And after taunting us in various ways, they one by one went into an examination of us, with intent to ascertain our value. They would impudently ask us if we would not like to have them for our masters. We would make them no answer, and leave them to find out as best they could. Then they would curse and swear at us, telling us that they could take the devil out of us in a very little while, if we were only in their hands.

While in jail, we found ourselves in much more comfortable quarters than we expected when we went there. We did not get much to eat, nor that which was very good; but we had a good clean room, from the windows of which we could see what was going on in the street, which was very much better than though we had been placed in one of the dark, damp cells. Upon the whole, we got along very well, so far as the jail and its keeper were concerned. Immediately after the holidays were over, contrary to all our expectations, Mr. Hamilton and Mr. Freeland came up to Easton, and took Charles, the two Henrys, and John, out of jail, and carried them home, leaving me alone. I regarded this separation as a final one. It caused me more pain than anything else in the whole transaction. I was ready for anything rather than separation. I supposed that they had consulted together, and had decided that, as I was the whole cause of the intention of the others to run away, it was hard to make the innocent suffer with the guilty; and that they had, therefore, concluded to take the others home, and sell me, as a warning to the others that remained. It is due to the noble Henry to say, he seemed almost as reluctant at leaving the prison as at leaving home to come to the prison. But we knew we should, in all probability, be separated, if we were sold; and since he was in their hands, he concluded to go peaceably home.

I was now left to my fate. I was all alone, and within the walls of a stone prison. But a few days before, and I was full of hope. I expected to have been safe in a land of freedom; but now I was covered with gloom, sunk down to the utmost despair. I thought the possibility of freedom was gone. I was kept in this way about one week, at the end of which, Captain Auld, my master, to my surprise and utter astonishment, came up, and took me out, with the intention of sending me, with a gentleman of his acquaintance, into Alabama. But, from some cause or other, he did not send me to Alabama, but concluded to send me back to Baltimore, to live again with his brother Hugh, and to learn a trade.

Thus, after an absence of three years and one month, I was once more permitted to return to my old home at Baltimore. My master sent me away, because there existed against me a very great prejudice in the community, and he feared I might be killed.

In a few weeks after I went to Baltimore, Master Hugh hired me to Mr. William Gardner, an extensive ship-builder, on Fell's Point. I was put there to learn how to caulk. It, however, proved a very unfavorable place for the accomplishment of this object. Mr. Gardner was engaged that spring in building two large man-of-war brigs, professedly for the Mexican government. The vessels were to be launched in the July of that year, and in failure thereof, Mr. Gardner was to lose a considerable sum; so that when I entered, all was hurry. There was no time to learn anything. Every man had to do that which he knew how to do. In entering the ship-yard, my orders from Mr. Gardner were, to do whatever the carpenters commanded me to do. This was placing me at the beck and call of about seventy-five men. I was to regard all these as masters. Their word was to be my law. My situation was a most trying one. At times I needed a dozen pair of hands. I was called a dozen ways in the space of a single minute. Three or four voices would strike my ear at the same moment. It was—"Fred., come help me to cant this timber here."—"Fred., come carry this timber yonder."—"Fred., bring that roller here."—"Fred., go get a fresh can of water."—"Fred., come help saw off the end of this timber."—"Fred., go quick, and get the crowbar."—"Fred., hold on the end of this fall."—"Fred., go to the blacksmith's shop, and get a new punch."—"Hurra, Fred.! run and bring me a cold chisel."—"I say, Fred., bear a hand, and get up a fire as quick as lightning under that steam-box."—"Halloo, nigger! come, turn this grindstone."—"Come, come! move, move! and *bowse* this timber forward."—"I say, darky, blast your eyes, why don't you heat up some pitch?"—"Halloo! halloo! halloo!" (Three voices at the same time.) "Come here!—Go there!—Hold on where you are! Damn you, if you move, I'll knock your brains out!"

This was my school for eight months; and I might have remained there longer, but for a most horrid fight I had with four of the white apprentices, in which my left eye was nearly knocked out, and I was horribly mangled in other respects. The facts in the case were these: Until a very little while after I went there, white and black ship-carpenters worked side by side, and no one seemed to see any impropriety in it. All hands seemed to be very well satisfied. Many of the black carpenters were freemen. Things seemed to be going on very well. All at once, the white carpenters knocked off, and said they would not work with free colored workmen. Their reason for this, as alleged, was, that if free colored carpenters were encouraged, they would soon take the trade into their own hands, and poor white men would be thrown out of employment. They therefore felt called upon at once to put a stop to it. And, taking advantage of Mr. Gardner's necessities, they broke off, swearing they would work no longer, unless he would discharge his black carpenters. Now, though this did not extend to me in form, it did reach me in fact. My fellow-apprentices very soon began to feel it degrading to them to work with me. They began to put on airs, and talk about the "niggers" taking the country, saying we all ought to be killed; and, being encouraged by the journeymen, they commenced making my condition as hard as they could, by hectoring me around, and sometimes striking me. I, of course, kept the vow I made after the fight with Mr. Covey, and struck back again, regardless of consequences; and while I kept them from combining, I succeeded very well; for I could whip the whole of them, taking them separately. They, however, at length combined, and came upon me, armed with sticks, stones, and heavy handspikes. One came in front with a half brick. There was one at each side of me, and one behind me. While I was attending to those in front, and on either side, the one behind ran up with the handspike, and struck me a heavy blow upon the head. It stunned me. I fell, and with this they all ran upon me, and fell to beating me with their fists. I let them lay on for a while, gathering strength. In an instant, I gave a sudden surge, and rose to my hands and knees. Just as I did that, one of their number gave me, with his heavy boot, a powerful kick in the left eye. My eyeball seemed to have burst. When they saw my eye closed, and badly swollen, they left me. With this I seized the handspike, and for a time pursued them. But here the carpenters interfered, and I thought I might as well give it up. It was impossible to stand my hand against so many. All this took place in sight of not less than fifty white ship-carpenters, and not one interposed a friendly word; but some cried, "Kill the damned nigger! Kill him! kill him! He struck a white person." I found my only chance for life was in flight. I succeeded in getting away without an additional blow, and barely so; for to strike a white man is death by Lynch law,—and that was the law in Mr. Gardner's ship-yard; nor is there much of any other out of Mr. Gardner's ship-yard.

I went directly home, and told the story of my wrongs to Master Hugh; and I am happy to say of him, irreligious as he was, his conduct was heavenly, compared with that of his brother Thomas under similar circumstances. He listened attentively to my narration of the circumstances leading to the savage outrage, and gave many proofs of his strong indignation at it. The heart of my once overkind mistress was again melted into pity. My puffed-out eye and blood-covered face moved her to tears. She took a chair by me, washed the blood from my face, and, with a mother's tenderness, bound up my head, covering the wounded eye with a lean piece of fresh beef. It was almost compensation for my suffering to witness, once more, a manifestation of kindness from this, my once affectionate old mistress. Master Hugh was very much enraged. He gave expression to his feelings by pouring out curses upon the heads of those who did the deed. As soon as I got a little the better of my bruises, he took me with him to Esquire Watson's, on Bond Street, to see what could be done about the matter. Mr. Watson inquired who saw the assault committed. Master Hugh told him it was done in Mr. Gardner's ship-yard, at midday, where there were a large company of men at work. "As to that," he said, "the deed was done, and there was no question as to who did it." His answer was, he could do nothing in the case, unless some white man would come forward and testify. He could issue no warrant on my word. If I had been killed in the presence of a thousand colored people, their testimony combined would have been insufficient to have arrested one of the murderers. Master Hugh, for once, was compelled to say this state of things was too bad. Of course, it was impossible to get any white man to volunteer his testimony in my behalf, and against the white young men. Even those who may have sympathized with me were not prepared to do this. It required a degree of courage unknown to them to do so; for just at that time, the slightest manifestation of humanity toward a colored person was denounced as abolitionism, and that name subjected its bearer to frightful liabilities. The watchwords of the bloody-minded in that region, and in those days, were, "Damn the abolitionists!" and "Damn the niggers!" There was nothing done, and probably nothing would have been done if I had been killed. Such was, and such remains, the state of things in the Christian city of Baltimore.

Master Hugh, finding he could get no redress, refused to let me go back again to Mr. Gardner. He kept me himself, and his wife dressed my wound till I was again restored to health. He then took me into the ship-yard of which he was foreman, in the employment of Mr. Walter Price. There I was immediately set to caulking, and very soon learned the art of using my mallet and irons. In the course of one year from the time I left Mr. Gardner's, I was able to command the highest wages given to the most experienced caulkers. I was now of some importance to my master. I was bringing him from six to seven dollars per week. I sometimes brought him nine dollars per week: my wages were a dollar and a half a day. After learning how to caulk, I sought my own employment, made my own contracts, and collected the money which I earned. My pathway became much more smooth than before; my condition was now much more comfortable. When I could get no caulking to do, I did nothing. During these leisure times, those old notions about freedom would steal over me again. When in Mr. Gardner's employment, I was kept in such a perpetual whirl of excitement, I could think of nothing, scarcely, but my life; and in thinking of my life, I almost forgot my liberty. I have observed this in my experience of slavery,—that whenever my condition was improved, instead of its increasing my contentment, it only increased my desire to be free, and set me to thinking of plans to gain my freedom. I have found that, to make a contented slave, it is necessary to make a thoughtless one. It is necessary to darken his moral and mental vision, and, as far as possible, to annihilate the power of reason. He must be able to detect no inconsistencies in slavery; he must be made to feel that slavery is right; and he can be brought to that only when he ceases to be a man.

I was now getting, as I have said, one dollar and fifty cents per day. I contracted for it; I earned it; it was paid to me; it was rightfully my own; yet, upon each returning Saturday night, I was compelled to deliver every cent of that money to Master Hugh. And why? Not because he earned it,—not because he had any hand in earning it,—not because I owed it to him,—nor because he possessed the slightest shadow of a right to it; but solely because he had the power to compel me to give it up. The right of the grim-visaged pirate upon the high seas is exactly the same.

Chapter XI

I NOW come to that part of my life during which I planned, and finally succeeded in making, my escape from slavery. But before narrating any of the peculiar circumstances, I deem it proper to make known my intention not to state all the facts connected with the transaction. My reasons for pursuing this course may be understood from the following: First, were I to give a minute statement of all the facts, it is not only possible, but quite probable, that others would thereby be involved in the most embarrassing difficulties. Secondly, such a statement would most undoubtedly induce greater vigilance on the part of slaveholders than has existed heretofore among them; which would, of course, be the means of guarding a door whereby some dear brother bondman might escape his galling chains. I deeply regret the necessity that impels me to suppress anything of importance connected with my experience in slavery. It would afford me great pleasure indeed, as well as materially add to the interest of my narrative, were I at liberty to gratify a curiosity, which I know exists in the minds of many, by an accurate statement of all the facts pertaining to my most fortunate escape. But I must deprive myself of this pleasure, and the curious of the gratification which such a statement would afford. I would allow myself to suffer under the greatest imputations which evil-minded men might suggest, rather than exculpate myself, and thereby run the hazard of closing the slightest avenue by which a brother slave might clear himself of the chains and fetters of slavery.

I have never approved of the very public manner in which some of our western friends have conducted what they call the *underground railroad,* but which, I think, by their open declarations, has been made most emphatically the *upperground railroad.* I honor those good men and women for their noble daring, and applaud them for willingly subjecting themselves to bloody persecution, by openly avowing their participation in the escape of slaves. I, however, can see very little good resulting from such a course, either to themselves or the slaves escaping; while, upon the other hand, I see and feel assured that those open declarations are a positive evil to the slaves remaining, who are seeking to escape. They do nothing towards enlightening the slave, whilst they do much towards enlightening the master. They stimulate him to greater watchfulness, and enhance his power to capture his slave. We owe something to the slaves south of the line as well as to those north of it; and in aiding the latter on their way to freedom, we should be careful to do nothing which would be likely to hinder the former from escaping from slavery. I would keep the merciless slaveholder profoundly ignorant of the means of flight adopted by the slave. I would leave him to imagine himself surrounded by myriads of invisible tormentors, ever ready to snatch from his infernal grasp his trembling prey. Let him be left to feel his way in the dark; let darkness commensurate with his crime hover over him; and let him feel that at every step he takes, in pursuit of the flying bondman, he is running the frightful risk of having his hot brains dashed out by an invisible agency. Let us render the tyrant no aid; let us not hold the light by which he can trace the footprints of our flying brother. But enough of this. I will now proceed to the statement of those facts, connected with my escape, for which I am alone responsible, and for which no one can be made to suffer but myself.

In the early part of the year 1838, I became quite restless. I could see no reason why I should, at the end of each week, pour the reward of my toil into the purse of my master. When I carried to him my weekly wages, he would, after counting the money, look me in the face with a robber-like fierceness, and ask, "Is this all?" He was satisfied with nothing less than the last cent. He would, however, when I made him six dollars, sometimes give me six cents, to encourage me. It had the opposite effect. I regarded it as a sort of admission of my right to the whole. The fact that he gave me any part of my wages was proof, to my mind, that he believed me entitled to the whole of them. I always felt worse for having received anything; for I feared that the giving me a few cents would ease his conscience, and make him feel himself to be a pretty honorable sort of robber. My discontent grew upon me. I was ever on the look-out for means of escape; and, finding no direct means, I determined to try to hire my time, with a view of getting money with which to make my escape. In the spring of 1838, when Master Thomas came to Baltimore to purchase his spring goods, I got an opportunity, and applied to him to allow me to hire my time. He unhesitatingly refused my request, and told me this was another stratagem by which to escape. He told me I could go nowhere but that he could get me; and that, in the event of my running away, he should spare no pains in his efforts to catch me. He exhorted me to content myself, and be obedient. He told me, if I would be happy, I must lay out no plans for the future. He said, if I behaved myself properly, he would take care of me. Indeed, he advised me to complete thoughtlessness of the future, and taught me to depend solely upon him for happiness. He seemed to see fully the pressing necessity of setting aside my intellectual nature, in order to contentment in slavery. But in spite of him, and even in spite of myself, I continued to think, and to think about the injustice of my enslavement, and the means of escape.

About two months after this, I applied to Master Hugh for the privilege of hiring my time. He was not acquainted with the fact that I had applied to Master Thomas, and had been refused. He too, at first, seemed disposed to refuse; but, after some reflection, he granted me the privilege, and proposed the following terms: I was to be allowed all my time, make all contracts with those for whom I worked, and find my own employment; and, in return for this liberty, I was to pay him three dollars at the end of each week; find myself in caulking tools, and in board and clothing. My board was two dollars and a half per week. This, with the wear and tear of clothing and caulking tools, made my regular expenses about six dollars per week. This amount I was compelled to make up, or relinquish the privilege of hiring my time. Rain or shine, work or no work, at the end of each week the money must be forthcoming, or I must give up my privilege. This arrangement, it will be perceived, was decidedly in my master's favor. It relieved him of all need of looking after me. His money was sure. He received all the benefits of slaveholding without its evils; while I endured all the evils of a slave, and suffered all the care and anxiety of a freeman. I found it a hard bargain. But, hard as it was, I thought it better than the old mode of getting along. It was a step towards freedom to be allowed to bear the responsibilities of a freeman, and I was determined to hold on upon it. I bent myself to the work of making money. I was ready to work at night as well as day, and by the most untiring perseverance and industry, I made enough to meet my expenses, and lay up a little money every week. I went on thus from May till August. Master Hugh then refused to allow me to hire my time longer. The ground for his refusal was a failure on my part, one Saturday night, to pay him for my week's time. This failure was occasioned by my attending a camp meeting about ten miles from Baltimore. During the week, I had entered into an engagement with a number of young friends to start from Baltimore to the camp ground early Saturday evening; and being detained by my employer, I was unable to get down to Master Hugh's without disappointing the company. I knew that Master Hugh was in no special need of the money that night. I therefore decided to go to camp meeting, and upon my return pay him the three dollars. I stayed at the camp meeting one day longer than I intended when I left. But as soon as I returned, I called upon him to pay him what he considered his due. I found him very angry; he could scarce restrain his wrath. He said he had a great mind to give me a severe whipping. He wished to know how I dared go out of the city without asking his permission. I told him I hired my time, and while I paid him the price which he asked for it, I did not know that I was bound to ask him when and where I should go. This reply troubled him; and, after reflecting a few moments, he turned to me, and said I should hire my time no longer; that the next thing he should know of, I would be running away. Upon the same plea, he told me to bring my tools and clothing home forthwith. I did so; but instead of seeking work, as I had been accustomed to do previously to hiring my time, I spent the whole week without the performance of a single stroke of work. I did this in retaliation. Saturday night, he called upon me as usual for my week's wages. I told him I had no wages; I had done no work that week. Here we were upon the point of coming to blows. He raved, and swore his determination to get hold of me. I did not allow myself a single word; but was resolved, if he laid the weight of his hand upon me, it should be blow for blow. He did not strike me, but told me that he would find me in constant employment in future. I thought the matter over during the next day, Sunday, and finally resolved upon the third day of September, as the day upon which I would make a second attempt to secure my freedom. I now had three weeks during which to prepare for my journey. Early on Monday morning, before Master Hugh had time to make any engagement for me, I went out and got employment of Mr. Butler, at his ship-yard near the drawbridge, upon what is called the City Block, thus making it unnecessary for him to seek employment for me. At the end of the week, I brought him between eight and nine dollars. He seemed very well pleased, and asked me why I did not do the same the week before. He little knew what my plans were. My object in working steadily was to remove any suspicion he might entertain of my intent to run away; and in this I succeeded admirably. I suppose he thought I was never better satisfied with my condition than at the very time during which I was planning my escape. The second week passed, and again I carried him my full wages; and so well pleased was he, that he gave me twenty-five cents, (quite a large sum for a slaveholder to give a slave,) and bade me to make a good use of it. I told him I would.

Things went on without very smoothly indeed, but within there was trouble. It is impossible for me to describe my feelings as the time of my contemplated start drew near. I had a number of warm-hearted friends in Baltimore,—friends that I loved almost as I did my life,— and the thought of being separated from them forever was painful beyond expression. It is my opinion that thousands would escape from slavery, who now remain, but for the strong cords of affection that bind them to their friends. The thought of leaving my friends was decidedly the most painful thought with which I had to contend. The love of them was my tender point, and shook my decision more than all things else. Besides the pain of separation, the dread and apprehension of a failure exceeded what I had experienced at my first attempt. The appalling defeat I then sustained returned to torment me. I felt assured that, if I failed in this attempt, my case would be a hopeless one—it would seal my fate as a slave forever. I could not hope to get off with anything less than the severest punishment, and being placed beyond the means of escape. It required no very vivid imagination to depict the most frightful scenes through which I should have to pass, in case I failed. The wretchedness of slavery, and the blessedness of freedom, were perpetually before me. It was life and death with me. But I remained firm, and, according to my resolution, on the third day of September, 1838, I left my chains, and succeeded in reaching New York without the slightest interruption of any kind. How I did so,—what means I adopted,—what direction I travelled, and by what mode of conveyance,—I must leave unexplained, for the reasons before mentioned.

I have been frequently asked how I felt when I found myself in a free State. I have never been able to answer the question with any satisfaction to myself. It was a moment of the highest excitement I ever experienced. I suppose I felt as one may imagine the unarmed mariner to feel when he is rescued by a friendly man-of-war from the pursuit of a pirate. In writing to a dear friend, immediately after my arrival at New York, I said I felt like one who had escaped a den of hungry lions. This state of mind, however, very soon subsided; and I was again seized with a feeling of great insecurity and loneliness. I was yet liable to be taken back, and subjected to all the tortures of slavery. This in itself was enough to damp the ardor of my enthusiasm. But the loneliness overcame me. There I was in the midst of thousands, and yet a perfect stranger; without home and without friends, in the midst of thousands of my own brethren—children of a common Father, and yet I dared not to unfold to any one of them my sad condition. I was afraid to speak to anyone for fear of speaking to the wrong one, and thereby falling into the hands of money-loving kidnappers, whose business it was to lie in wait for the panting fugitive, as the ferocious beasts of the forest lie in wait for their prey. The motto which I adopted when I started from slavery was this—"Trust no man!" I saw in every white man an enemy, and in almost every colored man cause for distrust. It was a most painful situation; and, to understand it, one must needs experience it, or imagine himself in similar circumstances. Let him be a fugitive slave in a strange land—a land given up to be the hunting-ground for slaveholders—whose inhabitants are legalized kidnappers—where he is every moment subjected to the terrible liability of being seized upon by his fellow-men, as the hideous crocodile seizes upon his prey!—I say, let him place himself in my situation—without home or friends—without money or credit—wanting shelter, and no one to give it—wanting bread, and no money to buy it,—and at the same time let him feel that he is pursued by merciless men-hunters, and in total darkness as to what to do, where to go, or where to stay,—perfectly helpless both as to the means of defense and means of escape,—in the midst of plenty, yet suffering the terrible gnawings of hunger,—in the midst of houses, yet having no home,—among fellow-men, yet feeling as if in the midst of wild beasts, whose greediness to swallow up the trembling and half-famished fugitive is only equalled by that with which the monsters of the deep swallow up the helpless fish upon which they subsist,—I say, let him be placed in this most trying situation,—the situation in which I was placed,—then, and not till then, will he fully appreciate the hardships of, and know how to sympathize with, the toil-worn and whip-scarred fugitive slave.

Thank Heaven, I remained but a short time in this distressed situation. I was relieved from it by the humane hand of Mr. DAVID RUGGLES, whose vigilance, kindness, and perseverance, I shall never forget. I am glad of an opportunity to express, as far as words can, the love and gratitude I bear him. Mr. Ruggles is now afflicted with blindness, and is himself in need of the same kind offices which he was once so forward in the performance of toward others. I had been in New York but a few days, when Mr. Ruggles sought me out, and very kindly took me to his boarding-house at the corner of Church and Lespenard Streets. Mr. Ruggles was then very deeply engaged in the memorable *Darg* case, as well as attending to a number of other fugitive slaves, devising ways and means for their successful escape; and, though watched and hemmed in on almost every side, he seemed to be more than a match for his enemies.

Very soon after I went to Mr. Ruggles, he wished to know of me where I wanted to go; as he deemed it unsafe for me to remain in New York. I told him I was a caulker, and should like to go where I could get work. I thought of going to Canada; but he decided against it, and in favor of my going to New Bedford, thinking I should be able to get work there at my trade. At this time, Anna,★ my intended wife, came on; for I wrote to her immediately after my arrival at New York, (notwith-

★ She was free.

standing my homeless, houseless, and helpless condition,) informing her of my successful flight, and wishing her to come on forthwith. In a few days after her arrival, Mr. Ruggles called in the Rev. J. W. C. Pennington, who, in the presence of Mr. Ruggles, Mrs. Michaels, and two or three others, performed the marriage ceremony, and gave us a certificate, of which the following is an exact copy:—

"This may certify, that I joined together in holy matrimony Frederick Johnson* and Anna Murray, as man and wife, in the presence of Mr. David Ruggles and Mrs. Michaels.

"JAMES W. C. PENNINGTON.

"New York, Sept. 15, 1838."

Upon receiving this certificate, and a five-dollar bill from Mr. Ruggles, I shouldered one part of our baggage, and Anna took up the other, and we set out forthwith to take passage on board of the steamboat *John W. Richmond* for Newport, on our way to New Bedford. Mr. Ruggles gave me a letter to a Mr. Shaw in Newport, and told me, in case my money did not serve me to New Bedford, to stop in Newport and obtain further assistance; but upon our arrival at Newport, we were so anxious to get to a place of safety, that, notwithstanding we lacked the necessary money to pay our fare, we decided to take seats in the stage, and promise to pay when we got to New Bedford. We were encouraged to do this by two excellent gentlemen, residents of New Bedford, whose names I afterward ascertained to be Joseph Ricketson and William C. Taber. They seemed at once to understand our circumstances, and gave us such assurance of their friendliness as put us fully at ease in their presence. It was good indeed to meet with such friends, at such a time. Upon reaching New Bedford, we were directed to the house of Mr. Nathan Johnson, by whom we were kindly received, and hospitably provided for. Both Mr. and Mrs. Johnson took a deep and lively interest in our welfare. They proved themselves quite worthy of the name of abolitionists. When the stage-driver found us unable to pay our fare, he held on upon our baggage as security for the debt. I had but to mention the fact to Mr. Johnson, and he forthwith advanced the money.

We now began to feel a degree of safety, and to prepare ourselves for the duties and responsibilities of a life of freedom. On the morning after our arrival at New Bedford, while at the breakfast-table, the ques-

*I had changed my name from Frederick *Bailey* to that of *Johnson.*

tion arose as to what name I should be called by. The name given me by my mother was, "Frederick Augustus Washington Bailey." I, however, had dispensed with the two middle names long before I left Maryland, so that I was generally known by the name of "Frederick Bailey." I started from Baltimore bearing the name of "Stanley." When I got to New York, I again changed my name to "Frederick Johnson," and thought that would be the last change. But when I got to New Bedford, I found it necessary again to change my name. The reason of this necessity was, that there were so many Johnsons in New Bedford, it was already quite difficult to distinguish between them. I gave Mr. Johnson the privilege of choosing me a name, but told him he must not take from me the name of "Frederick." I must hold on to that, to preserve a sense of my identity. Mr. Johnson had just been reading the "Lady of the Lake," and at once suggested that my name be "Douglass." From that time until now I have been called "Frederick Douglass;" and as I am more widely known by that name than by either of the others, I shall continue to use it as my own.

I was quite disappointed at the general appearance of things in New Bedford. The impression which I had received respecting the character and condition of the people of the north, I found to be singularly erroneous. I had very strangely supposed, while in slavery, that few of the comforts, and scarcely any of the luxuries, of life were enjoyed at the north, compared with what were enjoyed by the slaveholders of the south. I probably came to this conclusion from the fact that northern people owned no slaves. I supposed that they were about upon a level with the non-slaveholding population of the south. I knew *they* were exceedingly poor, and I had been accustomed to regard their poverty as the necessary consequence of their being non-slaveholders. I had somehow imbibed the opinion that, in the absence of slaves, there could be no wealth, and very little refinement. And upon coming to the north, I expected to meet with a rough, hard-handed, and uncultivated population, living in the most Spartan-like simplicity, knowing nothing of the ease, luxury, pomp, and grandeur of southern slaveholders. Such being my conjectures, anyone acquainted with the appearance of New Bedford may very readily infer how palpably I must have seen my mistake.

In the afternoon of the day when I reached New Bedford, I visited the wharves, to take a view of the shipping. Here I found myself surrounded with the strongest proofs of wealth. Lying at the wharves, and riding in the stream, I saw many ships of the finest model, in the best order, and of the largest size. Upon the right and left, I was walled in by granite warehouses of the widest dimensions, stowed to their utmost capacity with the necessaries and comforts of life. Added to this, almost everybody seemed to be at work, but noiselessly so, compared with what I had been accustomed to in Baltimore. There were no loud songs heard from those engaged in loading and unloading ships. I heard no deep oaths or horrid curses on the laborer. I saw no whipping of men; but all seemed to go smoothly on. Every man appeared to understand his work, and went at it with a sober, yet cheerful earnestness, which betokened the deep interest which he felt in what he was doing, as well as a sense of his own dignity as a man. To me this looked exceedingly strange. From the wharves I strolled around and over the town, gazing with wonder and admiration at the splendid churches, beautiful dwellings, and finely-cultivated gardens; evincing an amount of wealth, comfort, taste, and refinement, such as I had never seen in any part of slaveholding Maryland.

Everything looked clean, new, and beautiful. I saw few or no dilapidated houses, with poverty-stricken inmates; no half-naked children and barefooted women, such as I had been accustomed to see in Hillsborough, Easton, St. Michael's, and Baltimore. The people looked more able, stronger, healthier, and happier, than those of Maryland. I was for once made glad by a view of extreme wealth, without being saddened by seeing extreme poverty. But the most astonishing as well as the most interesting thing to me was the condition of the colored people, a great many of whom, like myself, had escaped thither as a refuge from the hunters of men. I found many, who had not been seven years out of their chains, living in finer houses, and evidently enjoying more of the comforts of life, than the average of slaveholders in Maryland. I will venture to assert that my friend Mr. Nathan Johnson (of whom I can say with a grateful heart, "I was hungry, and he gave me meat; I was thirsty, and he gave me drink; I was a stranger, and he took me in") lived in a neater house; dined at a better table; took, paid for, and read, more newspapers; better understood the moral, religious, and political character of the nation,—than nine tenths of the slaveholders in Talbot county, Maryland. Yet Mr. Johnson was a working man. His hands were hardened by toil, and not his alone, but those also of Mrs. Johnson. I found the colored people much more spirited than I had supposed they would be. I found among them a determination to protect each other from the blood-thirsty kidnapper, at all hazards. Soon after my arrival, I was told of a circumstance which illustrated their spirit. A colored man and a fugitive slave were on unfriendly terms. The former was heard to threaten the latter with informing his master of his whereabouts. Straightway a meeting was called among the colored people, under the stereotyped notice, "Business of importance!" The betrayer was invited to attend. The people came at the appointed hour, and organized the meeting by appointing a very religious old gentleman as president, who, I believe, made a prayer, after which he addressed the meeting as follows: *"Friends, we have got him here, and I would recommend that you young men just take him outside the door, and kill him!"* With this, a number of them bolted at him; but they were intercepted by some more timid than themselves, and the betrayer escaped their vengeance, and has not been seen in New Bedford since. I believe there have been no more such threats, and should there be hereafter, I doubt not that death would be the consequence.

I found employment, the third day after my arrival, in stowing a sloop with a load of oil. It was new, dirty, and hard work for me; but I went at it with a glad heart and a willing hand. I was now my own master. It was a happy moment, the rapture of which can be understood only by those who have been slaves. It was the first work, the reward of which was to be entirely my own. There was no Master Hugh standing ready, the moment I earned the money, to rob me of it. I worked that day with a pleasure I had never before experienced. I was at work for myself and newly-married wife. It was to me the starting-point of a new existence. When I got through with that job, I went in pursuit of a job of caulking; but such was the strength of prejudice against color, among the white caulkers, that they refused to work with me, and of course I could get no employment.* Finding my trade of no immediate benefit, I threw off my caulking habiliments, and prepared myself to do any kind of work I could get to do. Mr. Johnson kindly let me have his wood-horse and saw, and I very soon found myself a plenty of work. There was no work too hard—none too dirty. I was ready to saw wood, shovel coal, carry the hod, sweep the chimney, or roll oil casks,—all of which I did for nearly three years in New Bedford, before I became known to the anti-slavery world.

In about four months after I went to New Bedford, there came a young man to me, and inquired if I did not wish to take the *Liberator*. I told him I did; but, just having made my escape from slavery, I remarked that I was unable to pay for it then. I, however, finally became

*I am told that colored persons can now get employment at caulking in New Bedford— a result of anti-slavery effort.

a subscriber to it. The paper came, and I read it from week to week with such feelings as it would be quite idle for me to attempt to describe. The paper became my meat and my drink. My soul was set all on fire. Its sympathy for my brethren in bonds—its scathing denunciations of slaveholders—its faithful exposures of slavery—and its powerful attacks upon the upholders of the institution—sent a thrill of joy through my soul, such as I had never felt before!

I had not long been a reader of the *Liberator,* before I got a pretty correct idea of the principles, measures and spirit of the anti-slavery reform. I took right hold of the cause. I could do but little; but what I could, I did with a joyful heart, and never felt happier than when in an anti-slavery meeting. I seldom had much to say at the meetings, because what I wanted to say was said so much better by others. But, while attending an anti-slavery convention at Nantucket, on the 11th of August, 1841, I felt strongly moved to speak, and was at the same time much urged to do so by Mr. William C. Coffin, a gentleman who had heard me speak in the colored people's meeting at New Bedford. It was a severe cross, and I took it up reluctantly. The truth was, I felt myself a slave, and the idea of speaking to white people weighed me down. I spoke but a few moments, when I felt a degree of freedom, and said what I desired with considerable ease. From that time until now, I have been engaged in pleading the cause of my brethren—with what success, and with what devotion, I leave those acquainted with my labors to decide.

APPENDIX.

I FIND, since reading over the foregoing Narrative that I have, in several instances, spoken in such a tone and manner, respecting religion, as may possibly lead those unacquainted with my religious views to suppose me an opponent of all religion. To remove the liability of such misapprehension, I deem it proper to append the following brief explanation. What I have said respecting and against religion, I mean strictly to apply to the *slaveholding religion* of this land, and with no possible reference to Christianity proper; for, between the Christianity of this land, and the Christianity of Christ, I recognize the widest possible difference—so wide, that to receive the one as good, pure, and holy, is of necessity to reject the other as bad, corrupt, and wicked. To be the friend of the one, is of necessity to be the enemy of the other. I love the pure, peaceable, and impartial Christianity of Christ: I therefore hate the corrupt, slaveholding, women-whipping, cradle-plundering, partial and hypocritical Christianity of this land. Indeed, I can see no reason, but the most deceitful one, for calling the religion of this land Christianity. I look upon it as the climax of all misnomers, the boldest of all frauds, and the grossest of all libels. Never was there a clearer case of "stealing the livery of the court of heaven to serve the devil in." I am filled with unutterable loathing when I contemplate the religious pomp and show, together with the horrible inconsistencies, which everywhere surround me. We have men-stealers for ministers, women-whippers for missionaries, and cradle-plunderers for church members. The man who wields the blood-clotted cowskin during the week fills the pulpit on Sunday, and claims to be a minister of the meek and lowly Jesus. The man who robs me of my earnings at the end of each week meets me as a class-leader on Sunday morning, to show me the way of life, and the path of salvation. He who sells my sister, for purposes of prostitution, stands forth as the pious advocate of purity. He who proclaims it a religious duty to read the Bible denies me the right of learning to read the name of the God who made me. He who is the religious advocate of marriage robs whole millions of its sacred influence, and leaves them to the ravages of wholesale pollution. The warm defender of the sacredness of the family relation is the same that scatters whole families,—sundering husbands and wives, parents and children, sisters and brothers,—leaving the hut vacant, and the hearth desolate. We see the thief preaching against theft, and the adulterer against adultery. We have men sold to build churches, women sold to support the gospel, and babes sold to purchase Bibles for the *poor heathen! all for the glory of God and the good of souls!* The slave auctioneer's bell and the church-going bell chime in with each other, and the bitter cries of the heart-broken slave are drowned in the religious shouts of his pious master. Revivals of religion and revivals in the slave-trade go hand in hand together. The slave prison and the church stand near each other. The clanking of fetters and the rattling of chains in the prison, and the pious psalm and solemn prayer in the church, may be heard at the same time. The dealers in the bodies and souls of men erect their stand in the presence of the pulpit, and they mutually help each other. The dealer gives his blood-stained gold to support the pulpit, and the pulpit, in return, covers his infernal business with the garb of Christianity. Here we have religion and robbery the allies of each other—devils dressed in angels' robes, and hell presenting the semblance of paradise.

> *"Just God! and these are they,*
> *Who minister at thine altar, God of right!*
> *Men who their hands, with prayer and blessing, lay*
> *On Israel's ark of light.*
>
> *"What! preach, and kidnap men?*
> *Give thanks, and rob thy own afflicted poor?*
> *Talk of thy glorious liberty, and then*
> *Bolt hard the captive's door?*
>
> *"What! servants of thy own*
> *Merciful Son, who came to seek and save*
> *The homeless and the outcast, fettering down*
> *The tasked and plundered slave!*
>
> *"Pilate and Herod friends!*
> *Chief priests and rulers, as of old, combine!*
> *Just God and holy! is that church which lends*
> *Strength to the spoiler thine?"*

The Christianity of America is a Christianity, of whose votaries it may be as truly said, as it was of the ancient scribes and Pharisees, "They bind heavy burdens, and grievous to be borne, and lay them on men's shoulders, but they themselves will not move them with one of their fingers. All their works they do for to be seen of men.———They love the uppermost rooms at feasts, and the chief seats in the synagogues, ... and to be called of men, Rabbi, Rabbi.———But woe unto you, scribes and Pharisees, hypocrites! for ye shut up the kingdom of heaven against men; for ye neither go in yourselves, neither suffer ye them that are entering to go in. Ye devour widows' houses, and for a pretense make long prayers; therefore ye shall receive the greater damnation. Ye compass sea and land to make one proselyte, and when he is made, ye make him twofold more the child of hell than yourselves.———Woe unto you, scribes and Pharisees, hypocrites! for ye pay tithe of mint, and anise, and cumin, and have omitted the weightier matters of the law, judgment, mercy, and faith; these ought ye to have done, and not to leave the other undone. Ye blind guides! which strain at a gnat, and swallow a camel. Woe unto you, scribes and Pharisees, hypocrites! for ye make clean the outside of the cup and of the platter; but within, they are full of extortion and excess.——— Woe unto you, scribes and Pharisees, hypocrites! for ye are like unto whited sepulchres, which indeed appear beautiful outward, but are within full of dead men's bones, and of all uncleanness. Even so ye also outwardly appear righteous unto men, but within ye are full of hypocrisy and iniquity."

Dark and terrible as is this picture, I hold it to be strictly true of the overwhelming mass of professed Christians in America. They strain at a gnat, and swallow a camel. Could anything be more true of our churches? They would be shocked at the proposition of fellowshipping a *sheep*-stealer; and at the same time they hug to their communion a *man*-stealer, and brand me with being an infidel, if I find fault with them for it. They attend with Pharisaical strictness to the outward forms of religion, and at the same time neglect the weightier matters of the law, judgment, mercy, and faith. They are always ready to sacrifice, but seldom to show mercy. They are they who are represented as professing to love God whom they have not seen, whilst they hate their brother whom they have seen. They love the heathen on the other side of the globe. They can pray for him, pay money to have the Bible put into his hand, and missionaries to instruct him; while they despise and totally neglect the heathen at their own doors.

Such is, very briefly, my view of the religion of this land; and to avoid any misunderstanding, growing out of the use of general terms, I mean, by the religion of this land, that which is revealed in the words, deeds, and actions, of those bodies, north and south, calling themselves Christian churches, and yet in union with slaveholders. It is against religion, as presented by these bodies, that I have felt it my duty to testify.

I conclude these remarks by copying the following portrait of the religion of the south, (which is, by communion and fellowship, the religion of the north,) which I soberly affirm is "true to the life," and without caricature or the slightest exaggeration. It is said to have been drawn, several years before the present anti-slavery agitation began, by a northern Methodist preacher, who, while residing at the south, had an opportunity to see slaveholding morals, manners, and piety, with his own eyes. "Shall I not visit for these things? saith the Lord. Shall not my soul be avenged on such a nation as this?"

"A PARODY.

"Come, saints and sinners, hear me tell
How pious priests whip Jack and Nell,
And women buy and children sell,
And preach all sinners down to hell,
And sing of heavenly union.

"They'll bleat and baa, dona like goats,
Gorge down black sheep, and strain at motes,
Array their backs in fine black coats,
Then seize their negroes by their throats,
And choke, for heavenly union.

"They'll church you if you sip a dram,
And damn you if you steal a lamb;
Yet rob old Tony, Doll, and Sam,
Of human rights, and bread and ham;
Kidnapper's heavenly union.

"They'll loudly talk of Christ's reward,
And bind his image with a cord,
And scold, and swing the lash abhorred,
And sell their brother in the Lord
To handcuffed heavenly union.

"They'll read and sing a sacred song,
And make a prayer both loud and long,
And teach the right and do the wrong,
Hailing the brother, sister throng,
With words of heavenly union.

"We wonder how such saints can sing,
Or praise the Lord upon the wing,
Who roar, and scold, and whip, and sting,
And to their slaves and mammon cling,
      In guilty conscience union.

"They'll raise tobacco, corn, and rye,
And drive, and thieve, and cheat, and lie,
And lay up treasures in the sky,
By making switch and cowskin fly,
      In hope of heavenly union.

"They'll crack old Tony on the skull,
And preach and roar like Bashan bull,
Or braying ass, of mischief full,
Then seize old Jacob by the wool,
      And pull for heavenly union.

"A roaring, ranting, sleek man-thief,
Who lived on mutton, veal, and beef,
Yet never would afford relief
To needy, sable sons of grief,
      Was big with heavenly union.

"'Love not the world,' the preacher said,
And winked his eye, and shook his head;
He seized on Tom, and Dick, and Ned,
Cut short their meat, and clothes, and bread,
      Yet still loved heavenly union.

"Another preacher whining spoke
Of One whose heart for sinners broke:
He tied old Nanny to an oak,
And drew the blood at every stroke,
      And prayed for heavenly union.

"Two others oped their iron jaws,
And waved their children-stealing paws;
There sat their children in gewgaws;
By stinting negroes' backs and maws,
      They kept up heavenly union.

"All good from Jack another takes,
And entertains their flirts and rakes,

Who dress as sleek as glossy snakes,
And cram their mouths with sweetened cakes;
And this goes down for union."

Sincerely and earnestly hoping that this little book may do something toward throwing light on the American slave system, and hastening the glad day of deliverance to the millions of my brethren in bonds—faithfully relying upon the power of truth, love, and justice, for success in my humble efforts—and solemnly pledging myself anew to the sacred cause,—I subscribe myself,

FREDERICK DOUGLASS.
Lynn, Mass., April 28, 1845.

THE END.

NARRATIVE

OF

WILLIAM W. BROWN,

An American Slave.

WRITTEN BY HIMSELF.

―――― *Is there not some chosen curse,*
Some hidden thunder in the stores of heaven,
Red with uncommon wrath, to blast the man
Who gains his fortune from the blood of souls?
Cowper.

ELEVENTH THOUSAND.

LONDON:
Charles Gilpin, Bishopgate-St. Without.
1849.

4

———

NARRATIVE OF

WILLIAM W. BROWN,

AN AMERICAN SLAVE,

WRITTEN BY HIMSELF

———

To Wells Brown, of Ohio.

THIRTEEN YEARS AGO, I came to your door, a weary fugitive from chains and stripes. I was a stranger, and you took me in. I was hungry, and you fed me. Naked was I, and you clothed me. Even a name by which to be known among men, slavery had denied me. You bestowed upon me your own. Base, indeed, should I be, if I ever forget what I owe to you, or do anything to disgrace that honored name!

As a slight testimony of my gratitude to my earliest benefactor, I take the liberty to inscribe to you this little narrative of the sufferings from which I was fleeing when you had compassion upon me. In the multitude that you have succored, it is very possible that you may not remember me; but until I forget God and myself, I can never forget you.

Your grateful friend,
William Wells Brown.

Fling Out the Anti-Slavery Flag.

BY W. W. BROWN.

Fling out the Anti-Slavery flag
  On every swelling breeze;
And let its folds wave o'er the land,
  And o'er the raging seas,
Till all beneath the standard sheet
  With new allegiance bow,
And pledge themselves to onward bear
  The emblem of their vow.

Fling out the Anti-Slavery flag,
  And let it onward wave
Till it shall float o'er every clime,
  And liberate the slave;
Till, like a meteor flashing far,
  It bursts with glorious light,
And with its heaven-born rays dispels
  The gloom of sorrow's night.

Fling out the Anti-Slavery flag,
  And let it not be furled,
Till, like a planet of the skies,
  It sweeps around the world.
And when each poor degraded slave
  Is gathered near and far,
O, fix it on the azure arch,
  As hope's eternal star.

Fling out the Anti-Slavery flag;
  Forever let it be
The emblem to a holy cause,
  The banner of the free.
And never from its guardian height
  Let it by man be driven,
But let it float forever there,
  Beneath the smiles of heaven.

NOTE TO THE FOURTH AMERICAN EDITION.

Three editions of this work, consisting in all of eight thousand copies, were sold in less than eighteen months from the time the first edition was published. No antislavery work has met with a more rapid sale in the United States than this narrative. The present edition is published to meet the demand now existing for the work.

The Publisher.

NOTE TO THE PRESENT EDITION.

The present Narrative was first published in Boston, (U. S.) in July, 1847, and eight thousand copies were sold in less than eighteen months from the time of its publication. This rapid sale may be attributed to the circumstance, that for three years preceding its publication, I had been employed as a lecturing agent by the American Antislavery Society; and I was thus very generally known throughout the Free States of the Great Republic, as one who had spent the first twenty years of his life as a slave, in her southern house of bondage.

In visiting Great Britain I had two objects in view. Firstly, I have been chosen as a delegate by "the American Peace Committee for a Congress of Nations," to attend the Peace Convention to be held in Paris during the last week of the present month, (August, 1849.) Many of the most distinguished American Abolitionists considered it a triumphant evidence of the progress of their principles, that one of the oppressed colored race—one who is even now, by the constitution of the United States, a slave—should have been selected for this honorable office; and were therefore very desirous that I should attend. Secondly, I wished to follow up the work of my friends and fellow-laborers, Charles Lenox Remond and Frederick Douglass, and to lay before the people of Great Britain and Ireland the wrongs that are still committed upon the slaves and the free colored people of America. The rapid increase of communication between the two sides of the Atlantic has brought them so close together, that the personal intercourse between the British people and American slaveowners is now very great; and the slaveholder, crafty and politic, as deliberate tyrants generally are, rarely leaves the shores of Europe without attempting at least to assuage the prevalent hostility against his beloved "peculiar institution." The influence of the Southern States of America is mainly directed to the maintenance and propagation of the system of slavery in their own and in other countries. In the pursuit of this object, every consideration of religion, liberty, national strength, and social order is made to give way, and hitherto they have been very successful. The actual number of the slaveholders is small, but their union is complete, so that they form a dominant oligarchy in the United States. It is my desire, in common with every abolitionist, to diminish their influence, and this can only be effected by the promulgation of truth, and the cultivation of a correct public sentiment at home and abroad. Slavery cannot be let alone. It is aggressive, and must either be succumbed to, or put down.

It has been suggested that my narrative is somewhat deficient in dates. From my total want of education previous to my escape from slavery, I am unable to give them with much accuracy. The ignorance of the American slaves is, with rare exceptions, intense; and the slaveholders generally do their utmost to perpetuate this mental darkness. The perpetuation of slavery depends upon it. Whatever may be said of the physical condition of the slaves, it is undeniable that if they were not kept in a state of intellectual, religious, and moral degradation, they could be retained as slaves no longer.

In conclusion, I ask the attention of the reader to the Resolutions of the colored citizens of Boston, and to the other documents in reference to myself, which will be found at the end of the book. Of the latter, two are from the pen of WILLIAM LLOYD GARRISON, that faithful and indefatigable friend of the oppressed, whose position, as the Pioneer of the anti-slavery movement, has secured to him—more than to any other American abolitionist—the gratitude of the colored race and a world-wide reputation.

William Wells Brown.
176, Great Brunswick-street, Dublin,
August 14th, 1849.

LETTER
from Edmund Quincy, Esq.

Dedham, July 1, 1847.

To WILLIAM W. BROWN.

My Dear Friend:—I heartily thank you for the privilege of reading the manuscript of your Narrative. I have read it with deep interest and strong emotion. I am much mistaken if it be not greatly successful and eminently useful. It presents a different phase of the infernal slave-system from that portrayed in the admirable story of Mr. Douglass, and gives us a glimpse of its hideous cruelties in other portions of its domain.

Your opportunities of observing the workings of this accursed system have been singularly great. Your experiences in the Field, in the House, and especially on the River in the service of the slave-trader, Walker, have been such as few individuals have had;—no one, certainly, who has been competent to describe them. What I have admired, and marvelled at, in your Narrative, is the simplicity and calmness with which you describe scenes and actions which might well "move the very stones to rise and mutiny" against the National Institution which makes them possible.

You will perceive that I have made very sparing use of your flattering permission to alter what you had written. To correct a few errors, which appeared to be merely clerical ones, committed in the hurry of composition under unfavorable circumstances, and to suggest a few curtailments, is all that I have ventured to do. I should be a bold man, as well as a vain one, if I should attempt to improve your descriptions of what you have seen and suffered. Some of the scenes are not unworthy of Defoe himself.

I trust and believe that your Narrative will have a wide circulation. I am sure it deserves it. At least, a man must be differently constituted from me, who can rise from the perusal of your Narrative without feeling that he understands slavery better, and hates it worse, than he ever did before.

I am, very faithfully and respectfully,

Your friend,
Edmund Quincy.

WHEN I FIRST published this Narrative, the public had no evidence whatever that I had been a slave, except my own story. As soon as the work came from the press, I sent several copies to slaveholders residing at the South, with whom I was acquainted; and among others, one to Mr. Enoch Price, the man who claims my body and soul as his property, and from whom I had run away. A few weeks after the Narrative was sent, Edmund Quincy, Esq., received the following letter from Mr. Price. It tells its own story, and forever settles the question of my having been a slave. Here is the letter:

St. Louis, Jan. 10th, 1848.

Sir:

I received a pamphlet, or a Narrative, so called on the title-page, of the Life of William W. Brown, a fugitive slave, purporting to have been written by himself; and in his book I see a letter from you to said William W. Brown. This said Brown is named Sanford; he is a slave belonging to me, and ran away from me the first day of January, 1834. Now I see many things in his book that are not true, and a part of it as near true as a man could recollect after so long a time. I purchased him of Mr. S. Willi, the last of September, 1833. I paid six hundred and fifty dollars for him. If I had wanted to speculate on him, I could have sold him for three times as much as I paid for him. I was offered two thousand dollars for him, in New Orleans, at one time, and fifteen hundred dollars for him, at another time, in Louisville, Kentucky. But I would not sell him. I was told that he was going to run away, the day before he ran away, but I did not believe the man, for I had so much confidence in Sanford. I want you to see him, and see if what I say is not the truth. I do not want him as a slave, but I think that his friends, who sustain him and give him the right hand of fellowship, or he himself, could afford to pay my agent in Boston three hundred and twenty-five dollars, and I will give him free papers, so that he may go wherever he wishes to. Then he can visit St. Louis, or any other place he may wish.

This amount is just half that I paid for him. Now, if this offer suits Mr. Brown, and the Anti-Slavery Society of Boston, or Massachusetts, let me know, and I will give you the name of my agent in Boston, and forward the papers, to be given to William W. Brown as soon as the money is paid.

Yours respectfully,
E. Price.
TO EDMUND QUINCY, ESQ.

Mr. Price says that he sees many things in my book which are not true, and a part of it as near true as a man could recollect after so long a time. As I was with Mr. Price only three months, and have devoted only six pages to him and his family, he can know but little about my narrative, except that part which speaks of him. But I am willing to avail myself of his testimony, for he says that a part of it is true.

But I cannot accept of Mr. Price's offer to become a purchaser of my body and soul. God made me as free as he did Enoch Price, and Mr. Price shall never receive a dollar from me, or my friends with my consent.

W. W. Brown.
Boston, October, 1848

Chapter I

I WAS BORN in Lexington, Ky. The man who stole me as soon as I was born, recorded the births of all the infants which he claimed to be born his property, in a book which he kept for that purpose. My mother's name was Elizabeth. She had seven children, viz.: Solomon, Leander, Benjamin, Joseph, Millford, Elizabeth, and myself. No two of us were children of the same father. My father's name, as I learned from my mother, was George Higgins. He was a white man, a relative of my master, and connected with some of the first families in Kentucky.

My master owned about forty slaves, twenty-five of whom were field hands. He removed from Kentucky to Missouri when I was quite young, and settled thirty or forty miles above St. Charles, on the Missouri, where, in addition to his practice as a physician, he carried on milling, merchandizing and farming. He had a large farm, the principal productions of which were tobacco and hemp. The slave cabins were situated on the back part of the farm, with the house of the overseer, whose name was Grove Cook, in their midst. He had the entire charge of the farm, and having no family, was allowed a woman to keep house for him, whose business it was to deal out the provisions for the hands.

A woman was also kept at the quarters to do the cooking for the field hands, who were summoned to their unrequited toil every morning at four o'clock, by the ringing of a bell, hung on a post near the house of the overseer. They were allowed half an hour to eat their breakfast, and get to the field. At half past four a horn was blown by the overseer, which was the signal to commence work; and everyone that was not on the spot at the time, had to receive ten lashes from the negro-whip, with which the overseer always went armed. The handle was about three feet long, with the butt-end filled with lead, and the lash, six or seven feet in length, made of cow-hide, with platted wire on the end of it. This whip was put in requisition very frequently and freely, and a small offense on the part of a slave furnished an occasion for its use. During the time that Mr. Cook was overseer, I was a house servant—a situation preferable to that of a field hand, as I was better fed, better clothed, and not obliged to rise at the ringing of the bell, but about half an hour after. I have often laid and heard the crack of the whip, and the screams of the slave. My mother was a field hand, and one morning was ten or fifteen minutes behind the others in getting into the field. As soon as she reached the spot where they were at work, the overseer commenced whipping her. She cried, "Oh! pray—Oh! pray—Oh! pray"—these are generally the words of slaves, when imploring mercy at the hands of their oppressors. I heard her voice, and knew it, and jumped out of my bunk, and went to the door. Though the field was some distance from the house, I could hear every crack of the whip, and every groan and cry of my poor mother. I remained at the door, not daring to venture any further. The cold chills ran over me, and I wept aloud. After giving her ten lashes, the sound of the whip ceased, and I returned to my bed, and found no consolation but in my tears. Experience has taught me that nothing can be more heart-rending than for one to see a dear and beloved mother or sister tortured, and to hear their cries, and not be able to render them assistance. But such is the position which an American slave occupies.

My master, being a politician, soon found those who were ready to put him into office, for the favors he could render them; and a few years after his arrival in Missouri he was elected to a seat in the legislature. In his absence from home everything was left in charge of Mr. Cook, the overseer, and he soon became more tyrannical and cruel. Among the slaves on the plantation was one by the name of Randall. He was a man about six feet high, and well-proportioned, and known as a man of great strength and power. He was considered the most valuable and able-bodied slave on the plantation; but no matter how good or useful a slave may be, he seldom escapes the lash. But it was not so with Randall. He had been on the plantation since my earliest recollection, and I had never known of his being flogged. No thanks were due to the master or overseer for this. I have often heard him declare that no white man should ever whip him—that he would die first.

Cook, from the time that he came upon the plantation, had frequently declared that he could and would flog any nigger that was put into the field to work under him. My master had repeatedly told him not to attempt to whip Randall, but he was determined to try it. As soon as he was left sole dictator, he thought the time had come to put his threats into execution. He soon began to find fault with Randall, and threatened to whip him if he did not do better. One day he gave him a very hard task—more than he could possibly do; and at night, the task not being performed, he told Randall that he should remember him the next morning. On the following morning, after the hands had taken breakfast, Cook called out to Randall, and told him that he intended to whip him, and ordered him to cross his hands and be tied. Randall asked why he wished to whip him. He answered, because he had not finished his task the day before. Randall said that the task was too great, or he should have done it. Cook said it made no difference—he should whip him. Randall stood silent for a moment, and then said, "Mr. Cook, I have always tried to please you since you have been on the plantation, and I find you are determined not to be satisfied with my work, let me do as well as I may. No man has laid hands on me, to whip me, for the last ten years, and I have long since come to the conclusion not to be whipped by any man living." Cook, finding by Randall's determined look and gestures, that he would resist, called three of the hands from their work, and commanded them to seize Randall, and tie him. The hands stood still;—they knew Randall—and they also knew him to be a powerful man, and were afraid to grapple with him. As soon as Cook had ordered the men to seize him, Randall turned to them, and said—"Boys, you all know me; you know that I can handle any three of you, and the man that lays hands on me shall die. This white man can't whip me himself, and therefore he has called you to help him." The overseer was unable to prevail upon them to seize and secure Randall, and finally ordered them all to go to their work together.

Nothing was said to Randall by the overseer for more than a week. One morning, however, while the hands were at work in the field, he came into it, accompanied by three friends of his, Thompson, Woodbridge and Jones. They came up to where Randall was at work, and Cook ordered him to leave his work, and go with them to the barn. He refused to go; whereupon he was attacked by the overseer and his companions, when he turned upon them, and laid them, one after another, prostrate on the ground. Woodbridge drew out his pistol, and fired at him, and brought him to the ground by a pistol ball. The others rushed upon him with their clubs, and beat him over the head and face, until they succeeded in tying him. He was then taken to the barn, and tied to a beam. Cook gave him over one hundred lashes with a heavy cowhide, had him washed with salt and water, and left him tied during the day. The next day he was untied, and taken to a blacksmith's shop, and had a ball and chain attached to his leg. He was compelled to labor in the field, and perform the same amount of work that the other hands did. When his master returned home, he was much pleased to find that Randall had been subdued in his absence.

Chapter II

SOON AFTERWARDS, my master removed to the city of St. Louis, and purchased a farm four miles from there, which he placed under the charge of an overseer by the name of Friend Haskell. He was a regular Yankee from New England. The Yankees are noted for making the most cruel overseers.

My mother was hired out in the city, and I was also hired out there to Major Freeland, who kept a public house. He was formerly from Virginia, and was a horse-racer, cock-fighter, gambler, and withal an inveterate drunkard. There were ten or twelve servants in the house, and when he was present, it was cut and slash—knock down and drag out. In his fits of anger, he would take up a chair, and throw it at a servant; and in his more rational moments, when he wished to chastise one, he would tie them up in the smoke-house, and whip them; after which, he would cause a fire to be made of tobacco stems, and smoke them. This he called *"Virginia play."*

I complained to my master of the treatment which I received from Major Freeland; but it made no difference. He cared nothing about it, so long as he received the money for my labor. After living with Major Freeland five or six months, I ran away, and went into the woods back of the city; and when night came on, I made my way to my master's farm, but was afraid to be seen, knowing that if Mr. Haskell, the overseer, should discover me, I should be again carried back to Major Freeland; so I kept in the woods. One day, while in the woods, I heard the barking and howling of dogs, and in a short time they came so near that I knew them to be the bloodhounds of Major Benjamin O'Fallon. He kept five or six, to hunt runaway slaves with.

As soon as I was convinced that it was them, I knew there was no chance of escape. I took refuge in the top of a tree, and the hounds were soon at its base, and there remained until the hunters came up in a half or three quarters of an hour afterwards. There were two men with the dogs, who, as soon as they came up, ordered me to descend. I came down, was tied, and taken to St. Louis jail. Major Freeland soon made his appearance, and took me out, and ordered me to follow him, which I did. After we returned home, I was tied up in the smoke-house, and was very severely whipped. After the major had flogged me to his satisfaction, he sent out his son Robert, a young man eighteen or twenty years of age, to see that I was well smoked. He made a fire of tobacco stems, which soon set me to coughing and sneezing. This, Robert told me, was the way his father used to do to his slaves in Virginia. After giving me what they conceived to be a decent smoking, I was untied and again set to work.

Robert Freeland was a "chip of the old block." Though quite young, it was not unfrequently that he came home in a state of intoxication. He is now, I believe, a popular commander of a steamboat on the Mississippi river. Major Freeland soon after failed in business, and I was put on board the steamboat *Missouri,* which plied between St. Louis and Galena. The commander of the boat was William B. Culver. I remained on her during the sailing season, which was the most pleasant time for me that I had ever experienced. At the close of navigation I was hired to Mr. John Colburn, keeper of the Missouri Hotel. He was from one of the free states; but a more inveterate hater of the negro I do not believe ever walked God's green earth. This hotel was at that time one of the largest in the city, and there were employed in it twenty or thirty servants, mostly slaves.

Mr. Colburn was very abusive, not only to the servants, but to his wife also, who was an excellent woman, and one from whom I never knew a servant to receive a harsh word; but never did I know a kind one to a servant from her husband. Among the slaves employed in the hotel was one by the name of Aaron, who belonged to Mr. John F. Darby, a lawyer. Aaron was the knife-cleaner. One day, one of the knives was put on the table, not as clean as it might have been. Mr. Colburn, for this offense, tied Aaron up in the wood-house, and gave him over fifty lashes on the bare back with a cow-hide, after which, he made me wash him down with rum. This seemed to put him into more agony than the whipping. After being untied he went home to his master, and complained of the treatment which he had received. Mr. Darby would give no heed to anything he had to say, but sent him directly back. Colburn, learning that he had been to his master with complaints, tied him up again, and gave him a more severe whipping than before. The poor fellow's back was literally cut to pieces; so much so, that he was not able to work for ten or twelve days.

There was, also, among the servants, a girl whose master resided in

the country. Her name was Patsey. Mr. Colburn tied her up one evening, and whipped her until several of the boarders came out and
begged him to desist. The reason for whipping her was this. She was
engaged to be married to a man belonging to Major William Christy,
who resided four or five miles north of the city. Mr. Colburn had forbid her to see John Christy. The reason of this was said to be the regard
which he himself had for Patsey. She went to meeting that evening,
and John returned home with her. Mr. Colburn had intended to flog
John, if he came within the inclosure; but John knew too well the temper of his rival, and kept at a safe distance:—so he took vengeance on
the poor girl. If all the slave-drivers had been called together, I do not
think a more cruel man than John Colburn—and he too a northern
man—could have been found among them.

While living at the Missouri hotel, a circumstance occurred which
caused me great unhappiness. My master sold my mother, and all her
children, except myself. They were sold to different persons in the city
of St. Louis.

Chapter III

I WAS SOON after taken from Mr. Colburn's, and hired to Elijah P.
Lovejoy, who was at that time publisher and editor of the *St. Louis
Times*. My work, while with him, was mainly in the printing office,
waiting on the hands, working the press, &c. Mr. Lovejoy was a very
good man, and decidedly the best master that I had ever had. I am
chiefly indebted to him, and to my employment in the printing office,
for what little learning I obtained while in slavery.

Though slavery is thought, by some, to be mild in Missouri, when
compared with the cotton, sugar and rice growing states, yet no part of
our slave-holding country is more noted for the barbarity of its inhabitants than St. Louis. It was here that Col. Harney, a United States
officer, whipped a slave woman to death. It was here that Francis Mc-
Intosh, a free colored man from Pittsburgh, was taken from the steamboat *Flora* and burned at the stake. During a residence of eight years in
this city, numerous cases of extreme cruelty came under my own observation;—to record them all would occupy more space than could
possibly be allowed in this little volume. I shall, therefore, give but a
few more in addition to what I have already related.

Capt. J. B. Brant, who resided near my master, had a slave named

John. He was his body servant, carriage driver, &c. On one occasion, while driving his master through the city—the streets being very muddy, and the horses going at a rapid rate—some mud spattered upon a gentleman by the name of Robert More. More was determined to be revenged. Some three or four months after this occurrence, he purchased John, for the express purpose, as he said, "to tame the d———d nigger." After the purchase he took him to a blacksmith's shop, and had a ball and chain fastened to his leg, and then put him to driving a yoke of oxen, and kept him at hard labor, until the iron around his leg was so worn into the flesh, that it was thought mortification would ensue. In addition to this, John told me that his master whipped him regularly three times a week for the first two months:—and all this to *"tame him."* A more noble-looking man than he was not to be found in all St. Louis, before he fell into the hands of More; and a more degraded and spirit-crushed looking being was never seen on a southern plantation, after he had been subjected to this *"taming"* process for three months. The last time that I saw him, he had nearly lost the entire use of his limbs.

While living with Mr. Lovejoy, I was often sent on errands to the office of the *Missouri Republican,* published by Mr. Edward Charless. Once, while returning to the office with type, I was attacked by several large boys, sons of slave-holders, who pelted me with snow-balls. Having the heavy form of type in my hands, I could not make my escape by running; so I laid down the type and gave them battle. They gathered around me, pelting me with stones and sticks, until they overpowered me, and would have captured me, if I had not resorted to my heels. Upon my retreat they took possession of the type; and what to do to regain it I could not devise. Knowing Mr. Lovejoy to be a very humane man, I went to the office and laid the case before him. He told me to remain in the office. He took one of the apprentices with him and went after the type, and soon returned with it; but on his return informed me that Samuel McKinney had told him he would whip me, because I had hurt his boy. Soon after, McKinney was seen making his way to the office by one of the printers, who informed me of the fact, and I made my escape through the back door.

McKinney not being able to find me on his arrival, left the office in a great rage, swearing that he would whip me to death. A few days after, as I was walking along Main street, he seized me by the collar, and struck me over the head five or six times with a large cane, which caused the blood to gush from my nose and ears in such a manner that my clothes were completely saturated with blood. After beating me to his satisfaction he let me go, and I returned to the office so weak from the loss of blood that Mr. Lovejoy sent me home to my master. It was five weeks before I was able to walk again. During this time it was necessary to have someone to supply my place at the office, and I lost the situation.

After my recovery, I was hired to Capt. Otis Reynolds, as a waiter on board the steamboat *Enterprise,* owned by Messrs. John and Edward Walsh, commission merchants at St. Louis. This boat was then running on the upper Mississippi. My employment on board was to wait on gentlemen, and the captain being a good man, the situation was a pleasant one to me;—but in passing from place to place, and seeing new faces every day, and knowing that they could go where they pleased, I soon became unhappy, and several times thought of leaving the boat at some landing-place, and trying to make my escape to Canada, which I had heard much about as a place where the slave might live, be free, and be protected.

But whenever such thoughts would come into my mind, my resolution would soon be shaken by the remembrance that my dear mother was a slave in St. Louis, and I could not bear the idea of leaving her in that condition. She had often taken me upon her knee, and told me how she had carried me upon her back to the field when I was an infant—how often she had been whipped for leaving her work to nurse me—and how happy I would appear when she would take me into her arms. When these thoughts came over me, I would resolve never to leave the land of slavery without my mother. I thought that to leave her in slavery, after she had undergone and suffered so much for me, would be proving recreant to the duty which I owed to her. Besides this, I had three brothers and a sister there—two of my brothers having died.

My mother, my brothers Joseph and Millford, and my sister Elizabeth, belonged to Mr. Isaac Mansfield, formerly from one of the free states, (Massachusetts, I believe.) He was a tinner by trade, and carried on a large manufacturing establishment. Of all my relatives, mother was first, and sister next. One evening, while visiting them, I made some allusion to a proposed journey to Canada, and sister took her seat by my side, and taking my hand in hers, said, with tears in her eyes—

"Brother, you are not going to leave mother and your dear sister here without a friend, are you?"

I looked into her face, as the tears coursed swiftly down her cheeks, and bursting into tears myself, said—

"No, I will never desert you and mother!"

She clasped my hand in hers, and said—

"Brother, you have often declared that you would not end your days in slavery. I see no possible way in which you can escape with us; and now, brother, you are on a steamboat where there is some chance for you to escape to a land of liberty. I beseech you not to let us hinder you. If we cannot get our liberty, we do not wish to be the means of keeping you from a land of freedom."

I could restrain my feelings no longer, and an outburst of my own feelings caused her to cease speaking upon that subject. In opposition to their wishes, I pledged myself not to leave them in the hand of the oppressor. I took leave of them, and returned to the boat, and laid down in my bunk; but "sleep departed from mine eyes, and slumber from mine eyelids."

A few weeks after, on our downward passage, the boat took on board, at Hannibal, a drove of slaves, bound for the New Orleans market. They numbered from fifty to sixty, consisting of men and women from eighteen to forty years of age. A drove of slaves on a southern steamboat, bound for the cotton or sugar regions, is an occurrence so common, that no one, not even the passengers, appear to notice it, though they clank their chains at every step. There was, however, one in this gang that attracted the attention of the passengers and crew. It was a beautiful girl, apparently about twenty years of age, perfectly white, with straight light hair and blue eyes. But it was not the whiteness of her skin that created such a sensation among those who gazed upon her—it was her almost unparalleled beauty. She had been on the boat but a short time, before the attention of all the passengers, including the ladies, had been called to her, and the common topic of conversation was about the beautiful slave-girl. She was not in chains. The man who claimed this article of human merchandise was a Mr. Walker—a well known slave-trader, residing in St. Louis. There was a general anxiety among the passengers and crew to learn the history of the girl. Her master kept close by her side, and it would have been considered impudent for any of the passengers to have spoken to her, and the crew were not allowed to have any conversation with them. When we reached St. Louis, the slaves were removed to a boat bound for New Orleans, and the history of the beautiful slave-girl remained a mystery.

I remained on the boat during the season, and it was not an unfrequent occurrence to have on board gangs of slaves on their way to the cotton, sugar and rice plantations of the south.

Toward the latter part of the summer Captain Reynolds left the boat, and I was sent home. I was then placed on the farm, under Mr. Haskell, the overseer. As I had been some time out of the field, and not accustomed to work in the burning sun, it was very hard; but I was compelled to keep up with the best of the hands.

I found a great difference between the work in a steamboat cabin and that in a corn-field.

My master, who was then living in the city, soon after removed to the farm, when I was taken out of the field to work in the house as a waiter. Though his wife was very peevish, and hard to please, I much preferred to be under her control than the overseer's. They brought with them Mr. Sloane, a Presbyterian minister; Miss Martha Tulley, a niece of theirs from Kentucky; and their nephew William. The latter had been in the family a number of years, but the others were all new-comers.

Mr. Sloane was a young minister, who had been at the south but a short time, and it seemed as if his whole aim was to please the slave-holders, especially my master and mistress. He was intending to make a visit during the winter, and he not only tried to please them, but I think he succeeded admirably. When they wanted singing, he sung; when they wanted praying, he prayed; when they wanted a story told, he told a story. Instead of his teaching my master theology, my master taught theology to him. While I was with Captain Reynolds my master "got religion," and new laws were made on the plantation. Formerly we had the privilege of hunting, fishing, making splint brooms, baskets, &c., on Sunday; but this was all stopped. Every Sunday we were all compelled to attend meeting. Master was so religious that he induced some others to join him in hiring a preacher to preach to the slaves.

Chapter IV

MY MASTER had family worship, night and morning. At night the slaves were called in to attend; but in the mornings they had to be at their work, and master did all the praying. My master and mistress were great lovers of mint julep, and every morning, a pitcher-full was made, of which they all partook freely, not excepting little master William. After drinking freely all round, they would have family worship, and then breakfast. I cannot say but I loved the julep as well as any of them, and during prayer was always careful to seat myself close to the table where it stood, so as to help myself when they were all busily engaged in their devotions. By the time prayer was over, I was about as happy as any of them. A sad accident happened one morning. In helping myself, and at the same time keeping an eye on my old mistress, I accidentally let the pitcher fall upon the floor, breaking it in pieces, and spilling the contents. This was a bad affair for me; for as soon as prayer was over, I was taken and severely chastised.

My master's family consisted of himself, his wife, and their nephew, William Moore. He was taken into the family when only a few weeks of age. His name being that of my own, mine was changed for the purpose of giving precedence to his, though I was his senior by ten or twelve years. The plantation being four miles from the city, I had to drive the family to church. I always dreaded the approach of the Sabbath; for, during service, I was obliged to stand by the horses in the hot, broiling sun, or in the rain, just as it happened.

One Sabbath, as we were driving past the house of D. D. Page, a gentleman who owned a large baking establishment, as I was sitting upon the box of the carriage, which was very much elevated, I saw Mr. Page pursuing a slave around the yard with a long whip, cutting him at every jump. The man soon escaped from the yard, and was followed by Mr. Page. They came running past us, and the slave, perceiving that he would be overtaken, stopped suddenly, and Page stumbled over him, and falling on the stone pavement, fractured one of his legs, which crippled him for life. The same gentleman, but a short time previous, tied up a woman of his, by the name of Delphia, and whipped her nearly to death; yet he was a deacon in the Baptist church, in good and regular standing. Poor Delphia! I was well acquainted with her, and called to see her while upon her sick bed; and I shall never forget her appearance. She was a member of the same church with her master.

Soon after this, I was hired out to Mr. Walker, the same man whom I have mentioned as having carried a gang of slaves down the river on the steamboat *Enterprise*. Seeing me in the capacity of a steward on the boat, and thinking that I would make a good hand to take care of slaves, he determined to have me for that purpose; and finding that my master would not sell me, he hired me for the term of one year.

When I learned the fact of my having been hired to a negro speculator, or a "soul driver," as they are generally called among slaves, no one can tell my emotions. Mr. Walker had offered a high price for me, as I afterwards learned, but I suppose my master was restrained from selling me by the fact that I was a near relative of his. On entering the service of Mr. Walker, I found that my opportunity of getting to a land of liberty was gone, at least for the time being. He had a gang of slaves in readiness to start for New Orleans, and in a few days we were on our journey. I am at a loss for language to express my feelings on that occasion. Although my master had told me that he had not sold me, and Mr. Walker had told me that he had not purchased me, I did not believe them; and not until I had been to New Orleans, and was on my return, did I believe that I was not sold.

There was on the boat a large room on the lower deck, in which the slaves were kept, men and women, promiscuously—all chained two and two, and a strict watch kept that they did not get loose; for cases have occurred in which slaves have got off their chains, and made their escape at landing-places, while the boats were taking in wood;—and with all our care, we lost one woman who had been taken from her husband and children, and having no desire to live without them, in the agony of her soul jumped overboard, and drowned herself. She was not chained.

It was almost impossible to keep that part of the boat clean.

On landing at Natchez, the slaves were all carried to the slave-pen, and there kept one week, during which time several of them were sold. Mr. Walker fed his slaves well. We took on board at St. Louis several hundred pounds of bacon (smoked meat) and corn-meal, and his slaves were better fed than slaves generally were in Natchez, so far as my observation extended.

At the end of a week, we left for New Orleans, the place of our final destination, which we reached in two days. Here the slaves were placed in a negro-pen, where those who wished to purchase could call and examine them. The negro-pen is a small yard, surrounded by buildings, from fifteen to twenty feet wide, with the exception of a large gate with iron bars. The slaves are kept in the buildings during the night, and turned out into the yard during the day. After the best of the stock was sold at private sale at the pen, the balance were taken to the Exchange Coffee-House Auction Rooms, kept by Isaac L. McCoy, and sold at public auction. After the sale of this lot of slaves, we left New Orleans for St. Louis.

Chapter V

ON OUR ARRIVAL at St. Louis I went to Dr. Young, and told him that I did not wish to live with Mr. Walker any longer. I was heart-sick at seeing my fellow-creatures bought and sold. But the Dr. had hired me for the year, and stay I must. Mr. Walker again commenced purchasing another gang of slaves. He bought a man of Colonel John O'Fallon, who resided in the suburbs of the city. This man had a wife and three children. As soon as the purchase was made, he was put in jail for safe keeping, until we should be ready to start for New Orleans. His wife visited him while there, several times, and several times when she went for that purpose was refused admittance.

In the course of eight or nine weeks Mr. Walker had his cargo of human flesh made up. There was in this lot a number of old men and women, some of them with gray locks. We left St. Louis in the steamboat *Carlton*, Captain Swan, bound for New Orleans. On our way down, and before we reached Rodney, the place where we made our first stop, I had to prepare the old slaves for market. I was ordered to have the old men's whiskers shaved off, and the grey hairs plucked out where they were not too numerous, in which case he had a preparation of blacking to color it, and with a blacking brush we would put it on. This was new business to me, and was performed in a room where the passengers could not see us. These slaves were also taught how old they were by Mr. Walker, and after going through the blacking process they looked ten or fifteen years younger; and I am sure that some of those who purchased slaves of Mr. Walker were dreadfully cheated, especially in the ages of the slaves which they bought.

We landed at Rodney, and the slaves were driven to the pen in the back part of the village. Several were sold at this place, during our stay of four or five days, when we proceeded to Natchez. There we landed at night, and the gang were put in the warehouse until morning, when they were driven to the pen. As soon as the slaves are put in these pens, swarms of planters may be seen in and about them. They knew when Walker was expected, as he always had the time advertised beforehand when he would be in Rodney, Natchez, and New Orleans. These were the principal places where he offered his slaves for sale.

When at Natchez the second time, I saw a slave very cruelly whipped. He belonged to a Mr. Broadwell, a merchant who kept a store on the wharf. The slave's name was Lewis. I had known him several years, as he was formerly from St. Louis. We were expecting a steamboat down the river, in which we were to take passage for New Orleans. Mr. Walker sent me to the landing to watch for the boat, ordering me to inform him on its arrival. While there I went into the store to see Lewis. I saw a slave in the store, and asked him where Lewis was. Said he, "They have got Lewis hanging between the heavens and the earth." I asked him what he meant by that. He told me to go into the warehouse and see. I went in, and found Lewis there. He was tied up to a beam, with his toes just touching the floor. As there was no one in the warehouse but himself, I inquired the reason of his being in that situation. He said Mr. Broadwell had sold his wife to a planter six miles from the city, and that he had been to visit her—that he went in the night, expecting to return before daylight, and went without his master's permission. The patrol had taken him up before he reached his wife. He was put in jail, and his master had to pay for his catching and keeping, and that was what he was tied up for.

Just as he finished his story, Mr. Broadwell came in, and inquired what I was doing there. I knew not what to say, and while I was thinking what reply to make he struck me over the head with the cow-hide, the end of which struck me over my right eye, sinking deep into the flesh, leaving a scar which I carry to this day. Before I visited Lewis he had received fifty lashes. Mr. Broadwell gave him fifty lashes more after I came out, as I was afterwards informed by Lewis himself.

The next day we proceeded to New Orleans, and put the gang in the same negro-pen which we occupied before. In a short time the planters came flocking to the pen to purchase slaves. Before the slaves were exhibited for sale, they were dressed and driven out into the yard. Some were set to dancing, some to jumping, some to singing, and some to playing cards. This was done to make them appear cheerful and happy. My business was to see that they were placed in those situations before the arrival of the purchasers, and I have often set them to dancing when their cheeks were wet with tears. As slaves were in good demand at that time, they were all soon disposed of, and we again set out for St. Louis.

On our arrival, Mr. Walker purchased a farm five or six miles from the city. He had no family, but made a housekeeper of one of his female slaves. Poor Cynthia! I knew her well. She was a quadroon, and one of the most beautiful women I ever saw. She was a native of St. Louis, and bore an irreproachable character for virtue and propriety of conduct. Mr. Walker bought her for the New Orleans market, and took her down with him on one of the trips that I made with him. Never shall I forget the circumstances of that voyage! On the first night that we were on board the steamboat, he directed me to put her into a state-room he had provided for her, apart from the other slaves. I had seen too much of the workings of slavery not to know what this meant. I accordingly watched him into the state-room, and listened to hear what passed between them. I heard him make his base offers, and her reject them. He told her that if she would accept his vile proposals, he would take her back with him to St. Louis, and establish her as his housekeeper on his farm. But if she persisted in rejecting them, he would sell her as a field hand on the worst plantation on the river. Neither threats nor bribes prevailed, however, and he retired, disappointed of his prey.

The next morning poor Cynthia told me what had passed, and bewailed her sad fate with floods of tears. I comforted and encouraged her all I could; but I foresaw but too well what the result must be. Without entering into any further particulars, suffice it to say that Walker performed his part of the contract at that time. He took her back to St. Louis, established her as his mistress and housekeeper at his farm, and before I left, he had two children by her. But, mark the end! Since I have been at the North, I have been credibly informed that Walker has been married, and, as a previous measure, sold poor Cynthia and her four children (she having had two more since I came away) into hopeless bondage!

He soon commenced purchasing to make up the third gang. We took steamboat, and went to Jefferson City, a town on the Missouri river. Here we landed, and took stage for the interior of the state. He bought a number of slaves as he passed the different farms and villages. After getting twenty-two or twenty-three men and women, we arrived at St. Charles, a village on the banks of the Missouri. Here he purchased a woman who had a child in her arms, appearing to be four or five weeks old.

We had been travelling by land for some days, and were in hopes to have found a boat at this place for St. Louis, but were disappointed. As no boat was expected for some days, we started for St. Louis by land. Mr. Walker had purchased two horses. He rode one, and I the other. The slaves were chained together, and we took up our line of march, Mr. Walker taking the lead, and I bringing up the rear. Though the distance was not more than twenty miles, we did not reach it the first day. The road was worse than any that I have ever travelled.

Soon after we left St. Charles the young child grew very cross, and kept up a noise during the greater part of the day. Mr. Walker complained of its crying several times, and told the mother to stop the child's d————d noise, or he would. The woman tried to keep the child from crying, but could not. We put up at night with an acquaintance of Mr. Walker, and in the morning, just as we were about to start, the child again commenced crying. Walker stepped up to her, and told her to give the child to him. The mother tremblingly obeyed. He took the child by one arm, as you would a cat by the leg, walked into the house, and said to the lady,

"Madam, I will make you a present of this little nigger; it keeps such a noise that I can't bear it."

"Thank you, sir," said the lady.

The mother, as soon as she saw that her child was to be left, ran up to Mr. Walker, and falling upon her knees, begged him to let her have her child; she clung around his legs, and cried, "Oh, my child! my child! master, do let me have my child! oh, do, do, do! I will stop its crying if you will only let me have it again." When I saw this woman crying for her child so piteously, a shudder—a feeling akin to horror—shot through my frame. I have often since in imagination heard her crying for her child:—

None but those who have been in a slave state, and who have seen the American slave-trader engaged in his nefarious traffic, can estimate the sufferings their victims undergo. If there is one feature of American slavery more abominable than another, it is that which sanctions the buying and selling of human beings. The African slave-trade was abolished by the American Congress some twenty years since; and now, by the laws of the country, if an American is found engaged in the African slave-trade, he is considered a pirate; and if found guilty of such, the penalty would be death.

Although the African slave-trader has been branded as a pirate, men are engaged in the traffic in slaves in this country, who occupy high positions in society, and hold offices of honor in the councils of the nation; and not a few have made their fortunes by this business.

After the woman's child had been given away, Mr. Walker commanded her to return into the ranks with the other slaves. Women who had children were not chained, but those that had none were. As soon as her child was disposed of she was chained in the gang.

The following song I have often heard the slaves sing, when about to be carried to the far south. It is said to have been composed by a slave.

"See these poor souls from Africa
Transported to America;
We are stolen, and sold to Georgia—
Will you go along with me?
We are stolen, and sold to Georgia—
Come sound the jubilee!

See wives and husbands sold apart,
Their children's screams will break my heart;—
There's a better day a coming—
Will you go along with me?
There's a better day a coming,
Go sound the jubilee!

O, gracious Lord! when shall it be,
That we poor souls shall all be free?
Lord, break them slavery powers—
Will you go along with me?
Lord, break them slavery powers,
Go sound the jubilee!

Dear Lord, dear Lord, when slavery'll cease,
Then we poor souls will have our peace;—
There's a better day a coming—
Will you go along with me?
There's a better day a coming,
Go sound the jubilee!"

We finally arrived at Mr. Walker's farm. He had a house built during our absence to put slaves in. It was a kind of domestic jail. The slaves were put in the jail at night, and worked on the farm during the day. They were kept here until the gang was completed, when we again started for New Orleans, on board the steamboat *North America*, Capt. Alexander Scott. We had a large number of slaves in this gang. One, by the name of Joe, Mr. Walker was training up to take my place, as my time was nearly out, and glad was I. We made our first stop at Vicksburg, where we remained one week and sold several slaves.

Mr. Walker, though not a good master, had not flogged a slave since I had been with him, though he had threatened me. The slaves were kept in the pen, and he always put up at the best hotel, and kept his wines in his room, for the accommodation of those who called to negotiate with him for the purchase of slaves. One day, while we were at

Vicksburg, several gentlemen came to see him for that purpose, and as usual the wine was called for. I took the tray and started around with it, and having accidentally filled some of the glasses too full, the gentlemen spilled the wine on their clothes as they went to drink. Mr. Walker apologized to them for my carelessness, but looked at me as though he would see me again on this subject.

After the gentlemen had left the room, he asked me what I meant by my carelessness, and said that he would attend to me. The next morning he gave me a note to carry to the jailer, and a dollar in money to give to him. I suspected that all was not right, so I went down near the landing, where I met with a sailor, and, walking up to him, asked him if he would be so kind as to read the note for me. He read it over, and then looked at me. I asked him to tell me what was in it. Said he,

"They are going to give you hell."

"Why?" said I.

He said, "This is a note to have you whipped, and says that you have a dollar to pay for it."

He handed me back the note, and off I started. I knew not what to do, but was determined not to be whipped. I went up to the jail—took a look at it, and walked off again. As Mr. Walker was acquainted with the jailer, I feared that I should be found out if I did not go, and be treated in consequence of it still worse.

While I was meditating on the subject, I saw a colored man about my size walk up, and the thought struck me in a moment to send him with my note. I walked up to him, and asked him who he belonged to. He said he was a free man, and had been in the city but a short time. I told him I had a note to go into the jail, and get a trunk to carry to one of the steamboats; but was so busily engaged that I could not do it, although I had a dollar to pay for it. He asked me if I would not give him the job. I handed him the note and the dollar, and off he started for the jail.

I watched to see that he went in, and as soon as I saw the door close behind him, I walked around the corner, and took my station, intending to see how my friend looked when he came out. I had been there but a short time, when a colored man came around the corner, and said to another colored man with whom he was acquainted—

"They are giving a nigger scissors in the jail."

"What for?" said the other. The man continued,

"A nigger came into the jail, and asked for the jailer. The jailer came out, and he handed him a note, and said he wanted to get a trunk. The jailer told him to go with him, and he would give him the trunk. So he took him into the room, and told the nigger to give up the dollar. He said a man had given him the dollar to pay for getting the trunk. But that lie would not answer. So they made him strip himself, and then they tied him down, and are now whipping him."

I stood by all the while listening to their talk, and soon found out that the person alluded to was my customer. I went into the street opposite the jail, and concealed myself in such a manner that I could not be seen by anyone coming out. I had been there but a short time, when the young man made his appearance, and looked around for me. I, unobserved, came forth from my hiding-place, behind a pile of brick, and he pretty soon saw me, and came up to me complaining bitterly, saying that I had played a trick upon him. I denied any knowledge of what the note contained, and asked him what they had done to him. He told me in substance what I heard the man tell who had come out of the jail.

"Yes," said he, "they whipped me and took my dollar, and gave me this note."

He showed me the note which the jailer had given him, telling him to give it to his master. I told him I would give him fifty cents for it—that being all the money I had. He gave it to me and took his money. He had received twenty lashes on his bare back, with the negro-whip.

I took the note and started for the hotel where I had left Mr. Walker. Upon reaching the hotel, I handed it to a stranger whom I had not seen before, and requested him to read it to me. As near as I can recollect, it was as follows:—

"Dear Sir:
By your direction, I have given your boy twenty lashes. He is a very saucy boy, and tried to make me believe that he did not belong to you, and I put it on to him well for lying to me.

"I remain
"Your obedient servant."

It is true that in most of the slave-holding cities, when a gentleman wishes his servants whipped, he can send him to the jail and have it done. Before I went in where Mr. Walker was, I wet my cheeks a little, as though I had been crying. He looked at me, and inquired what was the matter. I told him that I had never had such a whipping in my life, and handed him the note. He looked at it and laughed;—"And so you told him that you did not belong to me?" "Yes, sir," said I. "I did not know that there was any harm in that." He told me I must behave myself, if I did not want to be whipped again.

This incident shows how it is that slavery makes its victims lying and mean; for which vices it afterwards reproaches them, and uses them as arguments to prove that they deserve no better fate. Had I entertained the same views of right and wrong which I now do, I am sure I should never have practiced the deception upon that poor fellow which I did. I know of no act committed by me while in slavery which I have regretted more than that; and I heartily desire that it may be at some time or other in my power to make him amends for his vicarious sufferings in my behalf.

Chapter VI

IN A FEW DAYS we reached New Orleans, and arriving there in the night, remained on board until morning. While at New Orleans this time, I saw a slave killed; an account of which has been published by Theodore D. Weld, in his book entitled *Slavery as it is*. The circumstances were as follows. In the evening, between seven and eight o'clock, a slave came running down the levee, followed by several men and boys. The whites were crying out, "Stop that nigger! stop that nigger!" while the poor panting slave, in almost breathless accents, was repeating, "I did not steal the meat—I did not steal the meat." The poor man at last took refuge in the river. The whites who were in pursuit of him, run on board of one of the boats to see if they could discover him. They finally espied him under the bow of the steamboat *Trenton*. They got a pike-pole, and tried to drive him from his hiding place. When they would strike at him he would dive under the water. The water was so cold, that it soon became evident that he must come out or be drowned.

While they were trying to drive him from under the bow of the boat or drown him, he would in broken and imploring accents say, "I did not steal the meat; I did not steal the meat. My master lives up the river. I want to see my master. I did not steal the meat. Do let me go home to master." After punching him, and striking him over the head for some time, he at last sunk in the water, to rise no more alive.

On the end of the pike-pole with which they were striking him was a hook, which caught in his clothing, and they hauled him up on the bow of the boat. Some said he was dead; others said he was *"playing possum;"* while others kicked him to make him get up; but it was of no use—he was dead.

As soon as they became satisfied of this, they commenced leaving, one after another. One of the hands on the boat informed the captain that they had killed the man, and that the dead body was lying on the deck. The captain came on deck, and said to those who were remaining, "You have killed this nigger; now take him off of my boat." The captain's name was Hart. The dead body was dragged on shore and left there. I went on board of the boat where our gang of slaves were, and during the whole night my mind was occupied with what I had seen. Early in the morning I went on shore to see if the dead body remained there. I found it in the same position that it was left the night before. I watched to see what they would do with it. It was left there until between eight and nine o'clock, when a cart, which takes up the trash out of the streets, came along, and the body was thrown in, and in a few minutes more was covered over with dirt which they were removing from the streets. During the whole time, I did not see more than six or seven persons around it, who, from their manner, evidently regarded it as no uncommon occurrence.

During our stay in the city I met with a young white man with whom I was well acquainted in St. Louis. He had been sold into slavery, under the following circumstances. His father was a drunkard, and very poor, with a family of five or six children. The father died, and left the mother to take care of and provide for the children as best she might. The eldest was a boy, named Burrill, about thirteen years of age, who did chores in a store kept by Mr. Riley, to assist his mother in procuring a living for the family. After working with him two years, Mr. Riley took him to New Orleans to wait on him while in that city on a visit, and when he returned to St. Louis, he told the mother of the boy that he had died with the yellow fever. Nothing more was heard from him, no one supposing him to be alive. I was much astonished when Burrill told me his story. Though I sympathized with him I could not assist him. We were both slaves. He was poor, uneducated, and without friends; and, if living, is, I presume, still held as a slave.

After selling out this cargo of human flesh, we returned to St. Louis, and my time was up with Mr. Walker. I had served him one year, and it was the longest year I ever lived.

Chapter VII

I WAS SENT HOME, and was glad enough to leave the service of one who was tearing the husband from the wife, the child from the mother, and the sister from the brother—but a trial more severe and heart-rending than any which I had yet met with awaited me. My dear sister had been sold to a man who was going to Natchez, and was lying in jail awaiting the hour of his departure. She had expressed her determination to die, rather than go to the far south, and she was put in jail for safe-keeping. I went to the jail the same day that I arrived, but as the jailer was not in I could not see her.

I went home to my master, in the country, and the first day after my return he came where I was at work, and spoke to me very politely. I knew from his appearance that something was the matter. After talking to me about my several journeys to New Orleans with Mr. Walker, he told me that he was hard pressed for money, and as he had sold my mother and all her children except me, he thought it would be better to sell me than any other one, and that as I had been used to living in the city, he thought it probable that I would prefer it to a country life. I raised up my head, and looked him full in the face. When my eyes caught his he immediately looked to the ground. After a short pause, I said,

"Master, mother has often told me that you are a near relative of mine, and I have often heard you admit the fact; and after you have hired me out, and received, as I once heard you say, nine hundred dollars for my services—after receiving this large sum, will you sell me to be carried to New Orleans or some other place?"

"No," said he, "I do not intend to sell you to a negro-trader. If I had wished to have done that, I might have sold you to Mr. Walker for a large sum, but I would not sell you to a negro-trader. You may go to the city, and find you a good master."

"But," said I, "I cannot find a good master in the whole city of St. Louis."

"Why?" said he.

"Because there are no good masters in the state."

"Do you not call me a good master?"

"If you were you would not sell me."

"Now I will give you one week to find a master in, and surely you can do it in that time."

The price set by my evangelical master upon my soul and body was the trifling sum of five hundred dollars. I tried to enter into some arrangement by which I might purchase my freedom; but he would enter into no such arrangement.

I set out for the city with the understanding that I was to return in a week with someone to become my new master. Soon after reaching the city, I went to the jail, to learn if I could once more see my sister; but could not gain admission. I then went to mother, and learned from her that the owner of my sister intended to start for Natchez in a few days.

I went to the jail again the next day, and Mr. Simonds, the keeper, allowed me to see my sister for the last time. I cannot give a just description of the scene at that parting interview. Never, never can be erased from my heart the occurrences of that day! When I entered the room where she was, she was seated in one corner, alone. There were four other women in the same room, belonging to the same man. He had purchased them, he said, for his own use. She was seated with her face towards the door where I entered, yet she did not look up until I walked up to her. As soon as she observed me she sprung up, threw her arms around my neck, leaned her head upon my breast, and, without uttering a word, burst into tears. As soon as she recovered herself sufficiently to speak, she advised me to take mother, and try to get out of slavery. She said there was no hope for herself—that she must live and die a slave. After giving her some advice, and taking from my finger a ring and placing it upon hers, I bade her farewell forever, and returned to my mother, and then and there made up my mind to leave for Canada as soon as possible.

I had been in the city nearly two days, and as I was to be absent only a week, I thought best to get on my journey as soon as possible. In conversing with mother, I found her unwilling to make the attempt to reach a land of liberty, but she counselled me to get my liberty if I could. She said, as all her children were in slavery, she did not wish to leave them. I could not bear the idea of leaving her among those pirates, when there was a prospect of being able to get away from them. After much persuasion I succeeded in inducing her to make the attempt to get away.

The time fixed for our departure was the next night. I had with me a little money that I had received, from time to time, from gentlemen for whom I had done errands. I took my scanty means and purchased some dried beef, crackers and cheese, which I carried to mother, who had provided herself with a bag to carry it in. I occasionally thought of my old master, and of my mission to the city to find a new one. I waited with the most intense anxiety for the appointed time to leave the land of slavery, in search of a land of liberty.

The time at length arrived, and we left the city just as the clock struck nine. We proceeded to the upper part of the city, where I had been two or three times during the day, and selected a skiff to carry us across the river. The boat was not mine, nor did I know to whom it did belong; neither did I care. The boat was fastened with a small pole, which, with the aid of a rail, I soon loosened from its moorings. After hunting round and finding a board to use as an oar, I turned to the city, and bidding it a long farewell, pushed off my boat. The current running very swift, we had not reached the middle of the stream before we were directly opposite the city.

We were soon upon the Illinois shore, and, leaping from the boat, turned it adrift, and the last I saw of it it was going down the river at good speed. We took the main road to Alton, and passed through just at daylight, when we made for the woods, where we remained during the day. Our reason for going into the woods was, that we expected that Mr. Mansfield (the man who owned my mother) would start in pursuit of her as soon as he discovered that she was missing. He also knew that I had been in the city looking for a new master, and we thought probably he would go out to my master's to see if he could find my mother, and in so doing, Dr. Young might be led to suspect that I had gone to Canada to find a purchaser.

We remained in the woods during the day, and as soon as darkness overshadowed the earth, we started again on our gloomy way, having no guide but the North Star. We continued to travel by night, and secrete ourselves in the woods by day; and every night, before emerging from our hiding-place, we would anxiously look for our friend and leader—the North Star. And in the language of Pierpont we might have exclaimed,

> "*Star of the North! while blazing day*
> *Pours round me its full tide of light,*
> *And hides thy pale but faithful ray,*
> *I, too, lie hid, and long for night.*
> *For night;—I dare not walk at noon,*
> *Nor dare I trust the faithless moon,*
> *Nor faithless man, whose burning lust*
> *For gold hath riveted my chain;*

No other leader can I trust
But thee, of even the starry train;
For, all the host around thee burning,
Like faithless man, keep turning, turning.

In the dark top of southern pines
I nestled, when the driver's horn
Called to the field, in lengthening lines,
My fellows, at the break of morn.
And there I lay, till thy sweet face
Looked in upon my 'hiding place,'
Star of the North!
Thy light, that no poor slave deceiveth,
Shall set me free."

Chapter VIII

AS WE TRAVELLED towards a land of liberty, my heart would at times leap for joy. At other times, being, as I was, almost constantly on my feet, I felt as though I could travel no further. But when I thought of slavery, with its democratic whips—its republican chains—its evangelical blood-hounds, and its religious slave-holders—when I thought of all this paraphernalia of American democracy and religion behind me, and the prospect of liberty before me, I was encouraged to press forward, my heart was strengthened, and I forgot that I was tired or hungry.

On the eighth day of our journey, we had a very heavy rain, and in a few hours after it commenced we had not a dry thread upon our bodies. This made our journey still more unpleasant. On the tenth day, we found ourselves entirely destitute of provisions, and how to obtain any we could not tell. We finally resolved to stop at some farm-house, and try to get something to eat. We had no sooner determined to do this, than we went to a house, and asked them for some food. We were treated with great kindness, and they not only gave us something to eat, but gave us provisions to carry with us. They advised us to travel by day and lie by at night. Finding ourselves about one hundred and fifty miles from St. Louis, we concluded that it would be safe to travel by daylight, and did not leave the house until the next morning. We travelled on that day through a thickly settled country, and through one small village. Though we were fleeing from a land of oppression, our hearts were still there. My dear sister and two beloved brothers were behind us, and the idea of giving them up, and leaving them forever, made us feel sad. But with all this depression of heart, the thought that I should one day be free, and call my body my own, buoyed me up, and made my heart leap for joy. I had just been telling my mother how I should try to get employment as soon as we reached Canada, and how I intended to purchase us a little farm, and how I would earn money enough to buy sister and brothers, and how happy we would be in our own FREE HOME—when three men came up on horseback, and ordered us to stop.

I turned to the one who appeared to be the principal man, and asked him what he wanted. He said he had a warrant to take us up. The three immediately dismounted, and one took from his pocket a handbill, advertising us as runaways, and offering a reward of two hundred dollars for our apprehension and delivery in the city of St. Louis. The advertisement had been put out by Isaac Mansfield and John Young.

While they were reading the advertisement, mother looked me in the face, and burst into tears. A cold chill ran over me, and such a sensation I never experienced before, and I hope never to again. They took out a rope and tied me, and we were taken back about six miles, to the house of the individual who appeared to be the leader. We reached there about seven o'clock in the evening, had supper, and were separated for the night. Two men remained in the room during the night. Before the family retired to rest, they were all called together to attend prayers. The man who but a few hours before had bound my hands together with a strong cord, read a chapter from the Bible, and then offered up prayer, just as though God had sanctioned the act he had just committed upon a poor, panting, fugitive slave.

The next morning a blacksmith came in, and put a pair of handcuffs on me, and we started on our journey back to the land of whips, chains and Bibles. Mother was not tied, but was closely watched at night. We were carried back in a wagon, and after four days' travel, we came in sight of St. Louis. I cannot describe my feelings upon approaching the city.

As we were crossing the ferry, Mr. Wiggins, the owner of the ferry, came up to me, and inquired what I had been doing that I was in chains. He had not heard that I had run away. In a few minutes we were on the Missouri side, and were taken directly to the jail. On the way thither, I saw several of my friends, who gave me a nod of recognition as I passed them. After reaching the jail, we were locked up in different apartments.

Chapter IX

I HAD BEEN IN JAIL but a short time when I heard that my master was sick, and nothing brought more joy to my heart than that intelligence. I prayed fervently for him—not for his recovery, but for his death. I knew he would be exasperated at having to pay for my apprehension, and knowing his cruelty, I feared him. While in jail, I learned that my sister Elizabeth, who was in prison when we left the city, had been carried off four days before our arrival.

I had been in jail but a few hours when three negro-traders, learning that I was secured thus for running away, came to my prison-house and looked at me, expecting that I would be offered for sale. Mr. Mansfield, the man who owned mother, came into the jail as soon as Mr. Jones, the man who arrested us, informed him that he had brought her back. He told her that he would not whip her, but would sell her to a negro-trader, or take her to New Orleans himself. After being in jail about one week, master sent a man to take me out of jail, and send me home. I was taken out and carried home, and the old man was well enough to sit up. He had me brought into the room where he was, and as I entered, he asked me where I had been? I told him I had acted according to his orders. He had told me to look for a master, and I had been to look for one. He answered that he did not tell me to go to Canada to look for a master. I told him that as I had served him faithfully, and had been the means of putting a number of hundreds of dollars into his pocket, I thought I had a right to my liberty. He said he had promised my father that I should not be sold to supply the New Orleans market, or he would sell me to a negro-trader.

I was ordered to go into the field to work, and was closely watched by the overseer during the day, and locked up at night. The overseer gave me a severe whipping on the second day that I was in the field. I had been at home but a short time, when master was able to ride to the city; and on his return he informed me that he had sold me to Samuel Willi, a merchant tailor. I knew Mr. Willi. I had lived with him three or four months some years before, when he hired me of my master.

Mr. Willi was not considered by his servants as a very bad man, nor was he the best of masters. I went to my new home, and found my new mistress very glad to see me. Mr. Willi owned two servants before he purchased me—Robert and Charlotte. Robert was an excellent white-washer, and hired his time from his master, paying him one dollar per day, besides taking care of himself. He was known in the city by the name of Bob Music. Charlotte was an old woman, who attended to the cooking, washing, &c. Mr. Willi was not a wealthy man, and did not feel able to keep many servants around his house; so he soon decided to hire me out, and as I had been accustomed to service in steamboats, he gave me the privilege of finding such employment.

I soon secured a situation on board the steamer *Otto,* Capt. J. B. Hill, which sailed from St. Louis to Independence, Missouri. My former master, Dr. Young, did not let Mr. Willi know that I had run away, or he would not have permitted me to go on board a steamboat. The boat was not quite ready to commence running, and therefore I had to re-main with Mr. Willi. But during this time, I had to undergo a trial for which I was entirely unprepared. My mother, who had been in jail since her return until the present time, was now about being carried to New Orleans, to die on a cotton, sugar, or rice plantation!

I had been several times to the jail, but could obtain no interview with her. I ascertained, however, the time the boat in which she was to embark would sail, and as I had not seen mother since her being thrown into prison, I felt anxious for the hour of sailing to come. At last, the day arrived when I was to see her for the first time after our painful separation, and, for aught that I knew, for the last time in this world!

At about ten o'clock in the morning I went on board of the boat, and found her there in company with fifty or sixty other slaves. She was chained to another woman. On seeing me, she immediately dropped her head upon her heaving bosom. She moved not, neither did she weep. Her emotions were too deep for tears. I approached, threw my arms around her neck, kissed her, and fell upon my knees, begging her forgiveness, for I thought myself to blame for her sad condition; for if I had not persuaded her to accompany me, she would not then have been in chains.

She finally raised her head, looked me in the face, (and such a look none but an angel can give!) and said, *"My dear son, you are not to blame for my being here. You have done nothing more nor less than your duty. Do not, I pray you, weep for me. I cannot last long upon a cotton plantation. I feel that my heavenly Master will soon call me home, and then I shall be out of the hands of the slave-holders!"*

I could bear no more—my heart struggled to free itself from the human form. In a moment she saw Mr. Mansfield coming toward that part of the boat, and she whispered into my ear, *"My child, we must soon part to meet no more this side of the grave. You have ever said that you would not die a slave; that you would be a freeman. Now try to get your liberty! You will soon have no one to look after but yourself!"* and just as she whispered the last sentence into my ear, Mansfield came up to me, and with an oath, said, "Leave here this instant; you have been the means of my losing one hundred dollars to get this wench back"—at the same time kicking me with a heavy pair of boots. As I left her, she gave one shriek, saying, "God be with you!" It was the last time that I saw her, and the last word I heard her utter.

I walked on shore. The bell was tolling. The boat was about to start. I stood with a heavy heart, waiting to see her leave the wharf. As I thought of my mother, I could but feel that I had lost

> "———the glory of my life,
> My blessing and my pride!
> I half forgot the name of slave,
> When she was by my side."

The love of liberty that had been burning in my bosom had well-nigh gone out. I felt as though I was ready to die. The boat moved gently from the wharf, and while she glided down the river, I realized that my mother was indeed

> "Gone—gone—sold and gone,
> To the rice swamp, dank and lone!"

After the boat was out of sight I returned home; but my thoughts were so absorbed in what I had witnessed, that I knew not what I was about half of the time. Night came, but it brought no sleep to my eyes.

In a few days, the boat upon which I was to work being ready, I went on board to commence. This employment suited me better than living in the city, and I remained until the close of navigation; though it proved anything but pleasant. The captain was a drunken, profligate, hard-hearted creature, not knowing how to treat himself, or any other person.

The boat, on its second trip, brought down Mr. Walker, the man of whom I have spoken in a previous chapter, as hiring my time. He had between one and two hundred slaves, chained and manacled. Among them was a man that formerly belonged to my old master's brother, Aaron Young. His name was Solomon. He was a preacher, and belonged to the same church with his master. I was glad to see the old man. He wept like a child when he told me how he had been sold from his wife and children.

The boat carried down, while I remained on board, four or five gangs of slaves. Missouri, though a comparatively new state, is very much engaged in raising slaves to supply the southern market. In a former chapter, I have mentioned that I was once in the employ of a slave-trader, or driver, as he is called at the south. For fear that some may think that I have misrepresented a slave-driver, I will here give an extract from a paper published in a slave-holding state, Tennessee, called the *Millennial Trumpeter.*

"Droves of negroes, chained together in dozens and scores, and hand-cuffed, have been driven through our country in numbers far surpassing any previous year, and these vile slave-drivers and dealers are swarming like buzzards around a carrion. Through this county, you cannot pass a few miles in the great roads without having every feeling of humanity insulted and lacerated by this spectacle, nor can you go into any county or any neighborhood, scarcely, without seeing or hearing of some of these despicable creatures, called negro-drivers.

"Who is a negro-driver? One whose eyes dwell with delight on lacerated bodies of helpless men, women and children; whose soul feels diabolical raptures at the chains, and hand-cuffs, and cart-whips, for inflicting tortures on weeping mothers torn from helpless babes, and on husbands and wives torn asunder forever!"

Dark and revolting as is the picture here drawn, it is from the pen of one living in the midst of slavery. But though these men may cant about negro-drivers, and tell what despicable creatures they are, who is it, I ask, that supplies them with the human beings that they are tearing asunder? I answer, as far as I have any knowledge of the state where I came from, that those who raise slaves for the market are to be found among all classes, from Thomas H. Benton down to the lowest political demagogue who may be able to purchase a woman for the purpose of raising stock, and from the doctor of divinity down to the most humble lay member in the church.

It was not uncommon in St. Louis to pass by an auction-stand, and behold a woman upon the auction-block, and hear the seller crying out, "*How much is offered for this woman? She is a good cook, good washer, a good obedient servant. She has got religion!"* Why should this man tell the purchasers that she has religion? I answer, because in Missouri, and as far as I have any knowledge of slavery in the other states, the religious teaching consists in teaching the slave that he must never strike a white man; that God made him for a slave; and that, when whipped, he must not find fault—for the Bible says, "He that knoweth his master's will and doeth it not, shall be beaten with many stripes!" And slaveholders find such religion very profitable to them.

After leaving the steamer *Otto,* I resided at home, in Mr. Willi's family, and again began to lay my plans for making my escape from slavery. The anxiety to be a freeman would not let me rest day or night. I would think of the northern cities that I had heard so much about;—of Canada, where so many of my acquaintances had found a refuge. I would dream at night that I was in Canada, a freeman, and on waking in the morning, weep to find myself so sadly mistaken.

> *"I would think of Victoria's domain,*
> *And in a moment I seemed to be there!*
> *But the fear of being taken again,*
> *Soon hurried me back to despair."*

Mr. Willi treated me better than Dr. Young ever had; but instead of making me contented and happy, it only rendered me the more miserable, for it enabled me better to appreciate liberty. Mr. Willi was a man who loved money as most men do, and without looking for an opportunity to sell me, he found one in the offer of Captain Enoch Price, a steamboat owner and commission merchant, living in the city of St. Louis. Captain Price tendered seven hundred dollars, which was two hundred more than Mr. Willi had paid. He therefore thought best to accept the offer. I was wanted for a carriage driver, and Mrs. Price was very much pleased with the captain's bargain. His family consisted of himself, wife, one child, and three servants, besides myself,—one man and two women.

Mrs. Price was very proud of her servants, always keeping them well dressed, and as soon as I had been purchased, she resolved to have a new carriage. And soon one was procured, and all preparations were made for a turn-out in grand style, I being the driver.

One of the female servants was a girl some eighteen or twenty years of age, named Maria. Mrs. Price was very soon determined to have us united, if she could so arrange matters. She would often urge upon me the necessity of having a wife, saying that it would be so pleasant for me to take one in the same family! But getting married, while in slavery, was the last of my thoughts; and had I been ever so inclined, I should not have married Maria, as my love had already gone in another quarter. Mrs. Price soon found out that her efforts at this matchmaking between Maria and myself would not prove successful. She also discovered (or thought she had) that I was rather partial to a girl named Eliza, who was owned by Dr. Mills. This induced her at once to endeavor the purchase of Eliza, so great was her desire to get me a wife!

Before making the attempt, however, she deemed it best to talk to me a little upon the subject of love, courtship, and marriage. Accordingly, one afternoon she called me into her room—telling me to take a chair and sit down. I did so, thinking it rather strange, for servants are not very often asked thus to sit down in the same room with the master or mistress. She said that she had found out that I did not care enough about Maria to marry her. I told her that was true. She then asked me if there was not a girl in the city that I loved. Well, now, this was coming into too close quarters with me! People, generally, don't like to tell their love stories to everybody that may think fit to ask about them, and it was so with me. But, after blushing a while and recovering myself, I told her that I did not want a wife. She then asked me if I did not think something of Eliza. I told her that I did. She then said that if I wished to marry Eliza, she would purchase her if she could.

I gave but little encouragement to this proposition, as I was determined to make another trial to get my liberty, and I knew that if I should have a wife, I should not be willing to leave her behind; and if I should attempt to bring her with me, the chances would be difficult for success. However, Eliza was purchased, and brought into the family.

Chapter X

BUT THE MORE I thought of the trap laid by Mrs. Price to make me satisfied with my new home, by getting me a wife, the more I determined never to marry any woman on earth until I should get my liberty. But this secret I was compelled to keep to myself, which placed me in a very critical position. I must keep upon good terms with Mrs. Price and Eliza. I therefore promised Mrs. Price that I would marry Eliza; but said that I was not then ready. And I had to keep upon good terms with Eliza, for fear that Mrs. Price would find out that I did not intend to get married.

I have here spoken of marriage, and it is very common among slaves themselves to talk of it. And it is common for slaves to be married; or at least to have the marriage ceremony performed. But there is no such thing as slaves being lawfully married. There has never yet a case occurred where a slave has been tried for bigamy. The man may have as many women as he wishes, and the women as many men; and the law takes no cognizance of such acts among slaves. And in fact some masters, when they have sold the husband from the wife, compel her to take another.

There lived opposite Captain Price's, Doctor Farrar, well known in St. Louis. He sold a man named Ben, to one of the traders. He also owned Ben's wife, and in a few days he compelled Sally (that was her name) to marry Peter, another man belonging to him. I asked Sally "why she married Peter so soon after Ben was sold." She said, "because master made her do it."

Mr. John Calvert, who resided near our place, had a woman named Lavinia. She was quite young, and a man to whom she was about to be married was sold, and carried into the country near St. Charles, about twenty miles from St. Louis. Mr. Calvert wanted her to get a husband; but she had resolved not to marry any other man, and she refused. Mr. Calvert whipped her in such a manner that it was thought she would die. Some of the citizens had him arrested, but it was soon hushed up. And that was the last of it. The woman did not die, but it would have been the same if she had.

Captain Price purchased me in the month of October, and I remained with him until December, when the family made a voyage to New Orleans, in a boat owned by himself, and named the *Chester*. I served on board as one of the stewards. On arriving at New Orleans, about the middle of the month, the boat took in freight for Cincinnati; and it was decided that the family should go up the river in her, and what was of more interest to me, I was to accompany them.

The long looked for opportunity to make my escape from slavery was near at hand.

Captain Price had some fears as to the propriety of taking me near a free state, or a place where it was likely I could run away, with a prospect of liberty. He asked me if I had ever been in a free state. "Oh yes," said I, "I have been in Ohio; my master carried me into that state once, but I never liked a free state."

It was soon decided that it would be safe to take me with them, and what made it more safe, Eliza was on the boat with us, and Mrs. Price, to try me, asked if I thought as much as ever of Eliza. I told her that Eliza was very dear to me indeed, and that nothing but death should part us. It was the same as if we were married. This had the desired effect. The boat left New Orleans, and proceeded up the river.

I had at different times obtained little sums of money, which I had reserved for a "rainy day." I procured some cotton cloth, and made me a bag to carry provisions in. The trials of the past were all lost in hopes for the future. The love of liberty, that had been burning in my bosom for years, and had been well-nigh extinguished, was now resuscitated. At night, when all around was peaceful, I would walk the decks, meditating upon my happy prospects.

I should have stated, that, before leaving St. Louis, I went to an old man named Frank, a slave, owned by a Mr. Sarpee. This old man was very distinguished (not only among the slave population, but also the whites) as a fortune-teller. He was about seventy years of age, something over six feet high, and very slender. Indeed, he was so small around his body, that it looked as though it was not strong enough to hold up his head.

Uncle Frank was a very great favorite with the young ladies, who would go to him in great numbers to get their fortunes told. And it was generally believed that he could really penetrate into the mysteries of futurity. Whether true or not, he had the *name*, and that is about half of what one needs in this gullible age. I found Uncle Frank seated in the chimney corner, about ten o'clock at night. As soon as I entered, the old man left his seat. I watched his movement as well as I could by the dim light of the fire. He soon lit a lamp, and coming up, looked me full in the face, saying, "Well, my son, you have come to get uncle to tell your fortune, have you?" "Yes," said I. But how the old man should know what I came for, I could not tell. However, I paid the fee of twenty-five cents, and he commenced by looking into a gourd, filled with water. Whether the old man was a prophet, or the son of a prophet, I cannot say; but there is one thing certain, many of his predictions were verified.

I am no believer in soothsaying; yet I am sometimes at a loss to know how Uncle Frank could tell so accurately what would occur in the future. Among the many things he told was one which was enough to pay me for all the trouble of hunting him up. It was that I *should be free!* He further said, that in trying to get my liberty I would meet with many severe trials. I thought to myself any fool could tell me that!

The first place in which we landed in a free state was Cairo, a small village at the mouth of the Ohio river. We remained here but a few hours, when we proceeded to Louisville. After unloading some of the cargo, the boat started on her upward trip. The next day was the first of January. I had looked forward to New Year's day as the commencement of a new era in the history of my life. I had decided upon leaving the peculiar institution that day.

During the last night that I served in slavery I did not close my eyes a single moment. When not thinking of the future, my mind dwelt on the past. The love of a dear mother, a dear sister, and three dear brothers, yet living, caused me to shed many tears. If I could only have been assured of their being dead, I should have felt satisfied; but I imagined I saw my dear mother in the cotton-field, followed by a merciless taskmaster, and no one to speak a consoling word to her! I beheld my dear sister in the hands of a slave-driver, and compelled to submit to his cruelty! None but one placed in such a situation can for a moment imagine the intense agony to which these reflections subjected me.

Chapter XI

AT LAST THE TIME for action arrived. The boat landed at a point which appeared to me the place of all others to start from. I found that it would be impossible to carry anything with me but what was upon my person. I had some provisions, and a single suit of clothes, about half worn. When the boat was discharging her cargo, and the passengers engaged carrying their baggage on and off shore, I improved the opportunity to convey myself with my little effects on land. Taking up a trunk, I went up the wharf, and was soon out of the crowd. I made directly for the woods, where I remained until night, knowing well that I could not travel, even in the state of Ohio, during the day, without danger of being arrested.

I had long since made up my mind that I would not trust myself in the hands of any man, white or colored. The slave is brought up to look upon every white man as an enemy to him and his race; and twenty-one years in slavery had taught me that there were traitors, even among colored people. After dark, I emerged from the woods into a narrow path, which led me into the main travelled road. But I knew not which way to go. I did not know north from south, east from west. I looked in vain for the North Star; a heavy cloud hid it from my view. I walked up and down the road until near midnight, when the clouds disappeared, and I welcomed the sight of my friend—truly the slave's friend—the North Star!

As soon as I saw it, I knew my course, and before daylight I travelled twenty or twenty-five miles. It being in the winter, I suffered intensely from the cold; being without an overcoat, and my other clothes rather thin for the season. I was provided with a tinder-box, so that I could make up a fire when necessary. And but for this, I should certainly have frozen to death; for I was determined not to go to any house for shelter. I knew of a man belonging to Gen. Ashly, of St. Louis, who had run away near Cincinnati, on the way to Washington, but had been caught and carried back into slavery; and I felt that a similar fate awaited me, should I be seen by anyone. I travelled at night, and lay by during the day.

On the fourth day my provisions gave out, and then what to do I could not tell. Have something to eat I must; but how to get it was the question! On the first night after my food was gone, I went to a barn on the road-side and there found some ears of corn. I took ten or twelve of them, and kept on my journey. During the next day, while in the woods, I roasted my corn and feasted upon it, thanking God that I was so well provided for.

My escape to a land of freedom now appeared certain, and the prospects of the future occupied a great part of my thoughts. What should be my occupation, was a subject of much anxiety to me; and the next thing what should be my name? I have before stated that my old master, Dr. Young, had no children of his own, but had with him a nephew, the son of his brother, Benjamin Young. When this boy was brought to Dr. Young, his name being William, the same as mine, my mother was ordered to change mine to something else. This, at the time, I thought to be one of the most cruel acts that could be committed upon my rights; and I received several very severe whippings for telling people that my name was William, after orders were given to change it. Though young, I was old enough to place a high appreciation upon my name. It was decided, however, to call me "Sandford," and this name I was known by, not only upon my master's plantation, but up to the time that I made my escape. I was sold under the name of Sandford.

But as soon as the subject came to my mind, I resolved on adopting my old name of William, and let Sandford go by the board, for I always hated it. Not because there was anything peculiar in the name; but because it had been forced upon me. It is sometimes common, at the south, for slaves to take the name of their masters. Some have a legitimate right to do so. But I always detested the idea of being called by the name of either of my masters. And as for my father, I would rather have adopted the name of "Friday," and been known as the servant of some Robinson Crusoe, than to have taken his name. So I was not only hunting for my liberty, but also hunting for a name; though I regarded the latter as of little consequence, if I could but gain the former. Travelling along the road, I would sometimes speak to myself, sounding my name over, by way of getting used to it, before I should arrive among civilized human beings. On the fifth or sixth day, it rained very fast, and froze about as fast as it fell, so that my clothes were one glare of ice. I travelled on at night until I became so chilled and benumbed—the wind blowing into my face—that I found it impossible to go any further, and accordingly took shelter in a barn, where I was obliged to walk about to keep from freezing.

I have ever looked upon that night as the most eventful part of my escape from slavery. Nothing but the providence of God, and that old barn, saved me from freezing to death. I received a very severe cold, which settled upon my lungs, and from time to time my feet had been frostbitten, so that it was with difficulty I could walk. In this situation I travelled two days, when I found that I must seek shelter somewhere, or die.

The thought of death was nothing frightful to me, compared with that of being caught, and again carried back into slavery. Nothing but the prospect of enjoying liberty could have induced me to undergo such trials, for

> *"Behind I left the whips and chains,*
> *Before me were sweet Freedom's plains!"*

This, and this alone, cheered me onward. But I at last resolved to seek protection from the inclemency of the weather, and therefore I secured myself behind some logs and brush, intending to wait there until someone should pass by; for I thought it probable that I might see some colored person, or, if not, someone who was not a slave-holder; for I had an idea that I should know a slave-holder as far as I could see him.

The first person that passed was a man in a buggy-wagon. He looked too genteel for me to hail him. Very soon another passed by on horseback. I attempted to speak to him, but fear made my voice fail me. As he passed, I left my hiding-place, and was approaching the road, when I observed an old man walking towards me, leading a white horse. He had on a broad-brimmed hat and a very long coat, and was evidently walking for exercise. As soon as I saw him, and observed his dress, I thought to myself, "You are the man that I have been looking for!" Nor was I mistaken. He was the very man!

On approaching me, he asked me, "if I was not a slave." I looked at him some time, and then asked him "if he knew of anyone who would help me, as I was sick." He answered that he would; but again asked, if I was not a slave. I told him I was. He then said that I was in a very pro-slavery neighborhood, and if I would wait until he went home, he would get a covered wagon for me. I promised to remain. He mounted his horse, and was soon out of sight.

After he was gone, I meditated whether to wait or not; being apprehensive that he had gone for someone to arrest me. But I finally concluded to remain until he should return; removing some few rods to watch his movements. After a suspense of an hour and a half or more, he returned with a two-horse covered wagon, such as are usually seen under the shed of a Quaker meeting-house on Sundays and Thursdays; for the old man proved to be a Quaker of the George Fox stamp.

He took me to his house, but it was some time before I could be induced to enter it; not until the old lady came out, did I venture into the house. I thought I saw something in the old lady's cap that told me I was not only safe, but welcome, in her house. I was not, however, prepared to receive their hospitalities. The only fault I found with them was their being too kind. I had never had a white man to treat me as an equal, and the idea of a white lady waiting on me at the table was still worse! Though the table was loaded with the good things of this life, I could not eat. I thought if I could only be allowed the privilege of eating in the kitchen I should be more than satisfied!

Finding that I could not eat, the old lady, who was a "Thompsonian," made me a cup of "composition," or "number six;" but it was so strong and hot, that I called it *"number seven!"* However, I soon found myself at home in this family. On different occasions, when telling these facts, I have been asked how I felt upon finding myself regarded as a man by a white family; especially just having run away from one. I cannot say that I have ever answered the question yet.

The fact that I was in all probability a freeman, sounded in my ears like a charm. I am satisfied that none but a slave could place such an appreciation upon liberty as I did at that time. I wanted to see mother and sister, that I might tell them "I was free!" I wanted to see my fellow-slaves in St. Louis, and let them know that the chains were no longer upon my limbs. I wanted to see Captain Price, and let him learn from my own lips that I was no more a chattel, but a man! I was anxious, too, thus to inform Mrs. Price that she must get another coachman. And I wanted to see Eliza more than I did either Mr. or Mrs. Price!

The fact that I was a freeman—could walk, talk, eat and sleep, as a man, and no one to stand over me with the blood-clotted cow-hide—all this made me feel that I was not myself.

The kind friend that had taken me in was named Wells Brown. He was a devoted friend of the slave; but was very old, and not in the enjoyment of good health. After being by the fire awhile, I found that my feet had been very much frozen. I was seized with a fever, which threatened to confine me to my bed. But my Thompsonian friends soon raised me, treating me as kindly as if I had been one of their own children. I remained with them twelve or fifteen days, during which time they made me some clothing, and the old gentleman purchased me a pair of boots.

I found that I was about fifty or sixty miles from Dayton, in the State of Ohio, and between one and two hundred miles from Cleveland, on Lake Erie, a place I was desirous of reaching on my way to Canada. This I know will sound strangely to the ears of people in foreign lands, but it is nevertheless true. An American citizen was fleeing from a democratic, republican, Christian government, to receive protection under the monarchy of Great Britain. While the people of the United States boast of their freedom, they at the same time keep three millions of their own citizens in chains; and while I am seated here in sight of Bunker Hill Monument, writing this narrative, I am a slave, and no law, not even in Massachusetts, can protect me from the hands of the slave-holder!

Before leaving this good Quaker friend, he inquired what my name was besides William. I told him that I had no other name. "Well," said he, "thee must have another name. Since thee has got out of slavery, thee has become a man, and men always have two names."

I told him that he was the first man to extend the hand of friendship to me, and I would give him the privilege of naming me.

"If I name thee," said he, "I shall call thee Wells Brown, after myself."

"But," said I, "I am not willing to lose my name of William. As it was taken from me once against my will, I am not willing to part with it again upon any terms."

"Then," said he, "I will call thee William Wells Brown."

"So be it," said I; and I have been known by that name ever since I left the house of my first white friend, Wells Brown.

After giving me some little change, I again started for Canada. In four days I reached a public house, and went in to warm myself. I there learned that some fugitive slaves had just passed through the place. The men in the bar-room were talking about it, and I thought that it must have been myself they referred to, and I was therefore afraid to start, fearing they would seize me; but I finally mustered courage enough, and took my leave. As soon as I was out of sight, I went into the woods, and remained there until night, when I again regained the road, and travelled on until next day.

Not having had any food for nearly two days, I was faint with hunger, and was in a dilemma what to do, as the little cash supplied me by my adopted father, and which had contributed to my comfort, was now all gone. I however concluded to go to a farm-house, and ask for something to eat. On approaching the door of the first one presenting itself, I knocked, and was soon met by a man who asked me what I wanted. I told him that I would like something to eat. He asked me where I was from, and where I was going. I replied that I had come some way, and was going to Cleveland.

After hesitating a moment or two, he told me that he could give me nothing to eat, adding, "that if I would work, I could get something to eat."

I felt bad, being thus refused something to sustain nature, but did not dare tell him that I was a slave.

Just as I was leaving the door, with a heavy heart, a woman, who proved to be the wife of this gentleman, came to the door, and asked her husband what I wanted. He did not seem inclined to inform her. She therefore asked me herself. I told her that I had asked for something to eat. After a few other questions, she told me to come in, and that she would give me something to eat.

I walked up to the door, but the husband remained in the passage, as if unwilling to let me enter.

She asked him two or three times to get out of the way, and let me in. But as he did not move, she pushed him on one side, bidding me walk in! I was never before so glad to see a woman push a man aside! Ever since that act, I have been in favor of "woman's rights!"

After giving me as much food as I could eat, she presented me with ten cents, all the money then at her disposal, accompanied with a note to a friend, a few miles further on the road. Thanking this angel of mercy from an overflowing heart, I pushed on my way, and in three days arrived at Cleveland, Ohio.

Being an entire stranger in this place, it was difficult for me to find where to stop. I had no money, and the lake being frozen, I saw that I must remain until the opening of the navigation, or go to Canada by way of Buffalo. But believing myself to be somewhat out of danger, I secured an engagement at the Mansion House, as a table waiter, in payment for my board. The proprietor, however, whose name was E. M. Segur, in a short time, hired me for twelve dollars a month; on which terms I remained until spring, when I found good employment on board a lake steamboat.

I purchased some books, and at leisure moments perused them with considerable advantage to myself. While at Cleveland, I saw, for the first time, an anti-slavery newspaper. It was the *Genius of Universal Emancipation*, published by Benjamin Lundy; and though I had no home, I subscribed for the paper. It was my great desire, being out of slavery myself, to do what I could for the emancipation of my brethren yet in chains, and while on Lake Erie, I found many opportunities of "helping their cause along."

It is well known that a great number of fugitives make their escape to Canada, by way of Cleveland; and while on the lakes, I always made arrangement to carry them on the boat to Buffalo or Detroit, and thus effect their escape to the "promised land." The friends of the slave, knowing that I would transport them without charge, never failed to have a delegation when the boat arrived at Cleveland. I have sometimes had four or five on board at one time.

In the year 1842, I conveyed, from the first of May to the first of December, sixty-nine fugitives over Lake Erie to Canada. In 1843, I visited Malden, in Upper Canada, and counted seventeen in that small village, whom I had assisted in reaching Canada. Soon after coming north I subscribed for the *Liberator,* edited by that champion of freedom, William Lloyd Garrison. I had heard nothing of the anti-slavery movement while in slavery, and as soon as I found that my enslaved countrymen had friends who were laboring for their liberation, I felt anxious to join them, and give what aid I could to the cause.

I early embraced the temperance cause, and found that a temperance reformation was needed among my colored brethren. In company with a few friends, I commenced a temperance reformation among the colored people in the city of Buffalo, and labored three years, in which time a society was built up, numbering over five hundred out of a population of less than seven hundred.

In the autumn, 1843, impressed with the importance of spreading anti-slavery truth, as a means to bring about the abolition of slavery, I commenced lecturing as an agent of the western New York Anti-Slavery Society, and have ever since devoted my time to the cause of my enslaved countrymen.

Chapter XII

DURING THE AUTUMN of 1836, a slaveholder by the name of Bacon Tate, from the State of Tennessee, came to the north in search of fugitives from slavery. On his arrival at Buffalo he heard of two of the most valuable of the slaves that he was in pursuit of. They were residing in St. Catharine's, in Upper Canada, some twenty-five miles from Buffalo. After hearing that they were in Canada, one would have supposed that Tate would have given up all hope of getting them. But not so. Bacon Tate was a man who had long been engaged in the slave-trade, and previous to that had been employed as a negro-driver. In these two situations he had gained the name of being the most complete "negro-breaker" in that part of Tennessee where he resided. He was as unfeeling and as devoid of principle as a man could possibly be. This made him the person, above all others, to be selected to be put on the track of the fugitive slave. He had not only been commissioned to catch Stanford and his wife, the two valuable slaves already alluded to, but he had the names of some twenty others.

Many slaves had made their escape from the vicinity of Nashville, and the slaveholders were anxious to have some caught, that they might make an example of them. And Tate, anxious to sustain his high reputation as a negro-catcher, left no stone unturned to carry out his nefarious objects.

Stanford and his little family were as happily situated as fugitives can be, who make their escape to Canada in the cold season of the year. Tate, on his arrival at Buffalo, took lodgings at the Eagle Tavern, the best house at that time in the city. And here he began to lay his plans to catch and carry back into slavery those men and women who had undergone so much to get their freedom. He soon became acquainted with a profligate colored woman, who was a servant in the hotel, and who was as unprincipled as himself. This woman was sent to St. Catharine's, to spy out the situation of Stanford's family. Under the pretense of wishing to get board in the family, and at the same time offering to pay a week's board in advance, she was taken in. After remaining with them three or four days, the spy returned to Buffalo, and informed Tate how they were situated. By the liberal use of money, Tate soon found those who were willing to do his bidding. A carriage was hired, and four men employed to go with it to St. Catharine's, and to secure their victims during the night.

The carriage, with the kidnappers, crossed the Niagara river at Black Rock, on Saturday evening, about seven o'clock, and went on its way towards St. Catharine's; no one suspecting in the least that they were after fugitive slaves. About twelve o'clock that night they attacked Stanford's dwelling by breaking in the door. They found the family asleep, and of course met with no obstacle whatever in tying, gagging, and forcing them into the carriage.

The family had one child about six weeks old. That was kept at its mother's breast, to keep it quiet. The carriage re-crossed the river, at the same place, the next morning at sunrise, and proceeded to Buffalo, where it remained a short time, and after changing horses and leaving some of its company, it proceeded on its journey. The carriage being closely covered, no one had made the least discovery as to its contents. But some time during the morning, a man, who was neighbor to Stanford, and who resided but a short distance from him, came on an errand; and finding the house deserted, and seeing the most of the family's clothes lying on the floor, and seeing here and there stains of blood, soon gave the alarm, and the neighbors started in every direction, to see if they could find the kidnappers. One man got on the track of the carriage, and followed it to the ferry at Black Rock, where he heard that it had crossed some three hours before. He went on to Buffalo, and gave the alarm to the colored people of that place. The colored people of Buffalo are noted for their promptness in giving aid to the fugitive slave. The alarm was given just as the bells were ringing for church. I was in company with five or six others, when I heard that a brother slave with his family had been seized and dragged from his home during the night previous. We started on a run for the livery-stable, where we found as many more of our own color trying to hire horses to go in search of the fugitives. There were two roads which the kidnappers could take, and we were at some loss to know which to take ourselves. But we soon determined to be on the right track, and so divided our company,—one half taking the road to Erie, the other taking the road leading to Hamburgh. I was among those who took the latter.

We travelled on at a rapid rate, until we came within half a mile of Hamburgh Corners, when we met a man on the side of the road on foot, who made signs to us to stop. We halted for a moment, when he informed us that the carriage that we were in pursuit of was at the public house, and that he was then in search of some of his neighbors, to assemble and to demand of the kidnappers the authority by which they were taking these people into slavery.

We proceeded to the tavern, where we found the carriage standing in front of the door, with a pair of fresh horses ready to proceed on their journey. The kidnappers, seeing us coming, took their victims into a room, and locked the door and fastened down the windows. We all dismounted, fastened our horses, and entered the house. We found four or five persons in the bar-room, who seemed to rejoice as we entered.

One of our company demanded the opening of the door, while others went out and surrounded the house. The kidnappers stationed one of their number at the door, and another at the window. They refused to let us enter the room, and the tavern-keeper, who was more favorable to us than we had anticipated, said to us, "Boys, get into the room in any way that you can; the house is mine, and I give you the liberty to break in through the door or window." This was all that we wanted, and we were soon making preparations to enter the room at all hazards. Those within had warned us that if we should attempt to enter, they would "shoot the first one." One of our company, who had obtained a crow-bar, went to the window, and succeeded in getting it under the sash, and soon we had the window up, and the kidnappers, together with their victims, in full view.

One of the kidnappers, while we were raising the window, kept crying at the top of his voice, "I'll shoot, I'll shoot!" but no one seemed to mind him. As soon as they saw that we were determined to rescue the slaves at all hazards, they gave up, one of their number telling us that we might "come in."

The door was thrown open, and we entered, and there found Stanford seated in one corner of the room, with his hands tied behind him, and his clothing, what little he had on, much stained with blood. Near him was his wife, with her child, but a few weeks old, in her arms. Neither of them had anything on except their night-clothes. They had both been gagged, to keep them from alarming the people, and had been much beaten and bruised when first attacked by the kidnappers. Their countenances lighted up the moment we entered the room.

The most of those who made up our company were persons who had made their escape from slavery, and who knew its horrors from personal experience, and who had left near and dear relatives behind them. And we knew how to "feel for those in bonds as bound with them."

The woman who had betrayed them, and who was in the house at the time they were taken, had been persuaded by Tate to go on with him to Tennessee. She had accompanied them from Canada, and we found her in the same room with Stanford and his wife. As soon as she found that we were about to enter the room, she ran under the bed. We knew nothing of her being in the room until Stanford pointed to the bed and said, "Under there is our betrayer." She was soon hauled out, and it was as much as some of us could do to keep the others from lynching her upon the spot. The curses came thick and fast from a majority of the company. But nothing attracted my attention at the time more than the look of Mrs. Stanford at the betrayer, as she sat before her. She did not say a word to her, but her countenance told the feelings of her inmost soul, and we could but think, that had she spoken to her, she would have said, "May the world deny thee a shelter! earth a home! the dust a grave! the sun his light! and Heaven her God!"

The betrayer begged us to let her go. I was somewhat disposed to comply with her request, but I found many to oppose me; in fact, I was entirely alone. My main reason for wishing to let her escape was that I was afraid that her life would be in danger. I knew that, if she was taken back to Buffalo or Canada, she would fall into the hands of an excited people, the most of whom had themselves been slaves. And they, being comparatively ignorant of the laws, would be likely to take the law into their own hands.

However, the woman was not allowed to escape, but was put into the coach, together with Stanford and his wife; and after an hour and a half's drive, we found ourselves in the city of Buffalo. The excitement which the alarm had created in the morning had broken up the meetings of the colored people for that day; and on our arrival in the city we were met by some forty or fifty colored persons. The kidnappers had not been inactive; for, on our arrival in the city, we learned that the man who had charge of the carriage and fugitives when we caught up with them, returned to the city immediately after giving the slaves up to us, and had informed Tate, who had remained behind, of what had occurred. Tate immediately employed the sheriff and his posse to re-take the slaves. So, on our arrival in Buffalo, we found that the main battle had yet to be fought. Stanford and his wife and child were soon provided with clothing and some refreshment, while we were pre-paring ourselves with clubs, pistols, knives, and other weapons of de-fense. News soon come to us that the sheriff, with his under officers, together with some sixty or seventy men who were at work on the ca-nal, were on the road between Buffalo and Black Rock, and that they intended to re-take the slaves when we should attempt to take them to the ferry to convey them to Canada. This news was anything but pleasant to us, but we prepared for the worst.

We returned to the city about two o'clock in the afternoon, and about four we started for Black Rock ferry, which is about three miles below Buffalo. We had in our company some fifty or more able-bodied, resolute men, who were determined to stand by the slaves, and who had resolved, before they left the city, that if the sheriff and his men took the slaves, they should first pass over their dead bodies.

We started, and when about a mile below the city, the sheriff and his men came upon us, and surrounded us. The slaves were in a carriage, and the horses were soon stopped, and we found it advisable to take them out of the carriage, and we did so. The sheriff came forward, and read something purporting to be a "Riot Act," and at the same time called upon all good citizens to aid him in keeping the "peace." This was a trick of his, to get possession of the slaves. His men rushed upon us with their clubs and stones, and a general fight ensued. Our com-pany had surrounded the slaves, and had succeeded in keeping the sheriff and his men off. We fought, and at the same time kept pushing on towards the ferry.

In the midst of the fight, a little white man made his appearance among us, and proved to be a valuable friend. His name was Pepper; and he proved himself a *pepper* to the sheriff and his posse that day. He was a lawyer; and as the officers would arrest any of our company, he would step up and ask the officer if he had a "warrant to take that man;" and as none of them had warrants, and could not answer affirmatively, he would say to the colored man, "He has no right to take you; knock him down." The command was no sooner given than the man would fall. If the one who had been arrested was not able to knock him down, some who were close by, and who were armed with a club or other weapon, would come to his assistance.

After it became generally known in our company that the "little man" was a lawyer, he had a tremendous influence with them. You could hear them cry out occasionally, "That's right, knock him down; the little man told you to do it, and he is a lawyer; he knows all about the law; that's right,—hit him again! he is a white man, and he has done our color enough."

Such is but a poor representation of what was said by those who were engaged in the fight. After a hard-fought battle, of nearly two hours, we arrived at the ferry, the slaves still in our possession. On arriving at the ferry, we found that some of the sheriff's gang had taken possession of the ferry-boat. Here another battle was to be fought, before the slaves could reach Canada. The boat was fastened at each end by a chain, and in the scuffle for the ascendency, one party took charge of one end of the boat, while the other took the other end. The blacks were commanding the ferryman to carry them over, while the whites were commanding him not to. While each party was contending for power, the slaves were pushed on board, and the boat shoved from the wharf. Many of the blacks jumped on board of the boat, while the whites jumped on shore. And the swift current of the Niagara soon carried them off, amid the shouts of the blacks, and the oaths and imprecations of the whites. We on shore swung our hats and gave three cheers, just as a reinforcement came to the whites. Seeing the odds entirely against us in numbers, and having gained the great victory, we gave up without resistance, and suffered ourselves to be arrested by the sheriff's posse. However, we all remained on the shore until the ferry-boat had landed on the Canada side. As the boat landed, Stanford leaped on shore, and rolled over in the sand, and even rubbed it into his hair.

I did not accompany the boat over, but those who did informed us that Mrs. Stanford, as she stepped on the shore, with her child in her arms, exclaimed, "I thank God that I am again in Canada!" We returned to the city, and some forty of our company were lodged in jail, to await their trial the next morning.

And now I will return to the betrayer. On our return to Buffalo, she was given over to a committee of women, who put her in a room, and put a guard over her. Tate, who had been very active from the time that he heard that we had recaptured the carriage with the slaves, was still in the city. He was not with the slaves when we caught up with them at Hamburgh, nor was he to be found in the fight. He sent his hirelings, while he remained at the hotel drinking champagne. As soon as he found the slaves were out of his reach, he then made an offer of fifty dollars to any person who would find the betrayer. He pretended that he wished to save her from the indignation of the colored people. But the fact is, he had promised her that if she would accompany him to the south, that he would put her in a situation where she would be a lady. Poor woman! She was foolish enough to believe him; and now that the people had lost all sympathy for her, on account of her traitorous act, he still thought that, by pretending to be her friend, he could induce her to go to the south, that he might sell her. But those who had her in charge were determined that she should be punished for being engaged in this villainous transaction.

Several meetings were held to determine what should be done with her. Some were in favor of hanging her, others for burning her, but a majority were for taking her to the Niagara river, tying a fifty-six pound weight to her, and throwing her in. There seemed to be no way in which she could be reached by the civil law. She was kept in confinement three days, being removed to different places each night.

So conflicting were the views of those who had her in charge, that they could not decide upon what should be done with her. However, there seemed to be such a vast majority in favor of throwing her into the Niagara river, that some of us, who were opposed to taking life, succeeded in having her given over to another committee, who, after reprimanding her, let her go.

Tate, in the meantime, hearing that the colored people had resolved to take vengeance on him, thought it best to leave the city. On Monday, at ten o'clock, we were all carried before Justice Grosvenor; and of the forty who had been committed the evening before, twenty-five were held to bail to answer to a higher court. When the trials came on, we were fined more or less, from five to fifty dollars each.

During the fight no one was killed, though there were many broken noses and black eyes; one young man, who was attached to a theatrical corps, was so badly injured in the conflict that he died some three months after.

Thus ended one of the most fearful fights for human freedom that I ever witnessed. The reader will observe that this conflict took place on the Sabbath, and that those who were foremost in getting it up were officers of justice. The plea of the sheriff and his posse was, that we were breaking the Sabbath by assembling in such large numbers to protect a brother slave and his wife and child from being dragged back into slavery, which is far worse than death itself.

From the *Liberty Bell* of 1848.

THE AMERICAN SLAVE-TRADE.

BY WILLIAM WELLS BROWN.

OF THE MANY FEATURES which American slavery presents, the most cruel is that of the slave-trade. A traffic in the bodies and souls of native-born Americans is carried on in the slave-holding states to an extent little dreamed of by the great mass of the people in the non-slave-holding states. The precise number of slaves carried from the slave-raising to the slave-consuming states we have no means of knowing. But it must be very great, as forty thousand were sold and carried out of the State of Virginia in one single year!

This heart-rending and cruel traffic is not confined to any particular class of persons. No person forfeits his or her character or standing in society by being engaged in raising and selling slaves to supply the cotton, sugar, and rice plantations of the south. Few persons who have visited the slave states have not, on their return, told of the gangs of slaves they had seen on their way to the southern market. This trade presents some of the most revolting and atrocious scenes which can be imagined. Slave-prisons, slave-auctions, handcuffs, whips, chains, bloodhounds, and other instruments of cruelty, are part of the furniture which belongs to the American slave-trade. It is enough to make humanity bleed at every pore, to see these implements of torture.

Known to God only is the amount of human agony and suffering which sends its cry from these slave-prisons, unheard or unheeded by man, up to His ear; mothers weeping for their children—breaking the night-silence with the shrieks of their breaking hearts. We wish no human being to experience emotions of needless pain, but we do wish that every man, woman, and child in New England, could visit a southern slave-prison and auction-stand.

I shall never forget a scene which took place in the city of St. Louis, while I was in slavery. A man and his wife, both slaves, were brought from the country to the city, for sale. They were taken to the rooms of AUSTIN & SAVAGE, auctioneers. Several slave-speculators, who are always to be found at auctions where slaves are to be sold, were present. The man was first put up, and sold to the highest bidder. The wife was next ordered to ascend the platform. I was present. She slowly obeyed the order. The auctioneer commenced, and soon several hundred dollars were bid. My eyes were intensely fixed on the face of the woman, whose cheeks were wet with tears. But a conversation between the slave and his new master attracted my attention. I drew near them to listen. The slave was begging his new master to purchase his wife. Said he, "Master, if you will only buy Fanny, I know you will get the worth of your money. She is a good cook, a good washer, and her last mistress liked her very much. If you will only buy her how happy I shall be." The new master replied that he did not want her but if she sold cheap he would purchase her. I watched the countenance of the man while the different persons were bidding on his wife. When his new master bid on his wife you could see the smile upon his countenance, and the tears stop; but as soon as another would bid, you could see the countenance change and the tears start afresh. From this change of countenance one could see the workings of the inmost soul. But this suspense did not last long; the wife was struck off to the highest bidder, who proved not to be the owner of her husband. As soon as they became aware that they were to be separated, they both burst into tears; and as she descended from the auction-stand, the husband, walking up to her and taking her by the hand, said, "Well, Fanny, we are to part forever, on earth; you have been a good wife to me. I did all that I could to get my new master to buy you; but he did not want you, and all I have to say is, I hope you will try to meet me in heaven. I shall try to meet you there." The wife made no reply, but her sobs and cries told, too well, her own feelings. I saw the countenances of a number of whites who were present, and whose eyes were dim with tears at hearing the man bid his wife farewell.

Such are but common occurrences in the slave states. At these auction-stands, bones, muscles, sinews, blood and nerves, of human beings, are sold with as much indifference as a farmer in the north sells a horse or sheep. And this great American nation is, at the present time, engaged in the slave-trade. I have before me now the Washington *Union*, the organ of the government, in which I find an advertisement of several slaves to be sold for the benefit of the government. They will, in all human probability, find homes among the rice-swamps of Georgia, or the cane-brakes of Mississippi.

With every disposition on the part of those who are engaged in it to veil the truth, certain facts have, from time to time, transpired, sufficient to show, if not the full amount of the evil, at least that it is one of prodigious magnitude. And what is more to be wondered at, is the fact that the greatest slave-market is to be found at the capital of the country! The American slave-trader marches by the capitol with his "coffle-gang,"—the stars and stripes waving over their heads, and the constitution of the United States in his pocket!

The *Alexandria Gazette,* speaking of the slave-trade at the capital, says, "Here you may behold fathers and brothers leaving behind them the dearest objects of affection, and moving slowly along in the mute agony of despair; there, the young mother, sobbing over the infant whose innocent smile seems but to increase her misery. From some you will hear the burst of bitter lamentation, while from others, the loud hysteric laugh breaks forth, denoting still deeper agony. Such is but a faint picture of the American slave-trade."

Boston, Massachusetts.

Flight of the Bondman.
Dedicated to William W. Brown,
And sung by the Hutchinsons.
BY ELIAS SMITH.

From the crack of the rifle and baying of hound,
   Takes the poor panting bondman his flight;
His couch through the day is the cold damp ground,
   But northward he runs through the night.

O, God speed the flight of the desolate slave,
   Let his heart never yield to despair;
There is room 'mong our hills for the true and the brave,
   Let his lungs breathe our free northern air!

O sweet to the storm-driven sailor the light,
   Streaming far o'er the dark swelling wave:
But sweeter by far 'mong the lights of the night,
   Is the star of the north to the slave.

Cold and bleak are our mountains and chilling our winds,
   But warm as the soft southern gales
Be the hands and the hearts which the hunted one finds,
   'Mong our hills and our own winter vales.

Then list to the 'plaint of the heart-broken thrall,
   Ye blood-hounds, go back to your lair;
May a free northern soil soon give freedom to all,
   Who shall breathe in its pure mountain air.

Freedom's Star.

Respectfully Dedicated to William Wells Brown, as a testimony of
regard for his uncompromising advocacy of the cause of his
enslaved brothers and sisters, by D. B. Harris.

As I strayed from my cot at the close of the day,
    I turned my fond gaze to the sky;
I beheld all the stars as so sweetly they lay,
    And but one fixed my heart or my eye.
Shine on, northern star, thou 'rt beautiful and bright
    To the slave on his journey afar;
For he speeds from his foes in the darkness of night,
    Guided on by thy light, freedom's star.

On thee he depends when he threads the dark woods,
    Ere the bloodhounds have hunted him back;
Thou leadest him on over mountains and floods,
    With thy beams shining full on his track.

Unwelcome to him is the bright orb of day,
    As it glides o'er the earth and the sea;
He seeks then to hide like a wild beast of prey,
    But with hope, rests his heart upon thee.

May never a cloud overshadow thy face,
    While the slave flies before his pursuer;
Gleam steadily on to the end of his race,
    Till his body and soul are secure.

Lament of the Fugitive Slave.

"My child, we must soon part, to meet no more this side of the grave.
You have ever said that you would not die a slave; that you would be a free man.
Now try to get your liberty!"—W. W. Brown's Narrative.

I've wandered out beneath the moonlit heaven,
    Lost mother! loved and dear,
To every beam a magic power seems given
    To bring thy spirit near;
For though the breeze of freedom fans my brow,
My soul still turns to thee! oh, where art thou?

Where art thou, mother! I am weary thinking;
    A heritage of pain and woe

Was thine,—beneath it art thou slowly sinking,
    Or hast thou perished long ago?
And doth thy spirit 'mid the quivering leaves above me,
Hover, dear mother, to guard and love me?

I murmur at my lot; in the white man's dwelling
    The mother there is found;
Or he may tell where spring-buds first are swelling
    Above her lowly mound;
But thou,—lost mother, every trace of thee
In the vast sepulchre of Slavery!

Long years have fled, since sad, faint-hearted,
    I stood on Freedom's shore,
And knew, dear mother, from thee I was parted,
    To meet thee never more;
And deemed the tyrant's chain with thee were better
Than stranger hearts and limbs without a fetter.

Yet blessings on thy Roman-mother spirit;
    Could I forget it, then,
The parting scene, and struggle not to inherit
    A freeman's birth-right once again?
O noble words! O holy love, which gave
Thee strength to utter them, a poor, heart-broken slave!

Be near me, mother, be thy spirit near me,
    Wherever thou may'st be;
In hours like this bend near that I may hear thee,
    And know that thou art free;
Summoned at length from bondage, toil and pain,
To God's free world, a world without a chain!

Appendix.

In giving a history of my own sufferings in slavery, as well as the sufferings of others with which I was acquainted, or which came under my immediate observation, I have spoken harshly of slaveholders, in church and state.

Nor am I inclined to apologize for anything which I have said. There are exceptions among slaveholders, as well as among other sinners; and the fact that a slaveholder feeds his slaves better, clothes them better, than another, does not alter the case; he is a slaveholder. I do not ask the slaveholder to feed, clothe, or to treat his victim better as a slave. I am not waging a warfare against the collateral evils, or what are sometimes called the abuses, of slavery. I wage a war against slavery itself, because it takes man down from the lofty position which God intended he should occupy, and places him upon a level with the beasts of the field. It decrees that the slave shall not worship God according to the dictates of his own conscience; it denies him the word of God; it makes him a chattel, and sells him in the market to the highest bidder; it decrees that he shall not protect the wife of his bosom; it takes from him every right which God gave him. Clothing and food are as nothing compared with liberty. What care I for clothing or food, while I am the slave of another? You may take me and put cloth upon my back, boots upon my feet, a hat upon my head, and cram a beef-steak down my throat, and all of this will not satisfy me as long as I know that you have the power to tear me from my dearest relatives. All I ask of the slaveholder is to give the slave his liberty. It is freedom I ask for the *slave*. And that the American slave will eventually get his freedom, no one can doubt. You cannot keep the human mind forever locked up in darkness. A ray of light, a spark from freedom's altar, the idea of inherent right, each, all, will become fixed in the soul; and that moment his "limbs swell beyond the measure of his chains," that moment he is free; then it is that the slave dies to become a freeman; then it is felt that one hour of virtuous liberty is worth an eternity of bondage; then it is, in the madness and fury of his blood, that the excited soul exclaims,

"From life without freedom, oh! who would not fly;
For one day of freedom, oh! who would not die?"

The rising of the slaves in Southampton, Virginia, in 1831, has not been forgotten by the American people. Nat Turner, a slave for life,— a Baptist minister,—entertained the idea that he was another Moses, whose duty it was to lead his people out of bondage. His soul was fired with the love of liberty, and he declared to his fellow-slaves that the time had arrived, and that "They who would be free, themselves must strike the blow." He knew that it would be "liberty or death" with his little band of patriots, numbering less than three hundred. He commenced the struggle for liberty; he knew his cause was just, and he loved liberty more than he feared death. He did not wish to take the lives of the whites; he only demanded that himself and brethren might be free. The slaveholders found that men whose souls were burning for liberty, however small their numbers, could not be put down at their pleasure; that something more than water was wanted to extinguish the flame. They trembled at the idea of meeting men in open combat, whose backs they had lacerated, whose wives and daughters they had torn from their bosoms, whose hearts were bleeding from the wounds inflicted by them. They appealed to the United States government for assistance. A company of United States troops was sent into Virginia to put down men whose only offense was, that they wanted to be free. Yes! northern men, men born and brought up in the free states, at the demand of slavery, marched to its rescue. They succeeded in reducing the poor slave again to his chains; but they did not succeed in crushing his spirit.

Not the combined powers of the American Union, not the slaveholders, with all their northern allies, can extinguish that burning desire of freedom in the slave's soul! Northern men may stand by as the body-guard of slaveholders. They may succeed for the time being in keeping the slave in his chains; but unless the slaveholders liberate their victims, and that, too, speedily, some modern Hannibal will make his appearance in the southern states, who will trouble the slaveholders as the noble Carthaginian did the Romans. Abolitionists deprecate the shedding of blood; they have warned the slaveholders again and again. Yet they will not give heed, but still persist in robbing the slave of liberty.

"But for the fear of northern bayonets, pledged for the master's protection, the slaves would long since have wrung a peaceful emancipation from the fears of their oppressors, or sealed their own redemption in blood." To the shame of the northern people, the slaveholders confess that to them they are "indebted for a permanent safe-guard against insurrection;" that "a million of their slaves stand ready to strike for liberty at the first tap of the drum;" and but for the aid of the north they would be too weak to keep them in their chains. I ask in the language of the slave's poet,

> "What! shall ye guard your neighbor still,
> While woman shrieks beneath his rod,
> And while he tramples down at will
> The image of a common God?
> Shall watch and ward be 'round him set,
> Of northern nerve and bayonet?"

The countenance of the people at the north has quieted the fears of the slaveholders, especially the countenance which they receive from northern churches. "But for the countenance of the northern church, the southern conscience would have long since awakened to its guilt: and the impious sight of a church made up of slaveholders, and called the church of Christ, been scouted from the world." So says a distinguished writer.

Slaveholders hide themselves behind the church. A more praying, preaching, psalm-singing people cannot be found than the slaveholders at the south. The religion of the south is referred to every day, to prove that slaveholders are good, pious men. But with all their pretensions, and all the aid which they get from the northern church, they cannot succeed in deceiving the Christian portion of the world. Their child-robbing, man-stealing, woman-whipping, chain-forging, marriage-destroying, slave-manufacturing, man-slaying religion, will not be received as genuine; and the people of the free states cannot expect to live in union with slaveholders, without becoming contaminated with slavery. They are looked upon as one people; they *are* one people; the people in the free and slave states form the "American Union." Slavery is a national institution. The nation licenses men to traffic in the bodies and souls of men; it supplies them with public buildings at the capital of the country to keep their victims in. For a paltry sum it gives the auctioneer a license to sell American men, women, and children, upon the auction-stand. The American slave-trader, with the constitution in his hat and his license in his pocket, marches his gang of chained men and women under the very eaves of the nation's capitol. And this, too, in a country professing to be the freest nation in the world. They profess to be democrats, republicans, and to believe in the natural equality of men; that they are "all created

with certain inalienable rights, among which are life, liberty, and the
pursuit of happiness." They call themselves a Christian nation; they
rob three millions of their countrymen of their liberties, and then talk
of their piety, their democracy, and their love of liberty; and, in the language of Shakespeare, say,

> *"And thus I clothe my naked villainy,*
> *And seem a saint when most I play the devil."*

The people of the United States, with all their high professions, are
forging chains for unborn millions, in their wars for slavery. With all
their democracy, there is not a foot of land over which the "stars and
stripes" fly, upon which the American slave can stand and claim protection. Wherever the United States constitution has jurisdiction, and
the American flag is seen flying, they point out the slave as a chattel, a
thing, a piece of property. But I thank God there is one spot in America upon which the slave can stand and be a man. No matter whether
the claimant be a United States president, or a doctor of divinity; no
matter with what solemnities some American court may have pronounced him a slave; the moment he makes his escape from under the
"stars and stripes," and sets foot upon the soil of CANADA, "the altar
and the god sink together in the dust; his soul walks abroad in her own
majesty; his body swells beyond the measure of his chains, that burst
from around him; and he stands redeemed, regenerated, and disen-
thralled, by the irresistible genius of universal emancipation."

But slavery must and will be banished from the United States soil:

> *"Let tyrants scorn, while tyrants dare,*
> *The shrieks and writhings of despair;*
> *The end will come, it will not wait,*
> *Bonds, yokes, and scourges have their date;*
> *Slavery itself must pass away,*
> *And be a tale of yesterday."*

But I will now stop, and let the slaveholders speak for themselves. I
shall here present some evidences of the treatment which slaves receive from their masters; after which I will present a few of the slave-
laws. And it has been said, and I believe truly, that no people were ever
found to be better than their laws. And, as an American slave,—as one
who is identified with the slaves of the south by the scars which I carry
on my back,—as one identified with them by the tenderest ties of nature,—as one whose highest aspirations are to serve the cause of truth

and freedom,—I beg of the reader not to lay this book down until he or she has read every page it contains. I ask it not for my own sake, but for the sake of three millions who cannot speak for themselves.

From the *Livingston County* (Alabama) *Whig* of Nov. 16, 1845:

"NEGRO DOGS.—The undersigned having bought the entire pack of Negro Dogs, (of the Hays & Allen stock,) he now proposes to catch runaway Negroes. His charge will be three dollars per day for hunting, and fifteen dollars for catching a runaway. He resides three and a half miles north of Livingston, near the lower Jones' Bluff road.

"William Gambrel.
"Nov. 6, 1845."

The *Wilmington* [North Carolina] *Advertiser* of July 13, 1838, contains the following advertisement:

"Ranaway, my Negro man Richard. A reward of $25 will be paid for his apprehension, DEAD or ALIVE. Satisfactory proof will only be required of his being killed. He has with him, in all probability, his wife Eliza, who ran away from Col. Thompson, now a resident of Alabama, about the time he commenced his journey to that state.

"D. H. Rhodes."

The *St. Louis Gazette* says—

"A wealthy man here had a boy named Reuben, almost white, whom he caused to be branded in the face with the words 'A slave for life.'"

From the *N. C. Standard,* July 28, 1838:

"TWENTY DOLLARS REWARD.—Ranaway from the subscriber, a negro woman and two children; the woman is tall and black, and *a few days before she went off* I BURNT HER ON THE LEFT SIDE OF HER FACE: I TRIED TO MAKE THE LETTER M, *and she kept a cloth over her head and face, and a fly bonnet over her head, so as to cover the burn;* her children are both boys, the oldest is in his seventh year; he is a *mulatto* and has blue eyes; the youngest is a black, and is in his fifth year.

"Micajah Ricks, Nash County."

"One of my neighbors sold to a speculator a negro boy, about 14 years old. It was more than his poor mother could bear. Her reason fled, and she became a perfect *maniac,* and had to be kept in close confinement. She would occasionally get out and run off to the neighbors. On one of these occasions she came to my house. With tears rolling down her cheeks, and her frame shaking with agony, she would cry out, *'Don't you hear him—they are whipping him now, and he is calling for me!'* This neighbor of mine, who tore the boy away from his poor mother, and thus broke her heart, was a *member of the Presbyterian church."—Rev. Francis Hawley, Baptist minister, Cole-brook, Ct.*

A colored man in the city of St. Louis was taken by a mob, and burnt alive at the stake. A bystander gives the following account of the scene:—

"After the flames had surrounded their prey, and when his clothes were in a blaze all over him, his eyes burnt out of his head, and his mouth seemingly parched to a cinder, someone in the *crowd,* more compassionate than the rest, proposed to put an end to his misery by shooting him, when it was replied, that it would be of no use, since he was already out of his pain. 'No,' said the wretch, 'I am not, I am suffering as much as ever,—shoot me, shoot me.' 'No, no,' said one of the fiends, who was standing about the sacrifice they were roasting, 'he shall not be shot; I would sooner slacken the fire, if that would increase his misery;' and the man who said this was, we understand, an *officer of justice."—Alton Telegraph.*

"We have been informed that the slave William, who murdered his master (Huskey) some weeks since, was taken by a party a few days since *from the sheriff* of Hot Spring, and *burned alive!* yes, tied up to the limb of a tree and a fire built under him, and consumed in a slow lingering torture."—*Arkansas Gazette,* Oct. 29, 1836.

The Natchez Free Trader, 16th June, 1842, gives a horrible account of the execution of the negro Joseph on the 5th of that month for murder.

"The body," says that paper, "was taken and chained to a tree immediately on the bank of the Mississippi, on what is called Union Point. The torches were lighted and placed in the pile. He watched unmoved the curling flame as it grew, until it began to entwine itself around and feed upon his body; then he sent forth cries of agony painful to the ear, begging someone to blow his brains out; at the same time surging with almost superhuman strength, until the staple with which the chain was fastened to the tree, not being well secured, drew out, and he leaped from the burning pile. At that moment the sharp ring of several rifles was heard, and the body of the negro fell a corpse to the ground. He was picked up by two or three, and again thrown into the fire and consumed."

"ANOTHER NEGRO BURNED.—We learn from the clerk of the Highlander, that, while wooding a short distance below the mouth of Red river, they were *invited to stop a short time and see another negro burned."—New Orleans Bulletin.*

"We can assure the Bostonians, one and all, who have embarked in the nefarious scheme of abolishing slavery at the south, that lashes will hereafter be spared the backs of their emissaries. Let them send out their men to Louisiana; they will never return to tell their sufferings, but they shall expiate the crime of interfering in our domestic institutions by being BURNED AT THE STAKE."—*New Orleans True American.*

"The cry of the whole south should be death, instant death, to the abolitionist, wherever he is caught."—*Augusta (Geo.) Chronicle.*

"Let us declare through the public journals of our country, that the question of slavery is not and shall not be open for discussion: that the system is too deep-rooted among us, and must remain forever; that the very moment any private individual attempts to lecture us upon its evils and immorality, and the necessity of putting means in operation to secure us from them, in the same moment his tongue shall be cut out and cast upon the dunghill."—*Columbia (S.C.) Telescope.*

From the *St. Louis Republican:*

"On Friday last the coroner held an inquest at the house of Judge Dunica, a few miles south of the city, over the body of a negro girl, about 8 years of age, belonging to Mr. Cordell. The body exhibited evidence of the most cruel whipping and beating we have ever heard of. The flesh on the back and limbs was beaten to a jelly—one shoulder-bone was laid bare—there were several cuts, apparently from a club, on the head—and around the neck was the indentation of a cord, by which it is supposed she had been confined to a tree. She had been hired by a man by the name of Tanner, residing in the neighborhood, and was sent home in this condition. After coming home, her constant request, until her death, was for bread, by which it would seem that she had been starved as well as unmercifully whipped. The jury returned a verdict that she came to her death by the blows inflicted by some persons unknown whilst she was in the employ of Mr. Tanner. Mrs. Tanner has been tried and acquitted."

A correspondent of the *N. Y. Herald* writes from St. Louis, Oct. 19:

"I yesterday visited the cell of Cornelia, the slave charged with being the accomplice of Mrs. Ann Tanner (recently acquitted) in the murder of a little negro girl, by whipping and starvation. She admits her participancy, but says she was compelled to take the part she did in the affair. On one occasion she says the child was tied to a tree from Monday morning till Friday night, exposed by day to the scorching rays of the sun, and by night to the stinging of myriads of mosquitoes; and that during all this time the child had nothing to eat, but was whipped daily. The child told the same story to Dr. McDowell."

From the *Carroll County Mississippian,* May 4th, 1844:

"Committed to jail in this place, on the 29th of April last, a runaway slave named Creesy, and says she belongs to William Barrow, of Carroll county, Mississippi. Said woman is stout built, five feet four inches high, and appears to be about twenty years of age; she has a band of iron on each ankle, and a trace chain around her neck, fastened with a common padlock.

"J. N. Spencer, Jailer.
"May 15, 1844."

The Savannah, Ga, *Republican* of the 13th of March, 1845, contains an advertisement, one item of which is as follows:—

"Also, at the same time and place, the following negro slaves, to wit: Charles, Peggy, Antonnett, Davy, September, Maria, Jenny, and Isaac—levied on as the property of Henry T. Hall, to satisfy a mortgage fi. fia. issued out of McIntosh Superior Court, in favor of the board of directors of the *Theological Seminary of the Synod of South Carolina and Georgia,* said Henry T. Hall. Conditions, cash.
"C. O'Neal, Deputy Sheriff, M. C."

In the *Macon* (Georgia) *Telegraph,* May 28, is the following:

"About the first of March last, the negro man RANSOM left me, without the least provocation whatever. I will give a reward of $20 dollars for said negro, if taken DEAD or ALIVE,—and if killed in any attempt an advance of $5 will be paid.

"Bryant Johnson.
"Crawford Co., Ga."

From the *Apalachicola Gazette*, May 9:

"ONE HUNDRED AND FIFTY DOLLARS REWARD.—Ranaway from my plantation on the 6th inst., three negro men, all of dark complexion.

"BILL is about five feet four inches high, aged about twenty-six, *a scar on his upper lip,* also *one on his shoulder,* and has been *badly cut on his arm*; speaks quick and broken, and a venomous look.

"DANIEL is about the same height, chunky and well set, broad, flat mouth, with a pleasing countenance, rather inclined to show his teeth when talking, no particular marks recollected, aged about twenty-three.

"NOAH is about six feet three or four inches high, twenty-eight years old, with rather a down, impudent look, insolent in his discourse, with a large mark on his breast, *a good many large scars,* caused by the whip, on his back—*has been shot in the back of his arm* with small shot. The above reward will be paid to anyone who will KILL the three, or fifty for either one, or twenty dollars apiece for them delivered to me at my plantation alive, on Chattahoochie, Early county.

"J. McDonald."

From the *Alabama Beacon*, June 14, 1845:

"Ranaway, on the 15th of May, from me, a negro woman named Fanny. Said woman is twenty years old; is rather tall, can read and write, and so forge passes for herself. Carried away with her a pair of ear-rings, a Bible with a red cover, is very pious. She prays a great deal, and was, as supposed, contented and happy. She is as white as most white women, with straight light hair, and blue eyes, and can pass herself for a white woman. I will give five hundred dollars for her apprehension and delivery to me. She is very intelligent.

"John Balch.
"Tuscaloosa, May, 29, 1845."

From the *N. O. Commercial Bulletin*, Sept. 30:

"TEN DOLLARS REWARD.—Ranaway from the subscribers, on the 15th of last month, the negro man Charles, about 45 years of age, 5 feet 6 inches high; red complexion, has had the *upper lid of his right eye torn*, and *a scar on his forehead*; speaks English only, and stutters when spoken to; he had on when he left, *an iron collar, the prongs of which he broke off before absconding*. The above reward will be paid for the arrest of said slave.

W. E. & R. Murphy,
"132 Old Raisin."

From the *N. O. Bee*, Oct. 5:

"Ranaway from the residence of Messrs. F. Duncom & Co., the negro Francois, aged from 25 to 30 years, about 5 feet 1 inch in height; the *upper front teeth are missing*; he had *chains on both of his legs*, dressed with a kind of blouse made of sackcloth. A proportionate reward will be given to whoever will bring him back to the bakery, No. 74, Bourbon street."

From the *N. O. Picayune* of Sunday, Dec. 17:

"COCK-PIT.—*Benefit of Fire Company No. 1, Lafayette.*—A cock-fight will take place on Sunday, the 17th inst., at the well-known house of the subscriber. As the entire proceeds are for the benefit of the fire company, a full attendance is respectfully solicited.

Adam Israng.
"Corner of Josephine and Tchoupitolas streets, Lafayette."

From the *N. O. Picayune:*

"TURKEY SHOOTING.—This day, Dec. 17, from 10 o'clock, A. M., until 6 o'clock, P. M., and the following Sundays, at M'Donoughville, opposite the Second Municipality Ferry."

The next is an advertisement from the *New Orleans Bee*, an equally popular paper.

"A BULL FIGHT, between a ferocious bull and a number of dogs, will take place on Sunday next, at 4¼ o'clock, P. M., on the other side of the river, at Algiers, opposite Canal street. After the bull fight, a fight will take place between a bear and some dogs. The whole to conclude by a combat between an ass and several dogs.

"Amateurs bringing dogs to participate in the fight will be admitted gratis. Admittance—Boxes, 50 cts.; Pit, 30 cts. The spectacle will be repeated every Sunday, weather permitting.

"Pepe Llulla."

The following is from the *Christian Index*, published at Penfield, Ga.:

"EXECUTORS' SALE.—Will be sold at the late residence of Jesse Perkins, deceased, late of Greene county, on Wednesday, the 1st of March next, the following property, VIZ:

Allen, about 30 years old; Claiborn, 25; Dick, 25; Anderson, 20; Asa, 15; Israel, 14; Harrison, 13; Nathan, 13; Sirena, 14; Adaline, 12; and Wesley, 10.

"Also, stock of hogs, stock of cattle, horses, corn, fodder and oats, plantation tools, &c.

"All sold as the property of the said Jesse Perkins, deceased, under his last will, in order to make a division among the legatees of said estate. Terms on day of sale.

> Vincent Sanford,
> Nicholas Perkins,
> Ex'rs."
> Jan. 15, 1848.

"The sale of about one hundred and sixty negroes, 44 mules and horses, 250 or 300 pork hogs, stock hogs, cattle, corn, fodder, oats, plantation tools, cooking utensils, &c., &c., will commence on Friday, the 10th of December, at the plantation of John Jones, deceased, near Warsaw, Sumter county.

"The sale will be continued on Monday, 13th of December, at the late residence of John Jones, deceased, in Greene county—say *one hundred and fourteen or fifteen negroes,* 33 mules and horses, 7 yoke of oxen, pork hogs, stock hogs, cattle, road-wagon, ox-wagon, horse-carts, cart-wheels, cotton-gins, corn, fodder, oats, plantation tools, &c.

"The terms of sale, twelve months credit. Notes with two approved securities—interest to be added from sale. All sums under $20, cash.

> William Jones, Jr.,
> John P. Evans,
> Adm'rs."
> ———*Eutaw (Ala.) Whig.*

268 The Civitas Anthology of African American Slave Narratives

"$100 REWARD—Will be given for the apprehension of my ne-gro (!) Edmund Kenney. He has *straight* hair, and complexion so nearly WHITE, that it is believed a stranger would suppose *there was no African blood in him.* He was with my boy Dick a short time since in Norfolk, *and offered him for sale,* and was apprehended, but es-caped under pretense of being a WHITE MAN.

Anderson Bowles."

————*Richmond Whig, 6th Jan.,* 1836.

"$50 REWARD will be given for the apprehension and delivery to me of the following slaves: Samuel, and Judy his wife, with their four children, belonging to the estate of Sacker Dubberly, deceased.

"I will give ten dollars for the apprehension of William Dubberly, a slave belonging to the estate. William is about nineteen years old, QUITE WHITE, and would not readily be mistaken for a slave.

John T. Lane."

————*Newbern Spectator,* 13*th March,* 1837.

"$100 REWARD.—Ran away from the subscriber, a bright mu-latto man slave, named Sam. *Light sandy hair, blue eyes, ruddy com-plexion*—is so WHITE as easily to pass for a free WHITE MAN.

Edwin Peck.

"Mobile, April 22, 1837."

"$50 REWARD.—I will give the above reward of fifty dollars for the apprehension and securing in any jail, so that I get him again, or delivering to me in Dandridge, E. Tennessee, my mulatto boy named Preston, about twenty years old. It is supposed he will try to pass as a *free* WHITE MAN.

John Roper.

"Oct. 12, 1838."

"RAN AWAY from the subscriber, working on the plantation of Colonel H. Tinker, a bright mulatto boy named Alfred. Alfred is about eighteen years of age, pretty well grown, has *blue eyes, light flaxen hair, skin disposed to freckle.* He will try to pass as FREE BORN.

S. G. Stewart.

"Greene County, Alabama."

"NOTICE.—The subscriber, living on Carroway Lake, on Hoe's Bayou, in Carroll Parish, sixteen miles on the road leading from

Bayou Mason to Lake Providence, is ready with a pack of dogs to hunt runaway negroes at any time. These dogs are well trained, and are known throughout the parish. Letters addressed to me at Providence will secure immediate attention.

"My terms are five dollars per day for hunting the trails, whether the negro is caught or not. Where a twelve hours' trail is shown and the negro not taken, no charge is made. For taking a negro, twenty-five dollars, and no charge made for hunting.

"James W. Hall."

The above advertisement we cut from the *Madison Journal*, published in Richmond, La., Nov. 26, 1847.

The following advertisement is from the Charleston. S. C., *Courier*, of Feb. 12, 1835:—

"FIELD NEGROES. By Thomas Gadsden. On Tuesday, the 17th inst., will be sold, at the north of the Exchange, at ten o'clock, A. M., a prime gang of *ten negroes*, accustomed to the culture of cotton and provisions, belonging to the Independent Church, in Christ's Church Parish. Feb. 6th."

In 1833, the Rev. Dr. Furman, of North Carolina, addressed a lengthy communication to the Governor of that State, expressing the sentiments of the Baptist church and clergy on the subject of slavery. This brief extract contains the essence of the whole:—"The right of holding slaves is clearly established in the Holy Scriptures, both by precept and example."

Not long after, Dr. Furman died. His legal representative thus advertises his property:—

"NOTICE. On the first Monday of February next, will be put up at *public auction*, before the *court-house*, the *following property*, belonging to the estate of the late Rev. Dr. Furman, viz:—

"A plantation or tract of land, on and in the Wataree Swamp. A tract of the first quality of fine land, on the waters of Black River. A lot of land in the town of Camden. A LIBRARY of a miscellaneous character, chiefly THEOLOGICAL. TWENTY-SEVEN NEGROES, some of them very prime. Two mules, one horse, and an old wagon."

EXTRACTS FROM THE AMERICAN SLAVE CODE.

The following are mostly abridged selections from the statutes of the slave states and of the United States. They give but a faint view of the cruel oppression to which the slaves are subject, but a strong one enough, it is thought, to fill every honest heart with a deep abhorrence of the atrocious system. Most of the important provisions here cited, though placed under the name of only one state, prevail in nearly all the states, with slight variations in language, and some diversity in the penalties. The extracts have been made in part from Stroud's *Sketch of the Slave Laws*, but chiefly from authorized editions of the statute books referred to, found in the Philadelphia Law Library. As the compiler has not had access to many of the later enactments of the several states, nearly all he has cited are acts of an earlier date than that of the present anti-slavery movement, so that their severity cannot be ascribed to its influence.

The cardinal principle of slavery, that the slave is not to be ranked among *sentient beings,* but among things—is an article of property, a chattel personal—obtains as undoubted law in all the slave states.*— *Stroud's Sketch,* p. 22.

The dominion of the master is as unlimited as is that which is tolerated by the laws of any civilized country in relation to brute animals— to *quadrupeds;* to use the words of the civil law.—*Ib.* 24.

Slaves cannot even contract matrimony.†—*Ib.* 61.

LOUISIANA.—A slave is one who is in the power of his master, to whom he belongs. The master may sell him, dispose of his person, his industry and his labor; he can do nothing, possess nothing, nor acquire anything, but what must belong to his master.—*Civil Code,* Art. 35.

Slaves are incapable of inheriting or transmitting property.—*Civil Code,* Art. 945; also Art. 175, and *Code of Practice,* Art. 103.

Martin's Digest, Act of June 7, 1806.—Slaves shall always be reputed and considered real estate; shall be as such subject to be mortgaged, according to the rules prescribed by law, and they shall be seized and sold as real estate.—*Vol. I.,* p. 612.

Dig. Stat. Sec 13.—No owner of slaves shall hire his slaves to themselves, under a penalty of twenty-five dollars for each offense.—*Vol. I.,* p. 102.

Sec. 15.—No slave can possess anything in his own right, or dispose

---

*In accordance with this doctrine, an act of Maryland, 1798, enumerates among articles of property, "*slaves, working beasts, animals of any kind, stock, furniture, plate, and so forth.*"—*Ib.* 23.
†A slave is not admonished for incontinence, punished for adultery, nor prosecuted for bigamy.—*Attorney General of Maryland, Md. Rep. Vol. I.* 561.

of the produce of his own industry, without the consent of his master.—p. 103.

Sec. 16.—No slave can be party in a civil suit, or witness in a civil or criminal matter, against any white person.—p. 103. *See also Civil Code*, Art. 117, p. 28.

Sec. 18.—A slave's subordination to his master is susceptible of no restriction, (except in what incites to crime,) and he owes to him and all his family, respect without bounds, and absolute obedience.—p. 103.

Sec. 25.—Every slave found on horseback, without a written permission from his master, shall receive twenty-five lashes.—p. 105.

Sec. 32.—Any freeholder may seize and correct any slave found absent from his usual place of work or residence, without some white person, and if the slave resist or try to escape, he may use arms, and if the slave *assault** and strike him, he may *kill* the slave.—p. 109.

Sec. 35.—It is lawful to fire upon runaway negroes who are armed, and upon those who, when pursued, refuse to surrender.—p. 109.

Sec. 38.—No slave may buy, sell, or exchange any kind of goods, or hold any boat, or bring up for his own use any horses or cattle, under a penalty of forfeiting the whole.—p. 110.

Sec. 7.—Slaves or free colored persons are punished with *death* for willfully burning or destroying any stack of produce or any building.—p. 115.

Sec. 15.—The punishment of a slave for striking a white person, shall be for the first and second offenses at the discretion of the court,[†] but not extending to life or limb, and for the third offense *death;* but for grievously wounding or mutilating a white person, *death* for the first offense; provided, if the blow or wound is given in defense of the person or *property of his master*, or the person having charge of him, he is entirely justified.

Act of Feb. 22, 1824, Sec. 2.—A slave for willfully striking his master or mistress, or the child of either, or his white overseer, so as to cause a bruise or shedding of blood, *shall be punished with death.*—p. 125.

Act of March 6, 1819.—Any person cutting or breaking any iron chain or collar used to prevent the escape of slaves, shall be fined not less than two hundred dollars, nor more than one thousand dollars,

---

*The legal meaning of assault is to *offer* to do personal violence.
[†]A court for the trial of slaves consists of one justice of the peace, and three freeholders, and the justice and one freeholder, i. e., *one half the court, may convict, though the other two are for acquittal.—Martin's Dig., I.* 646.

and be imprisoned not more than two years nor less than six months.—p. 64 of the session.

Law of January 8, 1813, Sec. 71.—All slaves sentenced to death or perpetual imprisonment, in virtue of existing laws, shall be paid for out of the public treasury, provided the sum paid shall not exceed $300 for each slave.

Law of March 16, 1830, Sec. 93.—The state treasurer shall pay the owners the value of all slaves whose punishment has been commuted from that of death to that of imprisonment for life, &c.

If any slave shall *happen* to be slain for refusing to surrender him or herself, contrary to law, or in unlawfully resisting any officer or *other person*, who shall apprehend, or endeavor to apprehend, such slave or slaves, &c., such officer or *other person so killing such slave as aforesaid*, making resistance, shall be, and he is by this act, *indemnified*, from any prosecution for such killing aforesaid, &c.—*Maryland Laws, act of* 1751, *chap* xiv., §9.

And by the negro act of 1740, of South Carolina, it is declared:

If any slave, who shall be out of the house or plantation where such slave shall live, or shall be usually employed, or without some white person in company with such slave, shall *refuse to submit* to undergo the examination of *any white* person, it shall be lawful for such white person to pursue, apprehend, and moderately correct such slave; and if such slave shall assault and strike such white person, such slave may be *lawfully killed!!*—2 *Brevard's Digest*, 231.

MISSISSIPPI. *Chapt.* 92, Sec. 110.—Penalty for any slave or free colored person exercising the functions of a minister of the gospel, thirty-nine lashes; but any master may permit his slave to preach on his own premises, no slaves but his own being permitted to assemble.—*Digest of Stat.*, p. 770.

Act of June 18, 1822, Sec. 21.—No negro or mulatto can be a witness in any case, except against negroes or mulattoes.—p. 749. *New Code*, 372.

Sec. 25.—Any master licensing his slave to go at large and trade as a freeman, shall forfeit fifty dollars to the state for the literary fund.

Penalty for teaching a slave to read, imprisonment one year. For using language having a *tendency* to promote discontent among free colored people, or insubordination among slaves, imprisonment at *hard labor*, not less than three, nor more than twenty-one years, or DEATH, at the discretion of the court.—*L. M. Child's Appeal*, p. 70.

Sec. 26.—It is *lawful* for *any* person, and the duty of every sheriff, deputy-sheriff, coroner and constable to apprehend any slave going at large, or hired out by him, or herself, and take him or her before a justice of the peace, who shall impose a penalty of not less than twenty dollars, nor more than fifty dollars, on the owner, who has permitted such slave to do so.

Sec. 32.—Any negro or mulatto, for using abusive language, or lifting his hand in opposition to any white person, (except in self-defense against a wanton assault,) shall, on proof of the offense by oath of such person, receive such punishment as a justice of the peace may order, not exceeding thirty-nine lashes.

Sec. 41—Forbids the holding of cattle, sheep or hogs by slaves, even with consent of the master, under penalty of forfeiture, half to the county, and half to the *informer.*

Sec. 42—Forbids a slave keeping a dog, under a penalty of twenty-five stripes; and requires any master who permits it to pay a fine of five dollars, and make good all damages done by such dog.

Sec. 43—Forbids slaves cultivating cotton for their own use, and imposes a fine of fifty dollars on the master or overseer who permits it.

Revised Code.—Every negro or mulatto found in the state, not able to show himself entitled to freedom, may be sold as a slave.—p. 389. The owner of any plantation, on which a slave comes without written leave from his master, and not on lawful business, may inflict ten lashes for every such offense.—p. 371.

ALABAMA.—*Aiken's Digest.* Tit. *Slaves, &c.,* Sec. 31.—For *attempting* to teach any free colored person, or slave, to spell, read or write, a fine of not less than two hundred and fifty dollars, nor more than five hundred dollars!—p. 397.

Sec. 35 and 36.—Any free colored person found with slaves in a kitchen, outhouse or negro quarter, without a written permission from the master or overseer of said slaves, and any slave found without such permission with a free negro on his premises, shall receive fifteen lashes for the first offense, and thirty-nine for each subsequent offense; to be inflicted by master, overseer, or member of any patrol company.—p. 397.

Toulmin's Digest.—No slave can be emancipated but by a *special* act of the Legislature.—p. 623.

Act Jan. 1st, 1823—Authorizes an agent to be appointed by the governor of the state, *to sell for the benefit of the state* all persons of color brought into the United States and within the jurisdiction of Alabama, *contrary to the laws of congress prohibiting the slave trade.*—p. 643.

GEORGIA.—*Prince's Digest*. Act Dec. 19, 1818.—Penalty for any free person of color (except regularly articled seamen) coming into the state, a fine of one hundred dollars, and on failure of payment to be sold as a slave.—p. 465.

Penalty for permitting a slave to labor or do business for himself, except on his master's premises, thirty dollars per week.—p. 457.

No slave can be a party to any suit against a white man, except on claim of his freedom, *and every colored person is presumed to be a slave, unless he can prove himself free.*—p. 446.

Act Dec. 13, 1792—Forbids the assembling of negroes under pretense of divine worship, contrary to the act regulating patrols, p. 342. This act provides that any justice of the peace may disperse any assembly of slaves which *may* endanger the peace; and every slave found at such meeting shall receive, *without trial,* twenty-five stripes!—p. 447.

Any person who sees more than seven men slaves without any white person, in a high road, may whip each slave *twenty* lashes.—p. 454.

Any slave who harbors a runaway, may suffer punishment to *any extent,* not affecting life or limb.—p. 452.

SOUTH CAROLINA.—*Brevard's Digest.*—Slaves shall be deemed sold, taken, reputed, and adjudged in law to be *chattels personal* in the hands of their owners and possessors, and their executors, administrators, and assigns, *to all intents, constructions and purposes whatever.*—Vol. ii., p. 229.

Act of 1740, in the preamble, states that "*many* owners of slaves and others that have the management of them do confine them *so closely to hard labor,* that they have *not sufficient time for natural rest,*" and enacts that no slave shall be compelled to labor more than *fifteen* hours in the twenty-four, from March 25th to Sept. 25th, or *fourteen* in the twenty-four for the rest of the year. Penalty from £5 to £20.—Vol. ii., p. 243.

[Yet, in several of the slave states, the time of work for *criminals* whose *punishment* is hard labor, is eight hours a day for three months, nine hours for two months, and ten for the rest of the year.]

A slave endeavoring to entice another slave to run away, if provision be prepared for the purpose of aiding or abetting such endeavor, shall suffer *death.*—pp. 233 and 244.

Penalty for cruelly scalding or burning a slave, cutting out his tongue, putting out his eye, or depriving him of any limb, a fine of £100. For beating with a *horse*-whip, cow-skin, switch or small stick, or putting irons on, or imprisoning a slave, *no penalty or prohibition.*— p. 241.

Any person who, not having lawful authority to do so, shall beat a slave, so as to disable him from *working,* shall pay fifteen shillings a day *to the owner,* for the slave's lost time, and the charge of his cure.—pp. 231 and 232.

A slave claiming his freedom may sue for it by some friend who will act as guardian, but if the action be judged groundless, said guardian shall pay *double* costs of suit, and such damages to the owner as the court may decide.—p. 260.

Any assembly of slaves or free colored persons, in a secret or confined place, for mental instruction, (even if white persons *are* present,) is an unlawful meeting, and magistrates must disperse it, breaking doors if necessary, and may inflict *twenty lashes* upon each slave or colored person present.—pp. 254 and 255.

Meetings for religious worship, before sunrise, or after 9 o'clock, P. M., unless a majority are white persons, are forbidden; and magistrates are required to disperse them.—p. 261.

A slave who lets loose any boat from the place where the owner has fastened it, for the first *offense shall receive thirty-nine lashes, and for the second shall have one ear cut off.*—p. 228.

James' Digest.—Penalty for *killing* a slave, on *sudden heat of passion,* or by *undue correction,* a fine of $500 and imprisonment not over six months.—p. 392.

NORTH CAROLINA.—*Haywood's Manual.*—Act of 1798, Sec. 3, enacts, that the killing of a slave shall be punished like that of a free man; *except* in the case of a slave *out-lawed,** or a slave *offering to resist* his master, or a slave *dying under moderate correction.*—p. 530.

Act of 1799.—Any slave set free, except for meritorious services, to be adjudged of by the county court, may be seized by any freeholder, committed to jail, *and sold to the highest bidder.*†—p. 525.

Patrols are not liable to the master for punishing his slave, unless their conduct clearly shows malice *against the master.*—*Hawk's Reps.,* vol. i., p. 418.

TENNESSEE.—*Stat. Law,* Chap. 57, Sec. 1.—Penalty on master for hiring to any slave his own time, a fine of not less than one dollar nor more than two dollars a day, *half* to the informer.—p. 679.

---

*A slave may be out-lawed when he runs away, conceals himself, and, to sustain life, kills a hog, or any animal of the cattle kind.—*Haywood's Manual,* p. 521.

†In South Carolina, *any* person may seize such freed man and keep him as his property.

Chap. 2, Sec. 102.—No slave can be emancipated but on condition of immediately removing from the state, and the person emancipating shall give bond, in a sum equal to the slave's value, to have him removed.—p. 279.

Laws of 1813. Chap. 35.—In the trial of slaves, the sheriff chooses the court, which must consist of three justices and twelve *slaveholders* to serve as jurors.

ARKANSAS.—*Rev. Stat.,* Sec. 4, requires the patrol to visit all places suspected of unlawful assemblages of slaves; and sec. 5 provides that any slave found at such assembly, or strolling about without a pass, *shall receive* any number of *lashes,* at the discretion of the patrol, not exceeding twenty.—p. 604.

MISSOURI.—*Laws, I.*—Any master may commit to jail, there to remain, at *his pleasure,* any slave who refuses to obey him or his overseer.—p. 309.

Whether a slave claiming freedom may even commence a suit for it, may depend on the decision of a single judge.—*Stroud's Sketch,* p. 78, note which refers to Missouri laws, I., 404.

KENTUCKY.—*Dig. of Stat.,* Act Feb. 8, 1798, Sec. 5.—No colored person may *keep* or *carry* gun, powder, shot, *club* or *other weapon,* on penalty of *thirty-nine lashes,* and forfeiting the weapon, which any person is authorized to take.

VIRGINIA.—*Rev. Code.*—Any emancipated slave remaining in the state more than a year, may be sold by the overseers of the *poor,* for the benefit of the *literary fund!*—Vol. i., p. 436.

Any slave or free colored person found at any school for teaching reading or writing, by day or night, may be whipped, at the discretion of a justice, not exceeding twenty lashes.—p. 424.

Suppl. Rev. Code.—Any white person assembling with slaves, for the *purpose* of teaching them to read or write, shall be fined, not less than 10 dollars, nor more than 100 dollars; or with free colored persons, shall be fined not more than fifty dollars, and imprisoned not more than two months.—p. 245.

By the revised code, *seventy-one* offenses are punished with *death* when committed by slaves, and by nothing more than imprisonment when by the whites.—*Stroud's Sketch,* p. 107.

Rev. Code.—In the trial of slaves, the court consists of five justices without juries, even in capital cases.—I., p. 420.

MARYLAND.—*Stat. Law,* Sec. 8.—Any slave, for rambling in the night, or riding horses by day without leave, or running away, may be punished by whipping, cropping, or branding in the cheek, or otherwise, not rendering him unfit for labor.—p. 237.

Any slave convicted of petty treason, murder, or *willful burning of dwelling houses,* may be sentenced *to have the right hand cut off, to be hanged in the usual manner, the head severed from the body, the body divided into four quarters, and the head and quarters set up in the most public place in the country where such fact was committed!!*—p. 190.

Act 1717, Chap. 13, Sec. 5—Provides that any free colored person marrying a slave, becomes a slave for life, except mulattoes born of white women.

DELAWARE.—*Laws.*—More than six men slaves, meeting together, not belonging to one master, unless on lawful business of their owners, may be whipped to the extent of twenty-one lashes each.—p 104.

UNITED STATES.—*Constitution.*—The chief proslavery provisions of the constitution, as is generally known, are, 1st, that by virtue of which the slave states are represented in congress for three-fifths of their slaves;* 2nd, that requiring the giving up of any runaway slaves to their masters; 3rd, that pledging the physical force of the whole country to suppress insurrections, i. e., attempts to gain freedom by such means as the framers of the instrument themselves used.

Act of Feb. 12, 1793—Provides that any master or his agent may seize any person whom he claims as a "fugitive from service," and take him before a judge of the U. S. court, or magistrate of the city or county where he is taken, and the magistrate, on proof, in support of the claim, to his satisfaction, must give the claimant a certificate authorizing the removal of such fugitive to the state he fled from.†

DISTRICT OF COLUMBIA.—The act of congress incorporating Washington city, gives the corporation power to prescribe the terms and conditions on which free negroes and mulattoes may reside in the city. *City Laws,* 6 and 11. By this authority, the city in 1827 enacted that any free colored person coming there to reside, should give the mayor satisfactory evidence of his freedom, and enter into bond with two freehold sureties, in the sum of five hundred dollars, for his good conduct, to be renewed each year for three years; or failing to do

---

*By the operation of this provision, twelve slaveholding states, whose white population only equals that of New York and Ohio, send to congress 24 senators and 102 representatives, while these two states only send 4 senators and 59 representatives.

†Thus it may be seen that a *man* may be doomed to slavery by an authority not considered sufficient to settle a claim of *twenty dollars.*

so, must leave the city, or be committed to the workhouse, for not more than one year, and if he still refuse to go, may be again committed for the same period, and so on.—*Ib.* 198.

Colored persons residing in the city, who cannot prove their title to freedom, shall be imprisoned as absconding slaves.—*Ib.* 198.

Colored persons found without free papers may be arrested as runaway slaves, and after two months' notice, if no claimant appears, must be advertised ten days, and sold to pay their jail fees.*—*Stroud,* 85, note.

The city of Washington grants a license to *trade in slaves,* for profit, as agent, or otherwise, for four hundred dollars.—*City Laws,* p. 249.

READER, you uphold these laws *while you do nothing for their repeal.* You *can do* much. You can take and read the antislavery journals. They will give you an impartial history of the cause, and arguments with which to convert its enemies. You can countenance and aid those who are laboring for its promotion. You can petition against slavery; you can refuse to vote for slaveholders or pro-slavery men, constitutions and compacts; can abstain from products of slave labor; and can use your social influence to spread right principles and awaken a right feeling. Be as earnest for freedom as its foes are for slavery, and you can diffuse an anti-slavery sentiment through your whole neighborhood, and merit "the blessing of them that are ready to perish."

THE FOLLOWING is from the old colonial law of North Carolina:

Notice of the commitment of runaways—viz., 1741, c. 24, §29. "An act concerning servants and slaves."

Copy of notice containing a full description of such runaway and his clothing.—The sheriff is to "cause a copy of such notice to be sent to the clerk or reader of each church or chapel within his county, who are hereby required to make publication thereof by setting up the same in some open and convenient place, near the said church or chapel, on every Lord's day, during the space of two months from the date thereof."

---

*The prisons of the district, built with the money of the nation, are used as storehouses of the slaveholder's human merchandize. "From the statement of the keeper of a jail at Washington, it appears that in five years, upwards of 450 colored persons were committed to the national prison in that city, for safe keeping, i. e., until they could be disposed of in the course of the *slave trade* besides nearly 300 who had been taken up as runaways."—*Miner's Speech in H. Rep.,* 1829.

1741, c. 24, §45.—"Which proclamation shall be published on a Sabbath day at the door of every church or chapel, or, for want of such, at the place where divine service shall be performed in the said county, by the parish clerk or reader, immediately after divine service; and if any slave or slaves, against whom proclamation hath been thus issued, stay out and do not immediately return home, it shall be lawful for any person or persons whatsoever to kill and destroy such slave or slaves by such way or means as he or she shall think fit, without accusation or impeachment of any crime for the same."

An Act in Relation to Free Negroes and Mulattoes.
Be it enacted by the General Assembly of the State of Missouri, as follows:

§1. No person shall keep or teach any school for the instruction of negroes or mulattoes, in reading or writing, in this state.

§2. No meeting or assemblage of negroes or mulattoes, for the purpose of religious worship or preaching, shall be held or permitted, where the services are performed or conducted by negroes, unless some sheriff, constable, marshal, police officer, or justice of the peace, shall be present during all the time of such assemblage, in order to prevent all seditious speeches, and disorderly and unlawful conduct of every kind.

§3. All meetings of negroes or mulattoes, for the purposes mentioned in the preceding sections, shall be considered unlawful assemblies, and shall be suppressed by sheriffs, constables, and other public officers.

§5. If any person shall violate the provisions of this act, he shall, for every such offense, be indicted and punished by fine not exceeding five hundred dollars, or by both fine and imprisonment.

Approved, February 16, 1847.

Mental Instruction Prohibited.
South Carolina may lay claim to the earliest movement in legislation on this subject. In 1740, while yet a province, she enacted this law:

"Whereas, the having of slaves taught to write, or suffering them to be employed in writing, may be attended with great inconveniences, Be it enacted, That all and every person and persons whatsoever, who shall hereafter teach, or cause any slave or slaves to be taught to write, or shall use or employ any slave as a scribe in any manner of writing whatsoever, hereafter taught to write, every such person or persons shall, for every such offense, forfeit the sum of one hundred pounds current money."—2 *Brevard's Digest*, 243.

Similar in Georgia, *by act of* 1770, except as to the penalty, which is twenty pounds sterling.—*Prince's Digest*, 455.

In the same state the following additional restraints were enacted in 1800:

"That assemblies of slaves, free negroes, mulattoes and mestizos, whether composed of all or any of such description of persons, or of all or any of the same and of a proportion of white persons, met together for the purpose of *mental instruction* in a confined or secret place, &c. &c., is (are) declared to be an unlawful meeting; and magistrates, &c. &c., are hereby required, &c., to enter into such confined places, &c. &c., to break doors, &c., if resisted, and to disperse such slaves, free negroes, &c. &c.; and the officers dispersing such unlawful assemblies *may inflict such corporal punishment, not exceeding twenty lashes, upon such slaves, free negroes, &c., as they may judge necessary, for* DETERRING THEM FROM THE LIKE UNLAWFUL ASSEMBLAGE IN FUTURE."—*Brevard's Digest*, 254.

TESTIMONIALS.

Boston, July 17, 1849.

In consequence of the departure for England of their esteemed friend and faithful co-laborer in the cause of the American slave, William W. Brown, the Board of Managers of the Massachusetts Anti-Slavery Society would commend him to the confidence, respect, esteem, and hospitality of the friends of emancipation wherever he may travel:—

1. Because he is a fugitive slave from the American house of bondage, and on the soil which gave him birth can find no spot on which he can stand in safety from his pursuers, protected by law.

2. Because he is a man, and not a chattel; and while as the latter he may at any time be sold at public vendue under the American star-spangled banner, we rejoice to know that he will be recognized and protected as the former under the flag of England.

3. Because for several years past, he has nobly consecrated his time and talents, at great personal hazard, and under the most adverse circumstances, to the uncompromising advocacy of the cause of his enslaved countrymen.

4. Because he visits England for the purpose of increasing, consolidating, and directing British humanity and piety against that horrible system of slavery in America, by which three millions of human beings, by creation the children of God, are ranked with four-footed beasts, and treated as marketable commodities.

5. Because he has long been in their employment as a lecturing agent in Massachusetts, and has labored to great acceptance and with great success; and from the acquaintance thus formed, they are enabled to certify that he has invariably conducted himself with great circumspection, and won for himself the sympathy, respect, and friendship of a very large circle of acquaintance.

In behalf of the Board of Managers,

Wm. Lloyd Garrison,
Robert F. Wallcut,
Samuel May, Jun.

Boston, July 18, 1849.

My dear friend,

Today you leave the land of your nativity, in which you have been reared and treated as a slave—a chattel personal—a marketable commodity—though it claims to be a republican and Christian land, the freest of the free, the most pious of the pious—for the shores of Europe; on touching which, your shackles will instantly fall, your limbs expand, your spirit exult in absolute personal freedom, as a man, and nothing less than a man. Since your escape from bondage, a few years since, you have nobly devoted yourself to the cause of the three millions of our countrymen who are yet clanking their chains in hopeless bondage—pleading their cause eloquently and effectively, by day and by night, in season and out of season, before the people of the Free States (falsely so called) of America, at much personal hazard of being seized and hurried back to slavery. Not to forsake that cause, but still more powerfully to aid it, by enlisting the sympathies, and consolidating the feelings and opinions of the friends of freedom and universal emancipation in the old world in its favor and against the atrocious slave system, do you bid farewell to the land of whips and chains today. God—the God of the oppressed, the poor, the needy, the defenseless—be with you, to guide, strengthen, aid and bless you abundantly! Three millions of slaves are your constituents, and you are their legitimate and faithful representative. With a mother, sister, and three brothers yet pining in hopeless servitude, with the marks of the slavedriver's lash upon your body, you cannot but "remember them that are in bonds as bound with them." Speak in trumpet tones to Europe, and call upon the friends of "liberty, equality, and fraternity" there, to cry, "Shame upon recreant and apostate America, which flourishes the Declaration of Independence in one hand, and the whip of the negro overseer in the other!" Challenge all that is free, all that is humane, all that is pious, across the Atlantic, to raise a united testimony against American slaveholders and their abettors, as the enemies of God and the human race! So shall that cry and that testimony cause the knees of the oppressor to smite together, the Bastille of slavery to tremble to its foundation, and the hearts of the American abolitionists to be filled with joy and inspired afresh! Tell Europe that our watchword is, "Immediate, unconditional emancipation for the slave"—and the motto we have placed on our anti-slavery banner is, "No Union with Slaveholders, religiously or politically!"

You have secured the respect, confidence, and esteem of thousands of the best portion of the American people; and may you continue faithful to the end, neither corrupted by praise, nor cast down by opposition, nor intimidated by any earthly power!

Accept the assurances of my warm personal regard, and believe me to be,

Your faithful co-laborer and unwearied advocate of the best of causes,

Wm. Lloyd Garrison,
President of the American Anti-slavery Society.

RESOLUTIONS OF THE COLORED CITIZENS OF BOSTON,
ADOPTED AT THE FAREWELL MEETING FOR
WILLIAM WELLS BROWN, JULY 16, 1849.

At a very large Meeting, held under the auspices of the Colored Citizens of Boston, at the Washingtonian Hall, on Monday evening, July 16th, 1849, a Silver Pitcher was presented to WM. LLOYD GARRISON, in grateful testimony of his undeviating devotion to the cause of universal emancipation. A Farewell was then tendered our brother, William Wells Brown, which was responded to on his part in an eloquent and affecting manner. The following Resolutions were adopted unanimously by the Meeting:—

Resolved,—That we bid our brother, William Wells Brown, God speed in his mission to Europe, and commend him to the hospitality and encouragement of all true friends of humanity.

Resolved,—That we forward by him our renewed protest against the American Colonization Society; and invoke for him a candid hearing before the British public, in reply to the efforts put forth there by Rev. Mr. Miller, or any other agent of said society.

Resolved,—That the views entertained by WILLIAM LLOYD GARRISON of the American Colonization Society meets the entire approbation and hearty concurrence of the Colored Citizens of Boston.

John T. Hilton, President.
Isaac H. Snowden,
Wm. T. Raymond,
Secretaries.

OPINIONS OF THE AMERICAN PRESS.

"NARRATIVE OF THE LIFE OF WILLIAM WELLS BROWN, A FUGITIVE SLAVE, WRITTEN BY HIMSELF."—We have received a copy of the above book, and have read it. Wells Brown, the Christian philanthropist, who fed, clothed, and otherwise assisted this panting fugitive, and to whom this little book is dedicated, is truly a happy man. This act of humanity, though among perhaps the hundreds in his life of a similar character, and in defiance of the law solemnly made, will, we doubt not, redound even to his everlasting happiness. The thoughts and feelings which naturally arise from the perusal of this little narrative, make all questions of party and sectarian rivalry appear utterly insignificant. We would that a copy of this book could be placed in every school library in Massachusetts. We hope and believe that it will be widely circulated.—*Boston Whig.*

"NARRATIVE OF THE LIFE OF WM. W. BROWN, A FUGITIVE SLAVE, WRITTEN BY HIMSELF."—This is the title of a book that has just made its appearance, and a copy of which is upon our table. The author is well known in this community as an able advocate of his enslaved countrymen, and his narrative will, we doubt not, get an extensive circulation. We have read the narrative, and consider it a fair history of the author's life and of slavery at the South. It is an interesting narrative, and should be read by every person in the country. We commend it to the public, and venture the assertion, that no one who takes it up and reads a chapter will lay it down until he has finished it.—*New Bedford Bulletin.*

"WILLIAM W. BROWN ON SLAVERY."—This talented American slave has delivered three lectures in this town, to crowded and very attentive audiences. We did not attend the lectures, but a friend informed us that they evinced much ability, and though rather spicy for the tender ears of those who despise a man on account of the color of his skin, they were not as much so as might to have been expected from one who has himself felt the scourge of involuntary servitude; not as much so as might have been expected from one who is hunted as a fugitive slave from one end of this notable "land of the free" to the other. We have read Mr. Brown's *Narrative* with great interest, and found it a thrilling tale. We would recommend it to all who feel any interest in the cause of the American slaves—it will quicken their devotion to the cause. We would advise the indifferent to read it—it will touch them with sympathy for the oppressed bondman.—*Lawrence Courier.*

NARRATIVE

OF THE

LIFE AND ADVENTURES

OF

HENRY BIBB,

AN AMERICAN SLAVE

WRITTEN BY HIMSELF.

WITH

AN INTRODUCTION

BY LUCIUS C. MATLACK.

NEW YORK:
PUBLISHED BY THE AUTHOR; 5 SPRUCE STREET.
1849.

5

———————

NARRATIVE OF THE LIFE

AND ADVENTURES OF

HENRY BIBB,

AN AMERICAN SLAVE,

WRITTEN BY HIMSELF

———————

INTRODUCTION

by Lucius C. Matlack

FROM THE MOST obnoxious substances we often see spring forth, beautiful and fragrant, flowers of every hue, to regale the eye, and perfume the air. Thus, frequently, are results originated which are wholly unlike the cause that gave them birth. An illustration of this truth is afforded by the history of American slavery.

Naturally and necessarily the enemy of literature, it has become the prolific theme of much that is profound in argument, sublime in poetry, and thrilling in narrative. From the soil of slavery itself have sprung forth some of the most brilliant productions, whose logical levers will ultimately upheave and overthrow the system. Gushing fountains of poetic thought, have started from beneath the rod of violence, that will long continue to slake the feverish thirst of humanity outraged, until swelling to a flood it shall rush with wasting violence over the ill-gotten heritage of the oppressor. Startling incidents authenticated, far excelling fiction in their touching pathos, from the pen of self-emancipated slaves, do now exhibit slavery in such revolting aspects as to secure the execrations of all good men and become a monument more enduring than marble, in testimony strong as sacred writ against it.

Of the class last named, is the narrative of the life of Henry Bibb, which is equally distinguished as a revolting portrait of the hideous slave system, a thrilling narrative of individual suffering, and a triumphant vindication of the slave's manhood and mental dignity. And all this is associated with unmistakable traces of originality and truthfulness.

To many, the elevated style, purity of diction, and easy flow of language, frequently exhibited, will appear unaccountable and contradictory, in view of his want of early mental culture. But to the thousands who have listened with delight to his speeches on anniversary and other occasions, these same traits will be noted as unequivocal evidence of originality. Very few men present in their written composition so perfect a transcript of their style as is exhibited by Mr. Bibb.

Moreover, the writer of this introduction is well acquainted with his handwriting and style. The entire manuscript I have examined and prepared for the press. Many of the closing pages of it were written by Mr. Bibb in my office. And the whole is preserved for inspection now. An examination of it will show that no alteration of sentiment, language, or style was necessary to make it what it now is, in the hands of the reader. The work of preparation for the press was that of orthography and punctuation merely, an arrangement of the chapters, and a table of contents—little more than falls to the lot of publishers generally.

The fidelity of the narrative is sustained by the most satisfactory and ample testimony. Time has proved its claims to truth. Thorough investigation has sifted and analyzed every essential fact alleged, and demonstrated clearly that this thrilling and eloquent narrative, though stranger than fiction, is undoubtedly true.

It is only necessary to present the following documents to the reader to sustain this declaration. For convenience of reference, and that they may be more easily understood, the letters will be inserted consecutively, with explanations following the last.

The best preface to these letters is the report of a committee appointed to investigate the truth of Mr. Bibb's narrative as he has delivered it in public for years past.

REPORT
of the undersigned, Committee appointed by the Detroit Liberty Association to investigate the truth of the narrative of Henry Bibb, a fugitive from Slavery, and report thereon:

Mr. Bibb has addressed several assemblies in Michigan, and his narrative is generally known. Some of his hearers, among whom were Liberty men, felt doubt as to the truth of his statements. Respect for their scruples and the obligation of duty to the public induced the formation of the present Committee.

The Committee entered on the duty confided to them, resolved on a searching scrutiny, and an unreserved publication of its result. Mr. Bibb acquiesced in the inquiry with a praiseworthy spirit. He attended before the Committee and gave willing aid to its object. He was subjected to a rigorous examination. Facts—dates—persons— and localities were demanded and cheerfully furnished. Proper inquiry—either by letter, or personally, or through the medium of friends was then made from *every* person, and in *every* quarter likely to elucidate the truth. In fact no test for its ascertainment, known to the sense or experience of the Committee, was omitted. The result was the collection of a large body of testimony from very diversified quarters. Slave owners, slave dealers, fugitives from slavery, political friends and political foes contributed to a mass of testimony, every part of which pointed to a common conclusion—the undoubted truth of Mr. Bibb's statements.

In the Committee's opinion no individual can substantiate the events of his life by testimony more conclusive and harmonious than is now before them in confirmation of Mr. Bibb. The main facts of his narrative, and many of the minor ones are corroborated beyond all question. No inconsistency has been disclosed nor anything revealed to create suspicion. The Committee have no hesitation in declaring their conviction that Mr. Bibb is amply sustained, and is entitled to public confidence and high esteem.

The bulk of testimony precludes its publication, but it is in the Committee's hands for the inspection of any applicant.

A. L. Porter,
C. H. Stewart,
Silas M. Holmes.
Committee.
Detroit, April 22, 1845.

FROM THE bulk of testimony obtained, a part only is here introduced. The remainder fully corroborates and strengthens that.

[NO. I. AN EXTRACT]
Dawn Mills, Feb. 19th, 1845.

Charles H. Stewart, Esq.
My Dear Brother:
Your kind communication of the 13th came to hand yesterday. I have made inquiries respecting Henry Bibb which may be of service to you. Mr. Wm. Harrison, to whom you allude in your letter, is here. He is a respectable and worthy man—a man of piety. I have just had an interview with him this evening. He testifies, that he was well acquainted with Henry Bibb in Trimble County, Ky., and that he sent a letter to him by Thomas Henson, and got one in return from him. He says that Bibb came out to Canada some three years ago, and went back to get his wife up, but was betrayed at Cincinnati by a col-

ored man—that he was taken to Louisville but got away—was taken again and lodged in jail, and sold off to New Orleans, or he, (Harrison,) understood that he was taken to New Orleans. He testifies that Bibb is a Methodist man, and says that two persons who came on with him last Summer, knew Bibb. One of these, Simpson Young, is now at Malden. ⋆ ⋆ ⋆

Very respectfully, thy friend,
Hiram Wilson.

[NO. 2.]
Bedford, Trimble Co., Kentucky.
March 4, 1845.

Sir:
Your letter under date of the 13th ult., is now before me, making some inquiry about a person supposed to be a fugitive from the South, "who is lecturing to your religious community on Slavery and the South."

I am pleased to inform you that I have it in my power to give you the information you desire. The person spoken of by you I have no doubt is Walton, a yellow man, who once belonged to my father, William Gatewood. He was purchased by him from John Sibly, and by John Sibly of his brother Albert G. Sibly, and Albert G. Sibly became possessed of him by his marriage with Judge David White's daughter, he being born Judge White's slave.

The boy Walton at the time he belonged to John Sibly, married a slave of my father's, a mulatto girl, and sometime afterwards solicited him to buy him; the old man after much importuning from Walton, consented to do so; and accordingly paid Sibly eight hundred and fifty dollars. He did not buy him because he needed him, but from the fact that he had a wife there, and Walton on his part promising everything that my father could desire.

It was not long, however, before Walton became indolent and neglectful of his duty; and in addition to this, he was guilty, as the old man thought, of worse offenses. He watched his conduct more strictly, and found he was guilty of disposing of articles from the farm for his own use, and pocketing the money.

He actually caught him one day stealing wheat—he had conveyed one sack full to a neighbor and whilst he was delivering the other my father caught him in the very act.

He confessed his guilt and promised to do better for the future— and on his making promises of this kind my father was disposed to keep him still, not wishing to part him from his wife, for whom he professed to entertain the strongest affection. When the Christmas Holidays came on, the old man, as is usual in this country, gave his negroes a week Holiday. Walton, instead of regaling himself by going about visiting his colored friends, took up his line of march for her Britannic Majesty's dominions.

He was gone about two years I think, when I heard of him in Cincinnati; I repaired thither, with some few friends to aid me, and succeeded in securing him.

He was taken to Louisville, and on the next morning after our arrival there, he escaped, almost from before our face, while we were on the street before the Tavern. He succeeded in eluding our pursuit, and again reached Canada in safety.

Nothing daunted he returned, after a lapse of some twelve or eighteen months, with the intention, as I have since learned, of conducting off his wife and eight or ten more slaves to Canada.

I got news of his whereabouts, and succeeded in recapturing him. I took him to Louisville and together with his wife and child, (she going along with him at her owner's request,) sold him. He was taken from thence to New Orleans—and from hence to Red River, Arkansas—and the next news I had of him he was again wending his way to Canada, and I suppose now is at or near Detroit.

In relation to his character, it was the general opinion here that he was a notorious liar, and a rogue. These things I can procure any number of respectable witnesses to prove.

In proof of it, he says his mother belonged to James Bibb, which is a lie, there not having been such a man about here, much less brother of Secretary Bibb. He says that Bibb's daughter married A. G. Sibly, when the fact is Sibly married Judge David White's daughter, and his mother belonged to White also and is now here, free.

So you will perceive he is guilty of lying for no effect, and what might it not be supposed he would do where he could effect anything by it.

I have been more tedious than I should have been, but being anxious to give you his rascally conduct in full, must be my apology. You are at liberty to publish this letter, or make any use you see proper of it. If you do publish it, let me have a paper containing the publication—at any rate let me hear from you again.

> Respectfully yours, &c.,
> Silas Gatewood.

To C. H. STEWART, ESQ.

[NO. 3. AN EXTRACT.]
Cincinnati, March 10, 1845.

My Dear Sir:
Mrs. Path, Nickens and Woodson did not see Bibb on his first visit, in 1837, when he stayed with Job Dundy, but were subsequently told of it by Bibb. They first saw him in May, 1838. Mrs. Path remembers this date because it was the month in which she removed from Broadway to Harrison street, and Bibb assisted her to remove. Mrs. Path's garden adjoined Dundy's back yard. While engaged in digging up flowers, she was addressed by Bibb, who was staying with Dundy, and who offered to dig them up for her. She hired him to do it. Mrs. Dundy shortly after called over and told Mrs. Path that he was a slave. After that Mrs. Path took him into her house and concealed him. While concealed, he astonished his good protectress by his ingenuity in bottoming chairs with cane. When the furniture was removed, Bibb insisted on helping, and was, after some remonstrances, permitted. At the house on Harrison street, he was employed for several days in digging a cellar, and was so employed when seized on Saturday afternoon by the constables. He held frequent conversations with Mrs. Path and others, in which he gave them the same account which he has given you.

On Saturday afternoon, two noted slave-catching constables, E. V. Brooks and O'Neil, surprised Bibb as he was digging in the cellar. Bibb sprang for the fence and gained the top of it, where he was seized and dragged back. They took him immediately before William Doty, a Justice of infamous notoriety as an accomplice of kidnappers, proved property, paid charges and took him away.

His distressed friends were surprised by his re-appearance in a few days after, the Wednesday following, as they think. He reached the house of Dr. Woods, (a colored man since deceased,) before daybreak, and stayed until dusk. Mrs. Path, John Woodson and others made up about twelve dollars for him. Woodson accompanied him out of town a mile and bid him "God speed." He has never been here since. Woodson and Clark saw him at Detroit two years ago.

Yours truly,
William Birney.

[NO. 4.]
Louisville, March 14, 1845.

Mr. Stewart.

Yours of the 1st came to hand on the 13th inst. You wished me to inform you what became of a boy that was in the work-house in the fall of '39. The boy you allude to went by the name of Walton; he had ran away from Kentucky some time before, and returned for his wife— was caught and sold to Garrison; he was taken to Louisiana, I think—he was sold on Red River to a planter. As Garrison is absent in the City of New Orleans at this time, I cannot inform you who he was sold to. Garrison will be in Louisville some time this Spring; if you wish me, I will inquire of Garrison and inform you to whom he was sold, and where his master lives at this time.

Yours,
W. Porter.

[NO. 5.]
Bedford, Trimble County, Ky.

C. H. Stewart, Esq.,

Sir.—I received your note on the 16th inst., and in accordance with it I write you these lines. You stated that you would wish to know something about Walton H. Bibb, and whether he had a wife and child, and whether they were sold to New Orleans. Sir, before I answer these inquiries, I should like to know who Charles H. Stewart is, and why you should make these inquiries of me, and how you knew who I was, as you are a stranger to me and I must be to you. In your next if you will tell me the intention of your inquiries, I will give you a full history of the whole case.

I have a boy in your county by the name of King, a large man and very black; if you are acquainted with him, give him my compliments, and tell him I am well, and all of his friends. W. H. Bibb is acquainted with him.

I wait your answer.

Your most obedient,
W. H. Gatewood.
March 17, 1845.

[NO. 6.]
Bedford, Kentucky, April 6th, 1845.

Mr. Charles H. Stewart.

Sir:—Yours of the 1st March is before me, inquiring if one Walton Bibb, a colored man, escaped from me at Louisville, Ky., in the Spring of 1839. To that inquiry I answer, he did. The particulars are these: He ran off from William Gatewood some time in 1838 I think, and was heard of in Cincinnati. Myself and some others went there and took him, and took him to Louisville for sale, by the directions of his master. While there he made his escape and was gone some time, I think about one year or longer. He came back it was said, to get his wife and child, so report says. He was again taken by his owner; he together with his wife and child was taken to Louisville and sold to a man who traded in negroes, and was taken by him to New Orleans and sold with his wife and child to some man up Red River, so I was informed by the man who sold him. He then ran off and left his wife and child and got back, it seems, to your country. I can say for Gatewood he was a good master, and treated him well. Gatewood bought him from a Mr. Sibly, who was going to send him down the river. Walton, to my knowledge, influenced Gatewood to buy him, and promised if he would, never to disobey him or run off. Who he belongs to now, I do not know. I know Gatewood sold his wife and child at a great sacrifice, to satisfy him. If any other information is necessary I will give it, if required. You will please write me again what he is trying to do in your country, or what he wishes the inquiry from me for.

Yours, truly,
Daniel S. Lane.

THESE LETTERS need little comment. Their testimony combined is most harmonious and conclusive. Look at the points established.

1. Hiram Wilson gives the testimony of reputable men now in Canada, who knew Henry Bibb as a slave in Kentucky.

2. Silas Gatewood, with a peculiar relish, fills three pages of foolscap, "being anxious to give his rascally conduct in full," as he says. But he vaults over the saddle and lands on the other side. His testimony is invaluable as an endorsement of Mr. Bibb's truthfulness. He illustrates all the essential facts of this narrative. He also labors to prove him deceitful and a liar.

Deceit in a slave is only a slight reflex of the stupendous fraud practiced by his master. And its indulgence has far more logic in its favor than the ablest plea ever written for slave holding, under ever such peculiar circumstances. The attempt to prove Mr. Bibb in the lie is a signal failure, as he never affirmed what Gatewood denies. With this offset, the letter under notice is a triumphant vindication of one whom he thought thereby to injure sadly. As Mr. Bibb has most happily acknowledged the wheat (see page [396],) I pass the charge of stealing by referring to the logic there used, which will be deemed convincing.

3. William Birney, Esq., attests the facts of Mr. Bibb's arrest in Cincinnati, and the subsequent escape, as narrated by him, from the declaration of eyewitnesses.

4. W. Porter, Jailor, states that Bibb was in the workhouse at Louisville, held and sold afterwards to the persons and at the places named in this volume.

5. W. H. Gatewood, with much Southern dignity, will answer no questions, but shows his relation to these matters by naming "King"— saying, "W. H. Bibb is acquainted with him," and promising "a full history of the case."

6. Daniel S. Lane, with remarkable straightforwardness and stupidity, tells all he knows, and then wants to know what they ask him for. The writer will answer that question. He wanted to prove by two or more witnesses the truth of his own statements; which has most surely been accomplished.

Having thus presented an array of testimony sustaining the facts alleged in this narrative, the introduction will be concluded by introducing a letter signed by respectable men of Detroit, and endorsed by Judge Wilkins, showing the high esteem in which Mr. Bibb is held by those who know him well where he makes his home. Their testimony expresses their present regard as well as an opinion of his past character. It is introduced here with the greatest satisfaction, as the writer is assured, from an intimate acquaintance with Henry Bibb, that all who know him hereafter will entertain the same sentiments toward him:

Detroit, March 10, 1845.
The undersigned have pleasure in recommending Henry Bibb to the kindness and confidence of Anti-slavery friends in every State. He has resided among us for some years. His deportment, his conduct, and his christian course have won our esteem and affection. The narrative of his sufferings and more early life has been thoroughly investigated by a Committee appointed for the purpose. They sought evidence respecting it in every proper quarter, and their report attested its undoubted truth. In this conclusion we all cordially unite.

H. Bibb has for some years publicly made this narrative to assemblies, whose number cannot be told; it has commanded public attention in this State, and provoked inquiry. Occasionally too we see persons from the South, who knew him in early years, yet not a word or fact worthy of impairing its truth has reached us; but on the contrary, everything tended to its corroboration.

Mr. Bibb's Anti-slavery efforts in this State have produced incalculable benefit. The Lord has blessed him into an instrument of great power. He has labored much, and for very inadequate compensation. Lucrative offers for other quarters did not tempt him to a more profitable field. His sincerity and disinterestedness are therefore beyond suspicion.

We bid him "God-speed," on his route. We bespeak for him every kind consideration.

> *H. Hallock, President of the Detroit Lib. Association.*
> *Cullen Brown, Vice-President.*
> *S. M. Holmes, Secretary.*
> *J. D. Baldwin,*
> *Charles H. Stewart,*
> *Martin Wilson,*
> *William Barnum.*

Detroit, Nov. 11, 1845.
The undersigned, cheerfully concurs with Mr. Hallock and others in their friendly recommendation of Mr. Henry Bibb. The undersigned has known him for many months in the Sab-

bath School in this City, partly under his charge, and can certify to his correct deportment, and commend him to the sympathies of Christian benevolence.

Ross Wilkins.

THE TASK now performed, in preparing for the press and introducing to the public the narrative of Henry Bibb, has been one of the most
pleasant ever required at my hands. And I conclude it with an expression of the hope that it may afford interest to the reader, support to the
author in his efforts against slavery, and be instrumental in advancing
the great work of emancipation in this country.

New York City, July 1st, 1849.

AUTHOR'S PREFACE

This work has been written during irregular intervals, while I have
been travelling and laboring for the emancipation of my enslaved
countrymen. The reader will remember that I make no pretension to
literature; for I can truly say, that I have been educated in the school of
adversity, whips, and chains. Experience and observation have been
my principal teachers, with the exception of three weeks schooling
which I have had the good fortune to receive since my escape from the
"grave yard of the mind," or the dark prison of human bondage. And
nothing but untiring perseverance has enabled me to prepare this volume for the public eye; and I trust by the aid of Divine Providence to
be able to make it intelligible and instructive. I thank God for the blessings of Liberty—the contrast is truly great between freedom and slavery. To be changed from a chattel to a human being, is no light matter,
though the process with myself practically was very simple. And if I
could reach the ears of every slave today, throughout the whole continent of America, I would teach the same lesson, I would sound it in the
ears of every hereditary bondman, "break your chains and fly for
freedom!"

It may be asked why I have written this work, when there has been so
much already written and published of the same character from other
fugitives? And, why publish it after having told it publicly all through
New England and the Western States to multiplied thousands?

My answer is, that in no place have I given orally the detail of my narrative; and some of the most interesting events of my life have never reached the public ear. Moreover, it was at the request of many friends of down-trodden humanity, that I have undertaken to write the following sketch, that light and truth might be spread on the sin and evils of slavery as far as possible. I also wanted to leave my humble testimony on record against this man-destroying system, to be read by succeeding generations when my body shall lie mouldering in the dust.

But I would not attempt by any sophistry to misrepresent slavery in order to prove its dreadful wickedness. For, I presume there are none who may read this narrative through, whether Christians or slavehold-ers, males or females, but what will admit it to be a system of the most high-handed oppression and tyranny that ever was tolerated by an en-lightened nation.

Henry Bibb

I

Sketch of my Parentage.—Early separation from my Mother.—Hard
Fare.—First Experiments at running away.—Earnest longing for Free-
dom.—Abhorrent nature of Slavery.*

I WAS BORN May 1815, of a slave mother, in Shelby County, Kentucky, and was claimed as the property of David White Esq. He came
into possession of my mother long before I was born. I was brought up
in the Counties of Shelby, Henry, Oldham, and Trimble. Or, more
correctly speaking, in the above counties, I may safely say, I was *flogged*
up; for where I should have received moral, mental, and religious instruction, I received stripes without number, the object of which was
to degrade and keep me in subordination. I can truly say, that I drank
deeply of the bitter cup of suffering and woe. I have been dragged
down to the lowest depths of human degradation and wretchedness,
by Slaveholders.

My mother was known by the name of Milldred Jackson. She is the
mother of seven slaves only, all being sons, of whom I am the eldest.
She was also so fortunate or unfortunate, as to have some of what is
called the slaveholding blood flowing in her veins. I know not how
much; but not enough to prevent her children though fathered by
slaveholders, from being bought and sold in the slave markets of the
South. It is almost impossible for slaves to give a correct account of
their male parentage. All that I know about it is, that my mother informed me that my father's name was JAMES BIBB. He was doubtless
one of the present Bibb family of Kentucky; but I have no personal
knowledge of him at all, for he died before my recollection.

The first time I was separated from my mother, I was young and
small. I knew nothing of my condition then as a slave. I was living with
Mr. White, whose wife died and left him a widower with one little girl,
who was said to be the legitimate owner of my mother, and all her children. This girl was also my playmate when we were children.

I was taken away from my mother, and hired out to labor for various
persons, eight or ten years in succession; and all my wages were expended for the education of Harriet White, my playmate. It was then
my sorrows and sufferings commenced. It was then I first commenced
seeing and feeling that I was a wretched slave, compelled to work un-

**Editor's note:* Bibb's *Narrative* was first published by the author, at 5 Spruce Street in
New York City, in 1849.

der the lash without wages, and often without clothes enough to hide my nakedness. I have often worked without half enough to eat, both late and early, by day and by night. I have often laid my wearied limbs down at night to rest upon a dirt floor, or a bench, without any covering at all, because I had nowhere else to rest my wearied body, after having worked hard all the day. I have also been compelled in early life, to go at the bidding of a tyrant, through all kinds of weather, hot or cold, wet or dry, and without shoes frequently, until the month of December, with my bare feet on the cold frosty ground, cracked open and bleeding as I walked. Reader, believe me when I say, that no tongue, nor pen ever has or can express the horrors of American Slavery. Consequently I despair in finding language to express adequately the deep feeling of my soul, as I contemplate the past history of my life. But although I have suffered much from the lash, and for want of food and raiment; I confess that it was no disadvantage to be passed through the hands of so many families, as the only source of information that I had to enlighten my mind, consisted in what I could see and hear from others. Slaves were not allowed books, pen, ink, nor paper, to improve their minds. But it seems to me now, that I was particularly observing, and apt to retain what came under my observation. But more especially, all that I heard about liberty and freedom to the slaves, I never forgot. Among other good trades I learned the art of running away to perfection. I made a regular business of it, and never gave it up, until I had broken the bands of slavery, and landed myself safely in Canada, where I was regarded as a man, and not as a thing.

The first time in my life that I ran away, was for ill treatment, in 1835. I was living with a Mr. Vires, in the village of Newcastle. His wife was a very cross woman. She was every day flogging me, boxing, pulling my ears, and scolding, so that I dreaded to enter the room where she was. This first started me to running away from them. I was often gone several days before I was caught. They would abuse me for going off, but it did no good. The next time they flogged me, I was off again; but after awhile they got sick of their bargain, and returned me back into the hands of my owners. By this time Mr. White had married his second wife. She was what I call a tyrant. I lived with her several months, but she kept me almost half of my time in the woods, running from under the bloody lash. While I was at home she kept me all the time rubbing furniture, washing, scrubbing the floors; and when I was not doing this, she would often seat herself in a large rocking chair, with two pillows about her, and would make me rock her, and keep off the flies. She was too lazy to scratch her own head, and would often make me scratch and comb it for her. She would at other times lie on her bed, in warm weather, and make me fan her while she slept, scratch and rub her feet; but after awhile she got sick of me, and preferred a maiden servant to do such business. I was then hired out again; but by this time I had become much better skilled in running away, and would make calculation to avoid detection, by taking with me a bridle. If anybody should see me in the woods, as they have, and asked "what are you doing here sir? you are a runaway?"—I said, "no, sir, I am looking for our old mare;" at other times, "looking for our cows." For such excuses I was let pass. In fact, the only weapon of self defense that I could use successfully, was that of deception. It is useless for a poor helpless slave, to resist a white man in a slaveholding State. Public opinion and the law is against him; and resistance in many cases is death to the slave, while the law declares, that he shall submit or die.

The circumstances in which I was then placed, gave me a longing desire to be free. It kindled a fire of liberty within my breast which has never yet been quenched. This seemed to be a part of my nature; it was first revealed to me by the inevitable laws of nature's God. I could see that the All-wise Creator, had made man a free, moral, intelligent and accountable being; capable of knowing good and evil. And I believed then, as I believe now, that every man has a right to wages for his labor; a right to his own wife and children; a right to liberty and the pursuit of happiness; and a right to worship God according to the dictates of his own conscience. But here, in the light of these truths, I was a slave, a prisoner for life; I could possess nothing, nor acquire anything but what must belong to my keeper. No one can imagine my feelings in my reflecting moments, but he who has himself been a slave. Oh! I have often wept over my condition, while sauntering through the forest, to escape cruel punishment.

> *No arm to protect me from tyrants aggression;*
> *No parents to cheer me when laden with grief.*
> *Man may picture the bounds of the rocks and the rivers,*
> *The hills and the valleys, the lakes and the ocean,*
> *But the horrors of slavery, he never can trace.*

The term slave to this day sounds with terror to my soul,—a word too obnoxious to speak—a system too intolerable to be endured. I know this from long and sad experience. I now feel as if I had just been aroused from sleep, and looking back with quickened perception at the state of torment from whence I fled. I was there held and claimed as a slave; as such I was subjected to the will and power of my keeper, in all respects whatsoever. That the slave is a human being, no one can deny. It is his lot to be exposed in common with other men, to the calamities of sickness, death, and the misfortunes incident to life. But unlike other men, he is denied the consolation of struggling against external difficulties, such as destroy the life, liberty, and happiness of himself and family. A slave may be bought and sold in the market like an ox. He is liable to be sold off to a distant land from his family. He is bound in chains hand and foot; and his sufferings are aggravated a hundred fold, by the terrible thought, that he is not allowed to struggle against misfortune, corporeal punishment, insults and outrages committed upon himself and family; and he is not allowed to help himself, to resist or escape the blow, which he sees impending over him.

This idea of utter helplessness, in perpetual bondage, is the more distressing, as there is no period even with the remotest generation when it shall terminate.

II

A fruitless effort for education.—The Sabbath among Slaves.—Degrading amusements.—Why religion is rejected.—Condition of poor white people.—Superstition among slaves.—Education forbidden.

IN 1833, I had some very serious religious impressions, and there was quite a number of slaves in that neighborhood, who felt very desirous to be taught to read the Bible. There was a Miss Davis, a poor white girl, who offered to teach a Sabbath School for the slaves, notwithstanding public opinion and the law was opposed to it. Books were furnished and she commenced the school; but the news soon got to our owners that she was teaching us to read. This caused quite an excitement in the neighborhood. Patrols* were appointed to go and break it up the next Sabbath. They were determined that we should not have a Sabbath School in operation. For slaves this was called an incendiary movement.

The Sabbath is not regarded by a large number of the slaves as a day of rest. They have no schools to go to; no moral nor religious instruc-

*Police peculiar to the South.

tion at all in many localities where there are hundreds of slaves. Hence they resort to some kind of amusement. Those who make no profession of religion, resort to the woods in large numbers on that day to gamble, fight, get drunk, and break the Sabbath. This is often encouraged by slaveholders. When they wish to have a little sport of that kind, they go among the slaves and give them whiskey, to see them dance, "pat juber," sing and play on the banjo. Then get them to wrestling, fighting, jumping, running foot races, and butting each other like sheep. This is urged on by giving them whiskey; making bets on them; laying chips on one slave's head, and daring another to tip it off with his hand; and if he tipped it off, it would be called an insult, and cause a fight. Before fighting, the parties choose their seconds to stand by them while fighting; a ring or a circle is formed to fight in, and no one is allowed to enter the ring while they are fighting, but their seconds, and the white gentlemen. They are not allowed to fight a duel, nor to use weapons of any kind. The blows are made by kicking, knocking, and butting with their heads; they grab each other by their ears, and jam their heads together like sheep. If they are likely to hurt each other very bad, their masters would rap them with their walking canes, and make them stop. After fighting, they make friends, shake hands, and take a dram together, and there is no more of it.

But this is all principally for want of moral instruction. This is where they have no Sabbath Schools; no one to read the Bible to them; no one to preach the gospel who is competent to expound the Scriptures, except slaveholders. And the slaves, with but few exceptions, have no confidence at all in their preaching, because they preach a proslavery doctrine. They say, "Servants be obedient to your masters;— and he that knoweth his master's will and doeth it not, shall be beaten with many stripes;—means that God will send them to hell, if they disobey their masters. This kind of preaching has driven thousands into infidelity. They view themselves as suffering unjustly under the lash, without friends, without protection of law or gospel, and the green eyed monster tyranny staring them in the face. They know that they are destined to die in that wretched condition, unless they are delivered by the arm of Omnipotence. And they cannot believe or trust in such a religion, as above named.

The poor and loafering class of whites, are about on a par in point of morals with the slaves at the South. They are generally ignorant, intemperate, licentious, and profane. They associate much with the slaves; are often found gambling together on the Sabbath; encouraging slaves to steal from their owners, and sell to them, corn, wheat, sheep, chickens, or anything of the kind which they can well conceal. For such offenses there is no law to reach a slave but lynch law. But if both parties are caught in the act by a white person, the slave is punished with the lash, while the white man is often punished with both lynch and common law. But there is another class of poor white people in the South, who, I think would be glad to see slavery abolished in self defense; they despise the institution because it is impoverishing and degrading to them and their children.

The slaveholders are generally rich, aristocratic, overbearing; and they look with utter contempt upon a poor laboring man, who earns his bread by the "sweat of his brow," whether he be moral or immoral, honest or dishonest. No matter whether he is white or black; if he performs manual labor for a livelihood, he is looked upon as being inferior to a slaveholder, and but little better off than the slave, who toils without wages under the lash. It is true, that the slaveholder, and non-slaveholder, are living under the same laws in the same State. But the one is rich, the other is poor; one is educated, the other is uneducated; one has houses, land and influence, the other has none. This being the case, that class of the non-slaveholders would be glad to see slavery abolished, but they dare not speak it aloud.

There is much superstition among the slaves. Many of them believe in what they call "conjuration," tricking, and witchcraft; and some of them pretend to understand the art, and say that by it they can prevent their masters from exercising their will over their slaves. Such are often applied to by others, to give them power to prevent their masters from flogging them. The remedy is most generally some kind of bitter root; they are directed to chew it and spit towards their masters when they are angry with their slaves. At other times they prepare certain kinds of powders, to sprinkle about their masters' dwellings. This is all done for the purpose of defending themselves in some peaceable manner, although I am satisfied that there is no virtue at all in it. I have tried it to perfection when I was a slave at the South. I was then a young man, full of life and vigor, and was very fond of visiting our neighbors' slaves, but had no time to visit only Sundays, when I could get a permit to go, or after night, when I could slip off without being seen. If it was found out, the next morning I was called up to give an account of myself for going off without permission; and would very often get a flogging for it.

I got myself into a scrape at a certain time, by going off in this way, and I expected to be severely punished for it. I had a strong notion of running off, to escape being flogged, but was advised by a friend to go to one of those conjurers, who could prevent me from being flogged. I went and informed him of the difficulty. He said if I would pay him a small sum, he would prevent my being flogged. After I had paid him, he mixed up some alum, salt and other stuff into a powder, and said I must sprinkle it about my master, if he should offer to strike me; this would prevent him. He also gave me some kind of bitter root to chew, and spit towards him, which would certainly prevent my being flogged. According to order I used his remedy, and for some cause I was let pass without being flogged that time.

I had then great faith in conjuration and witchcraft. I was led to believe that I could do almost as I pleased, without being flogged. So on the next Sabbath my conjuration was fully tested by my going off, and staying away until Monday morning, without permission. When I returned home, my master declared that he would punish me for going off; but I did not believe that he could do it, while I had this root and dust; and as he approached me, I commenced talking saucy to him. But he soon convinced me that there was no virtue in them. He became so enraged at me for saucing him, that he grasped a handful of switches and punished me severely, in spite of all my roots and powders.

But there was another old slave in that neighborhood, who professed to understand all about conjuration, and I thought I would try his skill. He told me that the first one was only a quack, and if I would only pay him a certain amount in cash, that he would tell me how to prevent any person from striking me. After I had paid him his charge, he told me to go to the cow-pen after night, and get some fresh cow manure, and mix it with red pepper and white people's hair, all to be put into a pot over the fire, and scorched until it could be ground into snuff. I was then to sprinkle it about my master's bedroom, in his hat and boots, and it would prevent him from ever abusing me in any way. After I got it all ready prepared, the smallest pinch of it scattered over a room, was enough to make a horse sneeze from the strength of it; but it did no good. I tried it to my satisfaction. It was my business to make fires in my master's chamber, night and morning. Whenever I could get a chance, I sprinkled a little of this dust about the linen of the bed, where they would breathe it on retiring. This was to act upon them as what is called a kind of love powder, to change their sentiments of anger, to those of love, towards me, but this all proved to be vain imagination. The old man had my money, and I was treated no better for it.

One night when I went in to make a fire, I availed myself of the opportunity of sprinkling a very heavy charge of this powder about my master's bed. Soon after their going to bed, they began to cough and sneeze. Being close around the house, watching and listening, to know what the effect would be, I heard them ask each other what in the world it could be, that made them cough and sneeze so. All the while, I was trembling with fear, expecting every moment I should be called and asked if I knew anything about it. After this, for fear they might find me out in my dangerous experiments upon them, I had to give them up, for the time being. I was then convinced that running away was the most effectual way by which a slave could escape cruel punishment.

As all the instrumentalities which I as a slave, could bring to bear upon the system, had utterly failed to palliate my sufferings, all hope and consolation fled. I must be a slave for life, and suffer under the lash or die. The influence which this had only tended to make me more unhappy. I resolved that I would be free if running away could make me so. I had heard that Canada was a land of liberty, somewhere in the North; and every wave of trouble that rolled across my breast, caused me to think more and more about Canada, and liberty. But more especially after having been flogged, I have fled to the highest hills of the forest, pressing my way to the North for refuge; but the river Ohio was my limit. To me it was an impassable gulf. I had no rod wherewith to smite the stream, and thereby divide the waters. I had no Moses to go before me and lead the way from bondage to a promised land. Yet I was in a far worse state than Egyptian bondage; for they had houses and land; I had none; they had oxen and sheep; I had none; they had a wise counsel, to tell them what to do, and where to go, and even to go with them; I had none. I was surrounded by opposition on every hand. My friends were few and far between. I have often felt when running away as if I had scarcely a friend on earth.

Sometimes standing on the Ohio River bluff, looking over on a free State, and as far north as my eyes could see, I have eagerly gazed upon the blue sky of the free North, which at times constrained me to cry out from the depths of my soul, Oh! Canada, sweet land of rest—Oh! when shall I get there? Oh, that I had the wings of a dove, that I might soar away to where there is no slavery; no clanking of chains, no captives, no lacerating of backs, no parting of husbands and wives; and where man ceases to be the property of his fellow man. These thoughts have revolved in my mind a thousand times. I have stood upon the lofty banks of the river Ohio, gazing upon the splendid steamboats, wafted with all their magnificence up and down the river, and I thought of the fishes of the water, the fowls of the air, the wild beasts of the forest, all appeared to be free, to go just where they pleased, and I was an unhappy slave!

But my attention was gradually turned in a measure from this subject, by being introduced into the society of young women. This for the time being took my attention from running away, as waiting on the girls appeared to be perfectly congenial to my nature. I wanted to be well thought of by them, and would go to great lengths to gain their affection. I had been taught by the old superstitious slaves, to believe in conjuration, and it was hard for me to give up the notion, for all I had been deceived by them. One of these conjurers, for a small sum agreed to teach me to make any girl love me that I wished. After I had paid him, he told me to get a bull frog, and take a certain bone out of the frog, dry it, and when I got a chance I must step up to any girl whom I wished to make love me, and scratch her somewhere on her naked skin with this bone, and she would be certain to love me, and would follow me in spite of herself; no matter who she might be engaged to, nor who she might be walking with.

So I got me a bone for a certain girl, whom I knew to be under the influence of another young man. I happened to meet her in the company of her lover, one Sunday evening, walking out; so when I got a chance, I fetched her a tremendous rasp across her neck with this bone, which made her jump. But in place of making her love me, it only made her angry with me. She felt more like running after me to retaliate on me for thus abusing her, than she felt like loving me. After I found there was no virtue in the bone of a frog, I thought I would try some other way to carry out my object. I then sought another counsellor among the old superstitious influential slaves; one who professed to be a great friend of mine, told me to get a lock of hair from the head of any girl, and wear it in my shoes: this would cause her to love me above all other persons. As there was another girl whose affections I was anxious to gain, but could not succeed, I thought, without trying the experiment of this hair. I slipped off one night to see the girl, and asked her for a lock of her hair; but she refused to give it. Believing that my success depended greatly upon this bunch of hair, I was bent on having a lock before I left that night let it cost what it might. As it was time for me to start home in order to get any sleep that night, I grasped hold of a lock of her hair, which caused her to screech, but I never let go until I had pulled it out. This of course made the girl mad with me, and I accomplished nothing but gained her displeasure.

Such are the superstitious notions of the great masses of southern slaves. It is given to them by tradition, and can never be erased, while the doors of education are bolted and barred against them. But there is a prohibition by law, of mental and religious instruction. The state of Georgia, by an act of 1770, declared "that it shall not be lawful for any number of free negroes, mulattoes or mestizos, or even slaves in company with white persons, to meet together for the purpose of mental instruction, either before the rising of the sun or after the going down of the same." *2d Brevard's Digest*, 254–5. Similar laws exist in most of the slave States, and patrols are sent out after night and on the Sabbath day to enforce them. They go through their respective towns to prevent slaves from meeting for religious worship or mental instruction.

This is the regulation and law of American Slavery, as sanctioned by the Government of the United States, and without which it could not exist. And almost the whole moral, political, and religious power of the nation are in favor of slavery and aggression, and against liberty and justice. I only judge by their actions, which speak louder than words. Slaveholders are put into the highest offices in the gift of the people in both Church and State, thereby making slaveholding popular and reputable.

III

My Courtship and Marriage.—Change of owner.—My first born.—
Its sufferings.—My wife abused.—My own anguish.

THE CIRCUMSTANCES of my courtship and marriage, I consider to be among the most remarkable events of my life while a slave. To think that after I had determined to carry out the great idea which is so universally and practically acknowledged among all the civilized nations of the earth, that I would be free or die, I suffered myself to be turned aside by the fascinating charms of a female, who gradually won my attention from an object so high as that of liberty; and an object which I held paramount to all others.

But when I had arrived at the age of eighteen, which was in the year of 1833, it was my lot to be introduced to the favor of a mulatto slave girl named Malinda, who lived in Oldham County, Kentucky, about four miles from the residence of my owner. Malinda was a medium sized girl, graceful in her walk, of an extraordinary make, and active in business. Her skin was of a smooth texture, red cheeks, with dark and penetrating eyes. She moved in the highest circle★ of slaves, and free people of color. She was also one of the best singers I ever heard, and was much esteemed by all who knew her, for her benevolence, talent and industry. In fact, I considered Malinda to be equalled by few, and surpassed by none, for the above qualities, all things considered.

It is truly marvellous to see how sudden a man's mind can be changed by the charms and influence of a female. The first two or three visits that I paid this dear girl, I had no intention of courting or marrying her, for I was aware that such a step would greatly obstruct my way to the land of liberty. I only visited Malinda because I liked her company, as a highly interesting girl. But in spite of myself, before I was aware of it, I was deeply in love; and what made this passion so effectual and almost irresistable, I became satisfied that it was reciprocal. There was a union of feeling, and every visit made the impression stronger and stronger. One or two other young men were paying attention to Malinda, at the same time; one of whom her mother was anxious to have her marry. This of course gave me a fair opportunity of testing Malinda's sincerity. I had just about opposition enough to make the subject interesting. That Malinda loved me above all others on earth, no one could deny. I could read it by the warm reception with which the dear girl always met me, and treated me in her mother's house. I could read it by the warm and affectionate shake of the hand, and gentle smile upon her lovely cheek. I could read it by her always giving me the preference of her company; by her pressing invitations to visit even in opposition to her mother's will. I could read it in the language of her bright and sparkling eye, penciled by the unchangeable finger of nature, that spake but could not lie. These strong temptations gradually diverted my attention from my actual condition and from liberty, though not entirely.

But oh! that I had only then been enabled to have seen as I do now, or to have read the following slave code, which is but a stereotyped law

★The distinction among slaves is as marked, as the classes of society are in any aristocratic community. Some refusing to associate with others whom they deem beneath them in point of character, color, condition, or the superior importance of their respective masters.

of American slavery. It would have saved me I think from having to lament that I was a husband and am the father of slaves who are still left to linger out their days in hopeless bondage. The laws of Kentucky, my native State, with Maryland and Virginia, which are said to be the mildest slave States in the Union, noted for their humanity, Christianity and democracy, declare that "Any slave, for rambling in the night, or riding horseback without leave, or running away, may be punished by whipping, cropping and branding in the cheek, or otherwise, not rendering him unfit for labor." "Any slave convicted of petty larceny, murder, or willfully burning of dwelling houses, may be sentenced to have his right hand cut off; to be hanged in the usual manner, or the head severed from the body, the body divided into four quarters, and head and quarters stuck up in the most public place in the county, where such act was committed."

At the time I joined my wife in holy wedlock, I was ignorant of these ungodly laws; I knew not that I was propagating victims for this kind of torture and cruelty. Malinda's mother was free, and lived in Bedford, about a quarter of a mile from her daughter; and we often met and passed off the time pleasantly. Agreeable to promise, on one Saturday evening, I called to see Malinda, at her mother's residence, with an intention of letting her know my mind upon the subject of marriage. It was a very bright moonlight night; the dear girl was standing in the door, anxiously waiting my arrival. As I approached the door she caught my hand with an affectionate smile, and bid me welcome to her mother's fireside. After having broached the subject of marriage, I informed her of the difficulties which I conceived to be in the way of our marriage; and that I could never engage myself to marry any girl only on certain conditions; near as I can recollect the substance of our conversation upon the subject, it was, that I was religiously inclined; that I intended to try to comply with the requisitions of the gospel, both theoretically and practically through life. Also that I was decided on becoming a free man before I died; and that I expected to get free by running away, and going to Canada, under the British Government. Agreement on those two cardinal questions I made my test for marriage.

I said, "I never will give my heart nor hand to any girl in marriage, until I first know her sentiments upon the all-important subjects of Religion and Liberty. No matter how well I might love her, nor how great the sacrifice in carrying out these God-given principles. And I here pledge myself from this course never to be shaken while a single pulsation of my heart shall continue to throb for Liberty." With this idea Malinda appeared to be well pleased, and with a smile she looked me in the face and said, "I have long entertained the same views, and this has been one of the greatest reasons why I have not felt inclined to enter the married state while a slave; I have always felt a desire to be free; I have long cherished a hope that I should yet be free, either by purchase or running away. In regard to the subject of Religion, I have always felt that it was a good thing, and something that I would seek for at some future period." After I found that Malinda was right upon these all-important questions, and that she truly loved me well enough to make me an affectionate wife, I made proposals for marriage. She very modestly declined answering the question then, considering it to be one of a grave character, and upon which our future destiny greatly depended. And notwithstanding she confessed that I had her entire affections, she must have some time to consider the matter. To this I of course consented, and was to meet her on the next Saturday night to decide the question. But for some cause I failed to come, and the next week she sent for me, and on the Sunday evening following I called on her again; she welcomed me with all the kindness of an affectionate lover, and seated me by her side. We soon broached the old subject of marriage, and entered upon a conditional contract of matrimony, viz: that we would marry if our minds should not change within one year; that after marriage we would change our former course and live a pious life; and that we would embrace the earliest opportunity of running away to Canada for our liberty. Clasping each other by the hand, pledging our sacred honor that we would be true, we called on high heaven to witness the rectitude of our purpose. There was nothing that could be more binding upon us as slaves than this; for marriage among American slaves, is disregarded by the laws of this country. It is counted a mere temporary matter; it is a union which may be continued or broken off, with or without the consent of a slaveholder, whether he is a priest or a libertine.

There is no legal marriage among the slaves of the South; I never saw nor heard of such a thing in my life, and I have been through seven of the slave states. A slave marrying according to law, is a thing unknown in the history of American Slavery. And be it known to the disgrace of our country that every slaveholder, who is the keeper of a number of slaves of both sexes, is also the keeper of a house or houses of ill-fame. Licentious white men, can and do, enter at night or day the lodging places of slaves; break up the bonds of affection in families; destroy all their domestic and social union for life; and the laws of the country afford them no protection. Will any man count, if they can be counted, the churches of Maryland, Kentucky, and Virginia, which have slaves connected with them, living in an open state of adultery, never having been married according to the laws of the State, and yet regular members of these various denominations, but more especially the Baptist and Methodist churches? And I hazard nothing in saying, that this state of things exists to a very wide extent in the above states.

I am happy to state that many fugitive slaves, who have been enabled by the aid of an over-ruling providence to escape to the free North with those whom they claim as their wives, notwithstanding all their ignorance and superstition, are not at all disposed to live together like brutes, as they have been compelled to do in slaveholding Churches. But as soon as they get free from slavery they go before some anti-slavery clergyman, and have the solemn ceremony of marriage performed according to the laws of the country. And if they profess religion, and have been baptized by a slaveholding minister, they repudiate it after becoming free, and are rebaptized by a man who is worthy of doing it according to the gospel rule.

The time and place of my marriage, I consider one of the most trying of my life. I was opposed by friends and foes; my mother opposed me because she thought I was too young, and marrying she thought would involve me in trouble and difficulty. My mother-in-law opposed me, because she wanted her daughter to marry a slave who belonged to a very rich man living nearby, and who was well known to be the son of his master. She thought no doubt that his master or father might chance to set him free before he died, which would enable him to do a better part by her daughter than I could! And there was no prospect then of my ever being free. But his master has neither died nor yet set his son free, who is now about forty years of age, toiling under the lash, waiting and hoping that his master may die and will him to be free.

The young men are opposed to our marriage for the same reason that Paddy opposed a match when the clergyman was about to pronounce the marriage ceremony of a young couple. He said "if there be any present who have any objections to this couple being joined together in holy wedlock, let them speak now, or hold their peace henceforth." At this time Paddy sprang to his feet and said, "Sir, I object to this." Every eye was fixed upon him. "What is your objection?" said the clergyman. "Faith," replied Paddy, "Sir I want her myself."

The man to whom I belonged was opposed, because he feared my taking off from his farm some of the fruits of my own labor for Malinda to eat, in the shape of pigs, chickens, or turkeys, and would count it not robbery. So we formed a resolution, that if we were prevented from joining in wedlock, that we would run away, and strike for Canada, let the consequences be what they might. But we had one consolation; Malinda's master was very much in favor of the match, but entirely upon selfish principles. When I went to ask his permission to marry Malinda, his answer was in the affirmative with but one condition, which I consider to be too vulgar to be written in this book. Our marriage took place one night during the Christmas holydays; at which time we had quite a festival given us. All appeared to be wide awake, and we had quite a jolly time at my wedding party. And notwithstanding our marriage was without license or sanction of law, we believed it to be honorable before God, and the bed undefiled. Our Christmas holydays were spent in matrimonial visiting among our friends, while it should have been spent in running away to Canada, for our liberty. But freedom was little thought of by us, for several months after marriage. I often look back to that period even now as one of the most happy seasons of my life; notwithstanding all the contaminating and heart-rending features with which the horrid system of slavery is marked, and must carry with it to its final grave, yet I still look back to that season with sweet remembrance and pleasure, that yet hath power to charm and drive back dull cares which have been accumulated by a thousand painful recollections of slavery. Malinda was to me an affectionate wife. She was with me in the darkest hours of adversity. She was with me in sorrow, and joy, in fasting and feasting, in trial and persecution, in sickness and health, in sunshine and in shade.

Some months after our marriage, the unfeeling master to whom I belonged, sold his farm with the view of moving his slaves to the State of Missouri, regardless of the separation of husbands and wives forever; but for fear of my resuming my old practice of running away, if he should have forced me to leave my wife, by my repeated requests, he was constrained to sell me to his brother, who lived within seven miles of Wm. Gatewood, who then held Malinda as his property. I was permitted to visit her only on Saturday nights, after my work was done, and I had to be at home before sunrise on Monday mornings or take a flogging. He proved to be so oppressive, and so unreasonable in punishing his victims, that I soon found that I should have to run away in self-defense. But he soon began to take the hint, and sold me to Wm.

Gatewood the owner of Malinda. With my new residence I confess that I was much dissatisfied. Not that Gatewood was a more cruel master than my former owner—not that I was opposed to living with Malinda, who was then the center and object of my affections—but to live where I must be eye witness to her insults, scourgings and abuses, such as are common to be inflicted upon slaves, was more than I could bear. If my wife must be exposed to the insults and licentious passions of wicked slavedrivers and overseers; if she must bear the stripes of the lash laid on by an unmerciful tyrant; if this is to be done with impunity, which is frequently done by slaveholders and their abettors, Heaven forbid that I should be compelled to witness the sight.

Not many months after I took up my residence on Wm. Gatewood's plantation, Malinda made me a father. The dear little daughter was called Mary Frances. She was nurtured and caressed by her mother and father, until she was large enough to creep over the floor after her parents, and climb up by a chair before I felt it to be my duty to leave my family and go into a foreign country for a season. Malinda's business was to labor out in the field the greater part of her time, and there was no one to take care of poor little Frances, while her mother was toiling in the field. She was left at the house to creep under the feet of an unmerciful old mistress, whom I have known to slap with her hand the face of little Frances, for crying after her mother, until her little face was left black and blue. I recollect that Malinda and myself came from the field one summer's day at noon, and poor little Frances came creeping to her mother smiling, but with large tear drops standing in her dear little eyes, sobbing and trying to tell her mother that she had been abused, but was not able to utter a word. Her little face was bruised black with the whole print of Mrs. Gatewood's hand. This print was plainly to be seen for eight days after it was done. But oh! this darling child was a slave; born of a slave mother. Who can imagine what could be the feelings of a father and mother, when looking upon their infant child whipped and tortured with impunity, and they placed in a situation where they could afford it no protection. But we were all claimed and held as property; the father and mother were slaves!

On this same plantation I was compelled to stand and see my wife shamefully scourged and abused by her master; and the manner in which this was done, was so violently and inhumanly committed upon the person of a female, that I despair in finding decent language to describe the bloody act of cruelty. My happiness or pleasure was then all blasted; for it was sometimes a pleasure to be with my little family even in slavery. I loved them as my wife and child. Little Frances was a pretty child; she was quiet, playful, bright, and interesting. She had a keen black eye, and the very image of her mother was stamped upon her cheek; but I could never look upon the dear child without being filled with sorrow and fearful apprehensions, of being separated by slaveholders, because she was a slave, regarded as property. And unfortunately for me, I am the father of a slave, a word too obnoxious to be spoken by a fugitive slave. It calls fresh to my mind the separation of husband and wife; of stripping, tying up and flogging; of tearing children from their parents, and selling them on the auction block. It calls to mind female virtue trampled under foot with impunity. But oh! when I remember that my daughter, my only child, is still there, destined to share the fate of all these calamities, it is too much to bear. If ever there was any one act of my life while a slave, that I have to lament over, it is that of being a father and a husband of slaves. I have the satisfaction of knowing that I am only the father of one slave. She is bone of my bone, and flesh of my flesh; poor unfortunate child. She was the first and shall be the last slave that ever I will father, for chains and slavery on this earth.

IV

My first adventure for liberty.—Parting Scene.—Journey up the river.—Safe arrival in Cincinnati.—Journey to Canada.—Suffering from cold and hunger.—Denied food and shelter by some.—One noble exception.—Subsequent success.—Arrival at Perrysburgh.—I obtained employment through the winter.—My return to Kentucky to get my family.

IN THE FALL or winter of 1837 I formed a resolution that I would escape, if possible, to Canada, for my Liberty. I commenced from that hour making preparations for the dangerous experiment of breaking the chains that bound me as a slave. My preparation for this voyage consisted in the accumulation of a little money, perhaps not exceeding two dollars and fifty cents, and a suit which I had never been seen or known to wear before; this last was to avoid detection.

On the twenty-fifth of December, 1837, my long anticipated time had arrived when I was to put into operation my former resolution, which was to bolt for Liberty or consent to die a Slave. I acted upon the former, although I confess it to be one of the most self-denying acts of my whole life, to take leave of an affectionate wife, who stood before me on my departure, with dear little Frances in her arms, and with tears of sorrow in her eyes as she bid me a long farewell. It required all the moral courage that I was master of to suppress my feelings while taking leave of my little family.

Had Malinda known my intention at that time, it would not have been possible for me to have got away, and I might have to this day been a slave. Notwithstanding every inducement which was held out to me to run away if I would be free, and the voice of liberty was thundering in my very soul, "Be free, oh, man! be free," I was struggling against a thousand obstacles which had clustered around my mind to bind my wounded spirit still in the dark prison of mental degradation. My strong attachments to friends and relatives, with all the love of home and birth-place which is so natural among the human family, twined about my heart and were hard to break away from. And withal, the fear of being pursued with guns and blood-hounds, and of being killed, or captured and taken to the extreme South, to linger out my days in hopeless bondage on some cotton or sugar plantation, all combined to deter me. But I had counted the cost, and was fully prepared to make the sacrifice. The time for fulfilling my pledge was then at hand. I must forsake friends and neighbors, wife and child, or consent to live and die a slave.

By the permission of my keeper, I started out to work for myself on Christmas. I went to the Ohio River, which was but a short distance from Bedford. My excuse for wanting to go there was to get work. High wages were offered for hands to work in a slaughter-house. But in place of my going to work there, according to promise, when I arrived at the river I managed to find a conveyance to cross over into a free state. I was landed in the village of Madison, Indiana, where steamboats were landing every day and night, passing up and down the river, which afforded me a good opportunity of getting a boat passage to Cincinnati. My anticipation being worked up to the highest pitch, no sooner was the curtain of night dropped over the village, than I secreted myself where no one could see me, and changed my suit ready for the passage. Soon I heard the welcome sound of a Steamboat coming up the river Ohio, which was soon to waft me beyond the limits of the human slave markets of Kentucky. When the boat had landed at Madison, notwithstanding my strong desire to get off, my heart trembled within me in view of the great danger to which I was exposed in taking passage on board of a Southern steamboat; hence before I took passage, I kneeled down before the Great I Am, and prayed for his aid and protection, which He bountifully bestowed even beyond my expectation; for I felt myself to be unworthy. I then stept boldly on the deck of this splendid swift-running Steamer, bound for the city of Cincinnati. This being the first voyage that I had ever taken on board of a Steamboat, I was filled with fear and excitement, knowing that I was surrounded by the vilest enemies of God and man, liable to be seized and bound hand and foot, by any white man, and taken back into captivity. But I crowded myself back from the light among the deck passengers, where it would be difficult to distinguish me from a white man. Every time during the night that the mate came round with a light after the hands, I was afraid he would see I was a colored man, and take me up; hence I kept from the light as much as possible. Some men love darkness rather than light, because their deeds are evil; but this was not the case with myself; it was to avoid detection in doing right. This was one of the instances of my adventures that my affinity with the Anglo-Saxon race, and even slaveholders, worked well for my escape. But no thanks to them for it. While in their midst they have not only robbed me of my labor and liberty, but they have almost entirely robbed me of my dark complexion. Being so near the color of a slaveholder, they could not, or did not find me out that night among the white passengers. There was one of the deck hands on board called out on his watch, whose hammock was swinging up near by me. I asked him if he would let me lie in it. He said if I would pay him twenty-five cents that I might lie in it until day. I readily paid him the price and got into the hammock. No one could see my face to know whether I was white or colored, while I was in the hammock; but I never closed my eyes for sleep that night. I had often heard of explosions on board of Steamboats; and every time the boat landed, and blowed off steam, I was afraid the boilers had bursted and we should all be killed; but I lived through the night amid the many dangers to which I was exposed. I still maintained my position in the hammock, until the next morning about 8 o'clock, when I heard the passengers saying the boat was near Cincinnati; and by this time I supposed that the attention of the people would be turned to the city, and I might pass off unnoticed.

There were no questions asked me while on board the boat. The boat landed about 9 o'clock in the morning in Cincinnati, and I waited until after most of the passengers had gone off of the boat; I then walked as gracefully up street as if I was not running away, until I had got pretty well up Broadway. My object was to go to Canada, but having no knowledge of the road, it was necessary for me to make some inquiry before I left the city. I was afraid to ask a white person, and I could see no colored person to ask. But fortunately for me I found a company of little boys at play in the street, and through these little boys, by asking them indirect questions, I found the residence of a colored man.

"Boys, can you tell me where that old colored man lives who saws wood, and works at jobs around the streets?"

"What is his name?" said one of the boys.

"I forget."

"Is it old Job Dundy?"

"Is Dundy a colored man?"

"Yes, sir."

"That is the very man I am looking for; will you show me where he lives?"

"Yes," said the little boy, and pointed me out the house.

Mr. D. invited me in, and I found him to be a true friend. He asked me if I was a slave from Kentucky, and if I ever intended to go back into slavery? Not knowing yet whether he was truly in favor of slaves running away, I told him I had just come over to spend my Christmas Holydays, and that I was going back. His reply was, "my son, I would never go back if I was in your place; you have a right to your liberty." I then asked him how I should get my freedom? He referred me to Canada, over which waved freedom's flag, defended by the British Government, upon whose soil there cannot be the foot print of a slave.

He then commenced telling me of the facilities for my escape to Canada; of the Abolitionists; of the Abolition Societies, and of their fidelity to the cause of suffering humanity. This was the first time in my life that ever I had heard of such people being in existence as the Abolitionists. I supposed that they were a different race of people. He conducted me to the house of one of these warm-hearted friends of God and the slave. I found him willing to aid a poor fugitive on his way to Canada, even to the dividing of the last cent, or morsel of bread if necessary.

These kind friends gave me something to eat, and started me on my way to Canada, with a recommendation to a friend on my way. This was the commencement of what was called the under ground rail road to Canada. I walked with bold courage, trusting in the arm of Omnipotence; guided by the unchangeable North Star by night, and inspired by an elevated thought that I was fleeing from a land of slavery and oppression, bidding farewell to handcuffs, whips, thumb-screws and chains.

I travelled on until I had arrived at the place where I was directed to call on an Abolitionist, but I made no stop: so great were my fears of being pursued by the pro-slavery hunting dogs of the South. I prosecuted my journey vigorously for nearly forty-eight hours without food or rest, struggling against external difficulties such as no one can imagine who has never experienced the same: not knowing what moment I might be captured while travelling among strangers, through cold and fear, breasting the north winds, being thinly clad, pelted by the snow storms through the dark hours of the night, and not a house in which I could enter to shelter me from the storm.

The second night from Cincinnati, about midnight, I thought that I should freeze; my shoes were worn through, and my feet were exposed to the bare ground. I approached a house on the roadside, knocked at the door, and asked admission to their fire, but was refused. I went to the next house, and was refused the privilege of their fireside, to prevent my freezing. This I thought was hard treatment among the human family. But—

"Behind a frowning Providence there was a smiling face,"

which soon shed beams of light upon unworthy me.

The next morning I was still found struggling on my way, faint, hungry, lame, and rest-broken. I could see people taking breakfast from the roadside, but I did not dare to enter their houses to get my breakfast, for neither love nor money. In passing a low cottage, I saw the breakfast table spread with all its bounties, and I could see no male person about the house; the temptation for food was greater than I could resist.

I saw a lady about the table, and I thought that if she was ever so much disposed to take me up, that she would have to catch and hold me, and that would have been impossible. I stepped up to the door with my hat off, and asked her if she would be good enough to sell me a sixpence worth of bread and meat. She cut off a piece and brought it to me; I thanked her for it, and handed her the pay, but instead of receiving it, she burst into tears, and said "never mind the money," but gently turned away bidding me go on my journey. This was altogether unexpected to me: I had found a friend in the time of need among strangers, and nothing could be more cheering in the day of trouble than this. When I left that place I started with bolder courage. The next night I put up at a tavern, and continued stopping at public houses until my means were about gone. When I got to the Black Swamp in the county of Wood, Ohio, I stopped one night at a hotel, after travelling all day through mud and snow; but I soon found that I should not be able to pay my bill. This was about the time that the "wild-cat banks" were in a flourishing state, and "shin plasters"* in abundance; they would charge a dollar for one night's lodging.

After I had found out this, I slipped out of the bar room into the kitchen where the landlady was getting supper; as she had quite a number of travellers to cook for that night, I told her if she would accept my services, I would assist her in getting supper; that I was a cook. She very readily accepted the offer, and I went to work.

She was very much pleased with my work, and the next morning I helped her to get breakfast. She then wanted to hire me for all winter, but I refused for fear I might be pursued. My excuse to her was that I had a brother living in Detroit, whom I was going to see on some important business, and after I got that business attended to, I would come back and work for them all winter.

When I started the second morning they paid me fifty cents beside my board, with the understanding that I was to return; but I have not gone back yet.

I arrived the next morning in the village of Perrysburgh, where I found quite a settlement of colored people, many of whom were fugitive slaves. I made my case known to them and they sympathized with me. I was a stranger, and they took me in and persuaded me to spend the winter in Perrysburgh, where I could get employment and go to Canada the next spring, in a steamboat which ran from Perrysburgh, if I thought it proper so to do.

I got a job of chopping wood during that winter which enabled me to purchase myself a suit, and after paying my board the next spring, I had saved fifteen dollars in cash. My intention was to go back to Kentucky after my wife.

When I got ready to start, which was about the first of May, my friends all persuaded me not to go, but to get some other person to go, for fear I might be caught and sold off from my family into slavery for-

*Nickname for temporary paper money.

ever. But I could not refrain from going back myself, believing that I could accomplish it better than a stranger.

The money that I had would not pass in the South, and for the purpose of getting it off to a good advantage, I took a steamboat passage to Detroit, Michigan, and there I spent all my money for dry goods, to peddle out on my way back through the State of Ohio. I also purchased myself a pair of false whiskers to put on when I got back to Kentucky, to prevent anyone from knowing me after night, should they see me. I then started back after my little family.

V

My safe arrival at Kentucky.—Surprise and delight to find my family.—Plan for their escape projected.—Return to Cincinnati.—My betrayal by traitors.—Imprisonment in Covington, Kentucky.—Return to slavery.—Infamous proposal of the slave catchers.—My reply.

I SUCCEEDED very well in selling out my goods, and when I arrived in Cincinnati, I called on some of my friends who had aided me on my first escape. They also opposed me in going back only for my own good. But it has ever been characteristic of me to persevere in what I undertake.

I took a Steamboat passage which would bring me to where I should want to land about dark, so as to give me a chance to find my family during the night if possible. The boat landed me at the proper place, and at the proper time accordingly. This landing was about six miles from Bedford, where my mother and wife lived, but with different families. My mother was the cook at a tavern, in Bedford. When I approached the house where mother was living, I remembered where she slept in the kitchen; her bed was near the window.

It was a bright moonlight night, and in looking through the kitchen window, I saw a person lying in bed about where my mother had formerly slept. I rapped on the glass which awakened the person in whom I recognized my dear mother, but she knew me not, as I was dressed in disguise with my false whiskers on; but she came to the window and asked who I was and what I wanted. But when I took off my false whiskers, and spoke to her, she knew my voice, and quickly sprang to the door, clasping my hand, exclaiming, "Oh! is this my son," drawing me into the room; where I was so fortunate as to find Malinda, and little Frances, my wife and child, whom I had left to find the fair climes of liberty, and whom I was then seeking to rescue from perpetual slavery.

They never expected to see me again in this life. I am entirely unable to describe what my feelings were at that time. It was almost like the return of the prodigal son. There was weeping and rejoicing. They were filled with surprise and fear; with sadness and joy. The sensation of joy at that moment flashed like lightning over my afflicted mind, mingled with a thousand dreadful apprehensions, that none but a heart-wounded slave father and husband like myself can possibly imagine. After talking the matter over, we decided it was not best to start with my family that night, as it was very uncertain whether we should get a boat passage immediately. And in case of failure, if Malinda should get back even before daylight the next morning, it would have excited suspicion against her, as it was not customary for slaves to leave home at that stage of the week without permission. Hence we thought it would be the most effectual way for her to escape, to start on Saturday night; this being a night on which the slaves of Kentucky are permitted to visit around among their friends, and are often allowed to stay until the afternoon on Sabbath day.

I gave Malinda money to pay her passage on board of a Steamboat to Cincinnati, as it was not safe for me to wait for her until Saturday night; but she was to meet me in Cincinnati, if possible, the next Sunday. Her father was to go with her to the Ohio River on Saturday night, and if a boat passed up during the night she was to get on board at Madison, and come to Cincinnati. If she should fail in getting off that night, she was to try it the next Saturday night. This was the understanding when we separated. This we thought was the best plan for her escape, as there had been so much excitement caused by my running away.

The owners of my wife were very much afraid that she would follow me; and to prevent her they had told her and other slaves that I had been persuaded off by the Abolitionists, who had promised to set me free, but had sold me off to New Orleans. They told the slaves to beware of the abolitionists, that their object was to decoy off slaves and then sell them off in New Orleans. Some of them believed this, and others believed it not; and the owners of my wife were more watchful over her than they had ever been before as she was unbelieving.

This was in the month of June, 1838. I left Malinda on a bright but lonesome Wednesday night. When I arrived at the river Ohio, I found a small craft chained to a tree, in which I ferried myself across the stream.

I succeeded in getting a Steamboat passage back to Cincinnati, where I put up with one of my abolition friends who knew that I had gone after my family, and who appeared to be much surprised to see me again. I was soon visited by several friends who knew of my having gone back after my family. They wished to know why I had not brought back my family with me; but after they understood the plan, and that my family was expected to be in Cincinnati within a few days, they thought it the best and safest plan for us to take a stage passage out to Lake Erie. But being short of money, I was not able to pay my passage in the stage, even if it would have prevented me from being caught by the slave hunters of Cincinnati, or save me from being taken back into bondage for life.

These friends proposed helping me by subscription; I accepted their kind offer, but in going among friends to solicit aid for me, they happened to get among traitors, and kidnappers, both white and colored men, who made their living by that kind of business. Several persons called on me and made me small donations, and among them two white men came in professing to be my friends. They told me not to be afraid of them, they were abolitionists. They asked me a great many questions. They wanted to know if I needed any help? and they wanted to know if it could be possible that a man so near white as myself could be a slave? Could it be possible that men would make slaves of their own children? They expressed great sympathy for me, and gave me fifty cents each; by this they gained my confidence. They asked my master's name; where he lived, &c. After which they left the room, bidding me God speed. These traitors, or land pirates, took passage on board of the first Steamboat down the river, in search of my owners. When they found them, they got a reward of three hundred dollars offered for the re-capture of this "stray" which they had so long and faithfully been hunting, by day and by night, by land and by water, with dogs and with guns, but all without success. This being the last and only chance for dragging me back into hopeless bondage, time and money was no object when they saw a prospect of my being re-taken.

Mr. Gatewood got two of his slaveholding neighbors to go with him to Cincinnati, for the purpose of swearing to anything which might be necessary to change me back into property. They came on to Cincinnati, and with but little effort they soon rallied a mob of ruffians who were willing to become the watch-dogs of slaveholders, for a dram, in connection with a few slavehunting petty constables.

While I was waiting the arrival of my family, I got a job of digging a cellar for the good lady where I was stopping, and while I was digging under the house, all at once I heard a man enter the house; another stept up to the cellar door to where I was at work; he looked in and saw me with my coat off at work. He then rapped over the cellar door on the house side, to notify the one who had entered the house to look for me that I was in the cellar. This strange conduct soon excited suspicion so strong in me, that I could not stay in the cellar and started to come out, but the man who stood by the door, rapped again on the house side, for the other to come to his aid, and told me to stop. I attempted to pass out by him, and he caught hold of me, and drew a pistol, swearing if I did not stop he would shoot me down. By this time I knew I was betrayed.

I asked him what crime I had committed that I should be murdered. "I will let you know, very soon," said he.

By this time there were others coming to his aid, and I could see no way by which I could possibly escape the jaws of that hell upon earth.

All my flattering prospects of enjoying my own fire-side, with my little family, were then blasted and gone; and I must bid farewell to friends and freedom forever.

In vain did I look to the infamous laws of the Commonwealth of Ohio, for that protection against violence and outrage, that even the vilest criminal with a white skin might enjoy. But oh! the dreadful thought, that after all my sacrifice and struggling to rescue my family from the hands of the oppressor; that I should be dragged back into cruel bondage to suffer the penalty of a tyrant's law, to endure stripes and imprisonment, and to be shut out from all moral as well as intellectual improvement, and linger out almost a living death.

When I saw a crowd of blood-thirsty, unprincipled slave hunters rushing upon me armed with weapons of death, it was no use for me to undertake to fight my way through against such fearful odds.

But I broke away from the man who stood by with his pistol drawn to shoot me if I should resist, and reached the fence and attempted to jump over it before I was overtaken; but the fence being very high I was caught by my legs before I got over.

I kicked and struggled with all my might to get away, but without success. I kicked a new cloth coat off of his back, while he was holding on to my leg. I kicked another in his eye; but they never let me go until they got more help. By this time, there was a crowd on the outside of the fence with clubs to beat me back. Finally, they succeeded in dragging me from the fence and overpowered me by numbers and choked me almost to death.

These ruffians dragged me through the streets of Cincinnati, to what was called a justice office. But it was more like an office of injustice.

When I entered the room I was introduced to three slaveholders, one of whom was a son of Wm. Gatewood, who claimed me as his property. They pretended to be very glad to see me.

They asked me if I did not want to see my wife and child; but I made no reply to anything that was said until I was delivered up as a slave. After they were asked a few questions by the court, the old pro-slavery squire very gravely pronounced me to be the property of Mr. Gatewood.

The office being crowded with spectators, many of whom were colored persons, Mr. G. was afraid to keep me in Cincinnati, two or three hours even, until a steamboat got ready to leave for the South. So they took me across the river, and locked me up in Covington jail, for safe keeping. This was the first time in my life that I had been put into a jail. It was truly distressing to my feelings to be locked up in a cold dungeon for no crime. The jailor not being at home, his wife had to act in his place. After my owners had gone back to Cincinnati, the jailor's wife, in company with another female, came into the jail and talked with me very friendly.

I told them all about my situation, and these ladies said they hoped that I might get away again, and went so far as to tell me if I should be kept in the jail that night, there was a hole under the wall of the jail where a prisoner had got out. It was only filled up with loose dirt, they said, and I might scratch it out and clear myself.

This I thought was a kind word from an unexpected friend: I had power to have taken the key from those ladies, in spite of them, and have cleared myself; but knowing that they would have to suffer perhaps for letting me get away, I thought I would wait until after dark, at which time I should try to make my escape, if they should not take me out before that time. But within two or three hours, they came after me, and conducted me on board of a boat, on which we all took passage down to Louisville. I was not confined in any way, but was well guarded by five men, three of whom were slaveholders, and the two young men from Cincinnati, who had betrayed me.

After the boat had got fairly under way, with these vile men standing around me on the upper deck of the boat, and she under full speed carrying me back into a land of torment, I could see no possible way of escape. Yet, while I was permitted to gaze on the beauties of nature, on free soil, as I passed down the river, things looked to me uncommonly pleasant: The green trees and wild flowers of the forest; the ripening harvest fields waving with the gentle breezes of Heaven; and the honest farmers tilling their soil and living by their own toil. These things seem to light upon my vision with a peculiar charm. I was conscious of what must be my fate; a wretched victim for Slavery without limit; to be sold like an ox, into hopeless bondage, and to be worked under the flesh-devouring lash during life, without wages.

This was to me an awful thought; every time the boat ran near the shore, I was tempted to leap from the deck down into the water, with a hope of making my escape. Such was then my feeling.

But on a moment's reflection, reason with her warning voice overcame this passion by pointing out the dreadful consequences of one's committing suicide. And this I thought would have a very striking resemblance to the act, and I declined putting into practice this dangerous experiment, though the temptation was great.

These kidnapping gentlemen, seeing that I was much dissatisfied, commenced talking to me, by saying that I must not be cast down; they were going to take me back home to live with my family, if I would promise not to run away again.

To this I agreed, and told them that this was all that I could ask, and more than I had expected.

But they were not satisfied with having recaptured me, because they had lost other slaves and supposed that I knew their whereabouts; and truly I did. They wanted me to tell them; but before telling I wanted them to tell who it was that had betrayed me into their hands. They said that I was betrayed by two colored men in Cincinnati, whose names they were backward in telling, because their business in connection with themselves was to betray and catch fugitive slaves for the reward offered. They undertook to justify the act by saying if they had not betrayed me, that somebody else would, and if I would tell them where they could catch a number of other runaway slaves, they would pay for me and set me free, and would then take me in as one of the Club. They said I would soon make money enough to buy my wife and child out of slavery.

But I replied, "No, gentlemen, I cannot commit or do an act of that kind, even if it were in my power so to do. I know that I am now in the power of a master who can sell me from my family for life, or punish me for the crime of running away, just as he pleases: I know that I am a prisoner for life, and have no way of extricating myself; and I also know that I have been deceived and betrayed by men who professed to be my best friends; but can all this justify me in becoming a traitor to others? Can I do that which I complain of others for doing unto me? Never, I trust, while a single pulsation of my heart continues to beat, can I consent to betray a fellow man like myself back into bondage, who has escaped. Dear as I love my wife and little child, and as much as I should like to enjoy freedom and happiness with them, I am unwilling to bring this about by betraying and destroying the liberty and happiness of others who have never offended me!"

I then asked them again if they would do me the kindness to tell me who it was betrayed me into their hands at Cincinnati? They agreed to tell me with the understanding that I was to tell where there was living, a family of slaves at the North, who had run away from Mr. King of Kentucky. I should not have agreed to this, but I knew the slaves were in Canada, where it was not possible for them to be captured. After they had told me the names of the persons who betrayed me, and how it was done, then I told them their slaves were in Canada, doing well. The two white men were Constables, who claimed the right of taking up any strange colored person as a slave; while the two colored kidnappers, under the pretext of being abolitionists, would find out all the fugitives they could, and inform these Constables for which they got a part of the reward, after they had found out where the slaves were from, the name of his master, &c. By the agency of these colored men, they were seized by a band of white ruffians, locked up in jail, and their master sent for. These colored kidnappers, with the Constables, were getting rich by betraying fugitive slaves. This was told to me by one of the Constables, while they were all standing around trying to induce me to engage in the same business for the sake of regaining my own liberty, and that of my wife and child. But my answer even there, under the most trying circumstances, surrounded by the strongest enemies of God and man, was most emphatically in the negative. "Let my punishment be what it may, either with the lash or by selling me away from my friends and home; let my destiny be what you please, I can never engage in this business for the sake of getting free."

They said I should not be sold nor punished with the lash for what

I had done, but I should be carried back to Bedford, to live with my wife. Yet when the boat got to where we should have landed, she wafted by without making any stop. I felt awful in view of never seeing my family again; they asked what was the matter? what made me look so cast down? I informed them that I knew I was to be sold in the Louisville slave market, or in New Orleans, and I never expected to see my family again. But they tried to pacify me by promising not to sell me to a slave trader who would take me off to New Orleans; cautioning me at the same time not to let it be known that I had been a runaway. This would very much lessen the value of me in market. They would not punish me by putting irons on my limbs, but would give me a good name, and sell me to some gentleman in Louisville for a house servant. They thought I would soon make money enough to buy myself, and would not part with me if they could get along without. But I had cost them so much in advertising and looking for me, that they were involved by it. In the first place they paid eight hundred and fifty dollars for me; and when I first run away, they paid one hundred for advertising and looking after me; and now they had to pay about forty dollars, expenses travelling to and from Cincinnati, in addition to the three hundred dollars reward; and they were not able to pay the reward without selling me.

I knew then the only alternative left for me to extricate myself was to use deception, which is the most effective defense a slave can use. I pretended to be satisfied for the purpose of getting an opportunity of giving them the slip.

But oh, the distress of mind, the lamentable thought that I should never again see the face nor hear the gentle voice of my nearest and dearest friends in this life. I could imagine what must be my fate from my peculiar situation. To be sold to the highest bidder, and then wear the chains of slavery down to the grave. The day star of liberty which had once cheered and gladdened my heart in freedom's land, had then hidden itself from my vision, and the dark and dismal frown of slavery had obscured the sunshine of freedom from me, as they supposed for all time to come.

But the understanding between us was, I was not to be tied, chained, nor flogged; for if they should take me into the city handcuffed and guarded by five men the question might be asked what crime I had committed? And if it should be known that I had been a runaway to Canada, it would lessen the value of me at least one hundred dollars.

VI

Arrival at Louisville, Ky.—Efforts to sell me.—Fortunate escape from the man-stealers in the public street.—I return to Bedford, Ky.—The rescue of my family again attempted.—I started alone expecting them to follow.—After waiting some months I resolve to go back again to Kentucky.

WHEN THE BOAT ARRIVED at Louisville, the day being too far spent for them to dispose of me, they had to put up at a Hotel. When we left the boat, they were afraid of my bolting from them in the street, and to prevent this they took hold of my arms, one on each side of me, gallanting me up to the hotel with as much propriety as if I had been a white lady. This was to deceive the people, and prevent my getting away from them.

They called for a bed-room to which I was conducted and locked within. That night three of them lodged in the same room to guard me. They locked the door and put the key under the head of their bed. I could see no possible way for my escape without jumping out of a three-story house window.

It was almost impossible for me to sleep that night in my peculiar situation. I passed the night in prayer to our Heavenly Father, asking that He would open to me even the smallest chance for escape.

The next morning after they had taken breakfast, four of them left me in the care of Dan Lane. He was what might be called one of the watch dogs of Kentucky. There was nothing too mean for him to do. He never blushed to rob a slave mother of her children, no matter how young or small. He was also celebrated for slave selling, kidnapping, and negro hunting. He was well known in that region by the slaves as well as the slaveholders, to have all the qualifications necessary for his business. He was a drunkard, a gambler, a profligate, and a slaveholder.

While the other four were looking around through the city for a purchaser, Dan was guarding me with his bowie knife and pistols. After a while the others came in with two persons to buy me, but on seeing me they remarked that they thought I would run away, and asked me if I had ever run away. Dan sprang to his feet and answered the question for me, by telling one of the most palpable falsehoods that ever came from the lips of a slaveholder. He declared that I had never run away in my life!

Fortunately for me, Dan, while the others were away, became unwell; and from taking salts, or from some other cause, was compelled to leave his room. Off he started to the horse stable which was located on one of the most public streets of Louisville, and of course I had to accompany him. He gallanted me into the stable by the arm, and placed himself back in one of the horses' stalls and ordered me to stand by until he was ready to come out.

At this time a thousand thoughts were flashing through my mind with regard to the propriety of trying the springs of my heels, which nature had so well adapted for taking the body out of danger, even in the most extraordinary emergencies. I thought in the attempt to get away by running, if I should not succeed, it could make my condition no worse, for they could but sell me and this they were then trying to do. These thoughts impelled me to keep edging towards the door, though very cautiously. Dan kept looking around after me as if he was not satisfied at my getting so near to the door. But the last I saw of him in the stable was just as he turned his eyes from me; I nerved myself with all the moral courage I could command and bolted for the door, perhaps with the fleetness of a much frightened deer, who never looks behind in time of peril. Dan was left in the stable to make ready for the race, or jump out into the street half dressed, and thereby disgrace himself before the public eye.

It would be impossible for me to set forth the speed with which I ran to avoid my adversary; I succeeded in turning a corner before Dan got sight of me, and by fast running, turning corners, and jumping high fences, I was enabled to effect my escape.

In running so swiftly through the public streets, I thought it would be a safer course to leave the public way, and as quick as thought I spied a high board fence by the way and attempted to leap over it. The top board broke and down I came into a hen-coop which stood by the fence. The dogs barked, and the hens flew and cackled so, that I feared it would lead to my detection before I could get out of the yard.

The reader can only imagine how great must have been the excited state of my mind while exposed to such extraordinary peril and danger on every side. In danger of being seized by a savage dog, which sprang at me when I fell into the hen-coop; in danger of being apprehended by the tenants of the lot; in danger of being shot or wounded by anyone who might have attempted to stop me, a runaway slave; and in danger on the other hand of being overtaken and getting in conflict with my adversary. With these fearful apprehensions, caution dictated me not to proceed far by daylight in this slaveholding city.

At this moment every nerve and muscle of my whole system was in full stretch; and every facility of the mind brought into action striving to save myself from being re-captured. I dared not go to the forest, knowing that I might be tracked by bloodhounds, and overtaken. I was so fortunate as to find a hiding place in the city which seemed to be pointed out by the finger of Providence. After running across lots, turning corners, and shunning my fellow men, as if they were wild ferocious beasts, I found a hiding place in a pile of boards or scantling, where I kept concealed during that day.

No tongue nor pen can describe the dreadful apprehensions under which I labored for the space of ten or twelve hours. My hiding place happened to be between two workshops, where there were men at work within six or eight feet of me. I could imagine that I heard them talking about me, and at other times thought I heard the footsteps of Daniel Lane in close pursuit. But I retained my position there until 9 or 10 o'clock at night, without being discovered; after which I attempted to find my way out, which was exceedingly difficult. The night being very dark, in a strange city, among slaveholders and slave hunters, to me it was like a person entering a wilderness among wolves and vipers, blindfolded. I was compelled from necessity to enter this place for refuge under the most extraordinary state of excitement, without regard to its geographical position. I found myself surrounded with a large block of buildings, which comprised a whole square, built up mostly on three sides, so that I could see no way to pass out without exposing myself perhaps to the gaze of patrols, or slave catchers.

In wandering around through the dark, I happened to find a calf in a back yard, which was bawling after the cow; the cow was also lowing in another direction, as if they were trying to find each other. A thought struck me that there must be an outlet somewhere about, where the cow and calf were trying to meet. I started in the direction where I heard the lowing of the cow, and I found an arch or tunnel extending between two large brick buildings, where I could see nothing of the cow but her eyes, shining like balls of fire through the dark tunnel, between the walls, through which I passed to where she stood. When I entered the streets I found them well lighted up. My heart was gladdened to know there was another chance for my escape. No bird ever let out of a cage felt more like flying, than I felt like running.

Before I left the city, I chanced to find by the way, an old man of color. Supposing him to be a friend, I ventured to make known my situation, and asked him if he would get me a bite to eat. The old man most cheerfully complied with my request. I was then about forty miles from the residence of Wm. Gatewood, where my wife, whom I sought to rescue from slavery, was living. This was also in the direction it was necessary for me to travel in order to get back to the free North. Knowing that the slave catchers would most likely be watching the public highway for me, to avoid them I made my way over the rocky hills, woods and plantations, back to Bedford.

I travelled all that night, guided on my way by the shining stars of heaven alone. The next morning just before the break of day, I came right to a large plantation, about which I secreted myself, until the darkness of the next night began to disappear. The morning larks commenced to chirp and sing merrily—pretty soon I heard the whip crack, and the voice of the ploughman driving in the corn field. About breakfast time, I heard the sound of a horn; saw a number of slaves in the field with a white man, who I supposed to be their overseer. He started to the house before the slaves, which gave me an opportunity to get the attention of one of the slaves, whom I met at the fence, before he started to his breakfast, and made known to him my wants and distresses. I also requested him to bring me a piece of bread if he could when he came back to the field.

The hospitable slave complied with my request. He came back to the field before his fellow laborers, and brought me something to eat, and as an equivalent for his kindness, I instructed him with regard to liberty, Canada, the way of escape, and the facilities by the way. He pledged his word that himself and others would be in Canada, in less than six months from that day. This closed our interview, and we separated. I concealed myself in the forest until about sunset, before I pursued my journey; and the second night from Louisville, I arrived again in the neighborhood of Bedford, where my little family were held in bondage, whom I so earnestly strove to rescue.

I concealed myself by the aid of a friend in that neighborhood, intending again to make my escape with my family. This confidential friend then carried a message to Malinda, requesting her to meet me on one side of the village.

We met under the most fearful apprehensions, for my pursuers had returned from Louisville, with the lamentable story that I was gone, and yet they were compelled to pay three hundred dollars to the Cincinnati slave catchers for re-capturing me there.

Daniel Lane's account of my escape from him, looked so unreasonable to slaveholders, that many of them charged him with selling me and keeping the money; while others believed that I had got away from him, and was then in the neighborhood, trying to take off my wife and child, which was true. Lane declared that in less than five minutes after I ran out of the stable in Louisville, he had over twenty men running and looking in every direction after me; but all without success. They could hear nothing of me. They had turned over several tons of hay in a large loft, in search, and I was not to be found there. Dan imputed my escape to my godliness! He said that I must have gone up in a chariot of fire, for I went off by flying; and that he should never again have anything to do with a praying negro.

Great excitement prevailed in Bedford, and many were out watching for me at the time Malinda was relating to me these facts. The excitement was then so great among the slaveholders—who were anxious to have me re-captured as a means of discouraging other slaves from running away—that time and money were no object while there was the least prospect of their success. I therefore declined making an effort just at that time to escape with my little family. Malinda managed to get me into the house of a friend that night, in the village, where I kept concealed several days seeking an opportunity to escape with Malinda and Frances to Canada.

But for some time Malinda was watched so very closely by white and by colored persons, both day and night, that it was not possible for us to escape together. They well knew that my little family was the only object of attraction that ever had or ever would induce me to come back and risk my liberty over the threshold of slavery—therefore this point was well guarded by the watch dogs of slavery, and I was compelled again to forsake my wife for a season, or surrender, which was suicidal to the cause of freedom, in my judgment.

The next day after my arrival in Bedford, Daniel Lane came to the very house wherein I was concealed and talked in my hearing to the family about my escape from him out of the stable in Louisville. He was near enough for me to have laid my hands on his head while in that house—and the intimidation which this produced on me was more than I could bear. I was also aware of the great temptation of the reward offered to white or colored persons for my apprehension; I was exposed to other calamities which rendered it altogether unsafe for me to stay longer under that roof.

One morning about 2 o'clock, I took leave of my little family and started for Canada. This was almost like tearing off the limbs from my body. When we were about to separate, Malinda clasped my hand exclaiming, "oh my soul! my heart is almost broken at the thought of this dangerous separation. This may be the last time we shall ever see each other's faces in this life, which will destroy all my future prospects of life and happiness forever." At this time the poor unhappy woman burst into tears and wept loudly; and my eyes were not dry. We separated with the understanding that she was to wait until the excitement was all over; after which she was to meet me at a certain place in the State of Ohio; which would not be longer than two months from that time.

I succeeded that night in getting a steamboat conveyance back to Cincinnati, or within ten miles of the city. I was apprehensive that there were slave-hunters in Cincinnati, watching the arrival of every boat up the river, expecting to catch me; and the boat landing to take in wood ten miles below the city, I got off and walked into Cincinnati, to avoid detection.

On my arrival at the house of a friend, I heard that the two young men who betrayed me for the three hundred dollars had returned and were watching for me. One of my friends in whom they had great confidence, called on the traitors, after he had talked with me, and asked them what they had done with me. Their reply was that I had given them the slip, and that they were glad of it, because they believed that I was a good man, and if they could see me on my way to Canada, they would give me money to aid me on my escape. My friend assured them that if they would give anything to aid me on my way, much or little, if they would put the same into his hands, he would give it to me that night, or return it to them the next morning.

They then wanted to know where I was and whether I was in the city; but he would not tell them, but one of them gave him one dollar for me, promising that if I was in the city, and he would let him know the next morning, he would give me ten dollars.

But I never waited for the ten dollars. I received one dollar of the amount which they got for betraying me, and started that night for the north. Their excuse for betraying me, was, that catching runaways was their business, and if they had not done it somebody else would, but since they had got the reward they were glad that I had made my escape.

Having travelled the road several times from Cincinnati to Lake Erie, I travelled through without much fear or difficulty. My friends in Perrysburgh, who knew that I had gone back into the very jaws of slavery after my family, were much surprised at my return, for they had heard that I was re-captured.

After I had waited three months for the arrival of Malinda and she came not, it caused me to be one of the most unhappy fugitives that ever left the South. I had waited eight or nine months without hearing from my family. I felt it to be my duty, as a husband and father, to make one more effort. I felt as if I could not give them up to be sacrificed on the "bloody altar of slavery." I felt as if love, duty, humanity and justice, required that I should go back, putting my trust in the God of Liberty for success.

VII

My safe return to Kentucky.—The perils I encountered there.—Again betrayed, and taken by a mob; ironed and imprisoned.—Narrow escape from death.—Life in a slave prison.

I PREPARED MYSELF for the journey before named, and started back in the month of July, 1839.

My intention was, to let no person know my business until I returned back to the North. I went to Cincinnati, and got a passage down on board of a boat just as I did the first time, without any misfortune or delay. I called on my mother, and the raising of a dead body from the grave could not have been more surprising to anyone than my arrival was to her, on that sad summer's night. She was not able to suppress her feelings. When I entered the room, there was but one other person in the house with my mother, and this was a little slave girl who was asleep when I entered. The impulsive feeling which is ever ready to act itself out at the return of a long absent friend, was more than my bereaved mother could suppress. And unfortunately for me, the loud shouts of joy at that late hour of the night, awakened the little slave girl, who afterwards betrayed me. She kept perfectly still, and never let either of us know that she was awake, in order that she might hear our conversation and report it. Mother informed me where my family was living, and that she would see them the next day, and would make arrangements for us to meet the next night at that house after the people in the village had gone to bed. I then went off and concealed myself during the next day, and according to promise came back the next night about eleven o'clock.

When I got near the house, moving very cautiously, filled with fearful apprehensions, I saw several men walking around the house as if they were looking for some person. I went back and waited about one hour, before I returned, and the number of men had increased. They were still to be seen lurking about this house, with dogs following them. This strange movement frightened me off again, and I never returned until after midnight, at which time I slipped up to the window, and rapped for my mother, who sprang to it and informed me that I was betrayed by the girl who overheard our conversation the night before. She thought that if I could keep out of the way for a few days, the white people would think that this girl was mistaken, or had lied. She had told her old mistress that I was there that night, and had made a plot with my mother to get my wife and child there the next night, and that I was going to take them off to Canada.

I went off to a friend of mine, who rendered me all the aid that one slave could render another, under the circumstances. Thank God he is now free from slavery, and is doing well. He was a messenger for me to my wife and mother, until at the suggestion of my mother, I changed an old friend for a new one, who betrayed me for the sum of five dollars.

We had set the time when we were to start for Canada, which was to be on the next Saturday night. My mother had an old friend whom she thought was true, and she got him to conceal me in a barn, not over two miles from the village. This man brought provisions to me, sent by my mother, and would tell me the news which was in circulation about me, among the citizens. But the poor fellow was not able to withstand the temptation of money.

My owners had about given me up, and thought the report of the slave girl was false; but they had offered a little reward among the slaves for my apprehension. The night before I was betrayed, I met with my mother and wife, and we had set up nearly all night plotting to start on the next Saturday night. I hid myself away in the flax in the barn, and being much rest broken I slept until the next morning about 9 o'clock. Then I was awakened by a mob of blood thirsty slaveholders, who had come armed with all the implements of death, with a determination to reduce me again to a life of slavery, or murder me on the spot.

When I looked up and saw that I was surrounded, they were exclaiming at the top of their voices, "shoot him down! shoot him down!" "If he offers to run, or to resist, kill him!"

I saw it was no use then for me to make any resistance, as I should be murdered. I felt confident that I had been betrayed by a slave, and all my flattering prospects of rescuing my family were gone forever, and the grim monster slavery with all its horrors was staring me in the face.

I surrendered myself to this hostile mob at once. The first thing done, after they had laid violent hands on me, was to bind my hands behind me with a cord, and rob me of all I possessed.

In searching my pockets, they found my certificate from the Methodist E. Church, which had been given me by my classleader, testifying to my worthiness as a member of that church. And what made the matter look more disgraceful to me, many of this mob were members of the M. E. Church, and they were the persons who took away my church ticket, and then robbed me also of fourteen dollars in cash, a silver watch for which I paid ten dollars, a pocket knife for which I paid seventy-five cents, and a Bible for which I paid sixty-two and one half cents. All this they tyrannically robbed me of, and yet my owner, Wm. Gatewood, was a regular member of the same church to which I belonged.

He then had me taken to a blacksmith's shop, and most wickedly had my limbs bound with heavy irons, and then had my body locked within the cold dungeon walls of the Bedford jail, to be sold to a Southern slave trader.

My heart was filled with grief—my eyes were filled with tears. I could see no way of escape. I could hear no voice of consolation. Slaveholders were coming to the dungeon window in great numbers to ask me questions. Some were rejoicing—some swearing, and others saying that I ought to be hung; while others were in favor of sending both me and my wife to New Orleans. They supposed that I had informed her all about the facilities for slaves to escape to Canada, and that she would tell other slaves after I was gone; hence we must all be sent off to where we could neither escape ourselves, nor instruct others the way.

In the afternoon of the same day Malinda was permitted to visit the prison wherein I was locked, but was not permitted to enter the door. When she looked through the dungeon grates and saw my sad situation, which was caused by my repeated adventures to rescue her and my little daughter from the grasp of slavery, it was more than she could bear without bursting in tears. She plead for admission into the cold dungeon where I was confined, but without success. With manacled limbs; with wounded spirit; with sympathizing tears and with bleeding heart, I entreated Malinda to weep not for me, for it only added to my grief, which was greater than I could bear.

I have often suffered from the sting of the cruel slave driver's lash on my quivering flesh—I have suffered from corporeal punishment in its various forms—I have mingled my sorrows with those that were bereaved by the ungodly soul drivers—and I also know what it is to shed the sympathetic tear at the grave of a departed friend; but all this is but a mere trifle compared with my sufferings from then to the end of six months subsequent.

The second night while I was in jail, two slaves came to the dungeon grates about the dead hour of night, and called me to the grates to have some conversation about Canada, and the facilities for getting there. They knew that I had travelled over the road, and they were determined to run away and go where they could be free. I of course took great pleasure in giving them directions how and where to go, and they started in less than a week from that time and got clear to Canada. I have seen them both since I came back to the north myself. They were known by the names of King and Jack.

The third day I was brought out of the prison to be carried off with my little family to the Louisville slave market. My hands were fastened together with heavy irons, and two men to guard me with loaded rifles, one of whom led the horse upon which I rode. My wife and child were set upon another nag. After we were all ready to start my old master thought I was not quite safe enough, and ordered one of the boys to bring him a bed cord from the store. He then tied my feet together under the horse, declaring that if I flew off this time, I should fly off with the horse.

Many tears were shed on that occasion by our friends and relatives, who saw us dragged off in irons to be sold in the human flesh market. No tongue could express the deep anguish of my soul when I saw the silent tear drops streaming down the sable cheeks of an aged slave mother, at my departure; and that too, caused by a black hearted traitor who was himself a slave:

> *I love the man with a feeling soul,*
> *Whose passions are deep and strong;*
> *Whose cords, when touched with a kindred power,*
> *Will vibrate loud and long:*
>
> *The man whose word is bond and law—*
> *Who ne'er for gold or power,*
> *Would kiss the hand that would stab the heart*
> *In adversity's trying hour.*

I love the man who delights to help
The panting, struggling poor:
The man that will open his heart,
Nor close against the fugitive at his door.

Oh give me a heart that will firmly stand,
When the storm of affliction shall lower—
A hand that will never shrink, if grasped,
In misfortune's darkest hour.

As we approached the city of Louisville, we attracted much attention, my being tied and handcuffed, and a person leading the horse upon which I rode. The horse appeared to be much frightened at the appearance of things in the city, being young and skittish. A carriage passing by jammed against the nag, which caused him to break from the man who was leading him, and in his fright throw me off backwards. My hands being confined with irons, and my feet tied under the horse with a rope, I had no power to help myself. I fell back off of the horse and could not extricate myself from this dreadful condition; the horse kicked with all his might while I was tied so close to his rump that he could only strike me with his legs by kicking.

The breath was kicked out of my body, but my bones were not broken. No one who saw my situation would have given five dollars for me. It was thought by all that I was dead and would never come to life again. When the horse was caught the cords were cut from my limbs, and I was rubbed with whiskey, camphor, &c., which brought me to life again.

Many bystanders expressed sympathy for me in my deplorable condition, and contempt for the tyrant who tied me to the young horse.

I was then driven through the streets of the city with my little family on foot, to jail, wherein I was locked with handcuffs yet on. A physician was then sent for, who doctored me several days before I was well enough to be sold in market.

The jail was one of the most disagreeable places I ever was confined in. It was not only disagreeable on account of the filth and dirt of the most disagreeable kind; but there were bed-bugs, fleas, lice and mosquitoes in abundance, to contend with. At night we had to lie down on the floor in this filth. Our food was very scanty, and of the most inferior quality. No gentleman's dog would eat what we were compelled to eat or starve.

I had not been in this prison many days before Madison Garrison, the soul driver, bought me and my family to sell again in the New Orleans slave market. He was buying up slaves to take to New Orleans. So he took me and my little family to the work-house, to be kept under lock and key at work until he had bought up as many as he wished to take off to the South.

The work-house of Louisville was a very large brick building, built on the plan of a jail or State's prison, with many apartments to it, divided off into cells wherein prisoners were locked up after night. The upper apartments were occupied by females, principally. This prison was enclosed by a high stone wall, upon which stood watchmen with loaded guns to guard the prisoners from breaking out, and on either side there were large iron gates.

When Garrison conducted me with my family to the prison in which we were to be confined until he was ready to take us to New Orleans, I was shocked at the horrid sight of the prisoners on entering the yard. When the large iron gate or door was thrown open to receive us, it was astonishing to see so many whites as well as colored men loaded down with irons, at hard labor, under the supervision of overseers.

Some were sawing stone, some cutting stone, and others breaking stone. The first impression which was made on my mind when I entered this place of punishment, made me think of hell, with all its terrors of torment; such as "weeping, wailing, and gnashing of teeth," which was then the idea that I had of the infernal regions from oral instruction. And I doubt whether there can be a better picture of it drawn, than may be sketched from an American slave prison.

In this prison almost every prisoner had a heavy log chain riveted about his leg. It would indeed be astonishing to a Christian man to stand in that prison one half hour and hear and see the contaminating influence of Southern slavery on the body and mind of man—you may there find almost every variety of character to look on. Some singing, some crying, some praying, and others swearing. The people of color who were in there were slaves, there without crime, but for safe keeping, while the whites were some of the most abandoned characters living. The keeper took me up to the anvil block and fastened a chain about my leg, which I had to drag after me both day and night during three months. My labor was sawing stone; my food was coarse corn bread and beef shanks and cows heads with pot liquor, and a very scanty allowance of that.

I have often seen the meat spoiled when brought to us, covered with flies and fly blows, and even worms crawling over when we were compelled to eat it, or go without any at all. It was all spread out on a long table in separate plates; and at the sound of a bell, everyone would take his plate, asking no questions. After hastily eating, we were hurried back to our work, each man dragging a heavy log chain after him to his work.

About a half hour before night they were commanded to stop work, take a bite to eat, and then be locked up in a small cell until the next morning after sunrise. The prisoners were locked in, two together. My bed was a cold stone floor with but little bedding! My visitors were bed-bugs and mosquitoes.

VIII

Character of my prison companions.—Jail breaking contemplated.—Defeat of our plan.—My wife and child removed.—Disgraceful proposal to her, and cruel punishment.—Our departure in a coffle for New Orleans.—Events of our journey.

MOST OF THE INMATES of this prison I have described, were white men who had been sentenced there by the law, for depredations committed by them. There was in that prison, gamblers, and even murderers. There were also in the female department, harlots, pickpockets, and adulteresses. In such company, and under such influences, where there was constant swearing, lying, cheating, and stealing, it was almost impossible for a virtuous person to avoid pollution, or to maintain their virtue. No place or places in this country can be better calculated to inculcate vice of every kind than a Southern work-house or house of correction.

After a profligate, thief, or a robber, has learned all that they can out of prison, they might go in one of those prisons and learn something more—they might properly be called robber colleges; and if slaveholders understood this they would never let their slaves enter them. No man would give much for a slave who had been kept long in one of these prisons.

I have often heard them telling each other how they robbed houses, and persons on the high way, by knocking them down, and would rob them, pick their pockets, and leave them half dead. Others would tell of stealing horses, cattle, sheep, and slaves; and when they would be sometimes apprehended, by the aid of their friends, they would break jail. But they could most generally find enough to swear them clear of any kind of villainy. They seemed to take great delight in telling of their exploits in robbery. There was a regular combination of them who had determined to resist law, wherever they went, to carry out their purposes.

In conversing with myself, they learned that I was notorious for running away, and professed sympathy for me. They thought that I might yet get to Canada, and be free, and suggested a plan by which I might accomplish it; and one way was, to learn to read and write, so that I might write myself a pass ticket, to go just where I pleased, when I was taken out of the prison; and they taught me secretly all they could while in the prison.

But there was another plan which they suggested to me to get away from slavery; that was to break out of the prison and leave my family. I consented to engage in this plot, but not to leave my family.

By my conduct in the prison, after having been there several weeks, I had gained the confidence of the keeper, and the turnkey. So much so, that when I wanted water or anything of the kind, they would open my door and hand it in to me. One of the turnkeys was an old colored man, who swept and cleaned up the cells, supplied the prisoners with water, &c.

On Sundays in the afternoon, the watchmen of the prison were most generally off, and this old slave, whose name was Stephen, had the prisoners to attend to. The white prisoners formed a plot to break out on Sunday in the afternoon, by making me the agent to get the prison keys from old Stephen.

I was to prepare a stone that would weigh about one pound, tie it up in a rag, and keep it in my pocket to strike poor old Stephen with, when he should open my cell door. But this I would not consent to do, without he should undertake to betray me.

I gave old Stephen one shilling to buy me a water melon, which he was to bring to me in the afternoon. All the prisoners were to be ready to strike, just as soon as I opened their doors. When Stephen opened my door to hand me the melon, I was to grasp him by the collar, raise the stone over his head, and say to him, that if he made any alarm that I should knock him down with the stone. But if he would be quiet he should not be hurt. I was then to take all the keys from him, lock him up in the cell—take a chisel and cut the chain from my own leg, then unlock all the cells below, and let out the other prisoners, who were all to cut off their chains. We were then to go and let out old Stephen, and make him go off with us. We were to form a line and march to the front gate of the prison with a sledge hammer, and break it open, and if we should be discovered, and there should be any out-cry, we were all to run and raise the alarm of fire, so as to avoid detection. But while we were all listening for Stephen to open the door with the melon, he came and reported that he could not get one, and handed me back the money through the window. All were disappointed, and nothing done. I looked upon it as being a fortunate thing for me, for it was certainly a very dangerous experiment for a slave, and they could never get me to consent to be the leader in that matter again.

A few days after, another plot was concocted to break prison, but it was betrayed by one of the party, which resulted in the most cruel punishment to the prisoners concerned in it; and I felt thankful that my name was not connected with it. They were not only flogged, but they were kept on bread and water alone, for many days. A few days after we were put in this prison, Garrison came and took my wife and child out, I knew not for what purpose, nor to what place, but after the absence of several days I supposed that he had sold them. But one morning, the outside door was thrown open, and Malinda thrust in by the ruthless hand of Garrison, whose voice was pouring forth the most bitter oaths and abusive language that could be dealt out to a female; while her heart-rending shrieks and sobbing, was truly melting to the soul of a father and husband.

The language of Malinda was, "Oh! my dear little child is gone? What shall I do? my child is gone." This most distressing sound struck a sympathetic chord through all the prison among the prisoners. I was not permitted to go to my wife and inquire what had become of little Frances. I never expected to see her again, for I supposed that she was sold.

That night, however, I had a short interview with my much abused wife, who told me the secret. She said that Garrison had taken her to a private house where he kept female slaves for the basest purposes. It was a resort for slave trading profligates and soul drivers, who were interested in the same business.

Soon after she arrived at this place, Garrison gave her to understand what he brought her there for, and made a most disgraceful assault on her virtue, which she promptly repelled; and for which Garrison punished her with the lash, threatening her that if she did not submit that he would sell her child. The next day he made the same attempt, which she resisted, declaring that she would not submit to it; and again he tied her up and flogged her until her garments were stained with blood.

He then sent our child off to another part of the city, and said he meant to sell it and that she should never see it again. He then drove Malinda before him to the work-house, swearing by his Maker that she should submit to him or die. I have already described her entrance in the prison.

Two days after this he came again and took Malinda out of the prison. It was several weeks before I saw her again, and learned that he had not sold her or the child. At the same time he was buying up other slaves to take to New Orleans. At the expiration of three months he was ready to start with us for the New Orleans slave market, but we never knew when we were to go, until the hour had arrived for our departure.

One Sabbath morning Garrison entered the prison and commanded that our limbs should be made ready for the coffles. They called us up to an anvil block, and the heavy log chains which we had been wearing on our legs during three months, were cut off. I had been in the prison over three months; but he had other slaves who had not been there so long. The hand-cuffs were then put on to our wrists. We were coupled together two and two—the right hand of one to the left hand of another, and a long chain to connect us together.

The other prisoners appeared to be sorry to see us start off in this way. We marched off to the river Ohio, to take passage on board of the steamboat *Water Witch*. But this was at a very low time of water, in the fall of 1839. The boat got aground, and did not get off that night; and Garrison had to watch us all night to keep any from getting away. He also had a very large savage dog, which was trained up to catch runaway slaves.

We were more than six weeks getting to the city of New Orleans, in consequence of low water. We were shifted on to several boats before we arrived at the mouth of the river Ohio. But we got but very little rest at night. As all were chained together night and day, it was impossible to sleep, being annoyed by the bustle and crowd of the passengers on board; by the terrible thought that we were destined to be sold in market as sheep or oxen; and annoyed by the galling chains that cramped our wearied limbs, on the tedious voyage. But I had several opportunities to have run away from Garrison before we got to the mouth of the Ohio River. While they were shifting us from one boat to another, my hands were sometimes loosed, until they got us all on board—and I know that I should have broke away had it not been for the sake of my wife and child who was with me. I could see no chance to get them off, and I could not leave them in that condition—and Garrison was not so much afraid of my running away from him while he held on to my family, for he knew from the great sacrifices which I had made to rescue them from slavery, that my attachment was too strong to run off and leave them in his hands, while there was the least hope of ever getting them away with me.

IX

Our arrival and examination at Vicksburg.—An account of slave sales.—Cruel punishment with the paddle.—Attempts to sell myself by Garrison's direction.—Amusing interview with a slave buyer.—Deacon Whitfield's examination.—He purchases the family.—Character of the Deacon.

WHEN WE ARRIVED at the city of Vicksburg, he intended to sell a portion of his slaves there, and stopped for three weeks trying to sell. But he met with very poor success.

We had there to pass through an examination or inspection by a city officer, whose business it was to inspect slave property that was brought to that market for sale. He examined our backs to see if we had been much scarred by the lash. He examined our limbs, to see whether we were inferior.

As it is hard to tell the ages of slaves, they look in their mouths at their teeth, and prick up the skin on the back of their hands, and if the person is very far advanced in life, when the skin is pricked up, the pucker will stand so many seconds on the back of the hand.

But the most rigorous examinations of slaves by those slave inspectors, is on the mental capacity. If they are found to be very intelligent, this is pronounced the most objectionable of all other qualities connected with the life of a slave. In fact, it undermines the whole fabric of his chattelhood; it prepares for what slaveholders are pleased to pronounce the unpardonable sin when committed by a slave. It lays the foundation for running away, and going to Canada. They also see in it a love for freedom, patriotism, insurrection, bloodshed, and exterminating war against American slavery.

Hence they are very careful to inquire whether a slave who is for sale can read or write. This question has been asked me often by slave traders, and cotton planters, while I was there for market. After conversing with me, they have sworn by their Maker, that they would not have me among their negroes; and that they saw the devil in my eye; I would run away, &c.

I have frequently been asked also, if I had ever run away; but Garrison would generally answer this question for me in the negative. He could have sold my little family without any trouble, for the sum of one thousand dollars. But for fear he might not get me off at so great an advantage, as the people did not like my appearance, he could do better by selling us all together. They all wanted my wife, but while very few wanted me. He asked for me and my family twenty-five hundred dollars, but was not able to get us off at that price.

He tried to speculate on my Christian character. He tried to make it appear that I was so pious and honest that I would not run away for ill treatment; which was a gross mistake, for I never had religion enough to keep me from running away from slavery in my life.

But we were taken from Vicksburg, to the city of New Orleans, where we were to be sold at any rate. We were taken to a trader's yard or a slave prison on the corner of St. Joseph street. This was a common resort for slave traders, and planters who wanted to buy slaves; and all classes of slaves were kept there for sale, to be sold in private or public—young or old, males or females, children or parents, husbands or wives.

Every day at 10 o'clock they were exposed for sale. They had to be in trim for showing themselves to the public for sale. Everyone's head had to be combed, and their faces washed, and those who were inclined to look dark and rough, were compelled to wash in greasy dish water, in order to make them look slick and lively.

When spectators would come in the yard, the slaves were ordered out to form a line. They were made to stand up straight, and look as sprightly as they could; and when they were asked a question, they had to answer it as promptly as they could, and try to induce the spectators to buy them. If they failed to do this, they were severely paddled after the spectators were gone. The object for using the paddle in the place of a lash was, to conceal the marks which would be made by the flogging. And the object for flogging under such circumstances, is to make the slaves anxious to be sold.

The paddle is made of a piece of hickory timber, about one inch thick, three inches in width, and about eighteen inches in length. The part which is applied to the flesh is bored full of quarter inch auger holes, and every time this is applied to the flesh of the victim, the blood gushes through the holes of the paddle, or a blister makes its appearance. The persons who are thus flogged, are always stripped naked, and their hands tied together. They are then bent over double, their knees are forced between their elbows, and a stick is put through between the elbows and the bend of the legs, in order to hold the victim in that position, while the paddle is applied to those parts of the body which would not be so likely to be seen by those who wanted to buy slaves.

I was kept in this prison for several months, and no one would buy me for fear I would run away. One day while I was in this prison, Garrison got mad with my wife, and took her off in one of the rooms, with his paddle in hand, swearing that he would paddle her; and I could afford her no protection at all, while the strong arm of the law, public opinion and custom, were all against me. I have often heard Garrison say, that he had rather paddle a female, than eat when he was hungry—that it was music for him to hear them scream, and to see their blood run.

After the lapse of several months, he found that he could not dispose of my person to a good advantage, while he kept me in that prison confined among the other slaves. I do not speak with vanity when I say the contrast was so great between myself and ordinary slaves, from the fact that I had enjoyed superior advantages, to which I have already referred. They have their slaves classed off and numbered.

Garrison came to me one day and informed me that I might go out through the city and find myself a master. I was to go to the Hotels, boarding houses, &c.—tell them that my wife was a good cook, washwoman, &c.,—and that I was a good dining room servant, carriage driver, or porter—and in this way I might find some gentleman who would buy us both; and that this was the only hope of our being sold together.

But before starting me out, he dressed me up in a suit of his old clothes, so as to make me look respectable, and I was so much better dressed than usual that I felt quite gay. He would not allow my wife to go out with me however, for fear we might get away. I was out every day for several weeks, three or four hours in each day, trying to find a new master, but without success.

Many of the old French inhabitants have taken slaves for their wives, in this city, and their own children for their servants. Such commonly are called Creoles. They are better treated than other slaves, and I resembled this class in appearance so much that the French did not want me. Many of them set their mulatto children free, and make slaveholders of them.

At length one day I heard that there was a gentleman in the city from the State of Tennessee, to buy slaves. He had brought down two rafts of lumber for market, and I thought if I could get him to buy me with my family, and take us to Tennessee, from there, I would stand a better opportunity to run away again and get to Canada, than I would from the extreme South.

So I brushed up myself and walked down to the river's bank, where the man was pointed out to me standing on board of his raft, I approached him, and after passing the usual compliments I said:

"Sir, I understand that you wish to purchase a lot of servants and I have called to know if it is so."

He smiled and appeared to be much pleased at my visit on such laudable business, supposing me to be a slave trader. He commenced rubbing his hands together, and replied by saying: "Yes sir, I am glad to see you. It is a part of my business here to buy slaves, and if I could get you to take my lumber in part pay I should like to buy four or five of your slaves at any rate. What kind of slaves have you, sir?"

After I found that he took me to be a slave trader I knew that it would be of no use for me to tell him that I was myself a slave looking for a master, for he would have doubtless brought up the same objection that others had brought up,—that I was too white; and that they were afraid that I could read and write; and would never serve as a slave, but run away. My reply to the question respecting the quality of my slaves was, that I did not think his lumber would suit me—that I must have the cash for my negroes, and turned on my heel and left him!

I returned to the prison and informed my wife of the fact that I had been taken to be a slaveholder. She thought that in addition to my light complexion my being dressed up in Garrison's old slave trading clothes might have caused the man to think that I was a slave trader, and she was afraid that we should yet be separated if I should not succeed in finding somebody to buy us.

Every day to us was a day of trouble, and every night brought new and fearful apprehensions that the golden link which binds together husband and wife might be broken by the heartless tyrant before the light of another day.

Deep has been the anguish of my soul when looking over my little family during the silent hours of the night, knowing the great danger of our being sold off at auction the next day and parted forever. That this might not come to pass, many have been the tears and prayers which I have offered up to the God of Israel that we might be preserved.

While waiting here to be disposed of, I heard of one Francis Whitfield, a cotton planter, who wanted to buy slaves. He was represented to be a very pious soul, being a deacon of a Baptist church. As the regulations, as well as public opinion generally, were against slaves meeting for religious worship, I thought it would give me a better opportunity to attend to my religious duties should I fall into the hands of this deacon.

So I called on him and tried to show to the best advantage, for the purpose of inducing him to buy me and my family. When I approached him, I felt much pleased at his external appearance—I addressed him in the following words as well as I can remember:

"Sir, I understand you are desirous of purchasing slaves?"

With a very pleasant smile, he replied, "Yes, I do want to buy some, are you for sale?"

"Yes sir, with my wife and one child."

Garrison had given me a note to show wherever I went, that I was for sale, speaking of my wife and child, giving us a very good character of course—and I handed him the note.

After reading it over he remarked, "I have a few questions to ask you, and if you will tell me the truth like a good boy, perhaps I may buy you with your family. In the first place, my boy, you are a little too near white. I want you to tell me now whether you can read or write?"

My reply was in the negative.

"Now I want you to tell me whether you have run away? Don't tell me no stories now, like a good fellow, and perhaps I may buy you."

But as I was not under oath to tell him the whole truth, I only gave him a part of it, by telling him that I had run away once.

He appeared to be pleased at that, but cautioned me to tell him the truth, and asked me how long I stayed away, when I ran off?

I told him that I was gone a month.

He assented to this by a bow of his head, and making a long grunt saying, "That's right, tell me the truth like a good boy."

The whole truth was that I had been off in the state of Ohio, and other free states, and even to Canada; besides this I was notorious for running away, from my boyhood.

I never told him that I had been a runaway longer than one month—neither did I tell him that I had not run away more than once in my life; for these questions he never asked me.

I afterwards found him to be one of the basest hypocrites that I ever saw. He looked like a saint—talked like the best of slave holding Christians, and acted at home like the devil.

When he saw my wife and child, he concluded to buy us. He paid for me twelve hundred dollars, and one thousand for my wife and child. He also bought several other slaves at the same time, and took home with him. His residence was in the parish of Claiborn, fifty miles up from the mouth of Red River.

When we arrived there, we found his slaves poor, ragged, stupid, and half-starved. The food he allowed them per week, was one peck of corn for each grown person, one pound of pork, and sometimes a quart of molasses. This was all that they were allowed, and if they got more they stole it.

He had one of the most cruel overseers to be found in that section of the country. He weighed and measured out to them, their week's allowance of food every Sabbath morning. The overseer's horn was sounded two hours before daylight for them in the morning, in order that they should be ready for work before daylight. They were worked from daylight until after dark, without stopping but one half hour to eat or rest, which was at noon. And at the busy season of the year, they were compelled to work just as hard on the Sabbath, as on any other day.

X

Cruel treatment on Whitfield's farm.—Exposure of the children.— Mode of extorting extra labor.—Neglect of the sick.—Strange medicine used.—Death of our second child.

MY FIRST IMPRESSIONS when I arrived on the Deacon's farm, were that he was far more like what the people call the devil, than he was like a deacon. Not many days after my arrival there, I heard the Deacon tell one of the slave girls, that he had bought her for a wife for his boy Stephen, which office he compelled her fully to perform against her will. This he enforced by a threat. At first the poor girl neglected to do this, having no sort of affection for the man—but she was finally forced to it by an application of the driver's lash, as threatened by the Deacon.

The next thing I observed was that he made the slave driver strip his own wife, and flog her for not doing just as her master had ordered. He had a white overseer, and a colored man for a driver, whose business it was to watch and drive the slaves in the field, and do the flogging according to the orders of the overseer.

Next a mulatto girl who waited about the house, on her mistress, displeased her, for which the Deacon stripped and tied her up. He then handed me the lash and ordered me to put it on—but I told him I never had done the like, and hoped he would not compel me to do it. He then informed me that I was to be his overseer, and that he had bought me for that purpose. He was paying a man eight hundred dollars a year to oversee, and he believed I was competent to do the same business, and if I would do it up right he would put nothing harder on me to do; and if I knew not how to flog a slave, he would set me an example by which I might be governed. He then commenced on this poor girl, and gave her two hundred lashes before he had her untied.

After giving her fifty lashes, he stopped and lectured her a while, asking her if she thought that she could obey her mistress, &c. She promised to do all in her power to please him and her mistress, if he would have mercy on her. But this plea was all vain. He commenced on her again; and this flogging was carried on in the most inhuman manner until she had received two hundred stripes on her naked quivering flesh, tied up and exposed to the public gaze of all. And this was the example that I was to copy after.

He then compelled me to wash her back off with strong salt brine, before she was untied, which was so revolting to my feelings, that I could not refrain from shedding tears.

For some cause he never called on me again to flog a slave. I presume he saw that I was not savage enough. The above was about the first items of the Deacon's conduct which struck me with peculiar disgust.

After having enjoyed the blessings of civil and religious liberty for a season, to be dragged into that horrible place with my family, to linger out my existence without the aid of religious societies, or the light of revelation, was more than I could endure. I really felt as if I had got into one of the darkest corners of the earth. I thought I was almost out of humanity's reach, and should never again have the pleasure of hearing the gospel sound, as I could see no way by which I could extricate myself; yet I never omitted to pray for deliverance. I had faith to believe that the Lord could see our wrongs and hear our cries.

I was not used quite as bad as the regular field hands, as the greater part of my time was spent working about the house; and my wife was the cook.

This country was full of pine timber, and every slave had to prepare a light wood torch, over night, made of pine knots, to meet the overseer with, before daylight in the morning. Each person had to have his torch lit, and come with it in his hand to the gin house, before the overseer and driver, so as to be ready to go to the cotton field by the time they could see to pick out cotton. These lights looked beautiful at a distance.

The object of blowing the horn for them two hours before day, was, that they should get their bite to eat, before they went to the field, that they need not stop to eat but once during the day. Another object was, to do up their flogging which had been omitted over night. I have often heard the sound of the slave driver's lash on the backs of the slaves, and their heart-rending shrieks, which were enough to melt the heart of humanity, even among the most barbarous nations of the earth.

But the Deacon would keep no overseer on his plantation, who neglected to perform this every morning. I have heard him say that he was no better pleased than when he could hear the overseer's loud complaining voice, long before daylight in the morning, and the sound of the driver's lash among the toiling slaves.

This was a very warm climate, abounding with mosquitoes, galinippers and other insects which were exceedingly annoying to the poor slaves by night and day, at their quarters and in the field. But more especially to their helpless little children, which they had to carry with them to the cotton fields, where they had to set on the damp ground alone from morning till night, exposed to the scorching rays of the sun, liable to be bitten by poisonous rattle snakes which are plenty in that section of the country, or to be devoured by large alligators, which are often seen creeping through the cotton fields going from swamp to swamp seeking their prey.

The cotton planters generally, never allow a slave mother time to go to the house, or quarter during the day to nurse her child; hence they have to carry them to the cotton fields and tie them in the shade of a tree, or in clusters of high weeds about in the fields, where they can go to them at noon, when they are allowed to stop work for one half hour. This is the reason why so very few slave children are raised on these cotton plantations, the mothers have no time to take care of them— and they are often found dead in the field and in the quarter for want of the care of their mothers. But I never was eye witness to a case of this kind, but have heard many narrated by my slave brothers and sisters, some of which occurred on the Deacon's plantation.

Their plan of getting large quantities of cotton picked is not only to extort it from them by the lash, but hold out an inducement and deceive them by giving small prizes. For example; the overseer will offer something worth one or two dollars to any slave who will pick out the most cotton in one day; dividing the hands off in three classes and offering a prize to the one who will pick out the most cotton in each of the classes. By this means they are all interested in trying to get the prize.

After making them try it over several times and weighing what cotton they pick every night, the overseer can tell just how much every hand can pick. He then gives the present to those that pick the most cotton, and then if they do not pick just as much afterward they are flogged.

I have known the slaves to be so much fatigued from labor that they could scarcely get to their lodging places from the field at night. And then they would have to prepare something to eat before they could lie down to rest. Their corn they had to grind on a hand mill for bread stuff, or pound it in a mortar; and by the time they would get their suppers it would be midnight; then they would herd down all together and take but two or three hours rest, before the overseer's horn called them up again to prepare for the field.

At the time of sickness among slaves they had but very little attention. The master was to be the judge of their sickness, but never had studied the medical profession. He always pronounced a slave who said he was sick, a liar and a hypocrite; said there was nothing the matter, and he only wanted to keep from work.

His remedy was most generally strong red pepper tea, boiled till it was red. He would make them drink a pint cup full of it at one dose. If he should not get better very soon after it, the dose was repeated. If that should not accomplish the object for which it was given, or have the desired effect, a pot or kettle was then put over the fire with a large quantity of chimney soot, which was boiled down until it was as strong as the juice of tobacco, and the poor sick slave was compelled to drink a quart of it.

This would operate on the system like salts, or castor oil. But if the slave should not be very ill, he would rather work as long as he could stand up, than to take this dreadful medicine.

If it should be a very valuable slave, sometimes a physician was sent for and something done to save him. But no special aid is afforded the suffering slave even in the last trying hour, when he is called to grapple with the grim monster death. He has no Bible, no family altar, no minister to address to him the consolations of the gospel, before he launches into the spirit world. As to the burial of slaves, but very little more care is taken of their dead bodies than if they were dumb beasts.

My wife was very sick while we were both living with the Deacon. We expected every day would be her last. While she was sick, we lost our second child, and I was compelled to dig my own child's grave and bury it myself without even a box to put it in.

XI

I attend a prayer meeting.—Punishment therefor threatened.—I attempt to escape alone.—My return to take my family.—Our sufferings.—Dreadful attack of wolves.—Our recapture.

SOME MONTHS AFTER Malinda had recovered from her sickness, I got permission from the Deacon, on one Sabbath day, to attend a prayer meeting, on a neighboring plantation, with a few old superannuated slaves, although this was contrary to the custom of the country—for slaves were not allowed to assemble for religious worship. Being more numerous than the whites there was fear of rebellion, and the overpowering of their oppressors in order to obtain freedom.

But this gentleman on whose plantation I attended the meeting was not a Deacon nor a professor of religion. He was not afraid of a few old Christian slaves rising up to kill their master because he allowed them to worship God on the Sabbath day.

We had a very good meeting, although our exercises were not conducted in accordance with an enlightened Christianity; for we had no Bible—no intelligent leader—but a conscience, prompted by our own reason, constrained us to worship God the Creator of all things.

When I returned home from meeting I told the other slaves what a good time we had at our meeting, and requested them to go with me to meeting there on the next Sabbath. As no slave was allowed to go from the plantation on a visit without a written pass from his master, on the next Sabbath several of us went to the Deacon, to get permission to attend that prayer meeting; but he refused to let any go. I thought I would slip off and attend the meeting and get back before he would miss me, and would not know that I had been to the meeting.

When I returned home from the meeting as I approached the house I saw Malinda, standing out at the fence looking in the direction in which I was expected to return. She hailed my approach, not with joy, but with grief. She was weeping under great distress of mind, but it was hard for me to extort from her the reason why she wept. She finally informed me that her master had found out that I had violated his law, and I should suffer the penalty, which was five hundred lashes, on my naked back.

I asked her how he knew that I had gone?

She said I had not long been gone before he called for me and I was not to be found. He then sent the overseer on horseback to the place where we were to meet to see if I was there. But when the overseer got to the place, the meeting was over and I had gone back home, but had gone a nearer route through the woods and the overseer happened not to meet me. He heard that I had been there and hurried back home before me and told the Deacon, who ordered him to take me on the next morning, strip off my clothes, drive down four stakes in the ground and fasten my limbs to them; then strike me five hundred lashes for going to the prayer meeting. This was what distressed my poor companion. She thought it was more than I could bear, and that it would be the death of me. I concluded then to run away—but she thought they would catch me with the blood hounds by their taking my track. But to avoid them I thought I would ride off on one of the Deacon's mules. She thought if I did, they would sell me.

"No matter, I will try it," said I, "let the consequences be what they may. The matter can be no worse than it now is." So I tackled up the Deacon's best mule with his saddle, &c., and started that night and went off eight or ten miles from home. But I found the mule to be rather troublesome, and was like to betray me by braying, especially when he would see cattle, horses, or anything of the kind in the woods.

The second night from home I camped in a cane brake down in the Red River swamp not a great way off from the road, perhaps not twenty rods, exposed to wild ferocious beasts which were numerous in that section of country. On that night about the middle of the night the mule heard the sound of horses' feet on the road, and he commenced stamping and trying to break away. As the horses seemed to come nearer, the mule commenced trying to bray, and it was all that I could do to prevent him from making a loud bray there in the woods, which would have betrayed me.

I supposed that it was the overseer out with the dogs looking for me, and I found afterwards that I was not mistaken. As soon as the people had passed by, I mounted the mule and took him home to prevent his betraying me. When I got near by home I stripped off the tackling and turned the mule loose. I then slipt up to the cabin wherein my wife laid and found her awake, much distressed about me. She informed me that they were then out looking for me, and that the Deacon was bent on flogging me nearly to death, and then selling me off from my family. This was truly heart-rending to my poor wife; the thought of our being torn apart in a strange land after having been sold away from all her friends and relations, was more than she could bear.

The Deacon had declared that I should not only suffer for the crime of attending a prayer meeting without his permission, and for running away, but for the awful crime of stealing a jackass, which was death by the law when committed by a negro.

But I well knew that I was regarded as property, and so was the ass; and I thought if one piece of property took off another, there could be no law violated in the act; no more sin committed in this than if one jackass had rode off another.

But after consultation with my wife I concluded to take her and my little daughter with me and they would be guilty of the same crime that I was, so far as running away was concerned; and if the Deacon sold one he might sell us all, and perhaps to the same person.

So we started off with our child that night, and made our way down to the Red River swamps among the buzzing insects and wild beasts of the forest. We wandered about in the wilderness for eight or ten days before we were apprehended, striving to make our way from slavery; but it was all in vain. Our food was parched corn, with wild fruit such as pawpaws, persimmons, grapes, &c. We did at one time chance to find a sweet potato patch where we got a few potatoes; but most of the time, while we were out, we were lost. We wanted to cross the Red River but could find no conveyance to cross in.

I recollect one day of finding a crooked tree which bent over the river or over one fork of the river, where it was divided by an island. I should think that the tree was at least twenty feet from the surface of the water. I picked up my little child, and my wife followed me, saying, "if we perish let us all perish together in the stream." We succeeded in crossing over. I often look back to that dangerous event even now with astonishment, and wonder how I could have run such a risk. What would induce me to run the same risk now? What could induce me now to leave home and friends and go to the wild forest and lay out on the cold ground night after night without covering, and live on parched corn?

What would induce me to take my family and go into the Red River swamps of Louisiana among the snakes and alligators, with all the liabilities of being destroyed by them, hunted down with blood hounds, or lay myself liable to be shot down like the wild beasts of the forest? Nothing I say, nothing but the strongest love of liberty, humanity, and justice to myself and family, would induce me to run such a risk again.

When we crossed over on the tree we supposed that we had crossed over the main body of the river, but we had not proceeded far on our journey before we found that we were on an Island surrounded by water on either side. We made our bed that night in a pile of dry leaves which had fallen from off the trees. We were much rest-broken, wearied from hunger and travelling through briers, swamps and cane brakes—consequently we soon fell asleep after lying down. About the dead hour of the night I was aroused by the awful howling of a gang of blood-thirsty wolves, which had found us out and surrounded us as their prey, there in the dark wilderness many miles from any house or settlement.

My dear little child was so dreadfully alarmed that she screamed loudly with fear—my wife trembling like a leaf on a tree, at the thought of being devoured there in the wilderness by ferocious wolves.

The wolves kept howling, and were near enough for us to see their glaring eyes, and hear their chattering teeth. I then thought that the hour of death for us was at hand; that we should not live to see the light of another day; for there was no way for our escape. My little family were looking up to me for protection, but I could afford them none. And while I was offering up my prayers to that God who never forsakes those in the hour of danger who trust in him, I thought of Deacon Whitfield; I thought of his profession, and doubted his piety. I thought of his hand-cuffs, of his whips, of his chains, of his stocks, of his thumb-screws, of his slave driver and overseer, and of his religion; I also thought of his opposition to prayer meetings, and of his five hundred lashes promised me for attending a prayer meeting. I thought of God, I thought of the devil, I thought of hell; and I thought of heaven, and wondered whether I should ever see the Deacon there. And I calculated that if heaven was made up of such Deacons, or such persons, it could not be filled with love to all mankind, and with glory and eternal happiness, as we know it is from the truth of the Bible.

The reader may perhaps think me tedious on this topic, but indeed it is one of so much interest to me, that I find myself entirely unable to describe what my own feelings were at that time. I was so much excited by the fierce howling of the savage wolves, and the frightful screams of my little family, that I thought of the future; I thought of the past; I thought the time of my departure had come at last.

My impression is, that all these thoughts and thousands of others, flashed through my mind, while I was surrounded by those wolves. But it seemed to be the will of a merciful providence, that our lives should be spared, and that we should not be destroyed by them.

I had no weapon of defense but a long bowie knife which I had slipped from the Deacon. It was a very splendid blade, about two feet in length, and about two inches in width. This used to be a part of his armor of defense while walking about the plantation among his slaves.

The plan which I took to expel the wolves was a very dangerous one, but it proved effectual. While they were advancing to me, prancing and accumulating in number, apparently of all sizes and grades, who had come to the feast, I thought just at this time, that there was no alternative left but for me to make a charge with my bowie knife. I well knew from the action of the wolves, that if I made no further resistance, they would soon destroy us, and if I made a break at them, the matter could be no worse. I thought if I must die, I would die striving to protect my little family from destruction, die striving to escape from slavery. My wife took a club in one hand, and her child in the other, while I rushed forth with my bowie knife in hand, to fight off the savage wolves. I made one desperate charge at them, and at the same time making a loud yell at the top of my voice, that caused them to retreat and scatter, which was equivalent to a victory on our part. Our prayers were answered, and our lives spared through the night. We slept no more that night, and the next morning there were no wolves to be seen or heard, and we resolved not to stay on that island another night.

We travelled up and down the river side trying to find a place where we could cross. Finally we found a lot of drift wood clogged together, extending across the stream at a narrow place in the river, upon which we crossed over. But we had not yet surmounted our greatest difficulty. We had to meet one which was far more formidable than the first. Not many days after I had to face the Deacon.

We had been wandering about through the cane brakes, bushes, and briers, for several days, when we heard the yelping of blood hounds, a great way off, but they seemed to come nearer and nearer to us. We thought after awhile that they must be on our track; we listened attentively at the approach. We knew it was no use for us to undertake to escape from them, and as they drew nigh, we heard the voice of a man hissing on the dogs.

After awhile we saw the hounds coming in full speed on our track, and the soul drivers close after them on horse back, yelling like tigers, as they came in sight. The shrill yelling of the savage blood hounds as they drew nigh made the woods echo.

The first impulse was to run to escape the approaching danger of ferocious dogs, and blood-thirsty slave hunters, who were so rapidly approaching me with loaded muskets and bowie knives, with a determination to kill or capture me and my family. I started to run with my little daughter in my arms, but stumbled and fell down and scratched the arm of little Frances with a brier, so that it bled very much; but the dear child never cried, for she seemed to know the danger to which we were exposed.

But we soon found that it was no use for us to run. The dogs were soon at our heels, and we were compelled to stop, or be torn to pieces by them. By this time, the soul drivers came charging up on their horses, commanding us to stand still or they would shoot us down.

Of course I surrendered up for the sake of my family. The most abusive terms to be found in the English language were poured forth on us with bitter oaths. They tied my hands behind me, and drove us home before them, to suffer the penalty of a slaveholder's broken law.

As we drew nigh the plantation my heart grew faint. I was aware that we should have to suffer almost death for running off. I was filled with dreadful apprehensions at the thought of meeting a professed follower of Christ, whom I knew to be a hypocrite! No tongue, no pen can ever describe what my feelings were at that time.

XII

My sad condition before Whitfield.—My terrible punishment.—Incidents of a former attempt to escape.—Jack at a farm house.—Six pigs and a turkey.—Our surprise and arrest.

THE READER MAY PERHAPS IMAGINE what must have been my feelings when I found myself surrounded on the island with my little family, at midnight, by a gang of savage wolves. This was one of those trying emergencies in my life when there was apparently but one step between us and the grave. But I had no cords wrapped about my limbs to prevent my struggling against the impending danger to which I was then exposed. I was not denied the consolation of resisting in self defense, as was now the case. There was no Deacon standing before me, with a loaded rifle, swearing that I should submit to the torturing lash, or be shot down like a dumb beast.

I felt that my chance was by far better among the howling wolves in the Red River Swamp, than before Deacon Whitfield, on the cotton plantation. I was brought before him as a criminal before a bar, without counsel, to be tried and condemned by a tyrant's law. My arms were bound with a cord, my spirit broken, and my little family standing by weeping. I was not allowed to plead my own cause, and there was no one to utter a word in my behalf.

He ordered that the field hands should be called together to witness my punishment, that it might serve as a caution to them never to attend a prayer meeting, or run away as I had, lest they should receive the same punishment.

At the sound of the overseer's horn, all the slaves came forward and witnessed my punishment. My clothing was stripped off and I was compelled to lie down on the ground with my face to the earth. Four stakes were driven in the ground, to which my hands and feet were tied. Then the overseer stood over me with the lash and laid it on according to the Deacon's order. Fifty lashes were laid on before stopping. I was then lectured with reference to my going to prayer meeting without his orders, and running away to escape flogging.

While I suffered under this dreadful torture, I prayed, and wept, and implored mercy at the hand of slavery, but found none. After I was marked from my neck to my heels, the Deacon took the gory lash, and said he thought there was a spot on my back yet where he could put in a few more. He wanted to give me something to remember him by, he said.

After I was flogged almost to death in this way, a paddle was brought forward and eight or ten blows given me with it, which was by far worse than the lash. My wounds were then washed with salt brine, after which I was let up. A description of such paddles I have already given in another page. I was so badly punished that I was not able to work for several days. After being flogged as described, they took me off several miles to a shop and had a heavy iron collar riveted on my neck with prongs extending above my head, on the end of which there was a small bell. I was not able to reach the bell with my hand. This heavy load of iron I was compelled to wear for six weeks. I never was allowed to lie in the same house with my family again while I was a slave of Whitfield. I either had to sleep with my feet in the stocks, or be chained with a large log chain to a log over night, with no bed or bedding to rest my wearied limbs on, after toiling all day in the cotton field. I suffered almost death while kept in this confinement; and he had ordered the overseer never to let me loose again; saying that I thought of getting free by running off, but no negro should ever get away from him alive.

I have omitted to state that this was the second time I had run away from him; while I was gone the first time, he extorted from my wife the fact that I had been in the habit of running away, before we left Kentucky; that I had been to Canada, and that I was trying to learn the art of reading and writing. All this was against me.

It is true that I was striving to learn myself to write. I was a kind of a house servant and was frequently sent off on errands, but never without a written pass; and on Sundays I have sometimes got permission to visit our neighbor's slaves, and I have often tried to write myself a pass.

Whenever I got hold of an old letter that had been thrown away, or a piece of white paper, I would save it to write on. I have often gone off in the woods and spent the greater part of the day alone, trying to learn to write myself a pass, by writing on the backs of old letters; copying after the pass that had been written by Whitfield; by so doing I got the use of the pen and could form letters as well as I can now, but knew not what they were.

The Deacon had an old slave by the name of Jack whom he bought about the time that he bought me. Jack was born in the State of Virginia. He had some idea of freedom; had often run away, but was very ignorant; knew not where to go for refuge; but understood all about providing something to eat when unjustly deprived of it.

So for ill treatment, we concluded to take a tramp together. I was to be the pilot, while Jack was to carry the baggage and keep us in provisions. Before we started, I managed to get hold of a suit of clothes the Deacon possessed, with his gun, ammunition and bowie knife. We also procured a blanket, a joint of meat, and some bread.

We started in a northern direction, being bound for the city of Little Rock, State of Arkansas. We travelled by night and laid by in the day, being guided by the unchangeable North Star; but at length, our provisions gave out, and it was Jack's place to get more. We came in sight of a large plantation one morning, where we saw people of color, and Jack said he could get something there, among the slaves, that night, for us to eat. So we concealed ourselves, in sight of this plantation until about bed time, when we saw the lights extinguished.

During the day we saw a female slave passing from the dwelling house to the kitchen as if she was the cook; the house being about three rods from the landlord's dwelling. After we supposed the whites were all asleep, Jack slipped up softly to the kitchen to try his luck with the cook, to see if he could get anything from her to eat.

I would remark that the domestic slaves are often found to be traitors to their own people, for the purpose of gaining favor with their masters; and they are encouraged and trained up by them to report every plot they know of being formed about stealing anything, or running away, or anything of the kind; and for which they are paid. This is one of the principal causes of the slaves being divided among themselves, and without which they could not be held in bondage one year, and perhaps not half that time.

I now proceed to describe the unsuccessful attempt of poor Jack to obtain something from the female slave to satisfy hunger. The planter's house was situated on an elevated spot on the side of a hill. The fencing about the house and garden was very crookedly laid up with rails. The night was rather dark and rainy, and Jack left me with the understanding that I was to stay at a certain place until he returned. I cautioned him before he left me to be very careful—and after he started, I left the place where he was to find me when he returned, for fear something might happen which might lead to my detection, should I remain at that spot. So I left it and went off where I could see the house, and that place too.

Jack had not long been gone, before I heard a great noise; a man, crying out with a loud voice, "Catch him! Catch him!" and hissing the dogs on, and they were close after Jack. The next thing I saw, was Jack running for life, and an old white man after him, with a gun, and his dogs. The fence being on sidling ground, and wet with the rain, when Jack ran against it he knocked down several panels of it and fell, tumbling over and over to the foot of the hill; but soon recovered and ran to where he had left me; but I was gone. The dogs were still after him.

There happened to be quite a thicket of small oak shrubs and bushes in the direction he ran. I think he might have been heard running and straddling bushes a quarter of a mile! the poor fellow hurt himself considerably in straddling over bushes in that way, in making his escape.

Finally the dogs relaxed their chase and poor Jack and myself again met in the thick forest. He said when he rapped on the cookhouse door, the colored woman came to the door. He asked her if she would let him have a bite of bread if she had it, that he was a poor hungry absconding slave. But she made no reply to what he said but immediately sounded the alarm by calling loudly after her master, saying, "here is a runaway negro!" Jack said that he was going to knock her down but her master was out within one moment, and he had to run for his life.

As soon as we got our eyes fixed on the North Star again, we started on our way. We travelled on a few miles and came to another large plantation, where Jack was determined to get something to eat. He left me at a certain place while he went up to the house to find something if possible.

He was gone some time before he returned, but when I saw him coming, he appeared to be very heavy loaded with a bag of something. We walked off pretty fast until we got some distance in the woods. Jack then stopped and opened his bag in which he had six small pigs. I asked him how he got them without making any noise; and he said that he found a bed of hogs, in which there were the pigs with their mother. While the pigs were sucking he crawled up to them without being discovered by the sow, and took them by their necks one after another, and choked them to death, and slipped them into his bag!

We intended to travel on all that night and lay by the next day in the forest and cook up our pigs. We fell into a large road leading on the direction which we were travelling, and had not proceeded over three miles before I found a white hat lying in the road before me. Jack being a little behind me I stopped until he came up, and showed it to him. He picked it up. We looked a few steps farther and saw a man lying by the way, either asleep or intoxicated, as we supposed.

I told Jack not to take the hat, but he would not obey me. He had only a piece of a hat himself, which he left in exchange for the other. We travelled on about five miles farther, and in passing a house discovered a large turkey sitting on the fence, which temptation was greater than Jack could resist. Notwithstanding he had six very nice fat little pigs on his back, he stepped up and took the turkey off the fence.

By this time it was getting near daylight and we left the road and went off a mile or so among the hills of the forest, where we struck camp for the day. We then picked our turkey, dressed our pigs, and cooked two of them. We got the hair off by singeing them over the fire, and after we had eaten all we wanted, one of us slept while the other watched. We had flint, punk, and powder to strike fire with. A little after dark the next night, we started on our way.

But about ten o'clock that night just as we were passing through a thick skirt of woods, five men sprang out before us with fire-arms, swearing if we moved another step, they would shoot us down; and each man having his gun drawn up for shooting we had no chance to make any defense, and surrendered sooner than run the risk of being killed.

They had been lying in wait for us there, for several hours. They had seen a reward out, for notices were put up in the most public places, that fifty dollars would be paid for me, dead or alive, if I should not return home within so many days. And the reader will remember that neither Jack nor myself was able to read the advertisement. It was of very little consequence with the slave catchers, whether they killed us or took us alive, for the reward was the same to them.

After we were taken and tied, one of the men declared to me that he would have shot me dead just as sure as he lived, if I had moved one step after they commanded us to stop. He had his gun leveled at my breast, already cocked, and his finger on the trigger. The way they came to find us out was from the circumstance of Jack's taking the man's hat in connection with the advertisement. The man whose hat was taken was drunk; and the next morning when he came to look for his hat it was gone and Jack's old hat lying in the place of it; and in looking round he saw the tracks of two persons in the dust, who had passed during the night, and one of them having but three toes on one foot. He followed these tracks until they came to a large mud pond, in a lane on one side of which a person might pass dry shod; but the man with three toes on one foot had plunged through the mud. This led the man to think there must be runaway slaves, and from out of that neighborhood; for all persons in that settlement knew which side of that mud hole to go. He then got others to go with him, and they followed us until our track left the road. They supposed that we had gone off in the woods to lay by until night, after which we should pursue our course.

After we were captured they took us off several miles to where one of them lived, and kept us over night. One of our pigs was cooked for us to eat that night; and the turkey the next morning. But we were both tied that night with our hands behind us, and our feet were also tied. The doors were locked, and a bedstead was set against the front door, and two men slept in it to prevent our getting out in the night. They said that they knew how to catch runaway negroes, and how to keep them after they were caught.

They remarked that after they found we had stopped to lay by until night, and they saw from our tracks what direction we were travelling, they went about ten miles on that direction, and hid by the road side until we came up that night. That night after all had got fast to sleep, I though I would try to get out, and I should have succeeded, if I could have moved the bed from the door. I managed to untie myself and crawled under the bed which was placed at the door, and strove to remove it, but in so doing I awakened the men and they got up and confined me again, and watched me until daylight, each with a gun in hand.

The next morning they started with us back to Deacon Whitfield's plantation; but when they got within ten miles of where he lived they stopped at a public house to stay over night; and who should we meet there but the Deacon, who was then out looking for me.

The reader may well imagine how I felt to meet him. I had almost as soon come in contact with Satan himself. He had two long poles or sticks of wood brought in to confine us to. I was compelled to lie on my back across one of those sticks with my arms out, and have them lashed fast to the log with a cord. My feet were also tied to the other, and there I had to lie all that night with my back across this stick of wood, and my feet and hands tied. I suffered that night under the most excruciating pain. From the tight binding of the cord the circulation of the blood in my arms and feet was almost entirely stopped. If the night had been much longer I must have died in that confinement.

The next morning we were taken back to the Deacon's farm, and both flogged for going off, and set to work. But there was some allowance made for me on account of my being young. They said that they knew old Jack had pursuaded me off, or I never would have gone. And the Deacon's wife begged that I might be favored some, for that time, as Jack had influenced me, so as to bring up my old habits of running away that I had entirely given up.

XIII

I am sold to gamblers.—They try to purchase my family.—Our parting scene.—My good usage.—I am sold to an Indian.—His confidence in my integrity manifested.

THE READER WILL REMEMBER that this brings me back to the time the Deacon had ordered me to be kept in confinement until he got a chance to sell me, and that no negro should ever get away from him and live. Some days after this we were all out at the gin house ginning cotton, which was situated on the road side, and there came along a company of men, fifteen or twenty in number, who were Southern sportsmen. Their attention was attracted by the load of iron which was fastened about my neck with a bell attached. They stopped and asked the Deacon what that bell was put on my neck for? and he said it was to keep me from running away, &c.

They remarked that I looked as if I might be a smart negro, and asked if he wanted to sell me. The reply was, yes. They then got off their horses and struck a bargain with him for me. They bought me at a reduced price for speculation.

After they had purchased me, I asked the privilege of going to the house to take leave of my family before I left, which was granted by the sportsmen. But the Deacon said I should never again step my foot inside of his yard; and advised the sportsmen not to take the irons from my neck until they had sold me; that if they gave me the least chance I would run away from them, as I did from him. So I was compelled to mount a horse and go off with them as I supposed, never again to meet my family in this life.

We had not proceeded far before they informed me that they had bought me to sell again, and if they kept the irons on me it would be detrimental to the sale, and that they would therefore take off the irons and dress me up like a man and throw away the old rubbish which I then had on; and they would sell me to someone who would treat me better than Deacon Whitfield. After they had cut off the irons and dressed me up, they crossed over Red River into Texas, where they spent some time horse racing and gambling; and although they were wicked blacklegs of the basest character, it is but due to them to say, that they used me far better than ever the Deacon did. They gave me plenty to eat and put nothing hard on me to do. They expressed much sympathy for me in my bereavement; and almost every day they gave me money more or less, and by my activity in waiting on them, and upright conduct, I got into the good graces of them all, but they could not get any person to buy me on account of the amount of intelligence which they supposed me to have; for many of them thought that I could read and write. When they left Texas, they intended to go to the Indian Territory west of the Mississippi, to attend a great horse race which was to take place. Not being much out of their way to go past Deacon Whitfield's again, I prevailed on them to call on him for the purpose of trying to purchase my wife and child; and I promised them that if they would buy my wife and child, I would get some person to purchase us from them. So they tried to grant my request by calling on the Deacon, and trying to make the purchase. As we approached the Deacon's plantation, my heart was filled with a thousand painful and fearful apprehensions. I had the fullest confidence in the blacklegs with whom I travelled, believing that they would do according to promise, and go to the fullest extent of their ability to restore peace and consolation to a bereaved family—to re-unite husband and wife, parent and child, who had long been severed by slavery through the agency of Deacon Whitfield. But I knew his determination in relation to myself, and I feared his wicked opposition to a restoration of myself and little family, which he had divided, and soon found that my fears were not without foundation.

When we rode up and walked into his yard, the Deacon came out and spoke to all but myself; and not finding me in tattered rags as a substitute for clothes, nor having an iron collar or bell about my neck, as was the case when he sold me, he appeared to be much displeased.

"What did you bring that negro back here for?" said he.

"We have come to try to buy his wife and child; for we can find no one who is willing to buy him alone; and we will either buy or sell so that the family may be together," said they.

While this conversation was going on, my poor bereaved wife, who never expected to see me again in this life, spied me and came rushing to me through the crowd, throwing her arms about my neck exclaiming in the most sympathetic tones, "Oh! my dear husband! I never expected to see you again!" The poor woman was bathed with tears of sorrow and grief. But no sooner had she reached me, than the Deacon peremptorily commanded her to go to her work. This she did not obey, but prayed that her master would not separate us again, as she was there alone, far from friends and relations whom she should never meet again. And now to take away her husband, her last and only true friend, would be like taking her life!

But such appeals made no impression on the unfeeling Deacon's heart. While he was storming with abusive language, and even using the gory lash with hellish vengeance to separate husband and wife, I could see the sympathetic tear-drop, stealing its way down the cheek of the profligate and blackleg, whose object it now was to bind up the broken heart of a wife, and restore to the arms of a bereaved husband, his companion.

They were disgusted at the conduct of Whitfield and cried out shame, even in his presence. They told him that they would give a thousand dollars for my wife and child, or anything in reason. But no! he would sooner see me to the devil than indulge or gratify me after my having run away from him; and if they did not remove me from his presence very soon, he said he should make them suffer for it.

But all this, and even the gory lash had yet failed to break the grasp of poor Malinda, whose prospect of connubial, social, and future happiness was all at stake. When the dear woman saw there was no help for us, and that we should soon be separated forever, in the name of Deacon Whitfield, and American slavery to meet no more as husband and wife, parent and child—the last and loudest appeal was made on our knees. We appealed to the God of justice and to the sacred ties of humanity; but this was all in vain. The louder we prayed the harder he whipped, amid the most heart-rending shrieks from the poor slave mother and child, as little Frances stood by, sobbing at the abuse inflicted on her mother.

"Oh! how shall I give my husband the parting hand never to meet again? This will surely break my heart," were her parting words.

I can never describe to the reader the awful reality of that separation—for it was enough to chill the blood and stir up the deepest feeling of revenge in the hearts of slaveholding blacklegs, who as they stood by, were threatening, some weeping, some swearing and others declaring vengeance against such treatment being inflicted on a human being. As we left the plantation, as far as we could see and hear, the Deacon was still laying on the gory lash, trying to prevent poor Malinda from weeping over the loss of her departed husband, who was then, by the hellish laws of slavery, to her, theoretically and practically dead. One of the blacklegs exclaimed that hell was full of just such deacons as Whitfield. This occurred in December, 1840. I have never seen Malinda, since that period. I never expect to see her again.

The sportsmen to whom I was sold, showed their sympathy for me not only by word but by deeds. They said that they had made the most liberal offer to Whitfield, to buy or sell for the sole purpose of reuniting husband and wife. But he stood out against it—they felt sorry for me. They said they had bought me to speculate on, and were not able to lose what they had paid for me. But they would make a bargain with me, if I was willing, and would lay a plan, by which I might yet get free. If I would use my influence so as to get some person to buy me while traveling about with them, they would give me a portion of the money for which they sold me, and they would also give me directions by which I might yet run away and go to Canada.

This offer I accepted, and the plot was made. They advised me to act very stupid in language and thought, but in business I must be spry; and that I must persuade men to buy me, and promise them that I would be smart.

We passed through the State of Arkansas and stopped at many places, horse-racing and gambling. My business was to drive a wagon in which they carried their gambling apparatus, clothing, &c. I had also to black boots and attend to horses. We stopped at Fayetteville, where they almost lost me, betting on a horse race.

They went from thence to the Indian Territory, among the Cherokee Indians, to attend the great races which were to take place there. During the races there was a very wealthy half Indian of that tribe, who became much attached to me, and had some notion of buying me, after hearing that I was for sale, being a slaveholder. The idea struck me rather favorable, for several reasons. First, I thought I should stand a better chance to get away from an Indian than from a white man. Second, he wanted me only for a kind of body servant to wait on him—and in this case I knew that I should fare better than I should in the field. And my owners also told me that it would be an easy place to get away from. I took their advice for fear I might not get another chance so good as that, and prevailed on the man to buy me. He paid them nine hundred dollars, in gold and silver, for me. I saw the money counted out.

After the purchase was made, the sportsmen got me off to one side, and according to promise they gave me a part of the money, and directions how to get from there to Canada. They also advised me how to act until I got a good chance to run away. I was to embrace the earliest opportunity of getting away, before they should become acquainted with me. I was never to let it be known where I was from, nor where I was born. I was to act quite stupid and ignorant. And when I started I was to go up the boundary line, between the Indian Territory and the States of Arkansas and Missouri, and this would fetch me out on the Missouri River, near Jefferson City, the capital of Missouri. I was to travel at first by night, and to lay by in daylight, until I got out of danger.

The same afternoon that the Indian bought me, he started with me to his residence, which was fifty or sixty miles distant. And so great was his confidence in me, that he entrusted me to carry his money. The amount must have been at least five hundred dollars, which was all in gold and silver; and when we stopped over night the money and horses were all left in my charge.

It would have been a very easy matter for me to have taken one of the best horses, with the money, and run off. And the temptation was truly great to a man like myself, who was watching for the earliest opportunity to escape; and I felt confident that I should never have a better opportunity to escape full handed than then.

XIV

Character of my Indian Master.—Slavery among the Indians less cruel.—Indian carousal.—Enfeebled health of my Indian Master.— His death.—My escape.—Adventure in a wigwam.—Successful progress toward liberty.

THE NEXT MORNING I went home with my new master; and by the way it is only doing justice to the dead to say, that he was the most reasonable, and humane slaveholder that I have ever belonged to. He was the last man that pretended to claim property in my person; and although I have freely given the names and residences of all others who have held me as a slave, for prudential reasons I shall omit giving the name of this individual.

He was the owner of a large plantation and quite a number of slaves. He raised corn and wheat for his own consumption only. There was no cotton, tobacco, or anything of the kind produced among them for market. And I found this difference between negro slavery among the Indians, and the same thing among the white slaveholders of the

South. The Indians allow their slaves enough to eat and wear. They have no overseers to whip nor drive them. If a slave offends his master, he sometimes, in the heat of passion, undertakes to chastise him; but it is as often the case as otherwise, that the slave gets the better of the fight, and even flogs his master;* for which there is no law to punish him; but when the fight is over that is the last of it. So far as religious instruction is concerned, they have it on terms of equality, the bond and the free; they have no respect of persons, they have neither slave laws nor negro pews. Neither do they separate husbands and wives, nor parents and children. All things considered, if I must be a slave, I had by far, rather be a slave to an Indian, than to a white man, from the experience I have had with both.

A majority of the Indians were uneducated, and still followed up their old heathen traditional notions. They made it a rule to have an Indian dance or frolic, about once a fortnight; and they would come together far and near to attend these dances. They would most generally commence about the middle of the afternoon; and would give notice by the blowing of horns. One would commence blowing and another would answer, and so it would go all round the neighborhood. When a number had got together, they would strike a circle about twenty rods in circumference, and kindle up fires about twenty feet apart, all around, in this circle. In the center they would have a large fire to dance around, and at each one of the small fires there would be a squaw to keep up the fire, which looked delightful off at a distance.

But the most degrading practice of all, was the use of intoxicating drinks, which were used to a great excess by all that attended these stump dances. At almost all of these fires there was someone with rum to sell. There would be some dancing, some singing, some gambling, some fighting, and some yelling; and this was kept up often for two days and nights together.

Their dress for the dance was most generally a great bunch of bird feathers, coon tails, or something of the kind stuck in their heads, and a great many shells tied about their legs to rattle while dancing. Their manner of dancing is taking hold of each other's hands and forming a ring around the large fire in the center, and go stomping around it until they would get drunk or their heads would get to swimming, and they would go off and drink, and another set come on. Such were some of the practices indulged in by these Indian slaveholders.

*This singular fact is corroborated in a letter read by the publisher, from an acquaintance while passing through this country in 1849.

My last owner was in a declining state of health when he bought me; and not long after he bought me he went off forty or fifty miles from home to be doctored by an Indian doctor, accompanied by his wife. I was taken along also to drive the carriage and to wait upon him during his sickness. But he was then so feeble, that his life was of but short duration after the doctor commenced on him.

While he lived, I waited on him according to the best of my ability. I watched over him night and day until he died, and even prepared his body for the tomb, before I left him. He died about midnight and I understood from his friends that he was not to be buried until the second day after his death. I pretended to be taking on at a great rate about his death, but I was more excited about running away, than I was about that, and before daylight the next morning I proved it, for I was on my way to Canada.

I never expected a better opportunity would present itself for my escape. I slipped out of the room as if I had gone off to weep for the deceased, knowing that they would not feel alarmed about me until after my master was buried and they had returned back to his residence. And even then, they would think that I was somewhere on my way home; and it would be at least four or five days before they would make any stir in looking after me. By that time, if I had no bad luck, I should be out of much danger.

After the first day, I laid by in the day and traveled by night for several days and nights, passing in this way through several tribes of Indians. I kept pretty near the boundary line. I recollect getting lost one dark rainy night. Not being able to find the road I came into an Indian settlement at the dead hour of the night. I was wet, wearied, cold and hungry; and yet I felt afraid to enter any of their houses or wigwams, not knowing whether they would be friendly or not. But I knew the Indians were generally drunkards, and that occasionally a drunken white man was found straggling among them, and that such an one would be more likely to find friends from sympathy than an upright man.

So I passed myself off that night as a drunkard among them. I walked up to the door of one of their houses, and fell up against it, making a great noise like a drunken man; but no one came to the door. I opened it and staggered in, falling about, and making a great noise. But finally an old woman got up and gave me a blanket to lie down on.

There was quite a number of them lying about on the dirt floor, but not one could talk or understand a word of the English language. I made signs so as to let them know that I wanted something to eat, but they had nothing, so I had to go without that night. I laid down and pretended to be asleep, but I slept none that night, for I was afraid that they would kill me if I went to sleep. About one hour before day, the next morning, three of the females got up and put into a tin kettle a lot of ashes with water, to boil, and then poured into it about one quart of corn. After letting it stand a few moments, they poured it into a trough, and pounded it into thin hominy. They washed it out, and boiled it down, and called me up to eat my breakfast of it.

After eating, I offered them six cents, but they refused to accept it. I then found my way to the main road, and traveled all that day on my journey, and just at night arrived at a public house kept by an Indian, who also kept a store. I walked in and asked if I could get lodging, which was granted; but I had not been there long before three men came riding up about dusk, or between sunset and dark. They were white men, and I supposed slaveholders. At any rate when they asked if they could have lodging, I trembled for fear they might be in pursuit of me. But the landlord told them that he could not lodge them, but they could get lodging about two miles off, with a white man, and they turned their horses and started.

The landlord asked me where I was traveling to, and where I was from. I told him that I had been out looking at the country; that I had thought of buying land, and that I lived in the State of Ohio, in the village of Perrysburgh. He then said that he had lived there himself, and that he had acted as an interpreter there among the Maumee tribe of Indians for several years. He then asked who I was acquainted with there? I informed him that I knew Judge Hollister, Francis Hollister, J. W. Smith, and others. At this he was so much pleased that he came up and took me by the hand, and received me joyfully, after seeing that I was acquainted with those of his old friends.

I could converse with him understandingly from personal acquaintance, for I had lived there when I first ran away from Kentucky. But I felt it to be my duty to start off the next morning before breakfast, or sunrise. I bought a dozen of eggs, and had them boiled to carry with me to eat on the way. I did not like the looks of those three men, and thought I would get on as fast as possible for fear I might be pursued by them.

I was then about to enter the territory of another slave State, Missouri. I had passed through the fiery ordeal of Sibley, Gatewood, and Garrison, and had even slipped through the fingers of Deacon Whitfield. I had doubtless gone through great peril in crossing the Indian territory, in passing through the various half civilized tribes, who seemed to look upon me with astonishment as I passed along. Their hands were almost invariably filled with bows and arrows, tomahawks, guns, butcher knives, and all the various implements of death which are used by them. And what made them look still more frightful, their faces were often painted red, and their heads muffled with birds' feathers, bushes, coons' tails and owls' heads. But all this I had passed through, and my long enslaved limbs and spirit were then in full stretch for emancipation. I felt as if one more short struggle would set me free.

XV

Adventure on the Prairie.—I borrow a horse without leave.—Rapid traveling one whole night.—Apology for using other men's horses.—My manner of living on the road.

EARLY IN THE MORNING I left the Indian territory as I have already said, for fear I might be pursued by the three white men whom I had seen there over night; but I had not proceeded far before my fears were magnified a hundred fold.

I always dreaded to pass through a prairie, and on coming to one which was about six miles in width, I was careful to look in every direction to see whether there was any person in sight before I entered it; but I could see no one. So I started across with a hope of crossing without coming in contact with anyone on the prairie. I walked as fast as I could, but when I got about midway of the prairie, I came to a high spot where the road forked, and three men came up from a low spot as if they had been there concealed. They were all on horse back, and I supposed them to be the same men that had tried to get lodging where I stopped over night. Had this been in timbered land, I might have stood some chance to have dodged them, but there I was, out in the open prairie, where I could see no possible way by which I could escape.

They came along slowly up behind me, and finally passed, and spoke or bowed their heads on passing, but they traveled in a slow walk and kept but a very few steps before me, until we got nearly across the prairie. When we were coming near a plantation a piece off from the road on the skirt of the timbered land, they whipped up their horses and left the road as if they were going across to this plantation. They soon got out of my sight by going down into a valley which lay between us and the plantation. Not seeing them rise the hill to go up to the farm, excited greater suspicion in my mind, so I stepped over on the brow of the hill, where I could see what they were doing, and to my surprise I saw them going right back in the direction they had just come, and they were going very fast. I was then satisfied that they were after me and that they were only going back to get more help to assist them in taking me, for fear that I might kill some of them if they undertook it. The first impression was that I had better leave the road immediately; so I bolted from the road and ran as fast as I could for some distance in the thick forest, and concealed myself for about fifteen or twenty minutes, which were spent in prayer to God for his protecting care and guidance.

My impression was that when they should start in pursuit of me again, they would follow on in the direction which I was going when they left me; and not finding or hearing of me on the road, they would come back and hunt through the woods around, and if they could find no track they might go and get dogs to trace me out.

I thought my chance of escape would be better, if I went back to the same side of the road that they first went, for the purpose of deceiving them; as I supposed that they would not suspect my going in the same direction that they went, for the purpose of escaping from them.

So I traveled all that day square off from the road through the wild forest without any knowledge of the country whatever for I had nothing to travel by but the sun by day, and the moon and stars by night. Just before night I came in sight of a large plantation, where I saw quite a number of horses running at large in a field, and knowing that my success in escaping depended upon my getting out of that settlement within twenty-four hours, to save myself from everlasting slavery, I thought I should be justified in riding one of those horses, that night, if I could catch one. I cut a grape vine with my knife, and made it into a bridle; and shortly after dark I went into the field and tried to catch one of the horses. I got a bunch of dry blades of fodder and walked up softly towards the horses, calling to them "cope," "cope," "cope;" but there was only one out of the number that I was able to get my hand on, and that was an old mare, which I supposed to be the mother of all the rest; and I knew that I could walk faster than she could travel. She had a bell on and was very thin in flesh; she looked gentle and walked on three legs only. The young horses pranced and galloped off. I was not able to get near them, and the old mare being of no use to me, I left them all. After fixing my eyes on the north star I pursued my journey, holding on to my bridle with a hope of finding a horse upon which I might ride that night.

I found a road leading pretty nearly in the direction which I wanted travel, and I kept it. After traveling several miles I found another large plantation where there was a prospect of finding a horse. I stepped up to the barn-yard, wherein I found several horses. There was a little barn standing with the door open, and I found it quite an easy task to get the horses into the barn, and select out the best looking one of them. I pulled down the fence, led the noble beast out and mounted him, taking a northern direction, being able to find a road which led that way. But I had not gone over three or four miles before I came to a large stream of water which was past fording; yet I could see that it had been forded by the road track, but from high water it was then impassable. As the horse seemed willing to go in I put him through; but before he got in far, he was in water up to his sides and finally the water came over his back and he swam over. I got as wet as could be, but the horse carried me safely across at the proper place. After I got out a mile or so from the river, I came into a large prairie, which I think must have been twenty or thirty miles in width, and the road ran across it about in the direction that I wanted to go. I laid whip to the horse, and I think he must have carried me not less than forty miles that night, or before sun rise the next morning. I then stopped him in a spot of high grass in an old field, and took off the bridle. I thanked God, and thanked the horse for what he had done for me, and wished him a safe journey back home.

I know the poor horse must have felt stiff, and tired from his speedy jaunt, and I felt very bad myself, riding at that rate all night without a saddle; but I felt as if I had too much at stake to favor either horse flesh or man flesh. I could indeed afford to crucify my own flesh for the sake of redeeming myself from perpetual slavery.

Some may be disposed to find fault with my taking the horse as I did; but I did nothing more than nine out of ten would do if they were placed in the same circumstances. I had no disposition to steal a horse from any man. But I ask, if a white man had been captured by the Cherokee Indians and carried away from his family for life into slavery, and could see a chance to escape and get back to his family; should the Indians pursue him with a determination to take him back or take his life, would it be a crime for the poor fugitive, whose life, liberty and future happiness were all at stake, to mount any man's horse by the way side, and ride him without asking any questions, to effect his escape? Or who would not do the same thing to rescue a wife, child, father, or mother? Such an act committed by a white man under the same circumstances would not only be pronounced proper, but praiseworthy; and if he neglected to avail himself of such a means of escape he would be pronounced a fool. Therefore from this act I have nothing to regret, for I have done nothing more than any other reasonable person would have done under the same circumstances. But I had good luck from the morning I left the horse until I got back into the State of Ohio. About two miles from where I left the horse, I found a public house on the road, where I stopped and took breakfast. Being asked where I was traveling, I replied that I was going home to Perrysburgh, Ohio, and that I had been out to look at the land in Missouri, with a view of buying. They supposed me to be a native of Ohio, from the fact of my being so well acquainted with its location, its principal cities, inhabitants, &c.

The next night I put up at one of the best hotels in the village where I stopped, and acted with as much independence as if I was worth a million of dollars; talked about buying land, stock and village property, and contrasting it with the same kind of property in the State of Ohio. In this kind of talk they were most generally interested, and I was treated just like other travelers. I made it a point to travel about thirty miles each day on my way to Jefferson City. On several occasions I have asked the landlords where I have stopped over night, if they could tell me who kept the best house where I would stop the next night, which was most generally in a small village. But for fear I might forget, I would get them to give me the name on a piece of paper as a kind of recommend. This would serve as an introduction through which I have always been well received from one landlord to another, and I have always stopped at the best houses, eaten at the first tables, and slept in the best beds. No man ever asked me whether I was bond or free, black or white, rich or poor; but I always presented a bold front and showed the best side out, which was all the pass I had. But when I got within about one hundred miles of Jefferson City, where I expected to take a steamboat passage to St. Louis, I stopped over night at a hotel, where I met with a young white man who was traveling on to Jefferson City on horse back, and was also leading a horse with a saddle and bridle on.

I asked him if he would let me ride the horse which he was leading, as I was going to the same city? He said that it was a hired horse, that he was paying at the rate of fifty cents per day for it, but if I would pay the same I could ride him. I accepted the offer and we rode together to the city. We were on the road together two or three days; stopped and ate and slept together at the same hotels.

XVI

Stratagem to get on board the steamer.—My Irish friends.—My success in reaching Cincinnati.—Reflections on again seeing Kentucky.—I get employment in a hotel.—My fright at seeing the gambler who sold me.— I leave Ohio with Mr. Smith.—His letter.—My education.

THE GREATEST OF my adventures came off when I arrived at Jefferson City. There I expected to meet an advertisement for my person; it was there I must cross the river or take a steamboat down; it was there I expected to be interrogated and required to prove whether I was actually a free man or a slave. If I was free, I should have to show my free papers; and if I was a slave I should be required to tell who my master was.

I stopped at a hotel, however, and ascertained that there was a steamboat expected down the river that day for St. Louis. I also found out that there were several passengers at that house who were going down on board of the first boat. I knew that the captain of a steamboat could not take a colored passenger on board of his boat from a slave state without first ascertaining whether such person was bond or free; I knew that this was more than he would dare to do by the laws of the slave states—and now to surmount this difficulty it brought into exercise all the powers of my mind. I would have got myself boxed up as freight, and have been forwarded to St. Louis, but I had no friend that I could trust to do it for me. This plan has since been adopted by some with success. But finally I thought I might possibly pass myself off as a body servant to the passengers going from the hotel down.

So I went to a store and bought myself a large trunk, and took it to the hotel. Soon, a boat came in which was bound to St. Louis, and the passengers started down to get on board. I took up my large trunk, and started along after them as if I was their servant. My heart trembled in view of the dangerous experiment which I was then about to try. It required all the moral courage that I was master of to bear me up in view of my critical condition. The white people that I was following walked on board and I after them. I acted as if the trunk was full of clothes, but I had not a stitch of clothes in it. The passengers went up into the cabin and I followed them with the trunk. I suppose this made the captain think that I was their slave.

I not only took the trunk in the cabin but stood by it until after the boat had started as if it belonged to my owners; and I was taking care of it for them; but as soon as the boat got fairly under way, I knew that some account would have to be given of me; so I then took my trunk down on the deck among the deck passengers to prepare myself to meet the clerk of the boat, when he should come to collect fare from the deck passengers.

Fortunately for me there was quite a number of deck passengers on board, among whom there were many Irish. I insinuated myself among them so as to get into their good graces, believing that if I should get into a difficulty they would stand by me. I saw several of these persons going up to the saloon buying whiskey, and I thought this might be the most effectual way by which I could gain speedily their respect and sympathy. So I participated with them pretty freely for awhile, or at least until after I got my fare settled. I placed myself in a little crowd of them, and invited them all up to the bar with me, stating that it was my treat. This was responded to, and they walked up and drank and I footed the bill. This, of course, brought us into a kind of union. We sat together and laughed and talked freely. Within ten or fifteen minutes I remarked that I was getting dry again, and invited them up and treated again. By this time I was thought to be one of the most liberal and gentlemanly men on board, by these deck passengers; they were ready to do anything for me—they got to singing songs, and telling long yarns in which I took quite an active part; but it was all for effect.

By this time the porter came around ringing his bell for all passengers who had not paid their fare, to walk up to the captain's office and settle it. Some of my Irish friends had not yet settled, and I asked one of them if he would be good enough to take my money and get me a ticket when he was getting one for himself, and he quickly replied, "yes, sir, I will get you a ticket." So he relieved me of my greatest trouble. When they came round to gather the tickets before we got to St. Louis, my ticket was taken with the rest, and no questions were asked me.

The next day the boat arrived at St. Louis; my object was to take passage on board of the first boat which was destined for Cincinnati, Ohio; and as there was a boat going out that day for Pittsburgh, I went on board to make some inquiry about the fare &c., and found the steward to be a colored man with whom I was acquainted. He lived in Cincinnati, and had rendered me some assistance in making my escape to Canada, in the summer of 1838, and he also very kindly aided me then in getting back into a land of freedom. The swift running steamer started that afternoon on her voyage, which soon wafted my body beyond the tyrannical limits of chattel slavery. When the boat struck the mouth of the river Ohio, and I had once more the pleasure of looking on that lovely stream, my heart leaped up for joy at the glorious prospect that I should again be free. Every revolution of the mighty steam-engine seemed to bring me nearer and nearer the "promised land." Only a few days had elapsed, before I was permitted by the smiles of a good providence, once more to gaze on the green hill-tops and valleys of old Kentucky, the State of my nativity. And notwithstanding I was deeply interested while standing on the deck of the steamer looking at the beauties of nature on either side of the river, as she pressed her way up the stream, my very soul was pained to look upon the slaves in the fields of Kentucky, still toiling under their task-masters without pay. It was on this soil I first breathed the free air of Heaven, and felt the bitter pangs of slavery—it was here that I first learned to abhor it. It was here I received the first impulse of human rights—it was here that I first entered my protest against the bloody institution of slavery, by running away from it, and declared that I would no longer work for any man as I had done, without wages.

When the steamboat arrived at Portsmouth, Ohio, I took off my trunk with the intention of going to Canada. But my funds were almost exhausted, so I had to stop and go to work to get money to travel on. I hired myself at the American Hotel to a Mr. McCoy to do the work of a porter, to black boots, &c., for which he was to pay me $12 per month. I soon found the landlord to be bad pay, and not only that, but he would not allow me to charge for blacking boots, although I had to black them after everybody had gone to bed at night, and set them in the bar-room, where the gentlemen could come and get them in the morning while I was at other work. I had nothing extra for this, neither would he pay me my regular wages; so I thought this was a little too much like slavery, and devised a plan by which I got some pay for my work.

I made it a point never to blacken all the boots and shoes overnight, neither would I put any of them in the bar-room, but lock them up in a room where no one could get them without calling for me. I got a piece of broken vessel, placed it in the room just before the boots, and put into it several pieces of small change, as if it had been given me for boot blacking; and almost everyone that came in after their boots, would throw some small trifle into my contribution box, while I was there blacking away. In this way, I made more than my landlord paid me, and I soon got a good stock of cash again. One morning I blacked a gentleman's boots who came in during the night by a steamboat. After he had put on his boots, I was called into the bar-room to button his straps; and while I was performing this service, not thinking to see anybody that knew me, I happened to look up at the man's face and who should it be but one of the very gamblers who had recently sold me. I dropped his foot and bolted from the room as if I had been struck by an electric shock. The man happened not to recognize me, but this strange conduct on my part excited the landlord, who followed me out to see what was the matter. He found me with my hand to my breast, groaning at a great rate. He asked me what was the matter; but I was not able to inform him correctly, but said that I felt very bad indeed. He of course thought I was sick with the colic and ran in the house and got some hot stuff for me, with spice, ginger, &c. But I never got able to go into the bar-room until long after breakfast time, when I knew this man was gone; then I got well.

And yet I have no idea that the man would have hurt a hair of my head; but my first thought was that he was after me. I then made up my mind to leave Portsmouth; its location being right on the border of a slave State.

A short time after this a gentleman put up there over night named Smith, from Perrysburgh, with whom I was acquainted in the North. He was on his way to Kentucky to buy up a drove of fine horses, and he wanted me to go and help him to drive his horses out to Perrysburgh, and said he would pay all my expenses if I would go. So I made a contract to go and agreed to meet him the next week, on a set day, in Washington, Ky., to start with his drove to the north. Accordingly at the time I took a steamboat passage down to Maysville, near where I was to meet Mr. Smith with my trunk. When I arrived at Maysville, I found that Washington was still six miles back from the river. I stopped at a hotel and took my breakfast, and who should I see there but a captain of a boat, who saw me but two years previous going down the river Ohio with handcuffs on, in a chain gang; but he happened not to know me. I left my trunk at the hotel and went out to Washington, where I found Mr. Smith, and learned that he was not going to start off with his drove until the next day.

The following letter which was addressed to the committee to investigate the truth of my narrative, will explain this part of it to the reader and corroborate my statements:

Maumee City, April 5, 1845.

Chas. H. Stewart, Esq.

Dear Sir:—Your favor of 13th February, addressed to me at Perrysburgh, was not received until yesterday; having removed to this place, the letter was not forwarded as it should have been. In reply to your inquiry respecting Henry Bibb, I can only say that about the year 1838 I became acquainted with him at Perrysburgh—employed him to do some work by the job which he performed well, and from his apparent honesty and candor, I became much interested in him. About that time he went South for the purpose, as was said, of getting his wife, who was there in slavery. In the spring of 1841, I found him at Portsmouth on the Ohio River, and after much persuasion, employed him to assist my man to drive home some horses and cattle which I was about purchasing near Maysville, Ky. My confidence in him was such that when about half way home I separated the horses from the cattle, and left him with the latter, with money and instructions to hire what help he wanted to get to Perrysburgh. This he accomplished to my entire satisfaction. He worked for me during the summer, and I was unwilling to part with him, but his desire to go to school and mature plans for the liberation of his wife, were so strong that he left for Detroit, where he could enjoy the society of his colored brethren. I have heard his story and must say that I have not the least reason to suspect it being otherwise than true, and furthermore, I firmly believe, and have for a long time, that he has the foundation to make himself useful. I shall always afford him all the facilities in my power to assist him, until I hear of something in relation to him to alter my mind.

Yours in the cause of truth.

J. W. Smith

When I arrived at Perrysburgh, I went to work for Mr. Smith for several months. This family I found to be one of the most kind-hearted, and unprejudiced that I ever lived with. Mr. and Mrs. Smith lived up to their profession.

I resolved to go to Detroit, that winter, and go to school, in January 1842. But when I arrived at Detroit I soon found that I was not able to give myself a very thorough education. I was among strangers, who were not disposed to show me any great favors. I had everything to pay for, and clothing to buy, so I graduated within three weeks! And this was all the schooling that I have ever had in my life.

W. C. Monroe was my teacher; to him I went about two weeks only. My occupation varied according to circumstances, as I was not settled in mind about the condition of my bereaved family for several years, and could not settle myself down at any permanent business. I saw occasionally, fugitives from Kentucky, some of whom I knew, but none of them were my relatives; none could give me the information which I desired most.

XVII

Letter from W. H. Gatewood.—My reply.—My efforts as a public lecturer.—Singular incident in Steubenville.—Meeting with a friend of Whitfield in Michigan.—Outrage on a canal packet.—Fruitless efforts to find my wife.

THE FIRST DIRECT information that I received concerning any of my relations, after my last escape from slavery, was communicated in a letter from Wm. H. Gatewood, my former owner, which I here insert word for word, without any correction:

Bedford, Trimble County, Ky.

Mr. H. Bibb,

Dear Sir:

After my respects to you and yours &c., I received a small book which you sent to me that I peroseed and found it was sent by H. Bibb I am a stranger in Detroit and know no man there without it is Walton H. Bibb if this be the man please to write to me and tell me all about that place and the people I will tell you the news here as well as I can your mother is still living here and she is well the people are generally well in this cuntry times are dull and produce low give my compliments to King, Jack, and all my friends in that cuntry I read that book you sent me and think it will do very well—George is sold, I do not know any thing about him I have nothing more at present, but remain yours &c

> W. H. Gatewood
> February 9th, 1844.

P.S. You will please to answer this letter.

Never was I more surprised than at the reception of this letter, it came so unexpected to me. There had just been a State Convention held in Detroit, by the free people of color, the proceedings of which were published in pamphlet form. I forwarded several of them to distinguished slaveholders in Kentucky—one among others was Mr. Gatewood, and gave him to understand who sent it. After showing this letter to several of my anti-slavery friends, and asking their opinions about the propriety of my answering it, I was advised to do it, as Mr. Gatewood had no claim on me as a slave, for he had sold and got the money for me and my family. So I wrote him an answer, as near as I can recollect, in the following language:

Dear Sir:

I am happy to inform you that you are not mistaken in the man whom you sold as property, and received pay for as such. But I thank God that I am not property now, but am regarded as a man like yourself, and although I live far north, I am enjoying a comfortable living by my own industry. If you should ever chance to be traveling this way, and will call on me, I will use you better than you did me while you held me as a slave. Think not that I have any malice against you, for the cruel treatment which you inflicted on me while I was in your power. As it was the custom of your country, to treat your fellow men as you did me and my little family, I can freely forgive you.

I wish to be remembered in love to my aged mother, and friends; please tell her that if we should never meet again in this life, my prayer shall be to God that we may meet in Heaven, where parting shall be no more.

You wish to be remembered to King and Jack. I am pleased, sir, to inform you that they are both here, well, and doing well. They are both living in Canada West. They are now the owners of better farms than the men are who once owned them.

You may perhaps think hard of us for running away from slavery, but as to myself, I have but one apology to make for it, which is this: I have only to regret that I did not start at an earlier period. I might have been free long before I was. But you had it in your power to have kept me there much longer than you did. I think it is very probable that I should have been a toiling slave on your plantation today, if you had treated me differently.

To be compelled to stand by and see you whip and slash my wife without mercy, when I could afford her no protection, not even by offering myself to suffer the lash in her place, was more than I felt it to be the duty of a slave husband to endure, while the way was open to Canada. My infant child was also frequently flogged by Mrs. Gatewood, for crying, until its skin was bruised literally purple. This kind of treatment was what drove me from home and family, to seek a better home for them. But I am willing to forget the past. I should be pleased to hear from you again, on the reception of this, and should also be very happy to correspond with you often, if it should be agreeable to yourself. I subscribe myself a friend to the oppressed, and Liberty forever.

> Henry Bibb.
> William Gatewood.
> Detroit, March 23d, 1844.

The first time that I ever spoke before a public audience, was to give a narration of my own sufferings and adventures, connected with slavery. I commenced in the village of Adrian, State of Michigan, May, 1844. From that up to the present period, the principle part of my time has been faithfully devoted to the cause of freedom—nerved up and encouraged by the sympathy of anti-slavery friends on the one hand, and prompted by a sense of duty to my enslaved countrymen on the other, especially, when I remembered that slavery had robbed me of my freedom—deprived me of education—banished me from my native State, and robbed me of my family.

I went from Michigan to the State of Ohio, where I traveled over some of the Southern counties of that State, in company with Samuel Brooks, and Amos Dresser, lecturing upon the subject of American Slavery. The prejudice of the people at that time was very strong against the abolitionists; so much so that they were frequently mobbed for discussing the subject.

We appointed a series of meetings along on the Ohio River, in sight of the State of Virginia; and in several places we had Virginians over to hear us upon the subject. I recollect our having appointed a meeting in the city of Steubenville, which is situated on the bank of the river Ohio. There was but one known abolitionist living in that city, named George Ore. On the day of our meeting, when we arrived in this splendid city there was not a church, school house, nor hall, that we could get for love or money, to hold our meeting in. Finally, I believe that the Whigs consented to let us have the use of their club room, to hold the meeting in; but before the hour had arrived for us to commence, they re-considered the matter, and informed us that we could not have the use of their house for an abolition meeting.

We then got permission to hold forth in the public market house, and even then so great was the hostility of the rabble, that they tried to bluff us off, by threats and epithets. Our meeting was advertised to take place at nine o'clock, A.M. The pro-slavery parties hired a colored man to take a large auction bell, and go all over the city ringing it, and crying, "ho ye! ho ye! Negro auction to take place in the market house, at nine o'clock, by George Ore!" This cry was sounded all over the city, which called out many who would not otherwise have been present. They came to see if it was really the case. The object of the rabble in having the bell rung was, to prevent us from attempting to speak. But at the appointed hour, Bro. Dresser opened the meeting with prayer, and Samuel Brooks mounted the block and spoke for fifteen or twenty minutes, after which Mr. Dresser took the block and talked about one hour upon the wickedness of slaveholding. There were not yet many persons present. They were standing off I suppose to see if I was to be offered for sale. Many windows were hoisted and store doors open, and they were looking and listening to what was said. After Mr. Dresser was through, I was called to take the stand. Just at this moment there was no small stir in rushing forward; so much indeed, that I thought they were coming up to mob me. I should think that in less than fifteen minutes there were about one thousand persons standing around, listening. I saw many of them shedding tears while I related the sad story of my wrongs. At twelve o'clock we adjourned the meeting, to meet again at the same place at two P.M. Our afternoon meeting was well attended until nearly sunset, at which time, we saw some signs of a mob and adjourned. The mob followed us that night to the house of Mr. Ore, and they were yelling like tigers, until late that night, around the house, as if they wanted to tear it down.

In the fall of 1844, S. B. Treadwell, of Jackson, and myself, spent two or three months in lecturing through the State of Michigan, upon the abolition of slavery, in a section of country where abolitionists were few and far between. Our meetings were generally appointed in small log cabins, school houses, among the farmers, which were sometimes crowded full; and where they had no horse teams, it was often the case that there would be four or five ox teams come, loaded down with men, women and children, to attend our meetings.

But the people were generally poor, and in many places not able to give us a decent night's lodging. We most generally carried with us a few pounds of candles to light up the houses wherein we held our meetings after night; for in many places, they had neither candles nor candlesticks. After meeting was out, we have frequently gone from three to eight miles to get lodging, through the dark forest, where there was scarcely any road for a wagon to run on.

I have traveled for miles over swamps, where the roads were covered with logs, without any dirt over them, which has sometimes shook and jostled the wagon to pieces, where we could find no shop or any place to mend it. We would have to tie it up with bark, or take the lines to tie it with, and lead the horse by the bridle. At other times we were in mud up to the hubs of the wheels. I recollect one evening, we lectured in a little village where there happened to be a Southerner present, who was a personal friend of Deacon Whitfield, who became much offended at what I said about his "Bro. Whitfield," and complained about it after the meeting was out.

He told the people not to believe a word that I said, that it was all a humbug. They asked him how he knew? "Ah!" said he, "he has slandered Bro. Whitfield. I am well acquainted with him, we both belonged to one church; and Whitfield is one of the most respectable men in all that region of country." They asked if he (Whitfield) was a slaveholder?

The reply was, "Yes, but he treated his slaves well."

"Well," said one, "that only proves that he has told us the truth; for all we wish to know, is that there is such a man as Whitfield, as represented by Bibb, and that he is a slaveholder."

On the 2d Sept., 1847, I started from Toledo on board the canal packet *Erie*, for Cincinnati, Ohio. But before going on board, I was waited on by one of the boat's crew, who gave me a card of the boat, upon which was printed, that no pains would be spared to render all passengers comfortable who might favor them with their patronage to Cincinnati. This card I slipped into my pocket, supposing it might be of some use to me. There were several drunken loafers on board going through as passengers, one of whom used the most vulgar language in the cabin, where there were ladies, and even vomited! But he was called a white man, and a Southerner, which made it all right. I of course took my place in the cabin with the rest, and there was nothing said against it that night. When the passengers went forward to settle their fare I paid as much as any other man, which entitled me to the same privileges. The next morning at the ringing of the breakfast bell, the proprietor of the packet line, Mr. Samuel Doyle, being on board, invited the passengers to sit up to breakfast. He also invited me personally to sit up to the table. But after we were all seated, and some had begun to eat, he came and ordered me up from the table, and said I must wait until the rest were done.

I left the table without making any reply, and walked out on the deck of the boat. After breakfast the passengers came up, and the cabin boy was sent after me to come to breakfast, but I refused. Shortly after, this man who had ordered me from the table, came up with the ladies. I stepped up and asked him if he was the captain of the boat. His answer was no, that he was one of the proprietors. I then informed him that I was going to leave his boat at the first stopping place, but before leaving I wanted to ask him a few questions: "Have I misbehaved to anyone on board of this boat? Have I disobeyed any law of this boat?"

"No," said he.

"Have I not paid you as much as any other passenger through to Cincinnati?"

"Yes," said he.

"Then I am sure that I have been insulted and imposed upon, on board of this boat, without any just cause whatever."

"No one has misused you, for you ought to have known better than to have come to the table where there were white people."

"Sir, did you not ask me to come to the table?"

"Yes, but I did not know that you was a colored man, when I asked you; and then it was better to insult one man than all the passengers on board of the boat."

"Sir, I do not believe that there is a gentleman or lady on board of this boat who would have considered it an insult for me to have taken my breakfast, and you have imposed upon me by taking my money and promising to use me well, and then to insult me as you have."

"I don't want any of your jaw," said he.

"Sir, with all due respect to your elevated station, you have imposed upon me in a way which is unbecoming a gentleman. I have paid my money, and behaved myself as well as any other man, and I am determined that no man shall impose on me as you have, by deceiving me, without my letting the world know it. I would rather a man should rob me of my money at midnight, than to take it in that way."

I left this boat at the first stopping place, and took the next boat to Cincinnati. On the last boat I had no cause to complain of my treatment. When I arrived at Cincinnati, I published a statement of this affair in the *Daily Herald*.

The next day Mr. Doyle called on the editor in a great passion. "Here," said he, "what does this mean."

"What, sir?" said the editor quietly.

"Why, the stuff here, read it and see."

"Read it yourself," answered the editor.

"Well, I want to know if you sympathize with this nigger here."

"Who, Mr. Bibb? Why yes, I think he is a gentleman, and should be used as such."

"Why this is all wrong—all of it."

"Put your finger on the place, and I will right it."

"Well, he says that we took his money, when we paid part back. And if you take his part, why I'll have nothing to do with your paper."

So ended his wrath.

In 1845, the anti-slavery friends of Michigan employed me to take the field as an anti-slavery Lecturer, in that State, during the Spring, Summer, and Fall, pledging themselves to restore to me my wife and child, if they were living, and could be reached by human agency, which may be seen by the following circular from the *Signal of Liberty:*

To LIBERTY FRIENDS:—In the *Signal* of the 28th inst. is a report from the undersigned respecting Henry Bibb. His narrative always excites deep sympathy for himself and favorable bias for the cause, which seeks to abolish the evils he so powerfully portrays. Friends and foes attest his efficiency.

Mr. Bibb has labored much in lecturing, yet has collected but a bare pittance. He has received from Ohio lucrative offers, but we have prevailed on him to remain in this State.

We think that a strong obligation rests on the friends in this state to sustain Mr. Bibb, and restore to him his wife and child. Under the expectation that Michigan will yield to these claims; will support their laborer, and re-unite the long severed ties of husband and wife, parent and child, Mr. Bibb will lecture through the whole State.

Our object is to prepare friends for the visit of Mr. Bibb, and to suggest an effective mode of operations for the whole State.

Let friends in each vicinity appoint a collector—pay to him all contributions for the freedom of Mrs. Bibb and child; then transmit them to us. We will acknowledge them in the *Signal,* and be responsible for them. We will see that the proper measures for the freedom of Mrs. Bibb and child are taken, and if it be within our means we will accomplish it—nay we will accomplish it, if the objects be living and the friends sustain us. But should we fail, the contributions will be held subject to the order of the donors, less however, by a proportionate deduction of expenses from each.

The hope of this re-union will nerve the heart and body of Mr. Bibb to re-doubled effort in a cause otherwise dear to him. And as he will devote his whole time systematically to the anti-slavery cause, he must also depend on friends for the means of livelihood. We bespeak for him your hospitality, and such pecuniary contributions as you can afford, trusting that the latter may be sufficient to enable him to keep the field.

> *A. L. Porter,*
> *C. H. Stewart,*
> *Silas M. Holmes*
> Detroit, April 22, 1845.

I have every reason to believe that they acted faithfully in the matter, but without success. They wrote letters in every quarter where they would be likely to gain any information respecting her. There were also two men sent from Michigan in the summer of 1845, down South, to find her if possible, and report—and whether they found out her condition, and refused to report, I am not able to say—but suffice it to say that they never have reported. They were respectable men and true friends of the cause, one of whom was a Methodist minister, and the other a cabinet maker, and both white men.

The small spark of hope which had still lingered about my heart had almost become extinct.

XVIII

My last effort to recover my family.—Sad tidings of my wife.—Her degradation.—I am compelled to regard our relation as dissolved forever.

IN VIEW OF the failure to hear anything of my wife, many of my best friends advised me to get married again, if I could find a suitable person. They regarded my former wife as dead to me, and all had been done that could be.

But I was not yet satisfied myself, to give up. I wanted to know certainly what had become of her. So in the winter of 1845, I resolved to go back to Kentucky, my native State, to see if I could hear anything from my family. And against the advice of all my friends, I went back to Cincinnati, where I took passage on board of a Southern steamboat to Madison, in the State of Indiana, which was only ten miles from where Wm. Gatewood lived, who was my former owner. No sooner had I landed in Madison, than I learned, on inquiry, and from good authority, that my wife was living in a state of adultery with her master, and had been for the last three years. This message she sent back to Kentucky, to her mother and friends. She also spoke of the time and manner of our separation by Deacon Whitfield, my being taken off by the Southern blacklegs, to where she knew not; and that she had finally given me up. The child she said was still with her. Whitfield had sold her to this man for the above purposes at a high price, and she was better used than ordinary slaves. This was a death blow to all my hopes and pleasant plans. While I was in Madison I hired a white man to go over to Bedford, in Kentucky, where my mother was then living, and bring her over into a free State to see me. I hailed her approach with unspeakable joy. She informed me too, on inquiring whether my family had ever been heard from, that the report which I had just heard in relation to Malinda was substantially true, for it was the same message that she had sent to her mother and friends. And my mother thought it was no use for me to run any more risks, or to grieve myself any more about her.

From that time I gave her up into the hands of an all-wise Providence. As she was then living with another man, I could no longer regard her as my wife. After all the sacrifices, sufferings, and risks which I had run, striving to rescue her from the grasp of slavery; every prospect and hope was cut off. She has ever since been regarded as theoretically and practically dead to me as a wife, for she was living in a state of adultery, according to the law of God and man.

Poor unfortunate woman, I bring no charge of guilt against her, for I know not all the circumstances connected with the case. It is consistent with slavery, however, to suppose that she became reconciled to it, from the fact of her sending word back to her friends and relatives that she was much better treated than she had ever been before, and that she had also given me up. It is also reasonable to suppose that there might have been some kind of attachment formed by living together in this way for years; and it is quite probable that they have other children according to the law of nature, which would have a tendency to unite them stronger together.

In view of all the facts and circumstances connected with this matter, I deem further comments and explanations unnecessary on my part. Finding myself thus isolated in this peculiarly unnatural state, I resolved, in 1846, to spend my days in traveling, to advance the anti-slavery cause. I spent the summer in Michigan, but in the subsequent fall I took a trip to New England, where I spent the winter. And there I found a kind reception wherever I traveled among the friends of freedom.

While traveling about in this way among strangers, I was sometimes sick, with no permanent home, or bosom friend to sympathize or take that care of me which an affectionate wife would. So I conceived the idea that it would be better for me to change my position, provided I should find a suitable person.

In the month of May, 1847, I attended the anti-slavery anniversary in the city of New York, where I had the good fortune to be introduced to the favor of a Miss Mary E. Miles, of Boston; a lady whom I had frequently heard very highly spoken of, for her activity and devotion to the anti-slavery cause, as well as her talents and learning, and benevolence in the cause of reforms, generally. I was very much impressed with the personal appearance of Miss Miles, and was deeply interested in our first interview, because I found that her principles and my own were nearly one and the same. I soon found by a few visits, as well as by letters, that she possessed moral principle, and frankness of disposition, which is often sought for but seldom found. These, in connection with other amiable qualities, soon won my entire confidence and affection. But this secret I kept to myself until I was fully satisfied that this feeling was reciprocal; that there was indeed a congeniality of principles and feeling, which time nor eternity could never change.

When I offered myself for matrimony, we mutually engaged ourselves to each other, to marry in one year, with this condition, viz: that if either party should see any reason to change their mind within that time, the contract should not be considered binding. We kept up a regular correspondence during the time, and in June, 1848, we had the happiness to be joined in holy wedlock. Not in slaveholding style, which is a mere farce, without the sanction of law or gospel; but in accordance with the laws of God and our country. My beloved wife is a bosom friend, a help-meet, a loving companion in all the social, moral, and religious relations of life. She is to me what a poor slave's wife can never be to her husband while in the condition of a slave; for she can not be true to her husband contrary to the will of her master. She can neither be pure nor virtuous, contrary to the will of her master. She dare not refuse to be reduced to a state of adultery at the will of her master; from the fact that the slaveholding law, customs and teachings are all against the poor slaves.

I presume there are no class of people in the United States who so highly appreciate the legality of marriage as those persons who have been held and treated as property. Yes, it is that fugitive who knows from sad experience, what it is to have his wife tyrannically snatched from his bosom by a slaveholding professor of religion, and finally reduced to a state of adultery, that knows how to appreciate the law that repels such high-handed villainy. Such as that to which the writer has been exposed. But thanks be to God, I am now free from the hand of the cruel oppressor, no more to be plundered of my dearest rights; the wife of my bosom, and my poor unoffending offspring. Of Malinda I will only add a word in conclusion. The relation once subsisting between us, to which I clung, hoping against hope, for years, after we were torn asunder, not having been sanctioned by any loyal power, cannot be cancelled by a legal process. Voluntarily assumed without law mutually, it was by her relinquished years ago without my knowledge, as before named; during which time I was making every effort to secure her restoration. And it was not until after living alone in the world for more than eight years without a companion known in law or morals, that I changed my condition.

XIX

Comments on S. Gatewood's letter about slaves stealing.—Their conduct vindicated.—Comments on W. Gatewood's letter.

BUT IT SEEMS that I am not now beyond the reach of the foul slander of slaveholders. They are not satisfied with selling and banishing me from my native State. As soon as they got news of my being in the Free North, exposing their peculiar Institution, a libelous letter was written by Silas Gatewood of Kentucky, a son of one of my former owners, to a Northern Committee, for publication, which he thought would destroy my influence and character.

He has charged me with the awful crime of taking from my keeper and oppressor, some of the fruits of my own labor for the benefit of myself and family.

But while writing this letter he seems to have overlooked the disgraceful fact that he was guilty himself of what would here be regarded highway robbery, in his conduct to me as narrated [earlier in] this narrative.

A word in reply to Silas Gatewood's letter. I am willing to admit all that is true, but shall deny that which is so basely false. In the first place, he puts words in my mouth that I never used. He says that I represented that "my mother belonged to James Bibb." I deny ever having said so in private or public. He says that I stated that Bibb's daughter married a Sibley. I deny it. He also says that the first time that I left Kentucky for my liberty, I was gone about two years, before I went back to rescue my family. I deny it. I was gone from Dec. 25th, 1837, to May, or June, 1838. He says that I went back the second time for the purpose of taking off my family, and eight or ten more slaves to Canada. This I will not pretend to deny. He says I was guilty of disposing of articles from the farm for my own use, and pocketing the money, and that his father caught me stealing a sack full of wheat. I admit the fact. I acknowledge the wheat.

And who had a better right to eat of the fruits of my own hard earnings than myself? Many a long summer's day have I toiled with my wife and other slaves, cultivating his father's fields, and gathering in his harvest, under the scorching rays of the sun, without half enough to eat, or clothes to wear, and at the same time his meat-house was filled with bacon and bread stuff; his dairy with butter and cheese; his barn with grain, husbanded by the unrequited toil of the slaves. And yet if a slave presumed to take a little from the abundance which he had made by his own sweat and toil, to supply the demands of nature, to quiet the craving appetite which is sometimes almost irresistible, it is called stealing by slaveholders.

But I did not regard it as stealing then, I do not regard it as such now. I hold that a slave has a moral right to eat, drink and wear all that he needs, and that it would be a sin on his part to suffer and starve in a country where there is a plenty to eat and wear within his reach. I consider that I had a just right to what I took, because it was the labor of my own hands. Should I take from a neighbor as a freeman, in a free country, I should consider myself guilty of doing wrong before God and man. But was I the slave of Wm. Gatewood today, or any other slaveholder, working without wages, and suffering with hunger or for clothing, I should not stop to inquire whether my master would approve of my helping myself to what I needed to eat or wear. For while the slave is regarded as property, how can he steal from his master? It is contrary to the very nature of the relation existing between master and slave, from the fact that there is no law to punish a slave for theft, but lynch law; and the way they avoid that is to hide well. For illustration, a slave from the State of Virginia, for cruel treatment left the State between daylight and dark, being borne off by one of his master's finest horses, and finally landed in Canada, where the British laws recognize no such thing as property in a human being. He was pursued by his owners, who expected to take advantage of the British law by claiming him as a fugitive from justice, and as such he was arrested and brought before the court of Queen's Bench. They swore that he was, at a certain time, the slave of Mr. A., and that he ran away at such a time and stole and brought off a horse. They enquired who the horse belonged to, and it was ascertained that the slave and horse both belonged to the same person. The court therefore decided that the horse and the man were both recognized, in the State of Virginia, alike, as articles of property, belonging to the same person—therefore, if there was theft committed on either side, the former must have stolen off the latter—the horse brought away the man, and not the man the horse. So the man was discharged and pronounced free according to the laws of Canada. There are several other letters published in this work upon the same subject, from slaveholders, which it is hardly necessary for me to notice. However, I feel thankful to the writers for the endorsement and confirmation which they have given to my story. No matter what their motives were, they have done me and the anti-slavery cause good service in writing those letters—but more especially the Gatewood's. Silas Gatewood has done more for me than all the rest. He has labored so hard in his long communication in trying to expose me, that he has proved everything that I could have asked of him; and for which I intend to reward him by forwarding him one of my books, hoping that it may be the means of converting him from a slaveholder to an honest man, and an advocate of liberty for all mankind.

The reader will see in the introduction that Wm. Gatewood writes a more cautious letter upon the subject than his son Silas. "It is not a very easy matter to catch old birds with chaff," and I presume if Silas had the writing of his letter over again, he would not be so free in telling all he knew, and even more, for the sake of making out a strong case. The object of his writing such a letter will doubtless be understood by the reader. It was to destroy public confidence in the victims of slavery, that the system might not be exposed—it was to gag a poor fugitive who had undertaken to plead his own cause and that of his enslaved brethren. It was a feeble attempt to suppress the voice of universal freedom which is now thundering on every gale. But thank God it is too late in the day.

> *Go stop the mighty thunder's roar,*
> *Go hush the ocean's sound,*
> *Or upward like the eagle soar*
> *To skies' remotest bound.*

> *And when thou hast the thunder stopped,*
> *And hushed the ocean's waves,*
> *Then, freedom's spirit bind in chains,*
> *And ever hold us slaves.*

> *And when the eagle's boldest feat,*
> *Thou canst perform with skill,*
> *Then, think to stop proud freedom's march,*
> *And hold the bondman still.*

XX

Review of my narrative.—Licentiousness a prop of slavery.—A case of mild slavery given.—Its revolting features.—Times of my purchase and sale by professed Christians.—Concluding remarks.

I NOW CONCLUDE my narrative, by reviewing briefly what I have written. This little work has been written without any personal aid or a knowledge of the English grammar, which must in part be my apology for many of its imperfections.

I find in several places, where I have spoken out the deep feelings of my soul, in trying to describe the horrid treatment which I have so often received at the hands of slaveholding professors of religion, that I might possibly make a wrong impression on the minds of some northern freemen, who are unacquainted theoretically or practically with the customs and treatment of American slaveholders to their slaves. I hope that it may not be supposed by any, that I have exaggerated in the least, for the purpose of making out the system of slavery worse than it really is, for, to exaggerate upon the cruelties of this system, would be almost impossible; and to write herein the most horrid features of it would not be in good taste for my book.

I have long thought from what has fallen under my own observation while a slave, that the strongest reason why southerners stick with such tenacity to their "peculiar institution," is because licentious white men could not carry out their wicked purposes among the defenseless colored population as they now do, without being exposed and punished by law, if slavery was abolished. Female virtue could not be trampled under foot with impunity, and marriage among the people of color kept in utter obscurity.

On the other hand, lest it should be said by slaveholders and their apologists, that I have not done them the justice to give a sketch of the best side of slavery, if there can be any best side to it; therefore in conclusion, they may have the benefit of the following case, that fell under the observation of the writer. And I challenge America to show a milder state of slavery than this. I once knew a Methodist in the state of Ky., by the name of Young, who was the owner of a large number of slaves, many of whom belonged to the same church with their master. They worshipped together in the same church.

Mr. Young never was known to flog one of his slaves or sell one. He fed and clothed them well, and never over-worked them. He allowed each family a small house to themselves with a little garden spot, whereon to raise their own vegetables; and a part of the day on Saturdays was allowed them to cultivate it.

In process of time he became deeply involved in debt by endorsing notes, and his property was all advertised to be sold by the sheriff at public auction. It consisted in slaves, many of whom were his brothers and sisters in the church.

On the day of sale there were slave traders and speculators on the ground to buy. The slaves were offered on the auction block one after another, until they were all sold before their old master's face. The first man offered on the block was an old gray-headed slave by the name of Richard. His wife followed him up to the block, and when they had bid him up to seventy or eighty dollars one of the bidders asked Mr. Young what he could do, as he looked very old and infirm? Mr. Young replied by saying, "he is not able to accomplish much manual labor, from his extreme age and hard labor in early life. Yet I would rather have him than many of those who are young and vigorous; who are able to perform twice as much labor—because I know him to be faithful and trustworthy, a Christian in good standing in my church. I can trust him anywhere with confidence. He has toiled many long years on my plantation and I have always found him faithful."

This giving him a good Christian character caused them to run him up to near two hundred dollars. His poor old companion stood by weeping and pleading that they might not be separated. But the marriage relation was soon dissolved by the sale, and they were separated never to meet again.

Another man was called up whose wife followed him with her infant in her arms, beseeching to be sold with her husband, which proved to be all in vain. After the men were all sold they then sold the women and children. They ordered the first woman to lay down her child and mount the auction block; she refused to give up her little one and clung to it as long as she could, while the cruel lash was applied to her back for disobedience. She pleaded for mercy in the name of God. But the child was torn from the arms of its mother amid the most heart-rending shrieks from the mother and child on the one hand, and bitter oaths and cruel lashes from the tyrants on the other. Finally the poor little child was torn from the mother while she was sacrificed to the highest bidder. In this way the sale was carried on from beginning to end.

There was each speculator with his hand-cuffs to bind his victims after the sale; and while they were doing their writings, the Christian portion of the slaves asked permission to kneel in prayer on the ground before they separated, which was granted. And while bathing each other with tears of sorrow on the verge of their final separation, their eloquent appeals in prayer to the Most High seemed to cause an unpleasant sensation upon the ears of their tyrants, who ordered them to rise and make ready their limbs for the coffles. And as they happened not to bound at the first sound, they were soon raised from their knees by the sound of the lash, and the rattle of the chains, in which they were soon taken off by their respective masters,—husbands from wives, and children from parents, never expecting to meet until the judgment of the great day. Then Christ shall say to the slaveholding professors of religion, "Inasmuch as ye did it unto one of the least of these little ones, my brethren, ye did it unto me."

Having thus tried to show the best side of slavery that I can conceive of, the reader can exercise his own judgment in deciding whether a man can be a Bible Christian, and yet hold his Christian brethren as property, so that they may be sold at any time in market, as sheep or oxen, to pay his debts.

During my life in slavery I have been sold by professors of religion several times. In 1836 "Bro." Albert G. Sibley, of Bedford, Kentucky, sold me for $850 to "Bro." John Sibley; and in the same year he sold me to "Bro." Wm. Gatewood of Bedford, for $850. In 1839 "Bro." Gatewood sold me to Madison Garrison, a slave trader, of Louisville, Kentucky, with my wife and child—at a depreciated price because I was a runaway. In the same year he sold me with my family to "Bro." Whitfield, in the city of New Orleans, for $1200. In 1841 "Bro." Whitfield sold me from my family to Thomas Wilson and Co., blacklegs. In the same year they sold me to a "Bro." in the Indian Territory. I think he was a member of the Presbyterian Church. F. E. Whitfield was a deacon in regular standing in the Baptist Church. A. Sibley was a Methodist exhorter of the M. E. Church in good standing. J. Sibley was a class-leader in the same church; and Wm. Gatewood was also an acceptable member of the same church.

Is this Christianity? Is it honest or right? Is it doing as we would be done by? Is it in accordance with the principles of humanity or justice?

I believe slaveholding to be a sin against God and man under all circumstances. I have no sympathy with the person or persons who tolerate and support the system willingly and knowingly, morally, religiously or politically.

Prayerfully and earnestly relying on the power of truth, and the aid of the divine providence, I trust that this little volume will bear some humble part in lighting up the path of freedom and revolutionizing public opinion upon this great subject. And I here pledge myself, God being my helper, ever to contend for the natural equality of the human family, without regard to color, which is but fading *matter,* while *mind* makes the man.

New York City, *May* 1, 1849.

Henry Bibb.

RUNNING A THOUSAND MILES

FOR FREEDOM

OR, THE ESCAPE

OF

WILLIAM AND ELLEN CRAFT

FROM SLAVERY.

"Slaves cannot breathe in England: if their lungs
Receive our air, that moment they are free;
They touch our country, and their shackles fall."

COWPER.

LONDON:
WILLIAM TWEEDIE, 337, STRAND.

———

1860.

6

RUNNING A THOUSAND MILES

FOR FREEDOM;

OR,

THE ESCAPE OF

WILLIAM AND

ELLEN CRAFT

FROM SLAVERY

PREFACE.

HAVING HEARD while in Slavery that "God made of one blood all nations of men," and also that the American Declaration of Independence says, that "We hold these truths to be self-evident, that all men are created equal; that they are endowed by their Creator with certain inalienable rights; that among these, are life, liberty, and the pursuit of happiness;" we could not understand by what right we were held as "chattels." Therefore, we felt perfectly justified in undertaking the dangerous and exciting task of "running a thousand miles" in order to obtain those rights which are so vividly set forth in the Declaration.

I beg those who would know the particulars of our journey, to peruse these pages.

This book is not intended as a full history of the life of my wife, nor of myself; but merely as an account of our escape; together with other matter which I hope may be the means of creating in some minds a deeper abhorrence of the sinful and abominable practice of enslaving and brutifying our fellow-creatures.

Without stopping to write a long apology for offering this little volume to the public, I shall commence at once to pursue my simple story.

W. CRAFT.
12, Cambridge Road,
Hammersmith,
London.

Running a Thousand Miles

for Freedom.

PART I.

"God gave us only over beast, fish, fowl,
Dominion absolute; that right we hold
By his donation. But man over man
He made not lord; such title to himself
Reserving, human left from human free."
MILTON.

MY WIFE AND MYSELF were born in different towns in the State of Georgia, which is one of the principal slave States. It is true, our condition as slaves was not by any means the worst; but the mere idea that we were held as chattels, and deprived of all legal rights—the thought that we had to give up our hard earnings to a tyrant, to enable him to live in idleness and luxury—the thought that we could not call the bones and sinews that God gave us our own: but above all, the fact that another man had the power to tear from our cradle the new-born babe and sell it in the shambles like a brute, and then scourge us if we dared to lift a finger to save it from such a fate, haunted us for years.

But in December, 1848, a plan suggested itself that proved quite successful, and in eight days after it was first thought of we were free from the horrible trammels of slavery, rejoicing and praising God in the glorious sunshine of liberty.

My wife's first master was her father, and her mother his slave, and the latter is still the slave of his widow.

Notwithstanding my wife being of African extraction on her mother's side, she is almost white—in fact, she is so nearly so that the tyrannical old lady to whom she first belonged became so annoyed, at finding her frequently mistaken for a child of the family, that she gave her when eleven years of age to a daughter, as a wedding present. This separated my wife from her mother, and also from several other dear friends. But the incessant cruelty of her old mistress made the change of owners or treatment so desirable, that she did not grumble much at this cruel separation.

It may be remembered that slavery in America is not at all confined to persons of any particular complexion; there are a very large number of slaves as white as anyone; but as the evidence of a slave is not admitted in court against a free white person, it is almost impossible for a white child, after having been kidnapped and sold into or reduced to slavery, in a part of the country where it is not known (as often is the case), ever to recover its freedom.

I have myself conversed with several slaves who told me that their parents were white and free; but that they were stolen away from them and sold when quite young. As they could not tell their address, and also as the parents did not know what had become of their lost and dear little ones, of course all traces of each other were gone.

The following facts are sufficient to prove, that he who has the power, and is inhuman enough to trample upon the sacred rights of the weak, cares nothing for race or color:—

In March, 1818, three ships arrived at New Orleans, bringing several hundred German emigrants from the province of Alsace, on the lower Rhine. Among them were Daniel Muller and his two daughters, Dorothea and Salomé, whose mother had died on the passage. Soon after his arrival, Muller, taking with him his two daughters, both young children, went up the river to Attakapas parish, to work on the plantation of John F. Miller. A few weeks later, his relatives, who had remained at New Orleans, learned that he had died of the fever of the country. They immediately sent for the two girls; but they had disappeared, and the relatives, notwithstanding repeated and persevering inquiries and researches, could find no traces of them. They were at length given up for dead. Dorothea was never again heard of; nor was anything known of Salomé from 1818 till 1843.

In the summer of that year, Madame Karl, a German woman who had come over in the same ship with the Mullers, was passing through a street in New Orleans, and accidentally saw Salomé in a wine-shop, belonging to Louis Belmonte, by whom she was held as a slave. Madame Karl recognized her at once, and carried her to the house of another German woman, Mrs. Schubert, who was Salomé's cousin and godmother, and who no sooner set eyes on her than, without having any intimation that the discovery had been previously made, she unhesitatingly exclaimed, "My God! here is the long-lost Salomé Muller."

The *Law Reporter,* in its account of this case, says:—

"As many of the German emigrants of 1818 as could be gathered together were brought to the house of Mrs. Schubert, and everyone of the number who had any recollection of the little girl upon the passage, or any acquaintance with her father and mother, immediately identified the woman before them as the long-lost Salomé Muller. By all these witnesses, who appeared at the trial, the identity was fully established. The family resemblance in every feature was declared to be so remarkable, that some of the witnesses did not hesitate to say that they should know her among ten thousand; that they were as certain the plaintiff was Salomé Muller, the daughter of Daniel and Dorothea Muller, as of their own existence."

Among the witnesses who appeared in Court was the midwife who had assisted at the birth of Salomé. She testified to the existence of certain peculiar marks upon the body of the child, which were found, exactly as described, by the surgeons who were appointed by the Court to make an examination for the purpose.

There was no trace of African descent in any feature of Salomé Muller. She had long, straight, black hair, hazel eyes, thin lips, and a Roman nose. The complexion of her face and neck was as dark as that of the darkest brunette. It appears, however, that, during the twenty-five years of her servitude, she had been exposed to the sun's rays in the hot climate of Louisiana, with head and neck unsheltered, as is customary with the female slaves, while laboring in the cotton or the sugar field. Those parts of her person which had been shielded from the sun were comparatively white.

Belmonte, the pretended owner of the girl, had obtained possession of her by an act of sale from John F. Miller, the planter in whose service Salomé's father died. This Miller was a man of consideration and substance, owning large sugar estates, and bearing a high reputation for honor and honesty, and for indulgent treatment of his slaves. It was testified on the trial that he had said to Belmonte, a few weeks after the sale of Salomé, "that she was white, and had as much right to her freedom as anyone, and was only to be retained in slavery by care and kind treatment." The broker who negotiated the sale from Miller to Belmonte, in 1838, testified in Court that he then thought, and still thought, that the girl was white!

The case was elaborately argued on both sides, but was at length decided in favor of the girl, by the Supreme Court declaring that "she was free and white, and therefore unlawfully held in bondage."

The Rev. George Bourne, of Virginia, in his *Picture of Slavery*, published in 1834, relates the case of a white boy who, at the age of seven, was stolen from his home in Ohio, tanned and stained in such a way that he could not be distinguished from a person of color, and then sold as a slave in Virginia. At the age of twenty, he made his escape, by running away, and happily succeeded in rejoining his parents.

I have known worthless white people to sell their own free children into slavery; and, as there are good-for-nothing white as well as colored persons everywhere, no one, perhaps, will wonder at such inhuman transactions: particularly in the Southern States of America, where I believe there is a greater want of humanity and high principle amongst the whites, than among any other civilized people in the world.

I know that those who are not familiar with the working of "the peculiar institution," can scarcely imagine anyone so totally devoid of all natural affection as to sell his own offspring into returnless bondage. But Shakespeare, that great observer of human nature, says:—

> "With caution judge of probabilities.
> Things deemed unlikely, e'en impossible,
> Experience often shows us to be true."

My wife's new mistress was decidedly more humane than the majority of her class. My wife has always given her credit for not exposing her to many of the worst features of slavery. For instance, it is a common practice in the slave States for ladies, when angry with their maids, to send them to the calybuce sugar-house, or to some other place established for the purpose of punishing slaves, and have them severely flogged; and I am sorry it is a fact, that the villains to whom those defenseless creatures are sent, not only flog them as they are ordered, but frequently compel them to submit to the greatest indignity. Oh! if there is any one thing under the wide canopy of heaven, horrible enough to stir a man's soul, and to make his very blood boil, it is the thought of his dear wife, his unprotected sister, or his young and virtuous daughters, struggling to save themselves from falling a prey to such demons!

It always appears strange to me that anyone who was not born a slaveholder, and steeped to the very core in the demoralizing atmosphere of the Southern States, can in any way palliate slavery. It is still more surprising to see virtuous ladies looking with patience upon and remaining indifferent to, the existence of a system that exposes nearly two millions of their own sex in the manner I have mentioned, and that too in a professedly free and Christian country. There is, however,

great consolation in knowing that God is just, and will not let the oppressor of the weak, and the spoiler of the virtuous, escape unpunished here and hereafter.

I believe a similar retribution to that which destroyed Sodom is
hanging over the slaveholders. My sincere prayer is that they may not
provoke God, by persisting in a reckless course of wickedness, to pour
out his consuming wrath upon them.

I must now return to our history.

My old master had the reputation of being a very humane and
Christian man, but he thought nothing of selling my poor old father,
and dear aged mother, at separate times, to different persons, to be
dragged off never to behold each other again, till summoned to appear
before the great tribunal of heaven. But, oh! what a happy meeting it
will be on that great day for those faithful souls. I say a happy meeting,
because I never saw persons more devoted to the service of God than
they. But how will the case stand with those reckless traffickers in human flesh and blood, who plunged the poisonous dagger of separation
into those loving hearts which God had for so many years closely
joined together—nay, sealed as it were with his own hands for the eternal courts of heaven? It is not for me to say what will become of those
heartless tyrants. I must leave them in the hands of an all-wise and just
God, who will, in his own good time, and in his own way, avenge the
wrongs of his oppressed people.

My old master also sold a dear brother and a sister, in the same manner as he did my father and mother. The reason he assigned for disposing of my parents, as well as of several other aged slaves, was, that "they
were getting old, and would soon become valueless in the market, and
therefore he intended to sell off all the old stock, and buy in a young
lot." A most disgraceful conclusion for a man to come to, who made
such great professions of religion!

This shameful conduct gave me a thorough hatred, not for true
Christianity, but for slaveholding piety.

My old master, then, wishing to make the most of the rest of his
slaves, apprenticed a brother and myself out to learn trades: he to a
blacksmith, and myself to a cabinet-maker. If a slave has a good trade,
he will let or sell for more than a person without one, and many slaveholders have their slaves taught trades on this account. But before our
time expired, my old master wanted money; so he sold my brother, and
then mortgaged my sister, a dear girl about fourteen years of age, and

myself, then about sixteen, to one of the banks, to get money to speculate in cotton. This we knew nothing of at the moment; but time rolled
on, the money became due, my master was unable to meet his pay-
ments; so the bank had us placed upon the auction stand and sold to
the highest bidder.

My poor sister was sold first: she was knocked down to a planter who
resided at some distance in the country. Then I was called upon the
stand. While the auctioneer was crying the bids, I saw the man that
had purchased my sister getting her into a cart, to take her to his home.
I at once asked a slave friend who was standing near the platform, to
run and ask the gentleman if he would please to wait till I was sold, in
order that I might have an opportunity of bidding her goodbye. He
sent me word back that he had some distance to go, and could not wait.

I then turned to the auctioneer, fell upon my knees, and humbly
prayed him to let me just step down and bid my last sister farewell. But,
instead of granting me this request, he grasped me by the neck, and in
a commanding tone of voice, and with a violent oath, exclaimed, "Get
up! You can do the wench no good; therefore there is no use in your
seeing her."

On rising, I saw the cart in which she sat moving slowly off; and, as
she clasped her hands with a grasp that indicated despair, and looked
pitifully round towards me, I also saw the large silent tears trickling
down her cheeks. She made a farewell bow, and buried her face in her
lap. This seemed more than I could bear. It appeared to swell my aching heart to its utmost. But before I could fairly recover, the poor girl
was gone;—gone, and I have never had the good fortune to see her
from that day to this! Perhaps I should have never heard of her again,
had it not been for the untiring efforts of my good old mother, who became free a few years ago by purchase, and, after a great deal of difficulty, found my sister residing with a family in Mississippi. My
mother at once wrote to me, informing me of the fact, and requesting
me to do something to get her free; and I am happy to say that, partly
by lecturing occasionally, and through the sale of an engraving of my
wife in the disguise in which she escaped, together with the extreme
kindness and generosity of Miss Burdett Coutts, Mr. George Rich-
ardson of Plymouth, and a few other friends, I have nearly accomplished this. It would be to me a great and ever-glorious achievement
to restore my sister to our dear mother, from whom she was forcibly
driven in early life.

I was knocked down to the cashier of the bank to which we were mortgaged, and ordered to return to the cabinet shop where I previously worked.

But the thought of the harsh auctioneer not allowing me to bid my dear sister farewell, sent red-hot indignation darting like lightning through every vein. It quenched my tears, and appeared to set my brain on fire, and made me crave for power to avenge our wrongs! But, alas! we were only slaves, and had no legal rights; consequently we were compelled to smother our wounded feelings, and crouch beneath the iron heel of despotism.

I must now give the account of our escape; but, before doing so, it may be well to quote a few passages from the fundamental laws of slavery; in order to give some idea of the legal as well as the social tyranny from which we fled.

According to the law of Louisiana, "A slave is one who is in the power of a master to whom he belongs. The master may sell him, dispose of his person, his industry, and his labor; he can do nothing, possess nothing, nor acquire anything but what must belong to his master."—*Civil Code, art.* 35.

In South Carolina it is expressed in the following language:— "Slaves shall be deemed, sold, taken, reputed and judged in law to be *chattels personal* in the hands of their owners and possessors, and their executors, administrators, and assigns, *to all intents, constructions, and purposes whatsoever.*—2 *Brevard's Digest,* 229.

The Constitution of Georgia has the following (Art. 4, sec. 12):— "Any person who shall maliciously dismember or deprive a slave of life, shall suffer such punishment as would be inflicted in case the like offense had been committed on a free white person, and on the like proof, except in case of insurrection of such slave, and unless SUCH DEATH SHOULD HAPPEN BY ACCIDENT IN GIVING SUCH SLAVE MODERATE CORRECTION."—*Prince's Digest,* 559.

I have known slaves to be beaten to death, but as they died under "moderate correction," it was quite lawful; and of course the murderers were not interfered with.

"If any slave, who shall be out of the house or plantation where such slave shall live, or shall be usually employed, or without some white person in company with such slave, shall *refuse to submit* to undergo the examination of *any white* person, (let him be ever so drunk or crazy), it shall be lawful for such white person to pursue, apprehend, and moderately correct such slave; and if such slave shall assault and strike such white person, such slave may be *lawfully killed.*"—2 *Brevard's Digest,* 231.

"Provided always," says the law, "that such striking be not done by the command and in the defense of the person or property of the owner, or other person having the government of such slave; in which case the slave shall be wholly excused."

According to this law, if a slave, by the direction of his overseer, strike a white person who is beating said overseer's pig, "the slave shall be wholly excused." But, should the bondman, of his own accord, fight to defend his wife, or should his terrified daughter instinctively raise her hand and strike the wretch who attempts to violate her chastity, he or she shall, saith the model republican law, suffer death.

From having been myself a slave for nearly twenty-three years, I am quite prepared to say, that the practical working of slavery is worse than the odious laws by which it is governed.

At an early age we were taken by the persons who held us as property to Maçon, the largest town in the interior of the State of Georgia, at which place we became acquainted with each other for several years before our marriage; in fact, our marriage was postponed for some time simply because one of the unjust and worse than Pagan laws under which we lived compelled all children of slave mothers to follow their condition. That is to say, the father of the slave may be the President of the Republic; but if the mother should be a slave at the infant's birth, the poor child is ever legally doomed to the same cruel fate.

It is a common practice for gentlemen (if I may call them such), moving in the highest circles of society, to be the fathers of children by their slaves, whom they can and do sell with the greatest impunity; and the more pious, beautiful, and virtuous the girls are, the greater the price they bring, and that too for the most infamous purposes.

Any man with money (let him be ever such a rough brute), can buy a beautiful and virtuous girl, and force her to live with him in a criminal connection; and as the law says a slave shall have no higher appeal than the mere will of the master, she cannot escape, unless it be by flight or death.

In endeavoring to reconcile a girl to her fate, the master sometimes says that he would marry her if it was not unlawful.* However, he will

---

*It is unlawful in the slave States for anyone of purely European descent to intermarry with a person of African extraction; though a white man may live with as many colored women as he pleases without materially damaging his reputation in Southern society.

always consider her to be his wife, and will treat her as such; and she, on the other hand, may regard him as her lawful husband; and if they have any children, they will be free and well educated.

I am in duty bound to add, that while a great majority of such men care nothing for the happiness of the women with whom they live, nor for the children of whom they are the fathers, there are those to be found, even in that heterogeneous mass of licentious monsters, who are true to their pledges. But as the woman and her children are legally the property of the man, who stands in the anomalous relation to them of husband and father, as well as master, they are liable to be seized and sold for his debts, should he become involved.

There are several cases on record where such persons have been sold and separated for life. I know of some myself, but I have only space to glance at one.

I knew a very humane and wealthy gentleman, that bought a woman, with whom he lived as his wife. They brought up a family of children, among whom were three nearly white, well educated, and beautiful girls.

On the father being suddenly killed it was found that he had not left a will; but, as the family had always heard him say that he had no surviving relatives, they felt that their liberty and property were quite secured to them, and, knowing the insults to which they were exposed, now their protector was no more, they were making preparations to leave for a free State.

But, poor creatures, they were soon sadly undeceived. A villain residing at a distance, hearing of the circumstance, came forward and swore that he was a relative of the deceased; and as this man bore, or assumed, Mr. Slator's name, the case was brought before one of those horrible tribunals, presided over by a second Judge Jeffreys, and calling itself a court of justice, but before whom no colored person, nor an abolitionist, was ever known to get his full rights.

A verdict was given in favor of the plaintiff, whom the better portion of the community thought had willfully conspired to cheat the family.

The heartless wretch not only took the ordinary property, but actually had the aged and friendless widow, and all her fatherless children, except Frank, a fine young man about twenty-two years of age, and Mary, a very nice girl, a little younger than her brother, brought to the auction stand and sold to the highest bidder. Mrs. Slator had cash enough, that her husband and master left, to purchase the liberty of herself and children; but on her attempting to do so, the pusillanimous scoundrel, who had robbed them of their freedom, claimed the money as his property; and, poor creature, she had to give it up. According to law, as will be seen hereafter, a slave cannot own anything. The old lady never recovered from her sad affliction.

At the sale she was brought up first, and after being vulgarly criticized, in the presence of all her distressed family, was sold to a cotton planter, who said he wanted the "proud old critter to go to his plantation, to look after the little woolly heads, while their mammies were working in the field."

When the sale was over, then came the separation, and

> *"O, deep was the anguish of that slave mother's heart,*
> *When called from her darlings forever to part;*
> *The poor mourning mother of reason bereft,*
> *Soon ended her sorrows, and sank cold in death."*

Antoinette, the flower of the family, a girl who was much beloved by all who knew her, for her Christ-like piety, dignity of manner, as well as her great talents and extreme beauty, was bought by an uneducated and drunken slave-dealer.

I cannot give a more correct description of the scene, when she was called from her brother to the stand, than will be found in the following lines—

> *"Why stands she near the auction stand?*
> *That girl so young and fair;*
> *What brings her to this dismal place?*
> *Why stands she weeping there?*
>
> *Why does she raise that bitter cry?*
> *Why hangs her head with shame,*
> *As now the auctioneer's rough voice*
> *So rudely calls her name!*
>
> *But see! she grasps a manly hand,*
> *And in a voice so low,*
> *As scarcely to be heard, she says,*
> *'My brother, must I go?'*
>
> *A moment's pause: then, midst a wail*
> *Of agonizing woe,*

His answer falls upon the ear.—
    'Yes, sister, you must go!

No longer can my arm defend,
    No longer can I save
My sister from the horrid fate
    That waits her as a SLAVE!'

Blush, Christian, blush! for e'en the dark
    Untutored heathen see
Thy inconsistency, and lo!
    They scorn thy God, and thee!"

The low trader said to a kind lady who wished to purchase Antoinette out of his hands, "I reckon I'll not sell the smart critter for ten thousand dollars; I always wanted her for my own use." The lady, wishing to remonstrate with him, commenced by saying, "You should remember, Sir, that there is a just God." Hoskens not understanding Mrs. Huston, interrupted her by saying, "I does, and guess its monstrous kind an' him to send such likely niggers for our convenience." Mrs. Huston finding that a long course of reckless wickedness, drunkenness, and vice, had destroyed in Hoskens every noble impulse, left him.

Antoinette, poor girl, also seeing that there was no help for her, became frantic. I can never forget her cries of despair, when Hoskens gave the order for her to be taken to his house, and locked in an upper room. On Hoskens entering the apartment, in a state of intoxication, a fearful struggle ensued. The brave Antoinette broke loose from him, pitched herself head foremost through the window, and fell upon the pavement below.

Her bruised but unpolluted body was soon picked up—restoratives brought—doctor called in; but, alas! it was too late: her pure and noble spirit had fled away to be at rest in those realms of endless bliss, "where the wicked cease from troubling, and the weary are at rest."

Antoinette like many other noble women who are deprived of liberty, still

"Holds something sacred, something undefiled;
    Some pledge and keepsake of their higher nature.
And, like the diamond in the dark, retains
    Some quenchless gleam of the celestial light."

On Hoskens fully realizing the fact that his victim was no more, he exclaimed "By thunder I am a used-up man!" The sudden disappointment, and the loss of two thousand dollars, was more than he could endure: so he drank more than ever, and in a short time died, raving mad with *delirium tremens*.

The villain Slator said to Mrs. Huston, the kind lady who endeavored to purchase Antoinette from Hoskins, "Nobody needn't talk to me 'bout buying them ar likely niggers, for I'm not going to sell em." "But Mary is rather delicate," said Mrs. Huston, "and, being unaccustomed to hard work cannot do you much service on a plantation." "I don't want her for the field," replied Slator, "but for another purpose." Mrs. Huston understood what this meant, and instantly exclaimed, "Oh, but she is your cousin!" "The devil she is!" said Slator; and added, "Do you mean to insult me Madam, by saying that I am related to niggers?" "No," replied Mrs. Huston, "I do not wish to offend you, Sir. But wasn't Mr. Slator, Mary's father, your uncle?" "Yes, I calculate he was," said Slator; "but I want you and everybody to understand that I'm no kin to his niggers." "Oh, very well," said Mrs. Huston; adding, "Now what will you take for the poor girl?" "Nothin'," he replied; "for, as I said before, I'm not goin' to sell, so you needn't trouble yourself no more. If the critter behaves herself, I'll do as well by her as any man."

Slator spoke up boldly, but his manner and sheepish look clearly indicated that

> "*His heart within him was at strife*
> *With such accursed gains;*
> *For he knew whose passions gave her life,*
> *Whose blood ran in her veins.*"

> "*The monster led her from the door,*
> *He led her by the hand,*
> *To be his slave and paramour*
> *In a strange and distant land!*"

Poor Frank and his sister were handcuffed together, and confined in prison. Their dear little twin brother and sister were sold, and taken where they knew not. But it often happens that misfortune causes those whom we counted dearest to shrink away; while it makes friends of those whom we least expected to take any interest in our affairs.

Among the latter class Frank found two comparatively new but faithful friends to watch the gloomy paths of the unhappy little twins.

In a day or two after the sale, Slator had two fast horses put to a large light van, and placed in it a good many small but valuable things belonging to the distressed family. He also took with him Frank and Mary, as well as all the money for the spoil; and after treating all his low friends and bystanders, and drinking deeply himself, he started in high glee for his home in South Carolina. But they had not proceeded many miles, before Frank and his sister discovered that Slator was too drunk to drive. But he, like most tipsy men, thought he was all right; and as he had with him some of the ruined family's best brandy and wine, such as he had not been accustomed to, and being a thirsty soul, he drank till the reins fell from his fingers, and in attempting to catch them he tumbled out of the vehicle, and was unable to get up. Frank and Mary there and then contrived a plan by which to escape. As they were still handcuffed by one wrist each, they alighted, took from the drunken assassin's pocket the key, undid the iron bracelets, and placed them upon Slator, who was better fitted to wear such ornaments. As the demon lay unconscious of what was taking place, Frank and Mary took from him the large sum of money that was realized at the sale, as well as that which Slator had so very meanly obtained from their poor mother. They then dragged him into the woods, tied him to a tree, and left the inebriated robber to shift for himself, while they made good their escape to Savannah. The fugitives being white, of course no one suspected that they were slaves.

Slator was not able to call anyone to his rescue till late the next day; and as there were no railroads in that part of the country at that time, it was not until late the following day that Slator was able to get a party to join him for the chase. A person informed Slator that he had met a man and woman, in a trap, answering to the description of those whom he had lost, driving furiously towards Savannah. So Slator and several slavehunters on horseback started off in full tilt, with their bloodhounds, in pursuit of Frank and Mary.

On arriving at Savannah, the hunters found that the fugitives had sold the horses and trap, and embarked as free white persons, for New York. Slator's disappointment and rascality so preyed upon his base mind, that he, like Judas, went and hanged himself.

As soon as Frank and Mary were safe, they endeavored to redeem their good mother. But, alas! she was gone; she had passed on to the realm of spirit life.

In due time Frank learned from his friends in Georgia where his little brother and sister dwelt. So he wrote at once to purchase them, but the persons with whom they lived would not sell them. After failing in several attempts to buy them, Frank cultivated large whiskers and moustachios, cut off his hair, put on a wig and glasses, and went down as a white man, and stopped in the neighborhood where his sister was; and after seeing her and also his little brother, arrangements were made for them to meet at a particular place on a Sunday, which they did, and got safely off.

I saw Frank myself, when he came for the little twins. Though I was then quite a lad, I well remember being highly delighted by hearing him tell how nicely he and Mary had served Slator.

Frank had so completely disguised or changed his appearance that his little sister did not know him, and would not speak till he showed their mother's likeness; the sight of which melted her to tears,—for she knew the face. Frank might have said to her

> "'O, Emma! O, my sister, speak to me!
> Dost thou not know me, that I am thy brother?
> Come to me, little Emma, thou shalt dwell
> With me henceforth, and know no care or want.'
> Emma was silent for a space, as if
> 'Twere hard to summon up a human voice."

Frank and Mary's mother was my wife's own dear aunt.

After this great diversion from our narrative, which I hope, dear reader, you will excuse, I shall return at once to it.

My wife was torn from her mother's embrace in childhood, and taken to a distant part of the country. She had seen so many other children separated from their parents in this cruel manner, that the mere thought of her ever becoming the mother of a child, to linger out a miserable existence under the wretched system of American slavery, appeared to fill her very soul with horror; and as she had taken what I felt to be an important view of her condition, I did not, at first, press the marriage, but agreed to assist her in trying to devise some plan by which we might escape from our unhappy condition, and then be married.

We thought of plan after plan, but they all seemed crowded with insurmountable difficulties. We knew it was unlawful for any public conveyance to take us as passengers, without our master's consent. We were also perfectly aware of the startling fact, that had we left without this consent the professional slave-hunters would have soon had their ferocious bloodhounds baying on our track, and in a short time we should have been dragged back to slavery, not to fill the more favorable situations which we had just left, but to be separated for life, and put to the very meanest and most laborious drudgery; or else have been tortured to death as examples, in order to strike terror into the hearts of others, and thereby prevent them from even attempting to escape from their cruel taskmasters. It is a fact worthy of remark, that nothing seems to give the slaveholders so much pleasure as the catching and torturing of fugitives. They had much rather take the keen and poisonous lash, and with it cut their poor trembling victims to atoms, than allow one of them to escape to a free country, and expose the infamous system from which he fled.

The greatest excitement prevails at a slave-hunt. The slaveholders and their hired ruffians appear to take more pleasure in this inhuman pursuit than English sportsmen do in chasing a fox or a stag. Therefore, knowing what we should have been compelled to suffer, if caught and taken back, we were more than anxious to hit upon a plan that would lead us safely to a land of liberty.

But, after puzzling our brains for years, we were reluctantly driven to the sad conclusion, that it was almost impossible to escape from slavery in Georgia, and travel 1,000 miles across the slave States. We therefore resolved to get the consent of our owners, be married, settle down in slavery, and endeavor to make ourselves as comfortable as possible under that system; but at the same time ever to keep our dim eyes steadily fixed upon the glimmering hope of liberty, and earnestly pray God mercifully to assist us to escape from our unjust thraldom.

We were married, and prayed and toiled on till December, 1848, at which time (as I have stated) a plan suggested itself that proved quite successful, and in eight days after it was first thought of we were free from the horrible trammels of slavery, and glorifying God who had brought us safely out of a land of bondage.

Knowing that slaveholders have the privilege of taking their slaves to any part of the country they think proper, it occurred to me that, as my wife was nearly white, I might get her to disguise herself as an invalid gentleman, and assume to be my master, while I could attend as his slave, and that in this manner we might effect our escape. After I thought of the plan, I suggested it to my wife, but at first she shrank from the idea. She thought it was almost impossible for her to assume that disguise, and travel a distance of 1,000 miles across the slave States. However, on the other hand, she also thought of her condition. She saw that the laws under which we lived did not recognize her to be a woman, but a mere chattel, to be bought and sold, or otherwise dealt with as her owner might see fit. Therefore the more she contemplated her helpless condition, the more anxious she was to escape from it. So she said, "I think it is almost too much for us to undertake; however, I feel that God is on our side, and with his assistance, notwithstanding all the difficulties, we shall be able to succeed. Therefore, if you will purchase the disguise, I will try to carry out the plan."

But after I concluded to purchase the disguise, I was afraid to go to anyone to ask him to sell me the articles. It is unlawful in Georgia for a white man to trade with slaves without the master's consent. But, notwithstanding this, many persons will sell a slave any article that he can get the money to buy. Not that they sympathize with the slave, but merely because his testimony is not admitted in court against a free white person.

Therefore, with little difficulty I went to different parts of the town, at odd times, and purchased things piece by piece, (except the trousers which she found necessary to make,) and took them home to the house where my wife resided. She being a ladies' maid, and a favorite slave in the family, was allowed a little room to herself; and amongst other pieces of furniture which I had made in my overtime, was a chest of drawers; so when I took the articles home, she locked them up carefully in these drawers. No one about the premises knew that she had anything of the kind. So when we fancied we had everything ready the time was fixed for the flight. But we knew it would not do to start off without first getting our masters' consent to be away for a few days. Had we left without this, they would soon have had us back into slavery, and probably we should never have got another fair opportunity of even attempting to escape.

Some of the best slaveholders will sometimes give their favorite slaves a few days' holiday at Christmas time; so, after no little amount of perseverance on my wife's part, she obtained a pass from her mistress, allowing her to be away for a few days. The cabinet-maker with whom I worked gave me a similar paper, but said that he needed my services very much, and wished me to return as soon as the time granted was up. I thanked him kindly; but somehow I have not been able to make it convenient to return yet; and, as the free air of good old

England agrees so well with my wife and our dear little ones, as well as with myself, it is not at all likely we shall return at present to the "peculiar institution" of chains and stripes.

On reaching my wife's cottage she handed me her pass, and I showed mine, but at that time neither of us were able to read them. It is not only unlawful for slaves to be taught to read, but in some of the States there are heavy penalties attached, such as fines and imprisonment, which will be vigorously enforced upon anyone who is humane enough to violate the so-called law.

The following case will serve to show how persons are treated in the most enlightened slaveholding community.

"INDICTMENT.
Commonwealth of Virginia, Norfolk County, ss.
In the Circuit Court.

The Grand Jurors empanelled and sworn to inquire of offenses committed in the body of the said County on their oath present, that Margaret Douglass, being an evil disposed person, not having the fear of God before her eyes, but moved and instigated by the devil, wickedly, maliciously, and feloniously, on the fourth day of July, in the year of our Lord one thousand eight hundred and fifty-four, at Norfolk, in said County, did teach a certain black girl named Kate to read in the Bible, to the great displeasure of Almighty God, to the pernicious example of others in like case offending, contrary to the form of the statute in such case made and provided, and against the peace and dignity of the Commonwealth of Virginia.

"Victor Vagabond, *Prosecuting Attorney*."

"On this indictment Mrs. Douglass was arraigned as a necessary matter of form, tried, found guilty of course; and Judge Scalawag, before whom she was tried, having consulted with Dr. Adams, ordered the sheriff to place Mrs. Douglass in the prisoner's box, when he addressed her as follows: 'Margaret Douglass, stand up. You are guilty of one of the vilest crimes that ever disgraced society; and the jury have found you so. You have taught a slave girl to read in the Bible. No enlightened society can exist where such offenses go unpunished. The Court, in your case, do not feel for you one solitary ray of sympathy, and they will inflict on you the utmost penalty of the law. In any other civilized country you would have paid the forfeit of your crime with your life, and the Court have only to regret that such is not the law in this country. The sentence for your offense is, that you be imprisoned one month in the county jail, and that you pay the costs of this prosecution. Sheriff, remove the prisoner to jail.' On the publication of these proceedings, the Doctors of Divinity preached each a sermon on the necessity of obeying the laws; the *New York Observer* noticed with much pious gladness a revival of religion on Dr. Smith's plantation in Georgia, among his slaves; while the *Journal of Commerce* commended this political preaching of the Doctors of Divinity because it favored slavery. Let us do nothing to offend our Southern brethren."

However, at first, we were highly delighted at the idea of having gained permission to be absent for a few days; but when the thought flashed across my wife's mind, that it was customary for travellers to register their names in the visitors' book at hotels, as well as in the clearance or Custom-house book at Charleston, South Carolina—it made our spirits droop within us.

So, while sitting in our little room upon the verge of despair, all at once my wife raised her head, and with a smile upon her face, which was a moment before bathed in tears, said, "I think I have it!" I asked what it was. She said, "I think I can make a poultice and bind up my right hand in a sling, and with propriety ask the officers to register my name for me." I thought that would do.

It then occurred to her that the smoothness of her face might betray her; so she decided to make another poultice, and put it in a white handkerchief to be worn under the chin, up the cheeks, and to tie over the head. This nearly hid the expression of the countenance, as well as the beardless chin.

The poultice is left off in the engraving, because the likeness could not have been taken well with it on.

My wife, knowing that she would be thrown a good deal into the company of gentlemen, fancied that she could get on better if she had something to go over the eyes; so I went to a shop and bought a pair of green spectacles. This was in the evening.

We sat up all night discussing the plan, and making preparations. Just before the time arrived, in the morning, for us to leave, I cut off my wife's hair square at the back of the head, and got her to dress in the disguise and stand out on the floor. I found that she made a most respectable looking gentleman.

My wife had no ambition whatever to assume this disguise, and would not have done so had it been possible to have obtained our liberty by more simple means; but we knew it was not customary in the South for ladies to travel with male servants; and therefore, notwithstanding my wife's fair complexion, it would have been a very difficult task for her to have come off as a free white lady, with me as her slave; in fact, her not being able to write would have made this quite impossible. We knew that no public conveyance would take us, or any other slave, as a passenger, without our master's consent. This consent could never be obtained to pass into a free State. My wife's being muffled in the poultices, &c., furnished a plausible excuse for avoiding general conversation, of which most Yankee travellers are passionately fond.

There are a large number of free negroes residing in the southern States; but in Georgia (and I believe in all the slave States,) every colored person's complexion is *primâ facie* evidence of his being a slave; and the lowest villain in the country, should he be a white man, has the legal power to arrest, and question, in the most inquisitorial and insulting manner, any colored person, male or female, that he may find at large, particularly at night and on Sundays, without a written pass, signed by the master or someone in authority; or stamped free papers, certifying that the person is the rightful owner of himself.

If the colored person refuses to answer questions put to him, he may be beaten, and his defending himself against this attack makes him an outlaw, and if he be killed on the spot, the murderer will be exempted from all blame; but after the colored person has answered the questions put to him, in a most humble and pointed manner, he may then be taken to prison; and should it turn out, after further examination, that he was caught where he had no permission or legal right to be, and that he has not given what they term a satisfactory account of himself, the master will have to pay a fine. On his refusing to do this, the poor slave may be legally and severely flogged by public officers. Should the prisoner prove to be a free man, he is most likely to be both whipped and fined.

The great majority of slaveholders hate this class of persons with a hatred that can only be equalled by the condemned spirits of the infernal regions. They have no mercy upon, nor sympathy for, any negro whom they cannot enslave. They say that God made the black man to be a slave for the white, and act as though they really believed that all free persons of color are in open rebellion to a direct command from heaven, and that they (the whites) are God's chosen agents to pour out upon them unlimited vengeance. For instance, a Bill has been introduced in the Tennessee Legislature to prevent free negroes from travelling on the railroads in that State. It has passed the first reading. The bill provides that the President who shall permit a free negro to travel on any road within the jurisdiction of the State under his supervision shall pay a fine of 500 dollars; any conductor permitting a violation of the Act shall pay 250 dollars; provided such free negro is not under the control of a free white citizen of Tennessee, who will vouch for the character of said free negro in a penal bond of one thousand dollars. The State of Arkansas has passed a law to banish all free negroes from its bounds, and it came into effect on the 1st day of January, 1860. Every free negro found there after that date will be liable to be sold into slavery, the crime of freedom being unpardonable. The Missouri Senate has before it a bill providing that all free negroes above the age of eighteen years who shall be found in the State after September, 1860, shall be sold into slavery; and that all such negroes as shall enter the State after September, 1861, and remain there twenty-four hours, shall also be sold into slavery forever. Mississippi, Kentucky, and Georgia, and in fact, I believe, all the slave States, are legislating in the same manner. Thus the slaveholders make it almost impossible for free persons of color to get out of the slave States, in order that they may sell them into slavery if they don't go. If no white persons travelled upon railroads except those who could get someone to vouch for their character in a penal bond of one thousand dollars, the railroad companies would soon go to the "wall." Such mean legislation is too low for comment; therefore I leave the villainous acts to speak for themselves.

But the Dred Scott decision is the crowning act of infamous Yankee legislation. The Supreme Court, the highest tribunal of the Republic, composed of nine Judge Jeffries's, chosen both from the free and slave States, has decided that no colored person, or persons of African extraction, can ever become a citizen of the United States, or have any rights which white men are bound to respect. That is to say, in the opinion of this Court, robbery, rape, and murder are not crimes when committed by a white upon a colored person.

Judges who will sneak from their high and honorable position down into the lowest depths of human depravity, and scrape up a decision like this, are wholly unworthy the confidence of any people. I believe such men would, if they had the power, and were it to their temporal interest, sell their country's independence, and barter away every man's birthright for a mess of pottage. Well may Thomas Campbell say—

> *United States, your banner wears,*
> *Two emblems,—one of fame,*
> *Alas, the other that it bears*
> *Reminds us of your shame!*
> *The white man's liberty in types*
> *Stands blazoned by your stars;*
> *But what's the meaning of your stripes?*
> *They mean your Negro-scars.*

When the time had arrived for us to start, we blew out the lights, knelt down, and prayed to our Heavenly Father mercifully to assist us, as he did his people of old, to escape from cruel bondage; and we shall ever feel that God heard and answered our prayer. Had we not been sustained by a kind, and I sometimes think special, providence, we could never have overcome the mountainous difficulties which I am now about to describe.

After this we rose and stood for a few moments in breathless silence,—we were afraid that someone might have been about the cottage listening and watching our movements. So I took my wife by the hand, stepped softly to the door, raised the latch, drew it open, and peeped out. Though there were trees all around the house, yet the foliage scarcely moved; in fact, everything appeared to be as still as death. I then whispered to my wife, "Come my dear, let us make a desperate leap for liberty!" But poor thing, she shrank back, in a state of trepidation. I turned and asked what was the matter; she made no reply, but burst into violent sobs, and threw her head upon my breast. This appeared to touch my very heart, it caused me to enter into her feelings more fully than ever. We both saw the many mountainous difficulties that rose one after the other before our view, and knew far too well what our sad fate would have been, were we caught and forced back into our slavish den. Therefore on my wife's fully realizing the solemn fact that we had to take our lives, as it were, in our hands, and contest every inch of the thousand miles of slave territory over which we had to pass, it made her heart almost sink within her, and, had I known them at that time I would have repeated the following encouraging lines, which may not be out of place here—

> *"The hill, though high, I covet to ascend,*
> *The* difficulty will not me offend;
> *For I perceive the way to life lies here:*
> *Come, pluck up heart, let's neither faint nor fear;*

> *Better, though difficult, the right way to go,—*
> *Than wrong, though easy, where the end is woe."*

However, the sobbing was soon over, and after a few moments of silent prayer she recovered her self-possession, and said, "Come, William, it is getting late, so now let us venture upon our perilous journey."

We then opened the door, and stepped as softly out as "moonlight upon the water." I locked the door with my own key, which I now have before me, and tiptoed across the yard into the street. I say tiptoed, because we were like persons near a tottering avalanche, afraid to move, or even breathe freely, for fear the sleeping tyrants should be aroused, and come down upon us with double vengeance, for daring to attempt to escape in the manner which we contemplated.

We shook hands, said farewell, and started in different directions for the railway station. I took the nearest possible way to the train, for fear I should be recognized by someone, and got into the negro car in which I knew I should have to ride; but my *master* (as I will now call my wife) took a longer way round, and only arrived there with the bulk of the passengers. He obtained a ticket for himself and one for his slave to Savannah, the first port, which was about two hundred miles off. My master then had the luggage stowed away, and stepped into one of the best carriages.

But just before the train moved off I peeped through the window, and, to my great astonishment, I saw the cabinet-maker with whom I had worked so long, on the platform. He stepped up to the ticket-seller, and asked some question, and then commenced looking rapidly through the passengers, and into the carriages. Fully believing that we were caught, I shrank into a corner, turned my face from the door, and expected in a moment to be dragged out. The cabinet-maker looked into my master's carriage, but did not know him in his new attire, and, as God would have it, before he reached mine the bell rang, and the train moved off.

I have heard since that the cabinet-maker had a presentiment that we were about to "make tracks for parts unknown;" but, not seeing me, his suspicions vanished, until he received the startling intelligence that we had arrived safely in a free State.

As soon as the train had left the platform, my master looked round in the carriage, and was terror-stricken to find a Mr. Cray—an old friend of my wife's master, who dined with the family the day before, and knew my wife from childhood—sitting on the same seat.

The doors of the American railway carriages are at the ends. The passengers walk up the aisle, and take seats on either side; and as my master was engaged in looking out of the window, he did not see who came in.

My master's first impression, after seeing Mr. Cray, was, that he was there for the purpose of securing him. However, my master thought it was not wise to give any information respecting himself, and for fear that Mr. Cray might draw him into conversation and recognize his voice, my master resolved to feign deafness as the only means of self-defense.

After a little while, Mr. Cray said to my master, "It is a very fine morning, sir." The latter took no notice, but kept looking out of the window. Mr. Cray soon repeated this remark, in a little louder tone, but my master remained as before. This indifference attracted the attention of the passengers near, one of whom laughed out. This, I suppose, annoyed the old gentleman; so he said, "I will make him hear;" and in a loud tone of voice repeated, "It is a very fine morning, sir."

My master turned his head, and with a polite bow said, "Yes," and commenced looking out of the window again.

One of the gentlemen remarked that it was a very great deprivation to be deaf. "Yes," replied Mr. Cray, "and I shall not trouble that fellow any more." This enabled my master to breathe a little easier, and to feel that Mr. Cray was not his pursuer after all.

The gentlemen then turned the conversation upon the three great topics of discussion in first-class circles in Georgia, namely, Niggers, Cotton, and the Abolitionists.

My master had often heard of abolitionists, but in such a connection as to cause him to think that they were a fearful kind of wild animal. But he was highly delighted to learn, from the gentlemen's conversation, that the abolitionists were persons who were opposed to oppression; and therefore, in his opinion, not the lowest, but the very highest, of God's creatures.

Without the slightest objection on my master's part, the gentlemen left the carriage at Gordon, for Milledgeville (the capital of the State).

We arrived at Savannah early in the evening, and got into an omnibus, which stopped at the hotel for the passengers to take tea. I stepped into the house and brought my master something on a tray to the omnibus, which took us in due time to the steamer, which was bound for Charleston, South Carolina.

Soon after going on board, my master turned in; and as the captain and some of the passengers seemed to think this strange, and also questioned me respecting him, my master thought I had better get out the flannels and opodeldoc which we had prepared for the rheumatism, warm them quickly by the stove in the gentleman's saloon, and bring them to his berth. We did this as an excuse for my master's retiring to bed so early.

While at the stove one of the passengers said to me, "Buck, what have you got there?" "Opodeldoc, sir," I replied. "I should think it's opo*devil*," said a lanky swell, who was leaning back in a chair with his heels upon the back of another, and chewing tobacco as if for a wager; "it stinks enough to kill or cure twenty men. Away with it, or I reckon I will throw it overboard!"

It was by this time warm enough, so I took it to my master's berth, remained there a little while, and then went on deck and asked the steward where I was to sleep. He said there was no place provided for colored passengers, whether slave or free. So I paced the deck till a late hour, then mounted some cotton bags, in a warm place near the funnel, sat there till morning, and then went and assisted my master to get ready for breakfast.

He was seated at the right hand of the captain, who, together with all the passengers, inquired very kindly after his health. As my master had one hand in a sling, it was my duty to carve his food. But when I went out the captain said, "You have a very attentive boy, sir; but you had better watch him like a hawk when you get on to the North. He seems all very well here, but he may act quite differently there. I know several gentlemen who have lost their valuable niggers among them d———d cut-throat abolitionists."

Before my master could speak, a rough slave-dealer, who was sitting opposite, with both elbows on the table, and with a large piece of broiled fowl in his fingers, shook his head with emphasis, and in a deep Yankee tone, forced through his crowded mouth the words, "Sound doctrine, captain, very sound." He then dropped the chicken into the plate, leant back, placed his thumbs in the armholes of his fancy waistcoat, and continued, "I would not take a nigger to the North under no consideration. I have had a deal to do with niggers in my time, but I never saw one who ever had his heel upon free soil that was worth a d———n." "Now stranger," addressing my master, "if you have made up your mind to sell that ere nigger, I am your man; just mention your price, and if it isn't out of the way, I will pay for him on this board with hard silver dollars." This hard-featured, bristly-bearded, wire-headed, red-eyed monster, staring at my master as the serpent did at Eve, said, "What do you say, stranger?" He replied, "I don't wish to sell, sir; I cannot get on well without him."

"You will have to get on without him if you take him to the North," continued this man; "for I can tell ye, stranger, as a friend, I am an older cove than you, I have seen lots of this ere world, and I reckon I have had more dealings with niggers than any man living or dead. I was once employed by General Wade Hampton, for ten years, in doing nothing but breaking 'em in; and everybody knows that the General would not have a man that didn't understand his business. So I tell ye, stranger, again, you had better sell, and let me take him down to Orleans. He will do you no good if you take him across Mason's and Dixon's line; he is a keen nigger, and I can see from the cut of his eye that he is certain to run away." My master said, "I think not, sir; I have great confidence in his fidelity." "Fi*devil*," indignantly said the dealer, as his fist came down upon the edge of the saucer and upset a cup of hot coffee in a gentleman's lap. (As the scalded man jumped up the trader quietly said, "Don't disturb yourself, neighbor; accidents will happen in the best of families.") "It always makes me mad to hear a man talking about fidelity in niggers. There isn't a d———d one on 'em who wouldn't cut sticks, if he had half a chance."

By this time we were near Charleston; my master thanked the captain for his advice, and they all withdrew and went on deck, where the trader fancied he became quite eloquent. He drew a crowd around him, and with emphasis said, "Cap'en, if I was the President of this mighty United States of America, the greatest and freest country under the whole univarse, I would never let no man, I don't care who he is, take a nigger into the North and bring him back here, filled to the brim, as he is sure to be, with d———d abolition vices, to taint all quiet niggers with the hellish spirit of running away. These air, cap'en, my flat-footed, every day, right up and down sentiments, and as this is a free country, cap'en, I don't care who hears 'em; for I am a Southern man, every inch on me to the backbone" "Good!" said an insignificant-looking individual of the slave-dealer stamp. "Three cheers for John C. Calhoun and the whole fair sunny South!" added the trader. So off went their hats, and out burst a terrific roar of irregular but continued cheering. My master took no more notice of the dealer. He merely said to the captain that the air on deck was too keen for him, and he would therefore return to the cabin.

While the trader was in the zenith of his eloquence, he might as well have said, as one of his kit did, at a great Filibustering meeting, that "When the great American Eagle gets one of his mighty claws upon Canada and the other into South America, and his glorious and starry wings of liberty extending from the Atlantic to the Pacific, oh! then, where will England be, ye gentlemen? I tell ye, she will only serve as a pocket-handkerchief for Jonathan to wipe his nose with."

On my master entering the cabin he found at the breakfast-table a young southern military officer, with whom he had travelled some distance the previous day.

After passing the usual compliments the conversation turned upon the old subject,—niggers.

The officer, who was also travelling with a manservant, said to my master, "You will excuse me, Sir, for saying I think you are very likely to spoil your boy by saying 'thank you' to him. I assure you, sir, nothing spoils a slave so soon as saying, 'thank you' and 'if you please' to him. The only way to make a nigger toe the mark, and to keep him in his place, is to storm at him like thunder, and keep him trembling like a leaf. Don't you see, when I speak to my Ned, he darts like lightning; and if he didn't I'd skin him."

Just then the poor dejected slave came in, and the officer swore at him fearfully, merely to teach my master what he called the proper way to treat me.

After he had gone out to get his master's luggage ready, the officer said, "That is the way to speak to them. If every nigger was drilled in this manner, they would be as humble as dogs, and never dare to run away."

The gentleman urged my master not to go to the North for the restoration of his health, but to visit the Warm Springs in Arkansas.

My master said, he thought the air of Philadelphia would suit his complaint best; and, not only so, he thought he could get better advice there.

The boat had now reached the wharf. The officer wished my master a safe and pleasant journey, and left the saloon.

There were a large number of persons on the quay waiting the arrival of the steamer: but we were afraid to venture out for fear that someone might recognize me; or that they had heard that we were gone, and had telegraphed to have us stopped. However, after remaining in the cabin till all the other passengers were gone, we had our luggage placed on a fly, and I took my master by the arm, and with a little difficulty he hobbled on shore, got in and drove off to the best hotel, which John C. Calhoun, and all the other great southern fire-eating statesmen, made their head-quarters while in Charleston.

On arriving at the house the landlord ran out and opened the door: but judging, from the poultices and green glasses, that my master was an invalid, he took him very tenderly by one arm and ordered his man to take the other.

My master then eased himself out, and with their assistance found no trouble in getting up the steps into the hotel. The proprietor made me stand on one side, while he paid my master the attention and homage he thought a gentleman of his high position merited.

My master asked for a bed-room. The servant was ordered to show a good one, into which we helped him. The servant returned. My master then handed me the bandages, I took them downstairs in great haste, and told the landlord my master wanted two hot poultices as quickly as possible. He rang the bell, the servant came in, to whom he said, "Run to the kitchen and tell the cook to make two hot poultices right off, for there is a gentleman upstairs very badly off indeed!"

In a few minutes the smoking poultices were brought in. I placed them in white handkerchiefs, and hurried upstairs, went into my master's apartment, shut the door, and laid them on the mantel-piece. As he was alone for a little while, he thought he could rest a great deal better with the poultices off. However, it was necessary to have them to complete the remainder of the journey. I then ordered dinner, and took my master's boots out to polish them. While doing so I entered into conversation with one of the slaves. I may state here, that on the sea-coast of South Carolina and Georgia the slaves speak worse English than in any other part of the country. This is owing to the frequent importation, or smuggling in, of Africans, who mingle with the natives. Consequently the language cannot properly be called English or African, but a corruption of the two.

The shrewd son of African parents to whom I referred said to me, "Say, brudder, way you come from, and which side you goin day wid dat ar little don up buckra" (white man)?

I replied, "To Philadelphia."

"What!" he exclaimed, with astonishment, "to Philumadelphy?"

"Yes," I said.

"By squash! I wish I was going wid you! I hears um say dat dare's no slaves way over in dem parts; is um so?"

I quietly said, "I have heard the same thing."

"Well," continued he, as he threw down the boot and brush, and, placing his hands in his pockets, strutted across the floor with an air of independence—"Gorra Mighty, dem is de parts for Pompey; and I hope when you get dare you will stay, and nebber follow dat buckra back to dis hot quarter no more, let him be eber so good."

I thanked him; and just as I took the boots up and started off, he caught my hand between his two, and gave it a hearty shake, and, with tears streaming down his cheeks, said:—

"God bless you, broder, and may de Lord be wid you. When you gets de freedom, and sitin under your own wine and fig-tree, don't forget to pray for poor Pompey."

I was afraid to say much to him, but I shall never forget his earnest request, nor fail to do what little I can to release the millions of unhappy bondmen, of whom he was one.

At the proper time my master had the poultices placed on, came down, and seated himself at a table in a very brilliant dining-room, to have his dinner. I had to have something at the same time, in order to be ready for the boat; so they gave me my dinner in an old broken plate, with a rusty knife and fork, and said, "Here, boy, you go in the kitchen." I took it and went out, but did not stay more than a few minutes, because I was in a great hurry to get back to see how the invalid was getting on. On arriving I found two or three servants waiting on him; but as he did not feel able to make a very hearty dinner, he soon finished, paid the bill, and gave the servants each a trifle, which caused one of them to say to me, "Your massa is a big bug"—meaning a gentleman of distinction—"he is the greatest gentleman dat has been dis way for dis six months." I said, "Yes, he is some pumpkins," meaning the same as "big bug."

When we left Maçon, it was our intention to take a steamer at Charleston through to Philadelphia; but on arriving there we found that the vessels did not run during the winter, and I have no doubt it was well for us they did not; for on the very last voyage the steamer made that we intended to go by, a fugitive was discovered secreted on board, and sent back to slavery. However, as we had also heard of the Overland Mail Route, we were all right. So I ordered a fly to the door, had luggage placed on; we got in, and drove down to the Customhouse Office, which was near the wharf where we had to obtain tickets, to take a steamer for Wilmington, North Carolina. When we reached the building, I helped my master into the office, which was crowded with passengers. He asked for a ticket for himself and one for his slave to Philadelphia. This caused the principal officer—a very mean-looking, cheese-colored fellow, who was sitting there—to look up at us very suspiciously, and in a fierce tone of voice he said to me, "Boy, do you belong to that gentleman?" I quickly replied, "Yes, sir" (which was quite correct). The tickets were handed out, and as my master was paying for them the chief man said to him, "I wish you to register your name here, sir, and also the name of your nigger, and pay a dollar duty on him."

My master paid the dollar, and pointing to the hand that was in the poultice, requested the officer to register his name for him. This seemed to offend the "high-bred" South Carolinian. He jumped up, shaking his head; and, cramming his hands almost through the bottom of his trousers pockets, with a slave-bullying air, said, "I shan't do it."

This attracted the attention of all the passengers. Just then the young military officer with whom my master travelled and conversed on the steamer from Savannah stepped in, somewhat the worse for brandy; he shook hands with my master, and pretended to know all about him. He said, "I know his kin (friends) like a book;" and as the officer was known in Charleston, and was going to stop there with friends, the recognition was very much in my master's favor.

The captain of the steamer, a good-looking jovial fellow, seeing that the gentleman appeared to know my master, and perhaps not wishing to lose us as passengers, said in an off-hand sailor-like manner, "I will register the gentleman's name, and take the responsibility upon myself." He asked my master's name. He said, "William Johnson." The names were put down, I think, "Mr. Johnson and slave." The captain said, "It's all right now, Mr. Johnson." He thanked him kindly, and the young officer begged my master to go with him, and have something to drink and a cigar; but as he had not acquired these accomplishments, he excused himself, and we went on board and came off to Wilmington, North Carolina. When the gentleman finds out his mistake, he will, I have no doubt, be careful in future not to pretend to have an intimate acquaintance with an entire stranger. During the voyage the captain said, "It was rather sharp shooting this morning, Mr. Johnson. It was not out of any disrespect to you, sir; but they make it a rule to be very strict at Charleston. I have known families to be detained there with their slaves till reliable information could be received respecting them. If they were not very careful, any d———d abolitionist might take off a lot of valuable niggers."

My master said, "I suppose so," and thanked him again for helping him over the difficulty.

We reached Wilmington the next morning, and took the train for Richmond, Virginia. I have stated that the American railway carriages (or cars, as they are called), are constructed differently to those in England. At one end of some of them, in the South, there is a little apartment with a couch on both sides for the convenience of families and invalids; and as they thought my master was very poorly, he was allowed to enter one of these apartments at Petersburg, Virginia, where an old gentleman and two handsome young ladies, his daughters, also got in, and took seats in the same carriage. But before the train started, the gentleman stepped into my car, and questioned me respecting my master. He wished to know what was the matter with him, where he was from, and where he was going. I told him where he came from, and said that he was suffering from a complication of complaints, and was going to Philadelphia, where he thought he could get more suitable advice than in Georgia.

The gentleman said my master could obtain the very best advice in Philadelphia. Which turned out to be quite correct, though he did not receive it from physicians, but from kind abolitionists who understood his case much better. The gentleman also said, "I reckon your master's father hasn't any more such faithful and smart boys as you." "O, yes, sir, he has," I replied, "lots on 'em." Which was literally true. This seemed all he wished to know. He thanked me, gave me a ten-cent piece, and requested me to be attentive to my good master. I promised that I would do so, and have ever since endeavored to keep my pledge. During the gentleman's absence, the ladies and my master had a little cosy chat. But on his return, he said, "You seem to be very much afflicted, sir." "Yes, sir," replied the gentleman in the poultices. "What seems to be the matter with you, sir; may I be allowed to ask?" "Inflammatory rheumatism, sir." "Oh! that is very bad, sir," said the kind gentleman: "I can sympathize with you; for I know from bitter experience what the rheumatism is." If he did, he knew a good deal more than Mr. Johnson.

The gentleman thought my master would feel better if he would lie down and rest himself; and as he was anxious to avoid conversation, he at once acted upon this suggestion. The ladies politely rose, took their extra shawls, and made a nice pillow for the invalid's head. My master wore a fashionable cloth cloak, which they took and covered him comfortably on the couch. After he had been lying a little while the ladies, I suppose, thought he was asleep; so one of them gave a long sigh, and said, in a quiet fascinating tone, "Papa, he seems to be a very nice young gentleman." But before papa could speak, the other lady quickly said, "Oh! dear me, I never felt so much for a gentleman in my life!" To use an American expression, "they fell in love with the wrong chap."

After my master had been lying a little while he got up, the gentleman assisted him in getting on his cloak, the ladies took their shawls, and soon all were seated. They then insisted upon Mr. Johnson taking some of their refreshments, which of course he did, out of courtesy to the ladies. All went on enjoying themselves until they reached Richmond, where the ladies and their father left the train. But, before doing so, the good old Virginian gentleman, who appeared to be much pleased with my master, presented him with a recipe, which he said was a perfect cure for the inflammatory rheumatism. But the invalid not being able to read it, and fearing he should hold it upside down in pretending to do so, thanked the donor kindly, and placed it in his waistcoat pocket. My master's new friend also gave him his card, and requested him the next time he travelled that way to do him the kindness to call; adding, "I shall be pleased to see you, and so will my daughters." Mr. Johnson expressed his gratitude for the proffered hospitality, and said he should feel glad to call on his return. I have not the slightest doubt that he will fulfil the promise whenever that return takes place. After changing trains we went on a little beyond Fredericksburg, and took a steamer to Washington.

At Richmond, a stout elderly lady, whose whole demeanor indicated that she belonged (as Mrs. Stowe's Aunt Chloe expresses it) to one of the "firstest families," stepped into the carriage, and took a seat near my master. Seeing me passing quickly along the platform, she sprang up as if taken by a fit, and exclaimed, "Bless my soul! there goes my nigger, Ned!"

My master said, "No; that is my boy."

The lady paid no attention to this; she poked her head out of the window, and bawled to me, "You Ned, come to me, sir, you runaway rascal!"

On my looking round she drew her head in, and said to my master, "I beg your pardon, sir, I was sure it was my nigger; I never in my life saw two black pigs more alike than your boy and my Ned."

After the disappointed lady had resumed her seat, and the train had moved off, she closed her eyes, slightly raising her hands, and in a sanctified tone said to my master, "Oh! I hope, sir, your boy will not turn out to be so worthless as my Ned has. Oh! I was as kind to him as if he had been my own son. Oh! sir, it grieves me very much to think that after all I did for him he should go off without having any cause whatever."

"When did he leave you?" asked Mr. Johnson.

"About eighteen months ago, and I have never seen hair or hide of him since."

"Did he have a wife?" enquired a very respectable-looking young gentleman, who was sitting near my master and opposite to the lady.

"No, sir; not when he left, though he did have one a little before that. She was very unlike him; she was as good and as faithful a nigger as anyone need wish to have. But, poor thing! she became so ill, that she was unable to do much work; so I thought it would be best to sell her, to go to New Orleans, where the climate is nice and warm."

"I suppose she was very glad to go South for the restoration of her health?" said the gentleman.

"No; she was not," replied the lady, "for niggers never know what is best for them. She took on a great deal about leaving Ned and the little nigger; but, as she was so weakly, I let her go."

"Was she good-looking?" asked the young passenger, who was evidently not of the same opinion as the talkative lady, and therefore wished her to tell all she knew.

"Yes; she was very handsome, and much whiter than I am; and therefore will have no trouble in getting another husband. I am sure I wish her well. I asked the speculator who bought her to sell her to a good master. Poor thing! she has my prayers, and I know she prays for me. She was a good Christian, and always used to pray for my soul. It was through her earliest prayers," continued the lady, "that I was first led to seek forgiveness of my sins, before I was converted at the great camp-meeting."

This caused the lady to snuffle and to draw from her pocket a richly embroidered handkerchief, and apply it to the corner of her eyes. But my master could not see that it was at all soiled.

The silence which prevailed for a few moments was broken by the gentleman's saying, "As your 'July' was such a very good girl, and had served you so faithfully before she lost her health, don't you think it would have been better to have emancipated her?"

"No, indeed I do not!" scornfully exclaimed the lady, as she impatiently crammed the fine handkerchief into a little work-bag. "I have no patience with people who set niggers at liberty. It is the very worst thing you can do for them. My dear husband just before he died willed all his niggers free. But I and all our friends knew very well that he was too good a man to have ever thought of doing such an unkind and foolish thing, had he been in his right mind, and, therefore we had the will altered as it should have been in the first place."

"Did you mean, madam," asked my master, "that willing the slaves free was unjust to yourself, or unkind to them?"

"I mean that it was decidedly unkind to the servants themselves. It always seems to me such a cruel thing to turn niggers loose to shift for themselves, when there are so many good masters to take care of them. As for myself," continued the considerate lady, "I thank the Lord my dear husband left me and my son well provided for. Therefore I care nothing for the niggers, on my own account, for they are a great deal more trouble than they are worth, I sometimes wish that there was not one of them in the world; for the ungrateful wretches are always running away. I have lost no less than ten since my poor husband died. It's ruinous, sir!"

"But as you are well provided for, I suppose you do not feel the loss very much," said the passenger.

"I don't feel it at all," haughtily continued the good soul; "but that is no reason why property should be squandered. If my son and myself had the money for those valuable niggers, just see what a great deal of good we could do for the poor, and in sending missionaries abroad to the poor heathen, who have never heard the name of our blessed Redeemer. My dear son who is a good Christian minister has advised me not to worry and send my soul to hell for the sake of niggers; but to sell every blessed one of them for what they will fetch, and go and live in peace with him in New York. This I have concluded to do. I have just been to Richmond and made arrangements with my agent to make clean work of the forty that are left."

"Your son being a good Christian minister," said the gentleman, "It's strange he did not advise you to let the poor negroes have their liberty and go North."

"It's not at all strange, sir; it's not at all strange. My son knows what's best for the niggers; he has always told me that they were much better off than the free niggers in the North. In fact, I don't believe there are any white laboring people in the world who are as well off as the slaves."

"You are quite mistaken, madam," said the young man. "For instance, my own widowed mother, before she died, emancipated all her slaves, and sent them to Ohio, where they are getting along well. I saw several of them last summer myself."

"Well," replied the lady, "freedom may do for your ma's niggers, but it will never do for mine; and, plague them, they shall never have it; that is the word, with the bark on it."

"If freedom will not do for your slaves," replied the passenger, "I have no doubt your Ned and the other nine negroes will find out their mistake, and return to their old home."

"Blast them!" exclaimed the old lady, with great emphasis, "if I ever get them, I will cook their infernal hash, and tan their accursed black hides well for them! God forgive me," added the old soul, "the niggers will make me lose all my religion!"

By this time the lady had reached her destination. The gentleman got out at the next station beyond. As soon as she was gone, the young Southerner said to my master, "What a d———d shame it is for that old whining hypocritical humbug to cheat the poor negroes out of their liberty! If she has religion, may the devil prevent me from ever being converted!"

For the purpose of somewhat disguising myself, I bought and wore a very good second-hand white beaver, an article which I had never indulged in before. So just before we arrived at Washington, an uncouth planter, who had been watching me very closely, said to my master, "I reckon, stranger, you are *'spiling'* that ere nigger of yourn, by letting him wear such a devilish fine hat. Just look at the quality on it; the President couldn't wear a better. I should just like to go and kick it overboard." His friend touched him, and said, "Don't speak so to a gentleman." "Why not?" exclaimed the fellow. He grated his short teeth, which appeared to be nearly worn away by the incessant chewing of tobacco, and said, "It always makes me itch all over, from head to toe, to get hold of every d———d nigger I see dressed like a white man. Washington is run away with *spiled* and free niggers. If I had my way I would sell every d———d rascal of 'em way down South, where the devil would be whipped out on 'em."

This man's fierce manner made my master feel rather nervous, and therefore he thought the less he said the better; so he walked off without making any reply. In a few minutes we were landed at Washington, where we took a conveyance and hurried off to the train for Baltimore.

We left our cottage on Wednesday morning, the 21st of December,

1848, and arrived at Baltimore, Saturday evening, the 24th (Christmas Eve). Baltimore was the last slave port of any note at which we stopped.

On arriving there we felt more anxious than ever, because we knew not what that last dark night would bring forth. It is true we were near the goal, but our poor hearts were still as if tossed at sea; and, as there was another great and dangerous bar to pass, we were afraid our liberties would be wrecked, and, like the ill-fated *Royal Charter,* go down forever just off the place we longed to reach.

They are particularly watchful at Baltimore to prevent slaves from escaping into Pennsylvania, which is a free State. After I had seen my master into one of the best carriages, and was just about to step into mine, an officer, a full-blooded Yankee of the lower order, saw me. He came quickly up, and, tapping me on the shoulder, said in his unmistakable native twang, together with no little display of his authority, "Where are you going, boy?" "To Philadelphia, sir," I humbly replied. "Well, what are you going there for?" "I am travelling with my master, who is in the next carriage, sir." "Well, I calculate you had better get him out; and be mighty quick about it, because the train will soon be starting. It is against my rules to let any man take a slave past here, unless he can satisfy them in the office that he has a right to take him along."

The officer then passed on and left me standing upon the platform, with my anxious heart apparently palpitating in the throat. At first I scarcely knew which way to turn. But it soon occurred to me that the good God, who had been with us thus far, would not forsake us at the eleventh hour. So with renewed hope I stepped into my master's carriage, to inform him of the difficulty. I found him sitting at the farther end, quite alone. As soon as he looked up and saw me, he smiled. I also tried to wear a cheerful countenance, in order to break the shock of the sad news. I knew what made him smile. He was aware that if we were fortunate we should reach our destination at five o'clock the next morning, and this made it the more painful to communicate what the officer had said; but, as there was no time to lose, I went up to him and asked him how he felt. He said "Much better," and that he thanked God we were getting on so nicely. I then said we were not getting on quite so well as we had anticipated. He anxiously and quickly asked what was the matter. I told him. He started as if struck by lightning, and exclaimed, "Good Heavens! William, is it possible that we are, after all, doomed to hopeless bondage?" I could say nothing, my heart was too full to speak, for at first I did not know what to do. However we knew it would never do to turn back to the "City of Destruction," like Bunyan's *Mistrust* and *Timorous,* because they saw lions in the narrow way after ascending the hill Difficulty; but press on, like noble *Christian* and *Hopeful,* to the great city in which dwelt a few "shining ones." So, after a few moments, I did all I could to encourage my companion, and we stepped out and made for the office: but how or where my master obtained sufficient courage to face the tyrants who had power to blast all we held dear, heaven only knows! Queen Elizabeth could not have been more terror-stricken, on being forced to land at the traitors' gate leading to the Tower, than we were on entering that office. We felt that our very existence was at stake, and that we must either sink or swim. But, as God was our present and mighty helper in this as well as in all former trials, we were able to keep our heads up and press forwards.

On entering the room we found the principal man, to whom my master said, "Do you wish to see me, sir?" "Yes," said this eagle-eyed officer; and he added, "It is against our rules, sir, to allow any person to take a slave out of Baltimore into Philadelphia, unless he can satisfy us that he has a right to take him along." "Why is that?" asked my master, with more firmness than could be expected. "Because, sir," continued he, in a voice and manner that almost chilled our blood, "if we should suffer any gentleman to take a slave past here into Philadelphia; and should the gentleman with whom the slave might be travelling turn out not to be his rightful owner; and should the proper master come and prove that his slave escaped on our road, we shall have him to pay for; and, therefore, we cannot let any slave pass here without receiving security to show, and to satisfy us, that it is all right."

This conversation attracted the attention of the large number of bustling passengers. After the officer had finished, a few of them said, "Chit, chit, chit;" not because they thought we were slaves endeavoring to escape, but merely because they thought my master was a slaveholder and invalid gentleman, and therefore it was wrong to detain him. The officer, observing that the passengers sympathized with my master, asked him if he was not acquainted with some gentleman in Baltimore that he could get to endorse for him, to show that I was his property, and that he had a right to take me off. He said, "No;" and added, "I bought tickets in Charleston to pass us through to Philadelphia, and therefore you have no right to detain us here." "Well, sir," said the man, indignantly, "right or no right, we shan't let you go."

These sharp words fell upon our anxious hearts like the crack of doom, and made us feel that hope only smiles to deceive.

For a few moments perfect silence prevailed. My master looked at me, and I at him, but neither of us dared to speak a word, for fear of making some blunder that would tend to our detection. We knew that the officers had power to throw us into prison, and if they had done so we must have been detected and driven back, like the vilest felons, to a life of slavery, which we dreaded far more than sudden death.

We felt as though we had come into deep waters and were about being overwhelmed, and that the slightest mistake would clip asunder the last brittle thread of hope by which we were suspended, and let us down forever into the dark and horrible pit of misery and degradation from which we were straining every nerve to escape. While our hearts were crying lustily unto Him who is ever ready and able to save, the conductor of the train that we had just left stepped in. The officer asked if we came by the train with him from Washington; he said we did, and left the room. Just then the bell rang for the train to leave; and had it been the sudden shock of an earthquake it could not have given us a greater thrill. The sound of the bell caused every eye to flash with apparent interest, and to be more steadily fixed upon us than before. But, as God would have it, the officer all at once thrust his fingers through his hair, and in a state of great agitation said, "I really don't know what to do; I calculate it is all right." He then told the clerk to run and tell the conductor to "let this gentleman and slave pass;" adding, "As he is not well, it is a pity to stop him here. We will let him go." My master thanked him, and stepped out and hobbled across the platform as quickly as possible. I tumbled him unceremoniously into one of the best carriages, and leaped into mine just as the train was gliding off towards our happy destination.

We thought of this plan about four days before we left Mâcon; and as we had our daily employment to attend to, we only saw each other at night. So we sat up the four long nights talking over the plan and making preparations.

We had also been four days on the journey; and as we travelled night and day, we got but very limited opportunities for sleeping. I believe nothing in the world could have kept us awake so long but the intense excitement, produced by the fear of being retaken on the one hand, and the bright anticipation of liberty on the other.

We left Baltimore about eight o'clock in the evening; and not being aware of a stopping-place of any consequence between there and Philadelphia, and also knowing that if we were fortunate we should be in the latter place early the next morning, I thought I might indulge in a few minutes' sleep in the car; but I, like Bunyan's Christian in the arbor, went to sleep at the wrong time, and took too long a nap. So, when the train reached Havre de Grace, all the first-class passengers had to get out of the carriages and into a ferry-boat, to be ferried across the Susquehanna river, and take the train on the opposite side.

The road was constructed so as to be raised or lowered to suit the tide. So they rolled the luggage-vans on to the boat, and off on the other side; and as I was in one of the apartments adjoining a baggage-car, they considered it unnecessary to awaken me, and tumbled me over with the luggage. But when my master was asked to leave his seat, he found it very dark, and cold, and raining. He missed me for the first time on the journey. On all previous occasions, as soon as the train stopped, I was at hand to assist him. This caused many slaveholders to praise me very much: they said they had never before seen a slave so attentive to his master: and therefore my absence filled him with terror and confusion; the children of Israel could not have felt more troubled on arriving at the Red Sea. So he asked the conductor if he had seen anything of his slave. The man being somewhat of an abolitionist, and believing that my master was really a slaveholder, thought he would tease him a little respecting me. So he said, "No, sir; I haven't seen anything of him for some time: I have no doubt he has run away, and is in Philadelphia, free, long before now." My master knew that there was nothing in this; so he asked the conductor if he would please to see if he could find me. The man indignantly replied, "I am no slave-hunter; and as far as I am concerned everybody must look after their own niggers." He went off and left the confused invalid to fancy whatever he felt inclined. My master at first thought I must have been kidnapped into slavery by someone, or left, or perhaps killed on the train. He also thought of stopping to see if he could hear anything of me, but he soon remembered that he had no money. That night all the money we had was consigned to my own pocket, because we thought, in case there were any pickpockets about, a slave's pocket would be the last one they would look for. However, hoping to meet me someday in a land of liberty, and as he had the tickets, he thought it best upon the whole to enter the boat and come off to Philadelphia, and endeavor to make his way alone in this cold and hollow world as best he could. The time was now up, so he went on board and came across with feelings that can be better imagined than described.

After the train had got fairly on the way to Philadelphia, the guard came into my car and gave me a violent shake, and bawled out at the same time, "Boy, wake up!" I started, almost frightened out of my wits. He said, "Your master is scared half to death about you." That frightened me still more—I thought they had found him out; so I anxiously inquired what was the matter. The guard said, "He thinks you have run away from him." This made me feel quite at ease. I said, "No, sir; I am satisfied my good master doesn't think that." So off I started to see him. He had been fearfully nervous, but on seeing me he at once felt much better. He merely wished to know what had become of me.

On returning to my seat, I found the conductor and two or three other persons amusing themselves very much respecting my running away. So the guard said, "Boy, what did your master want?"* I replied, "He merely wished to know what had become of me." "No," said the man, "that was not it; he thought you had taken French leave, for parts unknown. I never saw a fellow so badly scared about losing his slave in my life. Now," continued the guard, "let me give you a little friendly advice. When you get to Philadelphia, run away and leave that cripple, and have your liberty." "No, sir," I indifferently replied, "I can't promise to do that." "Why not?" said the conductor, evidently much surprised; "don't you want your liberty?" "Yes, sir," I replied; "but I shall never run away from such a good master as I have at present."

One of the men said to the guard, "Let him alone; I guess he will open his eyes when he gets to Philadelphia, and see things in another light." After giving me a good deal of information, which I afterwards found to be very useful, they left me alone.

I also met with a colored gentleman on this train, who recommended me to a boarding-house that was kept by an abolitionist, where he thought I would be quite safe, if I wished to run away from my master. I thanked him kindly, but of course did not let him know who we were. Late at night, or rather early in the morning, I heard a fearful whistling of the steam-engine; so I opened the window and looked out, and saw a large number of flickering lights in the distance, and heard a passenger in the next carriage—who also had his head out of the window—say to his companion, "Wake up, old horse, we are at Philadelphia!"

---

*I may state here that every man slave is called boy till he is very old, then the more respectable slaveholders call him uncle. The women are all girls till they are aged, then they are called aunts. This is the reason why Mrs. Stowe calls her characters Uncle Tom, Aunt Chloe, Uncle Tiff, &c.

The sight of those lights and that announcement made me feel almost as happy as Bunyan's Christian must have felt when he first caught sight of the cross. I, like him, felt that the straps that bound the heavy burden to my back began to pop, and the load to roll off. I also looked, and looked again, for it appeared very wonderful to me how the mere sight of our first city of refuge should have all at once made my hitherto sad and heavy heart become so light and happy. As the train speeded on, I rejoiced and thanked God with all my heart and soul for his great kindness and tender mercy, in watching over us, and bringing us safely through.

As soon as the train had reached the platform, before it had fairly stopped, I hurried out of my carriage to my master, whom I got at once into a cab, placed the luggage on, jumped in myself, and we drove off to the boarding-house which was so kindly recommended to me. On leaving the station, my master—or rather my wife, as I may now say— who had from the commencement of the journey borne up in a manner that much surprised us both, grasped me by the hand, and said, "Thank God, William, we are safe!" then burst into tears, leant upon me, and wept like a child. The reaction was fearful. So when we reached the house, she was in reality so weak and faint that she could scarcely stand alone. However, I got her into the apartments that were pointed out, and there we knelt down, on this Sabbath, and Christmas-day,—a day that will ever be memorable to us,—and poured out our heartfelt gratitude to God, for his goodness in enabling us to overcome so many perilous difficulties, in escaping out of the jaws of the wicked.

PART II.

AFTER MY WIFE had a little recovered herself, she threw off the disguise and assumed her own apparel. We then stepped into the sitting-room, and asked to see the landlord. The man came in, but he seemed thunderstruck on finding a fugitive slave and his wife, instead of a "young cotton planter and his nigger." As his eyes travelled round the room, he said to me, "Where is your master?" I pointed him out. The man gravely replied, "I am not joking, I really wish to see your master." I pointed him out again, but at first he could not believe his eyes; he said "he knew that was not the gentleman that came with me."

But, after some conversation, we satisfied him that we were fugitive slaves, and had just escaped in the manner I have described. We asked him if he thought it would be safe for us to stop in Philadelphia. He said he thought not, but he would call in some persons who knew more about the laws than himself. He then went out, and kindly brought in several of the leading abolitionists of the city, who gave us a most hearty and friendly welcome amongst them. As it was in December, and also as we had just left a very warm climate, they advised us not to go to Canada as we had intended, but to settle at Boston in the United States. It is true that the constitution of the Republic has always guaranteed the slaveholders the right to come into any of the so-called free States, and take their fugitives back to southern Egypt. But through the untiring, uncompromising, and manly efforts of Mr. Garrison, Wendell Phillips, Theodore Parker, and a host of other noble abolitionists of Boston and the neighborhood, public opinion in Massachusetts had become so much opposed to slavery and to kidnapping, that it was almost impossible for anyone to take a fugitive slave out of that State.

So we took the advice of our good Philadelphia friends, and settled at Boston. I shall have something to say about our sojourn there presently.

Among other friends we met with at Philadelphia, was Robert Purves, Esq., a well educated and wealthy colored gentleman, who introduced us to Mr. Barkley Ivens, a member of the Society of Friends, and a noble and generous-hearted farmer, who lived at some distance in the country.

This good Samaritan at once invited us to go and stop quietly with his family, till my wife could somewhat recover from the fearful reaction of the past journey. We most gratefully accepted the invitation, and at the time appointed we took a steamer to a place up the Delaware river, where our new and dear friend met us with his snug little cart, and took us to his happy home. This was the first act of great and disinterested kindness we had ever received from a white person.

The gentleman was not of the fairest complexion, and therefore, as my wife was not in the room when I received the information respecting him and his anti-slavery character, she thought of course he was a quadroon like herself. But on arriving at the house, and finding out her mistake, she became more nervous and timid than ever.

As the cart came into the yard, the dear good old lady, and her three charming and affectionate daughters, all came to the door to meet us. We got out, and the gentleman said, "Go in, and make yourselves at home; I will see after the baggage." But my wife was afraid to approach them. She stopped in the yard, and said to me, "William, I thought we were coming among colored people?" I replied, "It is all right; these are the same." "No," she said, "it is not all right, and I am not going to stop here; I have no confidence whatever in white people, they are only trying to get us back to slavery." She turned round and said, "I am going right off." The old lady then came out, with her sweet, soft, and winning smile, shook her heartily by the hand, and kindly said, "How art thou, my dear? We are all very glad to see thee and thy husband. Come in, to the fire; I dare say thou art cold and hungry after thy journey."

We went in, and the young ladies asked if she would like to go upstairs and "fix" herself before tea. My wife said, "No, I thank you; I shall only stop a little while." "But where art thou going this cold night?" said Mr. Ivens, who had just stepped in. "I don't know," was the reply. "Well, then," he continued, "I think thou hadst better take off thy things and sit near the fire; tea will soon be ready." "Yes, come Ellen," said Mrs. Ivens, "let me assist thee;" (as she commenced undoing my wife's bonnet-strings;) "don't be frightened, Ellen, I shall not hurt a single hair of thy head. We have heard with much pleasure of the marvellous escape of thee and thy husband, and deeply sympathize with thee in all that thou hast undergone. I don't wonder at thee, poor thing, being timid; but thou needs not fear us; we would as soon send one of our own daughters into slavery as thee; so thou mayest make thyself quite at ease!" These soft and soothing words fell like balm upon my wife's unstrung nerves, and melted her to tears; her fears and prejudices vanished, and from that day she has firmly believed that there are good and bad persons of every shade of complexion.

After seeing Sally Ann and Jacob, two colored domestics, my wife felt quite at home. After partaking of what Mrs. Stowe's Mose and Pete called a "busting supper," the ladies wished to know whether we could read. On learning we could not, they said if we liked they would teach us. To this kind offer, of course, there was no objection. But we looked rather knowingly at each other, as much as to say that they would have rather a hard task to cram anything into our thick and matured skulls.

However, all hands set to and quickly cleared away the tea-things, and the ladies and their good brother brought out the spelling and copy books and slates, &c., and commenced with their new and green pupils. We had, by stratagem, learned the alphabet while in slavery, but not the writing characters; and, as we had been such a time learning so little, we at first felt that it was a waste of time for anyone at our ages to undertake to learn to read and write. But, as the ladies were so anxious that we should learn, and so willing to teach us, we concluded to give our whole minds to the work, and see what could be done. By so doing, at the end of the three weeks we remained with the good family we could spell and write our names quite legibly. They all begged us to stop longer; but, as we were not safe in the State of Pennsylvania, and also as we wished to commence doing something for a livelihood, we did not remain.

When the time arrived for us to leave for Boston, it was like parting with our relatives. We have since met with many very kind and hospitable friends, both in America and England; but we have never been under a roof where we were made to feel more at home, or where the inmates took a deeper interest in our well-being, than Mr. Barkley Ivens and his dear family. May God ever bless them, and preserve each one from every reverse of fortune!

We finally, as I have stated, settled at Boston, where we remained nearly two years, I employed as cabinet-maker and furniture broker, and my wife at her needle; and, as our little earnings in slavery were not all spent on the journey, we were getting on very well, and would have made money, if we had not been compelled by the General Government, at the bidding of the slaveholders, to break up business, and fly from under the Stars and Stripes to save our liberties and our lives.

In 1850, Congress passed the Fugitive Slave Bill, an enactment too infamous to have been thought of or tolerated by any people in the world, except the unprincipled and tyrannical Yankees. The following are a few of the leading features of the above law; which requires, under heavy penalties, that the inhabitants of the *free* States should not only refuse food and shelter to a starving, hunted human being, but also should assist, if called upon by the authorities, to seize the unhappy fugitive and send him back to slavery.

In no case is a person's evidence admitted in Court, in defense of his liberty, when arrested under this law.

If the judge decides that the prisoner is a slave, he gets ten dollars; but if he sets him at liberty, he only receives five.

After the prisoner has been sentenced to slavery, he is handed over to the United States Marshal, who has the power, at the expense of the General Government, to summon a sufficient force to take the poor creature back to slavery, and to the lash, from which he fled.

Our old masters sent agents to Boston after us. They took out warrants, and placed them in the hands of the United States Marshal to execute. But the following letter from our highly esteemed and faithful friend, the Rev. Samuel May, of Boston, to our equally dear and much lamented friend, Dr. Estlin of Bristol, will show why we were not taken into custody.

"21, Cornhill, Boston,
"November 6th, 1850.

"My dear Mr Estlin,

"I trust that in God's good providence this letter will be handed to you in safety by our good friends, William and Ellen Craft. They have lived amongst us about two years, and have proved themselves worthy, in all respects, of our confidence and regard. The laws of this republican and Christian land (tell it not in Moscow, nor in Constantinople) regard them only as slaves—chattels—personal property. But they nobly vindicated their title and right to freedom, two years since, by winning their way to it; at least, so they thought. But now, the slave power, with the aid of Daniel Webster and a band of lesser traitors, has enacted a law, which puts their dearly-bought liberties in the most imminent peril; holds out a strong temptation to every mercenary and unprincipled ruffian to become their kidnapper; and has stimulated the slaveholders generally to such desperate acts for the recovery of their fugitive property, as have never before been enacted in the history of this government.

"Within a fortnight, two fellows from Maçon, Georgia, have been in Boston for the purpose of arresting our friends William and Ellen. A writ was served against them from the United States District Court; but it was not served by the United States Marshal; why not, is not certainly known: perhaps through fear, for a general feeling of indignation, and a cool determination not to allow this young couple to be taken from Boston into slavery, was aroused, and pervaded the city. It is understood that one of the judges told the Marshal that he would not be authorized in breaking the door of Craft's house. Craft kept himself close within the house, armed himself, and awaited with remarkable composure the event. Ellen, in the meantime, had been taken to a retired place out of the city. The Vigilance Committee (appointed at a late meeting in Faneuil Hall) enlarged their numbers, held an almost permanent session, and appointed various subcommittees to act in different ways. One of these committees called repeatedly on Messrs. Hughes and Knight, the slave-catchers, and requested and advised them to leave the city. At first they peremptorily refused to do so, ' 'till they got hold of the niggers.' On complaint of different persons, these two fellows were several times arrested, carried before one of our county courts, and held to bail on charges of 'conspiracy to kidnap,' and of 'defamation,' in calling William and Ellen *'slaves.'* At length, they became so alarmed, that they left the city by an indirect route, evading the vigilance of many persons who were on the look-out for them. Hughes, at one time, was near losing his life at the hands of an infuriated colored man. While these men remained in the city, a prominent whig gentleman sent word to William Craft, that if he would submit peaceably to an arrest, he and his wife should be bought from their owners, cost what it might. Craft replied, in effect, that he was in a measure the representative of all the other fugitives in Boston, some 200 or 300 in number; that, if he gave up, they would all be at the mercy of the slave-catchers, and must fly from the city at any sacrifice; and that, if his freedom could be bought for two cents, he would not consent to compromise the matter in such a way. This event has stirred up the slave spirit of the country, south and north; the United States government is determined to try its hand in enforcing the Fugitive Slave law; and William and Ellen Craft would be prominent objects of the slaveholders' vengeance. Under these circumstances, it is the almost unanimous opinion of their best friends, that they should quit America as speedily as possible, and seek an asylum in England! Oh! shame, shame upon us, that Americans, whose fathers fought against Great Britain, in order to be FREE, should have to acknowledge this disgraceful fact! God gave us a fair and goodly heritage in this land, but man has cursed it with his devices and crimes against human souls and human rights. Is America the 'land of the free, and the home of the brave?' God knows it is not; and we know it too. A brave young man and a virtuous young woman must fly the American shores, and seek, under the shadow of the British throne, the enjoyment of 'life, liberty, and the pursuit of happiness.'

"But I must pursue my plain, sad story. All day long, I have been busy planning a safe way for William and Ellen to leave Boston. We dare not allow them to go on board a vessel, even in the port of Boston; for the writ is yet in the Marshal's hands, and he *may* be waiting an opportunity to serve it; so I am expecting to accompany them tomorrow to Portland, Maine, which is beyond the reach of the

Marshal's authority; and there I hope to see them on board a British steamer.

"This letter is written to introduce them to you. I know your infirm health; but I am sure, if you were stretched on your bed in your last illness, and could lift your hand at all, you would extend it to welcome these poor hunted fellow-creatures. Henceforth, England is their nation and their home. It is with real regret for our personal loss in their departure, as well as burning shame for the land that is not worthy of them, that we send them away, or rather allow them to go. But, with all the resolute courage they have shown in a most trying hour, they themselves see it is the part of a foolhardy rashness to attempt to stay here longer.

"I must close; and with many renewed thanks for all your kind words and deeds towards us,

"I am, very respectfully yours,
"Samuel May, Jun."

Our old masters, having heard how their agents were treated at Boston, wrote to Mr. Fillmore, who was then President of the States, to know what he could do to have us sent back to slavery. Mr. Fillmore said that we should be returned. He gave instructions for military force to be sent to Boston to assist the officers in making the arrest. Therefore we, as well as our friends (among whom was George Thompson, Esq., late M.P. for the Tower Hamlets—the slave's long-tried, self-sacrificing friend, and eloquent advocate) thought it best, at any sacrifice, to leave the mock-free Republic, and come to a country where we and our dear little ones can be truly free.—"No one daring to molest or make us afraid." But, as the officers were watching every vessel that left the port to prevent us from escaping, we had to take the expensive and tedious overland route to Halifax.

We shall always cherish the deepest feelings of gratitude to the Vigilance Committee of Boston (upon which were many of the leading abolitionists), and also to our numerous friends, for the very kind and noble manner in which they assisted us to preserve our liberties and to escape from Boston, as it were like Lot from Sodom, to a place of refuge, and finally to this truly free and glorious country; where no tyrant, let his power be ever so absolute over his poor trembling victims at home, dare come and lay violent hands upon us or upon our dear little boys (who had the good fortune to be born upon British soil), and reduce us to the legal level of the beast that perisheth. Oh! may God bless the thousands of unflinching, disinterested abolitionists of America, who are laboring through evil as well as through good report, to cleanse their country's escutcheon from the foul and destructive blot of slavery, and to restore to every bondman his God-given rights; and may God ever smile upon England and upon England's good, much-beloved, and deservedly-honored Queen, for the generous protection that is given to unfortunate refugees of every rank, and of every color and clime.

On the passing of the Fugitive Slave Bill, the following learned doctors, as well as a host of lesser traitors, came out strongly in its defense.

The Rev. Dr. Gardiner Spring, an eminent Presbyterian Clergyman of New York, well known in this country by his religious publications, declared from the pulpit that, "if by one prayer he could liberate every slave in the world he would not dare to offer it."

The Rev. Dr. Joel Parker, of Philadelphia, in the course of a discussion on the nature of Slavery, says, "What, then, are the evils inseparable from slavery? There is not one that is not equally inseparable from depraved human nature in other lawful relations."

The Rev. Moses Stuart, D.D., (late Professor in the Theological College of Andover), in his vindication of this Bill, reminds his readers that "many Southern slaveholders are true *Christians.*" That "sending back a fugitive to them is not like restoring one to an idolatrous people." That "though we may *pity* the fugitive, yet the Mosaic Law does not authorize the rejection of the claims of the slaveholders to their stolen or strayed *property.*"

The Rev. Dr. Spencer, of Brooklyn, New York, has come forward in support of the "Fugitive Slave Bill," by publishing a sermon entitled the "Religious Duty of Obedience to the Laws," which has elicited the highest encomiums from Dr. Samuel H. Cox, the Presbyterian minister of Brooklyn (notorious both in this country and America for his sympathy with the slaveholder).

The Rev. W. M. Rogers, an orthodox minister of Boston, delivered a sermon in which he says, "When the slave asks me to stand between him and his master, what does he ask? He asks me to murder a nation's life; and I will not do it, because I have a conscience,—because there is a God." He proceeds to affirm that if resistance to the carrying out of the "Fugitive Slave Law" should lead the magistracy to call the citizens to arms, their duty was to obey and "if ordered to take human life, in the name of God to take it;" and he concludes by admonishing the fugitives to "hearken to the Word of God, and to count their own masters worthy of all honor."

The Rev. William Crowell, of Waterfield, State of Maine, printed a Thanksgiving Sermon of the same kind, in which he calls upon his hearers not to allow "excessive sympathies for a few hundred fugitives to blind them so as that they may risk increased suffering to the millions already in chains."

The Rev. Dr. Taylor, an Episcopal Clergyman of New Haven, Connecticut, made a speech at a Union Meeting, in which he deprecates the agitation on the law, and urges obedience to it; asking,—"Is that article in the Constitution contrary to the law of Nature, of nations, or to the will of God? Is it so? Is there a shadow of reason for saying it? I have not been able to discover it. Have I not shown you it is lawful to deliver up, in compliance with the laws, fugitive slaves, for the high, the great, the momentous interests of those [Southern] States?"

The Right Rev. Bishop Hopkins, of Vermont, in a Lecture at Lockport, says, "It was warranted by the Old Testament;" and inquires, "What effect had the Gospel in doing away with slavery? None whatever." Therefore he argues, as it is expressly permitted by the Bible, it does not in itself involve any sin; but that every Christian is authorized by the Divine Law to own slaves, provided they were not treated with unnecessary cruelty.

The Rev. Orville Dewey, D.D., of the Unitarian connection, maintained in his lectures that the safety of the Union is not to be hazarded for the sake of the African race. He declares that, for his part, he would send his own brother or child into slavery, if needed to preserve the Union between the free and the slaveholding States; and, counselling the slave to similar magnanimity, thus exhorts him:—"*Your right to be free is not absolute, unqualified, irrespective of all consequences.* If my espousal of your claim is likely to involve your race and mine together in disasters infinitely greater than your personal servitude, then you ought not to be free. In such a case personal rights ought to be sacrificed to the general good. You yourself ought to see this, and be willing to suffer for a while—one for many."

If the Doctor is prepared, he is quite at liberty to sacrifice his "personal rights to the general good." But, as I have suffered a long time in slavery, it is hardly fair for the Doctor to advise me to go back. According to his showing, he ought rather to take my place. That would be practically carrying out his logic, as respects "suffering awhile—one for many."

In fact, so eager were they to prostrate themselves before the great idol of slavery, and, like Balaam, to curse instead of blessing the people whom God had brought out of bondage, that they in bringing up obsolete passages from the Old Testament to justify their downward course, overlooked, or would not see, the following verses, which show very clearly, according to the Doctor's own textbook, that the slaves have a right to run away, and that it is unscriptural for anyone to send them back.

In the 23rd chapter of Deuteronomy, 15th and 16th verses, it is thus written:—"Thou shalt not deliver unto his master the servant which is escaped from his master unto thee. He shall dwell with thee, even among you, in that place which he shall choose in one of thy gates, where it liketh him best: thou shalt not oppress him."

"Hide the outcast. Bewray not him that wandereth. Let mine outcasts dwell with thee. Be thou a covert to them from the face of the spoiler."—(Isa. xvi. 3, 4.)

The great majority of the American ministers are not content with uttering sentences similar to the above, or remaining wholly indifferent to the cries of the poor bondman; but they do all they can to blast the reputation, and to muzzle the mouths, of the few good men who dare to beseech the God of mercy "to loose the bonds of wickedness, to undo the heavy burdens, and let the oppressed go free." These reverend gentlemen pour a terrible cannonade upon "Jonah," for refusing to carry God's message against Nineveh, and tell us about the whale in which he was entombed; while they utterly overlook the existence of the whales which trouble their republican waters, and know not that they themselves are the "Jonahs" who threaten to sink their ship of state, by steering in an unrighteous direction. We are told that the whale vomited up the runaway prophet. This would not have seemed so strange, had it been one of the above lukewarm Doctors of Divinity whom he had swallowed; for even a whale might find such a morsel difficult of digestion.

> *"I venerate the man whose heart is warm,*
> *Whose hands are pure; whose doctrines and whose life*
> *Coincident, exhibit lucid proof*
> *That he is honest in the sacred cause."*

"But grace abused brings forth the foulest deeds,
As richest soil the most luxuriant weeds."

I must now leave the reverend gentlemen in the hands of Him who knows best how to deal with a recreant ministry.

I do not wish it to be understood that all the ministers of the States are of the Balaam stamp. There are those who are as uncompromising with slaveholders as Moses was with Pharaoh, and, like Daniel, will never bow down before the great false God that has been set up.

On arriving at Portland, we found that the steamer we intended to take had run into a schooner the previous night, and was lying up for repairs; so we had to wait there, in fearful suspense, for two or three days. During this time, we had the honor of being the guest of the late and much lamented Daniel Oliver, Esq., one of the best and most hospitable men in the State. By simply fulfilling the Scripture injunction, to take in the stranger, &c., he ran the risk of incurring a penalty of 2,000 dollars, and twelve months' imprisonment.

But neither the Fugitive Slave Law, nor any other Satanic enactment, can ever drive the spirit of liberty and humanity out of such noble and generous-hearted men.

May God ever bless his dear widow, and eventually unite them in His courts above!

We finally got off to St. John's, New Brunswick, where we had to wait two days for the steamer that conveyed us to Windsor, Nova Scotia.

On going into a hotel at St. John's, we met the butler in the hall, to whom I said, "We wish to stop here tonight." He turned round, scratching his head, evidently much put about. But thinking that my wife was white, he replied, "We have plenty of room for the lady, but I don't know about yourself; we never take in colored folks." "Oh, don't trouble about me," I said; "if you have room for the lady, that will do; so please have the luggage taken to a bed-room." Which was immediately done, and my wife went upstairs into the apartment.

After taking a little walk in the town, I returned, and asked to see the "lady." On being conducted to the little sitting-room, where she then was, I entered without knocking, much to the surprise of the whole house. The "lady" then rang the bell, and ordered dinner for two. "Dinner for two, mum!" exclaimed the waiter, as he backed out of the door. "Yes, for two," said my wife. In a little while the stout, red-nosed butler, whom we first met, knocked at the door. I called out, "Come in." On entering, he rolled his whisky eyes at me, and then at my wife, and said, in a very solemn tone, "Did you order dinner for two, mum?" "Yes, for two," my wife again replied. This confused the chubby butler more than ever; and, as the landlord was not in the house, he seemed at a loss what to do.

When dinner was ready, the maid came in and said, "Please mum, the Missis wishes to know whether you will have dinner up now, or wait till your friend arrives?" "I will have it up at once, if you please." "Thank you, mum," continued the maid, and out she glided.

After a good deal of giggling in the passage, someone said, "You are in for it, butler, after all; so you had better make the best of a bad job." But before dinner was sent up, the landlord returned, and having heard from the steward of the steamer by which we came that we were bound for England, the proprietor's native country, he treated us in the most respectful manner.

At the above house, the boots (whose name I forget) was a fugitive slave, a very intelligent and active man, about forty-five years of age. Soon after his marriage, while in slavery, his bride was sold away from him, and he could never learn where the poor creature dwelt. So after remaining single for many years, both before and after his escape, and never expecting to see again, nor even to hear from, his long-lost partner, he finally married a woman at St. John's. But, poor fellow, as he was passing down the street one day, he met a woman; at the first glance they nearly recognized each other; they both turned round and stared, and unconsciously advanced, till she screamed and flew into his arms. Her first words were, "Dear, are you married?" On his answering in the affirmative, she shrank from his embrace, hung her head, and wept. A person who witnessed this meeting told me it was most affecting.

This couple knew nothing of each other's escape or whereabouts. The woman had escaped a few years before to the free States, by secreting herself in the hold of a vessel; but as they tried to get her back to bondage, she fled to New Brunswick for that protection which her native country was too mean to afford.

The man at once took his old wife to see his new one, who was also a fugitive slave, and as they all knew the workings of the infamous system of slavery, they could (as no one else can,) sympathize with each other's misfortune.

According to the rules of slavery, the man and his first wife were already divorced, but not morally; and therefore it was arranged between the three that he should live only with the lastly married wife, and allow the other one so much a week, as long as she requested his assistance.

After staying at St. John's two days, the steamer arrived, which took us to Windsor, where we found a coach bound for Halifax. Prejudice against color forced me on the top in the rain. On arriving within about seven miles of the town, the coach broke down and was upset. I fell upon the big crotchety driver, whose head stuck in the mud; and as he "always objected to niggers riding inside with white folks," I was not particularly sorry to see him deeper in the mire than myself. All of us were scratched and bruised more or less. After the passengers had crawled out as best they could, we all set off, and paddled through the deep mud and cold and rain, to Halifax.

On leaving Boston, it was our intention to reach Halifax at least two or three days before the steamer from Boston touched there, *en route* for Liverpool; but, having been detained so long at Portland and St. John's, we had the misfortune to arrive at Halifax at dark, just two hours after the steamer had gone; consequently we had to wait there a fortnight, for the *Cambria*.

The coach was patched up, and reached Halifax with the luggage, soon after the passengers arrived. The only respectable hotel that was then in the town had suspended business, and was closed; so we went to the inn, opposite the market, where the coach stopped: a most miserable, dirty hole it was.

Knowing that we were still under the influence of the low Yankee prejudice, I sent my wife in with the other passengers, to engage a bed for herself and husband. I stopped outside in the rain till the coach came up. If I had gone in and asked for a bed they would have been quite full. But as they thought my wife was white, she had no difficulty in securing apartments, into which the luggage was afterwards carried. The landlady, observing that I took an interest in the baggage, became somewhat uneasy, and went into my wife's room, and said to her, "Do you know the dark man downstairs?" "Yes, he is my husband." "Oh! I mean the black man—the *nigger?*" "I quite understand you; he is my husband." "My God!" exclaimed the woman as she flounced out and banged to the door. On going upstairs, I heard what had taken place: but, as we were there, and did not mean to leave that night, we did not disturb ourselves. On our ordering tea, the landlady sent word back to say that we must take it in the kitchen, or in our bed-room, as she had no other room for "niggers." We replied that we were not particular, and that they could send it up to our room,—which they did.

After the pro-slavery persons who were staying there heard that we were in, the whole house became agitated, and all sorts of oaths and fearful threats were heaped upon the "d———d niggers, for coming among white folks." Some of them said they would not stop there a minute if there was another house to go to.

The mistress came up the next morning to know how long we wished to stop. We said a fortnight. "Oh! dear me, it is impossible for us to accommodate you, and I think you had better go: you must understand, I have no prejudice myself; I think a good deal of the colored people, and have always been their friend; but if you stop here we shall lose all our customers, which we can't do no-how." We said we were glad to hear that she had "no prejudice," and was such a staunch friend to the colored people. We also informed her that we would be sorry for her "customers" to leave on our account; and as it was not our intention to interfere with anyone, it was foolish for them to be frightened away. However, if she would get us a comfortable place, we would be glad to leave. The landlady said she would go out and try. After spending the whole morning in canvassing the town, she came to our room and said, "I have been from one end of the place to the other, but everybody is full." Having a little foretaste of the vulgar prejudice of the town, we did not wonder at this result. However, the landlady gave me the address of some respectable colored families, whom she thought, "under the circumstances," might be induced to take us. And, as we were not at all comfortable—being compelled to sit, eat and sleep, in the same small room—we were quite willing to change our quarters.

I called upon the Rev. Mr. Cannady, a truly good-hearted Christian man, who received us at a word; and both he and his kind lady treated us handsomely, and for a nominal charge.

My wife and myself were both unwell when we left Boston, and, having taken fresh cold on the journey to Halifax, we were laid up there under the doctor's care, nearly the whole fortnight. I had much worry about getting tickets, for they baffled us shamefully at the Cunard office. They at first said that they did not book till the steamer came; which was not the fact. When I called again, they said they knew the steamer would come full from Boston, and therefore we had "better try to get to Liverpool by other means." Other mean Yankee excuses were made; and it was not till an influential gentleman, to whom Mr. Francis Jackson, of Boston, kindly gave us a letter, went and rebuked them, that we were able to secure our tickets. So when we went on board my wife was very poorly, and was also so ill on the voyage that I did not believe she could live to see Liverpool.

However, I am thankful to say she arrived; and, after laying up at Liverpool very ill for two or three weeks, gradually recovered.

It was not until we stepped upon the shore at Liverpool that we were free from every slavish fear.

We raised our thankful hearts to Heaven, and could have knelt down, like the Neapolitan exiles, and kissed the soil; for we felt that from slavery

> *"Heaven sure had kept this spot of earth uncurs'd,*
> *To show how all things were created first."*

In a few days after we landed, the Rev. Francis Bishop and his lady came and invited us to be their guests; to whose unlimited kindness and watchful care my wife owes, in a great degree, her restoration to health.

We enclosed our letter from the Rev. Mr. May to Mr. Estlin, who at once wrote to invite us to his house at Bristol. On arriving there, both Mr. and Miss Estlin received us as cordially as did our first good Quaker friends in Pennsylvania. It grieves me much to have to mention that he is no more. Everyone who knew him can truthfully say—

> *"Peace to the memory of a man of worth,*
> *A man of letters, and of manners too!*
> *Of manners sweet as Virtue always wears*
> *When gay Good-nature dresses her in smiles."*

It was principally through the extreme kindness of Mr. Estlin, the Right Hon. Lady Noel Byron, Miss Harriet Martineau, Mrs. Reid, Miss Sturch, and a few other good friends, that my wife and myself were able to spend a short time at a school in this country, to acquire a little of that education which we were so shamefully deprived of while in the house of bondage. The school is under the supervision of the Misses Lushington, daughters of the Right Hon. Stephen Lushington, D.C.L. During our stay at the school we received the greatest attention from everyone; and I am particularly indebted to Thomas Wilson, Esq., of Bradmore House, Chiswick, (who was then the master,) for the deep interest he took in trying to get me on in my studies. We shall ever fondly and gratefully cherish the memory of our endeared and departed friend, Mr. Estlin. We, as well as the Anti-Slavery cause, lost a good friend in him. However, if departed spirits in Heaven are conscious of the wickedness of this world, and are allowed to speak, he will never fail to plead in the presence of the angelic host, and before the great and just Judge, for downtrodden and outraged humanity.

> *"Therefore I cannot think thee wholly gone;*
> *The better part of thee is with us still;*
> *Thy soul its hampering clay aside hath thrown,*
> *And only freer wrestles with the ill.*
>
> *"Thou livest in the life of all good things;*
> *What words thou spak'st for Freedom shall not die;*
> *Thou sleepest not, for now thy Love hath wings*
> *To soar where hence thy hope could hardly fly.*
>
> *"And often, from that other world, on this*
> *Some gleams from great souls gone before may shine,*
> *To shed on struggling hearts a clearer bliss,*
> *And clothe the Right with lustre more divine.*
>
> *"Farewell! good man, good angel now! this hand*
> *Soon, like thine own, shall lose its cunning, too;*
> *Soon shall this soul, like thine, bewildered stand,*
> *Then leap to thread the free unfathomed blue."*

James Russell Lowell.

IN THE PRECEDING PAGES I have not dwelt upon the great barbarities which are practiced upon the slaves; because I wish to present the system in its mildest form, and to show that the "tender mercies of the wicked are cruel." But I do now, however, most solemnly declare, that a very large majority of the American slaves are over-worked, under-fed, and frequently unmercifully flogged.

I have often seen slaves tortured in every conceivable manner. I have seen them hunted down and torn by bloodhounds. I have seen them shamefully beaten, and branded with hot irons. I have seen them hunted, and even burned alive at the stake, frequently for offenses that would be applauded if committed by white persons for similar purposes.

In short, it is well known in England, if not all over the world, that the Americans, as a people, are notoriously mean and cruel towards all colored persons, whether they are bond or free.

> *"Oh, tyrant, thou who sleepest*
> *On a volcano, from whose pent-up wrath,*
> *Already some red flashes bursting up,*
> *Beware!"*

INCIDENTS

IN THE

LIFE OF A SLAVE GIRL.

WRITTEN BY HERSELF.

"Northerners know nothing at all about Slavery. They think it is perpetual bondage only. They have no conception of the depth of *degradation* involved in that word, SLAVERY; if they had, they would never cease their efforts until so horrible a system was overthrown."

A WOMAN OF NORTH CAROLINA.

"Rise up, ye women that are at ease! Hear my voice, ye careless daughters! Give ear unto my speech."

ISAIAH XXXII.9.

EDITED BY L. MARIA CHILD.

BOSTON:
PUBLISHED FOR THE AUTHOR.
1861.

7

INCIDENTS IN THE LIFE

OF A SLAVE GIRL,

WRITTEN BY HERSELF.

HARRIET A. JACOBS

PREFACE BY THE AUTHOR.

READER, BE ASSURED this narrative is no fiction. I am aware that some of my adventures may seem incredible; but they are, nevertheless, strictly true. I have not exaggerated the wrongs inflicted by Slavery; on the contrary, my descriptions fall far short of the facts. I have concealed the names of places, and given persons fictitious names. I had no motive for secrecy on my own account, but I deemed it kind and considerate towards others to pursue this course.

I wish I were more competent to the task I have undertaken. But I trust my readers will excuse deficiencies in consideration of circumstances. I was born and reared in Slavery; and I remained in a Slave State twenty-seven years. Since I have been at the North, it has been necessary for me to work diligently for my own support, and the education of my children. This has not left me much leisure to make up for the loss of early opportunities to improve myself; and it has compelled me to write these pages at irregular intervals, whenever I could snatch an hour from household duties.

When I first arrived in Philadelphia, Bishop Paine advised me to publish a sketch of my life, but I told him I was altogether incompetent to such an undertaking. Though I have improved my mind somewhat since that time, I still remain of the same opinion; but I trust my motives will excuse what might otherwise seem presumptuous. I have not written my experiences in order to attract attention to myself; on the contrary, it would have been more pleasant to me to have been silent about my own history. Neither do I care to excite sympathy for my own sufferings. But I do earnestly desire to arouse the women of the North to a realizing sense of the condition of two millions of women at the South, still in bondage, suffering what I suffered, and most of them far worse. I want to add my testimony to that of abler pens to convince the people of the Free States what Slavery really is. Only by experience can anyone realize how deep, and dark, and foul is that pit of abominations. May the blessing of God rest on this imperfect effort in behalf of my persecuted people!

Linda Brent.

INTRODUCTION BY THE EDITOR.

THE AUTHOR OF the following autobiography is personally known to me, and her conversation and manners inspire me with confidence. During the last seventeen years, she has lived the greater part of the time with a distinguished family in New York, and has so deported herself as to be highly esteemed by them. This fact is sufficient, without further credentials of her character. I believe those who know her will not be disposed to doubt her veracity, though some incidents in her story are more romantic than fiction.

At her request, I have revised her manuscript; but such changes as I have made have been mainly for purposes of condensation and orderly arrangement. I have not added anything to the incidents, or changed the import of her very pertinent remarks. With trifling exceptions, both the ideas and the language are her own. I pruned excrescences a little, but otherwise I had no reason for changing her lively and dramatic way of telling her own story. The names of both persons and places are known to me; but for good reasons I suppress them.

It will naturally excite surprise that a woman reared in Slavery should be able to write so well. But circumstances will explain this. In the first place, nature endowed her with quick perceptions. Secondly, the mistress, with whom she lived till she was twelve years old, was a kind, considerate friend, who taught her to read and spell. Thirdly, she was placed in favorable circumstances after she came to the North; having frequent intercourse with intelligent persons, who felt a friendly interest in her welfare, and were disposed to give her opportunities for self-improvement.

I am well aware that many will accuse me of indecorum for presenting these pages to the public; for the experiences of this intelligent and much-injured woman belong to a class which some call delicate subjects, and others indelicate. This peculiar phase of Slavery has generally been kept veiled; but the public ought to be made acquainted with its monstrous features, and I willingly take the responsibility of presenting them with the veil withdrawn. I do this for the sake of my sisters in bondage, who are suffering wrongs so foul, that our ears are too delicate to listen to them. I do it with the hope of arousing conscientious and reflecting women at the North to a sense of their duty in the exertion of moral influence on the question of Slavery, on all possible occasions. I do it with the hope that every man who reads this narrative will swear solemnly before God that, so far as he has power to prevent it, no fugitive from Slavery shall ever be sent back to suffer in that loathsome den of corruption and cruelty.

L. Maria Child.

Contents.

Incidents in the Life

of a Slave Girl,

Seven Years Concealed.

I

Childhood

I WAS BORN a slave; but I never knew it till six years of happy childhood had passed away. My father was a carpenter, and considered so intelligent and skillful in his trade, that, when buildings out of the common line were to be erected, he was sent for from long distances, to be head workman. On condition of paying his mistress two hundred dollars a year, and supporting himself, he was allowed to work at his trade, and manage his own affairs. His strongest wish was to purchase his children; but, though he several times offered his hard earnings for that purpose, he never succeeded. In complexion my parents were a light shade of brownish yellow, and were termed mulattoes. They lived together in a comfortable home; and, though we were all slaves, I was so fondly shielded that I never dreamed I was a piece of merchandise, trusted to them for safe keeping, and liable to be demanded of them at any moment. I had one brother, William, who was two years younger than myself—a bright, affectionate child. I had also a great treasure in my maternal grandmother, who was a remarkable woman in many respects. She was the daughter of a planter in South Carolina, who, at his death, left her mother and his three children free, with money to go to St. Augustine, where they had relatives. It was during the Revolutionary War; and they were captured on their passage, carried back, and sold to different purchasers. Such was the story my grandmother used to tell me; but I do not remember all the particulars. She was a little girl when she was captured and sold to the keeper of a large hotel. I have often heard her tell how hard she fared during childhood. But as she grew older she evinced so much intelligence, and was so faithful, that her master and mistress could not help seeing it was for their interest to take care of such a valuable piece of property. She became an indispensable personage in the household, officiating in all capacities, from cook and wet nurse to seamstress. She was much praised for her cooking; and her nice crackers became so famous in the neighborhood that many people were desirous of obtaining them. In consequence of numerous requests of this kind, she asked permission of her mistress to bake crackers at night, after all the household work was done; and she obtained leave to do it, provided she would clothe herself and her children from the profits. Upon these terms, after working hard all day for her mistress, she began her midnight bakings, assisted by her two oldest children. The business proved profitable; and each year she laid by a little, which was saved for a fund to purchase her children. Her master died, and the property was divided among his heirs. The widow had her dower in the hotel, which she continued to keep open. My grandmother remained in her service as a slave; but her children were divided among her master's children. As she had five, Benjamin, the youngest one, was sold, in order that each heir might have an equal portion of dollars and cents. There was so little difference in our ages that he seemed more like my brother than my uncle. He was a bright, handsome lad, nearly white; for he inherited the complexion my grandmother had derived from Anglo-Saxon ancestors. Though only ten years old, seven hundred and twenty dollars were paid for him. His sale was a terrible blow to my grandmother; but she was naturally hopeful, and she went to work with renewed energy, trusting in time to be able to purchase some of her children. She had laid up three hundred dollars, which her mistress one day begged as a loan, promising to pay her soon. The reader probably knows that no promise or writing given to a slave is legally binding; for, according to Southern laws, a slave, *being* property, can *hold* no property. When my grandmother lent her hard earnings to her mistress, she trusted solely to her honor. The honor of a slaveholder to a slave!

To this good grandmother I was indebted for many comforts. My brother Willie and I often received portions of the crackers, cakes, and preserves, she made to sell; and after we ceased to be children we were indebted to her for many more important services.

Such were the unusually fortunate circumstances of my early childhood. When I was six years old, my mother died; and then, for the first time, I learned, by the talk around me, that I was a slave. My mother's mistress was the daughter of my grandmother's mistress. She was the foster sister of my mother; they were both nourished at my grandmother's breast. In fact, my mother had been weaned at three months old, that the babe of the mistress might obtain sufficient food. They played together as children; and, when they became women, my mother was a most faithful servant to her whiter foster sister. On her death-bed her mistress promised that her children should never suffer for anything; and during her lifetime she kept her word. They all spoke kindly of my dead mother, who had been a slave merely in name, but in nature was noble and womanly. I grieved for her, and my young mind was troubled with the thought who would now take care of me and my little brother. I was told that my home was now to be with her mistress; and I found it a happy one. No toilsome or disagreeable duties were imposed upon me. My mistress was so kind to me that I was always glad to do her bidding, and proud to labor for her as much as my young years would permit. I would sit by her side for hours, sewing diligently, with a heart as free from care as that of any free-born white child. When she thought I was tired, she would send me out to run and jump; and away I bounded, to gather berries or flowers to decorate her room. Those were happy days—too happy to last. The slave child had no thought for the morrow; but there came that blight, which too surely waits on every human being born to be a chattel.

When I was nearly twelve years old, my kind mistress sickened and died. As I saw the cheek grow paler, and the eye more glassy, how earnestly I prayed in my heart that she might live! I loved her; for she had been almost like a mother to me. My prayers were not answered. She died, and they buried her in the little churchyard, where, day after day, my tears fell upon her grave.

I was sent to spend a week with my grandmother. I was now old enough to begin to think of the future; and again and again I asked myself what they would do with me. I felt sure I should never find another mistress so kind as the one who was gone. She had promised my dying mother that her children should never suffer for anything; and when I remembered that, and recalled her many proofs of attachment to me, I could not help having some hopes that she had left me free. My friends were almost certain it would be so. They thought she would be sure to do it, on account of my mother's love and faithful service. But, alas! we all know that the memory of a faithful slave does not avail much to save her children from the auction block.

After a brief period of suspense, the will of my mistress was read, and we learned that she had bequeathed me to her sister's daughter, a child of five years old. So vanished our hopes. My mistress had taught me the precepts of God's Word: "Thou shalt love thy neighbor as thyself." "Whatsoever ye would that men should do unto you, do ye even so unto them." But I was her slave, and I suppose she did not recognize me as her neighbor. I would give much to blot out from my memory that one great wrong. As a child, I loved my mistress; and, looking back on the happy days I spent with her, I try to think with less bitterness of this act of injustice. While I was with her, she taught me to read and spell; and for this privilege, which so rarely falls to the lot of a slave, I bless her memory.

She possessed but few slaves; and at her death those were all distributed among her relatives. Five of them were my grandmother's children, and had shared the same milk that nourished her mother's children. Notwithstanding my grandmother's long and faithful service to her owners, not one of her children escaped the auction block. These God-breathing machines are no more, in the sight of their masters, than the cotton they plant, or the horses they tend.

II

The New Master and Mistress

DR. FLINT, a physician in the neighborhood, had married the sister of my mistress, and I was now the property of their little daughter. It was not without murmuring that I prepared for my new home; and what added to my unhappiness, was the fact that my brother William was purchased by the same family. My father, by his nature, as well as by the habit of transacting business as a skillful mechanic, had more of the feelings of a freeman than is common among slaves. My brother was a spirited boy; and being brought up under such influences, he early detested the name of master and mistress. One day, when his father and his mistress both happened to call him at the same time, he hesitated between the two; being perplexed to know which had the strongest claim upon his obedience. He finally concluded to go to his mistress. When my father reproved him for it, he said, "You both called me, and I didn't know which I ought to go to first."

"You are *my* child," replied our father, "and when I call you, you should come immediately, if you have to pass through fire and water."

Poor Willie! He was now to learn his first lesson of obedience to a master. Grandmother tried to cheer us with hopeful words, and they found an echo in the credulous hearts of youth.

When we entered our new home we encountered cold looks, cold words, and cold treatment. We were glad when the night came. On my narrow bed I moaned and wept, I felt so desolate and alone.

I had been there nearly a year, when a dear little friend of mine was buried. I heard her mother sob, as the clods fell on the coffin of her only child, and I turned away from the grave, feeling thankful that I still had something left to love. I met my grandmother, who said, "Come with me, Linda;" and from her tone I knew that something sad had happened. She led me apart from the people, and then said, "My child, your father is dead." Dead! How could I believe it? He had died so suddenly I had not even heard that he was sick. I went home with my grandmother. My heart rebelled against God, who had taken from me mother, father, mistress, and friend. The good grandmother tried to comfort me. "Who knows the ways of God?" said she. "Perhaps they have been kindly taken from the evil days to come." Years afterwards I often thought of this. She promised to be a mother to her grandchildren, so far as she might be permitted to do so; and strengthened by her love, I returned to my master's. I thought I should be allowed to go to my father's house the next morning; but I was ordered to go for flowers, that my mistress's house might be decorated for an evening party. I spent the day gathering flowers and weaving them into festoons, while the dead body of my father was lying within a mile of me. What cared my owners for that? he was merely a piece of property. Moreover, they thought he had spoiled his children, by teaching them to feel that they were human beings. This was blasphemous doctrine for a slave to teach; presumptuous in him, and dangerous to the masters.

The next day I followed his remains to a humble grave beside that of my dear mother. There were those who knew my father's worth, and respected his memory.

My home now seemed more dreary than ever. The laugh of the little slave-children sounded harsh and cruel. It was selfish to feel so about the joy of others. My brother moved about with a very grave face. I tried to comfort him, by saying, "Take courage, Willie; brighter days will come by and by."

"You don't know anything about it, Linda," he replied. "We shall have to stay here all our days; we shall never be free."

I argued that we were growing older and stronger, and that perhaps we might, before long, be allowed to hire our own time, and then we could earn money to buy our freedom. William declared this was much easier to say than to do; moreover, he did not intend to *buy* his freedom. We held daily controversies upon this subject.

Little attention was paid to the slaves' meals in Dr. Flint's house. If they could catch a bit of food while it was going, well and good. I gave myself no trouble on that score, for on my various errands I passed my grandmother's house, where there was always something to spare for me. I was frequently threatened with punishment if I stopped there; and my grandmother, to avoid detaining me, often stood at the gate with something for my breakfast or dinner. I was indebted to *her* for all my comforts, spiritual or temporal. It was *her* labor that supplied my scanty wardrobe. I have a vivid recollection of the linsey-woolsey dress given me every winter by Mrs. Flint. How I hated it! It was one of the badges of slavery.

While my grandmother was thus helping to support me from her hard earnings, the three hundred dollars she had lent her mistress were never repaid. When her mistress died, her son-in-law, Dr. Flint, was appointed executor. When grandmother applied to him for payment, he said the estate was insolvent, and the law prohibited payment. It did not, however, prohibit him from retaining the silver candelabra, which had been purchased with that money. I presume they will be handed down in the family, from generation to generation.

My grandmother's mistress had always promised her that, at her death, she should be free; and it was said that in her will she made good the promise. But when the estate was settled, Dr. Flint told the faithful old servant that, under existing circumstances, it was necessary she should be sold.

On the appointed day, the customary advertisement was posted up, proclaiming that there would be a "public sale of negroes, horses, &c." Dr. Flint called to tell my grandmother that he was unwilling to wound her feelings by putting her up at auction, and that he would prefer to dispose of her at private sale. My grandmother saw through his hypocrisy; she understood very well that he was ashamed of the job. She was a very spirited woman, and if he was base enough to sell her, when her mistress intended she should be free, she was determined the public should know it. She had for a long time supplied many families with crackers and preserves; consequently, "Aunt Marthy," as she was called, was generally known, and everybody who knew her respected her intelligence and good character. Her long and faithful service in the family was also well known, and the intention of her mistress to leave her free. When the day of sale came, she took her place among the chattels, and at the first call she sprang upon the auction-block. Many voices called out, "Shame! Shame! Who is going to sell *you*, aunt Marthy? Don't stand there! That is no place for *you*." Without saying a word, she quietly awaited her fate. No one bid for her. At last, a feeble voice said, "Fifty dollars." It came from a maiden lady, seventy years old, the sister of my grandmother's deceased mistress. She had lived forty years under the same roof with my grandmother; she knew how faithfully she had served her owners, and how cruelly she had been defrauded of her rights; and she resolved to protect her. The auctioneer waited for a higher bid; but her wishes were respected; no one bid above her. She could neither read nor write; and when the bill of sale was made out, she signed it with a cross. But what consequence was that, when she had a big heart overflowing with human kindness? She gave the old servant her freedom.

At that time, my grandmother was just fifty years old. Laborious years had passed since then; and now my brother and I were slaves to the man who had defrauded her of her money, and tried to defraud her of her freedom. One of my mother's sisters, called Aunt Nancy, was also a slave in his family. She was a kind, good aunt to me; and supplied the place of both housekeeper and waiting maid to her mistress. She was, in fact, at the beginning and end of everything.

Mrs. Flint, like many southern women, was totally deficient in energy. She had not strength to superintend her household affairs; but her nerves were so strong, that she could sit in her easy chair and see a woman whipped, till the blood trickled from every stroke of the lash. She was a member of the church; but partaking of the Lord's supper did not seem to put her in a Christian frame of mind. If dinner was not served at the exact time on that particular Sunday, she would station herself in the kitchen, and wait till it was dished, and then spit in all the kettles and pans that had been used for cooking. She did this to prevent the cook and her children from eking out their meager fare with the remains of the gravy and other scrapings. The slaves could get nothing to eat except what she chose to give them. Provisions were weighed out by the pound and ounce, three times a day. I can assure you she gave them no chance to eat wheat bread from her flour barrel. She knew how many biscuits a quart of flour would make, and exactly what size they ought to be.

Dr. Flint was an epicure. The cook never sent a dinner to his table without fear and trembling; for if there happened to be a dish not to his liking, he would either order her to be whipped, or compel her to eat every mouthful of it in his presence. The poor, hungry creature might not have objected to eating it; but she did object to having her master cram it down her throat till she choked.

They had a pet dog, that was a nuisance in the house. The cook was ordered to make some Indian mush for him. He refused to eat, and when his head was held over it, the froth flowed from his mouth into the basin. He died a few minutes after. When Dr. Flint came in, he said the mush had not been well cooked, and that was the reason the animal would not eat it. He sent for the cook, and compelled her to eat it. He thought that the woman's stomach was stronger than the dog's; but her sufferings afterwards proved that he was mistaken. This poor woman endured many cruelties from her master and mistress; sometimes she was locked up, away from her nursing baby, for a whole day and night.

When I had been in the family a few weeks, one of the plantation slaves was brought to town, by order of his master. It was near night when he arrived, and Dr. Flint ordered him to be taken to the work house, and tied up to the joist, so that his feet would just escape the ground. In that situation he was to wait till the doctor had taken his tea. I shall never forget that night. Never before, in my life, had I heard hundreds of blows fall, in succession, on a human being. His piteous groans, and his "O, pray don't, massa," rang in my ear for months afterwards. There were many conjectures as to the cause of this terrible punishment. Some said master accused him of stealing corn; others said the slave had quarrelled with his wife, in presence of the overseer, and had accused his master of being the father of her child. They were both black, and the child was very fair.

I went into the work house next morning, and saw the cowhide still wet with blood, and the boards all covered with gore. The poor man lived, and continued to quarrel with his wife. A few months afterwards Dr. Flint handed them both over to a slave-trader. The guilty man put their value into his pocket, and had the satisfaction of knowing that they were out of sight and hearing. When the mother was delivered into the trader's hands, she said, "You *promised* to treat me well." To which he replied, "You have let your tongue run too far; damn you!" She had forgotten that it was a crime for a slave to tell who was the father of her child.

From others than the master persecution also comes in such cases. I once saw a young slave girl dying soon after the birth of a child nearly white. In her agony she cried out, "O Lord, come and take me!" Her mistress stood by, and mocked at her like an incarnate fiend. "You suffer, do you?" she exclaimed. "I am glad of it. You deserve it all, and more too."

The girl's mother said, "The baby is dead, thank God; and I hope my poor child will soon be in heaven, too."

"Heaven!" retorted the mistress. "There is no such place for the like of her and her bastard."

The poor mother turned away, sobbing. Her dying daughter called her, feebly, and as she bent over her, I heard her say, "Don't grieve so, mother; God knows all about it; and HE will have mercy upon me."

Her sufferings, afterwards, became so intense, that her mistress felt unable to stay; but when she left the room, the scornful smile was still on her lips. Seven children called her mother. The poor black woman had but the one child, whose eyes she saw closing in death, while she thanked God for taking her away from the greater bitterness of life.

III

The Slaves' New Year's Day

DR. FLINT owned a fine residence in town, several farms, and about fifty slaves, besides hiring a number by the year.

Hiring-day at the south takes place on the 1st of January. On the 2d, the slaves are expected to go to their new masters. On a farm, they work until the corn and cotton are laid. They then have two holidays. Some masters give them a good dinner under the trees. This over, they work until Christmas eve. If no heavy charges are meantime brought against them, they are given four or five holidays, whichever the master or overseer may think proper. Then comes New Year's eve; and they gather together their little alls, or more properly speaking, their little nothings, and wait anxiously for the dawning of day. At the appointed hour the grounds are thronged with men, women, and children, waiting, like criminals, to hear their doom pronounced. The slave is sure to know who is the most humane, or cruel master, within forty miles of him.

It is easy to find out, on that day, who clothes and feeds his slaves well; for he is surrounded by a crowd, begging, "Please, massa, hire me this year. I will work *very* hard, massa."

If a slave is unwilling to go with his new master, he is whipped, or locked up in jail, until he consents to go, and promises not to run away during the year. Should he chance to change his mind, thinking it justifiable to violate an extorted promise, woe unto him if he is caught! The whip is used till the blood flows at his feet; and his stiffened limbs are put in chains, to be dragged in the field for days and days!

If he lives until the next year, perhaps the same man will hire him again, without even giving him an opportunity of going to the hiring-ground. After those for hire are disposed of, those for sale are called up.

O, you happy free women, contrast *your* New Year's day with that of the poor bond-woman! With you it is a pleasant season, and the light of the day is blessed. Friendly wishes meet you everywhere, and gifts are showered upon you. Even hearts that have been estranged from you soften at this season, and lips that have been silent echo back, "I wish you a happy New Year." Children bring their little offerings, and raise their rosy lips for a caress. They are your own, and no hand but that of death can take them from you.

But to the slave mother New Year's day comes laden with peculiar sorrows. She sits on her cold cabin floor, watching the children who may all be torn from her the next morning; and often does she wish that she and they might die before the day dawns. She may be an ignorant creature, degraded by the system that has brutalized her from childhood; but she has a mother's instincts, and is capable of feeling a mother's agonies.

On one of these sale days, I saw a mother lead seven children to the auction-block. She knew that *some* of them would be taken from her; but they took *all*. The children were sold to a slave-trader, and their mother was bought by a man in her own town. Before night her children were all far away. She begged the trader to tell her where he intended to take them; this he refused to do. How *could* he, when he knew he would sell them, one by one, wherever he could command the highest price? I met that mother in the street, and her wild, haggard face lives today in my mind. She wrung her hands in anguish, and exclaimed, "Gone! All gone! Why *don't* God kill me?" I had no words wherewith to comfort her. Instances of this kind are of daily, yea, of hourly occurrence.

Slaveholders have a method, peculiar to their institution, of getting rid of *old* slaves, whose lives have been worn out in their service. I knew an old woman, who for seventy years faithfully served her master. She had become almost helpless, from hard labor and disease. Her owners moved to Alabama, and the old black woman was left to be sold to anybody who would give twenty dollars for her.

IV

The Slave Who Dared to Feel Like a Man

TWO YEARS had passed since I entered Dr. Flint's family, and those years had brought much of the knowledge that comes from experience, though they had afforded little opportunity for any other kinds of knowledge.

My grandmother had, as much as possible, been a mother to her orphan grandchildren. By perseverance and unwearied industry, she was now mistress of a snug little home, surrounded with the necessaries of life. She would have been happy could her children have shared them with her. There remained but three children and two grandchildren, all slaves. Most earnestly did she strive to make us feel that it was the will of God: that He had seen fit to place us under such circumstances; and though it seemed hard, we ought to pray for contentment.

It was a beautiful faith, coming from a mother who could not call her children her own. But I, and Benjamin, her youngest boy, condemned it. We reasoned that it was much more the will of God that we should be situated as she was. We longed for a home like hers. There we always found sweet balsam for our troubles. She was so loving, so sympathizing! She always met us with a smile, and listened with patience to all our sorrows. She spoke so hopefully, that unconsciously the clouds gave place to sunshine. There was a grand big oven there, too, that baked bread and nice things for the town, and we knew there was always a choice bit in store for us.

But, alas! even the charms of the old oven failed to reconcile us to our hard lot. Benjamin was now a tall, handsome lad, strongly and gracefully made, and with a spirit too bold and daring for a slave. My brother William, now twelve years old, had the same aversion to the word master that he had when he was an urchin of seven years. I was his confidant. He came to me with all his troubles. I remember one instance in particular. It was on a lovely spring morning, and when I marked the sunlight dancing here and there, its beauty seemed to mock my sadness. For my master, whose restless, craving, vicious nature roved about day and night, seeking whom to devour, had just left me, with stinging, scorching words; words that scathed ear and brain like fire. O, how I despised him! I thought how glad I should be, if some day when he walked the earth, it would open and swallow him up, and disencumber the world of a plague.

When he told me that I was made for his use, made to obey his command in *every* thing; that I was nothing but a slave, whose will must and should surrender to his, never before had my puny arm felt half so strong.

So deeply was I absorbed in painful reflections afterwards, that I neither saw nor heard the entrance of anyone, till the voice of William sounded close beside me. "Linda," said he, "what makes you look so sad? I love you. O, Linda, isn't this a bad world? Everybody seems so cross and unhappy. I wish I had died when poor father did."

I told him that everybody was *not* cross, or unhappy; that those who had pleasant homes, and kind friends, and who were not afraid to love them, were happy. But we, who were slave-children, without father or mother, could not expect to be happy. We must be good; perhaps that would bring us contentment.

"Yes," he said, "I try to be good; but what's the use? They are all the time troubling me." Then he proceeded to relate his afternoon's difficulty with young master Nicholas. It seemed that the brother of master Nicholas had pleased himself with making up stories about William. Master Nicholas said he should be flogged, and he would do it. Whereupon he went to work; but William fought bravely, and the young master, finding he was getting the better of him, undertook to tie his hands behind him. He failed in that likewise. By dint of kicking and fisting, William came out of the skirmish none the worse for a few scratches.

He continued to discourse on his young master's *meanness;* how he whipped the *little* boys, but was a perfect coward when a tussle ensued between him and white boys of his own size. On such occasions he always took to his legs. William had other charges to make against him. One was his rubbing up pennies with quicksilver, and passing them off for quarters of a dollar on an old man who kept a fruit stall. William was often sent to buy fruit, and he earnestly inquired of me what he ought to do under such circumstances. I told him it was certainly wrong to deceive the old man, and that it was his duty to tell him of the impositions practiced by his young master. I assured him the old man would not be slow to comprehend the whole, and there the matter would end. William thought it might with the old man, but not with *him*. He said he did not mind the smart of the whip, but he did not like the *idea* of being whipped.

While I advised him to be good and forgiving I was not unconscious of the beam in my own eye. It was the very knowledge of my own short-comings that urged me to retain, if possible, some sparks of my brother's God-given nature. I had not lived fourteen years in slavery for nothing. I had felt, seen, and heard enough, to read the characters, and question the motives, of those around me. The war of my life had begun; and though one of God's most powerless creatures, I resolved never to be conquered. Alas, for me!

If there was one pure, sunny spot for me, I believed it to be in Benjamin's heart, and in another's, whom I loved with all the ardor of a girl's first love. My owner knew of it, and sought in every way to render me miserable. He did not resort to corporal punishment, but to all the petty, tyrannical ways that human ingenuity could devise.

I remember the first time I was punished. It was in the month of February. My grandmother had taken my old shoes, and replaced them with a new pair. I needed them; for several inches of snow had fallen, and it still continued to fall. When I walked through Mrs. Flint's room, their creaking grated harshly on her refined nerves. She called me to her, and asked what I had about me that made such a horrid noise. I told her it was my new shoes. "Take them off," said she; "and if you put them on again, I'll throw them into the fire."

I took them off, and my stockings also. She then sent me a long distance, on an errand. As I went through the snow, my bare feet tingled. That night I was very hoarse; and I went to bed thinking the next day would find me sick, perhaps dead. What was my grief on waking to find myself quite well!

I had imagined if I died, or was laid up for some time, that my mistress would feel a twinge of remorse that she had so hated "the little imp," as she styled me. It was my ignorance of that mistress that gave rise to such extravagant imaginings.

Dr. Flint occasionally had high prices offered for me; but he always said, "She don't belong to me. She is my daughter's property, and I have no right to sell her." Good, honest man! My young mistress was still a child, and I could look for no protection from her. I loved her, and she returned my affection. I once heard her father allude to her attachment to me; and his wife promptly replied that it proceeded from fear. This put unpleasant doubts into my mind. Did the child feign what she did not feel? or was her mother jealous of the mite of love she bestowed on me? I concluded it must be the latter. I said to myself, "Surely, little children are true."

One afternoon I sat at my sewing, feeling unusual depression of spirits. My mistress had been accusing me of an offense, of which I assured her I was perfectly innocent; but I saw, by the contemptuous curl of her lip, that she believed I was telling a lie.

I wondered for what wise purpose God was leading me through such thorny paths, and whether still darker days were in store for me. As I sat musing thus, the door opened softly, and William came in. "Well, brother," said I, "what is the matter this time?"

"O Linda, Ben and his master have had a dreadful time!" said he. My first thought was that Benjamin was killed. "Don't be frightened, Linda," said William; "I will tell you all about it."

It appeared that Benjamin's master had sent for him, and he did not immediately obey the summons. When he did, his master was angry, and began to whip him. He resisted. Master and slave fought, and finally the master was thrown. Benjamin had cause to tremble; for he had thrown to the ground his master—one of the richest men in town. I anxiously awaited the result.

That night I stole to my grandmother's house, and Benjamin also stole thither from his master's. My grandmother had gone to spend a day or two with an old friend living in the country.

"I have come," said Benjamin, "to tell you goodby. I am going away."

I inquired where.

"To the north," he replied.

I looked at him to see whether he was in earnest. I saw it all in his firm, set mouth. I implored him not to go, but he paid no heed to my words. He said he was no longer a boy, and every day made his yoke more galling. He had raised his hand against his master, and was to be publicly whipped for the offense. I reminded him of the poverty and hardships he must encounter among strangers. I told him he might be caught and brought back; and that was terrible to think of.

He grew vexed, and asked if poverty and hardships with freedom, were not preferable to our treatment in slavery. "Linda," he continued, "we are dogs here; foot-balls, cattle, everything that's mean. No, I will not stay. Let them bring me back. We don't die but once."

He was right; but it was hard to give him up. "Go," said I, "and break your mother's heart."

I repented of my words ere they were out.

"Linda," said he, speaking as I had not heard him speak that evening, "how *could* you say that? Poor mother! be kind to her, Linda; and you, too, cousin Fanny."

Cousin Fanny was a friend who had lived some years with us.

Farewells were exchanged, and the bright, kind boy, endeared to us by so many acts of love, vanished from our sight.

It is not necessary to state how he made his escape. Suffice it to say, he was on his way to New York when a violent storm overtook the vessel. The captain said he must put into the nearest port. This alarmed Benjamin, who was aware that he would be advertised in every port near his own town. His embarrassment was noticed by the captain. To port they went. There the advertisement met the captain's eye. Benjamin so exactly answered its description, that the captain laid hold on him, and bound him in chains. The storm passed, and they proceeded to New York. Before reaching that port Benjamin managed to get off his chains and throw them overboard. He escaped from the vessel, but was pursued, captured, and carried back to his master.

When my grandmother returned home and found her youngest child had fled, great was her sorrow; but, with characteristic piety, she said, "God's will be done." Each morning, she inquired if any news had been heard from her boy. Yes, news *was* heard. The master was rejoicing over a letter, announcing the capture of his human chattel.

That day seems but as yesterday, so well do I remember it. I saw him led through the streets in chains, to jail. His face was ghastly pale, yet full of determination. He had begged one of the sailors to go to his mother's house and ask her not to meet him. He said the sight of her distress would take from him all self-control. She yearned to see him, and she went; but she screened herself in the crowd, that it might be as her child had said.

We were not allowed to visit him; but we had known the jailer for years, and he was a kind-hearted man. At midnight he opened the jail door for my grandmother and myself to enter, in disguise. When we entered the cell not a sound broke the stillness. "Benjamin, Benjamin!" whispered my grandmother. No answer. "Benjamin!" she again faltered. There was a jingle of chains. The moon had just risen, and cast an uncertain light through the bars of the window. We knelt down and took Benjamin's cold hands in ours. We did not speak. Sobs were heard, and Benjamin's lips were unsealed; for his mother was weeping on his neck. How vividly does memory bring back that sad night!

Mother and son talked together. He asked her pardon for the suffering he had caused her. She said she had nothing to forgive; she could not blame his desire for freedom. He told her that when he was captured, he broke away, and was about casting himself into the river, when thoughts of *her* came over him, and he desisted. She asked if he did not also think of God. I fancied I saw his face grow fierce in the moonlight. He answered, "No, I did not think of him. When a man is hunted like a wild beast he forgets there is a God, a heaven. He forgets everything in his struggle to get beyond the reach of the bloodhounds."

"Don't talk so, Benjamin," said she. "Put your trust in God. Be humble, my child, and your master will forgive you."

"Forgive me for *what*, mother? For not letting him treat me like a dog? No! I will never humble myself to him. I have worked for him for nothing all my life, and I am repaid with stripes and imprisonment. Here I will stay till I die, or till he sells me."

The poor mother shuddered at his words. I think he felt it; for when he next spoke, his voice was calmer. "Don't fret about me, mother. I ain't worth it," said he. "I wish I had some of your goodness. You bear everything patiently, just as though you thought it was all right. I wish I could."

She told him she had not always been so; once, she was like him; but when sore troubles came upon her, and she had no arm to lean upon, she learned to call on God, and he lightened her burdens. She besought him to do likewise.

We overstayed our time, and were obliged to hurry from the jail.

Benjamin had been imprisoned three weeks, when my grand-mother went to intercede for him with his master. He was immovable. He said Benjamin should serve as an example to the rest of his slaves; he should be kept in jail till he was subdued, or be sold if he got but one dollar for him. However, he afterwards relented in some degree. The chains were taken off, and we were allowed to visit him.

As his food was of the coarsest kind, we carried him as often as pos-sible a warm supper, accompanied with some little luxury for the jailer.

Three months elapsed, and there was no prospect of release or of a purchaser. One day he was heard to sing and laugh. This piece of inde-corum was told to his master, and the overseer was ordered to re-chain him. He was now confined in an apartment with other prisoners, who were covered with filthy rags. Benjamin was chained near them, and was soon covered with vermin. He worked at his chains till he succeeded in getting out of them. He passed them through the bars of the window, with a request that they should be taken to his master, and he should be informed that he was covered with vermin.

This audacity was punished with heavier chains, and prohibition of our visits.

My grandmother continued to send him fresh changes of clothes. The old ones were burned up. The last night we saw him in jail his mother still begged him to send for his master, and beg his pardon. Neither persuasion nor argument could turn him from his purpose. He calmly answered, "I am waiting his time."

Those chains were mournful to hear.

Another three months passed, and Benjamin left his prison walls. We that loved him waited to bid him a long and last farewell. A slave-trader had bought him. You remember, I told you what price he brought when ten years of age. Now he was more than twenty years old, and sold for three hundred dollars. The master had been blind to his own interest. Long confinement had made his face too pale, his form too thin; moreover, the trader had heard something of his character, and it did not strike him as suitable for a slave. He said he would give any price if the handsome lad was a girl. We thanked God that he was not.

Could you have seen that mother clinging to her child, when they fastened the irons upon his wrists; could you have heard her heart-rending groans, and seen her bloodshot eyes wander wildly from face to face, vainly pleading for mercy; could you have witnessed that scene as I saw it, you would exclaim, *Slavery is damnable!*

Benjamin, her youngest, her pet, was forever gone! She could not realize it. She had had an interview with the trader for the purpose of ascertaining if Benjamin could be purchased. She was told it was impossible, as he had given bonds not to sell him till he was out of the state. He promised that he would not sell him till he reached New Orleans.

With a strong arm and unvaried trust, my grandmother began her work of love. Benjamin must be free. If she succeeded, she knew they would still be separated; but the sacrifice was not too great. Day and night she labored. The trader's price would treble that he gave; but she was not discouraged.

She employed a lawyer to write to a gentleman, whom she knew, in New Orleans. She begged him to interest himself for Benjamin, and he willingly favored her request. When he saw Benjamin, and stated his business, he thanked him; but said he preferred to wait a while before making the trader an offer. He knew he had tried to obtain a high price for him, and had invariably failed. This encouraged him to make another effort for freedom. So one morning, long before day, Benjamin was missing. He was riding over the blue billows, bound for Baltimore.

For once his white face did him a kindly service. They had no suspicion that it belonged to a slave; otherwise, the law would have been followed out to the letter, and the *thing* rendered back to slavery. The brightest skies are often overshadowed by the darkest clouds. Benjamin was taken sick, and compelled to remain in Baltimore three weeks. His strength was slow in returning; and his desire to continue his journey seemed to retard his recovery. How could he get strength without air and exercise? He resolved to venture on a short walk. A by-street was selected, where he thought himself secure of not being met by anyone that knew him; but a voice called out, "Halloo, Ben, my boy! what are you doing *here?*"

His first impulse was to run; but his legs trembled so that he could not stir. He turned to confront his antagonist, and behold, there stood his old master's next door neighbor! He thought it was all over with him now; but it proved otherwise. That man was a miracle. He possessed a goodly number of slaves, and yet was not quite deaf to that mystic clock, whose ticking is rarely heard in the slaveholder's breast.

"Ben, you are sick," said he. "Why, you look like a ghost. I guess I gave you something of a start. Never mind, Ben, I am not going to touch you. You had a pretty tough time of it, and you may go on your way rejoicing for all me. But I would advise you to get out of this place plaguy quick, for there are several gentlemen here from our town." He described the nearest and safest route to New York, and added, "I shall be glad to tell your mother I have seen you. Goodby, Ben."

Benjamin turned away, filled with gratitude, and surprised that the town he hated contained such a gem—a gem worthy of a purer setting.

This gentleman was a Northerner by birth, and had married a southern lady. On his return, he told my grandmother that he had seen her son, and of the service he had rendered him.

Benjamin reached New York safely, and concluded to stop there until he had gained strength enough to proceed further. It happened that my grandmother's only remaining son had sailed for the same city on business for his mistress. Through God's providence, the brothers met. You may be sure it was a happy meeting. "O Phil," exclaimed Benjamin, "I am here at last." Then he told him how near he came to dying, almost in sight of free land, and how he prayed that he might live to get one breath of free air. He said life was worth something now, and it would be hard to die. In the old jail he had not valued it; once, he was tempted to destroy it; but something, he did not know what, had prevented him; perhaps it was fear. He had heard those who profess to be religious declare there was no heaven for self-murderers; and as his life had been pretty hot here, he did not desire a continuation of the same in another world. "If I die now," he exclaimed, "thank God, I shall die a freeman!"

He begged my uncle Phillip not to return south; but stay and work with him, till they earned enough to but those at home. His brother told him it would kill their mother if he deserted her in her trouble. She had pledged her house, and with difficulty had raised money to buy him. Would he be bought?

"No, never!" he replied. "Do you suppose, Phil, when I have got so far out of their clutches, I will give them one red cent? No! And do you suppose I would turn mother out of her home in her old age? That I would let her pay all those hard-earned dollars for me, and never to see me? For you know she will stay south as long as her other children are slaves. What a good mother! Tell her to buy *you*, Phil. You have been a comfort to her, and I have been a trouble. And Linda, poor Linda; what'll become of her? Phil, you don't know what a life they lead her. She has told me something about it, and I wish old Flint was dead, or a better man. When I was in jail, he asked her if she didn't want *him* to ask my master to forgive me, and take me home again. She told him, No; that I didn't want to go back. He got mad, and said we were all alike. I never despised my own master half as much as I do that man. There is many a worse slaveholder than my master; but for all that I would not be his slave."

While Benjamin was sick, he had parted with nearly all his clothes to pay necessary expenses. But he did not part with a little pin I fastened in his bosom when we parted. It was the most valuable thing I owned, and I thought none more worthy to wear it. He had it still.

His brother furnished him with clothes, and gave him what money he had.

They parted with moistened eyes; and as Benjamin turned away, he said, "Phil, I part with all my kindred." And so it proved. We never heard from him again.

Uncle Phillip came home; and the first words he uttered when he entered the house were, "Mother, Ben is free! I have seen him in New

York." She stood looking at him with a bewildered air. "Mother, don't you believe it?" he said, laying his hand softly upon her shoulder. She raised her hands, and exclaimed, "God be praised! Let us thank him." She dropped on her knees, and poured forth her heart in prayer. Then Phillip must sit down and repeat to her every word Benjamin had said. He told her all; only he forbore to mention how sick and pale her darling looked. Why should he distress her when she could do him no good?

The brave old woman still toiled on, hoping to rescue some of her other children. After a while she succeeded in buying Phillip. She paid eight hundred dollars, and came home with the precious document that secured his freedom. The happy mother and son sat together by the old hearthstone that night, telling how proud they were of each other, and how they would prove to the world that they could take care of themselves, as they had long taken care of others. We all concluded by saying, "He that is *willing* to be a slave, let him be a slave."

V

The Trials of Girlhood

DURING the first years of my service in Dr. Flint's family, I was accustomed to share some indulgences with the children of my mistress. Though this seemed to me no more than right, I was grateful for it, and tried to merit the kindness by the faithful discharge of my duties. But I now entered on my fifteenth year—a sad epoch in the life of a slave girl. My master began to whisper foul words in my ear. Young as I was, I could not remain ignorant of their import. I tried to treat them with indifference or contempt. The master's age, my extreme youth, and the fear that his conduct would be reported to my grandmother, made him bear this treatment for many months. He was a crafty man, and resorted to many means to accomplish his purposes. Sometimes he had stormy, terrific ways, that made his victims tremble; sometimes he assumed a gentleness that he thought must surely subdue. Of the two, I preferred his stormy moods, although they left me trembling. He tried his utmost to corrupt the pure principles my grandmother had instilled. He peopled my young mind with unclean images, such as only a vile monster could think of. I turned from him with disgust and hatred. But he was my master. I was compelled to live under the same

roof with him—where I saw a man forty years my senior daily violating the most sacred commandments of nature. He told me I was his
property; that I must be subject to his will in all things. My soul re-
volted against the mean tyranny. But where could I turn for protection? No matter whether the slave girl be as black as ebony or as fair as
her mistress. In either case, there is no shadow of law to protect her
from insult, from violence, or even from death; all these are inflicted by
fiends who bear the shape of men. The mistress, who ought to protect
the helpless victim, has no other feelings towards her but those of jealousy and rage. The degradation, the wrongs, the vices, that grow out
of slavery, are more than I can describe. They are greater than you
would willingly believe. Surely, if you credited one half the truths that
are told you concerning the helpless millions suffering in this cruel
bondage, you at the north would not help to tighten the yoke. You
surely would refuse to do for the master, on your own soil, the mean
and cruel work which trained bloodhounds and the lowest class of
whites do for him at the south.

Everywhere the years bring to all enough of sin and sorrow; but in
slavery the very dawn of life is darkened by these shadows. Even the little child, who is accustomed to wait on her mistress and her children,
will learn, before she is twelve years old, why it is that her mistress hates
such and such a one among the slaves. Perhaps the child's own mother
is among those hated ones. She listens to violent outbreaks of jealous
passion, and cannot help understanding what is the cause. She will
become prematurely knowing in evil things. Soon she will learn to
tremble when she hears her master's footfall. She will be compelled to
realize that she is no longer a child. If God has bestowed beauty upon
her, it will prove her greatest curse. That which commands admiration
in the white woman only hastens the degradation of the female slave. I
know that some are too much brutalized by slavery to feel the humilia-
tion of their position; but many slaves feel it most acutely, and shrink
from the memory of it. I cannot tell how much I suffered in the presence of these wrongs, nor how I am still pained by the retrospect. My
master met me at every turn, reminding me that I belonged to him, and
swearing by heaven and earth that he would compel me to submit to
him. If I went out for a breath of fresh air, after a day of unwearied toil,
his footsteps dogged me. If I knelt by my mother's grave, his dark
shadow fell on me even there. The light heart which nature had given
me became heavy with sad forebodings. The other slaves in my master's house noticed the change. Many of them pitied me; but none

dared to ask the cause. They had no need to inquire. They knew too well the guilty practices under that roof; and they were aware that to speak of them was an offense that never went unpunished.

I longed for someone to confide in. I would have given the world to have laid my head on my grandmother's faithful bosom, and told her all my troubles. But Dr. Flint swore he would kill me, if I was not as silent as the grave. Then, although my grandmother was all in all to me, I feared her as well as loved her. I had been accustomed to look up to her with a respect bordering upon awe. I was very young, and felt shame-faced about telling her such impure things, especially as I knew her to be very strict on such subjects. Moreover, she was a woman of a high spirit. She was usually very quiet in her demeanor; but if her indignation was once roused, it was not very easily quelled. I had been told that she once chased a white gentleman with a loaded pistol, because he insulted one of her daughters. I dreaded the consequences of a violent outbreak; and both pride and fear kept me silent. But though I did not confide in my grandmother, and even evaded her vigilant watchfulness and inquiry, her presence in the neighborhood was some protection to me. Though she had been a slave, Dr. Flint was afraid of her. He dreaded her scorching rebukes. Moreover, she was known and patronized by many people; and he did not wish to have his villainy made public. It was lucky for me that I did not live on a distant plantation, but in a town not so large that the inhabitants were ignorant of each other's affairs. Bad as are the laws and customs in a slaveholding community, the doctor, as a professional man, deemed it prudent to keep up some outward show of decency.

O, what days and nights of fear and sorrow that man caused me! Reader, it is not to awaken sympathy for myself that I am telling you truthfully what I suffered in slavery. I do it to kindle a flame of compassion in your hearts for my sisters who are still in bondage, suffering as I once suffered.

I once saw two beautiful children playing together. One was a fair white child; the other was her slave, and also her sister. When I saw them embracing each other, and heard their joyous laughter, I turned sadly away from the lovely sight. I foresaw the inevitable blight that would fall on the little slave's heart. I knew how soon her laughter would be changed to sighs. The fair child grew up to be a still fairer woman. From childhood to womanhood her pathway was blooming with flowers, and overarched by a sunny sky. Scarcely one day of her life had been clouded when the sun rose on her happy bridal morning.

How had those years dealt with her slave sister, the little playmate of her childhood? She, also, was very beautiful; but the flowers and sunshine of love were not for her. She drank the cup of sin, and shame, and misery, whereof her persecuted race are compelled to drink.

In view of these things, why are ye silent, ye free men and women of the north? Why do your tongues falter in maintenance of the right? Would that I had more ability! But my heart is so full, and my pen is so weak! There are noble men and women who plead for us, striving to help those who cannot help themselves. God bless them! God give them strength and courage to go on! God bless those, everywhere, who are laboring to advance the cause of humanity!

VI

The Jealous Mistress

I WOULD ten thousand times rather that my children should be the half-starved paupers of Ireland than to be the most pampered among the slaves of America. I would rather drudge out my life on a cotton plantation, till the grave opened to give me rest, than to live with an unprincipled master and a jealous mistress. The felon's home in a penitentiary is preferable. He may repent, and turn from the error of his ways, and so find peace; but it is not so with a favorite slave. She is not allowed to have any pride of character. It is deemed a crime in her to wish to be virtuous.

Mrs. Flint possessed the key to her husband's character before I was born. She might have used this knowledge to counsel and to screen the young and the innocent among her slaves; but for them she had no sympathy. They were the objects of her constant suspicion and malevolence. She watched her husband with unceasing vigilance; but he was well practiced in means to evade it. What he could not find opportunity to say in words he manifested in signs. He invented more than were ever thought of in a deaf and dumb asylum. I let them pass, as if I did not understand what he meant; and many were the curses and threats bestowed on me for my stupidity. One day he caught me teaching myself to write. He frowned, as if he was not well pleased; but I suppose he came to the conclusion that such an accomplishment might help to advance his favorite scheme. Before long, notes were often slipped into my hand. I would return them, saying, "I can't read them, sir." "Can't you?" he replied; "then I must read them to you." He always finished the reading by asking, "Do you understand?" Sometimes he would complain of the heat of the tea room, and order his supper to be placed on a small table in the piazza. He would seat himself there with a well-satisfied smile, and tell me to stand by and brush away the flies. He would eat very slowly, pausing between the mouthfuls. These intervals were employed in describing the happiness I was so foolishly throwing away, and in threatening me with the penalty that finally awaited my stubborn disobedience. He boasted much of the forbearance he had exercised towards me, and reminded me that there was a limit to his patience. When I succeeded in avoiding opportunities for him to talk to me at home, I was ordered to come to his office, to do some errand. When there, I was obliged to stand and listen to such language as he saw fit to address to me. Sometimes I so openly expressed my contempt for him that he would become violently enraged, and I wondered why he did not strike me. Circumstanced as he was, he probably thought it was better policy to be forbearing. But the state of things grew worse and worse daily. In desperation I told him that I must and would apply to my grandmother for protection. He threatened me with death, and worse than death, if I made any complaint to her. Strange to say, I did not despair. I was naturally of a buoyant disposition, and always I had a hope of somehow getting out of his clutches. Like many a poor, simple slave before me, I trusted that some threads of joy would yet be woven into my dark destiny.

I had entered my sixteenth year, and every day it became more apparent that my presence was intolerable to Mrs. Flint. Angry words frequently passed between her and her husband. He had never punished me himself, and he would not allow anybody else to punish me. In that respect, she was never satisfied; but, in her angry moods, no terms were too vile for her to bestow upon me. Yet I, whom she detested so bitterly, had far more pity for her than he had, whose duty it was to make her life happy. I never wronged her, or wished to wrong her; and one word of kindness from her would have brought me to her feet.

After repeated quarrels between the doctor and his wife, he announced his intention to take his youngest daughter, then four years old, to sleep in his apartment. It was necessary that a servant should sleep in the same room, to be on hand if the child stirred. I was selected for that office, and informed for what purpose that arrangement had been made. By managing to keep within sight of people, as much as possible, during the day time, I had hitherto succeeded in eluding my master, though a razor was often held to my throat to force me to change this line of policy. At night I slept by the side of my great aunt, where I felt safe. He was too prudent to come into her room. She was an old woman, and had been in the family many years. Moreover, as a married man, and a professional man, he deemed it necessary to save appearances in some degree. But he resolved to remove the obstacle in the way of his scheme; and he thought he had planned it so that he should evade suspicion. He was well aware how much I prized my refuge by the side of my old aunt, and he determined to dispossess me of it. The first night the doctor had the little child in his room alone. The next morning, I was ordered to take my station as nurse the following night. A kind Providence interposed in my favor. During the day Mrs. Flint heard of this new arrangement, and a storm followed. I rejoiced to hear it rage.

After a while my mistress sent for me to come to her room. Her first question was, "Did you know you were to sleep in the doctor's room?"

"Yes, ma'am."

"Who told you?"

"My master."

"Will you answer truly all the questions I ask?"

"Yes, ma'am."

"Tell me, then, as you hope to be forgiven, are you innocent of what I have accused you?"

"I am."

She handed me a Bible, and said, "Lay your hand on your heart, kiss this holy book, and swear before God that you tell me the truth."

I took the oath she required, and I did it with a clear conscience.

"You have taken God's holy word to testify your innocence," said she. "If you have deceived me, beware! Now take this stool, sit down, look me directly in the face, and tell me all that has passed between your master and you."

I did as she ordered. As I went on with my account her color changed frequently, she wept, and sometimes groaned. She spoke in tones so sad, that I was touched by her grief. The tears came to my eyes; but I was soon convinced that her emotions arose from anger and wounded pride. She felt that her marriage vows were desecrated, her dignity insulted; but she had no compassion for the poor victim of her husband's perfidy. She pitied herself as a martyr; but she was incapable of feeling for the condition of shame and misery in which her unfortunate, helpless slave was placed.

Yet perhaps she had some touch of feeling for me; for when the conference was ended, she spoke kindly, and promised to protect me. I should have been much comforted by this assurance if I could have had confidence in it; but my experiences in slavery had filled me with distrust. She was not a very refined woman, and had not much control over her passions. I was an object of her jealousy, and, consequently, of her hatred; and I knew I could not expect kindness or confidence from her under the circumstances in which I was placed. I could not blame her. Slave-holders' wives feel as other women would under similar circumstances. The fire of her temper kindled from small sparks, and now the flame became so intense that the doctor was obliged to give up his intended arrangement.

I knew I had ignited the torch, and I expected to suffer for it afterwards; but I felt too thankful to my mistress for the timely aid she rendered me to care much about that. She now took me to sleep in a room adjoining her own. There I was an object of her especial care, though not of her especial comfort, for she spent many a sleepless night to watch over me. Sometimes I woke up, and found her bending over me. At other times she whispered in my ear, as though it was her husband who was speaking to me, and listened to hear what I would answer. If she startled me, on such occasions, she would glide stealthily away; and the next morning she would tell me I had been talking in my sleep, and ask who I was talking to. At last, I began to be fearful for my life. It had been often threatened; and you can imagine, better than I can describe, what an unpleasant sensation it must produce to wake up in the dead of night and find a jealous woman bending over you. Terrible as this experience was, I had fears that it would give place to one more terrible.

My mistress grew weary of her vigils; they did not prove satisfactory. She changed her tactics. She now tried the trick of accusing my master of crime, in my presence, and gave my name as the author of the accusation. To my utter astonishment, he replied, "I don't believe it; but if she did acknowledge it, you tortured her into exposing me." Tortured into exposing him! Truly, Satan had no difficulty in distinguishing the color of his soul! I understood his object in making this false representation. It was to show me that I gained nothing by seeking the protection of my mistress; that the power was still all in his own hands. I pitied Mrs. Flint. She was a second wife, many years the junior of her husband; and the hoary-headed miscreant was enough to try the patience of a wiser and better woman. She was completely foiled, and knew not how to proceed. She would gladly have had me flogged for my supposed false oath; but, as I have already stated, the doctor never allowed anyone to whip me. The old sinner was politic. The application of the lash might have led to remarks that would have exposed him in the eyes of his children and grandchildren. How often did I rejoice that I lived in a town where all the inhabitants knew each other! If I had been on a remote plantation, or lost among the multitude of a crowded city, I should not be a living woman at this day.

The secrets of slavery are concealed like those of the Inquisition. My master was, to my knowledge, the father of eleven slaves. But did the mothers dare to tell who was the father of their children? Did the other slaves dare to allude to it, except in whispers among themselves? No, indeed! They knew too well the terrible consequences.

My grandmother could not avoid seeing things which excited her suspicions. She was uneasy about me, and tried various ways to buy me; but the never-changing answer was always repeated: "Linda does not belong to *me*. She is my daughter's property, and I have no legal right to sell her." The conscientious man! He was too scrupulous to *sell* me; but he had no scruples whatever about committing a much greater wrong against the helpless young girl placed under his guardianship, as his daughter's property. Sometimes my persecutor would ask me whether I would like to be sold. I told him I would rather be sold to anybody than to lead such a life as I did. On such occasions he would assume the air of a very injured individual, and reproach me for my ingratitude. "Did I not take you into the house, and make you the companion of my own children?" he would say. "Have I ever treated you like a negro? I have never allowed you to be punished, not even to please your mistress. And this is the recompense I get, you ungrateful girl!" I answered that he had reasons of his own for screening me from punishment, and that the course he pursued made my mistress hate me and persecute me. If I wept, he would say, "Poor child! Don't cry! don't cry! I will make peace for you with your mistress. Only let me arrange matters in my own way. Poor, foolish girl! you don't know what is for your own good. I would cherish you. I would make a lady of you. Now go, and think of all I have promised you."

I did think of it.

Reader, I draw no imaginary pictures of southern homes. I am telling you the plain truth. Yet when victims make their escape from this wild beast of Slavery, northerners consent to act the part of bloodhounds, and hunt the poor fugitive back into his den, "full of dead

men's bones, and all uncleanness." Nay, more, they are not only willing, but proud, to give their daughters in marriage to slaveholders. The
poor girls have romantic notions of a sunny clime, and of the flowering
vines that all the year round shade a happy home. To what disappoint-
ments are they destined! The young wife soon learns that the husband
in whose hands she has placed her happiness pays no regard to his marriage vows. Children of every shade of complexion play with her own
fair babies, and too well she knows that they are born unto him of his
own household. Jealousy and hatred enter the flowery home, and it is
ravaged of its loveliness.

Southern women often marry a man knowing that he is the father
of many little slaves. They do not trouble themselves about it. They
regard such children as property, as marketable as the pigs on the
plantation; and it is seldom that they do not make them aware of this by
passing them into the slave-trader's hands as soon as possible, and thus
getting them out of their sight. I am glad to say there are some honorable exceptions.

I have myself known two southern wives who exhorted their husbands to free those slaves towards whom they stood in a "parental relation;" and their request was granted. These husbands blushed before
the superior nobleness of their wives' natures. Though they had only
counselled them to do that which it was their duty to do, it commanded
their respect, and rendered their conduct more exemplary. Concealment was at an end, and confidence took the place of distrust.

Though this bad institution deadens the moral sense, even in white
women, to a fearful extent, it is not altogether extinct. I have heard
southern ladies say of Mr. Such a one, "He not only thinks it no disgrace to be the father of those little niggers, but he is not ashamed to
call himself their master. I declare, such things ought not to be tolerated in any decent society!"

VII

The Lover

WHY DOES the slave ever love? Why allow the tendrils of the heart to
twine around objects which may at any moment be wrenched away by
the hand of violence? When separations come by the hand of death,
the pious soul can bow in resignation, and say, "Not my will, but thine

be done, O Lord!" But when the ruthless hand of man strikes the blow, regardless of the misery he causes, it is hard to be submissive. I did not reason thus when I was a young girl. Youth will be youth. I loved, and I indulged the hope that the dark clouds around me would turn out a bright lining. I forgot that in the land of my birth the shadows are too dense for light to penetrate. A land

> *"Where laughter is not mirth; nor thought the mind;*
> *Nor words a language; nor e'en men mankind.*
> *Where cries reply to curses, shrieks to blows,*
> *And each is tortured in his separate hell."*

There was in the neighborhood a young colored carpenter; a free born man. We had been well acquainted in childhood, and frequently met together afterwards. We became mutually attached, and he proposed to marry me. I loved him with all the ardor of a young girl's first love. But when I reflected that I was a slave, and that the laws gave no sanction to the marriage of such, my heart sank within me. My lover wanted to buy me; but I knew that Dr. Flint was too willful and arbitrary a man to consent to that arrangement. From him, I was sure of experiencing all sorts of opposition, and I had nothing to hope from my mistress. She would have been delighted to have got rid of me, but not in that way. It would have relieved her mind of a burden if she could have seen me sold to some distant state, but if I was married near home I should be just as much in her husband's power as I had previously been,—for the husband of a slave has no power to protect her. Moreover, my mistress, like many others, seemed to think that slaves had no right to any family ties of their own; that they were created merely to wait upon the family of the mistress. I once heard her abuse a young slave girl, who told her that a colored man wanted to make her his wife. "I will have you peeled and pickled, my lady," said she, "if I ever hear you mention that subject again. Do you suppose that I will have you tending *my* children with the children of that nigger?" The girl to whom she said this had a mulatto child, of course not acknowledged by its father. The poor black man who loved her would have been proud to acknowledge his helpless offspring.

Many and anxious were the thoughts I revolved in my mind. I was at a loss what to do. Above all things, I was desirous to spare my lover the insults that had cut so deeply into my own soul. I talked with my grandmother about it, and partly told her my fears. I did not dare to tell her the worst. She had long suspected all was not right, and if I confirmed her suspicions I knew a storm would rise that would prove the overthrow of all my hopes.

This love-dream had been my support through many trials; and I could not bear to run the risk of having it suddenly dissipated. There was a lady in the neighborhood, a particular friend of Dr. Flint's, who often visited the house. I had a great respect for her, and she had always manifested a friendly interest in me. Grandmother thought she would have great influence with the doctor. I went to this lady, and told her my story. I told her I was aware that my lover's being a free-born man would prove a great objection; but he wanted to buy me; and if Dr. Flint would consent to that arrangement, I felt sure he would be willing to pay any reasonable price. She knew that Mrs. Flint disliked me; therefore, I ventured to suggest that perhaps my mistress would approve of my being sold, as that would rid her of me. The lady listened with kindly sympathy, and promised to do her utmost to promote my wishes. She had an interview with the doctor, and I believe she pleaded my cause earnestly; but it was all to no purpose.

How I dreaded my master now! Every minute I expected to be summoned to his presence; but the day passed, and I heard nothing from him. The next morning, a message was brought to me: "Master wants you in his study." I found the door ajar, and I stood a moment gazing at the hateful man who claimed a right to rule me, body and soul. I entered, and tried to appear calm. I did not want him to know how my heart was bleeding. He looked fixedly at me, with an expression which seemed to say, "I have half a mind to kill you on the spot." At last he broke the silence, and that was a relief to both of us.

"So you want to be married, do you?" said he, "and to a free nigger."

"Yes, sir."

"Well, I'll soon convince you whether I am your master, or the nigger fellow you honor so highly. If you *must* have a husband, you may take up with one of my slaves."

What a situation I should be in, as the wife of one of *his* slaves, even if my heart had been interested!

I replied, "Don't you suppose, sir, that a slave can have some preference about marrying? Do you suppose that all men are alike to her?"

"Do you love this nigger?" said he, abruptly.

"Yes, sir."

"How dare you tell me so!" he exclaimed, in great wrath. After a slight pause, he added, "I supposed you thought more of yourself; that you felt above the insults of such puppies."

I replied, "If he is a puppy I am a puppy, for we are both of the negro race. It is right and honorable for us to love each other. The man you call a puppy never insulted me, sir; and he would not love me if he did not believe me to be a virtuous woman."

He sprang upon me like a tiger, and gave me a stunning blow. It was the first time he had ever struck me; and fear did not enable me to control my anger. When I had recovered a little from the effects, I exclaimed, "You have struck me for answering you honestly. How I despise you!"

There was silence for some minutes. Perhaps he was deciding what should be my punishment; or, perhaps, he wanted to give me time to reflect on what I had said, and to whom I had said it. Finally, he asked, "Do you know what you have said?"

"Yes, sir; but your treatment drove me to it."

"Do you know that I have a right to do as I like with you,—that I can kill you, if I please?"

"You have tried to kill me, and I wish you had; but you have no right to do as you like with me."

"Silence!" he exclaimed, in a thundering voice. "By heavens, girl, you forget yourself too far! Are you mad? If you are, I will soon bring you to your senses. Do you think any other master would bear what I have borne from you this morning? Many masters would have killed you on the spot. How would you like to be sent to jail for your in-solence?"

"I know I have been disrespectful, sir," I replied; "but you drove me to it; I couldn't help it. As for the jail, there would be more peace for me there than there is here."

"You deserve to go there," said he, "and to be under such treatment, that you would forget the meaning of the word *peace*. It would do you good. It would take some of your high notions out of you. But I am not ready to send you there yet, notwithstanding your ingratitude for all my kindness and forbearance. You have been the plague of my life. I have wanted to make you happy, and I have been repaid with the basest ingratitude; but though you have proved yourself incapable of appre-ciating my kindness, I will be lenient towards you, Linda. I will give you one more chance to redeem your character. If you behave yourself and do as I require, I will forgive you and treat you as I always have done; but if you disobey me, I will punish you as I would the meanest slave on my plantation. Never let me hear the fellow's name mentioned again. If I ever know of your speaking to him, I will cowhide you both;

and if I catch him lurking about my premises, I will shoot him as soon as I would a dog. Do you hear what I say? I'll teach you a lesson about marriage and free niggers! Now go, and let this be the last time I have occasion to speak to you on this subject."

Reader, did you ever hate? I hope not. I never did but once; and I trust I never shall again. Somebody has called it "the atmosphere of hell;" and I believe it is so.

For a fortnight the doctor did not speak to me. He thought to mortify me; to make me feel that I had disgraced myself by receiving the honorable addresses of a respectable colored man, in preference to the base proposals of a white man. But though his lips disdained to address me, his eyes were very loquacious. No animal ever watched its prey more narrowly than he watched me. He knew that I could write, though he had failed to make me read his letters; and he was now troubled lest I should exchange letters with another man. After a while he became weary of silence; and I was sorry for it. One morning, as he passed through the hall, to leave the house, he contrived to thrust a note into my hand. I thought I had better read it, and spare myself the vexation of having him read it to me. It expressed regret for the blow he had given me, and reminded me that I myself was wholly to blame for it. He hoped I had become convinced of the injury I was doing myself by incurring his displeasure. He wrote that he had made up his mind to go to Louisiana; that he should take several slaves with him, and intended I should be one of the number. My mistress would remain where she was; therefore I should have nothing to fear from that quarter. If I merited kindness from him, he assured me that it would be lavishly bestowed. He begged me to think over the matter, and answer the following day.

The next morning I was called to carry a pair of scissors to his room. I laid them on the table, with the letter beside them. He thought it was my answer, and did not call me back. I went as usual to attend my young mistress to and from school. He met me in the street, and ordered me to stop at his office on my way back. When I entered, he showed me his letter, and asked me why I had not answered it. I replied, "I am your daughter's property, and it is in your power to send me, or take me, wherever you please." He said he was very glad to find me so willing to go, and that we should start early in the autumn. He had a large practice in the town, and I rather thought he had made up the story merely to frighten me. However that might be, I was determined that I would never go to Louisiana with him.

Summer passed away, and early in the autumn Dr. Flint's eldest son was sent to Louisiana to examine the country, with a view to emigrating. That news did not disturb me. I knew very well that I should not be sent with *him*. That I had not been taken to the plantation before this time, was owing to the fact that his son was there. He was jealous of his son; and jealousy of the overseer had kept him from punishing me by sending me into the fields to work. Is it strange that I was not proud of these protectors? As for the overseer, he was a man for whom I had less respect that I had for a bloodhound.

Young Mr. Flint did not bring back a favorable report of Louisiana, and I heard no more of that scheme. Soon after this, my lover met me at the corner of the street, and I stopped to speak to him. Looking up, I saw my master watching us from his window. I hurried home, trembling with fear. I was sent for, immediately, to go to his room. He met me with a blow. "When is mistress to be married?" said he, in a sneering tone. A shower of oaths and imprecations followed. How thankful I was that my lover was a free man! that my tyrant had no power to flog him for speaking to me in the street!

Again and again I revolved in my mind how all this would end. There was no hope that the doctor would consent to sell me on any terms. He had an iron will, and was determined to keep me, and to conquer me. My lover was an intelligent and religious man. Even if he could have obtained permission to marry me while I was a slave, the marriage would give him no power to protect me from my master. It would have made him miserable to witness the insults I should have been subjected to. And then, if we had children, I knew they must "follow the condition of the mother." What a terrible blight that would be on the heart of a free, intelligent father! For *his* sake, I felt that I ought not to link his fate with my own unhappy destiny. He was going to Savannah to see about a little property left him by an uncle; and hard as it was to bring my feelings to it, I earnestly entreated him not to come back. I advised him to go to the Free States, where his tongue would not be tied, and where his intelligence would be of more avail to him. He left me, still hoping the day would come when I could be bought. With me the lamp of hope had gone out. The dream of my girlhood was over. I felt lonely and desolate.

Still I was not stripped of all. I still had my good grandmother, and my affectionate brother. When he put his arms round my neck, and looked into my eyes, as if to read there the troubles I dared not tell, I felt that I still had something to love. But even that pleasant emotion was chilled by the reflection that he might be torn from me at any moment, by some sudden freak of my master. If he had known how we loved each other, I think he would have exulted in separating us. We often planned together how we could get to the north. But, as William remarked, such things are easier said than done. My movements were very closely watched, and we had no means of getting any money to defray our expenses. As for grandmother, she was strongly opposed to her children's undertaking any such project. She had not forgotten poor Benjamin's sufferings, and she was afraid that if another child tried to escape, he would have a similar or a worse fate. To me, nothing seemed more dreadful than my present life. I said to myself, "William *must* be free. He shall go to the north, and I will follow him." Many a slave sister has formed the same plans.

VIII

What Slaves are Taught to Think of the North

SLAVEHOLDERS pride themselves upon being honorable men; but if you were to hear the enormous lies they tell their slaves, you would have small respect for their veracity. I have spoken plain English. Pardon me. I cannot use a milder term. When they visit the north, and return home, they tell their slaves of the runaways they have seen, and describe them to be in the most deplorable condition. A slaveholder once told me that he had seen a runaway friend of mine in New York, and that she besought him to take her back to her master, for she was literally dying of starvation; that many days she had only one cold potato to eat, and at other times could get nothing at all. He said he refused to take her, because he knew her master would not thank him for bringing such a miserable wretch to his house. He ended by saying to me, "This is the punishment she brought on herself for running away from a kind master."

This whole story was false. I afterwards stayed with that friend in New York, and found her in comfortable circumstances. She had never thought of such a thing as wishing to go back to slavery. Many of the slaves believe such stories, and think it is not worthwhile to exchange slavery for such a hard kind of freedom. It is difficult to persuade such that freedom could make them useful men, and enable them to protect their wives and children. If those heathen in our

Christian land had as much teaching as some Hindoos, they would think otherwise. They would know that liberty is more valuable than life. They would begin to understand their own capabilities, and exert themselves to become men and women.

But while the Free States sustain a law which hurls fugitives back into slavery, how can the slaves resolve to become men? There are some who strive to protect wives and daughters from the insults of their masters; but those who have such sentiments have had advantages above the general mass of slaves. They have been partially civilized and Christianized by favorable circumstances. Some are bold enough to *utter* such sentiments to their masters. O, that there were more of them!

Some poor creatures have been so brutalized by the lash that they will sneak out of the way to give their masters free access to their wives and daughters. Do you think this proves the black man to belong to an inferior order of beings? What would *you* be, if you had been born and brought up a slave, with generations of slaves for ancestors? I admit that the black man *is* inferior. But what is it that makes him so? It is the ignorance in which white men compel him to live; it is the torturing whip that lashes manhood out of him; it is the fierce bloodhounds of the South, and the scarcely less cruel human bloodhounds of the north, who enforce the Fugitive Slave Law. *They* do the work.

Southern gentlemen indulge in the most contemptuous expressions about the Yankees, while they, on their part, consent to do the vilest work for them, such as the ferocious bloodhounds and the despised negro-hunters are employed to do at home. When southerners go to the north, they are proud to do them honor; but the northern man is not welcome south of Mason and Dixon's line, unless he suppresses every thought and feeling at variance with their "peculiar institution." Nor is it enough to be silent. The masters are not pleased, unless they obtain a greater degree of subservience than that; and they are generally accomodated. Do they respect the northerner for this? I trow not. Even the slaves despise "a northern man with southern principles;" and that is the class they generally see. When northerners go to the south to reside, they prove very apt scholars. They soon imbibe the sentiments and disposition of their neighbors, and generally go beyond their teachers. Of the two, they are proverbially the hardest masters.

They seem to satisfy their consciences with the doctrine that God created the Africans to be slaves. What a libel upon the heavenly Father, who "made of one blood all nations of men!" And then who *are* Africans? Who can measure the amount of Anglo-Saxon blood coursing in the veins of American slaves?

I have spoken of the pains slaveholders take to give their slaves a bad opinion of the north; but, notwithstanding this, intelligent slaves are aware that they have many friends in the Free States. Even the most ignorant have some confused notions about it. They knew that I could read; and I was often asked if I had seen anything in the newspapers about white folks over in the big north, who were trying to get their freedom for them. Some believe that the abolitionists have already made them free, and that it is established by law, but that their masters prevent the law from going into effect. One woman begged me to get a newspaper and read it over. She said her husband told her that the black people had sent word to the queen of 'Merica that they were all slaves; that she didn't believe it, and went to Washington city to see the president about it. They quarrelled; she drew her sword upon him, and swore that he should help her to make them all free.

That poor, ignorant woman thought that America was governed by a Queen, to whom the President was subordinate. I wish the President was subordinate to Queen Justice.

IX

Sketches of Neighboring Slaveholders

THERE WAS A PLANTER in the country, not far from us, whom I will call Mr. Litch. He was an ill-bred, uneducated man, but very wealthy. He had six hundred slaves, many of whom he did not know by sight. His extensive plantation was managed by well-paid overseers. There was a jail and a whipping post on his grounds; and whatever cruelties were perpetrated there, they passed without comment. He was so effectually screened by his great wealth that he was called to no account for his crimes, not even for murder.

Various were the punishments resorted to. A favorite one was to tie a rope round a man's body, and suspend him from the ground. A fire was kindled over him, from which was suspended a piece of fat pork. As this cooked, the scalding drops of fat continually fell on the bare flesh. On his own plantation, he required very strict obedience to the eighth commandment. But depredations on the neighbors were allowable, provided the culprit managed to evade detection or suspicion. If a neighbor brought a charge of theft against any of his slaves, he was browbeaten by the master, who assured him that his slaves had enough of everything at home, and had no inducement to steal. No sooner was the neighbor's back turned, than the accused was sought out, and whipped for his lack of discretion. If a slave stole from him even a pound of meat or a peck of corn, if detection followed, he was put in chains and imprisoned, and so kept till his form was attenuated by hunger and suffering.

A freshet once bore his wine cellar and meat house miles away from the plantation. Some slaves followed, and secured bits of meat and bottles of wine. Two were detected; a ham and some liquor being found in their huts. They were summoned by their master. No words were used, but a club felled them to the ground. A rough box was their coffin, and their interment was a dog's burial. Nothing was said.

Murder was so common on his plantation that he feared to be alone after nightfall. He might have believed in ghosts.

His brother, if not equal in wealth, was at least equal in cruelty. His bloodhounds were well trained. Their pen was spacious, and a terror to the slaves. They were let loose on a runaway, and, if they tracked him, they literally tore the flesh from his bones. When this slaveholder died, his shrieks and groans were so frightful that they appalled his own friends. His last words were, "I am going to hell; bury my money with me."

After death his eyes remained open. To press the lids down, silver dollars were laid on them. These were buried with him. From this circumstance, a rumor went abroad that his coffin was filled with money. Three times his grave was opened, and his coffin taken out. The last time, his body was found on the ground, and a flock of buzzards were pecking at it. He was again interred, and a sentinel set over his grave. The perpetrators were never discovered.

Cruelty is contagious in uncivilized communities. Mr. Conant, a neighbor of Mr. Litch, returned from town one evening in a partial state of intoxication. His body servant gave him some offense. He was divested of his clothes, except his shirt, whipped, and tied to a large tree in front of the house. It was a stormy night in winter. The wind blew bitterly cold, and the boughs of the old tree crackled under falling sleet. A member of the family, fearing he would freeze to death, begged that he might be taken down; but the master would not relent. He remained there three hours; and, when he was cut down, he was more dead than alive. Another slave, who stole a pig from this master, to appease his hunger, was terribly flogged. In desperation, he tried to run away. But at the end of two miles, he was so faint with loss of blood, he thought he was dying. He had a wife, and he longed to see her once more. Too sick to walk, he crept back that long distance on his hands and knees. When he reached his master's, it was night. He had not strength to rise and open the gate. He moaned, and tried to call for help. I had a friend living in the same family. At last his cry reached her. She went out and found the prostrate man at the gate. She ran back to the house for assistance, and two men returned with her. They carried him in, and laid him on the floor. The back of his shirt was one clot of blood. By means of lard, my friend loosened it from the raw flesh. She bandaged him, gave him cool drink, and left him to rest. The master said he deserved a hundred more lashes. When his own labor was stolen from him, he had stolen food to appease his hunger. This was his crime.

Another neighbor was a Mrs. Wade. At no hour of the day was there cessation of the lash on her premises. Her labors began with the dawn, and did not cease till long after nightfall. The barn was her particular place of torture. There she lashed the slaves with the might of a man. An old slave of hers once said to me, "It is hell in missis's house. 'Pears I can never get out. Day and night I prays to die."

The mistress died before the old woman, and, when dying, entreated her husband not to permit any one of her slaves to look on her after death. A slave who had nursed her children, and had still a child in her care, watched her chance, and stole with it in her arms to the room where lay her dead mistress. She gazed a while on her, then raised her hand and dealt two blows on her face, saying, as she did so, "The devil is got you *now!*" She forgot that the child was looking on. She had just begun to talk; and she said to her father, "I did see ma, and mammy did strike ma, so," striking her own face with her little hand. The master was startled. He could not imagine how the nurse could obtain access to the room where the corpse lay; for he kept the door locked. He questioned her. She confessed that what the child had said was true, and told how she had procured the key. She was sold to Georgia.

In my childhood I knew a valuable slave, named Charity, and loved her, as all children did. Her young mistress married, and took her to Louisiana. Her little boy, James, was sold to a good sort of master. He became involved in debt, and James was sold again to a wealthy slaveholder, noted for his cruelty. With this man he grew up to manhood, receiving the treatment of a dog. After a severe whipping, to save himself from further infliction of the lash, with which he was threatened, he took to the woods. He was in a most miserable condition—cut by the cowskin, half naked, half starved, and without the means of procuring a crust of bread.

Some weeks after his escape, he was captured, tied, and carried back to his master's plantation. This man considered punishment in his jail, on bread and water, after receiving hundreds of lashes, too mild for the poor slave's offense. Therefore he decided, after the overseer should have whipped him to his satisfaction, to have him placed between the screws of the cotton gin, to stay as long as he had been in the woods. This wretched creature was cut with the whip from his head to his feet, then washed with strong brine, to prevent the flesh from mortifying, and make it heal sooner than it otherwise would. He was then put into the cotton gin, which was screwed down, only allowing him room to turn on his side when he could not lie on his back. Every morning a slave was sent with a piece of bread and bowl of water, which were placed within reach of the poor fellow. The slave was charged, under penalty of severe punishment, not to speak to him.

Four days passed, and the slave continued to carry the bread and water. On the second morning, he found the bread gone, but the water untouched. When he had been in the press four days and five nights, the slave informed his master that the water had not been used for four mornings, and that a horrible stench came from the gin house. The overseer was sent to examine into it. When the press was unscrewed, the dead body was found partly eaten by rats and vermin. Perhaps the rats that devoured his bread had gnawed him before life was extinct. Poor Charity! Grandmother and I often asked each other how her affectionate heart would bear the news, if she should ever hear of the murder of her son. We had known her husband, and knew that James was like him in manliness and intelligence. These were the qualities that made it so hard for him to be a plantation slave. They put him into a rough box, and buried him with less feeling than would have been manifested for an old house dog. Nobody asked any questions. He was a slave; and the feeling was that the master had a right to do what he pleased with his own property. And what did *he* care for the value of a slave? He had hundreds of them. When they had finished their daily toil, they must hurry to eat their little morsels, and be ready to extinguish their pine knots before nine o'clock, when the overseer went his patrol rounds. He entered every cabin, to see that men and their wives had gone to bed together, lest the men, from over-fatigue, should fall asleep in the chimney corner, and remain there till the morning horn called them to their daily task. Women are considered of no value, unless they continually increase their owner's stock. They are put on a par with animals. This same master shot a woman through the head, who had run away and been brought back to him. No one called him to account for it. If a slave resisted being whipped, the bloodhounds were unpacked, and set upon him, to tear his flesh from his bones. The master who did these things was highly educated, and styled a perfect gentleman. He also boasted the name and standing of a Christian, though Satan never had a truer follower.

I could tell of more slaveholders as cruel as those I have described. They are not exceptions to the general rule. I do not say there are no humane slaveholders. Such characters do exist, notwithstanding the hardening influences around them. But they are "like angels' visits— few and far between."

I knew a young lady who was one of these rare specimens. She was an orphan, and inherited as slaves a woman and her six children. Their father was a free man. They had a comfortable home of their own, parents and children living together. The mother and eldest daughter served their mistress during the day, and at night returned to their dwelling, which was on the premises. The young lady was very pious, and there was some reality in her religion. She taught her slaves to lead pure lives, and wished them to enjoy the fruit of their own industry. *Her* religion was not a garb put on for Sunday, and laid aside till Sunday returned again. The eldest daughter of the slave mother was promised in marriage to a free man; and the day before the wedding this good mistress emancipated her, in order that her marriage might have the sanction of *law.*

Report said that this young lady cherished an unrequited affection for a man who had resolved to marry for wealth. In the course of time a rich uncle of hers died. He left six thousand dollars to his two sons by a colored woman, and the remainder of his property to this orphan niece. The metal soon attracted the magnet. The lady and her weighty purse became his. She offered to manumit her slaves—telling them that her marriage might make unexpected changes in their destiny, and she wished to insure their happiness. They refused to take their freedom, saying that she had always been their best friend, and they could not be so happy anywhere as with her. I was not surprised. I had often seen them in their comfortable home, and thought that the whole town did not contain a happier family. They had never felt slavery; and, when it was too late, they were convinced of its reality.

When the new master claimed this family as his property, the father became furious, and went to his mistress for protection. "I can do nothing for you now, Harry," said she. "I no longer have the power I had a week ago. I have succeeded in obtaining the freedom of your wife; but I cannot obtain it for your children." The unhappy father swore that nobody should take his children from him. He concealed them in the woods for some days; but they were discovered and taken. The father was put in jail, and the two oldest boys sold to Georgia. One little girl, too young to be of service to her master, was left with the wretched mother. The other three were carried to their master's plantation. The eldest soon became a mother; and, when the slaveholder's wife looked at the babe, she wept bitterly. She knew that her own husband had violated the purity she had so carefully inculcated. She had a second child by her master, and then he sold her and his offspring to his brother. She bore two children to the brother, and was sold again. The next sister went crazy. The life she was compelled to lead drove her mad. The third one became the mother of five daughters. Before the birth of the fourth the pious mistress died. To the last, she rendered every kindness to the slaves that her unfortunate circumstances permitted. She passed away peacefully, glad to close her eyes on a life which had been made so wretched by the man she loved.

This man squandered the fortune he had received, and sought to retrieve his affairs by a second marriage; but, having retired after a night of drunken debauch, he was found dead in the morning. He was called a good master; for he fed and clothed his slaves better than most masters, and the lash was not heard on his plantation so frequently as on many others. Had it not been for slavery, he would have been a better man, and his wife a happier woman.

No pen can give an adequate description of the all-pervading corruption produced by slavery. The slave girl is reared in an atmosphere of licentiousness and fear. The lash and the foul talk of her master and his sons are her teachers. When she is fourteen or fifteen, her owner, or his sons, or the overseer, or perhaps all of them, begin to bribe her with presents. If these fail to accomplish their purpose, she is whipped or starved into submission to their will. She may have had religious principles inculcated by some pious mother or grandmother, or some good mistress; she may have a lover, whose good opinion and peace of mind are dear to her heart; or the profligate men who have power over her may be exceedingly odious to her. But resistance is hopeless.

> *"The poor worm*
> *Shall prove her contest vain. Life's little day*
> *Shall pass, and she is gone!"*

The slaveholder's sons are, of course, vitiated, even while boys, by the unclean influences everywhere around them. Nor do the master's daughters always escape. Severe retributions sometimes come upon him for the wrongs he does to the daughters of the slaves. The white daughters early hear their parents quarrelling about some female slave. Their curiosity is excited, and they soon learn the cause. They are attended by the young slave girls whom their father has corrupted; and they hear such talk as should never meet youthful ears, or any other ears. They know that the women slaves are subject to their father's authority in all things; and in some cases they exercise the same authority over the men slaves. I have myself seen the master of such a household whose head was bowed down in shame; for it was known in the neighborhood that his daughter had selected one of the meanest slaves on his plantation to be the father of his first grandchild. She did not make her advances to her equals, nor even to her father's more intelligent servants. She selected the most brutalized, over whom her authority could be exercised with less fear of exposure. Her father, half frantic with rage, sought to revenge himself on the offending black man; but his daughter, foreseeing the storm that would arise, had given him free papers, and sent him out of the state.

In such cases the infant is smothered, or sent where it is never seen by any who know its history. But if the white parent is the *father,* instead of the mother, the offspring are unblushingly reared for the market. If they are girls, I have indicated plainly enough what will be their inevitable destiny.

You may believe what I say; for I write only that whereof I know. I was twenty-one years in that cage of obscene birds. I can testify, from my own experience and observation, that slavery is a curse to the whites as well as to the blacks. It makes the white fathers cruel and sensual; the sons violent and licentious; it contaminates the daughters, and makes the wives wretched. And as for the colored race, it needs an abler pen than mine to describe the extremity of their sufferings, the depth of their degradation.

Yet few slaveholders seem to be aware of the widespread moral ruin occasioned by this wicked system. Their talk is of blighted cotton crops—not of the blight on their children's souls.

If you want to be fully convinced of the abominations of slavery, go on a southern plantation, and call yourself a negro trader. Then there will be no concealment; and you will see and hear things that will seem to you impossible among human beings with immortal souls.

X

A Perilous Passage in the Slave Girl's Life

AFTER MY LOVER went away, Dr. Flint contrived a new plan. He seemed to have an idea that my fear of my mistress was his greatest obstacle. In the blandest tones, he told me that he was going to build a small house for me, in a secluded place, four miles away from the town. I shuddered; but I was constrained to listen, while he talked of his intention to give me a home of my own, and to make a lady of me. Hitherto, I had escaped my dreaded fate, by being in the midst of people. My grandmother had already had high words with my master about me. She had told him pretty plainly what she thought of his character, and there was considerable gossip in the neighborhood about our affairs, to which the open-mouthed jealousy of Mrs. Flint contributed not a little. When my master said he was going to build a house for me, and that he could do it with little trouble and expense, I was in hopes something would happen to frustrate his scheme; but I soon heard that the house was actually begun. I vowed before my Maker that I would never enter it. I had rather toil on the plantation from dawn till dark; I had rather live and die in jail, than drag on, from day to day, through such a living death. I was determined that the master, whom I so hated and loathed, who had blighted the prospects of my youth, and made my life a desert, should not, after my long struggle with him, succeed at last in trampling his victim under his feet. I would do anything, everything, for the sake of defeating him. What *could* I do? I thought and thought, till I became desperate, and made a plunge into the abyss.

And now, reader, I come to a period in my unhappy life, which I would gladly forget if I could. The remembrance fills me with sorrow and shame. It pains me to tell you of it; but I have promised to tell you the truth, and I will do it honestly, let it cost me what it may. I will not try to screen myself behind the plea of compulsion from a master; for it was not so. Neither can I plead ignorance or thoughtlessness. For years, my master had done his utmost to pollute my mind with foul images, and to destroy the pure principles inculcated by my grandmother, and the good mistress of my childhood. The influences of slavery had had the same effect on me that they had on other young girls; they had made me prematurely knowing, concerning the evil ways of the world. I knew what I did, and I did it with deliberate calculation.

But, O, ye happy women, whose purity has been sheltered from childhood, who have been free to choose the objects of your affection, whose homes are protected by law, do not judge the poor desolate slave girl too severely! If slavery had been abolished, I, also, could have married the man of my choice; I could have had a home shielded by the laws; and I should have been spared the painful task of confessing what I am now about to relate; but all my prospects had been blighted by slavery. I wanted to keep myself pure; and, under the most adverse circumstances, I tried hard to preserve my self-respect; but I was struggling alone in the powerful grasp of the demon Slavery; and the monster proved too strong for me. I felt as if I was forsaken by God and man; as if all my efforts must be frustrated; and I became reckless in my despair.

I have told you that Dr. Flint's persecutions and his wife's jealousy had given rise to some gossip in the neighborhood. Among others, it chanced that a white unmarried gentleman had obtained some knowledge of the circumstances in which I was placed. He knew my grandmother, and often spoke to me in the street. He became interested for me, and asked questions about my master, which I answered in part. He expressed a great deal of sympathy, and a wish to aid me. He constantly sought opportunities to see me, and wrote to me frequently. I was a poor slave girl, only fifteen years old.

So much attention from a superior person was, of course, flattering; for human nature is the same in all. I also felt grateful for his sympathy, and encouraged by his kind words. It seemed to me a great thing to have such a friend. By degrees, a more tender feeling crept into my heart. He was an educated and eloquent gentleman; too eloquent, alas, for the poor slave girl who trusted in him. Of course I saw whither all this was tending. I knew the impassable gulf between us; but to be an object of interest to a man who is not married, and who is not her master, is agreeable to the pride and feelings of a slave, if her miserable situation has left her any pride or sentiment. It seems less degrading to give one's self, than to submit to compulsion. There is something akin to freedom in having a lover who has no control over you, except that which he gains by kindness and attachment. A master may treat you as rudely as he pleases, and you dare not speak; moreover, the wrong does not seem so great with an unmarried man, as with one who has a wife to be made unhappy. There may be sophistry in all this; but the condition of a slave confuses all principles of morality, and, in fact, renders the practice of them impossible.

When I found that my master had actually begun to build the lonely cottage, other feelings mixed with those I have described. Revenge, and calculations of interest, were added to flattered vanity and sincere gratitude for kindness. I knew nothing would enrage Dr. Flint so much as to know that I favored another; and it was something to triumph over my tyrant even in that small way. I thought he would revenge himself by selling me, and I was sure my friend, Mr. Sands, would buy me. He was a man of more generosity and feeling than my master, and I thought my freedom could be easily obtained from him. The crisis of my fate now came so near that I was desperate. I shuddered to think of being the mother of children that should be owned by my old tyrant. I knew that as soon as a new fancy took him, his victims were sold far off to get rid of them; especially if they had children. I had seen several women sold, with his babies at the breast. He never allowed his offspring by slaves to remain long in sight of himself and his wife. Of a man who was not my master I could ask to have my children well supported; and in this case, I felt confident I should obtain the boon. I also felt quite sure that they would be made free. With all these thoughts revolving in my mind, and seeing no other way of escaping the doom I so much dreaded, I made a headlong plunge. Pity me, and pardon me, O virtuous reader! You never knew what it is to be a slave; to be entirely unprotected by law or custom; to have the laws reduce you to the condition of a chattel, entirely subject to the will of another. You never exhausted your ingenuity in avoiding the snares, and eluding the power of a hated tyrant; you never shuddered at the sound of his footsteps, and trembled within hearing of his voice. I know I did wrong. No one can feel it more sensibly than I do. The painful and humiliating memory will haunt me to my dying day. Still, in looking back, calmly, on the events of my life, I feel that the slave woman ought not to be judged by the same standard as others.

The months passed on. I had many unhappy hours. I secretly mourned over the sorrow I was bringing on my grandmother, who had so tried to shield me from harm. I knew that I was the greatest comfort of her old age, and that it was a source of pride to her that I had not degraded myself, like most of the slaves. I wanted to confess to her that I was no longer worthy of her love; but I could not utter the dreaded words.

As for Dr. Flint, I had a feeling of satisfaction and triumph in the thought of telling *him*. From time to time he told me of his intended arrangements, and I was silent. At last, he came and told me the cottage was completed, and ordered me to go to it. I told him I would never enter it. He said, "I have heard enough of such talk as that. You shall go, if you are carried by force; and you shall remain there."

I replied, "I will never go there. In a few months I shall be a mother."

He stood and looked at me in dumb amazement, and left the house without a word. I thought I should be happy in my triumph over him. But now that the truth was out, and my relatives would hear of it, I felt wretched. Humble as were their circumstances, they had pride in my good character. Now, how could I look them in the face? My self-respect was gone! I had resolved that I would be virtuous, though I was a slave. I had said, "Let the storm beat! I will brave it till I die." And now, how humiliated I felt!

I went to my grandmother. My lips moved to make confession, but the words stuck in my throat. I sat down in the shade of a tree at her door and began to sew. I think she saw something unusual was the matter with me. The mother of slaves is very watchful. She knows there is no security for her children. After they have entered their teens she lives in daily expectation of trouble. This leads to many questions. If the girl is of a sensitive nature, timidity keeps her from answering truthfully, and this well-meant course has a tendency to drive her from maternal counsels. Presently, in came my mistress, like a mad woman, and accused me concerning her husband. My grandmother, whose suspicions had been previously awakened, believed what she said. She exclaimed, "O Linda! has it come to this? I had rather see you dead than to see you as you now are. You are a disgrace to your dead mother." She tore from my fingers my mother's wedding ring and her silver thimble. "Go away!" she exclaimed, "and never come to my house, again." Her reproaches fell so hot and heavy, that they left me no chance to answer. Bitter tears, such as the eyes never shed but once, were my only answer. I rose from my seat, but fell back again, sobbing. She did not speak to me; but the tears were running down her furrowed cheeks, and they scorched me like fire. She had always been so kind to me! *So* kind! How I longed to throw myself at her feet, and tell her all the truth! But she had ordered me to go, and never to come there again. After a few minutes, I mustered strength, and started to obey her. With what feelings did I now close that little gate, which I used to open with such an eager hand in my childhood! It closed upon me with a sound I never heard before.

Where could I go? I was afraid to return to my master's. I walked on recklessly, not caring where I went, or what would become of me. When I had gone four or five miles, fatigue compelled me to stop. I sat down on the stump of an old tree. The stars were shining through the boughs above me. How they mocked me, with their bright, calm light! The hours passed by, and as I sat there alone a chilliness and deadly sickness came over me. I sank on the ground. My mind was full of horrid thoughts. I prayed to die; but the prayer was not answered. At last, with great effort I roused myself, and walked some distance further, to the house of a woman who had been a friend of my mother. When I told her why I was there, she spoke soothingly to me; but I could not be comforted. I thought I could bear my shame if I could only be reconciled to my grandmother. I longed to open my heart to her. I thought if she could know the real state of the case, and all I had been bearing for years, she would perhaps judge me less harshly. My friend advised me to send for her. I did so; but days of agonizing suspense passed before she came. Had she utterly forsaken me? No. She came at last. I knelt before her, and told her the things that had poisoned my life; how long I had been persecuted; that I saw no way of escape; and in an hour of extremity I had become desperate. She listened in silence. I told her I would bear anything and do anything, if in time I had hopes of obtaining her forgiveness. I begged of her to pity me, for my dead mother's sake. And she did pity me. She did not say, "I forgive you;" but she looked at me lovingly, with her eyes full of tears. She laid her old hand gently on my head, and murmured, "Poor child! Poor child!"

XI

The New Tie to Life

I RETURNED to my good grandmother's house. She had an interview with Mr. Sands. When she asked him why he could not have left her one ewe lamb,—whether there were not plenty of slaves who did not care about character,—he made no answer; but he spoke kind and encouraging words. He promised to care for my child, and to buy me, be the conditions what they might.

I had not seen Dr. Flint for five days. I had never seen him since I made the avowal to him. He talked of the disgrace I had brought on myself; how I had sinned against my master, and mortified my old grandmother. He intimated that if I had accepted his proposals, he, as a physician, could have saved me from exposure. He even condescended to pity me. Could he have offered wormwood more bitter? He, whose persecutions had been the cause of my sin!

"Linda," said he, "though you have been criminal towards me, I feel for you, and I can pardon you if you obey my wishes. Tell me whether the fellow you wanted to marry is the father of your child. If you deceive me, you shall feel the fires of hell."

I did not feel as proud as I had done. My strongest weapon with him was gone. I was lowered in my own estimation, and had resolved to bear his abuse in silence. But when he spoke contemptuously of the lover who had always treated me honorably; when I remembered that but for *him* I might have been a virtuous, free, and happy wife, I lost my patience. "I have sinned against God and myself," I replied; "but not against you."

He clinched his teeth, and muttered, "Curse you!" He came towards me, with ill-suppressed rage, and exclaimed, "You obstinate girl! I could grind your bones to powder! You have thrown yourself away on some worthless rascal. You are weak-minded, and have been easily persuaded by those who don't care a straw for you. The future will settle accounts between us. You are blinded now; but hereafter you will be convinced that your master was your best friend. My lenity towards you is a proof of it. I might have punished you in many ways. I might have had you whipped till you fell dead under the lash. But I wanted you to live; I would have bettered your condition. Others cannot do it. You are my slave. Your mistress, disgusted by your conduct, forbids you to return to the house; therefore I leave you here for the present; but I shall see you often. I will call tomorrow."

He came with frowning brows, that showed a dissatisfied state of mind. After asking about my health, he inquired whether my board was paid, and who visited me. He then went on to say that he had neglected his duty; that as a physician there were certain things that he ought to have explained to me. Then followed talk such as would have made the most shameless blush. He ordered me to stand up before him. I obeyed. "I command you," said he, "to tell me whether the father of your child is white or black." I hesitated. "Answer me this instant!" he exclaimed. I did answer. He sprang upon me like a wolf, and grabbed my arm as if he would have broken it. "Do you love him?" said he, in a hissing tone.

"I am thankful that I do not despise him," I replied.

He raised his hand to strike me; but it fell again. I don't know what arrested the blow. He sat down, with lips tightly compressed. At last he spoke. "I came here," said he, "to make you a friendly proposition; but your ingratitude chafes me beyond endurance. You turn aside all my good intentions towards you. I don't know what it is that keeps me from killing you." Again he rose, as if he had a mind to strike me.

But he resumed. "On one condition I will forgive your insolence and crime. You must henceforth have no communication of any kind with the father of your child. You must not ask anything from him, or receive anything from him. I will take care of you and your child. You had better promise this at once, and not wait till you are deserted by him. This is the last act of mercy I shall show towards you."

I said something about being unwilling to have my child supported by a man who had cursed it and me also. He rejoined, that a woman who had sunk to my level had no right to expect anything else. He asked, for the last time, would I accept his kindness? I answered that I would not.

"Very well," said he; "then take the consequences of your wayward course. Never look to me for help. You are my slave, and shall always be my slave. I will never sell you, that you may depend upon."

Hope died away in my heart as he closed the door after him. I had calculated that in his rage he would sell me to a slave-trader; and I knew the father of my child was on the watch to buy me.

About this time my uncle Phillip was expected to return from a voyage. The day before his departure I had officiated as bridesmaid to a young friend. My heart was then ill at ease, but my smiling countenance did not betray it. Only a year had passed; but what fearful changes it had wrought! My heart had grown gray in misery. Lives that flash in sunshine, and lives that are born in tears, receive their hue from circumstances. None of us know what a year may bring forth.

I felt no joy when they told me my uncle had come. He wanted to see me, though he knew what had happened. I shrank from him at first; but at last consented that he should come to my room. He received me as he always had done. O, how my heart smote me when I felt his tears on my burning cheeks! The words of my grandmother came to my mind,—"Perhaps your mother and father are taken from the evil days to come." My disappointed heart could now praise God that it was so. But why, thought I, did my relatives ever cherish hopes for me? What was there to save me from the usual fate of slave girls? Many more beautiful and more intelligent than I had experienced a similar fate, or a far worse one. How could they hope that I should escape?

My uncle's stay was short, and I was not sorry for it. I was too ill in mind and body to enjoy my friends as I had done. For some weeks I was unable to leave my bed. I could not have any doctor but my master, and I would not have him sent for. At last, alarmed by my increasing illness, they sent for him. I was very weak and nervous; and as soon as he entered the room, I began to scream. They told him my state was very critical. He had no wish to hasten me out of the world, and he withdrew.

When my babe was born, they said it was premature. It weighed only four pounds; but God let it live. I heard the doctor say I could not survive till morning. I had often prayed for death; but now I did not want to die, unless my child could die too. Many weeks passed before I was able to leave my bed. I was a mere wreck of my former self. For a year there was scarcely a day when I was free from chills and fever. My babe also was sickly. His little limbs were often racked with pain. Dr. Flint continued his visits, to look after my health; and he did not fail to remind me that my child was an addition to his stock of slaves.

I felt too feeble to dispute with him, and listened to his remarks in silence. His visits were less frequent; but his busy spirit could not remain quiet. He employed my brother in his office, and he was made the medium of frequent notes and messages to me. William was a bright lad, and of much use to the doctor. He had learned to put up medicines, to leech, cup, and bleed. He had taught himself to read and spell. I was proud of my brother; and the old doctor suspected as much. One day, when I had not seen him for several weeks, I heard his steps approaching the door. I dreaded the encounter, and hid myself. He inquired for me, of course; but I was nowhere to be found. He went to his office, and despatched William with a note. The color mounted to my brother's face when he gave it to me; and he said, "Don't you hate me, Linda, for bringing you these things?" I told him I could not blame him; he was a slave, and obliged to obey his master's will. The note or-

dered me to come to his office. I went. He demanded to know where I
was when he called. I told him I was at home. He flew into a passion,
and said he knew better. Then he launched out upon his usual
themes,—my crimes against him, and my ingratitude for his forbearance. The laws were laid down to me anew, and I was dismissed. I felt
humiliated that my brother should stand by, and listen to such language as would be addressed only to a slave. Poor boy! He was powerless to defend me; but I saw the tears, which he vainly strove to keep
back. This manifestation of feeling irritated the doctor. William could
do nothing to please him. One morning he did not arrive at the office
so early as usual; and that circumstance afforded his master an opportunity to vent his spleen. He was put in jail. The next day my brother
sent a trader to the doctor, with a request to be sold. His master was
greatly incensed at what he called his insolence. He said he had put him
there to reflect upon his bad conduct, and he certainly was not giving
any evidence of repentance. For two days he harassed himself to find
somebody to do his office work; but everything went wrong without
William. He was released, and ordered to take his old stand, with many
threats, if he was not careful about his future behavior.

As the months passed on, my boy improved in health. When he was
a year old, they called him beautiful. The little vine was taking deep
root in my existence, though its clinging fondness excited a mixture of
love and pain. When I was most sorely oppressed I found a solace in his
smiles. I loved to watch his infant slumbers; but always there was a dark
cloud over my enjoyment. I could never forget that he was a slave.
Sometimes I wished that he might die in infancy. God tried me. My
darling became very ill. The bright eyes grew dull, and the little feet
and hands were so icy cold that I thought death had already touched
them. I had prayed for his death, but never so earnestly as I now prayed
for his life; and my prayer was heard. Alas, what mockery it is for a slave
mother to try to pray back her dying child to life! Death is better than
slavery. It was a sad thought that I had no name to give my child. His
father caressed him and treated him kindly, whenever he had a chance
to see him. He was not unwilling that he should bear his name; but he
had no legal claim to it; and if I had bestowed it upon him, my master
would have regarded it as a new crime, a new piece of insolence, and
would, perhaps, revenge it on the boy. O, the serpent of Slavery has
many and poisonous fangs!

XII

Fear of Insurrection

NOT FAR FROM this time Nat Turner's insurrection broke out; and the news threw our town into great commotion. Strange that they should be alarmed, when their slaves were so "contented and happy"! But so it was.

It was always the custom to have a muster every year. On that occasion every white man shouldered his musket. The citizens and the so-called country gentlemen wore military uniforms. The poor whites took their places in the ranks in everyday dress, some without shoes, some without hats. This grand occasion had already passed; and when the slaves were told there was to be another muster, they were surprised and rejoiced. Poor creatures! They thought it was going to be a holiday. I was informed of the true state of affairs, and imparted it to the few I could trust. Most gladly would I have proclaimed it to every slave; but I dared not. All could not be relied on. Mighty is the power of the torturing lash.

By sunrise, people were pouring in from every quarter within twenty miles of the town. I knew the houses were to be searched; and I expected it would be done by country bullies and the poor whites. I knew nothing annoyed them so much as to see colored people living in comfort and respectability; so I made arrangements for them with especial care. I arranged everything in my grandmother's house as neatly as possible. I put white quilts on the beds, and decorated some of the rooms with flowers. When all was arranged, I sat down at the window to watch. Far as my eye could reach, it rested on a motley crowd of soldiers. Drums and fifes were discoursing martial music. The men were divided into companies of sixteen, each headed by a captain. Orders were given, and the wild scouts rushed in every direction, wherever a colored face was to be found.

It was a grand opportunity for the low whites, who had no negroes of their own to scourge. They exulted in such a chance to exercise a little brief authority, and show their subserviency to the slaveholders; not reflecting that the power which trampled on the colored people also kept themselves in poverty, ignorance, and moral degradation. Those who never witnessed such scenes can hardly believe what I know was inflicted at this time on innocent men, women, and children, against whom there was not the slightest ground for suspicion. Colored people and slaves who lived in remote parts of the town suffered in an especial manner. In some cases the searchers scattered powder and shot among their clothes, and then sent other parties to find them, and bring them forward as proof that they were plotting insurrection. Everywhere men, women, and children were whipped till the blood stood in puddles at their feet. Some received five hundred lashes; others were tied hands and feet, and tortured with a bucking paddle, which blisters the skin terribly. The dwellings of the colored people, unless they happened to be protected by some influential white person, who was nigh at hand, were robbed of clothing and everything else the marauders thought worth carrying away. All day long these unfeeling wretches went round; like a troop of demons, terrifying and tormenting the helpless. At night, they formed themselves into patrol bands, and went wherever they chose among the colored people, acting out their brutal will. Many women hid themselves in woods and swamps, to keep out of their way. If any of the husbands or fathers told of these outrages, they were tied up to the public whipping post, and cruelly scourged for telling lies about white men. The consternation was universal. No two people that had the slightest tinge of color in their faces dared to be seen talking together.

I entertained no positive fears about our household, because we were in the midst of white families who would protect us. We were ready to receive the soldiers whenever they came. It was not long before we heard the tramp of feet and the sound of voices. The door was rudely pushed open; and in they tumbled, like a pack of hungry wolves. They snatched at everything within their reach. Every box, trunk, closet, and corner underwent a thorough examination. A box in one of the drawers containing some silver change was eagerly pounced upon. When I stepped forward to take it from them, one of the soldiers turned and said angrily, "What d'ye foller us fur? D'ye s'pose white folks is come to steal?"

I replied, "You have come to search; but you have searched that box, and I will take it, if you please."

At that moment I saw a white gentleman who was friendly to us; and I called to him, and asked him to have the goodness to come in and stay till the search was over. He readily complied. His entrance into the house brought in the captain of the company, whose business it was to guard the outside of the house, and see that none of the inmates left it. This officer was Mr. Litch, the wealthy slaveholder whom I mentioned, in the account of neighboring planters, as being notorious for his cruelty. He felt above soiling his hands with the search. He merely gave orders; and, if a bit of writing was discovered, it was carried to him by his ignorant followers, who were unable to read.

My grandmother had a large trunk of bedding and tablecloths. When that was opened, there was a great shout of surprise; and one exclaimed, "Where'd the damned niggers git all dis sheet an' table clarf?"

My grandmother, emboldened by the presence of our white protector, said, "You may be sure we didn't pilfer 'em from *your* houses."

"Look here, mammy," said a grim-looking fellow without any coat, "you seem to feel mighty gran' 'cause you got all them 'ere fixens. White folks oughter have 'em all."

His remarks were interrupted by a chorus of voices shouting, "We's got 'em! We's got 'em! Dis 'ere yaller gal's got letters!"

There was a general rush for the supposed letter, which, upon examination, proved to be some verses written to me by a friend. In packing away my things, I had overlooked them. When their captain informed them of their contents, they seemed much disappointed. He inquired of me who wrote them. I told him it was one of my friends. "Can you read them?" he asked. When I told him I could, he swore, and raved, and tore the paper into bits. "Bring me all your letters!" said he, in a commanding tone. I told him I had none. "Don't be afraid," he continued, in an insinuating way. "Bring them all to me. Nobody shall do you any harm." Seeing I did not move to obey him, his pleasant tone changed to oaths and threats. "Who writes to you? half free niggers?" inquired he. I replied, "O, no; most of my letters are from white people. Some request me to burn them after they are read, and some I destroy without reading."

An exclamation of surprise from some of the company put a stop to our conversation. Some silver spoons which ornamented an old-fashioned buffet had just been discovered. My grandmother was in the habit of preserving fruit for many ladies in the town, and of preparing suppers for parties; consequently she had many jars of preserves. The closet that contained these was next invaded, and the contents tasted. One of them, who was helping himself freely, tapped his neighbor on the shoulder, and said, "Wal done! Don't wonder de niggers want to kill all de white folks, when dey live on 'sarves" [meaning preserves]. I stretched out my hand to take the jar, saying, "You were not sent here to search for sweetmeats."

"And what *were* we sent for?" said the captain, bristling up to me. I evaded the question.

The search of the house was completed, and nothing found to condemn us. They next proceeded to the garden, and knocked about every bush and vine, with no better success. The captain called his men together, and, after a short consultation, the order to march was given. As they passed out of the gate, the captain turned back, and pronounced a malediction on the house. He said it ought to be burned to the ground, and each of its inmates receive thirty-nine lashes. We came out of this affair very fortunately; not losing anything except some wearing apparel.

Towards evening the turbulence increased. The soldiers, stimulated by drink, committed still greater cruelties. Shrieks and shouts continually rent the air. Not daring to go to the door, I peeped under the window curtain. I saw a mob dragging along a number of colored people, each white man, with his musket upraised, threatening instant death if they did not stop their shrieks. Among the prisoners was a respectable old colored minister. They had found a few parcels of shot in his house, which his wife had for years used to balance her scales. For this they were going to shoot him on Court House Green. What a spectacle was that for a civilized country! A rabble, staggering under intoxication, assuming to be the administrators of justice!

The better class of the community exerted their influence to save the innocent, persecuted people; and in several instances they succeeded, by keeping them shut up in jail till the excitement abated. At last the white citizens found that their own property was not safe from the lawless rabble they had summoned to protect them. They rallied the drunken swarm, drove them back into the country, and set a guard over the town.

The next day, the town patrols were commissioned to search colored people that lived out of the city; and the most shocking outrages were committed with perfect impunity. Every day for a fortnight, if I looked out, I saw horsemen with some poor panting negro tied to their saddles, and compelled by the lash to keep up with their speed, till they arrived at the jail yard. Those who had been whipped too unmercifully to walk were washed with brine, tossed into a cart, and carried to jail. One black man, who had not fortitude to endure scourging, promised to give information about the conspiracy. But it turned out that he knew nothing at all. He had not even heard the name of Nat Turner.

The poor fellow had, however, made up a story, which augmented his own sufferings and those of the colored people.

The day patrol continued for some weeks, and at sundown a night guard was substituted. Nothing at all was proved against the colored people, bond or free. The wrath of the slaveholders was somewhat appeased by the capture of Nat Turner. The imprisoned were released. The slaves were sent to their masters, and the free were permitted to return to their ravaged homes. Visiting was strictly forbidden on the plantations. The slaves begged the privilege of again meeting at their little church in the woods, with their burying ground around it. It was built by the colored people, and they had no higher happiness than to meet there and sing hymns together, and pour out their hearts in spontaneous prayer. Their request was denied, and the church was demolished. They were permitted to attend the white churches, a certain portion of the galleries being appropriated to their use. There, when everybody else had partaken of the communion, and the benediction had been pronounced, the minister said, "Come down, now, my colored friends." They obeyed the summons, and partook of the bread and wine, in commemoration of the meek and lowly Jesus, who said, "God is your Father, and all ye are brethren."

XIII

The Church and Slavery

AFTER THE ALARM caused by Nat Turner's insurrection had subsided, the slaveholders came to the conclusion that it would be well to give the slaves enough of religious instruction to keep them from murdering their masters. The Episcopal clergyman offered to hold a separate service on Sundays for their benefit. His colored members were very few, and also very respectable—a fact which I presume had some weight with him. The difficulty was to decide on a suitable place for them to worship. The Methodist and Baptist churches admitted them in the afternoon; but their carpets and cushions were not so costly as those at the Episcopal church. It was at last decided that they should meet at the house of a free colored man, who was a member.

I was invited to attend, because I could read. Sunday evening came, and, trusting to the cover of night, I ventured out. I rarely ventured out

by daylight, for I always went with fear, expecting at every turn to encounter Dr. Flint, who was sure to turn me back, or order me to his
office to inquire where I got my bonnet, or some other article of dress.
When the Rev. Mr. Pike came, there were some twenty persons present. The reverend gentleman knelt in prayer, then seated himself, and
requested all present, who could read, to open their books, while he
gave out the portions he wished them to repeat or respond to.

His text was, "Servants, be obedient to them that are your masters
according to the flesh, with fear and trembling, in singleness of your
heart, as unto Christ."

Pious Mr. Pike brushed up his hair till it stood upright, and, in deep,
solemn tones, began: "Hearken, ye servants! Give strict heed unto my
words. You are rebellious sinners. Your hearts are filled with all manner of evil. 'Tis the devil who tempts you. God is angry with you, and
will surely punish you, if you don't forsake your wicked ways. You that
live in town are eye-servants behind your master's back. Instead of
serving your masters faithfully, which is pleasing in the sight of your
heavenly Master, you are idle, and shirk your work. God sees you. You
tell lies. God hears you. Instead of being engaged in worshipping him,
you are hidden away somewhere, feasting on your master's substance;
tossing coffee-grounds with some wicked fortuneteller, or cutting
cards with another old hag. Your masters may not find you out, but
God sees you, and will punish you. O, the depravity of your hearts!
When your master's work is done, are you quietly together, thinking of
the goodness of God to such sinful creatures? No; you are quarrelling,
and tying up little bags of roots to bury under the door-steps to poison
each other with. God sees you. You men steal away to every grog shop
to sell your master's corn, that you may buy rum to drink. God sees
you. You sneak into the back streets, or among the bushes, to pitch
coppers. Although your masters may not find you out, God sees you;
and he will punish you. You must forsake your sinful ways, and be
faithful servants. Obey your old master and your young master—your
old mistress and your young mistress. If you disobey your earthly master, you offend your heavenly Master. You must obey God's commandments. When you go from here, don't stop at the corners of the
streets to talk, but go directly home, and let your master and mistress
see that you have come."

The benediction was pronounced. We went home, highly amused
at brother Pike's gospel teaching, and we determined to hear him
again. I went the next Sabbath evening, and heard pretty much a repe-

tition of the last discourse. At the close of the meeting, Mr. Pike informed us that he found it very inconvenient to meet at the friend's house, and he should be glad to see us, every Sunday evening, at his own kitchen.

I went home with the feeling that I had heard the Reverend Mr. Pike for the last time. Some of his members repaired to his house, and found that the kitchen sported two tallow candles; the first time, I am sure, since its present occupant owned it, for the servants never had anything but pine knots. It was so long before the reverend gentleman descended from his comfortable parlor that the slaves left, and went to enjoy a Methodist shout. They never seem so happy as when shouting and singing at religious meetings. Many of them are sincere, and nearer to the gate of heaven than sanctimonious Mr. Pike, and other long-faced Christians, who see wounded Samaritans, and pass by on the other side.

The slaves generally compose their own songs and hymns; and they do not trouble their heads much about the measure. They often sing the following verses:

> *"Old Satan is one busy ole man;*
> *He rolls dem blocks all in my way;*
> *But Jesus is my bosom friend;*
> *He rolls dem blocks away.*

> *"If I had died when I was young,*
> *Den how my stam'ring tongue would have sung;*
> *But I am ole, and now I stand*
> *A narrow chance for to tread dat heavenly land."*

I well remember one occasion when I attended a Methodist class meeting. I went with a burdened spirit, and happened to sit next a poor, bereaved mother, whose heart was still heavier than mine. The class leader was the town constable—a man who bought and sold slaves, who whipped his brethren and sisters of the church at the public whipping post, in jail or out of jail. He was ready to perform that Christian office anywhere for fifty cents. This white-faced, black-hearted brother came near us, and said to the stricken woman, "Sister, can't you tell us how the Lord deals with your soul? Do you love him as you did formerly?"

She rose to her feet, and said, in piteous tones, "My Lord and Master, help me! My load is more than I can bear. God has hid himself from me, and I am left in darkness and misery." Then, striking her breast, she continued, "I can't tell you what is in here! They've got all my children. Last week they took the last one. God only knows where they've sold her. They let me have her sixteen years, and then— O! O! Pray for her brothers and sisters! I've got nothing to live for now. God make my time short!"

She sat down, quivering in every limb. I saw that constable class leader become crimson in the face with suppressed laughter, while he held up his handkerchief, that those who were weeping for the poor woman's calamity might not see his merriment. Then, with assumed gravity, he said to the bereaved mother, "Sister, pray to the Lord that every dispensation of his divine will may be sanctified to the good of your poor needy soul!"

The congregation struck up a hymn, and sung as though they were as free as the birds that warbled round us,—

> *"Ole Satan thought he had a mighty aim;*
> *He missed my soul, and caught my sins.*
> *Cry Amen, cry Amen, cry Amen to God!*

> *"He took my sins upon his back;*
> *Went muttering and grumbling down to hell.*
> *Cry Amen, cry Amen, cry Amen to God!*

> *"Ole Satan's church is here below.*
> *Up to God's free church I hope to go.*
> *Cry Amen, cry Amen, cry Amen to God!"*

Precious are such moments to the poor slaves. If you were to hear them at such times, you might think they were happy. But can that hour of singing and shouting sustain them through the dreary week, toiling without wages, under constant dread of the lash?

The Episcopal clergyman, who, ever since my earliest recollection, had been a sort of god among the slaveholders, concluded, as his family was large, that he must go where money was more abundant. A very different clergyman took his place. The change was very agreeable to the colored people, who said, "God has sent us a good man this time." They loved him, and their children followed him for a smile or a kind word. Even the slaveholders felt his influence. He brought to the rectory five slaves. His wife taught them to read and write, and to be useful to her and themselves. As soon as he was settled, he turned his attention to the needy slaves around him. He urged upon his parishioners the duty of having a meeting expressly for them every Sunday, with a sermon adapted to their comprehension. After much argument and importunity, it was finally agreed that they might occupy the gallery of the church on Sunday evenings. Many colored people, hitherto unaccustomed to attend church, now gladly went to hear the gospel preached. The sermons were simple, and they understood them. Moreover, it was the first time they had ever been addressed as human beings. It was not long before his white parishioners began to be dissatisfied. He was accused of preaching better sermons to the negroes than he did to them. He honestly confessed that he bestowed more pains upon those sermons than upon any others; for the slaves were reared in such ignorance that it was a difficult task to adapt himself to their comprehension. Dissensions arose in the parish. Some wanted he should preach to them in the evening, and to the slaves in the afternoon. In the midst of these disputings his wife died, after a very short illness. Her slaves gathered round her dying bed in great sorrow. She said, "I have tried to do you good and promote your happiness; and if I have failed, it has not been for want of interest in your welfare. Do not weep for me; but prepare for the new duties that lie before you. I leave you all free. May we meet in a better world." Her liberated slaves were sent away, with funds to establish them comfortably. The colored people will long bless the memory of that truly Christian woman. Soon after her death her husband preached his farewell sermon, and many tears were shed at his departure.

Several years after, he passed through our town and preached to his former congregation. In his afternoon sermon he addressed the colored people. "My friends," said he, "it affords me great happiness to have an opportunity of speaking to you again. For two years I have been striving to do something for the colored people of my own parish; but nothing is yet accomplished. I have not even preached a sermon to them. Try to live according to the word of God, my friends. Your skin is darker than mine; but God judges men by their hearts, not by the color of their skins." This was strange doctrine from a southern pulpit. It was very offensive to slaveholders. They said he and his wife had made fools of their slaves, and that he preached like a fool to the negroes.

I knew an old black man, whose piety and child-like trust in God were beautiful to witness. At fifty-three years old he joined the Baptist church. He had a most earnest desire to learn to read. He thought he should know how to serve God better if he could only read the Bible.

He came to me, and begged me to teach him. He said he could not pay me, for he had no money; but he would bring me nice fruit when the season for it came. I asked him if he didn't know it was contrary to law; and that slaves were whipped and imprisoned for teaching each other to read. This brought the tears into his eyes. "Don't be troubled, uncle Fred," said I. "I have no thoughts of refusing to teach you. I only told you of the law, that you might know the danger, and be on your guard." He thought he could plan to come three times a week without its being suspected. I selected a quiet nook, where no intruder was likely to penetrate, and there I taught him his A, B, C. Considering his age, his progress was astonishing. As soon as he could spell in two syllables he wanted to spell out words in the Bible. The happy smile that illuminated his face put joy into my heart. After spelling out a few words, he paused, and said, "Honey, it 'pears when I can read dis good book I shall be nearer to God. White man is got all de sense. He can larn easy. It ain't easy for ole black man like me. I only wants to read dis book, dat I may know how to live; den I hab no fear 'bout dying."

I tried to encourage him by speaking of the rapid progress he had made. "Hab patience, child," he replied. "I larns slow."

I had no need of patience. His gratitude, and the happiness I imparted, were more than a recompense for all my trouble.

At the end of six months he had read through the New Testament, and could find any text in it. One day, when he had recited unusually well, I said, "Uncle Fred, how do you manage to get your lessons so well?"

"Lord bress you, chile," he replied. "You nebber gibs me a lesson dat I don't pray to God to help me to understan' what I spells and what I reads. And he *does* help me, chile. Bress his holy name!"

There are thousands, who, like good uncle Fred, are thirsting for the water of life; but the law forbids it, and the churches withhold it. They send the Bible to heathen abroad, and neglect the heathen at home. I am glad that missionaries go out to the dark corners of the earth; but I ask them not to overlook the dark corners at home. Talk to American slaveholders as you talk to savages in Africa. Tell *them* it is wrong to traffic in men. Tell them it is sinful to sell their own children, and atrocious to violate their own daughters. Tell them that all men are brethren, and that man has no right to shut out the light of knowledge from his brother. Tell them they are answerable to God for sealing up the Fountain of Life from souls that are thirsting for it.

There are men who would gladly undertake such missionary work as this; but, alas! their number is small. They are hated by the south, and would be driven from its soil, or dragged to prison to die, as others have been before them. The field is ripe for the harvest, and awaits the reapers. Perhaps the great-grandchildren of uncle Fred may have freely imparted to them the divine treasures, which he sought by stealth, at the risk of the prison and the scourge.

Are doctors of divinity blind, or are they hypocrites? I suppose some are the one, and some the other; but I think if they felt the interest in the poor and the lowly, that they ought to feel, they would not be so *easily* blinded. A clergyman who goes to the south, for the first time, has usually some feeling, however vague, that slavery is wrong. The slaveholder suspects this, and plays his game accordingly. He makes himself as agreeable as possible; talks on theology, and other kindred topics. The reverend gentleman is asked to invoke a blessing on a table loaded with luxuries. After dinner he walks round the premises, and sees the beautiful groves and flowering vines, and the comfortable huts of favored household slaves. The southerner invites him to talk with these slaves. He asks them if they want to be free, and they say, "O, no, massa." This is sufficient to satisfy him. He comes home to publish a "South-Side View of Slavery," and to complain of the exaggerations of abolitionists. He assures people that he has been to the south, and seen slavery for himself; that it is a beautiful "patriarchal institution;" that the slaves don't want their freedom; that they have hallelujah meetings, and other religious privileges.

What does *he* know of the half-starved wretches toiling from dawn till dark on the plantations? of mothers shrieking for their children, torn from their arms by slave-traders? of young girls dragged down into moral filth? of pools of blood around the whipping post? of hounds trained to tear human flesh? of men screwed into cotton gins to die? The slaveholder showed him none of these things, and the slaves dared not tell of them if he had asked them.

There is a great difference between Christianity and religion at the south. If a man goes to the communion table, and pays money into the treasury of the church, no matter if it be the price of blood, he is called religious. If a pastor has offspring by a woman not his wife, the church dismiss him, if she is a white woman; but if she is colored, it does not hinder his continuing to be their good shepherd.

When I was told that Dr. Flint had joined the Episcopal church, I was much surprised. I supposed that religion had a purifying effect on the character of men; but the worst persecutions I endured from him were after he was a communicant. The conversation of the doctor, the day after he had been confirmed, certainly gave *me* no indication that he had "renounced the devil and all his works." In answer to some of his usual talk, I reminded him that he had just joined the church. "Yes, Linda," said he. "It was proper for me to do so. I am getting in years, and my position in society requires it, and it puts an end to all the damned slang. You would do well to join the church, too, Linda."

"There are sinners enough in it already," rejoined I. "If I could be allowed to live like a Christian, I should be glad."

"You can do what I require; and if you are faithful to me, you will be as virtuous as my wife," he replied.

I answered that the Bible didn't say so.

His voice became hoarse with rage. "How dare you preach to me about your infernal Bible!" he exclaimed. "What right have you, who are my negro, to talk to me about what you would like, and what you wouldn't like? I am your master, and you shall obey me."

No wonder the slaves sing,—

> *"Ole Satan's church is here below;*
> *Up to God's free church I hope to go."*

XIV

Another Link to Life

I HAD NOT RETURNED to my master's house since the birth of my child. The old man raved to have me thus, removed from his immediate power; but his wife vowed, by all that was good and great, she would kill me if I came back; and he did not doubt her word. Sometimes he would stay away for a season. Then he would come and renew the old threadbare discourse about his forbearance and my ingratitude. He labored, most unnecessarily, to convince me that I had lowered myself. The venomous old reprobate had no need of descanting on that theme. I felt humiliated enough. My unconscious babe was the ever-present witness of my shame. I listened with silent contempt when he talked about my having forfeited *his* good opinion; but I shed bitter tears that I was no longer worthy of being respected by the good and pure. Alas! slavery still held me in its poisonous grasp. There was no chance for me to be respectable. There was no prospect of being able to lead a better life.

Sometimes, when my master found that I still refused to accept what he called his kind offers, he would threaten to sell my child. "Perhaps that will humble you," said he.

Humble *me!* Was I not already in the dust? But his threat lacerated my heart. I knew the law gave him power to fulfil it; for slaveholders have been cunning enough to enact that "the child shall follow the condition of the *mother*," not of the *father;* thus taking care that licentiousness shall not interfere with avarice. This reflection made me clasp my innocent babe all the more firmly to my heart. Horrid visions passed through my mind when I thought of his liability to fall into the slave trader's hands. I wept over him, and said, "O my child! perhaps they will leave you in some cold cabin to die, and then throw you into a hole, as if you were a dog."

When Dr. Flint learned that I was again to be a mother, he was exasperated beyond measure. He rushed from the house, and returned with a pair of shears. I had a fine head of hair; and he often railed about my pride of arranging it nicely. He cut every hair close to my head, storming and swearing all the time. I replied to some of his abuse, and he struck me. Some months before, he had pitched me downstairs in a fit of passion; and the injury I received was so serious that I was unable to turn myself in bed for many days. He then said, "Linda, I swear by God I will never raise my hand against you again;" but I knew that he would forget his promise.

After he discovered my situation, he was like a restless spirit from the pit. He came every day; and I was subjected to such insults as no pen can describe. I would not describe them if I could; they were too low, too revolting. I tried to keep them from my grandmother's knowledge as much as I could. I knew she had enough to sadden her life, without having my troubles to bear. When she saw the doctor treat me with violence, and heard him utter oaths terrible enough to palsy a man's tongue, she could not always hold her peace. It was natural and motherlike that she should try to defend me; but it only made matters worse.

When they told me my new-born babe was a girl, my heart was heavier than it had ever been before. Slavery is terrible for men; but it is far more terrible for women. Superadded to the burden common to all, *they* have wrongs, and sufferings, and mortifications peculiarly their own.

Dr. Flint had sworn that he would make me suffer, to my last day, for this new crime against *him*, as he called it; and as long as he had me in his power he kept his word. On the fourth day after the birth of my babe, he entered my room suddenly, and commanded me to rise and bring my baby to him. The nurse who took care of me had gone out of the room to prepare some nourishment, and I was alone. There was no alternative. I rose, took up my babe, and crossed the room to where he sat. "Now stand there," said he, "till I tell you to go back!" My child bore a strong resemblance to her father, and to the deceased Mrs. Sands, her grandmother. He noticed this; and while I stood before him, trembling with weakness, he heaped upon me and my little one every vile epithet he could think of. Even the grandmother in her grave did not escape his curses. In the midst of his vituperations I fainted at his feet. This recalled him to his senses. He took the baby from my arms, laid it on the bed, dashed cold water in my face, took me up, and shook me violently, to restore my consciousness before anyone entered the room. Just then my grandmother came in, and he hurried out of the house. I suffered in consequence of this treatment; but I begged my friends to let me die, rather than send for the doctor. There was nothing I dreaded so much as his presence. My life was spared; and I was glad for the sake of my little ones. Had it not been for these ties to life, I should have been glad to be released by death, though I had lived only nineteen years.

Always it gave me a pang that my children had no lawful claim to a name. Their father offered his; but, if I had wished to accept the offer, I dared not while my master lived. Moreover, I knew it would not be accepted at their baptism. A Christian name they were at least entitled to; and we resolved to call my boy for our dear good Benjamin, who had gone far away from us.

My grandmother belonged to the church; and she was very desirous of having the children christened. I knew Dr. Flint would forbid it, and I did not venture to attempt it. But chance favored me. He was called to visit a patient out of town, and was obliged to be absent during Sunday. "Now is the time," said my grandmother; "we will take the children to church, and have them christened."

When I entered the church, recollections of my mother came over me, and I felt subdued in spirit. There she had presented me for baptism, without any reason to feel ashamed. She had been married, and had such legal rights as slavery allows to a slave. The vows had at least been sacred to *her*, and she had never violated them. I was glad she was not alive, to know under what different circumstances her grandchildren were presented for baptism. Why had my lot been so different from my mother's? *Her* master had died when she was a child; and she remained with her mistress till she married. She was never in the power of any master; and thus she escaped one class of the evils that generally fall upon slaves.

When my baby was about to be christened, the former mistress of my father stepped up to me, and proposed to give it her Christian name. To this I added the surname of my father, who had himself no legal right to it; for my grandfather on the paternal side was a white gentleman. What tangled skeins are the genealogies of slavery! I loved my father; but it mortified me to be obliged to bestow his name on my children.

When we left the church, my father's old mistress invited me to go home with her. She clasped a gold chain round my baby's neck. I thanked her for this kindness; but I did not like the emblem. I wanted no chain to be fastened on my daughter, not even if its links were of gold. How earnestly I prayed that she might never feel the weight of slavery's chain, whose iron entereth into the soul!

XV

Continued Persecutions

MY CHILDREN GREW finely; and Dr. Flint would often say to me, with an exulting smile, "These brats will bring me a handsome sum of money one of these days."

I thought to myself that, God being my helper, they should never pass into his hands. It seemed to me I would rather see them killed than have them given up to his power. The money for the freedom of myself and my children could be obtained; but I derived no advantage from that circumstance. Dr. Flint loved money, but he loved power more. After much discussion, my friends resolved on making another trial. There was a slaveholder about to leave for Texas, and he was commissioned to buy me. He was to begin with nine hundred dollars, and go up to twelve. My master refused his offers. "Sir," said he, "she don't belong to me. She is my daughter's property, and I have no right to sell her. I mistrust that you come from her paramour. If so, you may tell him that he cannot buy her for any money; neither can he buy her children."

The doctor came to see me the next day, and my heart beat quicker as he entered. I never had seen the old man tread with so majestic a step. He seated himself and looked at me with withering scorn. My children had learned to be afraid of him. The little one would shut her eyes and hide her face on my shoulder whenever she saw him; and Benny, who was now nearly five years old, often inquired, "What makes that bad man come here so many times? Does he want to hurt us?" I would clasp the dear boy in my arms, trusting that he would be free before he was old enough to solve the problem. And now, as the doctor sat there so grim and silent, the child left his play and came and nestled up by me. At last my tormentor spoke. "So you are left in disgust, are you?" said he. "It is no more than I expected. You remember I told you years ago that you would be treated so. So he is tired of you? Ha! ha! ha! The virtuous madam don't like to hear about it, does she? Ha! ha! ha!" There was a sting in his calling me virtuous madam. I no longer had the power of answering him as I had formerly done. He continued: "So it seems you are trying to get up another intrigue. Your new paramour came to me, and offered to buy you; but you may be assured you will not succeed. You are mine; and you shall be mine for life. There lives no human being that can take you out of slavery. I would have done it; but you rejected my kind offer."

I told him I did not wish to get up any intrigue; that I had never seen the man who offered to buy me.

"Do you tell me I lie?" exclaimed he, dragging me from my chair. "Will you say again that you never saw that man?"

I answered, "I do say so."

He clinched my arm with a volley of oaths. Ben began to scream, and I told him to go to his grandmother.

"Don't you stir a step, you little wretch!" said he. The child drew nearer to me, and put his arms round me, as if he wanted to protect me. This was too much for my enraged master. He caught him up and hurled him across the room. I thought he was dead, and rushed towards him to take him up.

"Not yet!" exclaimed the doctor. "Let him lie there till he comes to."

"Let me go! Let me go!" I screamed, "or I will raise the whole house." I struggled and got away; but he clinched me again. Somebody opened the door, and he released me. I picked up my insensible child, and when I turned my tormentor was gone. Anxiously I bent over the little form, so pale and still; and when the brown eyes at last opened, I don't know whether I was very happy.

All the doctor's former persecutions were renewed. He came morning, noon, and night. No jealous lover ever watched a rival more closely than he watched me and the unknown slaveholder, with whom he accused me of wishing to get up an intrigue. When my grandmother was out of the way he searched every room to find him.

In one of his visits, he happened to find a young girl, whom he had sold to a trader a few days previous. His statement was, that he sold her because she had been too familiar with the overseer. She had had a bitter life with him, and was glad to be sold. She had no mother, and no near ties. She had been torn from all her family years before. A few friends had entered into bonds for her safety, if the trader would allow her to spend with them the time that intervened between her sale and the gathering up of his human stock. Such a favor was rarely granted. It saved the trader the expense of board and jail fees, and though the amount was small, it was a weighty consideration in a slave-trader's mind.

Dr. Flint always had an aversion to meeting slaves after he had sold them. He ordered Rose out of the house; but he was no longer her master, and she took no notice of him. For once the crushed Rose was the conqueror. His gray eyes flashed angrily upon her; but that was the extent of his power. "How came this girl here?" he exclaimed. "What right had you to allow it, when you knew I had sold her?"

I answered, "This is my grandmother's house, and Rose came to see her. I have no right to turn anybody out of doors, that comes here for honest purposes."

He gave me the blow that would have fallen upon Rose if she had still been his slave. My grandmother's attention had been attracted by loud voices, and she entered in time to see a second blow dealt. She was not a woman to let such an outrage, in her own house, go unrebuked. The doctor undertook to explain that I had been insolent. Her indignant feelings rose higher and higher, and finally boiled over in words. "Get out of my house!" she exclaimed. "Go home, and take care of your wife and children, and you will have enough to do, without watching my family."

He threw the birth of my children in her face, and accused her of sanctioning the life I was leading. She told him I was living with her by compulsion of his wife; that he needn't accuse her, for he was the one to blame; he was the one who had caused all the trouble. She grew more and more excited as she went on. "I tell you what, Dr. Flint," said she, "you ain't got many more years to live, and you'd better be saying your prayers. It will take 'em all, and more too, to wash the dirt off your soul."

"Do you know whom you are talking to?" he exclaimed.

She replied, "Yes, I know very well who I am talking to."

He left the house in a great rage. I looked at my grandmother. Our eyes met. Their angry expression had passed away, but she looked sorrowful and weary—weary of incessant strife. I wondered that it did not lessen her love for me; but if it did she never showed it. She was always kind, always ready to sympathize with my troubles. There might have been peace and contentment in that humble home if it had not been for the demon Slavery.

The winter passed undisturbed by the doctor. The beautiful spring came; and when Nature resumes her loveliness, the human soul is apt to revive also. My drooping hopes came to life again with the flowers. I was dreaming of freedom again; more for my children's sake than my own. I planned and I planned. Obstacles hit against plans. There seemed no way of overcoming them; and yet I hoped.

Back came the wily doctor. I was not at home when he called. A friend had invited me to a small party, and to gratify her I went. To my great consternation, a messenger came in haste to say that Dr. Flint was at my grandmother's, and insisted on seeing me. They did not tell him where I was, or he would have come and raised a disturbance in my friend's house. They sent me a dark wrapper; I threw it on and hurried home. My speed did not save me; the doctor had gone away in anger. I dreaded the morning, but I could not delay it; it came, warm and bright. At an early hour the doctor came and asked me where I had been last night. I told him. He did not believe me, and sent to my friend's house to ascertain the facts. He came in the afternoon to assure me he was satisfied that I had spoken the truth. He seemed to be in a facetious mood, and I expected some jeers were coming. "I suppose you need some recreation," said he, "but I am surprised at your being there, among those negroes. It was not the place for *you*. Are you *allowed* to visit such people?"

I understood this covert fling at the white gentleman who was my friend; but I merely replied, "I went to visit my friends, and any company they keep is good enough for me."

He went on to say, "I have seen very little of you of late, but my interest in you is unchanged. When I said I would have no more mercy on you I was rash. I recall my words. Linda, you desire freedom for yourself and your children, and you can obtain it only through me. If you agree to what I am about to propose, you and they shall be free. There must be no communication of any kind between you and their father. I will procure a cottage, where you and the children can live together. Your labor shall be light, such as sewing for my family. Think what is offered you, Linda—a home and freedom! Let the past be forgotten. If I have been harsh with you at times, your willfulness drove me to it. You know I exact obedience from my own children, and I consider you as yet a child."

He paused for an answer, but I remained silent.

"Why don't you speak?" said he. "What more do you wait for?"

"Nothing, sir."

"Then you accept my offer?"

"No, sir."

His anger was ready to break loose; but he succeeded in curbing it, and replied, "You have answered without thought. But I must let you know there are two sides to my proposition; if you reject the bright side, you will be obliged to take the dark one. You must either accept my offer, or you and your children shall be sent to your young master's plantation, there to remain till your young mistress is married; and your children shall fare like the rest of the negro children. I give you a week to consider of it."

He was shrewd; but I knew he was not to be trusted. I told him I was ready to give my answer now.

"I will not receive it now," he replied. "You act too much from impulse. Remember that you and your children can be free a week from today if you choose."

On what a monstrous chance hung the destiny of my children! I knew that my master's offer was a snare, and that if I entered it escape would be impossible. As for his promise, I knew him so well that I was sure if he gave me free papers, they would be so managed as to have no legal value. The alternative was inevitable. I resolved to go to the plantation. But then I thought how completely I should be in his power, and the prospect was appalling. Even if I should kneel before him, and implore him to spare me, for the sake of my children, I knew he would spurn me with his foot, and my weakness would be his triumph.

Before the week expired, I heard that young Mr. Flint was about to be married to a lady of his own stamp. I foresaw the position I should occupy in his establishment. I had once been sent to the plantation for punishment, and fear of the son had induced the father to recall me very soon. My mind was made up; I was resolved that I would foil my master and save my children, or I would perish in the attempt. I kept my plans to myself; I knew that friends would try to dissuade me from them, and I would not wound their feelings by rejecting their advice.

On the decisive day the doctor came, and said he hoped I had made a wise choice.

"I am ready to go to the plantation, sir," I replied.

"Have you thought how important your decision is to your children?" said he.

I told him I had.

"Very well. Go to the plantation, and my curse go with you," he replied. "Your boy shall be put to work, and he shall soon be sold; and your girl shall be raised for the purpose of selling well. Go your own ways!" He left the room with curses, not to be repeated.

As I stood rooted to the spot, my grandmother came and said, "Linda, child, what did you tell him?"

I answered that I was going to the plantation.

"*Must* you go?" said she. "Can't something be done to stop it?"

I told her it was useless to try; but she begged me not to give up. She said she would go to the doctor, and remind him how long and how faithfully she had served in the family, and how she had taken her own baby from her breast to nourish his wife. She would tell him I had been out of the family so long they would not miss me; that she would pay them for my time, and the money would procure a woman who had more strength for the situation than I had. I begged her not to go; but she persisted in saying, "He will listen to *me*, Linda." She went, and was treated as I expected. He coolly listened to what she said, but denied her request. He told her that what he did was for my good, that my feelings were entirely above my situation, and that on the plantation I would receive treatment that was suitable to my behavior.

My grandmother was much cast down. I had my secret hopes; but I must fight my battle alone. I had a woman's pride, and a mother's love for my children; and I resolved that out of the darkness of this hour a brighter dawn should rise for them. My master had power and law on his side; I had a determined will. There is might in each.

XVI

Scenes at the Plantation

EARLY THE NEXT MORNING I left my grandmother's with my youngest child. My boy was ill, and I left him behind. I had many sad thoughts as the old wagon jolted on. Hitherto, I had suffered alone; now, my little one was to be treated as a slave. As we drew near the great house, I thought of the time when I was formerly sent there out of revenge. I wondered for what purpose I was now sent. I could not tell. I resolved to obey orders so far as duty required; but within myself, I determined to make my stay as short as possible. Mr. Flint was waiting to receive us, and told me to follow him upstairs to receive orders for the day. My little Ellen was left below in the kitchen. It was a change for her, who had always been so carefully tended. My young master said she might amuse herself in the yard. This was kind of him, since the child was hateful to his sight. My task was to fit up the house for the reception of the bride. In the midst of sheets, tablecloths, towels, drapery, and carpeting, my head was as busy planning, as were my fingers with the needle. At noon I was allowed to go to Ellen. She had sobbed herself to sleep. I heard Mr. Flint say to a neighbor, "I've got her down here, and I'll soon take the town notions out of her head. My father is partly to blame for her nonsense. He ought to have broke her in long ago." The remark was made within my hearing, and it would have been quite as manly to have made it to my face. He *had* said things to my face which might, or might not, have surprised his neighbor if he had known of them. He was "a chip of the old block."

I resolved to give him no cause to accuse me of being too much of a lady, so far as work was concerned. I worked day and night, with wretchedness before me. When I lay down beside my child, I felt how much easier it would be to see her die than to see her master beat her about, as I daily saw him beat other little ones. The spirit of the mothers was so crushed by the lash, that they stood by, without courage to remonstrate. How much more must I suffer, before I should be "broke in" to that degree?

I wished to appear as contented as possible. Sometimes I had an opportunity to send a few lines home; and this brought up recollections that made it difficult, for a time, to seem calm and indifferent to my lot. Notwithstanding my efforts, I saw that Mr. Flint regarded me with a

suspicious eye. Ellen broke down under the trials of her new life. Separated from me, with no one to look after her, she wandered about, and
in a few days cried herself sick. One day, she sat under the window
where I was at work, crying that weary cry which makes a mother's
heart bleed. I was obliged to steel myself to bear it. After a while it
ceased. I looked out, and she was gone. As it was near noon, I ventured
to go down in search of her. The great house was raised two feet above
the ground. I looked under it, and saw her about midway, fast asleep. I
crept under and drew her out. As I held her in my arms, I thought how
well it would be for her if she never waked up; and I uttered my thought
aloud. I was startled to hear someone say, "Did you speak to me?" I
looked up, and saw Mr. Flint standing beside me. He said nothing further, but turned, frowning, away. That night he sent Ellen a biscuit and
a cup of sweetened milk. This generosity surprised me. I learned afterwards, that in the afternoon he had killed a large snake, which crept
from under the house; and I supposed that incident had prompted his
unusual kindness.

The next morning the old cart was loaded with shingles for town. I
put Ellen into it, and sent her to her grandmother. Mr. Flint said I
ought to have asked his permission. I told him the child was sick, and
required attention which I had no time to give. He let it pass; for he was
aware that I had accomplished much work in a little time.

I had been three weeks on the plantation, when I planned a visit
home. It must be at night, after everybody was in bed. I was six miles
from town, and the road was very dreary. I was to go with a young man,
who, I knew, often stole to town to see his mother. One night, when all
was quiet, we started. Fear gave speed to our steps, and we were not
long in performing the journey. I arrived at my grandmother's. Her
bed room was on the first floor, and the window was open, the weather
being warm. I spoke to her and she awoke. She let me in and closed the
window, lest some late passer-by should see me. A light was brought,
and the whole household gathered round me, some smiling and some
crying. I went to look at my children, and thanked God for their happy
sleep. The tears fell as I leaned over them. As I moved to leave, Benny
stirred. I turned back, and whispered, "Mother is here." After digging
at his eyes with his little fist, they opened, and he sat up in bed, looking
at me curiously. Having satisfied himself that it was I, he exclaimed,
"O mother! you ain't dead, are you? They didn't cut off your head at
the plantation, did they?"

My time was up too soon, and my guide was waiting for me. I laid

Benny back in his bed, and dried his tears by a promise to come again soon. Rapidly we retraced our steps back to the plantation. About half way we were met by a company of four patrols. Luckily we heard their horse's hoofs before they came in sight, and we had time to hide behind a large tree. They passed, hallooing and shouting in a manner that indicated a recent carousal. How thankful we were that they had not their dogs with them! We hastened our footsteps, and when we arrived on the plantation we heard the sound of the hand-mill. The slaves were grinding their corn. We were safely in the house before the horn summoned them to their labor. I divided my little parcel of food with my guide, knowing that he had lost the chance of grinding his corn, and must toil all day in the field.

Mr. Flint often took an inspection of the house, to see that no one was idle. The entire management of the work was trusted to me, because he knew nothing about it; and rather than hire a superintendent he contented himself with my arrangements. He had often urged upon his father the necessity of having me at the plantation to take charge of his affairs, and make clothes for the slaves; but the old man knew him too well to consent to that arrangement.

When I had been working a month at the plantation, the great aunt of Mr. Flint came to make him a visit. This was the good old lady who paid fifty dollars for my grandmother, for the purpose of making her free, when she stood on the auction block. My grandmother loved this old lady, whom we all called Miss Fanny. She often came to take tea with us. On such occasions the table was spread with a snow-white cloth, and the china cups and silver spoons were taken from the old-fashioned buffet. There were hot muffins, tea rusks, and delicious sweetmeats. My grandmother kept two cows, and the fresh cream was Miss Fanny's delight. She invariably declared that it was the best in town. The old ladies had cosey times together. They would work and chat, and sometimes, while talking over old times, their spectacles would get dim with tears, and would have to be taken off and wiped. When Miss Fanny bade us goodby, her bag was filled with grandmother's best cakes, and she was urged to come again soon.

There had been a time when Dr. Flint's wife came to take tea with us, and when her children were also sent to have a feast of "Aunt Marthy's" nice cooking. But after I became an object of her jealousy and spite, she was angry with grandmother for giving a shelter to me and my children. She would not even speak to her in the street. This wounded my grandmother's feelings, for she could not retain ill will against the woman whom she had nourished with her milk when a babe. The doctor's wife would gladly have prevented our intercourse with Miss Fanny if she could have done it, but fortunately she was not dependent on the bounty of the Flints. She had enough to be independent; and that is more than can ever be gained from charity, however lavish it may be.

Miss Fanny was endeared to me by many recollections, and I was rejoiced to see her at the plantation. The warmth of her large, loyal heart made the house seem pleasanter while she was in it. She stayed a week, and I had many talks with her. She said her principal object in coming was to see how I was treated, and whether anything could be done for me. She inquired whether she could help me in any way. I told her I believed not. She condoled with me in her own peculiar way; saying she wished that I and all my grandmother's family were at rest in our graves, for not until then should she feel any peace about us. The good old soul did not dream that I was planning to bestow peace upon her, with regard to myself and my children; not by death, but by securing our freedom.

Again and again I had traversed those dreary twelve miles, to and from the town; and all the way, I was meditating upon some means of escape for myself and my children. My friends had made every effort that ingenuity could devise to effect our purchase, but all their plans had proved abortive. Dr. Flint was suspicious, and determined not to loosen his grasp upon us. I could have made my escape alone; but it was more for my helpless children than for myself that I longed for freedom. Though the boon would have been precious to me, above all price, I would not have taken it at the expense of leaving them in slavery. Every trial I endured, every sacrifice I made for their sakes, drew them closer to my heart, and gave me fresh courage to beat back the dark waves that rolled and rolled over me in a seemingly endless night of storms.

The six weeks were nearly completed, when Mr. Flint's bride was expected to take possession of her new home. The arrangements were all completed, and Mr. Flint said I had done well. He expected to leave home on Saturday, and return with his bride the following Wednesday. After receiving various orders from him, I ventured to ask permission to spend Sunday in town. It was granted; for which favor I was thankful. It was the first I had ever asked of him, and I intended it should be the last. It needed more than one night to accomplish the project I had in view; but the whole of Sunday would give me an opportunity. I spent the Sabbath with my grandmother. A calmer, more beautiful day never came down out of heaven. To me it was a day of conflicting emotions. Perhaps it was the last day I should ever spend under that dear, old sheltering roof! Perhaps these were the last talks I should ever have with the faithful old friend of my whole life! Perhaps it was the last time I and my children should be together! Well, better so, I thought, than that they should be slaves. I knew the doom that awaited my fair baby in slavery, and I determined to save her from it, or perish in the attempt. I went to make this vow at the graves of my poor parents, in the burying-ground of the slaves. "There the wicked cease from troubling, and there the weary be at rest. There the prisoners rest together; they hear not the voice of the oppressor; the servant is free from his master." I knelt by the graves of my parents, and thanked God, as I had often done before, that they had not lived to witness my trials, or to mourn over my sins. I had received my mother's blessing when she died; and in many an hour of tribulation I had seemed to hear her voice, sometimes chiding me, sometimes whispering loving words into my wounded heart. I have shed many and bitter tears, to think that when I am gone from my children they cannot remember me with such entire satisfaction as I remembered my mother.

The graveyard was in the woods, and twilight was coming on. Nothing broke the death-like stillness except the occasional twitter of a bird. My spirit was overawed by the solemnity of the scene. For more than ten years I had frequented this spot, but never had it seemed to me so sacred as now. A black stump, at the head of my mother's grave, was all that remained of a tree my father had planted. His grave was marked by a small wooden board, bearing his name, the letters of which were nearly obliterated. I knelt down and kissed them, and poured forth a prayer to God for guidance and support in the perilous step I was about to take. As I passed the wreck of the old meeting house, where, before Nat Turner's time, the slaves had been allowed to meet for worship, I seemed to hear my father's voice come from it, bidding me not to tarry till I reached freedom or the grave. I rushed on with renovated hopes. My trust in God had been strengthened by that prayer among the graves.

My plan was to conceal myself at the house of a friend, and remain there a few weeks till the search was over. My hope was that the doctor would get discouraged, and, for fear of losing my value, and also of subsequently finding my children among the missing, he would consent to sell us; and I knew somebody would buy us. I had done all in my power to make my children comfortable during the time I expected to be separated from them. I was packing my things, when grandmother came into the room, and asked what I was doing. "I am putting my things in order," I replied. I tried to look and speak cheerfully; but her watchful eye detected something beneath the surface. She drew me towards her, and asked me to sit down. She looked earnestly at me, and said, "Linda, do you want to kill your old grandmother? Do you mean to leave your little, helpless children? I am old now, and cannot do for your babies as I once did for you."

I replied, that if I went away, perhaps their father would be able to secure their freedom.

"Ah, my child," said she, "don't trust too much to him. Stand by your own children, and suffer with them till death. Nobody respects a mother who forsakes her children; and if you leave them, you will never have a happy moment. If you go, you will make me miserable the short time I have to live. You would be taken and brought back, and your sufferings would be dreadful. Remember poor Benjamin. Do give it up, Linda. Try to bear a little longer. Things may turn out better than we expect."

My courage failed me, in view of the sorrow I should bring on that faithful, loving old heart. I promised that I would try longer, and that I would take nothing out of her house without her knowledge.

Whenever the children climbed on my knee, or laid their heads on my lap, she would say, "Poor little souls! what would you do without a mother? She don't love you as I do." And she would hug them to her own bosom, as if to reproach me for my want of affection; but she knew all the while that I loved them better than my life. I slept with her that night, and it was the last time. The memory of it haunted me for many a year.

On Monday I returned to the plantation, and busied myself with preparations for the important day. Wednesday came. It was a beautiful day, and the faces of the slaves were as bright as the sunshine. The poor creatures were merry. They were expecting little presents from the bride, and hoping for better times under her administration. I had no such hopes for them. I knew that the young wives of slaveholders often thought their authority and importance would be best established and maintained by cruelty; and what I had heard of young Mrs. Flint gave me no reason to expect that her rule over them would be less severe than that of the master and overseer. Truly, the colored race are the most cheerful and forgiving people on the face of the earth. That their masters sleep in safety is owing to their superabundance of heart; and yet they look upon their sufferings with less pity than they would bestow on those of a horse or a dog.

I stood at the door with others to receive the bridegroom and bride. She was a handsome, delicate-looking girl, and her face flushed with emotion at sight of her new home. I thought it likely that visions of a happy future were rising before her. It made me sad; for I knew how soon clouds would come over her sunshine. She examined every part of the house, and told me she was delighted with the arrangements I had made. I was afraid old Mrs. Flint had tried to prejudice her against me, and I did my best to please her.

All passed off smoothly for me until dinner time arrived. I did not mind the embarrassment of waiting on a dinner party, for the first time in my life, half so much as I did the meeting with Dr. Flint and his wife, who would be among the guests. It was a mystery to me why Mrs. Flint had not made her appearance at the plantation during all the time I was putting the house in order. I had not met her, face to face, for five years, and I had no wish to see her now. She was a praying woman, and, doubtless, considered my present position a special answer to her prayers. Nothing could please her better than to see me humbled and trampled upon. I was just where she would have me—in the power of a hard, unprincipled master. She did not speak to me when she took her seat at table; but her satisfied, triumphant smile, when I handed her plate, was more eloquent than words. The old doctor was not so quiet in his demonstrations. He ordered me here and there, and spoke with peculiar emphasis when he said "your *mistress.*" I was drilled like a disgraced soldier. When all was over, and the last key turned, I sought my pillow, thankful that God had appointed a season of rest for the weary.

The next day my new mistress began her housekeeping. I was not exactly appointed maid of all work; but I was to do whatever I was told. Monday evening came. It was always a busy time. On that night the slaves received their weekly allowance of food. Three pounds of meat, a peck of corn, and perhaps a dozen herring were allowed to each man. Women received a pound and a half of meat, a peck of corn, and the same number of herring. Children over twelve years old had half the allowance of the women. The meat was cut and weighed by the foreman of the field hands, and piled on planks before the meat house. Then the second foreman went behind the building, and when the first foreman called out, "Who takes this piece of meat?" he answered by calling somebody's name. This method was resorted to as a means of preventing partiality in distributing the meat. The young mistress came out to see how things were done on her plantation, and she soon gave a specimen of her character. Among those in waiting for their allowance was a very old slave, who had faithfully served the Flint family through three generations. When he hobbled up to get his bit of meat, the mistress said he was too old to have any allowance; that when niggers were too old to work, they ought to be fed on grass. Poor old man! He suffered much before he found rest in the grave.

My mistress and I got along very well together. At the end of a week, old Mrs. Flint made us another visit, and was closeted a long time with her daughter-in-law. I had my suspicions what was the subject of the conference. The old doctor's wife had been informed that I could leave the plantation on one condition, and she was very desirous to keep me there. If she had trusted me, as I deserved to be trusted by her, she would have had no fears of my accepting that condition. When she entered her carriage to return home, she said to young Mrs. Flint, "Don't neglect to send for them as quick as possible." My heart was on the watch all the time, and I at once concluded that she spoke of my children. The doctor came the next day, and as I entered the room to spread the tea table, I heard him say, "Don't wait any longer. Send for them tomorrow." I saw through the plan. They thought my children's being there would fetter me to the spot, and that it was a good place to break us all in to abject submission to our lot as slaves. After the doctor left, a gentleman called, who had always manifested friendly feelings towards my grandmother and her family. Mr. Flint carried him over the plantation to show him the results of labor performed by men and women who were unpaid, miserably clothed, and half famished. The cotton crop was all they thought of. It was duly admired, and the gentleman returned with specimens to show his friends. I was ordered to carry water to wash his hands. As I did so, he said, "Linda, how do you like your new home?" I told him I liked it as well as I expected. He replied, "They don't think you are contented, and tomorrow they are going to bring your children to be with you. I am sorry for you, Linda. I hope they will treat you kindly." I hurried from the room, unable to thank him. My suspicions were correct. My children were to be brought to the plantation to be "broke in."

To this day I feel grateful to the gentleman who gave me this timely information. It nerved me to immediate action.

XVII

The Flight

MR. FLINT WAS hard pushed for house servants, and rather than lose me he had restrained his malice. I did my work faithfully, though not, of course, with a willing mind. They were evidently afraid I should leave them. Mr. Flint wished that I should sleep in the great house instead of the servants' quarters. His wife agreed to the proposition, but said I mustn't bring my bed into the house, because it would scatter feathers on her carpet. I knew when I went there that they would never think of such a thing as furnishing a bed of any kind for me and my little one. I therefore carried my own bed, and now I was forbidden to use it. I did as I was ordered. But now that I was certain my children were to be put in their power, in order to give them a stronger hold on me, I resolved to leave them that night. I remembered the grief this step would bring upon my dear old grandmother; and nothing less than the freedom of my children would have induced me to disregard her advice. I went about my evening work with trembling steps. Mr. Flint twice called from his chamber door to inquire why the house was not locked up. I replied that I had not done my work. "You have had time enough to do it," said he. "Take care how you answer me!"

I shut all the windows, locked all the doors, and went up to the third story, to wait till midnight. How long those hours seemed, and how fervently I prayed that God would not forsake me in this hour of utmost need! I was about to risk everything on the throw of a die; and if I failed, O what would become of me and my poor children? They would be made to suffer for my fault.

At half past twelve I stole softly downstairs. I stopped on the second floor, thinking I heard a noise. I felt my way down into the parlor, and looked out of the window. The night was so intensely dark that I could see nothing. I raised the window very softly and jumped out. Large drops of rain were falling, and the darkness bewildered me. I dropped on my knees, and breathed a short prayer to God for guidance and protection. I groped my way to the road, and rushed towards the town with almost lightning speed. I arrived at my grandmother's house, but dared not see her. She would say, "Linda, you are killing me;" and I knew that would unnerve me. I tapped softly at the window of a room, occupied by a woman, who had lived in the house several years. I knew she was a faithful friend, and could be trusted with my secret. I tapped several times before she heard me. At last she raised the window, and I whispered, "Sally, I have run away. Let me in, quick." She opened the door softly, and said in low tones, "For God's sake, don't. Your grandmother is trying to buy you and de chillern. Mr. Sands was here last week. He tole her he was going away on business, but he wanted her to go ahead about buying you and de chillern, and he would help her all he could. Don't run away, Linda. Your grandmother is all bowed down wid trouble now."

I replied, "Sally, they are going to carry my children to the plantation tomorrow; and they will never sell them to anybody so long as they have me in their power. Now, would you advise me to go back?"

"No, chile, no," answered she. "When dey finds you is gone, dey won't want de plague ob de chillern; but where is you going to hide? Dey knows ebery inch ob dis house."

I told her I had a hiding-place, and that was all it was best for her to know. I asked her to go into my room as soon as it was light, and take all my clothes out of my trunk, and pack them in hers; for I knew Mr. Flint and the constable would be there early to search my room. I feared the sight of my children would be too much for my full heart; but I could not go out into the uncertain future without one last look. I bent over the bed where lay my little Benny and baby Ellen. Poor little ones! fatherless and motherless! Memories of their father came over me. He wanted to be kind to them; but they were not all to him, as they were to my womanly heart. I knelt and prayed for the innocent little sleepers. I kissed them lightly, and turned away.

As I was about to open the street door, Sally laid her hand on my shoulder, and said, "Linda, is you gwine all alone? Let me call your uncle."

"No, Sally," I replied, "I want no one to be brought into trouble on my account."

I went forth into the darkness and rain. I ran on till I came to the house of the friend who was to conceal me.

Early the next morning Mr. Flint was at my grandmother's inquiring for me. She told him she had not seen me, and supposed I was at the plantation. He watched her face narrowly, and said, "Don't you know anything about her running off?" She assured him that she did not. He went on to say, "Last night she ran off without the least provocation. We had treated her very kindly. My wife liked her. She will soon be found and brought back. Are her children with you?" When told that they were, he said, "I am very glad to hear that. If they are here, she cannot be far off. If I find out that any of my niggers have had anything to do with this damned business, I'll give 'em five hundred lashes." As he started to go to his father's, he turned round and added, persuasively, "Let her be brought back, and she shall have her children to live with her."

The tidings made the old doctor rave and storm at a furious rate. It was a busy day for them. My grandmother's house was searched from top to bottom. As my trunk was empty, they concluded I had taken my clothes with me. Before ten o'clock every vessel northward bound was thoroughly examined, and the law against harboring fugitives was read to all on board. At night a watch was set over the town. Knowing how distressed my grandmother would be, I wanted to send her a message; but it could not be done. Everyone who went in or out of her house was closely watched. The doctor said he would take my children, unless she became responsible for them; which of course she willingly did. The next day was spent in searching. Before night, the following advertisement was posted at every corner, and in every public place for miles round:—

"$300 REWARD! Ran away from the subscriber, an intelligent, bright, mulatto girl, named Linda, 21 years of age. Five feet four inches high. Dark eyes, and black hair inclined to curl; but it can be made straight. Has a decayed spot on a front tooth. She can read and write, and in all probability will try to get to the Free States. All persons are forbidden, under penalty of the law, to harbor or employ said slave. $150 will be given to whoever takes her in the state, and $300 if taken out of the state and delivered to me, or lodged in jail.

Dr. Flint."

XVIII

Months of Peril

THE SEARCH FOR ME was kept up with more perseverence than I had anticipated. I began to think that escape was impossible. I was in great anxiety lest I should implicate the friend who harbored me. I knew the consequences would be frightful; and much as I dreaded being caught, even that seemed better than causing an innocent person to suffer for

kindness to me. A week had passed in terrible suspense, when my pursuers came into such close vicinity that I concluded they had tracked
me to my hiding-place. I flew out of the house, and concealed myself in
a thicket of bushes. There I remained in an agony of fear for two hours.
Suddenly, a reptile of some kind seized my leg. In my fright, I struck a
blow which loosened its hold, but I could not tell whether I had killed
it; it was so dark, I could not see what it was; I only knew it was something cold and slimy. The pain I felt soon indicated that the bite was
poisonous. I was compelled to leave my place of concealment, and I
groped my way back into the house. The pain had become intense, and
my friend was startled by my look of anguish. I asked her to prepare a
poultice of warm ashes and vinegar, and I applied it to my leg, which
was already much swollen. The application gave me some relief, but
the swelling did not abate. The dread of being disabled was greater
than the physical pain I endured. My friend asked an old woman, who
doctored among the slaves, what was good for the bite of a snake or a
lizard. She told her to steep a dozen coppers in vinegar, over night, and
apply the cankered vinegar to the inflamed part.*

I had succeeded in cautiously conveying some messages to my relatives. They were harshly threatened, and despairing of my having a
chance to escape, they advised me to return to my master, ask his forgiveness, and let him make an example of me. But such counsel had no
influence with me. When I started upon this hazardous undertaking, I
had resolved that, come what would, there should be no turning back.
"Give me liberty, or give me death," was my motto. When my friend
contrived to make known to my relatives the painful situation I had
been in for twenty-four hours, they said no more about my going back
to my master. Something must be done, and that speedily; but where
to turn for help, they knew not. God in his mercy raised up "a friend
in need."

Among the ladies who were acquainted with my grandmother, was
one who had known her from childhood, and always been very
friendly to her. She had also known my mother and her children, and
felt interested for them. At this crisis of affairs she called to see my
grandmother, as she not unfrequently did. She observed the sad and
troubled expression of her face, and asked if she knew where Linda

---

*The poison of a snake is a powerful acid, and is counteracted by powerful alkalies,
such as potash, ammonia, &c. The Indians are accustomed to apply wet ashes, or
plunge the limb into strong lye. White men, employed to lay out railroads in snaky
places, often carry ammonia with them as an antidote.—EDITOR.

was, and whether she was safe. My grandmother shook her head, without answering. "Come, Aunt Martha," said the kind lady, "tell me all about it. Perhaps I can do something to help you." The husband of this lady held many slaves, and bought and sold slaves. She also held a number in her own name; but she treated them kindly, and would never allow any of them to be sold. She was unlike the majority of slaveholders' wives. My grandmother looked earnestly at her. Something in the expression of her face said "Trust me!" and she did trust her. She listened attentively to the details of my story, and sat thinking for a while. At last she said, "Aunt Martha, I pity you both. If you think there is any chance of Linda's getting to the Free States, I will conceal her for a time. But first you must solemnly promise that my name shall never be mentioned. If such a thing should become known, it would ruin me and my family. No one in my house must know of it, except the cook. She is so faithful that I would trust my own life with her; and I know she likes Linda. It is a great risk; but I trust no harm will come of it. Get word to Linda to be ready as soon as it is dark, before the patrols are out. I will send the housemaids on errands, and Betty shall go to meet Linda." The place where we were to meet was designated and agreed upon. My grandmother was unable to thank the lady for this noble deed; overcome by her emotions, she sank on her knees and sobbed like a child.

I received a message to leave my friend's house at such an hour, and go to a certain place where a friend would be waiting for me. As a matter of prudence no names were mentioned. I had no means of conjecturing who I was to meet, or where I was going. I did not like to move thus blindfolded, but I had no choice. It would not do for me to remain where I was. I disguised myself, summoned up courage to meet the worst, and went to the appointed place. My friend Betty was there; she was the last person I expected to see. We hurried along in silence. The pain in my leg was so intense that it seemed as if I should drop; but fear gave me strength. We reached the house and entered unobserved. Her first words were: "Honey, now you is safe. Dem devils ain't coming to search *dis* house. When I get you into missis' safe place, I will bring some nice hot supper. I specs you need it after all dis skeering." Betty's vocation led her to think eating the most important thing in life. She did not realize that my heart was too full for me to care much about supper.

The mistress came to meet us, and led me upstairs to a small room over her own sleeping apartment. "You will be safe here, Linda," said she; "I keep this room to store away things that are out of use. The girls are not accustomed to be sent to it, and they will not suspect anything unless they hear some noise. I always keep it locked, and Betty shall take care of the key. But you must be very careful, for my sake as well as your own; and you must never tell my secret; for it would ruin me and my family. I will keep the girls busy in the morning, that Betty may have a chance to bring your breakfast; but it will not do for her to come to you again till night. I will come to see you sometimes. Keep up your courage. I hope this state of things will not last long." Betty came with the "nice hot supper," and the mistress hastened downstairs to keep things straight till she returned. How my heart overflowed with gratitude! Words choked in my throat; but I could have kissed the feet of my benefactress. For that deed of Christian womanhood, may God forever bless her!

I went to sleep that night with the feeling that I was for the present the most fortunate slave in town. Morning came and filled my little cell with light. I thanked the heavenly Father for this safe retreat. Opposite my window was a pile of feather beds. On the top of these I could lie perfectly concealed, and command a view of the street through which Dr. Flint passed to his office. Anxious as I was, I felt a gleam of satisfaction when I saw him. Thus far I had outwitted him, and I triumphed over it. Who can blame slaves for being cunning? They are constantly compelled to resort to it. It is the only weapon of the weak and oppressed against the strength of their tyrants.

I was daily hoping to hear that my master had sold my children; for I knew who was on the watch to buy them. But Dr. Flint cared even more for revenge than he did for money. My brother William, and the good aunt who had served in his family twenty years, and my little Benny, and Ellen, who was a little over two years old, were thrust into jail, as a means of compelling my relatives to give some information about me. He swore my grandmother should never see one of them again till I was brought back. They kept these facts from me for several days. When I heard that my little ones were in a loathsome jail, my first impulse was to go to them. I was encountering dangers for the sake of freeing them, and must I be the cause of their death? The thought was agonizing. My benefactress tried to soothe me by telling me that my aunt would take good care of the children while they remained in jail. But it added to my pain to think that the good old aunt, who had always been so kind to her sister's orphan children, should be shut up in prison for no other crime than loving them. I suppose my friends feared a reckless movement on my part, knowing, as they did, that my life was bound up in my children. I received a note from my brother William. It was scarcely legible, and ran thus: "Wherever you are, dear sister, I beg of you not to come here. We are all much better off than you are. If you come, you will ruin us all. They would force you to tell where you had been, or they would kill you. Take the advice of your friends; if not for the sake of me and your children, at least for the sake of those you would ruin."

Poor William! He also must suffer for being my brother. I took his advice and kept quiet. My aunt was taken out of jail at the end of a month, because Mrs. Flint could not spare her any longer. She was tired of being her own housekeeper. It was quite too fatiguing to order her dinner and eat it too. My children remained in jail, where brother William did all he could for their comfort. Betty went to see them sometimes, and brought me tidings. She was not permitted to enter the jail; but William would hold them up to the grated window while she chatted with them. When she repeated their prattle, and told me how they wanted to see their ma, my tears would flow. Old Betty would exclaim, "Lors, chile! what's you crying 'bout? Dem young uns vil kill you dead. Don't be so chick'n hearted! If you does, you vil nebber git thro' dis world."

Good old soul! She had gone through the world childless. She had never had little ones to clasp their arms round her neck; she had never seen their soft eyes looking into hers; no sweet little voices had called her mother; she had never pressed her own infants to her heart, with the feeling that even in fetters there was something to live for. How could she realize my feelings? Betty's husband loved children dearly, and wondered why God had denied them to him. He expressed great sorrow when he came to Betty with the tidings that Ellen had been taken out of jail and carried to Dr. Flint's. She had the measles a short time before they carried her to jail, and the disease had left her eyes affected. The doctor had taken her home to attend to them. My children had always been afraid of the doctor and his wife. They had never been inside of their house. Poor little Ellen cried all day to be carried back to prison. The instincts of childhood are true. She knew she was loved in the jail. Her screams and sobs annoyed Mrs. Flint. Before night she called one of the slaves, and said, "Here, Bill, carry this brat back to the jail. I can't stand her noise. If she would be quiet I should like to keep the little minx. She would make a handy waiting-maid for my daughter by and by. But if she stayed here, with her white face, I suppose I should either kill her or spoil her. I hope the doctor will sell them as far as wind and water can carry them. As for their mother, her ladyship will find out yet what she gets by running away. She hasn't so much feeling for her children as a cow has for its calf. If she had, she would have come back long ago, to get them out of jail, and save all this expense and trouble. The good-for-nothing hussy! When she is caught, she shall stay in jail, in irons, for one six months, and then be sold to a sugar plantation. I shall see her broke in yet. What do you stand there for, Bill? Why don't you go off with the brat? Mind, now, that you don't let any of the niggers speak to her in the street!"

When these remarks were reported to me, I smiled at Mrs. Flint's saying that she should either kill my child or spoil her. I thought to myself there was very little danger of the latter. I have always considered it as one of God's special providences that Ellen screamed till she was carried back to jail.

That same night Dr. Flint was called to a patient, and did not return till near morning. Passing my grandmother's, he saw a light in the house, and thought to himself, "Perhaps this has something to do with Linda." He knocked, and the door was opened. "What calls you up so early?" said he. "I saw your light, and I thought I would just stop and tell you that I have found out where Linda is. I know where to put my hands on her, and I shall have her before twelve o'clock." When he had turned away, my grandmother and my uncle looked anxiously at each other. They did not know whether or not it was merely one of the doctor's tricks to frighten them. In their uncertainty, they thought it was best to have a message conveyed to my friend Betty. Unwilling to alarm her mistress, Betty resolved to dispose of me herself. She came to me, and told me to rise and dress quickly. We hurried downstairs, and across the yard, into the kitchen. She locked the door, and lifted up a plank in the floor. A buffalo skin and a bit of carpet were spread for me to lie on, and a quilt thrown over me. "Stay dar," said she, "till I sees if dey know 'bout you. Dey say dey vil put thar hans on you afore twelve o'clock. If dey *did* know whar you are, dey won't know *now*. Dey'll be disapinted dis time. Dat's all I got to say. If dey comes rummagin 'mong *my* tings, dey'll get one bressed sarssin from dis 'ere nigger." In my shallow bed I had but just room enough to bring my hands to my face to keep the dust out of my eyes; for Betty walked over me twenty times in an hour, passing from the dresser to the fireplace. When she was alone, I could hear her pronouncing anathemas over Dr. Flint and all his tribe, every now and then saying, with a chuckling laugh, "Dis nigger's too cute for 'em dis time." When the housemaids were about, she had sly ways of drawing them out, that I might hear what they would say. She would repeat stories she had heard about my being in this, or that, or the other place. To which they would answer, that I was not fool enough to be staying round there; that I was in Philadelphia or New York before this time. When all were abed and asleep, Betty raised the plank, and said, "Come out, chile; come out. Dey don't know nottin 'bout you. 'Twas only white folks' lies, to skeer de niggers."

Some days after this adventure I had a much worse fright. As I sat very still in my retreat above stairs, cheerful visions floated through my mind. I thought Dr. Flint would soon get discouraged, and would be willing to sell my children, when he lost all hopes of making them the means of my discovery. I knew who was ready to buy them. Suddenly I heard a voice that chilled my blood. The sound was too familiar to me, it had been too dreadful, for me not to recognize at once my old master. He was in the house, and I at once concluded he had come to seize me. I looked round in terror. There was no way of escape. The voice receded. I supposed the constable was with him, and they were searching the house. In my alarm I did not forget the trouble I was bringing on my generous benefactress. It seemed as if I were born to bring sorrow on all who befriended me, and that was the bitterest drop in the bitter cup of my life. After a while I heard approaching footsteps; the key was turned in my door. I braced myself against the wall to keep from falling. I ventured to look up, and there stood my kind benefactress alone. I was too much overcome to speak, and sunk down upon the floor.

"I thought you would hear your master's voice," she said; "and knowing you would be terrified, I came to tell you there is nothing to fear. You may even indulge in a laugh at the old gentleman's expense. He is so sure you are in New York, that he came to borrow five hundred dollars to go in pursuit of you. My sister had some money to loan on interest. He has obtained it, and proposes to start for New York tonight. So, for the present, you see you are safe. The doctor will merely lighten his pocket hunting after the bird he has left behind."

XIX

The Children Sold

THE DOCTOR CAME BACK from New York, of course without accomplishing his purpose. He had expended considerable money, and was rather disheartened. My brother and the children had now been in jail two months, and that also was some expense. My friends thought it was a favorable time to work on his discouraged feelings. Mr. Sands sent a speculator to offer him nine hundred dollars for my brother William, and eight hundred for the two children. These were high prices, as slaves were then selling; but the offer was rejected. If it had been merely a question of money, the doctor would have sold any boy of Benny's age for two hundred dollars; but he could not bear to give up the power of revenge. But he was hard pressed for money, and he revolved the matter in his mind. He knew that if he could keep Ellen till she was fifteen, he could sell her for a high price; but I presume he reflected that she might die, or might be stolen away. At all events, he came to the conclusion that he had better accept the slave-trader's offer. Meeting him in the street, he inquired when he would leave town. "Today, at ten o'clock," he replied. "Ah, do you go so soon?" said the doctor; "I have been reflecting upon your proposition, and I have concluded to let you have the three negroes if you will say nineteen hundred dollars." After some parley, the trader agreed to his terms. He wanted the bill of sale drawn up and signed immediately, as he had a great deal to attend to during the short time he remained in town. The doctor went to the jail and told William he would take him back into his service if he would promise to behave himself; but he replied that he would rather be sold. "And you *shall* be sold, you ungrateful rascal!" exclaimed the doctor. In less than an hour the money was paid, the papers were signed, sealed, and delivered, and my brother and children were in the hands of the trader.

It was a hurried transaction; and after it was over, the doctor's characteristic caution returned. He went back to the speculator, and said, "Sir, I have come to lay you under obligations of a thousand dollars not to sell any of those negroes in this state." "You come too late," replied the trader; "our bargain is closed." He had, in fact, already sold them to Mr. Sands, but he did not mention it. The doctor required him to put irons on "that rascal, Bill," and to pass through the back streets when he took his gang out of town. The trader was privately instructed to concede to his wishes. My good old aunt went to the jail to bid the children goodby, supposing them to be the speculator's property, and that she should never see them again. As she held Benny in her lap, he said, "Aunt Nancy, I want to show you something." He led her to the door and showed her a long row of marks, saying, "Uncle Will taught me to count. I have made a mark for every day I have been here, and it is sixty days. It is a long time; and the speculator is going to take me and Ellen away. He's a bad man. It's wrong for him to take grandmother's children. I want to go to my mother."

My grandmother was told that the children would be restored to her, but she was requested to act as if they were really to be sent away. Accordingly, she made up a bundle of clothes and went to the jail. When she arrived, she found William handcuffed among the gang, and the children in the trader's cart. The scene seemed too much like reality. She was afraid there might have been some deception or mistake. She fainted, and was carried home.

When the wagon stopped at the hotel, several gentlemen came out and proposed to purchase William, but the trader refused their offers, without stating that he was already sold. And now came the trying hour for that drove of human beings, driven away like cattle, to be sold they knew not where. Husbands were torn from wives, parents from children, never to look upon each other again this side the grave. There was wringing of hands and cries of despair.

Dr. Flint had the supreme satisfaction of seeing the wagon leave town, and Mrs. Flint had the gratification of supposing that my children were going "as far as wind and water would carry them." According to agreement, my uncle followed the wagon some miles, until they came to an old farm house. There the trader took the irons from William, and as he did so, he said, "You are a damned clever fellow. I should like to own you myself. Them gentlemen that wanted to buy you said you was a bright, honest chap, and I must git you a good home. I guess your old master will swear tomorrow, and call himself an old fool for selling the children. I reckon he'll never git their mammy back agin. I expect she's made tracks for the north. Goodby, old boy. Remember, I have done you a good turn. You must thank me by coaxing all the pretty gals to go with me next fall. That's going to be my last trip. This trading in niggers is a bad business for a fellow that's got any heart. Move on, you fellows!" And the gang went on, God alone knows where.

Much as I despise and detest the class of slave-traders, whom I regard as the vilest wretches on earth, I must do this man the justice to say that he seemed to have some feeling. He took a fancy to William in the jail, and wanted to buy him. When he heard the story of my children, he was willing to aid them in getting out of Dr. Flint's power, even without charging the customary fee.

My uncle procured a wagon and carried William and the children

back to town. Great was the joy in my grandmother's house! The cur-
tains were closed, and the candles lighted. The happy grandmother
cuddled the little ones to her bosom. They hugged her, and kissed her,
and clapped their hands, and shouted. She knelt down and poured
forth one of her heartfelt prayers of thanksgiving to God. The father
was present for a while; and though such a "parental relation" as existed between him and my children takes slight hold of the hearts or
consciences of slaveholders, it must be that he experienced some moments of pure joy in witnessing the happiness he had imparted.

I had no share in the rejoicings of that evening. The events of the day
had not come to my knowledge. And now I will tell you something that
happened to me; though you will, perhaps, think it illustrates the superstition of slaves. I sat in my usual place on the floor near the window, where I could hear much that was said in the street without being
seen. The family had retired for the night, and all was still. I sat there
thinking of my children, when I heard a low strain of music. A band of
serenaders were under the window, playing "Home, sweet home." I
listened till the sounds did not seem like music, but like the moaning of
children. It seemed as if my heart would burst. I rose from my sitting
posture, and knelt. A streak of moonlight was on the floor before me,
and in the midst of it appeared the forms of my two children. They
vanished; but I had seen them distinctly. Some will call it a dream, others a vision. I know not how to account for it, but it made a strong impression on my mind, and I felt certain something had happened to my
little ones.

I had not seen Betty since morning. Now I heard her softly turning
the key. As soon as she entered, I clung to her, and begged her to let me
know whether my children were dead, or whether they were sold; for
I had seen their spirits in my room, and I was sure something had
happened to them. "Lor, chile," said she, putting her arms round me,
"you's got de high-sterics. I'll sleep wid you to-night, 'cause you'll
make a noise, and ruin missis. Something has stirred you up mightily.
When you is done cryin, I'll talk wid you. De chillern is well, and
mighty happy. I seed 'em myself. Does dat satisfy you? Dar, chile, be
still! Somebody vill hear you." I tried to obey her. She lay down, and
was soon sound asleep; but no sleep would come to my eyelids.

At dawn, Betty was up and off to the kitchen. The hours passed on,
and the vision of the night kept constantly recurring to my thoughts.
After a while I heard the voices of two women in the entry. In one of

them I recognized the housemaid. The other said to her, "Did you know Linda Brent's children was sold to the speculator yesterday. They say ole massa Flint was mighty glad to see 'em drove out of town; but they say they've come back agin. I 'spect it's all their daddy's doings. They say he's bought William too. Lor! how it will take hold of ole massa Flint! I'm going roun' to aunt Marthy's to see 'bout it."

I bit my lips till the blood came to keep from crying out. Were my children with their grandmother, or had the speculator carried them off? The suspense was dreadful. Would Betty *never* come, and tell me the truth about it? At last she came, and I eagerly repeated what I had overheard. Her face was one broad, bright smile. "Lor, you foolish ting!" said she. "I'se gwine to tell you all 'bout it. De gals is eating thar breakfast, and missus tole me to let her tell you; but, poor creeter! t'aint right to keep you waitin', and I'se gwine to tell you. Brudder, chillern, all is bought by de daddy! I'se laugh more dan nuff, tinking 'bout ole massa Flint. Lor, how he *vill* swar! He's got ketched dis time, any how; but I must be getting out o' dis, or dem gals vill come and ketch *me*."

Betty went off laughing; and I said to myself, "Can it be true that my children are free? I have not suffered for them in vain. Thank God!"

Great surprise was expressed when it was known that my children had returned to their grandmother's. The news spread through the town, and many a kind word was bestowed on the little ones.

Dr. Flint went to my grandmother's to ascertain who was the owner of my children, and she informed him. "I expected as much," said he. "I am glad to hear it. I have had news from Linda lately, and I shall soon have her. You need never expect to see *her* free. She shall be my slave as long as I live, and when I am dead she shall be the slave of my children. If I ever find out that you or Phillip had anything to do with her running off I'll kill him. And if I meet William in the street, and he presumes to look at me, I'll flog him within an inch of his life. Keep those brats out of my sight!"

As he turned to leave, my grandmother said something to remind him of his own doings. He looked back upon her, as if he would have been glad to strike her to the ground.

I had my season of joy and thanksgiving. It was the first time since my childhood that I had experienced any real happiness. I heard of the old doctor's threats, but they no longer had the same power to trouble me. The darkest cloud that hung over my life had rolled away. Whatever slavery might do to me, it could not shackle my children. If I fell a sacrifice, my little ones were saved. It was well for me that my simple heart believed all that had been promised for their welfare. It is always better to trust than to doubt.

XX

New Perils

THE DOCTOR, more exasperated than ever, again tried to revenge himself on my relatives. He arrested uncle Phillip on the charge of having aided my flight. He was carried before a court, and swore truly that he knew nothing of my intention to escape, and that he had not seen me since I left my master's plantation. The doctor then demanded that he should give bail for five hundred dollars that he would have nothing to do with me. Several gentlemen offered to be security for him; but Mr. Sands told him he had better go back to jail, and he would see that he came out without giving bail.

The news of his arrest was carried to my grandmother, who conveyed it to Betty. In the kindness of her heart, she again stowed me away under the floor; and as she walked back and forth, in the performance of her culinary duties, she talked apparently to herself, but with the intention that I should hear what was going on. I hoped that my uncle's imprisonment would last but few days; still I was anxious. I thought it likely Dr. Flint would do his utmost to taunt and insult him, and I was afraid my uncle might lose control of himself, and retort in some way that would be construed into a punishable offense; and I was well aware that in court his word would not be taken against any white man's. The search for me was renewed. Something had excited suspicions that I was in the vicinity. They searched the house I was in. I heard their steps and their voices. At night, when all were asleep, Betty came to release me from my place of confinement. The fright I had undergone, the constrained posture, and the dampness of the ground, made me ill for several days. My uncle was soon after taken out of prison; but the movements of all my relatives, and of all our friends, were very closely watched.

We all saw that I could not remain where I was much longer. I had already stayed longer than was intended, and I knew my presence must be a source of perpetual anxiety to my kind benefactress. During this time, my friends had laid many plans for my escape, but the extreme vigilance of my persecutors made it impossible to carry them into effect.

One morning I was much startled by hearing somebody trying to get into my room. Several keys were tried, but none fitted. I instantly conjectured it was one of the housemaids; and I concluded she must either have heard some noise in the room, or have noticed the entrance of Betty. When my friend came, at her usual time, I told her what had happened. "I knows who it was," said she. " 'Pend upon it, 'twas dat Jenny. Dat nigger allers got de debble in her." I suggested that she might have seen or heard something that excited her curiosity.

"Tut! tut! chile!" exclaimed Betty, "she ain't seen notin', nor hearn notin'. She only 'spects someting. Dat's all. She wants to fine out who hab cut and make my gownd. But she won't nebber know. Dat's sartin. I'll git missis to fix her."

I reflected a moment, and said, "Betty, I must leave here tonight."

"Do as you tink best, poor chile," she replied. "I'se mighty 'fraid dat 'ere nigger vill pop on you some time."

She reported the incident to her mistress, and received orders to keep Jenny busy in the kitchen till she could see my uncle Phillip. He told her he would send a friend for me that very evening. She told him she hoped I was going to the north, for it was very dangerous for me to remain anywhere in the vicinity. Alas, it was not an easy thing, for one in my situation, to go to the north. In order to leave the coast quite clear for me, she went into the country to spend the day with her brother, and took Jenny with her. She was afraid to come and bid me goodby, but she left a kind message with Betty. I heard her carriage roll from the door, and I never again saw her who had so generously befriended the poor, trembling fugitive! Though she was a slaveholder, to this day my heart blesses her!

I had not the slightest idea where I was going. Betty brought me a suit of sailor's clothes,—jacket, trowsers, and tarpaulin hat. She gave me a small bundle, saying I might need it where I was going. In cheery tones, she exclaimed, "I'se *so* glad you is gwine to free parts! Don't forget ole Betty. P'raps I'll come 'long by and by."

I tried to tell her how grateful I felt for all her kindness, but she interrupted me. "I don't want no tanks, honey. I'se glad I could help you, and I hope de good Lord vill open de path for you. I'se gwine wid you to de lower gate. Put your hands in your pockets, and walk ricketty, like de sailors."

I performed to her satisfaction. At the gate I found Peter, a young colored man, waiting for me. I had known him for years. He had been an apprentice to my father, and had always borne a good character. I was not afraid to trust to him. Betty bade me a hurried goodby, and we walked off. "Take courage, Linda," said my friend Peter. "I've got a dagger, and no man shall take you from me, unless he passes over my dead body."

It was a long time since I had taken a walk out of doors, and the fresh air revived me. It was also pleasant to hear a human voice speaking to me above a whisper. I passed several people whom I knew, but they did not recognize me in my disguise. I prayed internally that, for Peter's sake, as well as my own, nothing might occur to bring out his dagger. We walked on till we came to the wharf. My aunt Nancy's husband was a seafaring man, and it had been deemed necessary to let him into our secret. He took me into his boat, rowed out to a vessel not far distant, and hoisted me on board. We three were the only occupants of the vessel. I now ventured to ask what they proposed to do with me. They said I was to remain on board till near dawn, and then they would hide me in Snaky Swamp, till my uncle Phillip had prepared a place of conceal-ment for me. If the vessel had been bound north, it would have been of no avail to me, for it would certainly have been searched. About four o'clock, we were again seated in the boat, and rowed three miles to the swamp. My fear of snakes had been increased by the venomous bite I had received, and I dreaded to enter this hiding-place. But I was in no situation to choose, and I gratefully accepted the best that my poor, persecuted friends could do for me.

Peter landed first, and with a large knife cut a path through bam-boos and briers of all descriptions. He came back, took me in his arms, and carried me to a seat made among the bamboos. Before we reached it, we were covered with hundreds of mosquitos. In an hour's time they had so poisoned my flesh that I was a pitiful sight to behold. As the light increased, I saw snake after snake crawling round us. I had been accus-tomed to the sight of snakes all my life, but these were larger than any I had ever seen. To this day I shudder when I remember that morning. As evening approached, the number of snakes increased so much that we were continually obliged to thrash them with sticks to keep them from crawling over us. The bamboos were so high and so thick that it was impossible to see beyond a very short distance. Just before it be-came dark we procured a seat nearer to the entrance of the swamp, be-ing fearful of losing our way back to the boat. It was not long before we heard the paddle of oars, and the low whistle, which had been agreed upon as a signal. We made haste to enter the boat, and were rowed back to the vessel. I passed a wretched night; for the heat of the swamp, the mosquitos, and the constant terror of snakes, had brought on a burning fever. I had just dropped asleep, when they came and told me it was time to go back to that horrid swamp. I could scarcely summon courage to rise. But even those large, venomous snakes were less dreadful to my imagination than the white men in that community called civilized. This time Peter took a quantity of tobacco to burn, to keep off the mosquitos. It produced the desired effect on them, but gave me nausea and severe headache. At dark we returned to the vessel. I had been so sick during the day, that Peter declared I should go home that night, if the devil himself was on patrol. They told me a place of concealment had been provided for me at my grandmother's. I could not imagine how it was possible to hide me in her house, every nook and corner of which was known to the Flint family. They told me to wait and see. We were rowed ashore, and went boldly through the streets, to my grandmother's. I wore my sailor's clothes, and had blackened my face with charcoal. I passed several people whom I knew. The father of my children came so near that I brushed against his arm; but he had no idea who it was.

"You must make the most of this walk," said my friend Peter, "for you may not have another very soon."

I thought his voice sounded sad. It was kind of him to conceal from me what a dismal hole was to be my home for a long, long time.

XXI

The Loophole of Retreat

A SMALL SHED had been added to my grandmother's house years ago. Some boards were laid across the joists at the top, and between these boards and the roof was a very small garret, never occupied by anything but rats and mice. It was a pent roof, covered with nothing but shingles, according to the southern custom for such buildings. The garret was only nine feet long and seven wide. The highest part was three feet high, and sloped down abruptly to the loose board floor. There was no admission for either light or air. My uncle Phillip, who was a carpenter, had very skillfully made a concealed trap-door, which communicated with the storeroom. He had been doing this while I was waiting in the swamp. The storeroom opened upon a piazza. To this hole I was conveyed as soon as I entered the house. The air was stifling; the darkness total. A bed had been spread on the floor. I could sleep quite comfortably on one side; but the slope was so sudden that I could not turn on the other without hitting the roof. The rats and mice ran over my bed; but I was weary, and I slept such sleep as the wretched may, when a tempest has passed over them. Morning came. I knew it only by the noises I heard; for in my small den day and night were all the same. I suffered for air even more than for light. But I was not comfortless. I heard the voices of my children. There was joy and there was sadness in the sound. It made my tears flow. How I longed to speak to them! I was eager to look on their faces; but there was no hole, no crack, through which I could peep. This continued darkness was oppressive. It seemed horrible to sit or lie in a cramped position day after day, without one gleam of light. Yet I would have chosen this, rather than my lot as a slave, though white people considered it an easy one; and it was so compared with the fate of others. I was never cruelly over-worked; I was never lacerated with the whip from head to foot; I was never so beaten and bruised that I could not turn from one side to the other; I never had my heel-strings cut to prevent my running away; I was never chained to a log and forced to drag it about, while I toiled in the fields from morning till night; I was never branded with hot iron, or torn by bloodhounds. On the contrary, I had always been kindly treated, and tenderly cared for, until I came into the hands of Dr. Flint. I had never wished for freedom till then. But though my life in slavery was comparatively devoid of hardships, God pity the woman who is compelled to lead such a life!

My food was passed up to me through the trap-door my uncle had contrived; and my grandmother, my uncle Phillip, and aunt Nancy would seize such opportunities as they could, to mount up there and chat with me at the opening. But of course this was not safe in the daytime. It must all be done in darkness. It was impossible for me to move in an erect position, but I crawled about my den for exercise. One day I hit my head against something, and found it was a gimlet. My uncle had left it sticking there when he made the trap-door. I was as rejoiced as Robinson Crusoe could have been at finding such a treasure. It put a lucky thought into my head. I said to myself, "Now I will have some light. Now I will see my children." I did not dare to begin my work during the daytime, for fear of attracting attention. But I groped round; and having found the side next the street, where I could frequently see my children, I stuck the gimlet in and waited for evening. I bored three rows of holes, one above another; then I bored out the interstices between. I thus succeeded in making one hole about an inch long and an inch broad. I sat by it till late into the night, to enjoy the little whiff of air that floated in. In the morning I watched for my children. The first person I saw in the street was Dr. Flint. I had a shuddering, superstitious feeling that it was a bad omen. Several familiar faces passed by. At last I heard the merry laugh of children, and presently two sweet little faces were looking up at me, as though they knew I was there, and were conscious of the joy they imparted. How I longed to *tell* them I was there!

My condition was now a little improved. But for weeks I was tormented by hundreds of little red insects, fine as a needle's point, that pierced through my skin, and produced an intolerable burning. The good grandmother gave me herb teas and cooling medicines, and finally I got rid of them. The heat of my den was intense, for nothing but thin shingles protected me from the scorching summer's sun. But I had my consolations. Through my peeping-hole I could watch the children, and when they were near enough, I could hear their talk. Aunt Nancy brought me all the news she could hear at Dr. Flint's. From her I learned that the doctor had written to New York to a colored woman, who had been born and raised in our neighborhood, and had breathed his contaminating atmosphere. He offered her a reward if she could find out anything about me. I know not what was the nature of her reply; but he soon after started for New York in haste, saying to his family that he had business of importance to transact. I peeped at him as he passed on his way to the steamboat. It was a satisfaction to have miles of land and water between us, even for a little while; and it was a still greater satisfaction to know that he believed me to be in the Free States. My little den seemed less dreary than it had done. He returned, as he did from his former journey to New York, without obtaining any satisfactory information. When he passed our house next morning, Benny was standing at the gate. He had heard them say that he had gone to find me, and he called out, "Dr. Flint, did you bring my mother home? I want to see her." The doctor stamped his foot at him in a rage, and exclaimed, "Get out of the way, you little damned rascal! If you don't, I'll cut off your head."

Benny ran terrified into the house, saying, "You can't put me in jail again. I don't belong to you now." It was well that the wind carried the words away from the doctor's ear. I told my grandmother of it, when we had our next conference at the trap-door; and begged of her not to allow the children to be impertinent to the irascible old man.

Autumn came, with a pleasant abatement of heat. My eyes had become accustomed to the dim light, and by holding my book or work in a certain position near the aperture I contrived to read and sew. That was a great relief to the tedious monotony of my life. But when winter came, the cold penetrated through the thin shingle roof, and I was dreadfully chilled. The winters there are not so long, or so severe, as in northern latitudes; but the houses are not built to shelter from cold, and my little den was peculiarly comfortless. The kind grandmother brought me bed-clothes and warm drinks. Often I was obliged to lie in bed all day to keep comfortable; but with all my precautions, my shoulders and feet were frostbitten. O, those long, gloomy days, with no object for my eye to rest upon, and no thoughts to occupy my mind, except the dreary past and the uncertain future! I was thankful when there came a day sufficiently mild for me to wrap myself up and sit at the loophole to watch the passers by. Southerners have the habit of stopping and talking in the streets, and I heard many conversations not intended to meet my ears. I heard slave-hunters planning how to catch some poor fugitive. Several times I heard allusions to Dr. Flint, myself, and the history of my children, who, perhaps, were playing near the gate. One would say, "I wouldn't move my little finger to catch her, as old Flint's property." Another would say, "I'll catch *any* nigger for the reward. A man ought to have what belongs to him, if he *is* a damned brute." The opinion was often expressed that I was in the Free States. Very rarely did anyone suggest that I might be in the vicinity. Had the least suspicion rested on my grandmother's house, it would have been burned to the ground. But it was the last place they thought of. Yet there was no place, where slavery existed, that could have afforded me so good a place of concealment.

Dr. Flint and his family repeatedly tried to coax and bribe my children to tell something they had heard said about me. One day the doctor took them into a shop, and offered them some bright little silver pieces and gay handkerchiefs if they would tell where their mother was. Ellen shrank away from him, and would not speak; but Benny spoke up, and said, "Dr. Flint, I don't know where my mother is. I guess she's in New York; and when you go there again, I wish you'd ask her to come home, for I want to see her; but if you put her in jail, or tell her you'll cut her head off, I'll tell her to go right back."

XXII

Christmas Festivities

CHRISTMAS WAS approaching. Grandmother brought me materials, and I busied myself making some new garments and little playthings for my children. Were it not that hiring day is near at hand, and many families are fearfully looking forward to the probability of separation in a few days, Christmas might be a happy season for the poor slaves. Even slave mothers try to gladden the hearts of their little ones on that occasion. Benny and Ellen had their Christmas stockings filled. Their imprisoned mother could not have the privilege of witnessing their surprise and joy. But I had the pleasure of peeping at them as they went into the street with their new suits on. I heard Benny ask a little playmate whether Santa Claus brought him anything. "Yes," replied the boy; "but Santa Claus ain't a real man. It's the children's mothers that put things into the stockings." "No, that can't be," replied Benny, "for Santa Claus brought Ellen and me these new clothes, and my mother has been gone this long time."

How I longed to tell him that his mother made those garments, and that many a tear fell on them while she worked!

Every child rises early on Christmas morning to see the Johnkannaus. Without them, Christmas would be shorn of its greatest attraction. They consist of companies of slaves from the plantations, generally of the lower class. Two athletic men, in calico wrappers, have a net thrown over them, covered with all manner of bright-colored stripes. Cows' tails are fastened to their backs, and their heads are decorated with horns. A box, covered with sheepskin, is called the gumbo box. A dozen beat on this, while others strike triangles and jawbones, to which bands of dancers keep time. For a month previous they are composing songs, which are sung on this occasion. These companies, of a hundred each, turn out early in the morning, and are allowed to go round till twelve o'clock, begging for contributions. Not a door is left unvisited where there is the least chance of obtaining a penny or a glass of rum. They do not drink while they are out, but carry the rum home in jugs, to have a carousal. These Christmas donations frequently amount to twenty or thirty dollars. It is seldom that any white man or child refuses to give them a trifle. If he does, they regale his ears with the following song:—

"Poor massa, so dey say;
Down in de heel, so dey say;
Got no money, so dey say;
Not one shillin, so dey say;
God A'mighty bress you, so dey say."

Christmas is a day of feasting, both with white and colored people. Slaves, who are lucky enough to have a few shillings, are sure to spend them for good eating; and many a turkey and pig is captured, without saying, "By your leave, sir." Those who cannot obtain these, cook a 'possum, or a raccoon, from which savory dishes can be made. My grandmother raised poultry and pigs for sale; and it was her established custom to have both a turkey and a pig roasted for Christmas dinner.

On this occasion, I was warned to keep extremely quiet, because two guests had been invited. One was the town constable, and the other was a free colored man, who tried to pass himself off for white, and who was always ready to do any mean work for the sake of currying favor with white people. My grandmother had a motive for inviting them. She managed to take them all over the house. All the rooms on the lower floor were thrown open for them to pass in and out; and after dinner, they were invited upstairs to look at a fine mocking bird my uncle had just brought home. There, too, the rooms were all thrown open, that they might look in. When I heard them talking on the piazza, my heart almost stood still. I knew this colored man had spent many nights hunting for me. Everybody knew he had the blood of a slave father in his veins; but for the sake of passing himself off for white, he was ready to kiss the slaveholders' feet. How I despised him! As for the constable, he wore no false colors. The duties of his office were despicable, but he was superior to his companion, inasmuch as he did not pretend to be what he was not. Any white man, who could raise money enough to buy a slave, would have considered himself degraded by being a constable; but the office enabled its possessor to exercise authority. If he found any slave out after nine o'clock, he could whip him as much as he liked; and that was a privilege to be coveted. When the guests were ready to depart, my grandmother gave each of them some of her nice pudding, as a present for their wives. Through my peephole I saw them go out of the gate, and I was glad when it closed after them. So passed the first Christmas in my den.

XXIII

Still in Prison

WHEN SPRING RETURNED, and I took in the little patch of green the aperture commanded, I asked myself how many more summers and winters I must be condemned to spend thus. I longed to draw in a plentiful draught of fresh air, to stretch my cramped limbs, to have room to stand erect, to feel the earth under my feet again. My relatives were constantly on the lookout for a chance of escape; but none offered that seemed practicable, and even tolerably safe. The hot summer came again, and made the turpentine drop from the thin roof over my head.

During the long nights I was restless for want of air, and I had no room to toss and turn. There was but one compensation; the atmosphere was so stifled that even mosquitos would not condescend to buzz in it. With all my detestation of Dr. Flint, I could hardly wish him a worse punishment, either in this world or that which is to come, than to suffer what I suffered in one single summer. Yet the laws allowed *him* to be out in the free air, while I, guiltless of crime, was pent up here, as the only means of avoiding the cruelties the laws allowed him to inflict upon me! I don't know what kept life within me. Again and again, I thought I should die before long; but I saw the leaves of another autumn whirl through the air, and felt the touch of another winter. In summer the most terrible thunder storms were acceptable, for the rain came through the roof, and I rolled up my bed that it might cool the hot boards under it. Later in the season, storms sometimes wet my clothes through and through, and that was not comfortable when the air grew chilly. Moderate storms I could keep out by filling the chinks with oakum.

But uncomfortable as my situation was, I had glimpses of things out of doors, which made me thankful for my wretched hiding-place. One day I saw a slave pass our gate, muttering, "It's his own, and he can kill it if he will." My grandmother told me that woman's history. Her mistress had that day seen her baby for the first time, and in the lineaments of its fair face she saw a likeness to her husband. She turned the bondwoman and her child out of doors, and forbade her ever to return. The slave went to her master, and told him what had happened. He promised to talk with her mistress, and make it all right. The next day she and her baby were sold to a Georgia trader.

Another time I saw a woman rush wildly by, pursued by two men. She was a slave, the wet nurse of her mistress's children. For some trifling offense her mistress ordered her to be stripped and whipped. To escape the degradation and the torture, she rushed to the river, jumped in, and ended her wrongs in death.

Senator Brown, of Mississippi, could not be ignorant of many such facts as these, for they are of frequent occurrence in every Southern State. Yet he stood up in the Congress of the United States, and declared that slavery was "a great moral, social, and political blessing; a blessing to the master, and a blessing to the slave!"

I suffered much more during the second winter than I did during the first. My limbs were benumbed by inaction, and the cold filled them with cramp. I had a very painful sensation of coldness in my head; even my face and tongue stiffened, and I lost the power of speech. Of course it was impossible, under the circumstances, to summon any physician. My brother William came and did all he could for me. Uncle Phillip also watched tenderly over me; and poor grandmother crept up and down to inquire whether there were any signs of returning life. I was restored to consciousness by the dashing of cold water in my face, and found myself leaning against my brother's arm, while he bent over me with streaming eyes. He afterwards told me he thought I was dying, for I had been in an unconscious state sixteen hours. I next became delirious, and was in great danger of betraying myself and my friends. To prevent this, they stupefied me with drugs. I remained in bed six weeks, weary in body and sick at heart. How to get medical advice was the question. William finally went to a Thompsonian doctor, and described himself as having all my pains and aches. He returned with herbs, roots, and ointment. He was especially charged to rub on the ointment by a fire; but how could a fire be made in my little den? Charcoal in a furnace was tried, but there was no outlet for the gas, and it nearly cost me my life. Afterwards coals, already kindled, were brought up in an iron pan, and placed on bricks. I was so weak, and it was so long since I had enjoyed the warmth of a fire, that those few coals actually made me weep. I think the medicines did me some good; but my recovery was very slow. Dark thoughts passed through my mind as I lay there day after day. I tried to be thankful for my little cell, dismal as it was, and even to love it, as part of the price I had paid for the redemption of my children. Sometimes I thought God was a compassionate Father, who would forgive my sins for the sake of my sufferings. At other times, it seemed to me there was no justice or mercy in the divine government. I asked why the curse of slavery was permitted to exist, and why I had been so persecuted and wronged from youth upward. These things took the shape of mystery, which is to this day not so clear to my soul as I trust it will be hereafter.

In the midst of my illness, grandmother broke down under the weight of anxiety and toil. The idea of losing her, who had always been my best friend and a mother to my children, was the sorest trial I had yet had. O, how earnestly I prayed that she might recover! How hard it seemed, that I could not tend upon her, who had so long and so tenderly watched over me!

One day the screams of a child nerved me with strength to crawl to my peeping-hole, and I saw my son covered with blood. A fierce dog, usually kept chained, had seized and bitten him. A doctor was sent for, and I heard the groans and screams of my child while the wounds were being sewed up. O, what torture to a mother's heart, to listen to this and be unable to go to him!

But childhood is like a day in spring, alternately shower and sunshine. Before night Benny was bright and lively, threatening the destruction of the dog; and great was his delight when the doctor told him the next day that the dog had bitten another boy and been shot. Benny recovered from his wounds; but it was long before he could walk.

When my grandmother's illness became known, many ladies, who were her customers, called to bring her some little comforts, and to inquire whether she had everything she wanted. Aunt Nancy one night asked permission to watch with her sick mother, and Mrs. Flint replied, "I don't see any need of your going. I can't spare you." But when she found other ladies in the neighborhood were so attentive, not wishing to be outdone in Christian charity, she also sallied forth, in magnificent condescension, and stood by the bedside of her who had loved her in her infancy, and who had been repaid by such grievous wrongs. She seemed surprised to find her so ill, and scolded uncle Phillip for not sending for Dr. Flint. She herself sent for him immediately, and he came. Secure as I was in my retreat, I should have been terrified if I had known he was so near me. He pronounced my grandmother in a very critical situation, and said if her attending physician wished it, he would visit her. Nobody wished to have him coming to the house at all hours, and we were not disposed to give him a chance to make out a long bill.

As Mrs. Flint went out, Sally told her the reason Benny was lame was, that a dog had bitten him. "I'm glad of it," replied she. "I wish he had killed him. It would be good news to send to his mother. *Her* day will come. The dogs will grab *her* yet." With these Christian words she and her husband departed, and, to my great satisfaction, returned no more.

I heard from uncle Phillip, with feelings of unspeakable joy and gratitude, that the crisis was passed and grandmother would live. I could now say from my heart, "God is merciful. He has spared me the anguish of feeling that I caused her death."

XXIV

The Candidate for Congress

THE SUMMER had nearly ended, when Dr. Flint made a third visit to New York, in search of me. Two candidates were running for Congress, and he returned in season to vote. The father of my children was the Whig candidate. The doctor had hitherto been a stanch Whig; but now he exerted all his energies for the defeat of Mr. Sands. He invited large parties of men to dine in the shade of his trees, and supplied them with plenty of rum and brandy. If any poor fellow drowned his wits in the bowl, and, in the openness of his convivial heart, proclaimed that he did not mean to vote the Democratic ticket, he was shoved into the street without ceremony.

The doctor expended his liquor in vain. Mr. Sands was elected; an event which occasioned me some anxious thoughts. He had not emancipated my children, and if he should die they would be at the mercy of his heirs. Two little voices, that frequently met my ear, seemed to plead with me not to let their father depart without striving to make their freedom secure. Years had passed since I had spoken to him. I had not even seen him since the night I passed him, unrecognized, in my disguise of a sailor. I supposed he would call before he left, to say something to my grandmother concerning the children, and I resolved what course to take.

The day before his departure for Washington I made arrangements, towards evening, to get from my hiding-place into the storeroom below. I found myself so stiff and clumsy that it was with great difficulty I could hitch from one resting place to another. When I reached the storeroom my ankles gave way under me, and I sank exhausted on the floor. It seemed as if I could never use my limbs again. But the purpose I had in view roused all the strength I had. I crawled on my hands and knees to the window, and, screened behind a barrel, I waited for his coming. The clock struck nine, and I knew the steamboat would leave between ten and eleven. My hopes were failing. But presently I heard his voice, saying to someone, "Wait for me a moment. I wish to see aunt Martha." When he came out, as he passed the window, I said, "Stop one moment, and let me speak for my children." He started, hesitated, and then passed on, and went out of the gate. I closed the shutter I had partially opened, and sank down behind the barrel. I had suffered much; but seldom had I experienced a keener pang than I then felt. Had my children, then, become of so little consequence to him? And had he so little feeling for their wretched mother that he would not listen a moment while she pleaded for them? Painful memories were so busy within me, that I forgot I had not hooked the shutter, till I heard someone opening it. I looked up. He had come back. "Who called me?" said he, in a low tone. "I did," I replied. "Oh, Linda," said he, "I knew your voice; but I was afraid to answer, lest my friend should hear me. Why do you come here? Is it possible you risk yourself in this house? They are mad to allow it. I shall expect to hear that you are all ruined." I did not wish to implicate him, by letting him know my place of concealment; so I merely said, "I thought you would come to bid grandmother goodby, and so I came here to speak a few words to you about emancipating my children. Many changes may take place during the six months you are gone to Washington, and it does not seem right for you to expose them to the risk of such changes. I want nothing for myself; all I ask is, that you will free my children, or authorize some friend to do it, before you go."

He promised he would do it, and also expressed a readiness to make any arrangements whereby I could be purchased.

I heard footsteps approaching, and closed the shutter hastily. I wanted to crawl back to my den, without letting the family know what I had done; for I knew they would deem it very imprudent. But he stepped back into the house, to tell my grandmother that he had spoken with me at the storeroom window, and to beg of her not to allow me to remain in the house over night. He said it was the height of madness for me to be there; that we should certainly all be ruined. Luckily, he was in too much of a hurry to wait for a reply, or the dear old woman would surely have told him all.

I tried to go back to my den, but found it more difficult to go up than

I had to come down. Now that my mission was fulfilled, the little strength that had supported me through it was gone, and I sank helpless on the floor. My grandmother, alarmed at the risk I had run, came into the storeroom in the dark, and locked the door behind her. "Linda," she whispered, "where are you?"

"I am here by the window," I replied. "I *couldn't* have him go away without emancipating the children. Who knows what may happen?"

"Come, come, child," said she, "it won't do for you to stay here another minute. You've done wrong; but I can't blame you, poor thing!"

I told her I could not return without assistance, and she must call my uncle. Uncle Phillip came, and pity prevented him from scolding me. He carried me back to my dungeon, laid me tenderly on the bed, gave me some medicine, and asked me if there was anything more he could do. Then he went away, and I was left with my own thoughts—starless as the midnight darkness around me.

My friends feared I should become a cripple for life; and I was so weary of my long imprisonment that, had it not been for the hope of serving my children, I should have been thankful to die; but, for their sakes, I was willing to bear on.

XXV

Competition in Cunning

DR. FLINT had not given me up. Every now and then he would say to my grandmother that I would yet come back, and voluntarily surrender myself; and that when I did, I could be purchased by my relatives, or anyone who wished to buy me. I knew his cunning nature too well not to perceive that this was a trap laid for me; and so all my friends understood it. I resolved to match my cunning against his cunning. In order to make him believe that I was in New York, I resolved to write him a letter dated from that place. I sent for my friend Peter, and asked him if he knew any trustworthy seafaring person, who would carry such a letter to New York, and put it in the post office there. He said he knew one that he would trust with his own life to the ends of the world. I reminded him that it was a hazardous thing for him to undertake. He said he knew it, but he was willing to do anything to help me. I expressed a wish for a New York paper, to ascertain the names of some of the streets. He run his hand into his pocket, and said, "Here is half a one, that was round a cap I bought of a pedlar yesterday." I told him the letter would be ready the next evening. He bade me goodby, adding, "Keep up your spirits, Linda; brighter days will come by and by."

My uncle Phillip kept watch over the gate until our brief interview was over. Early the next morning, I seated myself near the little aperture to examine the newspaper. It was a piece of the *New York Herald*; and, for once, the paper that systematically abuses the colored people, was made to render them a service. Having obtained what information I wanted concerning streets and numbers, I wrote two letters, one to my grandmother, the other to Dr. Flint. I reminded him how he, a gray-headed man, had treated a helpless child, who had been placed in his power, and what years of misery he had brought upon her. To my grandmother, I expressed a wish to have my children sent to me at the north, where I could teach them to respect themselves, and set them a virtuous example; which a slave mother was not allowed to do at the south. I asked her to direct her answer to a certain street in Boston, as I did not live in New York, though I went there sometimes. I dated these letters ahead, to allow for the time it would take to carry them, and sent a memorandum of the date to the messenger. When my friend came for the letters, I said, "God bless and reward you, Peter, for this disinterested kindness. Pray be careful. If you are detected, both you and I will have to suffer dreadfully. I have not a relative who would dare to do it for me." He replied, "You may trust to me, Linda. I don't forget that your father was my best friend, and I will be a friend to his children so long as God lets me live."

It was necessary to tell my grandmother what I had done, in order that she might be ready for the letter, and prepared to hear what Dr. Flint might say about my being at the north. She was sadly troubled. She felt sure mischief would come of it. I also told my plan to aunt Nancy, in order that she might report to us what was said at Dr. Flint's house. I whispered it to her through a crack, and she whispered back, "I hope it will succeed. I shan't mind being a slave all *my* life, if I can only see you and the children free."

I had directed that my letters should be put into the New York post office on the 20th of the month. On the evening of the 24th my aunt came to say that Dr. Flint and his wife had been talking in a low voice about a letter he had received, and that when he went to his office he promised to bring it when he came to tea. So I concluded I should hear my letter read the next morning. I told my grandmother Dr. Flint would be sure to come, and asked her to have him sit near a certain door, and leave it open, that I might hear what he said. The next morning I took my station within sound of that door, and remained motionless as a statue. It was not long before I heard the gate slam, and the well-known footsteps enter the house. He seated himself in the chair that was placed for him, and said, "Well, Martha, I've brought you a letter from Linda. She has sent me a letter, also. I know exactly where to find her; but I don't choose to go to Boston for her. I had rather she would come back of her own accord, in a respectable manner. Her uncle Phillip is the best person to go for her. With *him,* she would feel perfectly free to act. I am willing to pay his expenses going and returning. She shall be sold to her friends. Her children are free; at least I suppose they are; and when you obtain her freedom, you'll make a happy family. I suppose, Martha, you have no objection to my reading to you the letter Linda has written to you."

He broke the seal, and I heard him read it. The old villain! He had suppressed the letter I wrote to grandmother, and prepared a substitute of his own, the purport of which was as follows:—

> "Dear Grandmother:
> I have long wanted to write to you; but the disgraceful manner in which I left you and my children made me ashamed to do it. If you knew how much I have suffered since I ran away, you would pity and forgive me. I have purchased freedom at a dear rate. If any arrangement could be made for me to return to the south without being a slave, I would gladly come. If not, I beg of you to send my children to the north. I cannot live any longer without them. Let me know in time, and I will meet them in New York or Philadelphia, whichever place best suits my uncle's convenience. Write as soon as possible to your unhappy daughter,
>
> Linda."

"It is very much as I expected it would be," said the old hypocrite, rising to go. "You see the foolish girl has repented of her rashness, and wants to return. We must help her to do it, Martha. Talk with Phillip about it. If he will go for her, she will trust to him, and come back. I should like an answer tomorrow. Good morning, Martha."

As he stepped out on the piazza, he stumbled over my little girl. "Ah, Ellen, is that you?" he said, in his most gracious manner. "I didn't see you. How do you do?"

"Pretty well, sir," she replied. "I heard you tell grandmother that my mother is coming home. I want to see her."

"Yes, Ellen, I am going to bring her home very soon," rejoined he;

"and you shall see her as much as you like, you little curly-headed nigger."

This was as good as a comedy to me, who had heard it all; but grandmother was frightened and distressed, because the doctor wanted my uncle to go for me.

The next evening Dr. Flint called to talk the matter over. My uncle told him that from what he had heard of Massachusetts, he judged he should be mobbed if he went there after a runaway slave. "All stuff and nonsense, Phillip!" replied the doctor. "Do you suppose I want you to kick up a row in Boston? The business can all be done quietly. Linda writes that she wants to come back. You are her relative, and she would trust *you*. The case would be different if I went. She might object to coming with *me;* and the damned abolitionists, if they knew I was her master, would not believe me, if I told them she had begged to go back. They would get up a row; and I should not like to see Linda dragged through the streets like a common negro. She has been very ungrateful to me for all my kindness; but I forgive her, and want to act the part of a friend towards her. I have no wish to hold her as my slave. Her friends can buy her as soon as she arrives here."

Finding that his arguments failed to convince my uncle, the doctor "let the cat out of the bag," by saying that he had written to the mayor of Boston, to ascertain whether there was a person of my description at the street and number from which my letter was dated. He had omitted this date in the letter he had made up to read to my grandmother. If I had dated from New York, the old man would probably have made another journey to that city. But even in that dark region, where knowledge is so carefully excluded from the slave, I had heard enough about Massachusetts to come to the conclusion that slaveholders did not consider it a comfortable place to go to in search of a runaway. That was before the Fugitive Slave Law was passed; before Massachusetts had consented to become a "nigger hunter" for the south.

My grandmother, who had become skittish by seeing her family always in danger, came to me with a very distressed countenance, and said, "What will you do if the mayor of Boston sends him word that you haven't been there? Then he will suspect the letter was a trick; and maybe he'll find out something about it, and we shall all get into trouble. O Linda, I wish you had never sent the letters."

"Don't worry yourself, grandmother," said I. "The mayor of Boston won't trouble himself to hunt niggers for Dr. Flint. The letters will do good in the end. I shall get out of this dark hole some time or other."

"I hope you will, child," replied the good, patient old friend. "You have been here a long time; almost five years; but whenever you do go, it will break your old grandmother's heart. I should be expecting every day to hear that you were brought back in irons and put in jail. God help you, poor child! Let us be thankful that some time or other we shall go "where the wicked cease from troubling, and the weary are at rest." My heart responded, Amen.

The fact that Dr. Flint had written to the mayor of Boston convinced me that he believed my letter to be genuine, and of course that he had no suspicion of my being anywhere in the vicinity. It was a great object to keep up this delusion, for it made me and my friends feel less anxious, and it would be very convenient whenever there was a chance to escape. I resolved, therefore, to continue to write letters from the north from time to time.

Two or three weeks passed, and as no news came from the mayor of Boston, grandmother began to listen to my entreaty to be allowed to leave my cell, sometimes, and exercise my limbs to prevent my becoming a cripple. I was allowed to slip down into the small storeroom, early in the morning, and remain there a little while. The room was all filled up with barrels, except a small open space under my trap-door. This faced the door, the upper part of which was of glass, and purposely left uncurtained, that the curious might look in. The air of this place was close; but it was so much better than the atmosphere of my cell, that I dreaded to return. I came down as soon as it was light, and remained till eight o'clock, when people began to be about, and there was danger that someone might come on the piazza. I had tried various applications to bring warmth and feeling into my limbs, but without avail. They were so numb and stiff that it was a painful effort to move; and had my enemies come upon me during the first mornings I tried to exercise them a little in the small unoccupied space of the storeroom, it would have been impossible for me to have escaped.

XXVI

Important Era in My Brother's Life

I MISSED THE COMPANY and kind attentions of my brother William, who had gone to Washington with his master, Mr. Sands. We received several letters from him, written without any allusion to me, but expressed in such a manner that I knew he did not forget me. I disguised my hand, and wrote to him in the same manner. It was a long session; and when it closed, William wrote to inform us that Mr. Sands was going to the north, to be gone some time, and that he was to accompany him. I knew that his master had promised to give him his freedom, but no time had been specified. Would William trust to a slave's chances? I remembered how we used to talk together, in our young days, about obtaining our freedom, and I thought it very doubtful whether he would come back to us.

Grandmother received a letter from Mr. Sands, saying that William had proved a most faithful servant, and he would also say a valued friend; that no mother had ever trained a better boy. He said he had travelled through the Northern States and Canada; and though the abolitionists had tried to decoy him away, they had never succeeded. He ended by saying they should be at home shortly.

We expected letters from William, describing the novelties of his journey, but none came. In time, it was reported that Mr. Sands would return late in the autumn, accompanied by a bride. Still no letters from William. I felt almost sure I should never see him again on southern soil; but had he no word of comfort to send to his friends at home? to the poor captive in her dungeon? My thoughts wandered through the dark past, and over the uncertain future. Alone in my cell, where no eye but God's could see me, I wept bitter tears. How earnestly I prayed to him to restore me to my children, and enable me to be a useful woman and a good mother!

At last the day arrived for the return of the travellers. Grandmother had made loving preparations to welcome her absent boy back to the old hearthstone. When the dinner table was laid, William's plate occupied its old place. The stage coach went by empty. My grandmother waited dinner. She thought perhaps he was necessarily detained by his master. In my prison I listened anxiously, expecting every moment to hear my dear brother's voice and step. In the course of the afternoon a lad was sent by Mr. Sands to tell grandmother that William did not return with him; that the abolitionists had decoyed him away. But he begged her not to feel troubled about it, for he felt confident she would see William in a few days. As soon as he had time to reflect he would come back, for he could never expect to be so well off at the north as he had been with him.

If you had seen the tears, and heard the sobs, you would have thought the messenger had brought tidings of death instead of freedom. Poor old grandmother felt that she should never see her darling boy again. And I was selfish. I thought more of what I had lost, than of what my brother had gained. A new anxiety began to trouble me. Mr. Sands had expended a good deal of money, and would naturally feel irritated by the loss he had incurred. I greatly feared this might injure the prospects of my children, who were now becoming valuable property. I longed to have their emancipation made certain. The more so, because their master and father was now married. I was too familiar with slavery not to know that promises made to slaves, though with kind intentions, and sincere at the time, depend upon many contingencies for their fulfilment.

Much as I wished William to be free, the step he had taken made me sad and anxious. The following Sabbath was calm and clear; so beautiful that it seemed like a Sabbath in the eternal world. My grandmother brought the children out on the piazza, that I might hear their voices. She thought it would comfort me in my despondency; and it did. They chatted merrily, as only children can. Benny said, "Grandmother, do you think uncle Will has gone for good? Won't he ever come back again? Maybe he'll find mother. If he does, *won't* she be glad to see him! Why don't you and uncle Phillip, and all of us, go and live where mother is? I should like it; wouldn't you, Ellen?"

"Yes, I should like it," replied Ellen; "but how could we find her? Do you know the place, grandmother? I don't remember how mother looked—do you, Benny?"

Benny was just beginning to describe me when they were interrupted by an old slave woman, a near neighbor, named Aggie. This poor creature had witnessed the sale of her children, and seen them carried off to parts unknown, without any hopes of ever hearing from them again. She saw that my grandmother had been weeping, and she said, in a sympathizing tone, "What's the matter, aunt Marthy?"

"O Aggie," she replied, "it seems as if I shouldn't have any of my children or grandchildren left to hand me a drink when I'm dying, and lay my old body in the ground. My boy didn't come back with Mr. Sands. He stayed at the north."

Poor old Aggie clapped her hands for joy. "Is *dat* what you's crying fur?" she exclaimed. "Git down on your knees and bress de Lord! I don't know whar my poor chillern is, and I nebber 'spect to know. You don't know whar poor Linda's gone to; but you *do* know whar her brudder is. He's in free parts; and dat's de right place. Don't murmur at de Lord's doings, but git down on your knees and tank him for his goodness."

My selfishness was rebuked by what poor Aggie said. She rejoiced over the escape of one who was merely her fellow-bondman, while his own sister was only thinking what his good fortune might cost her children. I knelt and prayed God to forgive me; and I thanked him from my heart, that one of my family was saved from the grasp of slavery.

It was not long before we received a letter from William. He wrote that Mr. Sands had always treated him kindly, and that he had tried to do his duty to him faithfully. But ever since he was a boy, he had longed to be free; and he had already gone through enough to convince him he had better not lose the chance that offered. He concluded by saying, "Don't worry about me, dear grandmother. I shall think of you always; and it will spur me on to work hard and try to do right. When I have earned money enough to give you a home, perhaps you will come to the north, and we can all live happy together."

Mr. Sands told my uncle Phillip the particulars about William's leaving him. He said, "I trusted him as if he were my own brother, and treated him as kindly. The abolitionists talked to him in several places; but I had no idea they could tempt him. However, I don't blame William. He's young and inconsiderate, and those Northern rascals decoyed him. I must confess the scamp was very bold about it. I met him coming down the steps of the Astor House with his trunk on his shoulder, and I asked him where he was going. He said he was going to change his old trunk. I told him it was rather shabby, and asked if he didn't need some money. He said, No, thanked me, and went off. He did not return so soon as I expected; but I waited patiently. At last I went to see if our trunks were packed, ready for our journey. I found them locked, and a sealed note on the table informed me where I could find the keys. The fellow even tried to be religious. He wrote that he hoped God would always bless me, and reward me for my kindness; that he was not unwilling to serve me; but he wanted to be a free man; and that if I thought he did wrong, he hoped I would forgive him. I intended to give him his freedom in five years. He might have trusted me. He has shown himself ungrateful; but I shall not go for him, or send for him. I feel confident that he will soon return to me."

I afterwards heard an account of the affair from William himself. He had not been urged away by abolitionists. He needed no information they could give him about slavery to stimulate his desire for freedom. He looked at his hands, and remembered that they were once in irons. What security had he that they would not be so again? Mr. Sands was kind to him; but he might indefinitely postpone the promise he had made to give him his freedom. He might come under pecuniary embarrassments, and his property be seized by creditors; or he might die, without making any arrangements in his favor. He had too often known such accidents to happen to slaves who had kind masters, and he wisely resolved to make sure of the present opportunity to own himself. He was scrupulous about taking any money from his master on false pretenses; so he sold his best clothes to pay for his passage to Boston. The slaveholders pronounced him a base, ungrateful wretch, for thus requiting his master's indulgence. What would *they* have done under similar circumstances?

When Dr. Flint's family heard that William had deserted Mr. Sands, they chuckled greatly over the news. Mrs. Flint made her usual manifestations of Christian feeling, by saying, "I'm glad of it. I hope he'll never get him again. I like to see people paid back in their own coin. I reckon Linda's children will have to pay for it. I should be glad to see them in the speculator's hands again, for I'm tired of seeing those little niggers march about the streets."

XXVII

New Destination for the Children

MRS. FLINT proclaimed her intention of informing Mrs. Sands who was the father of my children. She likewise proposed to tell her what an artful devil I was; that I had made a great deal of trouble in her family; that when Mr. Sands was at the north, she didn't doubt I had followed him in disguise, and persuaded William to run away. She had some reason to entertain such an idea; for I had written from the north, from time to time, and I dated my letters from various places. Many of them fell into Dr. Flint's hands, as I expected they would; and he must have come to the conclusion that I travelled about a good deal. He kept a close watch over my children, thinking they would eventually lead to my detection.

A new and unexpected trial was in store for me. One day, when Mr. Sands and his wife were walking in the street, they met Benny. The lady took a fancy to him, and exclaimed, "What a pretty little negro! Whom does he belong to?"

Benny did not hear the answer; but he came home very indignant with the stranger lady, because she had called him a negro. A few days afterwards, Mr. Sands called on my grandmother, and told her he wanted her to take the children to his house. He said he had informed his wife of his relation to them, and told her they were motherless; and she wanted to see them.

When he had gone, my grandmother came and asked what I would do. The question seemed a mockery. What *could* I do? They were Mr. Sands's slaves, and their mother was a slave, whom he had represented to be dead. Perhaps he thought I was. I was too much pained and puzzled to come to any decision; and the children were carried without my knowledge.

Mrs. Sands had a sister from Illinois staying with her. This lady, who had no children of her own, was so much pleased with Ellen, that she offered to adopt her, and bring her up as she would a daughter. Mrs. Sands wanted to take Benjamin. When grandmother reported this to me, I was tried almost beyond endurance. Was this all I was to gain by what I had suffered for the sake of having my children free? True, the prospect *seemed* fair; but I knew too well how lightly slaveholders held such "parental relations." If pecuniary troubles should come, or if the new wife required more money than could conveniently be spared, my children might be thought of as a convenient means of raising funds. I had no trust in thee, O Slavery! Never should I know peace till my children were emancipated with all due formalities of law.

I was too proud to ask Mr. Sands to do anything for my own benefit; but I could bring myself to become a supplicant for my children. I resolved to remind him of the promise he had made me, and to throw myself upon his honor for the performance of it. I persuaded my grandmother to go to him, and tell him I was not dead, and that I earnestly entreated him to keep the promise he had made me; that I had heard of the recent proposals concerning my children, and did not feel easy to accept them; that he had promised to emancipate them, and it was time for him to redeem his pledge. I knew there was some risk in thus betraying that I was in the vicinity; but what will not a mother do for her children? He received the message with surprise, and said, "The children are free. I have never intended to claim them as slaves. Linda may decide their fate. In my opinion, they had better be sent to the north. I don't think they are quite safe here. Dr. Flint boasts that they are still in his power. He says they were his daughter's property, and as she was not of age when they were sold, the contract is not legally binding."

So, then, after all I had endured for their sakes, my poor children were between two fires; between my old master and their new master! And I was powerless. There was no protecting arm of the law for me to invoke. Mr. Sands proposed that Ellen should go, for the present, to some of his relatives, who had removed to Brooklyn, Long Island. It was promised that she should be well taken care of, and sent to school. I consented to it, as the best arrangement I could make for her. My grandmother, of course, negotiated it all; and Mrs. Sands knew of no other person in the transaction. She proposed that they should take Ellen with them to Washington, and keep her till they had a good chance of sending her, with friends, to Brooklyn. She had an infant daughter. I had had a glimpse of it, as the nurse passed with it in her arms. It was not a pleasant thought to me, that the bondwoman's child should tend her free-born sister; but there was no alternative. Ellen was made ready for the journey. O, how it tried my heart to send her away, so young, alone, among strangers! Without a mother's love to shelter her from the storms of life; almost without memory of a mother! I doubted whether she and Benny would have for me the natural affection that children feel for a parent. I thought to myself that I might perhaps never see my daughter again, and I had a great desire that she should look upon me, before she went, that she might take my image with her in her memory. It seemed to me cruel to have her brought to my dungeon. It was sorrow enough for her young heart to know that her mother was a victim of slavery, without seeing the wretched hiding-place to which it had driven her. I begged permission to pass the last night in one of the open chambers, with my little girl. They thought I was crazy to think of trusting such a young child with my perilous secret. I told them I had watched her character, and I felt sure she would not betray me; that I was determined to have an interview, and if they would not facilitate it, I would take my own way to obtain it. They remonstrated against the rashness of such a proceeding; but finding they could not change my purpose, they yielded. I slipped through the trap-door into the storeroom, and my uncle kept watch at the gate, while I passed into the piazza and went upstairs, to the room I used to occupy. It was more than five years since I had seen it; and how the memories crowded on me! There I had taken shelter when my mistress drove me from her house; there came my old tyrant, to mock, insult, and curse me; there my children were first laid in my arms; there I had watched over them, each day with a deeper and sadder love; there I had knelt to God, in anguish of heart, to forgive the wrong I had done.

How vividly it all came back! And after this long, gloomy interval, I stood there such a wreck!

In the midst of these meditations, I heard footsteps on the stairs. The door opened, and my uncle Phillip came in, leading Ellen by the hand. I put my arms round her, and said, "Ellen, my dear child, I am your mother." She drew back a little, and looked at me; then, with sweet confidence, she laid her cheek against mine, and I folded her to the heart that had been so long desolated. She was the first to speak. Raising her head, she said, inquiringly, "You really *are* my mother?" I told her I really was; that during all the long time she had not seen me, I had loved her most tenderly; and that now she was going away, I wanted to see her and talk with her, that she might remember me. With a sob in her voice, she said, "I'm glad you've come to see me; but why didn't you ever come before? Benny and I have wanted so much to see you! He remembers you, and sometimes he tells me about you. Why didn't you come home when Dr. Flint went to bring you?"

I answered, "I couldn't come before, dear. But now that I am with you, tell me whether you like to go away." "I don't know," said she, crying. "Grandmother says I ought not to cry; that I am going to a good place, where I can learn to read and write, and that by and by I can write her a letter. But I shan't have Benny, or grandmother, or uncle Phillip, or anybody to love me. Can't you go with me? O, *do* go, dear mother!"

I told her I couldn't go now; but sometime I would come to her, and then she and Benny and I would live together, and have happy times. She wanted to run and bring Benny to see me now. I told her he was going to the north, before long, with uncle Phillip, and then I would come to see him before he went away. I asked if she would like to have me stay all night and sleep with her. "O, yes," she replied. Then, turning to her uncle, she said, pleadingly, "*May* I stay? Please, uncle! She is my own mother." He laid his hand on her head, and said, solemnly, "Ellen, this is the secret you have promised grandmother never to tell. If you ever speak of it to anybody, they will never let you see your grandmother again, and your mother can never come to Brooklyn." "Uncle," she replied, "I will never tell." He told her she might stay with me; and when he had gone, I took her in my arms and told her I was a slave, and that was the reason she must never say she had seen me. I exhorted her to be a good child, to try to please the people where she was going, and that God would raise her up friends. I told her to say her prayers, and remember always to pray for her poor mother, and that God would permit us to meet again. She wept, and I did not check her tears. Perhaps she would never again have a chance to pour her tears into a mother's bosom. All night she nestled in my arms, and I had no inclination to slumber. The moments were too precious to lose any of them. Once, when I thought she was asleep, I kissed her forehead softly, and she said, "I am not asleep, dear mother."

Before dawn they came to take me back to my den. I drew aside the window curtain, to take a last look of my child. The moonlight shone on her face, and I bent over her, as I had done years before, that wretched night when I ran away. I hugged her close to my throbbing heart; and tears, too sad for such young eyes to shed, flowed down her cheeks, as she gave her last kiss, and whispered in my ear, "Mother, I will never tell." And she never did.

When I got back to my den, I threw myself on the bed and wept there alone in the darkness. It seemed as if my heart would burst. When the time for Ellen's departure drew nigh, I could hear neighbors and friends saying to her, "Goodby, Ellen. I hope your poor mother will find you out. *Won't* you be glad to see her!" She replied, "Yes, ma'am;" and they little dreamed of the weighty secret that weighed down her young heart. She was an affectionate child, but naturally very reserved, except with those she loved, and I felt secure that my secret would be safe with her. I heard the gate close after her, with such feelings as only a slave mother can experience. During the day my meditations were very sad. Sometimes I feared I had been very selfish not to give up all claim to her, and let her go to Illinois, to be adopted by Mrs. Sands's sister. It was my experience of slavery that decided me against it. I feared that circumstances might arise that would cause her to be sent back. I felt confident that I should go to New York myself; and then I should be able to watch over her, and in some degree protect her.

Dr. Flint's family knew nothing of the proposed arrangement till after Ellen was gone, and the news displeased them greatly. Mrs. Flint called on Mrs. Sands's sister to inquire into the matter. She expressed her opinion very freely as to the respect Mr. Sands showed for his wife, and for his own character, in acknowledging those "young niggers." And as for sending Ellen away, she pronounced it to be just as much stealing as it would be for him to come and take a piece of furniture out of her parlor. She said her daughter was not of age to sign the bill of sale, and the children were her property; and when she became of age, or was married, she could take them, wherever she could lay hands on them.

Miss Emily Flint, the little girl to whom I had been bequeathed, was now in her sixteenth year. Her mother considered it all right and honorable for her, or her future husband, to steal my children; but she did not understand how anybody could hold up their heads in respectable society, after they had purchased their own children, as Mr. Sands had done. Dr. Flint said very little. Perhaps he thought that Benny would be less likely to be sent away if he kept quiet. One of my letters, that fell into his hands, was dated from Canada; and he seldom spoke of me now. This state of things enabled me to slip down into the storeroom more frequently, where I could stand upright, and move my limbs more freely.

Days, weeks, and months passed, and there came no news of Ellen. I sent a letter to Brooklyn, written in my grandmother's name, to inquire whether she had arrived there. Answer was returned that she had not. I wrote to her in Washington; but no notice was taken of it. There was one person there, who ought to have had some sympathy with the anxiety of the child's friends at home; but the links of such relations as he had formed with me, are easily broken and cast away as rubbish. Yet how protectingly and persuasively he once talked to the poor, helpless slave girl! And how entirely I trusted him! But now suspicions darkened my mind. Was my child dead, or had they deceived me, and sold her?

If the secret memoirs of many members of Congress should be published, curious details would be unfolded. I once saw a letter from a member of Congress to a slave, who was the mother of six of his children. He wrote to request that she would send her children away from the great house before his return, as he expected to be accompanied by friends. The woman could not read, and was obliged to employ another to read the letter. The existence of the colored children did not trouble this gentleman, it was only the fear that friends might recognize in their features a resemblance to him.

At the end of six months, a letter came to my grandmother, from Brooklyn. It was written by a young lady in the family, and announced that Ellen had just arrived. It contained the following message from her: "I do try to do just as you told me to, and I pray for you every night and morning." I understood that these words were meant for me; and they were a balsam to my heart. The writer closed her letter by saying, "Ellen is a nice little girl, and we shall like to have her with us. My cousin, Mr. Sands, has given her to me, to be my little waiting maid. I shall send her to school, and I hope someday she will write to you herself." This letter perplexed and troubled me. Had my child's father merely placed her there till she was old enough to support herself? Or had he given her to his cousin, as a piece of property? If the last idea was correct, his cousin might return to the south at any time, and hold Ellen as a slave. I tried to put away from me the painful thought that such a foul wrong could have been done to us. I said to myself, "Surely there must be *some* justice in man;" then I remembered, with a sigh, how slavery perverted all the natural feelings of the human heart. It gave me a pang to look on my light-hearted boy. He believed himself free; and to have him brought under the yoke of slavery, would be more than I could bear. How I longed to have him safely out of the reach of its power!

XXVIII

Aunt Nancy

I HAVE MENTIONED my great-aunt, who was a slave in Dr. Flint's family, and who had been my refuge during the shameful persecutions I suffered from him. This aunt had been married at twenty years of age; that is, as far as slaves *can* marry. She had the consent of her master and mistress, and a clergyman performed the ceremony. But it was a mere form, without any legal value. Her master or mistress could annul it any day they pleased. She had always slept on the floor in the entry, near Mrs. Flint's chamber door, that she might be within call. When she was married, she was told she might have the use of a small room in an out-house. Her mother and her husband furnished it. He was a seafaring man, and was allowed to sleep there when he was at home. But on the wedding evening, the bride was ordered to her old post on the entry floor.

Mrs. Flint, at that time, had no children; but she was expecting to be a mother, and if she should want a drink of water in the night, what could she do without her slave to bring it? So my aunt was compelled to lie at her door, until one midnight she was forced to leave, to give premature birth to a child. In a fortnight she was required to resume her place on the entry floor, because Mrs. Flint's babe needed her attentions. She kept her station there through summer and winter, until she had given premature birth to six children; and all the while she was employed as night-nurse to Mrs. Flint's children. Finally, toiling all day, and being deprived of rest at night, completely broke down her constitution, and Dr. Flint declared it was impossible she could ever become the mother of a living child. The fear of losing so valuable a servant by death, now induced them to allow her to sleep in her little room in the out-house, except when there was sickness in the family. She afterwards had two feeble babes, one of whom died in a few days, and the other in four weeks. I well remember her patient sorrow as she held the last dead baby in her arms. "I wish it could have lived," she said; "it is not the will of God that any of my children should live. But I will try to be fit to meet their little spirits in heaven."

Aunt Nancy was housekeeper and waiting-maid in Dr. Flint's family. Indeed, she was the *factotum* of the household. Nothing went on well without her. She was my mother's twin sister, and, as far as was in her power, she supplied a mother's place to us orphans. I slept with her all the time I lived in my old master's house, and the bond between us was very strong. When my friends tried to discourage me from running away, she always encouraged me. When they thought I had better return and ask my master's pardon, because there was no possibility of escape, she sent me word never to yield. She said if I persevered I might, perhaps, gain the freedom of my children; and even if I perished in doing it, that was better than to leave them to groan under the same persecutions that had blighted my own life. After I was shut up in my dark cell, she stole away, whenever she could, to bring me the news and say something cheering. How often did I kneel down to listen to her words of consolation, whispered through a crack! "I am old, and have not long to live," she used to say; "and I could die happy if I could only see you and the children free. You must pray to God, Linda, as I do for you, that he will lead you out of this darkness." I would beg her not to worry herself on my account; that there was an end of all suffering sooner or later, and that whether I lived in chains or in freedom, I should always remember her as the good friend who had been the comfort of my life. A word from her always strengthened me; and not me only. The whole family relied upon her judgment, and were guided by her advice.

I had been in my cell six years when my grandmother was summoned to the bedside of this, her last remaining daughter. She was very ill, and they said she would die. Grandmother had not entered Dr. Flint's house for several years. They had treated her cruelly, but she thought nothing of that now. She was grateful for permission to watch by the death-bed of her child. They had always been devoted to each other; and now they sat looking into each other's eyes, longing to speak of the secret that had weighed so much on the hearts of both. My aunt had been stricken with paralysis. She lived but two days, and the last day she was speechless. Before she lost the power of utterance, she told her mother not to grieve if she could not speak to her; that she would try to hold up her hand, to let her know that all was well with her. Even the hard-hearted doctor was a little softened when he saw the dying woman try to smile on the aged mother, who was kneeling by her side. His eyes moistened for a moment, as he said she had always been a faithful servant, and they should never be able to supply her place. Mrs. Flint took to her bed, quite overcome by the shock. While my grandmother sat alone with the dead, the doctor came in, leading his youngest son, who had always been a great pet with aunt Nancy, and was much attached to her. "Martha," said he, "aunt Nancy loved this child, and when he comes where you are, I hope you will be kind to him, for her sake." She replied, "Your wife was my foster-child, Dr. Flint, the foster-sister of my poor Nancy, and you little know me if you think I can feel anything but good will for her children."

"I wish the past could be forgotten, and that we might never think of it," said he; "and that Linda would come to supply her aunt's place. She would be worth more to us than all the money that could be paid for her. I wish it for your sake also, Martha. Now that Nancy is taken away from you, she would be a great comfort to your old age."

He knew he was touching a tender chord. Almost choking with grief, my grandmother replied, "It was not I that drove Linda away. My grandchildren are gone; and of my nine children only one is left. God help me!"

To me, the death of this kind relative was an inexpressible sorrow. I knew that she had been slowly murdered; and I felt that my troubles had helped to finish the work. After I heard of her illness, I listened constantly to hear what news was brought from the great house; and the thought that I could not go to her made me utterly miserable. At last, as uncle Phillip came into the house, I heard someone inquire, "How is she?" and he answered, "She is dead." My little cell seemed whirling round, and I knew nothing more till I opened my eyes and found uncle Phillip bending over me. I had no need to ask any questions. He whispered, "Linda, she died happy." I could not weep. My fixed gaze troubled him. "Don't look *so*," he said. "Don't add to my poor mother's trouble. Remember how much she has to bear, and that we ought to do all we can to comfort her." Ah, yes, that blessed old grandmother, who for seventy-three years had borne the pelting storms of a slave-mother's life. She did indeed need consolation!

Mrs. Flint had rendered her poor foster-sister childless, apparently without any compunction; and with cruel selfishness had ruined her health by years of incessant, unrequited toil, and broken rest. But now she became very sentimental. I suppose she thought it would be a beautiful illustration of the attachment existing between slaveholder and slave, if the body of her old worn-out servant was buried at her feet. She sent for the clergyman and asked if he had any objection to burying aunt Nancy in the doctor's family burial-place. No colored person had ever been allowed interment in the white people's burying-ground, and the minister knew that all the deceased of our family reposed together in the old graveyard of the slaves. He therefore replied, "I have no objection to complying with your wish; but perhaps aunt Nancy's *mother* may have some choice as to where her remains shall be deposited."

It had never occurred to Mrs. Flint that slaves could have any feelings. When my grandmother was consulted, she at once said she wanted Nancy to lie with all the rest of her family, and where her own old body would be buried. Mrs. Flint graciously complied with her wish, though she said it was painful to her to have Nancy buried away from *her*. She might have added with touching pathos, "I was so long *used* to sleep with her lying near me, on the entry floor."

My uncle Phillip asked permission to bury his sister at his own expense; and slaveholders are always ready to grant *such* favors to slaves and their relatives. The arrangements were very plain, but perfectly respectable. She was buried on the Sabbath, and Mrs. Flint's minister read the funeral service. There was a large concourse of colored people, bond and free, and a few white persons who had always been friendly to our family. Dr. Flint's carriage was in the procession; and when the body was deposited in its humble resting place, the mistress dropped a tear, and returned to her carriage, probably thinking she had performed her duty nobly.

It was talked of by the slaves as a mighty grand funeral. Northern travellers, passing through the place, might have described this tribute of respect to the humble dead as a beautiful feature in the "patriarchal institution;" a touching proof of the attachment between slaveholders and their servants; and tender-hearted Mrs. Flint would have confirmed this impression, with handkerchief at her eyes. *We* could have told them a different story. We could have given them a chapter of wrongs and sufferings, that would have touched their hearts, if they *had* any hearts to feel for the colored people. We could have told them how the poor old slave-mother had toiled, year after year, to earn eight hundred dollars to buy her son Phillip's right to his own earnings; and how that same Phillip paid the expenses of the funeral, which they regarded as doing so much credit to the master. We could also have told them of a poor, blighted young creature, shut up in a living grave for years, to avoid the tortures that would be inflicted on her, if she ventured to come out and look on the face of her departed friend.

All this, and much more, I thought of, as I sat at my loophole, waiting for the family to return from the grave; sometimes weeping, sometimes falling asleep, dreaming strange dreams of the dead and the living.

It was sad to witness the grief of my bereaved grandmother. She had always been strong to bear, and now, as ever, religious faith supported her. But her dark life had become still darker, and age and trouble were leaving deep traces on her withered face. She had four places to knock for me to come to the trap-door, and each place had a different meaning. She now came oftener than she had done, and talked to me of her dead daughter, while tears trickled slowly down her furrowed cheeks. I said all I could to comfort her; but it was a sad reflection, that instead of being able to help her, I was a constant source of anxiety and trouble. The poor old back was fitted to its burden. It bent under it, but did not break.

XXIX

Preparations for Escape

I HARDLY EXPECT that the reader will credit me, when I affirm that I lived in that little dismal hole, almost deprived of light and air, and with no space to move my limbs, for nearly seven years. But it is a fact; and to me a sad one, even now; for my body still suffers from the effects of that long imprisonment, to say nothing of my soul. Members of my family, now living in New York and Boston, can testify to the truth of what I say.

Countless were the nights that I sat late at the little loophole scarcely large enough to give me a glimpse of one twinkling star. There, I heard the patrols and slave-hunters conferring together about the capture of runaways, well knowing how rejoiced they would be to catch me.

Season after season, year after year, I peeped at my children's faces, and heard their sweet voices, with a heart yearning all the while to say, "Your mother is here." Sometimes it appeared to me as if ages had rolled away since I entered upon that gloomy, monotonous existence. At times, I was stupefied and listless; at other times I became very impatient to know when these dark years would end, and I should again be allowed to feel the sunshine, and breathe the pure air.

After Ellen left us, this feeling increased. Mr. Sands had agreed that Benny might go to the north whenever his uncle Phillip could go with him; and I was anxious to be there also, to watch over my children, and protect them so far as I was able. Moreover, I was likely to be drowned out of my den, if I remained much longer; for the slight roof was getting badly out of repair, and uncle Phillip was afraid to remove the shingles, lest someone should get a glimpse of me. When storms occurred in the night, they spread mats and bits of carpet, which in the morning appeared to have been laid out to dry; but to cover the roof in the daytime might have attracted attention. Consequently, my clothes and bedding were often drenched; a process by which the pains and aches in my cramped and stiffened limbs were greatly increased. I revolved various plans of escape in my mind, which I sometimes imparted to my grandmother, when she came to whisper with me at the trap-door. The kind-hearted old woman had an intense sympathy for runaways. She had known too much of the cruelties inflicted on those who were captured. Her memory always flew back at once to the sufferings of her bright and handsome son, Benjamin, the youngest and dearest of her flock. So, whenever I alluded to the subject, she would groan out, "O, don't think of it, child. You'll break my heart." I had no good old aunt Nancy now to encourage me; but my brother William and my children were continually beckoning me to the north.

And now I must go back a few months in my story. I have stated that the first of January was the time for selling slaves, or leasing them out to new masters. If time were counted by heart-throbs, the poor slaves might reckon years of suffering during that festival so joyous to the free. On the New Year's day preceding my aunt's death, one of my friends, named Fanny, was to be sold at auction, to pay her master's debts. My thoughts were with her during all the day, and at night I anxiously inquired what had been her fate. I was told that she had been sold to one master, and her four little girls to another master, far distant;

that she had escaped from her purchaser, and was not to be found. Her mother was the old Aggie I have spoken of. She lived in a small tenement belonging to my grandmother, and built on the same lot with her own house. Her dwelling was searched and watched, and that brought the patrols so near me that I was obliged to keep very close in my den. The hunters were somehow eluded; and not long afterwards Benny accidentally caught sight of Fanny in her mother's hut. He told his grandmother, who charged him never to speak of it, explaining to him the frightful consequences; and he never betrayed the trust. Aggie little dreamed that my grandmother knew where her daughter was concealed, and that the stooping form of her old neighbor was bending under a similar burden of anxiety and fear; but these dangerous secrets deepened the sympathy between the two old persecuted mothers.

My friend Fanny and I remained many weeks hidden within call of each other; but she was unconscious of the fact. I longed to have her share my den, which seemed a more secure retreat than her own; but I had brought so much trouble on my grandmother, that it seemed wrong to ask her to incur greater risks. My restlessness increased. I had lived too long in bodily pain and anguish of spirit. Always I was in dread that by some accident, or some contrivance, slavery would succeed in snatching my children from me. This thought drove me nearly frantic, and I determined to steer for the North Star at all hazards. At this crisis, Providence opened an unexpected way for me to escape. My friend Peter came one evening, and asked to speak with me. "Your day has come, Linda," said he. "I have found a chance for you to go to the Free States. You have a fortnight to decide." The news seemed too good to be true; but Peter explained his arrangements, and told me all that was necessary was for me to say I would go. I was going to answer him with a joyful yes, when the thought of Benny came to my mind. I told him the temptation was exceedingly strong, but I was terribly afraid of Dr. Flint's alleged power over my child, and that I could not go and leave him behind. Peter remonstrated earnestly. He said such a good chance might never occur again; that Benny was free, and could be sent to me; and that for the sake of my children's welfare I ought not to hesitate a moment. I told him I would consult with uncle Phillip. My uncle rejoiced in the plan, and bade me go by all means. He promised, if his life was spared, that he would either bring or send my son to me as soon as I reached a place of safety. I resolved to go, but thought nothing had better be said to my grandmother till very near the time of departure. But my uncle thought she would feel it more keenly if I left her so suddenly. "I will reason with her," said he, "and convince her how necessary it is, not only for your sake, but for hers also. You cannot be blind to the fact that she is sinking under her burdens." I was not blind to it. I knew that my concealment was an ever-present source of anxiety, and that the older she grew the more nervously fearful she was of discovery. My uncle talked with her, and finally succeeded in persuading her that it was absolutely necessary for me to seize the chance so unexpectedly offered.

The anticipation of being a free woman proved almost too much for my weak frame. The excitement stimulated me, and at the same time bewildered me. I made busy preparations for my journey, and for my son to follow me. I resolved to have an interview with him before I went, that I might give him cautions and advice, and tell him how anxiously I should be waiting for him at the north. Grandmother stole up to me as often as possible to whisper words of counsel. She insisted upon my writing to Dr. Flint, as soon as I arrived in the Free States, and asking him to sell me to her. She said she would sacrifice her house, and all she had in the world, for the sake of having me safe with my children in any part of the world. If she could only live to know *that* she could die in peace. I promised the dear old faithful friend that I would write to her as soon as I arrived, and put the letter in a safe way to reach her; but in my own mind I resolved that not another cent of her hard earnings should be spent to pay rapacious slaveholders for what they called their property. And even if I had not been unwilling to buy what I had already a right to possess, common humanity would have prevented me from accepting the generous offer, at the expense of turning my aged relative out of house and home, when she was trembling on the brink of the grave.

I was to escape in a vessel; but I forbear to mention any further paticulars. I was in readiness, but the vessel was unexpectedly detained several days. Meantime, news came to town of a most horrible murder committed on a fugitive slave, named James. Charity, the mother of this unfortunate young man, had been an old acquaintance of ours. I have told the shocking particulars of his death, in my description of some of the neighboring slaveholders. My grandmother, always nervously sensitive about runaways, was terribly frightened. She felt sure that a similar fate awaited me, if I did not desist from my enterprise. She sobbed, and groaned, and entreated me not to go. Her excessive fear was somewhat contagious, and my heart was not proof against her extreme agony. I was grievously disappointed, but I promised to relinquish my project.

When my friend Peter was apprised of this, he was both disappointed and vexed. He said, that judging from our past experience, it would be a long time before I had such another chance to throw away. I told him it need not be thrown away; that I had a friend concealed nearby, who would be glad enough to take the place that had been provided for me. I told him about poor Fanny, and the kind-hearted, noble fellow, who never turned his back upon anybody in distress, white or black, expressed his readiness to help her. Aggie was much surprised when she found that we knew her secret. She was rejoiced to hear of such a chance for Fanny, and arrangements were made for her to go on board the vessel the next night. They both supposed that I had long been at the north, therefore my name was not mentioned in the transaction. Fanny was carried on board at the appointed time, and stowed away in a very small cabin. This accommodation had been purchased at a price that would pay for a voyage to England. But when one proposes to go to fine old England, they stop to calculate whether they can afford the cost of the pleasure; while in making a bargain to escape from slavery, the trembling victim is ready to say, "Take all I have, only don't betray me!"

The next morning I peeped through my loophole, and saw that it was dark and cloudy. At night I received news that the wind was ahead, and the vessel had not sailed. I was exceedingly anxious about Fanny, and Peter too, who was running a tremendous risk at my instigation. Next day the wind and weather remained the same. Poor Fanny had been half dead with fright when they carried her on board, and I could readily imagine how she must be suffering now. Grandmother came often to my den, to say how thankful she was I did not go. On the third morning she rapped for me to come down to the storeroom. The poor old sufferer was breaking down under her weight of trouble. She was easily flurried now. I found her in a nervous, excited state, but I was not aware that she had forgotten to lock the door behind her, as usual. She was exceedingly worried about the detention of the vessel. She was afraid all would be discovered, and then Fanny, and Peter, and I, would all be tortured to death, and Phillip would be utterly ruined, and her house would be torn down. Poor Peter! If he should die such a horrible death as the poor slave James had lately done, and all for his kindness in trying to help me, how dreadful it would be for us all! Alas, the thought was familiar to me, and had sent many a sharp pang through my heart. I tried to suppress my own anxiety, and speak soothingly to her. She brought in some allusion to aunt Nancy, the dear daughter she had recently buried, and then she lost all control of herself. As she stood there, trembling and sobbing, a voice from the piazza called out, "Whar is you, aunt Marthy?" Grandmother was startled, and in her agitation opened the door, without thinking of me. In stepped Jenny, the mischievous housemaid, who had tried to enter my room, when I was concealed in the house of my white benefactress. "I's bin huntin ebery whar for you, aunt Marthy," said she. "My missis wants you to send her some crackers." I had slunk down behind a barrel, which entirely screened me, but I imagined that Jenny was looking directly at the spot, and my heart beat violently. My grandmother immediately thought what she had done, and went out quickly with Jenny to count the crackers locking the door after her. She returned to me, in a few minutes, the perfect picture of despair. "Poor child!" she exclaimed, "my carelessness has ruined you. The boat ain't gone yet. Get ready immediately, and go with Fanny. I ain't got another word to say against it now; for there's no telling what may happen this day."

Uncle Phillip was sent for, and he agreed with his mother in thinking that Jenny would inform Dr. Flint in less than twenty-four hours. He advised getting me on board the boat, if possible; if not, I had better keep very still in my den, where they could not find me without tearing the house down. He said it would not do for him to move in the matter, because suspicion would be immediately excited; but he promised to communicate with Peter. I felt reluctant to apply to him again, having implicated him too much already; but there seemed to be no alternative. Vexed as Peter had been by my indecision, he was true to his generous nature, and said at once that he would do his best to help me, trusting I should show myself a stronger woman this time.

He immediately proceeded to the wharf, and found that the wind had shifted, and the vessel was slowly beating down stream. On some pretext of urgent necessity, he offered two boatmen a dollar apiece to catch up with her. He was of lighter complexion than the boatmen he hired, and when the captain saw them coming so rapidly, he thought officers were pursuing his vessel in search of the runaway slave he had on board. They hoisted sails, but the boat gained upon them, and the indefatigable Peter sprang on board.

The captain at once recognized him. Peter asked him to go below, to speak about a bad bill he had given him. When he told his errand, the captain replied, "Why, the woman's here already; and I've put her where you or the devil would have a tough job to find her."

"But it is another woman I want to bring," said Peter. "*She* is in great distress, too, and you shall be paid anything within reason, if you'll stop and take her."

"What's her name?" inquired the captain.

"Linda," he replied.

"That's the name of the woman already here," rejoined the captain. "By George! I believe you mean to betray me."

"O!" exclaimed Peter, "God knows I wouldn't harm a hair of your head. I am too grateful to you. But there really *is* another woman in great danger. Do have the humanity to stop and take her!"

After a while they came to an understanding. Fanny, not dreaming I was anywhere about in that region, had assumed my name, though she called herself Johnson. "Linda is a common name," said Peter, "and the woman I want to bring is Linda Brent."

The captain agreed to wait at a certain place till evening, being handsomely paid for his detention.

Of course, the day was an anxious one for us all. But we concluded that if Jenny had seen me, she would be too wise to let her mistress know of it; and that she probably would not get a chance to see Dr. Flint's family till evening, for I knew very well what were the rules in that household. I afterwards believed that she did not see me; for nothing ever came of it, and she was one of those base characters that would have jumped to betray a suffering fellow being for the sake of thirty pieces of silver.

I made all my arrangements to go on board as soon as it was dusk. The intervening time I resolved to spend with my son. I had not spoken to him for seven years, though I had been under the same roof, and seen him every day, when I was well enough to sit at the loophole. I did not dare to venture beyond the storeroom; so they brought him there, and locked us up together, in a place concealed from the piazza door. It was an agitating interview for both of us. After we had talked and wept together for a little while, he said, "Mother, I'm glad you're going away. I wish I could go with you. I knew you was here; and I have been *so* afraid they would come and catch you!"

I was greatly surprised, and asked him how he had found it out.

He replied, "I was standing under the eaves, one day, before Ellen went away, and I heard somebody cough up over the wood shed. I don't know what made me think it was you, but I did think so. I missed Ellen, the night before she went away; and grandmother brought her back into the room in the night; and I thought maybe she'd been to see *you*, before she went, for I heard grandmother whisper to her, 'Now go to sleep; and remember never to tell.'"

I asked him if he ever mentioned his suspicions to his sister. He said he never did; but after he heard the cough, if he saw her playing with other children on that side of the house, he always tried to coax her round to the other side, for fear they would hear me cough, too. He said he had kept a close lookout for Dr. Flint, and if he saw him speak to a constable, or a patrol, he always told grandmother. I now recollected that I had seen him manifest uneasiness, when people were on that side of the house, and I had at the time been puzzled to conjecture a motive for his actions. Such prudence may seem extraordinary in a boy of twelve years, but slaves, being surrounded by mysteries, deceptions, and dangers, early learn to be suspicious and watchful, and prematurely cautious and cunning. He had never asked a question of grandmother, or uncle Phillip, and I had often heard him chime in with other children, when they spoke of my being at the north.

I told him I was now really going to the Free States, and if he was a good, honest boy, and a loving child to his dear old grandmother, the Lord would bless him, and bring him to me, and we and Ellen would live together. He began to tell me that grandmother had not eaten anything all day. While he was speaking, the door was unlocked, and she came in with a small bag of money, which she wanted me to take. I begged her to keep a part of it, at least, to pay for Benny's being sent to the north; but she insisted, while her tears were falling fast, that I should take the whole. "You may be sick among strangers," she said, "and they would send you to the poorhouse to die." Ah, that good grandmother!

For the last time I went up to my nook. Its desolate appearance no longer chilled me, for the light of hope had risen in my soul. Yet, even with the blessed prospect of freedom before me, I felt very sad at leaving forever that old homestead, where I had been sheltered so long by the dear old grandmother; where I had dreamed my first young dream of love; and where, after that had faded away, my children came to twine themselves so closely round my desolate heart. As the hour approached for me to leave, I again descended to the storeroom. My grandmother and Benny were there. She took me by the hand, and said, "Linda, let us pray." We knelt down together, with my child pressed to my heart, and my other arm round the faithful, loving old friend I was about to leave forever. On no other occasion has it ever been my lot to listen to so fervent a supplication for mercy and protection. It thrilled through my heart, and inspired me with trust in God.

Peter was waiting for me in the street. I was soon by his side, faint in body, but strong of purpose. I did not look back upon the old place, though I felt that I should never see it again.

XXX

Northward Bound

I NEVER COULD TELL how we reached the wharf. My brain was all of a whirl, and my limbs tottered under me. At an appointed place we met my uncle Phillip, who had started before us on a different route, that he might reach the wharf first, and give us timely warning if there was any danger. A row-boat was in readiness. As I was about to step in, I felt something pull me gently, and turning round I saw Benny, looking pale and anxious. He whispered in my ear, "I've been peeping into the doctor's window, and he's at home. Goodby, mother. Don't cry; I'll come." He hastened away. I clasped the hand of my good uncle, to whom I owed so much, and of Peter, the brave, generous friend who had volunteered to run such terrible risks to secure my safety. To this day I remember how his bright face beamed with joy, when he told me he had discovered a safe method for me to escape. Yet that intelligent, enterprising, noble-hearted man was a chattel! liable, by the laws of a country that calls itself civilized, to be sold with horses and pigs! We parted in silence. Our hearts were all too full for words!

Swiftly the boat glided over the water. After a while, one of the sailors said, "Don't be down-hearted, madam. We will take you safely to your husband, in ———." At first I could not imagine what he meant; but I had presence of mind to think that it probably referred to something the captain had told him; so I thanked him, and said I hoped we should have pleasant weather.

When I entered the vessel the captain came forward to meet me. He was an elderly man, with a pleasant countenance. He showed me to a little box of a cabin, where sat my friend Fanny. She started as if she had seen a specter. She gazed on me in utter astonishment, and exclaimed, "Linda, can this be *you?* or is it your ghost?" When we were locked in each other's arms, my overwrought feelings could no longer be restrained. My sobs reached the ears of the captain, who came and very kindly reminded us, that for his safety, as well as our own, it would be prudent for us not to attract any attention. He said that when there was a sail in sight he wished us to keep below; but at other times, he had no objection to our being on deck. He assured us that he would keep a good lookout, and if we acted prudently, he thought we should be in no danger. He had represented us as women going to meet our husbands in ———. We thanked him, and promised to observe carefully all the directions he gave us.

Fanny and I now talked by ourselves, low and quietly, in our little cabin. She told me of the sufferings she had gone through in making her escape, and of her terrors while she was concealed in her mother's house. Above all, she dwelt on the agony of separation from all her children on that dreadful auction day. She could scarcely credit me, when I told her of the place where I had passed nearly seven years. "We have the same sorrows," said I. "No," replied she, "you are going to see your children soon, and there is no hope that I shall ever even hear from mine."

The vessel was soon under way, but we made slow progress. The wind was against us. I should not have cared for this, if we had been out of sight of the town; but until there were miles of water between us and our enemies, we were filled with constant apprehensions that the constables would come on board. Neither could I feel quite at ease with the captain and his men. I was an entire stranger to that class of people, and I had heard that sailors were rough, and sometimes cruel. We were so completely in their power, that if they were bad men, our situation would be dreadful. Now that the captain was paid for our passage, might he not be tempted to make more money by giving us up to those who claimed us as property? I was naturally of a confiding disposition, but slavery had made me suspicious of everybody. Fanny did not share my distrust of the captain or his men. She said she was afraid at first, but she had been on board three days while the vessel lay in the dock, and nobody had betrayed her, or treated her otherwise than kindly.

The captain soon came to advise us to go on deck for fresh air. His friendly and respectful manner, combined with Fanny's testimony, reassured me, and we went with him. He placed us in a comfortable seat, and occasionally entered into conversation. He told us he was a Southerner by birth, and had spent the greater part of his life in the Slave States, and that he had recently lost a brother who traded in slaves. "But," said he, "it is a pitiable and degrading business, and I always felt ashamed to acknowledge my brother in connection with it." As we passed Snaky Swamp, he pointed to it, and said, "There is a slave territory that defies all the laws." I thought of the terrible days I had spent there, and though it was not called Dismal Swamp, it made me feel very dismal as I looked at it.

I shall never forget that night. The balmy air of spring was so refreshing! And how shall I describe my sensations when we were fairly sailing on Chesapeake Bay? O, the beautiful sunshine! the exhilarating breeze! and I could enjoy them without fear or restraint. I had never realized what grand things air and sunlight are till I had been deprived of them.

Ten days after we left land we were approaching Philadelphia. The captain said we should arrive there in the night, but he thought we had better wait till morning, and go on shore in broad daylight, as the best way to avoid suspicion.

I replied, "You know best. But will you stay on board and protect us?"

He saw that I was suspicious, and he said he was sorry, now that he had brought us to the end of our voyage, to find I had so little confidence in him. Ah, if he had ever been a slave he would have known how difficult it was to trust a white man. He assured us that we might sleep through the night without fear; that he would take care we were not left unprotected. Be it said to the honor of this captain, Southerner as he was, that if Fanny and I had been white ladies, and our passage lawfully engaged, he could not have treated us more respectfully. My intelligent friend, Peter, had rightly estimated the character of the man to whose honor he had entrusted us.

The next morning I was on deck as soon as the day dawned. I called Fanny to see the sun rise, for the first time in our lives, on free soil; for such I *then* believed it to be. We watched the reddening sky, and saw the great orb come up slowly out of the water, as it seemed. Soon the waves began to sparkle, and everything caught the beautiful glow. Before us lay the city of strangers. We looked at each other, and the eyes of both were moistened with tears. We had escaped from slavery, and we supposed ourselves to be safe from the hunters. But we were alone in the world, and we had left dear ties behind us; ties cruelly sundered by the demon Slavery.

XXI

Incidents in Philadelphia

I HAD HEARD that the poor slave had many friends at the north. I trusted we should find some of them. Meantime, we would take it for granted that all were friends, till they proved to the contrary. I sought out the kind captain, thanked him for his attentions, and told him I should never cease to be grateful for the service he had rendered us. I gave him a message to the friends I had left at home, and he promised to deliver it. We were placed in a row-boat, and in about fifteen minutes were landed on a wood wharf in Philadelphia. As I stood looking round, the friendly captain touched me on the shoulder, and said, "There is a respectable-looking colored man behind you. I will speak to him about the New York trains, and tell him you wish to go directly on." I thanked him, and asked him to direct me to some shops where I could buy gloves and veils. He did so, and said he would talk with the colored man till I returned. I made what haste I could. Constant exercise on board the vessel, and frequent rubbing with salt water, had nearly restored the use of my limbs. The noise of the great city confused me, but I found the shops, and bought some double veils and gloves for Fanny and myself. The shopman told me they were so many levies. I had never heard the word before, but I did not tell him so. I thought if he knew I was a stranger he might ask me where I came from. I gave him a gold piece, and when he returned the change, I counted it, and found out how much a levy was. I made my way back to the wharf, where the captain introduced me to the colored man, as the Rev. Jeremiah Durham, minister of Bethel church. He took me by the hand, as if I had been an old friend. He told us we were too late for the morning cars to New York, and must wait until the evening, or the next morning. He invited me to go home with him, assuring me that his wife would give me a cordial welcome; and for my friend he would provide a home with one of his neighbors. I thanked him for so much kindness to strangers, and told him if I must be detained, I should like to hunt up some people who formerly went from our part of the country. Mr. Durham insisted that I should dine with him, and then he would assist me in finding my friends. The sailors came to bid us goodby. I shook their hardy hands, with tears in my eyes. They had all been kind to us, and they had rendered us a greater service than they could possibly conceive of.

I had never seen so large a city, or been in contact with so many people in the streets. It seemed as if those who passed looked at us with an expression of curiosity. My face was so blistered and peeled, by sitting on deck, in wind and sunshine, that I thought they could not easily decide to what nation I belonged.

Mrs. Durham met me with a kindly welcome, without asking any questions. I was tired, and her friendly manner was a sweet refreshment. God bless her! I was sure that she had comforted other weary hearts, before I received her sympathy. She was surrounded by her husband and children, in a home made sacred by protecting laws. I thought of my own children, and sighed.

After dinner Mr. Durham went with me in quest of the friends I had spoken of. They went from my native town, and I anticipated much pleasure in looking on familiar faces. They were not at home, and we retraced our steps through streets delightfully clean. On the way, Mr. Durham observed that I had spoken to him of a daughter I expected to meet; that he was surprised, for I looked so young he had taken me for a single woman. He was approaching a subject on which I was extremely sensitive. He would ask about my husband next, I thought, and if I answered him truly, what would he think of me? I told him I had two children, one in New York, the other at the south. He asked some further questions, and I frankly told him some of the most important events of my life. It was painful for me to do it; but I would not deceive him. If he was desirous of being my friend, I thought he ought to know how far I was worthy of it. "Excuse me, if I have tried your feelings," said he. "I did not question you from idle curiosity. I wanted to understand your situation, in order to know whether I could be of any service to you, or your little girl. Your straightforward answers do you credit; but don't answer everybody so openly. It might give some heartless people a pretext for treating you with contempt."

That word *contempt* burned me like coals of fire. I replied, "God alone knows how I have suffered; and He, I, trust, will forgive me. If I am permitted to have my children, I intend to be a good mother, and to live in such a manner that people cannot treat me with contempt."

"I respect your sentiments," said he. "Place your trust in God, and be governed by good principles, and you will not fail to find friends."

When we reached home, I went to my room, glad to shut out the world for a while. The words he had spoken made an indelible impression upon me. They brought up great shadows from the mournful past. In the midst of my meditations I was startled by a knock at the door. Mrs. Durham entered, her face all beaming with kindness, to say that there was an anti-slavery friend downstairs, who would like to see me. I overcame my dread of encountering strangers, and went with her. Many questions were asked concerning my experiences, and my escape from slavery; but I observed how careful they all were not to say anything that might wound my feelings. How gratifying this was, can be fully understood only by those who have been accustomed to be treated as if they were not included within the pale of human beings. The anti-slavery friend had come to inquire into my plans, and to offer assistance, if needed. Fanny was comfortably established, for the present, with a friend of Mr. Durham. The Anti-Slavery Society agreed to pay her expenses to New York. The same was offered to me, but I declined to accept it; telling them that my grandmother had given me sufficient to pay my expenses to the end of my journey. We were urged to remain in Philadelphia a few days, until some suitable escort could be found for us. I gladly accepted the proposition, for I had a dread of meeting slaveholders, and some dread also of railroads. I had never entered a railroad car in my life, and it seemed to me quite an important event.

That night I sought my pillow with feelings I had never carried to it before. I verily believed myself to be a free woman. I was wakeful for a long time, and I had no sooner fallen asleep, than I was roused by fire-bells. I jumped up, and hurried on my clothes. Where I came from, everybody hastened to dress themselves on such occasions. The white people thought a great fire might be used as a good opportunity for insurrection, and that it was best to be in readiness; and the colored people were ordered out to labor in extinguishing the flames. There was but one engine in our town, and colored women and children were often required to drag it to the river's edge and fill it. Mrs. Durham's daughter slept in the same room with me, and seeing that she slept through all the din, I thought it was my duty to wake her. "What's the matter?" said she, rubbing her eyes.

"They're screaming fire in the streets, and the bells are ringing," I replied.

"What of that?" said she, drowsily. "We are used to it. We never get up, without the fire is very near. What good would it do?"

I was quite surprised that it was not necessary for us to go and help fill the engine. I was an ignorant child, just beginning to learn how things went on in great cities.

At daylight, I heard women crying fresh fish, berries, radishes, and various other things. All this was new to me. I dressed myself at an early hour, and sat at the window to watch that unknown tide of life. Philadelphia seemed to me a wonderfully great place. At the breakfast table, my idea of going out to drag the engine was laughed over, and I joined in the mirth.

I went to see Fanny, and found her so well contented among her new friends that she was in no haste to leave. I was also very happy with my kind hostess. She had had advantages for education, and was vastly my superior. Every day, almost every hour, I was adding to my little stock of knowledge. She took me out to see the city as much as she deemed prudent. One day she took me to an artist's room, and showed me the portraits of some of her children. I had never seen any paintings of colored people before, and they seemed to me beautiful.

At the end of five days, one of Mrs. Durham's friends offered to accompany us to New York the following morning. As I held the hand of my good hostess in a parting clasp, I longed to know whether her husband had repeated to her what I had told him. I supposed he had, but she never made any allusion to it. I presume it was the delicate silence of womanly sympathy.

When Mr. Durham handed us our tickets, he said, "I am afraid you will have a disagreeable ride; but I could not procure tickets for the first-class cars."

Supposing I had not given him money enough, I offered more. "O, no," said he, "they could not be had for any money. They don't allow colored people to go in the first-class cars."

This was the first chill to my enthusiasm about the Free States. Colored people were allowed to ride in a filthy box, behind white people, at the south, but there they were not required to pay for the privilege. It made me sad to find how the north aped the customs of slavery.

We were stowed away in a large, rough car, with windows on each side, too high for us to look out without standing up. It was crowded with people, apparently of all nations. There were plenty of beds and cradles, containing screaming and kicking babies. Every other man had a cigar or pipe in his mouth, and jugs of whiskey were handed round freely. The fumes of the whiskey and the dense tobacco smoke were sickening to my senses, and my mind was equally nauseated by the coarse jokes and ribald songs around me. It was a very disagreeable ride. Since that time there has been some improvement in these matters.

XXXII

The Meeting of Mother and Daughter

WHEN WE ARRIVED in New York, I was half crazed by the crowd of coachmen calling out, "Carriage, ma'am?" We bargained with one to take us to Sullivan Street for twelve shillings. A burly Irishman stepped up and said, "I'll tak' ye for sax shillings." The reduction of half the price was an object to us, and we asked if he could take us right away. "Troth an I will, ladies," he replied. I noticed that the hackmen smiled at each other, and I inquired whether his conveyance was decent. "Yes, it's dacent it is, marm. Devil a bit would I be after takin' ladies in a cab that was not dacent." We gave him our checks. He went for the baggage, and soon reappeared, saying, "This way, if you plase, ladies." We followed, and found our trunks on a truck, and we were invited to take our seats on them. We told him that was not what we bargained for, and he must take the trunks off. He swore they should not be touched till we had paid him six shillings. In our situation it was not prudent to attract attention, and I was about to pay him what he required, when a man nearby shook his head for me not to do it. After a great ado we got rid of the Irishman, and had our trunks fastened on a hack. We had been recommended to a boarding-house in Sullivan Street, and thither we drove. There Fanny and I separated. The Anti-Slavery Society provided a home for her, and I afterwards heard of her in prosperous circumstances. I sent for an old friend from my part of the country, who had for some time been doing business in New York. He came immediately. I told him I wanted to go to my daughter, and asked him to aid me in procuring an interview.

I cautioned him not to let it be known to the family that I had just arrived from the south, because they supposed I had been at the north seven years. He told me there was a colored woman in Brooklyn who came from the same town I did, and I had better go to her house, and have my daughter meet me there. I accepted the proposition thankfully, and he agreed to escort me to Brooklyn. We crossed Fulton ferry, went up Myrtle Avenue, and stopped at the house he designated. I was just about to enter, when two girls passed. My friend called my attention to them. I turned, and recognized in the eldest, Sarah, the daughter of a woman who used to live with my grandmother, but who had left the south years ago. Surprised and rejoiced at this unexpected meeting, I threw my arms round her, and inquired concerning her mother.

"You take no notice of the other girl," said my friend. I turned, and there stood my Ellen! I pressed her to my heart, then held her away from me to take a look at her. She had changed a good deal in the two years since I parted from her. Signs of neglect could be discerned by eyes less observing than a mother's. My friend invited us all to go into the house; but Ellen said she had been sent of an errand, which she would do as quickly as possible, and go home and ask Mrs. Hobbs to let her come and see me. It was agreed that I should send for her the next day. Her companion, Sarah, hastened to tell her mother of my arrival. When I entered the house, I found the mistress of it absent, and I waited for her return. Before I saw her, I heard her saying, "Where is Linda Brent? I used to know her father and mother." Soon Sarah came with her mother. So there was quite a company of us, all from my grandmother's neighborhood. These friends gathered round me and questioned me eagerly. They laughed, they cried, and they shouted. They thanked God that I had got away from my persecutors and was safe on Long Island. It was a day of great excitement. How different from the silent days I had passed in my dreary den!

The next morning was Sunday. My first waking thoughts were occupied with the note I was to send to Mrs. Hobbs, the lady with whom Ellen lived. That I had recently come into that vicinity was evident; otherwise I should have sooner inquired for my daughter. It would not do to let them know I had just arrived from the south, for that would involve the suspicion of my having been harbored there, and might bring trouble, if not ruin, on several people.

I like a straightforward course, and am always reluctant to resort to subterfuges. So far as my ways have been crooked, I charge them all upon slavery. It was that system of violence and wrong which now left me no alternative but to enact a falsehood. I began my note by stating that I had recently arrived from Canada, and was very desirous to have my daughter come to see me. She came and brought a message from Mrs. Hobbs, inviting me to her house, and assuring me that I need not have any fears. The conversation I had with my child did not leave my mind at ease. When I asked if she was well treated, she answered yes; but there was no heartiness in the tone, and it seemed to me that she said it from an unwillingness to have me troubled on her account. Before she left me, she asked very earnestly, "Mother, when will you take me to live with you?" It made me sad to think that I could not give her a home till I went to work and earned the means; and that might take me a long time. When she was placed with Mrs. Hobbs, the agreement was that she should be sent to school. She had been there two years, and was now nine years old, and she scarcely knew her letters. There was no excuse for this, for there were good public schools in Brooklyn, to which she could have been sent without expense.

She stayed with me till dark, and I went home with her. I was received in a friendly manner by the family, and all agreed in saying that Ellen was a useful, good girl. Mrs. Hobbs looked me coolly in the face, and said, "I suppose you know that my cousin, Mr. Sands, has *given* her to my eldest daughter. She will make a nice waiting-maid for her when she grows up." I did not answer a word. How *could* she, who knew by experience the strength of a mother's love, and who was perfectly aware of the relation Mr. Sands bore to my children,—how *could* she look me in the face, while she thrust such a dagger into my heart?

I was no longer surprised that they had kept her in such a state of ignorance. Mr. Hobbs had formerly been wealthy, but he had failed, and afterwards obtained a subordinate situation in the Custom House. Perhaps they expected to return to the south someday; and Ellen's knowledge was quite sufficient for a slave's condition. I was impatient to go to work and earn money, that I might change the uncertain position of my children. Mr. Sands had not kept his promise to emancipate them. I had also been deceived about Ellen. What security had I with regard to Benjamin? I felt that I had none.

I returned to my friend's house in an uneasy state of mind. In order to protect my children, it was necessary that I should own myself. I called myself free, and sometimes felt so; but I knew I was insecure. I sat down that night and wrote a civil letter to Dr. Flint, asking him to state the lowest terms on which he would sell me; and as I belonged by law to his daughter, I wrote to her also, making a similar request.

Since my arrival at the north I had not been unmindful of my dear brother William. I had made diligent inquiries for him, and having heard of him in Boston, I went thither. When I arrived there, I found he had gone to New Bedford. I wrote to that place, and was informed he had gone on a whaling voyage, and would not return for some months. I went back to New York to get employment near Ellen. I received an answer from Dr. Flint, which gave me no encouragement. He advised me to return and submit myself to my rightful owners, and then any request I might make would be granted. I lent this letter to a friend, who lost it; otherwise I would present a copy to my readers.

XXXIII

A Home Found

MY GREATEST ANXIETY now was to obtain employment. My health was greatly improved, though my limbs continued to trouble me with swelling whenever I walked much. The greatest difficulty in my way was, that those who employed strangers required a recommendation; and in my peculiar position, I could, of course, obtain no certificates from the families I had so faithfully served.

One day an acquaintance told me of a lady who wanted a nurse for her babe, and I immediately applied for the situation. The lady told me she preferred to have one who had been a mother, and accustomed to the care of infants. I told her I had nursed two babes of my own. She asked me many questions, but, to my great relief, did not require a recommendation from my former employers. She told me she was an English woman, and that was a pleasant circumstance to me, because I had heard they had less prejudice against color than Americans entertained. It was agreed that we should try each other for a week. The trial proved satisfactory to both parties, and I was engaged for a month.

The heavenly Father had been most merciful to me in leading me to this place. Mrs. Bruce was a kind and gentle lady, and proved a true and sympathizing friend. Before the stipulated month expired, the necessity of passing up and down stairs frequently, caused my limbs to swell so painfully, that I became unable to perform my duties. Many ladies would have thoughtlessly discharged me; but Mrs. Bruce made arrangements to save me steps, and employed a physician to attend upon me. I had not yet told her that I was a fugitive slave. She noticed that I was often sad, and kindly inquired the cause. I spoke of being separated from my children, and from relatives who were dear to me; but I did not mention the constant feeling of insecurity which oppressed my spirits. I longed for someone to confide in; but I had been so deceived by white people, that I had lost all confidence in them. If they spoke kind words to me, I thought it was for some selfish purpose. I had entered this family with the distrustful feelings I had brought with me out of slavery; but ere six months had passed, I found that the gentle deportment of Mrs. Bruce and the smiles of her lovely babe were thawing my chilled heart. My narrow mind also began to expand under the influences of her intelligent conversation, and the opportunities for reading, which were gladly allowed me whenever I had leisure from my duties. I gradually became more energetic and more cheerful.

The old feeling of insecurity, especially with regard to my children, often threw its dark shadow across my sunshine. Mrs. Bruce offered me a home for Ellen; but pleasant as it would have been, I did not dare to accept it, for fear of offending the Hobbs family. Their knowledge of my precarious situation placed me in their power; and I felt that it was important for me to keep on the right side of them, till, by dint of labor and economy, I could make a home for my children. I was far from feeling satisfied with Ellen's situation. She was not well cared for. She sometimes came to New York to visit me; but she generally brought a request from Mrs. Hobbs that I would buy her a pair of shoes, or some article of clothing. This was accompanied by a promise of payment when Mr. Hobbs's salary at the Custom House became due; but somehow or other the pay-day never came. Thus many dollars of my earnings were expended to keep my child comfortably clothed. That, however, was a slight trouble, compared with the fear that their pecuniary embarrassments might induce them to sell my precious young daughter. I knew they were in constant communication with Southerners, and had frequent opportunities to do it. I have stated that when Dr. Flint put Ellen in jail, at two years old, she had an inflammation of the eyes, occasioned by measles. This disease still troubled her; and kind Mrs. Bruce proposed that she should come to New York for a while, to be under the care of Dr. Elliott, a well known oculist. It did not occur to me that there was anything improper in a mother's making such a request; but Mrs. Hobbs was very angry, and refused to let her go. Situated as I was, it was not politic to insist upon it. I made no complaint, but I longed to be entirely free to act a mother's part towards my children. The next time I went over to Brooklyn, Mrs. Hobbs, as if to apologize for her anger, told me she had employed her own physician to attend to Ellen's eyes, and that she had refused my request because she did not consider it safe to trust her in New York. I accepted the explanation in silence; but she had told me that my child *belonged* to her daughter, and I suspected that her real motive was a fear of my conveying her property away from her. Perhaps I did her injustice; but my knowledge of Southerners made it difficult for me to feel otherwise.

Sweet and bitter were mixed in the cup of my life, and I was thankful that it had ceased to be entirely bitter. I loved Mrs. Bruce's babe. When it laughed and crowed in my face, and twined its little tender arms confidingly about my neck, it made me think of the time when Benny and

Ellen were babies, and my wounded heart was soothed. One bright morning, as I stood at the window, tossing baby in my arms, my attention was attracted by a young man in sailor's dress, who was closely observing every house as he passed. I looked at him earnestly. Could it be my brother William? It *must* be he—and yet, how changed! I placed the baby safely, flew downstairs, opened the front door, beckoned to the sailor, and in less than a minute I was clasped in my brother's arms. How much we had to tell each other! How we laughed, and how we cried, over each other's adventures! I took him to Brooklyn, and again saw him with Ellen, the dear child whom he had loved and tended so carefully, while I was shut up in my miserable den. He stayed in New York a week. His old feelings of affection for me and Ellen were as lively as ever. There are no bonds so strong as those which are formed by suffering together.

XXXIV

The Old Enemy Again

MY YOUNG MISTRESS, Miss Emily Flint, did not return any answer to my letter requesting her to consent to my being sold. But after a while, I received a reply, which purported to be written by her younger brother. In order rightly to enjoy the contents of this letter, the reader must bear in mind that the Flint family supposed I had been at the north many years. They had no idea that I knew of the doctor's three excursions to New York in search of me; that I had heard his voice, when he came to borrow five hundred dollars for that purpose; and that I had seen him pass on his way to the steamboat. Neither were they aware that all the particulars of aunt Nancy's death and burial were conveyed to me at the time they occurred. I have kept the letter, of which I herewith subjoin a copy:—

"Your letter to sister was received a few days ago. I gather from it that you are desirous of returning to your native place, among your friends and relatives. We were all gratified with the contents of your letter; and let me assure you that if any members of the family have had any feeling of resentment towards you, they feel it no longer. We all sympathize with you in your unfortunate condition, and are ready to do all in our power to make you contented and happy. It is difficult for you to return home as a free person. If you were purchased by your grandmother, it is doubtful whether you would be permitted to remain, although it would be lawful for you to do so. If a servant should be allowed to purchase herself, after absenting herself so long from her owners, and return free, it would have an injurious effect. From your letter, I think your situation must be hard and uncomfortable. Come home. You have it in your power to be reinstated in our affections. We would receive you with open arms and tears of joy. You need not apprehend any unkind treatment, as we have not put ourselves to any trouble or expense to get you. Had we done so, perhaps we should feel otherwise. You know my sister was always attached to you, and that you were never treated as a slave. You were never put to hard work, nor exposed to field labor. On the contrary, you were taken into the house, and treated as one of us, and almost as free; and we, at least, felt that you were above disgracing yourself by running away. Believing you may be induced to come home voluntarily has induced me to write for my sister. The family will be rejoiced to see you; and your poor old grandmother expressed a great desire to have you come, when she heard your letter read. In her old age she needs the consolation of having her children round her. Doubtless you have heard of the death of your aunt. She was a faithful servant, and a faithful member of the Episcopal church. In her Christian life she taught us how to live—and, O, too high the price of knowledge, she taught us how to die! Could you have seen us round her death bed, with her mother, all mingling our tears in one common stream, you would have thought the same heartfelt tie existed between a master and his servant, as between a mother and her child. But this subject is too painful to dwell upon. I must bring my letter to a close. If you are contented to stay away from your old grandmother, your child, and the friends who love you, stay where you are. We shall never trouble ourselves to apprehend you. But should you prefer to come home, we will do all that we can to make you happy. If you do not wish to remain in the family, I know that father, by our persuasion, will be induced to let you be purchased by any person you may choose in our community. You will please answer this as soon as possible, and let us know your decision. Sister sends much love to you. In the mean time believe me your sincere friend and well wisher."

This letter was signed by Emily's brother, who was as yet a mere lad. I knew, by the style, that it was not written by a person of his age, and though the writing was disguised, I had been made too unhappy by it, in former years, not to recognize at once the hand of Dr. Flint. O, the hypocrisy of slaveholders! Did the old fox suppose I was goose enough to go into such a trap? Verily, he relied too much on "the stupidity of the African race." I did not return the family of Flints any thanks for their cordial invitation—a remissness for which I was, no doubt, charged with base ingratitude.

Not long afterwards I received a letter from one of my friends at the south, informing me that Dr. Flint was about to visit the north. The letter had been delayed, and I supposed he might be already on the way. Mrs. Bruce did not know I was a fugitive. I told her that important business called me to Boston, where my brother then was, and asked permission to bring a friend to supply my place as nurse, for a fort-night. I started on my journey immediately; and as soon as I arrived, I wrote to my grandmother that if Benny came, he must be sent to Boston. I knew she was only waiting for a good chance to send him north, and, fortunately, she had the legal power to do so, without asking leave of anybody. She was a free woman; and when my children were purchased, Mr. Sands preferred to have the bill of sale drawn up in her name. It was conjectured that he advanced the money, but it was not known. At the south, a gentleman may have a shoal of colored children without any disgrace; but if he is known to purchase them, with the view of setting them free, the example is thought to be dangerous to their "peculiar institution," and he becomes unpopular.

There was a good opportunity to send Benny in a vessel coming di-rectly to New York. He was put on board with a letter to a friend, who was requested to see him off to Boston. Early one morning, there was a loud rap at my door, and in rushed Benjamin, all out of breath. "O mother!" he exclaimed, "here I am! I run all the way; and I come all alone. How d'you do?"

O reader, can you imagine my joy? No, you cannot, unless you have been a slave mother. Benjamin rattled away as fast as his tongue could go. "Mother, why don't you bring Ellen here? I went over to Brooklyn to see her, and she felt very bad when I bid her goodby. She said, 'O Ben, I wish I was going too.' I thought she'd know ever so much; but she don't know so much as I do; for I can read, and she can't. And, mother, I lost all my clothes coming. What can I do to get some more? I 'spose free boys can get along here at the north as well as white boys."

I did not like to tell the sanguine, happy little fellow how much he was mistaken. I took him to a tailor, and procured a change of clothes. The rest of the day was spent in mutual asking and answering of questions, with the wish constantly repeated that the good old grandmother was with us, and frequent injunctions from Benny to write to her immediately, and be sure to tell her everything about his voyage, and his journey to Boston.

Dr. Flint made his visit to New York, and made every exertion to call upon me, and invite me to return with him; but not being able to ascertain where I was, his hospitable intentions were frustrated, and the affectionate family, who were waiting for me with "open arms," were doomed to disappointment.

As soon as I knew he was safely at home, I placed Benjamin in the care of my brother William, and returned to Mrs. Bruce. There I remained through the winter and spring, endeavoring to perform my duties faithfully, and finding a good degree of happiness in the attractions of baby Mary, the considerate kindness of her excellent mother, and occasional interviews with my darling daughter.

But when summer came, the old feeling of insecurity haunted me. It was necessary for me to take little Mary out daily, for exercise and fresh air, and the city was swarming with Southerners, some of whom might recognize me. Hot weather brings out snakes and slaveholders, and I like one class of the venomous creatures as little as I do the other. What a comfort it is, to be free to *say* so!

XXXV

Prejudice Against Color

IT WAS A RELIEF to my mind to see preparations for leaving the city. We went to Albany in the steamboat *Knickerbocker*. When the gong sounded for tea, Mrs. Bruce said, "Linda, it is late, and you and baby had better come to the table with me." I replied, "I know it is time baby had her supper, but I had rather not go with you, if you please. I am afraid of being insulted." "O no, not if you are with *me*," she said. I saw several white nurses go with their ladies, and I ventured to do the same. We were at the extreme end of the table. I was no sooner seated, than a gruff voice said, "Get up! You know you are not allowed to sit here." I looked up, and, to my astonishment and indignation, saw that the speaker was a colored man. If his office required him to enforce the by-laws of the boat, he might, at least, have done it politely. I replied, "I shall not get up, unless the captain comes and takes me up." No cup of tea was offered me, but Mrs. Bruce handed me hers and called for another. I looked to see whether the other nurses were treated in a similar manner. They were all properly waited on.

Next morning, when we stopped at Troy for breakfast, everybody was making a rush for the table. Mrs. Bruce said, "Take my arm, Linda, and we'll go in together." The landlord heard her, and said, "Madam, will you allow your nurse and baby to take breakfast with my family?" I knew this was to be attributed to my complexion; but he spoke courteously, and therefore I did not mind it.

At Saratoga we found the United States Hotel crowded, and Mr. Bruce took one of the cottages belonging to the hotel. I had thought, with gladness, of going to the quiet of the country, where I should meet few people, but here I found myself in the midst of a swarm of Southerners. I looked round me with fear and trembling, dreading to see someone who would recognize me. I was rejoiced to find that we were to stay but a short time.

We soon returned to New York, to make arrangements for spending the remainder of the summer at Rockaway. While the laundress was putting the clothes in order, I took an opportunity to go over to Brooklyn to see Ellen. I met her going to a grocery store, and the first words she said, were, "O, mother, don't go to Mrs. Hobbs's. Her brother, Mr. Thorne, has come from the south, and maybe he'll tell where you are." I accepted the warning. I told her I was going away with Mrs. Bruce the next day, and would try to see her when I came back.

Being in servitude to the Anglo-Saxon race, I was not put into a "Jim Crow car," on our way to Rockaway, neither was I invited to ride through the streets on the top of trunks in a truck; but everywhere I found the same manifestations of that cruel prejudice, which so discourages the feelings, and represses the energies of the colored people. We reached Rockaway before dark, and put up at the Pavilion—a large hotel, beautifully situated by the sea-side—a great resort of the fashionable world. Thirty or forty nurses were there, of a great variety of nations. Some of the ladies had colored waiting-maids and coachmen, but I was the only nurse tinged with the blood of Africa. When the tea bell rang, I took little Mary and followed the other nurses. Supper was served in a long hall. A young man, who had the ordering of things, took the circuit of the table two or three times, and finally pointed me to a seat at the lower end of it. As there was but one chair, I sat down and took the child in my lap. Whereupon the young man came to me and said, in the blandest manner possible, "Will you please to seat the little girl in the chair, and stand behind it and feed her? After they have done, you will be shown to the kitchen, where you will have a good supper."

This was the climax! I found it hard to preserve my self-control, when I looked round, and saw women who were nurses, as I was, and only one shade lighter in complexion, eyeing me with a defiant look, as if my presence were a contamination. However, I said nothing. I quietly took the child in my arms, went to our room, and refused to go to the table again. Mr. Bruce ordered meals to be sent to the room for little Mary and I. This answered for a few days; but the waiters of the establishment were white, and they soon began to complain, saying they were not hired to wait on negroes. The landlord requested Mr. Bruce to send me down to my meals, because his servants rebelled against bringing them up, and the colored servants of other boarders were dissatisfied because all were not treated alike.

My answer was that the colored servants ought to be dissatisfied with *themselves*, for not having too much self-respect to submit to such treatment; that there was no difference in the price of board for colored and white servants, and there was no justification for difference of treatment. I stayed a month after this, and finding I was resolved to stand up for my rights, they concluded to treat me well. Let every colored man and woman do this, and eventually we shall cease to be trampled under foot by our oppressors.

XXXVI

The Hairbreadth Escape

AFTER WE RETURNED to New York, I took the earliest opportunity to go and see Ellen. I asked to have her called downstairs; for I supposed Mrs. Hobbs's southern brother might still be there, and I was desirous to avoid seeing him, if possible. But Mrs. Hobbs came to the kitchen, and insisted on my going upstairs. "My brother wants to see you," said she, "and he is sorry you seem to shun him. He knows you are living in New York. He told me to say to you that he owes thanks to good old aunt Martha for too many little acts of kindness for him to be base enough to betray her grandchild."

This Mr. Thorne had become poor and reckless long before he left the south, and such persons had much rather go to one of the faithful old slaves to borrow a dollar, or get a good dinner, than to go to one whom they consider an equal. It was such acts of kindness as these for which he professed to feel grateful to my grandmother. I wished he had kept at a distance, but as he was here, and knew where I was, I concluded there was nothing to be gained by trying to avoid him; on the contrary, it might be the means of exciting his ill will. I followed his sister upstairs. He met me in a very friendly manner, congratulated me on my escape from slavery, and hoped I had a good place, where I felt happy.

I continued to visit Ellen as often as I could. She, good thoughtful child, never forgot my hazardous situation, but always kept a vigilant lookout for my safety. She never made any complaint about her own inconveniences and troubles; but a mother's observing eye easily perceived that she was not happy. On the occasion of one of my visits I found her unusually serious. When I asked her what was the matter, she said nothing was the matter. But I insisted upon knowing what made her look so very grave. Finally, I ascertained that she felt troubled about the dissipation that was continually going on in the house. She was sent to the store very often for rum and brandy, and she felt ashamed to ask for it so often; and Mr. Hobbs and Mr. Thorne drank a great deal, and their hands trembled so that they had to call her to pour out the liquor for them. "But for all that," said she, "Mr. Hobbs is good to me, and I can't help liking him. I feel sorry for him." I tried to comfort her, by telling her that I had laid up a hundred dollars, and that before long I hoped to be able to give her and Benjamin a home, and send them to school. She was always desirous not to add to my troubles more than she could help, and I did not discover till years afterwards that Mr. Thorne's intemperance was not the only annoyance she suffered from him. Though he professed too much gratitude to my grandmother to injure any of her descendants, he had poured vile language into the ears of her innocent great-grandchild.

I usually went to Brooklyn to spend Sunday afternoon. One Sunday, I found Ellen anxiously waiting for me near the house. "O, mother," said she, "I've been waiting for you this long time. I'm afraid Mr. Thorne has written to tell Dr. Flint where you are. Make haste and come in. Mrs. Hobbs will tell you all about it!"

The story was soon told. While the children were playing in the grapevine arbor, the day before, Mr. Thorne came out with a letter in his hand, which he tore up and scattered about. Ellen was sweeping the yard at the time, and having her mind full of suspicions of him, she picked up the pieces and carried them to the children, saying, "I wonder who Mr. Thorne has been writing to."

"I'm sure I don't know, and don't care," replied the oldest of the children; "and I don't see how it concerns you."

"But it does concern me," replied Ellen; "for I'm afraid he's been writing to the south about my mother."

They laughed at her, and called her a silly thing, but good-naturedly put the fragments of writing together, in order to read them to her. They were no sooner arranged, than the little girl exclaimed, "I declare, Ellen, I believe you are right."

The contents of Mr. Thorne's letter, as nearly as I can remember, were as follows: "I have seen your slave, Linda, and conversed with her. She can be taken very easily, if you manage prudently. There are enough of us here to swear to her identity as your property. I am a patriot, a lover of my country, and I do this as an act of justice to the laws." He concluded by informing the doctor of the street and number where I lived. The children carried the pieces to Mrs. Hobbs, who immediately went to her brother's room for an explanation. He was not to be found. The servants said they saw him go out with a letter in his hand, and they supposed he had gone to the post office. The natural inference was, that he had sent to Dr. Flint a copy of those fragments. When he returned, his sister accused him of it, and he did not deny the charge. He went immediately to his room, and the next morning he was missing. He had gone over to New York, before any of the family were astir.

It was evident that I had no time to lose; and I hastened back to the city with a heavy heart. Again I was to be torn from a comfortable home, and all my plans for the welfare of my children were to be frustrated by that demon Slavery! I now regretted that I never told Mrs. Bruce my story. I had not concealed it merely on account of being a fugitive; that would have made her anxious, but it would have excited sympathy in her kind heart. I valued her good opinion, and I was afraid of losing it, if I told her all the particulars of my sad story. But now I felt that it was necessary for her to know how I was situated. I had once left her abruptly, without explaining the reason, and it would not be proper to do it again. I went home resolved to tell her in the morning.

But the sadness of my face attracted her attention, and, in answer to her kind inquiries, I poured out my full heart to her, before bed time. She listened with true womanly sympathy, and told me she would do all she could to protect me. How my heart blessed her!

Early the next morning, Judge Vanderpool and Lawyer Hopper were consulted. They said I had better leave the city at once, as the risk would be great if the case came to trial. Mrs. Bruce took me in a carriage to the house of one of her friends, where she assured me I should be safe until my brother could arrive, which would be in a few days. In the interval my thoughts were much occupied with Ellen. She was mine by birth, and she was also mine by Southern law, since my grandmother held the bill of sale that made her so. I did not feel that she was safe unless I had her with me. Mrs. Hobbs, who felt badly about her brother's treachery, yielded to my entreaties, on condition that she should return in ten days. I avoided making any promise. She came to me clad in very thin garments, all outgrown, and with a school satchel on her arm, containing a few articles. It was late in October, and I knew the child must suffer; and not daring to go out in the streets to purchase any thing, I took off my own flannel skirt and converted it into one for her. Kind Mrs. Bruce came to bid me goodby, and when she saw that I had taken off my clothing for my child, the tears came to her eyes. She said, "Wait for me, Linda," and went out. She soon returned with a nice warm shawl and hood for Ellen. Truly, of such souls as hers are the kingdom of heaven.

My brother reached New York on Wednesday. Lawyer Hopper advised us to go to Boston by the Stonington route, as there was less Southern travel in that direction. Mrs. Bruce directed her servants to tell all inquirers that I formerly lived there, but had gone from the city.

We reached the steamboat *Rhode Island* in safety. That boat employed colored hands, but I knew that colored passengers were not admitted to the cabin. I was very desirous for the seclusion of the cabin, not only on account of exposure to the night air, but also to avoid observation. Lawyer Hopper was waiting on board for us. He spoke to the stewardess, and asked, as a particular favor, that she would treat us well. He said to me, "Go and speak to the captain yourself by and by. Take your little girl with you, and I am sure that he will not let her sleep on deck." With these kind words and a shake of the hand he departed.

The boat was soon on her way, bearing me rapidly from the friendly home where I had hoped to find security and rest. My brother had left me to purchase the tickets, thinking that I might have better success than he would. When the stewardess came to me, I paid what she asked, and she gave me three tickets with clipped corners. In the most unsophisticated manner I said, "You have made a mistake; I asked you for cabin tickets. I cannot possibly consent to sleep on deck with my little daughter." She assured me there was no mistake. She said on some of the routes colored people were allowed to sleep in the cabin, but not on this route, which was much travelled by the wealthy. I asked her to show me to the captain's office, and she said she would after tea. When the time came, I took Ellen by the hand and went to the captain, politely requesting him to change our tickets, as we should be very uncomfortable on deck. He said it was contrary to their custom, but he would see that we had berths below; he would also try to obtain comfortable seats for us in the cars; of that he was not certain, but he would speak to the conductor about it, when the boat arrived. I thanked him, and returned to the ladies' cabin. He came afterwards and told me that the conductor of the cars was on board, that he had spoken to him, and he had promised to take care of us. I was very much surprised at receiving so much kindness. I don't know whether the pleasing face of my little girl had won his heart, or whether the stewardess inferred from Lawyer Hopper's manner that I was a fugitive, and had pleaded with him in my behalf.

When the boat arrived at Stonington, the conductor kept his promise, and showed us to seats in the first car, nearest the engine. He asked us to take seats next the door, but as he passed through, we ventured to move on toward the other end of the car. No incivility was offered us, and we reached Boston in safety.

The day after my arrival was one of the happiest of my life. I felt as if I was beyond the reach of the bloodhounds; and, for the first time during many years, I had both my children together with me. They greatly enjoyed their reunion, and laughed and chatted merrily. I watched them with a swelling heart. Their every motion delighted me.

I could not feel safe in New York, and I accepted the offer of a friend, that we should share expenses and keep house together. I represented to Mrs. Hobbs that Ellen must have some schooling, and must remain with me for that purpose. She felt ashamed of being unable to read or spell at her age, so instead of sending her to school with Benny, I instructed her myself till she was fitted to enter an intermediate school. The winter passed pleasantly, while I was busy with my needle, and my children with their books.

XXXVII

A Visit to England

IN THE SPRING, sad news came to me. Mrs. Bruce was dead. Never again, in this world, should I see her gentle face, or hear her sympathizing voice. I had lost an excellent friend, and little Mary had lost a tender mother. Mr. Bruce wished the child to visit some of her mother's relatives in England, and he was desirous that I should take charge of her. The little motherless one was accustomed to me, and attached to me, and I thought she would be happier in my care than in that of a stranger. I could also earn more in this way than I could by my needle. So I put Benny to a trade, and left Ellen to remain in the house with my friend and go to school.

We sailed from New York, and arrived in Liverpool after a pleasant voyage of twelve days. We proceeded directly to London, and took lodgings at the Adelaide Hotel. The supper seemed to me less luxurious than those I had seen in American hotels; but my situation was indescribably more pleasant. For the first time in my life I was in a place where I was treated according to my deportment, without reference to my complexion. I felt as if a great millstone had been lifted from my breast. Ensconced in a pleasant room, with my dear little charge, I laid my head on my pillow, for the first time, with the delightful consciousness of pure, unadulterated freedom.

As I had constant care of the child, I had little opportunity to see the wonders of that great city; but I watched the tide of life that flowed through the streets, and found it a strange contrast to the stagnation in our Southern towns. Mr. Bruce took his little daughter to spend some days with friends in Oxford Crescent, and of course it was necessary for me to accompany her. I had heard much of the systematic method of English education, and I was very desirous that my dear Mary should steer straight in the midst of so much propriety. I closely observed her little playmates and their nurses, being ready to take any lessons in the science of good management. The children were more rosy than American children, but I did not see that they differed materially in other respects. They were like all children—sometimes docile and sometimes wayward.

We next went to Steventon, in Berkshire. It was a small town, said to be the poorest in the county. I saw men working in the fields for six shillings, and seven shillings, a week, and women for sixpence, and sevenpence, a day, out of which they boarded themselves. Of course they lived in the most primitive manner; it could not be otherwise, where a woman's wages for an entire day were not sufficient to buy a pound of meat. They paid very low rents, and their clothes were made of the cheapest fabrics, though much better than could have been procured in the United States for the same money. I had heard much about the oppression of the poor in Europe. The people I saw around me were, many of them, among the poorest poor. But when I visited them in their little thatched cottages, I felt that the condition of even the meanest and most ignorant among them was vastly superior to the condition of the most favored slaves in America. They labored hard; but they were not ordered out to toil while the stars were in the sky, and driven and slashed by an overseer, through heat and cold, till the stars shone out again. Their homes were very humble; but they were protected by law. No insolent patrols could come, in the dead of night, and flog them at their pleasure. The father, when he closed his cottage door, felt safe with his family around him. No master or overseer could come and take from him his wife, or his daughter. They must separate to earn their living; but the parents knew where their children were going, and could communicate with them by letters. The relations of husband and wife, parent and child, were too sacred for the richest noble in the land to violate with impunity. Much was being done to enlighten these poor people. Schools were established among them, and benevolent societies were active in efforts to ameliorate their condition. There was no law forbidding them to learn to read and write; and if they helped each other in spelling out the Bible, they were in no danger of thirty-nine lashes, as was the case with myself and poor, pious, old uncle Fred. I repeat that the most ignorant and the most destitute of these peasants was a thousand fold better off than the most pampered American slave.

I do not deny that the poor are oppressed in Europe. I am not disposed to paint their condition so rose-colored as the Hon. Miss Murray paints the condition of the slaves in the United States. A small portion of *my* experience would enable her to read her own pages with anointed eyes. If she were to lay aside her title, and, instead of visiting among the fashionable, become domesticated, as a poor governess, on some plantation in Louisiana or Alabama, she would see and hear things that would make her tell quite a different story.

My visit to England is a memorable event in my life, from the fact of my having there received strong religious impressions. The contemptuous manner in which the communion had been administered to colored people, in my native place; the church membership of Dr. Flint, and others like him; and the buying and selling of slaves, by professed ministers of the gospel, had given me a prejudice against the Episcopal church. The whole service seemed to me a mockery and a sham. But my home in Steventon was in the family of a clergyman, who was a true disciple of Jesus. The beauty of his daily life inspired me with faith in the genuineness of Christian professions. Grace entered my heart, and I knelt at the communion table, I trust, in true humility of soul.

I remained abroad ten months, which was much longer than I had anticipated. During all that time, I never saw the slightest symptom of prejudice against color. Indeed, I entirely forgot it, till the time came for us to return to America.

XXXVIII

Renewed Invitation to Go South

WE HAD A TEDIOUS winter passage, and from the distance specters seemed to rise up on the shores of the United States. It is a sad feeling to be afraid of one's native country. We arrived in New York safely, and I hastened to Boston to look after my children. I found Ellen well, and improving at her school; but Benny was not there to welcome me. He had been left at a good place to learn a trade, and for several months everything worked well. He was liked by the master, and was a favorite with his fellow-apprentices; but one day they accidentally discovered a fact they had never before suspected—that he was colored! This at once transformed him into a different being. Some of the apprentices were Americans, others American-born Irish; and it was offensive to their dignity to have a "nigger" among them, after they had been told that he *was* a "nigger." They began by treating him with silent scorn, and finding that he returned the same, they resorted to insults and abuse. He was too spirited a boy to stand that, and he went off. Being desirous to do something to support himself, and having no one to advise him, he shipped for a whaling voyage. When I received these tidings I shed many tears, and bitterly reproached myself for having left him so long. But I had done it for the best, and now all I could do was to pray to the heavenly Father to guide and protect him.

Not long after my return, I received the following letter from Miss Emily Flint, now Mrs. Dodge:—

"In this you will recognize the hand of your friend and mistress. Having heard that you had gone with a family to Europe, I have waited to hear of your return to write to you. I should have answered the letter you wrote to me long since, but as I could not then act independently of my father, I knew there could be nothing done satisfactory to you. There were persons here who were willing to buy you and run the risk of getting you. To this I would not consent. I have always been attached to you, and would not like to see you the slave of another, or have unkind treatment. I am married now, and can protect you. My husband expects to move to Virginia this spring, where we think of settling. I am very anxious that you should come and live with me. If you are not willing to come, you may purchase yourself; but I should prefer having you live with me. If you come, you may, if you like, spend a month with your grandmother and friends, then come to me in Norfolk, Virginia. Think this over, and write as soon as possible, and let me know the conclusion. Hoping that your children are well, I remain you friend and mistress."

Of course I did not write to return thanks for this cordial invitation. I felt insulted to be thought stupid enough to be caught by such professions.

> "'Come up into my parlor,' said the spider to the fly;
> ''Tis the prettiest little parlor that ever you did spy.'"

It was plain that Dr. Flint's family were apprised of my movements, since they knew of my voyage to Europe. I expected to have further trouble from them; but having eluded them thus far, I hoped to be as successful in future. The money I had earned, I was desirous to devote to the education of my children, and to secure a home for them. It seemed not only hard, but unjust, to pay for myself. I could not possibly regard myself as a piece of property. Moreover, I had worked many years without wages, and during that time had been obliged to depend on my grandmother for many comforts in food and clothing. My children certainly belonged to me; but though Dr. Flint had incurred no expense for their support, he had received a large sum of money for them. I knew the law would decide that I was his property, and would probably still give his daughter a claim to my children; but I regarded such laws as the regulations of robbers, who had no rights that I was bound to respect.

The Fugitive Slave Law had not then passed. The judges of Massachusetts had not then stooped under chains to enter her courts of justice, so called. I knew my old master was rather skittish of Massachusetts. I relied on her love of freedom, and felt safe on her soil. I am now aware that I honored the old Commonwealth beyond her deserts.

XXXIX

The Confession

FOR TWO YEARS my daughter and I supported ourselves comfortably in Boston. At the end of that time, my brother William offered to send Ellen to a boarding school. It required a great effort for me to consent to part with her, for I had few near ties, and it was her presence that made my two little rooms seem home-like. But my judgment prevailed over my selfish feelings. I made preparations for her departure. During the two years we had lived together I had often resolved to tell her something about her father; but I had never been able to muster sufficient courage. I had a shrinking dread of diminishing my child's love. I knew she must have curiosity on the subject, but she had never asked a question. She was always very careful not to say anything to remind me of my troubles. Now that she was going from me, I thought if I should die before she returned, she might hear my story from someone who did not understand the palliating circumstances; and that if she were entirely ignorant on the subject, her sensitive nature might receive a rude shock.

When we retired for the night, she said, "Mother, it is very hard to leave you alone. I am almost sorry I am going, though I do want to improve myself. But you will write to me often; won't you, mother?"

I did not throw my arms round her. I did not answer her. But in a calm, solemn way, for it cost me great effort, I said, "Listen to me, Ellen; I have something to tell you!" I recounted my early sufferings in slavery, and told her how nearly they had crushed me. I began to tell her how they had driven me into a great sin, when she clasped me in her arms, and exclaimed, "O, don't, mother! Please don't tell me any more."

I said, "But, my child, I want you to know about your father."

"I know all about it, mother," she replied; "I am nothing to my father, and he is nothing to me. All my love is for you. I was with him five months in Washington, and he never cared for me. He never spoke to me as he did to his little Fanny. I knew all the time he was my father, for

Fanny's nurse told me so; but she said I must never tell anybody, and I never did. I used to wish he would take me in his arms and kiss me, as he did Fanny; or that he would sometimes smile at me, as he did at her. I thought if he was my own father, he ought to love me. I was a little girl then, and didn't know any better. But now I never think anything about my father. All my love is for you." She hugged me closer as she spoke, and I thanked God that the knowledge I had so much dreaded to impart had not diminished the affection of my child. I had not the slightest idea she knew that portion of my history. If I had, I should have spoken to her long before; for my pent-up feelings had often longed to pour themselves out to someone I could trust. But I loved the dear girl better for the delicacy she had manifested towards her unfortunate mother.

The next morning, she and her uncle started on their journey to the village in New York, where she was to be placed at school. It seemed as if all the sunshine had gone away. My little room was dreadfully lonely. I was thankful when a message came from a lady, accustomed to employ me, requesting me to come and sew in her family for several weeks. On my return, I found a letter from brother William. He thought of opening an anti-slavery reading room in Rochester, and combining with it the sale of some books and stationery; and he wanted me to unite with him. We tried it, but it was not successful. We found warm anti-slavery friends there, but the feeling was not general enough to support such an establishment. I passed nearly a year in the family of Isaac and Amy Post, practical believers in the Christian doctrine of human brotherhood. They measured a man's worth by his character, not by his complexion. The memory of those beloved and honored friends will remain with me to my latest hour.

XL

The Fugitive Slave Law

MY BROTHER, being disappointed in his project, concluded to go to California; and it was agreed that Benjamin should go with him. Ellen liked her school, and was a great favorite there. They did not know her history, and she did not tell it, because she had no desire to make capital out of their sympathy. But when it was accidentally discovered that her mother was a fugitive slave, every method was used to increase her advantages and diminish her expenses.

I was alone again. It was necessary for me to be earning money, and I preferred that it should be among those who knew me. On my return from Rochester, I called at the house of Mr. Bruce, to see Mary, the darling little babe that had thawed my heart, when it was freezing into a cheerless distrust of all my fellow-beings. She was growing a tall girl now, but I loved her always. Mr. Bruce had married again, and it was proposed that I should become nurse to a new infant. I had but one hesitation, and that was my feeling of insecurity in New York, now greatly increased by the passage of the Fugitive Slave Law. However, I resolved to try the experiment. I was again fortunate in my employer. The new Mrs. Bruce was an American, brought up under aristocratic influences, and still living in the midst of them; but if she had any prejudice against color, I was never made aware of it; and as for the system of slavery, she had a most hearty dislike of it. No sophistry of Southerners could blind her to its enormity. She was a person of excellent principles and a noble heart. To me, from that hour to the present, she has been a true and sympathizing friend. Blessings be with her and hers!

About the time that I reëntered the Bruce family, an event occurred of disastrous import to the colored people. The slave Hamlin, the first fugitive that came under the new law, was given up by the bloodhounds of the north to the bloodhounds of the south. It was the beginning of a reign of terror to the colored population. The great city rushed on in its whirl of excitement, taking no note of the "short and simple annals of the poor." But while fashionables were listening to the thrilling voice of Jenny Lind in Metropolitan Hall, the thrilling voices of poor hunted colored people went up, in an agony of supplication, to the Lord, from Zion's church. Many families, who had lived in the city for twenty years, fled from it now. Many a poor washerwoman, who, by hard labor, had made herself a comfortable home, was obliged to sacrifice her furniture, bid a hurried farewell to friends, and seek her fortune among strangers in Canada. Many a wife discovered a secret she had never known before—that her husband was a fugitive, and must leave her to insure his own safety. Worse still, many a husband discovered that his wife had fled from slavery years ago, and as "the child follows the condition of its mother," the children of his love were liable to be seized and carried into slavery. Everywhere, in those humble homes, there was consternation and anguish. But what cared the legislators of the "dominant race" for the blood they were crushing out of trampled hearts?

When my brother William spent his last evening with me, before he went to California, we talked nearly all the time of the distress brought on our oppressed people by the passage of this iniquitous law; and never had I seen him manifest such bitterness of spirit, such stern hostility to our oppressors. He was himself free from the operation of the law; for he did not run from any Slaveholding State, being brought into the Free States by his master. But I was subject to it; and so were hundreds of intelligent and industrious people all around us. I seldom ventured into the streets; and when it was necessary to do an errand for Mrs. Bruce, or any of the family, I went as much as possible through back streets and by-ways. What a disgrace to a city calling itself free, that inhabitants, guiltless of offense, and seeking to perform their duties conscientiously, should be condemned to live in such incessant fear, and have nowhere to turn for protection! This state of things, of course, gave rise to many impromptu vigilance committees. Every colored person, and every friend of their persecuted race, kept their eyes wide open. Every evening I examined the newspapers carefully, to see what Southerners had put up at the hotels. I did this for my own sake, thinking my young mistress and her husband might be among the list; I wished also to give information to others, if necessary; for if many were "running to and fro," I resolved that "knowledge should be increased."

This brings up one of my Southern reminiscences, which I will here briefly relate. I was somewhat acquainted with a slave named Luke, who belonged to a wealthy man in our vicinity. His master died, leaving a son and daughter heirs to his large fortune. In the division of the slaves, Luke was included in the son's portion. This young man became a prey to the vices growing out of the "patriarchal institution," and when he went to the north, to complete his education, he carried his vices with him. He was brought home, deprived of the use of his limbs, by excessive dissipation. Luke was appointed to wait upon his bed-ridden master, whose despotic habits were greatly increased by exasperation at his own helplessness. He kept a cowhide beside him, and, for the most trivial occurrence, he would order his attendant to bare his back, and kneel beside the couch, while he whipped him till his strength was exhausted. Some days he was not allowed to wear anything but his shirt, in order to be in readiness to be flogged. A day seldom passed without his receiving more or less blows. If the slightest resistance was offered, the town constable was sent for to execute the punishment, and Luke learned from experience how much more the constable's strong arm was to be dreaded than the comparatively feeble one of his master. The arm of his tyrant grew weaker, and was finally palsied; and then the constable's services were in constant requisition. The fact that he was entirely dependent on Luke's care, and was obliged to be tended like an infant, instead of inspiring any gratitude or compassion towards his poor slave, seemed only to increase his irritability and cruelty. As he lay there on his bed, a mere degraded wreck of manhood, he took into his head the strangest freaks of despotism; and if Luke hesitated to submit to his orders, the constable was immediately sent for. Some of these freaks were of a nature too filthy to be repeated. When I fled from the house of bondage, I left poor Luke still chained to the bedside of this cruel and disgusting wretch.

One day, when I had been requested to do an errand for Mrs. Bruce, I was hurrying through back streets, as usual, when I saw a young man approaching, whose face was familiar to me. As he came nearer, I recognized Luke. I always rejoiced to see or hear of anyone who had escaped from the black pit; but, remembering this poor fellow's extreme hardships, I was peculiarly glad to see him on Northern soil, though I no longer called it *free* soil. I well remembered what a desolate feeling it was to be alone among strangers, and I went up to him and greeted him cordially. At first, he did not know me; but when I mentioned my name, he remembered all about me. I told him of the Fugitive Slave Law, and asked him if he did not know that New York was a city of kidnappers.

He replied, "De risk ain't so bad for me, as 'tis fur you. 'Cause I runned away from de speculator, and you runned away from de massa. Dem speculators vont spen dar money to come here fur a runaway, if dey ain't sartin sure to put dar hans right on him. An I tell you I's tuk good car 'bout dat. I had too hard times down dar, to let 'em ketch dis nigger."

He then told me of the advice he had received, and the plans he had laid. I asked if he had money enough to take him to Canada. " 'Pend upon it, I hab," he replied. "I tuk car fur dat. I'd bin workin all my days fur dem cussed whites, an got no pay but kicks and cuffs. So I tought dis nigger had a right to money nuff to bring him to de Free States. Massa Henry he lib till ebery body vish him dead; an ven he did die, I knowed de debbil would hab him, an vouldn't vant him to bring his money 'long too. So I tuk some of his bills, and put 'em in de pocket of his ole trousers. An ven he was buried, dis nigger ask fur dem ole trousers, an dey gub 'em to me." With a low, chuckling laugh, he added, "You see I didn't *steal* it; dey *gub* it to me. I tell you, I had mighty hard time to keep de speculator from findin it; but he didn't git it."

This is a fair specimen of how the moral sense is educated by slavery. When a man has his wages stolen from him, year after year, and the laws sanction and enforce the theft, how can he be expected to have more regard to honesty than has the man who robs him? I have become somewhat enlightened, but I confess that I agree with poor, ignorant, much-abused Luke, in thinking he had a *right* to that money, as a portion of his unpaid wages. He went to Canada forthwith, and I have not since heard from him.

All that winter I lived in a state of anxiety. When I took the children out to breathe the air, I closely observed the countenances of all I met. I dreaded the approach of summer, when snakes and slaveholders make their appearance. I was, in fact, a slave in New York, as subject to slave laws as I had been in a Slave State. Strange incongruity in a State called free!

Spring returned, and I received warning from the south that Dr. Flint knew of my return to my old place, and was making preparations to have me caught. I learned afterwards that my dress, and that of Mrs. Bruce's children, had been described to him by some of the Northern tools, which slaveholders employ for their base purposes, and then indulge in sneers at their cupidity and mean servility.

I immediately informed Mrs. Bruce of my danger, and she took prompt measures for my safety. My place as nurse could not be supplied immediately, and this generous, sympathizing lady proposed that I should carry her baby away. It was a comfort to me to have the child with me; for the heart is reluctant to be torn away from every object it loves. But how few mothers would have consented to have one of their own babes become a fugitive, for the sake of a poor, hunted nurse, on whom the legislators of the country had let loose the bloodhounds! When I spoke of the sacrifice she was making, in depriving herself of her dear baby, she replied, "It is better for you to have baby with you, Linda; for if they get on your track, they will be obliged to bring the child to me; and then, if there is a possibility of saving you, you shall be saved."

This lady had a very wealthy relative, a benevolent gentleman in many respects, but aristocratic and pro-slavery. He remonstrated with her for harboring a fugitive slave; told her she was violating the laws of her country; and asked her if she was aware of the penalty. She replied, "I am very well aware of it. It is imprisonment and one thousand dollars fine. Shame on my country that it *is* so! I am ready to incur the penalty. I will go to the state's prison, rather than have any poor victim torn from *my* house, to be carried back to slavery."

The noble heart! The brave heart! The tears are in my eyes while I write of her. May the God of the helpless reward her for her sympathy with my persecuted people!

I was sent into New England, where I was sheltered by the wife of a senator, whom I shall always hold in grateful remembrance. This honorable gentleman would not have voted for the Fugitive Slave Law, as did the senator in "Uncle Tom's Cabin;" on the contrary, he was strongly opposed to it; but he was enough under its influence to be afraid of having me remain in his house many hours. So I was sent into the country, where I remained a month with the baby. When it was supposed that Dr. Flint's emissaries had lost track of me, and given up the pursuit for the present, I returned to New York.

XLI

Free at Last

MRS. BRUCE, and every member of her family, were exceedingly kind to me. I was thankful for the blessings of my lot, yet I could not always wear a cheerful countenance. I was doing harm to no one; on the contrary, I was doing all the good I could in my small way; yet I could never go out to breathe God's free air without trepidation at my heart. This seemed hard; and I could not think it was a right state of things in any civilized country.

From time to time I received news from my good old grandmother. She could not write; but she employed others to write for her. The following is an extract from one of her last letters:—

"Dear Daughter:
I cannot hope to see you again on earth; but I pray to God to unite us above, where pain will no more rack this feeble body of mine; where sorrow and parting from my children will be no more. God has promised these things if we are faithful unto the end. My age and feeble health deprive me of going to church now; but God is with me

here at home. Thank your brother for his kindness. Give much love to him, and tell him to remember the Creator in the days of his youth, and strive to meet me in the Father's kingdom. Love to Ellen and Benjamin. Don't neglect him. Tell him for me, to be a good boy. Strive, my child; to train them for God's children. May he protect and provide for you, is the prayer of your loving old mother."

These letters both cheered and saddened me. I was always glad to have tidings from the kind, faithful old friend of my unhappy youth; but her messages of love made my heart yearn to see her before she died, and I mourned over the fact that it was impossible. Some months after I returned from my flight to New England, I received a letter from her, in which she wrote, "Dr. Flint is dead. He has left a distressed family. Poor old man! I hope he made his peace with God."

I remembered how he had defrauded my grandmother of the hard earnings she had loaned; how he had tried to cheat her out of the freedom her mistress had promised her, and how he had persecuted her children; and I thought to myself that she was a better Christian than I was, if she could entirely forgive him. I cannot say, with truth, that the news of my old master's death softened my feelings towards him. There are wrongs which even the grave does not bury. The man was odious to me while he lived, and his memory is odious now.

His departure from this world did not diminish my danger. He had threatened my grandmother that his heirs should hold me in slavery after he was gone; that I never should be free so long as a child of his survived. As for Mrs. Flint, I had seen her in deeper afflictions than I supposed the loss of her husband would be, for she had buried several children; yet I never saw any signs of softening in her heart. The doctor had died in embarrassed circumstances, and had little to will to his heirs, except such property as he was unable to grasp. I was well aware what I had to expect from the family of Flints; and my fears were confirmed by a letter from the south, warning me to be on my guard, because Mrs. Flint openly declared that her daughter could not afford to lose so valuable a slave as I was.

I kept close watch of the newspapers for arrivals; but one Saturday night, being much occupied, I forgot to examine the *Evening Express* as usual. I went down into the parlor for it, early in the morning, and found the boy about to kindle a fire with it. I took it from him and examined the list of arrivals. Reader, if you have never been a slave, you cannot imagine the acute sensation of suffering at my heart, when I read the names of Mr. and Mrs. Dodge, at a hotel in Courtland Street. It was a third-rate hotel, and that circumstance convinced me of the truth of what I had heard, that they were short of funds and had need of my value, as *they* valued me; and that was by dollars and cents. I hastened with the paper to Mrs. Bruce. Her heart and hand were always open to everyone in distress, and she always warmly sympathized with mine. It was impossible to tell how near the enemy was. He might have passed and repassed the house while we were sleeping. He might at that moment be waiting to pounce upon me if I ventured out of doors. I had never seen the husband of my young mistress, and therefore I could not distinguish him from any other stranger. A carriage was hastily ordered; and, closely veiled, I followed Mrs. Bruce, taking the baby again with me into exile. After various turnings and crossings, and returnings, the carriage stopped at the house of one of Mrs. Bruce's friends, where I was kindly received. Mrs. Bruce returned immediately, to instruct the domestics what to say if anyone came to inquire for me.

It was lucky for me that the evening paper was not burned up before I had a chance to examine the list of arrivals. It was not long after Mrs. Bruce's return to her house, before several people came to inquire for me. One inquired for me, another asked for my daughter Ellen, and another said he had a letter from my grandmother, which he was requested to deliver in person.

They were told, "She *has* lived here, but she has left."

"How long ago?"

"I don't know, sir."

"Do you know where she went?"

"I do not, sir." And the door was closed.

This Mr. Dodge, who claimed me as his property, was originally a Yankee pedlar in the south; then he became a merchant, and finally a slaveholder. He managed to get introduced into what was called the first society, and married Miss Emily Flint. A quarrel arose between him and her brother, and the brother cowhided him. This led to a family feud, and he proposed to remove to Virginia. Dr. Flint left him no property, and his own means had become circumscribed, while a wife and children depended upon him for support. Under these circumstances, it was very natural that he should make an effort to put me into his pocket.

I had a colored friend, a man from my native place, in whom I had the most implicit confidence. I sent for him, and told him that Mr. and

Mrs. Dodge had arrived in New York. I proposed that he should call upon them to make inquiries about his friends at the south, with whom Dr. Flint's family were well acquainted. He thought there was no impropriety in his doing so, and he consented. He went to the hotel, and knocked at the door of Mr. Dodge's room, which was opened by the gentleman himself, who gruffly inquired, "What brought you here? How came you to know I was in the city?"

"Your arrival was published in the evening papers, sir; and I called to ask Mrs. Dodge about my friends at home. I didn't suppose it would give any offense."

"Where's that negro girl, that belongs to my wife?"

"What girl, sir?"

"You know well enough. I mean Linda, that ran away from Dr. Flint's plantation, some years ago. I dare say you've seen her, and know where she is."

"Yes, sir, I've seen her, and know where she is. She is out of your reach, sir."

"Tell me where she is, or bring her to me, and I will give her a chance to buy her freedom."

"I don't think it would be of any use, sir. I have heard her say she would go to the ends of the earth, rather than pay any man or woman for her freedom, because she thinks she has a right to it. Besides, she couldn't do it, if she would, for she has spent her earnings to educate her children."

This made Mr. Dodge very angry, and some high words passed between them. My friend was afraid to come where I was; but in the course of the day I received a note from him. I supposed they had not come from the south, in the winter, for a pleasure excursion; and now the nature of their business was very plain.

Mrs. Bruce came to me and entreated me to leave the city the next morning. She said her house was watched, and it was possible that some clue to me might be obtained. I refused to take her advice. She pleaded with an earnest tenderness, that ought to have moved me; but I was in a bitter, disheartened mood. I was weary of flying from pillar to post. I had been chased during half my life, and it seemed as if the chase was never to end. There I sat, in that great city, guiltless of crime, yet not daring to worship God in any of the churches. I heard the bells ringing for afternoon service, and, with contemptuous sarcasm, I said, "Will the preachers take for their text, 'Proclaim liberty to the captive, and the opening of prison doors to them that are bound'? or will they preach from the text, 'Do unto others as ye would they should do unto you'?" Oppressed Poles and Hungarians could find a safe refuge in that city; John Mitchell was free to proclaim in the City Hall his desire for "a plantation well stocked with slaves;" but there I sat, an oppressed American, not daring to show my face. God forgive the black and bitter thoughts I indulged on that Sabbath day! The Scripture says, "Oppression makes even a wise man mad;" and I was not wise.

I had been told that Mr. Dodge said his wife had never signed away her right to my children, and if he could not get me, he would take them. This it was, more than anything else, that roused such a tempest in my soul. Benjamin was with his uncle William in California, but my innocent young daughter had come to spend a vacation with me. I thought of what I had suffered in slavery at her age, and my heart was like a tiger's when a hunter tries to seize her young.

Dear Mrs. Bruce! I seem to see the expression of her face, as she turned away discouraged by my obstinate mood. Finding her expostulations unavailing, she sent Ellen to entreat me. When ten o'clock in the evening arrived and Ellen had not returned, this watchful and unwearied friend became anxious. She came to us in a carriage, bringing a well-filled trunk for my journey—trusting that by this time I would listen to reason. I yielded to her, as I ought to have done before.

The next day, baby and I set out in a heavy snow storm, bound for New England again. I received letters from the City of Iniquity, addressed to me under an assumed name. In a few days one came from Mrs. Bruce, informing me that my new master was still searching for me, and that she intended to put an end to this persecution by buying my freedom. I felt grateful for the kindness that prompted this offer, but the idea was not so pleasant to me as might have been expected. The more my mind had become enlightened, the more difficult it was for me to consider myself an article of property; and to pay money to those who had so grievously oppressed me seemed like taking from my sufferings the glory of triumph. I wrote to Mrs. Bruce, thanking her, but saying that being sold from one owner to another seemed too much like slavery; that such a great obligation could not be easily cancelled; and that I preferred to go to my brother in California.

Without my knowledge, Mrs. Bruce employed a gentleman in New York to enter into negotiations with Mr. Dodge. He proposed to pay three hundred dollars down, if Mr. Dodge would sell me, and enter into obligations to relinquish all claim to me or my children forever after. He who called himself my master said he scorned so small an offer for such a valuable servant. The gentleman replied, "You can do as you choose, sir. If you reject this offer you will never get anything; for the woman has friends who will convey her and her children out of the country."

Mr. Dodge concluded that "half a loaf was better than no bread," and he agreed to the proffered terms. By the next mail I received this brief letter from Mrs. Bruce: "I am rejoiced to tell you that the money for your freedom has been paid to Mr. Dodge. Come home tomorrow. I long to see you and my sweet babe."

My brain reeled as I read these lines. A gentleman near me said, "It's true; I have seen the bill of sale." "The bill of sale!" Those words struck me like a blow. So I was *sold* at last! A human being *sold* in the free city of New York! The bill of sale is on record, and future generations will learn from it that women were articles of traffic in New York, late in the nineteenth century of the Christian religion. It may hereafter prove a useful document to antiquaries, who are seeking to measure the progress of civilization in the United States. I well know the value of that bit of paper; but much as I love freedom, I do not like to look upon it. I am deeply grateful to the generous friend who procured it, but I despise the miscreant who demanded payment for what never rightfully belonged to him or his.

I had objected to having my freedom bought, yet I must confess that when it was done I felt as if a heavy load had been lifted from my weary shoulders. When I rode home in the cars I was no longer afraid to unveil my face and look at people as they passed. I should have been glad to have met Daniel Dodge himself; to have had him seen me and known me, that he might have mourned over the untoward circumstances which compelled him to sell me for three hundred dollars.

When I reached home, the arms of my benefactress were thrown round me, and our tears mingled. As soon as she could speak, she said, "O Linda, I'm *so* glad it's all over! You wrote to me as if you thought you were going to be transferred from one owner to another. But I did not buy you for your services. I should have done just the same, if you had been going to sail for California tomorrow. I should, at least, have the satisfaction of knowing that you left me a free woman."

My heart was exceedingly full. I remembered how my poor father had tried to buy me, when I was a small child, and how he had been disappointed. I hoped his spirit was rejoicing over me now. I remembered how my good old grandmother had laid up her earnings to purchase me in later years, and how often her plans had been frustrated. How that faithful, loving old heart would leap for joy, if she could look on me and my children now that we were free! My relatives had been foiled in all their efforts, but God had raised me up a friend among strangers, who had bestowed on me the precious, long-desired boon. Friend! It is a common word, often lightly used. Like other good and beautiful things, it may be tarnished by careless handling; but when I speak of Mrs. Bruce as my friend, the word is sacred.

My grandmother lived to rejoice in my freedom; but not long after, a letter came with a black seal. She had gone "where the wicked cease from troubling, and the weary are at rest."

Time passed on, and a paper came to me from the south, containing an obituary notice of my uncle Phillip. It was the only case I ever knew of such an honor conferred upon a colored person. It was written by one of his friends, and contained these words: "Now that death has laid him low, they call him a good man and a useful citizen; but what are eulogies to the black man, when the world has faded from his vision? It does not require man's praise to obtain rest in God's kingdom." So they called a colored man a *citizen!* Strange words to be uttered in that region!

Reader, my story ends with freedom; not in the usual way, with marriage. I and my children are now free! We are as free from the power of slaveholders as are the white people of the north; and though that, according to my ideas, is not saying a great deal, it is a vast improvement in *my* condition. The dream of my life is not yet realized. I do not sit with my children in a home of my own. I still long for a hearthstone of my own, however humble. I wish it for my children's sake far more than for my own. But God so orders circumstances as to keep me with my friend Mrs. Bruce. Love, duty, gratitude, also bind me to her side. It is a privilege to serve her who pities my oppressed people, and who has bestowed the inestimable boon of freedom on me and my children.

It has been painful to me, in many ways, to recall the dreary years I passed in bondage. I would gladly forget them if I could. Yet the retrospection is not altogether without solace; for with those gloomy recollections come tender memories of my good old grandmother, like light, fleecy clouds floating over a dark and troubled sea.

Appendix.

The following statement is from Amy Post, a member of the Society of Friends in the State of New York, well known and highly respected by friends of the poor and the oppressed. As has been already stated, in the preceding pages, the author of this volume spent some time under her hospitable roof. L.M.C.

"The author of this book is my highly-esteemed friend. If its readers knew her as I know her, they could not fail to be deeply interested in her story. She was a beloved inmate of our family nearly the whole of the year 1849. She was introduced to us by her affectionate and conscientious brother, who had previously related to us some of the almost incredible events in his sister's life. I immediately became much interested in Linda; for her appearance was prepossessing, and her deportment indicated remarkable delicacy of feeling and purity of thought.

"As we became acquainted, she related to me, from time to time some of the incidents in her bitter experiences as a slave-woman. Though impelled by a natural craving for human sympathy, she passed through a baptism of suffering, even in recounting her trials to me, in private confidential conversations. The burden of these memories lay heavily upon her spirit—naturally virtuous and refined. I repeatedly urged her to consent to the publication of her narrative; for I felt that it would arouse people to a more earnest work for the disenthralment of millions still remaining in that soul-crushing condition, which was so unendurable to her. But her sensitive spirit shrank from publicity. She said, 'You know a woman can whisper her cruel wrongs in the ear of a dear friend much easier than she can record them for the world to read.' Even in talking with me, she wept so much, and seemed to suffer such mental agony, that I felt her story was too sacred to be drawn from her by inquisitive questions, and I left her free to tell as much, or as little, as she chose. Still, I urged upon her the duty of publishing her experience, for the sake of the good it might do; and, at last, she undertook the task.

"Having been a slave so large a portion of her life, she is unlearned; she is obliged to earn her living by her own labor, and she has worked untiringly to procure education for her children; several times she has been obliged to leave her employments, in order to fly from the man-hunters and woman-hunters of our land; but she pressed through all these obstacles and overcame them. After the labors of the day were over, she traced secretly and wearily, by the midnight lamp, a truthful record of her eventful life.

"This Empire State is a shabby place of refuge for the oppressed; but here, through anxiety, turmoil, and despair, the freedom of Linda and her children was finally secured, by the exertions of a generous friend. She was grateful for the boon; but the idea of having been *bought* was always galling to a spirit that could never acknowledge itself to be a chattel. She wrote to us thus, soon after the event: 'I thank you for your kind expressions in regard to my freedom; but the freedom I had before the money was paid was dearer to me. God gave me *that* freedom; but man put God's image in the scales with the paltry sum of three hundred dollars. I served for my liberty as faithfully as Jacob served for Rachel. At the end, he had large possessions; but I was robbed of my victory; I was obliged to resign my crown, to rid myself of a tyrant.'

"Her story, as written by herself, cannot fail to interest the reader. It is a sad illustration of the condition of this country, which boasts of its civilization, while it sanctions laws and customs which make the experiences of the present more strange than any fictions of the past.

Amy Post.
"Rochester, N. Y., Oct. 30th, 1859."

The following testimonial is from a man who is now a highly respectable colored citizen of Boston. L.M.C.

"This narrative contains some incidents so extraordinary, that, doubtless, many persons, under whose eyes it may chance to fall, will be ready to believe that it is colored highly, to serve a special purpose. But, however it may be regarded by the incredulous, I know that it is full of living truths. I have been well acquainted with the author from my boyhood. The circumstances recounted in her history are perfectly familiar to me. I knew of her treatment from her master; of the imprisonment of her children; of their sale and redemption; of her seven years' concealment; and of her subsequent escape to the North. I am now a resident of Boston, and am a living witness to the truth of this interesting narrative.

George W. Lowther."